Legal Analysis and Writing for Paralegals

William H. Putman

WEST PUBLISHING

an International Thomson Publishing company ITP®

Albany • Bonn • Boston • Cincinnati • Detroit • London • Madrid
Melbourne • Mexico City • Minneapolis/St. Paul • New York • Pacific Grove
Paris • San Francisco • Singapore • Tokyo • Toronto • Washington

NOTICE TO THE READER

Publisher does not warrant or guarantee any of the products described herein or perform any independent analysis in connection with any of the product information contained herein. Publisher does not assume, and expressly disclaims, any obligation to obtain and include information other than that provided to it by the manufacturer.

The reader is notified that this text is an educational tool, not a practice book. Since the law is in constant change, no rule or statement of law in this book should be relied upon for any service to any client. The reader should always refer to standard legal sources for the current rule or law. If legal advice or other expert assistance is required, the services of the appropriate professional should be sought.

The publisher makes no representations or warranties of any kind, including but not limited to, the warranties of fitness for particular purpose or merchantability, nor are any such representations implied with respect to the material set forth herein, and the publisher takes no responsibility with respect to such material. The publisher shall not be liable for any special, consequential, or exemplary damages resulting, in whole or in part, from the readers' use of, or reliance upon, this material.

Cover Photo: Stock Studios Photography
Cover Design: Scott Keidong

Delmar Staff

Publisher: Susan Simpfender
Acquisitions Editor: Elizabeth Hannan
Developmental Editor: Rhonda Kreshover
Project Editor: Eugenia L. Orlandi

Production Manager: Wendy A. Troeger
Art & Design Coordinator: Timothy J. Conners
Production Coordinator: Sandra Woods
Marketing Manager: Katherine M. Slezak

Printed in the United States of America

For more information, contact:

Delmar Publishers
3 Columbia Circle, Box 15015
Albany, New York 12212-5015

International Thomson Editores
Campos Eliseos 385, Piso 7
Col Polanco
11560 Mexico DF Mexico

International Thomson Publishing - Europe
Berkshire House
168-173 High Holborn
London, WC1V7AA
England

International Thomson Publishing GmbH
Königswinterer Strasse 418
53227 Bonn
Germany

Thomas Nelson Australia
102 Dodds Street
South Melbourne, 3205
Victoria, Australia

International Thomson Publishing – Asia
221 Henderson Road
#05-10 Henderson Building
Singapore 0315

Nelson Canada
1120 Birchmount Road
Scarborough, Ontario
Canada, M1K 5G4

International Thomson Publishing - Japan
Hirakawacho Kyowa Building, 3F
2-2-1 Hirakawacho
Chiyoda-ku, Tokyo 102
Japan

1 2 3 4 5 6 7 8 9 10 XXX 03 02 01 00 99 98 97

Library of Congress Cataloging-in-Publication Data

Putman, William H.
Legal analysis and writing for paralegals / William H. Putman. — 1st ed.
p. cm.
Includes bibliographical references and index.
ISBN 0-314-12830-1
1. Legal composition. 2. Law—United States—Interpretation and construction. 3. Legal assistants—United States—Handbooks, manuals, etc. I. Title.
KF250.P87 1998
808'.06634—dc21 97-10303
CIP

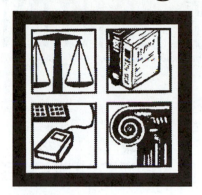

BRIEF CONTENTS

CONTENTS

CHAPTER 11 FUNDAMENTALS OF WRITING 208

CHAPTER 12 OFFICE LEGAL MEMORANDUM ASSIGNMENT—ISSUES AND FACTS 231

CHAPTER 13 OFFICE LEGAL MEMORANDUM ANALYSIS TO CONCLUSION 253

PREFACE

Paralegals are increasingly called upon to perform substantive legal analysis and legal writing tasks. These tasks range from the drafting of interoffice legal memoranda summarizing the research and analysis of issues involved in a client's case to the preparation of drafts of appellate court briefs. The goal of this text is to provide the student with in-depth knowledge of the fundamentals of legal analysis and legal writing. The hope is that the student will be better prepared to meet the challenges presented by substantive legal analysis and writing assignments.

The impetus for this book came from student requests for comprehensive information regarding many of the difficult areas of legal analysis and writing, such as:

- How to identify the issue
- How to state the issue
- How to determine if a case is on point
- How to identify the key facts in a case
- How to conduct counteranalysis
- How to prepare an interoffice memorandum and court brief

The text is designed to cover the topics of legal analysis and writing in general. It is organized in a manner to provide students with comprehensive information regarding the difficult areas of analysis and writing. The text is divided into the following three parts.

Part I Introduction to Analytical Principles and the Legal Process. Part I is composed of two introductory chapters. The first chapter presents an overview of the legal system and the legal process, and a summary of the basic legal principles involved in the process, such as authority, precedent, stare decisis, and so on. The second chapter introduces legal analysis and the IRAC analytical process.

Part II The Specifics of Legal Analysis. Part II consists of seven chapters that provide thorough coverage of the elements and tools used in the analysis and writing process. These chapters cover the difficult areas of legal analysis and writing that are not covered extensively in most texts:

- Statutory analysis
- Case law and case law briefing
- Key facts
- Issue identification
- Stating the issue
- Case law application (whether a case is "on point")
- Counteranalysis

Part III Legal Writing. The focus of Part III is on the application of the principles presented in the previous chapters to the drafting of legal research memoranda, court briefs, and legal correspondence. This part consists of chapters on the following topics:

- The legal writing process in general
- Fundamentals of writing
- Office legal memoranda (two chapters)
- Court briefs
- Correspondence

CHAPTER FEATURES

Each chapter is designed to help students completely understand and apply the concepts presented in the chapter. Chapters include the following features.

Hypothetical. Each chapter begins with a hypothetical that raises a question or questions involving the subject matter of the chapter. Following the hypothetical is a presentation of the principles, concepts, guidelines, and information concerning the subject matter. After the discussion of the subject matter, the principles and information discussed in the chapter are applied to answer the question or questions raised in the hypothetical.

The use of the hypothetical at the beginning of the chapter creates student interest in the subject matter of the chapter. The answer to the hypothetical toward the end of the chapter allows the student to see how the subject matter ties together and is applied.

Key Points. Each chapter has a list of key points that may be used as a quick reference and checklist when applying the concepts presented in the chapter. This checklist allows both the instructor and the student to make sure nothing is missed when reviewing or applying the principles presented in the chapter.

In-depth Coverage of Topics. The greatest advantage of this text for both teachers and students is the comprehensive and in-depth coverage of topics that are not thoroughly covered in most texts. These topics include the following:

- Issue stating
- Issue identification (issue spotting)
- Case law analysis (whether a case is "on point")
- Counteranalysis
- Statutory analysis
- Office legal memoranda preparation

Examples. A major advantage of the text is that every principle, concept, and so on is followed by an example that illustrates it. One of my students requested that there be "plenty of examples." This text has plenty of examples. These examples help the instructor teach principles and concepts and help the student understand them.

Assignments. There are assignments at the end of each chapter that range in difficulty. The assignments require students to apply the principles and techniques presented in the text. For example, among other assignments, there are eight case brief assignments in Chapter 4 (the cases are presented in Appendix A) and nine office legal memoranda assignments in Chapter 13 (based on the facts and law presented in the assignment and the court opinions in Appendix A). The answers to all the assignments are presented in the Teacher's Manual.

Appendices. The text has three appendices and a glossary of terms. Appendix A consists of court opinions that are necessary for the chapter assignments. Appendix B presents the brief of the appellee in a case filed in the Tenth Circuit Court of Appeals. The legal research, legal analysis, and initial drafts of this brief were performed by a paralegal who works in the Criminal Division of the United States Attorney's office for the District of New Mexico. Appendix C is a brief overview of the basic rules of legal citation. The overview uses the rules set forth in *A Uniform System of Citation* (Sixteenth Edition, 1996).

Readability. The text is written in a manner that a lay person can understand. Legalese is avoided, concepts are illustrated with examples, and the subject matter is presented simply and clearly.

SUPPORT MATERIAL

The text is accompanied by the following support material, which is designed to assist students in learning and instructors in teaching.

Teacher's Manual. Each chapter has several exercises ranging in difficulty. The Teacher's Manual provides *complete* answers to each exercise, general guides for the instructors, and suggested additional assignments. Among other things, the manual includes eight examples of briefs of court opinions, nine examples of office legal research memoranda, and two examples of appellate briefs.

Strategies and Tips for Paralegal Educators. This pamphlet, written by Anita Tebbe of Johnson County Community College, provides teaching strategies specifically designed for paralegal educators. It concentrates on how to teach and is organized in three parts: the *who* of paralegal education—students and teachers; the *what* of paralegal education—goals and objectives; and the *how* of paralegal education—methods of instruction, methods of evaluation, and other aspects of teaching. A copy of this pamphlet is available to each adopter. Quantities for distribution to adjunct instructors are available for purchase at a minimal price. A coupon in the pamphlet provides ordering information.

Citation-at-a-Glance. This handy reference card provides a quick, portable reference to the basic rules of citation for the most commonly cited legal sources, including judicial opinions, statutes, and secondary sources, such as legal encyclopedias and legal periodicals. *Citation-at-a-Glance* uses the rules set forth in *A Uniform System of Citation* (Sixteenth Edition, 1996). Classroom quantities are available free to adopters of the text.

WESTLAW. West's on-line computerized legal research system offers students hands-on experience with a system commonly used in law offices. Qualified adopters can receive ten free hours of WESTLAW. WESTLAW can be accessed with Macintosh and IBM PCs and compatibles. A modem is required.

WESTMATE Tutorial. This is an interactive tutorial that guides students through the process of accessing legal resources on WESTLAW by using WESTMATE, the special software that West has created for that purpose. There are two versions of the tutorial, one for DOS and one for Windows.

Video Library. West is proud to present an extensive paralegal video library for use in the classroom. Qualified adopters can choose and exchange videos from the library.

ACKNOWLEDGMENTS

I wish to gratefully acknowledge and express my deep appreciation to a number of individuals who took time and effort to assist in the development of this book. Without their expertise, suggestions, and support, this text would not have been remotely possible. I am particularly indebted to the following individuals:

Pamela A. Lambert, Esquire, who reviewed the text for intellectual and legal content and consistency. Her legal expertise, analytical skills, and input were invaluable. Pam's encouragement and positive attitude helped me through the rough spots.

Judith A. McCutcheon who reviewed this text for grammar and general compliance with the rules of English. Her efforts enhanced the quality of the writing. Her support helped keep me going.

Kate Arsenault who reviewed the text for general readability. Kate's patient support and encouragement helped ensure the text would be completed.

Jana Sorroche, my niece, who kept my computer in line and alive. Her computer expertise saved me many times when I thought the computer had eaten portions of the text.

Sheila McGlothlin, paralegal, who came up with the idea that this book should be written. Sheila's initial push, support, and comments on the text were essential.

Leigh Anne Chavez, Esquire, for assistance with several hypotheticals and ideas in general.

Robert T. Reeback, Esquire, for the ski resort hypothetical.

Elizabeth Hannan and Patricia Bryant of West Publishing Company for their encouragement and patience.

Finally, I would like to thank the reviewers who provided very valuable comments and suggestions for the text:

Melody K. Brown
College of Great Falls, MT

Wendy Edson
Hilbert College, NY

Vera Peaslee Haus
McIntosh College, NH

Mary Lowe
Westark Community College, AR

Joseph A. Marchesani
Winona State University, MN

Donna Kay Mettz
Southwestern Paralegal Institute, TX

Constance Ford Mungle
Oklahoma City University, OK

Diane Pevar
Manor Junior College, PA

Frances M. Rafferty
Peirce College, PA

Gail A. Randall
University of Maryland, University College, MD

Elizabeth Raulerson
Indian River Community College, FL

Brenda Rice
Johnson County Community College, KS

Vitonio San Juan
University of La Verne, CA

Martha Sartoris
North Hennepin Community College, MN

Pamela Poole Weber
Seminole Community College, FL

Christine A. Yared
Grand Valley State University, MI

ABOUT THE AUTHOR

William Putman received his Juris Doctor degree from the University of New Mexico School of Law and has been a member of the New Mexico Bar since 1975. He is an instructor in the Legal Assistant Studies Program at Albuquerque TVI, a community college, and the Paralegal Studies Program at Santa Fe Community College. Mr. Putman has taught legal analysis and legal writing since 1991. He has published several articles on legal analysis and writing in *Legal Assistant Today,* James Publishing Co. He maintains a private practice in Santa Fe, New Mexico.

DEDICATION

This book is dedicated to P.Y. whose love, inspiration, and guidance made this text possible. Thank you.

PART I

Introduction to Analytical Principles and the Legal Process

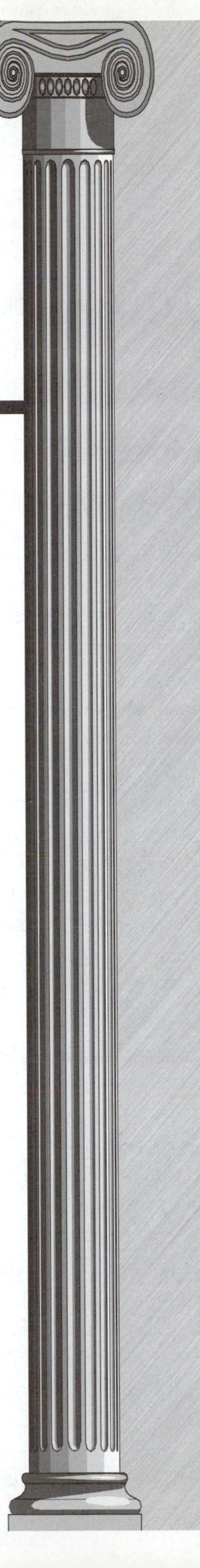

CHAPTER 1

Introduction to Legal Principles and Authorities

Renee has been working in a clerical position at the Addison law firm for the past seven years. Last fall she entered the paralegal program offered by the local community college. She has been an excellent employee. The firm, in support of her continued education, pays her tuition and allows her to leave work early so that she can attend a late afternoon class. The firm has reassigned her to work in the paralegal division and directed that she be assigned some substantive legal research and analysis tasks.

Two weeks ago Renee started working on a gender discrimination case. In the case, the client, Mary Stone, had been working for a company for eleven years. She always received excellent job performance evaluations. Her coworker, Tom, asked her on several occasions to go out with him. Ms. Stone always refused his invitations. The last time he asked her out was about one year ago. After she refused, he told her, "I'll get even with you." Nine months ago, Tom was promoted to the position of department supervisor. After his promotion, he did not ask Ms. Stone out again. On her evaluation three months ago, he rated her job performance as "poor" and stated that she was uncooperative and abrasive. He recommended that she be demoted or fired. Ms. Stone feels that she has been discriminated against and she wants the "poor" evaluation removed from her file.

Renee's assignment is to locate the pertinent state and federal law governing gender discrimination and any other relevant information on the subject and prepare a memo summarizing her research and how it applies to the case. Renee located a federal and a state statute prohibiting discrimination in employment on the basis of gender, a federal and a state court case with facts similar to those in Ms. Stone's case, and two law review articles discussing the type of gender discrimination encountered by Ms. Stone.

When analyzing the law and preparing her memo, Renee realizes that she must determine which authority applies and how. She asks herself, "Which court should the claim be filed in, federal or state? If a complaint is filed in state court, which of these authorities must the state court follow? Why?" General guidelines that assist you in determining when and how legal authorities apply are presented in this chapter; the application of the guidelines to Renee's questions are presented in the Application section of the chapter.

INTRODUCTION

As attorneys become more aware of the capabilities of paralegals, an increasing number of paralegals are being assigned substantive legal analysis and writing tasks. The goal of this text is to provide comprehensive coverage of the legal analysis and writing process. Emphasis is placed on in-depth coverage of many of the difficult areas of legal analysis and writing such as:

- Issue and key fact identification
- Issue stating (how to write the issue)
- Statutory and case law analysis
- Counteranalysis

Before considering these areas in subsequent chapters of the text, it is necessary to have a general understanding of the law and the legal system and some of the basic doctrines and principles that apply to legal analysis. This is essential because legal analysis involves a determination of how the law applies to a client's facts, which requires a knowledge of what the law is and the general principles that govern its application. This chapter presents an overview of the legal system and fundamental principles that guide its operation. The definitions, concepts, doctrines, and principles addressed are referred to and applied in the subsequent chapters of the text. A familiarity with them is essential when studying those chapters.

There are various definitions of the term *law,* depending on the philosophy and point of view of the individual defining it. Law can be defined from a political, moral, or ethical perspective. For the purposes of this text, *law* is defined as the enforceable rules that govern individual and group conduct in a society. The law establishes standards of conduct, the procedures governing the conduct, and the remedies available when the rules of conduct are not adhered to. The purpose of the law is to establish standards that allow individuals to interact with the greatest efficiency and the least amount of conflict. When conflicts or disputes occur, law provides a mechanism for a resolution that is predictable and peaceful.

law

The enforceable rules that govern individual and group conduct in a society. The law establishes standards of conduct, the procedures governing standards of conduct, and the remedies available when the standards are not adhered to.

The following sections focus on the various sources of law and the principles and concepts that impact on the analysis of these sources.

SOURCES OF LAW

The legal system of the United States, like the legal systems of most countries, is based upon history and has evolved with the passage of time. When America was settled, most of the colonies were governed by English law. As a result, the foundation of the American legal system is the English model, with influences from other European countries.

In England, after the Norman Conquest under William the Conqueror in 1066, a body of law called the common law developed. The common law consisted of the law created by the courts established by the king. When colonization of America took place, the law of England consisted primarily of the common law and the laws enacted by Parliament. At the time of the Revolution, the English model was adopted and firmly established in the colonies.

After the Revolution, the legal system of the colonies remained largely intact and remains so to the present time. It consists of two main categories of law:

1. Enacted law
2. Common law/case law

Enacted Law

enacted law
The body of law adopted by the people or legislative bodies, including constitutions, statutes, ordinances, and administrative rules and regulations.

As used in this text, the term *enacted law* encompasses all law that has been adopted by a legislative body or the people. It includes:

- Constitutions—adopted by the people
- Statutes, ordinances—laws passed by legislative bodies
- Regulations—actions of administrative bodies that have the force of law

In the United States, society is governed by laws established by two governing authorities: the federal government and the state governments. Local governments are a component of state governments and have the authority to govern local affairs. Each governing authority has the power to enact legislation affecting the rights and duties of members of society. It is necessary to keep this in mind when analyzing a problem, as the problem may be governed by more than one law. The categories of enacted law are addressed in the following.

Constitutions

A constitution is a governing document adopted by the people. It establishes the framework for the operation of government, defines the powers of government, and guarantees the fundamental rights of the people. Both the federal and state governments have constitutions.

constitution
A governing document adopted by the people that establishes the framework for the operation of the government, defines the powers of the government, and guarantees the fundamental rights of the people.

United States Constitution. The United States Constitution:

1. Establishes and defines the powers of the three branches of federal government: executive (president), legislative (Congress), and judicial (courts)
2. Establishes the broad powers of the federal and state governments and defines the relation between the federal and state governments
3. Defines in broad terms the rights of the members of society

State Constitutions. Each state has adopted a constitution that establishes the structure of the state government. In addition, each state constitution defines the powers and limits of the authority of the state government and the fundamental rights of the citizens of the state.

Statutes

statutes
Laws passed by legislative bodies that declare rights and duties, or command or prohibit certain conduct.

Statutes are laws passed by legislative bodies. Statutes declare rights and duties or command or prohibit certain conduct. As used here, *statute* includes any law passed by any legislative body: federal, state, or local. Such laws are referred to by various terms, such as *acts, codes, statutes,* or *ordinances.* The term *ordinance* usually refers to a law passed by a local government. Statutory law has assumed an increasing role in the United States as many matters once governed by the common law are now governed by statutory law.

For Example: Criminal law was once governed almost exclusively by the common law. Now a large part of the criminal law, such as the definition of crimes, is governed by statutory law.

Since statutes are usually designed to cover a broad range of present and future situations, they are written in general terms.

For Example: Section 335-1-4 of a state's Uniform Owner Resident Relations Act provides, "If a court, as a matter of law, finds that any provision of a rental agreement was inequitable when made, the court may limit the application of such inequitable provision to avoid an inequitable result." The statute is written in general terms so that cover a broad range of landlord/tenant rental situations and rental provisions. It is designed to cover all provisions of all rental agreements that may prove to be inequitable. The general terms of the statute allow a court a great deal of flexibility when addressing an issue involving an alleged inequitable lease provision. The court "may limit the application . . . to avoid an equitable result." How and to what degree the court limits the application of the lease provision is left to the court to decide.

Administrative Law

A third type of enacted law is administrative law. Legislative bodies are involved in determining what the law should be and enacting the appropriate legislation. They do not have the time and are not equipped to oversee the day-to-day running of the government and implementation of the laws. Legislatures delegate the task of administering the laws to administrative agencies.

When a law is passed, the legislature includes enabling legislation that establishes and authorizes administrative agencies to carry out the intent of the legislature. This enabling legislation usually includes a grant of authority to create rules and regulations necessary to carry out the law. These rules and regulations have the authority of law. The body of law that results is called administrative law. It is composed of the rules, regulations, orders, and decisions promulgated by the administrative agencies when carrying out their duties.

Administrative law is usually more specific than statutory law because it deals with the details of implementing the law.

For Example: The Environmental Protection Agency, in order to implement the Clean Air Act, has adopted various regulations setting air quality standards. Many of these regulations establish specific numerical standards for the amount of pollutants that may be emitted by manufacturing plants. The Clean Air Act is written in very broad terms, but the regulations enforcing it are very specific.

Enacted law covers a broad spectrum of the law. The process of analyzing enacted law is covered in detail in Chapter 3.

Common Law/Case Law

In a narrow sense, the term *common law* refers to the law created by courts in the absence of enacted law. Technically the term includes only the body of law created by courts when the legislative authority has not acted.

common law/case law
The body of law created by courts. It is composed of the general legal rules, doctrines, and principles adopted by courts when interpreting existing law or when creating law in the absence of controlling enacted law.

For Example: Most of the law of torts has been created by the courts. From the days of early England to the present, legislative bodies have not passed legislation establishing or defining most torts. In the absence of legislation, the courts have created and defined most torts and the rules and principles governing tort law.

The term *case law* encompasses a broader range of law than the term *common law.* Case law includes not only the law created by courts in the absence of enacted law but also the law created when courts interpret or apply enacted law.

Often the term *common law* is used in a very broad sense to encompass all law other than enacted law (*i.e.,* law enacted by legislatures or adopted by the people). In this text, *common law* is used in the broadest sense to include case law (often called judge-made law). Throughout the text, the terms *common law, case law,* and *judge-made law* are used interchangeably and should be interpreted to include all law other than enacted law.

As mentioned earlier, the common law system in the United States is based on the English common law, and much of the English common law has been adopted by the states. William the Conqueror established a king's court (Curia Regia) to unify the country through the establishment of a uniform set of rules and principles to govern social conduct throughout the country. The courts, in dealing with specific disputes, developed legal principles that could apply to all similar disputes. With the passage of time, these legal principles came to embody the common law. The common law process continues to the present day in both England and the United States, with new rules and principles continually being developed by the courts.

For Example: One hundred and fifty years ago, there was no remedy in tort law for strict products liability. The tort was developed by the courts in the twentieth century to address the needs of a modern industrial society.

Role of the Courts

Disputes in our society arise from specific fact situations. The courts are designed to resolve these disputes. When a dispute is before a court, it is called a case. The role of the court is to resolve the dispute in a peaceful manner through the application of the law to the facts of the case. To accomplish this resolution, the court must identify the law that controls the resolution of the dispute and apply that law to the facts of the case.

When there is no enacted or common law that governs a dispute, the court may be called upon to create new law. Where the meaning or application of an existing law is unclear or ambiguous, it may be necessary for the court to interpret the law. In interpreting and applying existing law, courts often announce new legal rules and principles. The creation of new law and the interpretation and application of existing law become law itself.

The result reached by a court is usually called a decision. The court's written decision, which includes the reasons for the decision, is called an opinion. The common law is composed of the general legal rules, doctrines, and principles contained in court opinions.

opinion
The written statement by the court expressing how it ruled in a case and the reasons for its ruling.

Court Systems

A basic understanding of court systems is necessary for anyone analyzing a legal problem. The approach to a problem and the direction of research may depend upon whether relief is available in federal or state court or both. A brief overview of the court systems is presented here.

There are two parallel court systems, the federal court system and the state court system. A concept that is common to both systems is the concept of jurisdiction. An understanding of this concept is essential to an understanding of the operation of both systems.

jurisdiction
The court's authority to hear and resolve specific disputes.

Jurisdiction. The types of cases that can come before a court of either system is determined by the jurisdiction of the court. Jurisdiction is the extent of a court's authority to hear and resolve specific disputes. A court's jurisdiction is usually limited to two main areas:

1. Over persons by geographic area—personal jurisdiction
2. Over subject matter by types of cases the court may hear and decide—subject matter jurisdiction

personal jurisdiction
The authority of the court over the parties to resolve a legal dispute involving the parties.

Personal Jurisdiction. The jurisdiction of state courts is limited to the geographic boundaries of the state or to matters that have some connection with the state.

For Example: New York state courts do not have authority to decide matters in the state of Ohio. Their authority is limited to the geographic boundaries of the state of New York. A New York state court does have jurisdiction over an Ohio resident if the resident is involved in a automobile accident in the state of New York.

Subject Matter Jurisdiction. In regard to subject matter jurisdiction, there are basically two types of courts in both the federal and state court systems:

subject matter jurisdiction
The types or kinds of cases the court has the authority to hear and decide.

1. Courts of general jurisdiction
2. Courts of limited jurisdiction

Courts of general jurisdiction have the authority to hear and decide any matter brought before them. There are some limitations, however. The authority of a state court of general jurisdiction is limited to matters involving state matters. The authority of a federal court of general jurisdiction is limited to questions involving federal matters or questions involving disputes between citizens of different states where the amount in controversy exceeds $50,000. The courts of general jurisdiction are the main trial courts in both systems.

For Example: The United States district courts are the courts of general jurisdiction in the federal system. They have the authority to hear and decide all matters with federal questions (involving the United States Constitution or federal law) or cases where the parties are citizens of different states and the amount in controversy exceeds $50,000. All states have state courts of general jurisdiction that have authority over state matters.

Courts of limited jurisdiction are limited in the types of cases they can hear and decide. There are courts of limited jurisdiction in both the federal and state court systems.

For Example: The United States Tax Court's authority is limited to matters involving disputes over federal taxes.

For Example: Most state courts have courts whose authority is limited by dollar amount. Such courts are limited to hearing and deciding matters where the amount in controversy does not exceed a certain amount, such as $5,000. These courts are called by various names: small claims, magistrate, and so on. Some state courts are limited to hearing specific types of cases, such as matters involving domestic relations or probate.

Jurisdiction is a very complex subject. An exhaustive and detailed treatment of jurisdiction is the subject of many texts and is properly addressed in a separate course of study. The brief discussion here is designed to acquaint the student with the fundamentals.

Federal Court System. The federal court system is composed of three basic levels of courts:

trial court
The court where the matter is heard and decided. Testimony is taken, the evidence is presented, and the decision is reached in the trial court.

appeals court
A court that reviews the decision of a trial court or other lower court to determine and correct any error that may have been made.

1. *Trial Courts.* The trial court is the court where the matter is heard and decided. The testimony is taken, the evidence presented, and the decision reached. Examples of trial courts in the federal court system are the United States District Court and the United States Tax Court. Each state has at least one United States District Court (see Figure 1–1).
2. *Court of Appeals.* A party aggrieved by the decision of a trial court has a right to appeal the decision to a court of appeals. The primary function of a court of appeals is to review the decision of a trial court to determine and correct any error that may have been made. A court of appeals only reviews what took place in the trial court. It does not hear new testimony, retry the case, or

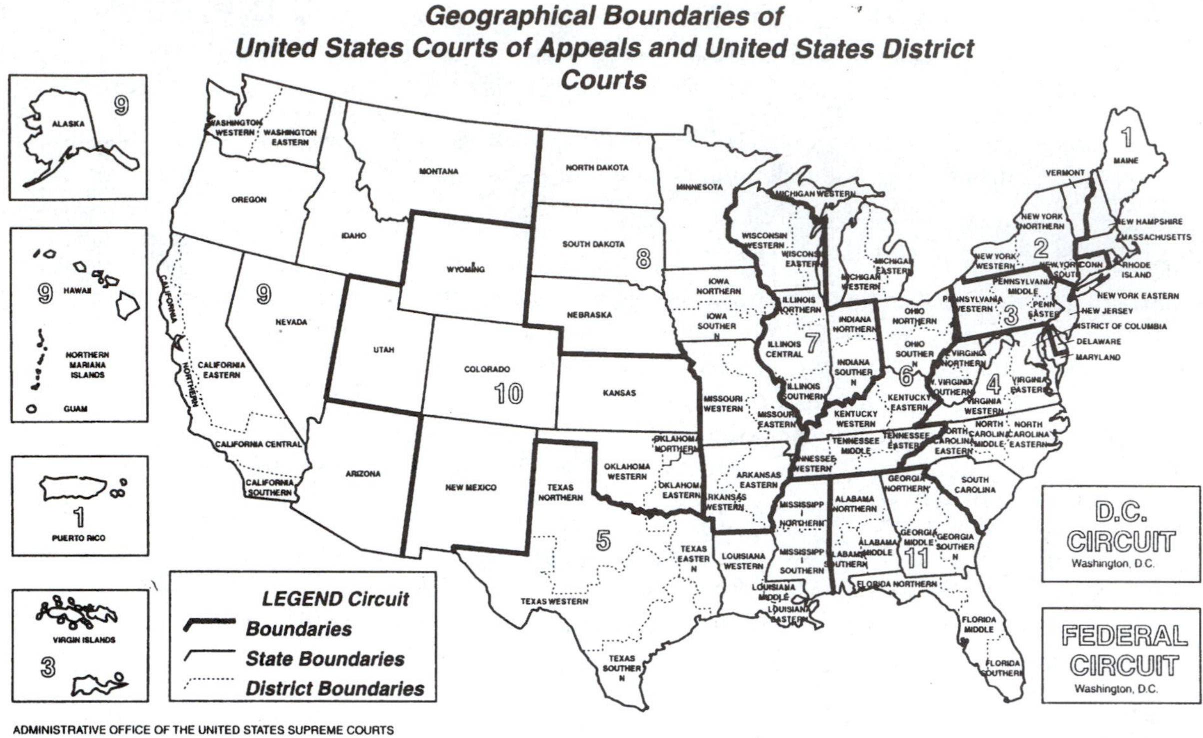

Figure 1-1

United States Circuit Courts of Appeals and United States District Courts

reconsider the evidence. A court of appeals reviews the record of the lower court and takes appropriate action to correct any errors made, such as ordering a new trial or reversing a decision of the trial court. The court of appeals in the federal system is called the United States Court of Appeals. These courts are also called circuit courts. There are thirteen federal courts of appeals (see Figure 1–1).

3. *United States Supreme Court.* The United States Supreme Court is the final court of appeals in the federal system. It is the highest court in the land. With few exceptions, an individual does not have an absolute right to have a matter reviewed by the Supreme Court. A party who disagrees with the decision of a court of appeals must ask (petition) the Supreme Court to review it. The request is called a petition for writ of certiorari. The Supreme Court has discretion to review or not review a decision of a court of appeals. If the Court denies the petition, the decision of the court of appeals stands. If the Court decides the matter involves important constitutional issues or if the challenged decision conflicts with federal court decisions, the Supreme Court may grant the petition and review the decision of the lower court.

The organization of the federal court system and the various federal courts is presented in Figure 1–2.

State Court System. Every state has its own state court system, each of which has unique features and variations. The names of the courts vary from state to state.

For Example: The highest court in many states is called the supreme court. In New York, however, the highest court is called the court of appeals.

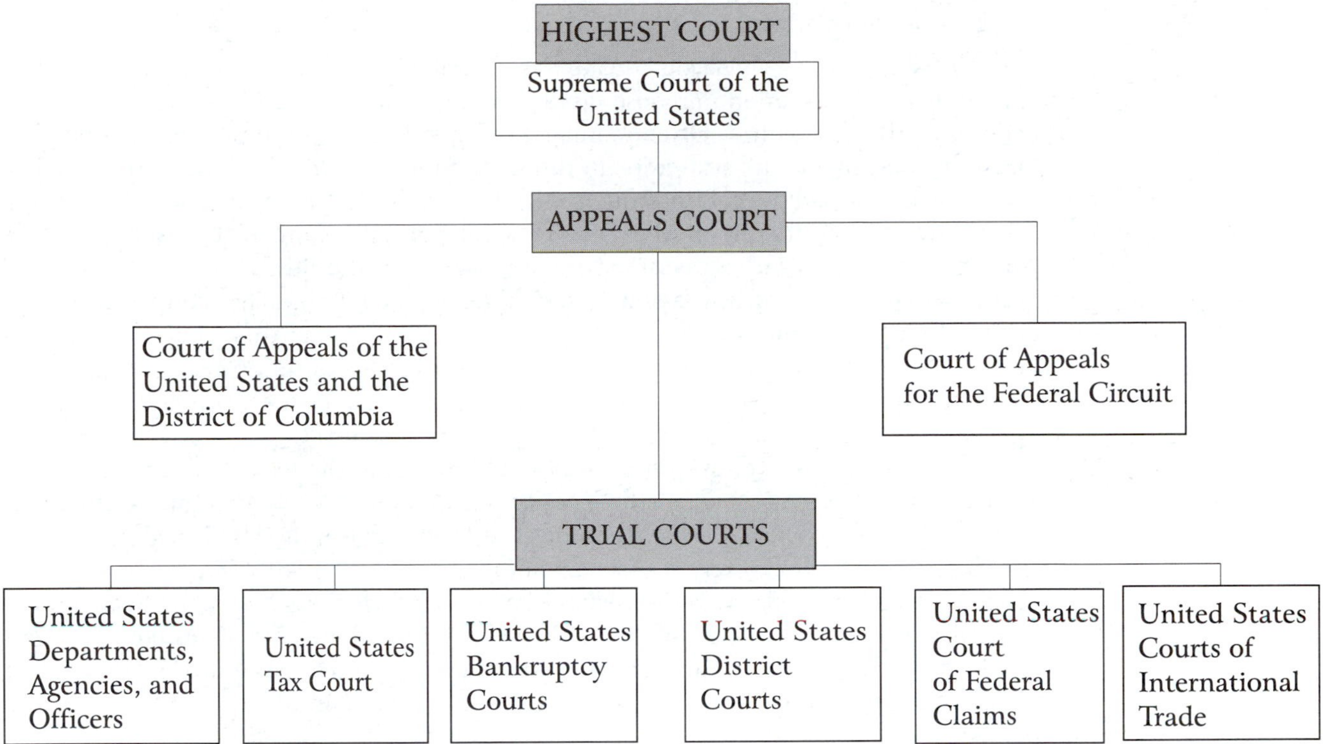

Figure 1-2
Organization of the Federal Court System

Because of the unique features of each state system, it is essential that you become familiar with the court system in your state.

Like the federal court system, most state court systems are composed of three basic levels of courts:

1. *Trial Courts.* All states have trial courts where the evidence is presented, testimony taken, and a decision reached. Usually there are trial courts of general jurisdiction and trial courts of limited jurisdiction. The court of general jurisdiction is often called a "district court." There are various courts of limited jurisdiction, such as probate courts, small claims courts, domestic relations courts, magistrate courts, and so on.
2. *Court of Appeals.* Many states have intermediary courts of appeals that function in the same manner and play the same role in the state court system as the federal court of appeals does in the federal system.
3. *State Supreme Court.* Every state has a highest appellate court, usually called the supreme court. This court is the highest court in the state, and its decisions are final on all questions involving state law. In states that have intermediary courts of appeals, the state supreme court often operates like the United States Supreme Court in that there is no automatic right of appeal. Like the federal Supreme Court, the state supreme court grants leave to appeal only in cases involving important questions of state law. In those states where there is no intermediary court of appeals, a party who disagrees with a trial court's decision has a right to appeal to the highest court. In either system, state or federal, all individuals have at least one opportunity to appeal the decision of a trial court to a higher court.

district court

In many states, the district court is the trial court of general jurisdiction. See also United States district court.

Precedent and Stare Decisis

It is apparent, when you consider the number of courts in the state and federal court systems, that an immense number of legal questions and problems are being addressed by the courts. Often, similar legal questions and similar facts situations arise in the same court system or in different court systems. If a court in an earlier case has developed a legal doctrine, principle, or rule that helps resolve a legal question, later courts addressing the same or a substantially similar question should be able to look to the earlier decision for guidance. Why should a court go through the process of determining how a matter should be decided if an earlier court has already gone through the process and developed a principle or rule that applies? The efficiency of the court system is greatly enhanced because courts do not have to "reinvent the wheel" in every case—they can rely on legal doctrines, principles, or rules developed over time in previous cases.

Reliance on doctrines, principles, or rules to guide the resolution of similar disputes in the future also makes the legal system more stable, predictable, and consistent. If the law governing a specific subject or legal question is established in an earlier case, individuals can rely on a court addressing the same or a similar question to base its decision on the principles established in the earlier case. Outcomes can be predicted to some extent, and stability and consistency become part of the court system.

Two complementary doctrines have developed to provide stability, predictability, and consistency to the common law. These doctrines are precedent and stare decisis.

precedent
An earlier court decision on an issue that applies to govern or guide a subsequent court in its determination of an identical or similar issue based upon identical or similar facts.

Precedent. Precedent is an earlier court decision on an issue that applies to govern or guide a subsequent court in its determination of an identical or similar issue based upon identical or similar facts.

For Example: Suppose that the state's highest court, in the case of *State v. Ahrens,* held that bail must be set in all criminal cases except where a court determines that the defendant poses a clear and present threat to the public at large or to an individual member or members of the public. If a case before a subsequent court involves a situation where the defendant has made threats against the life of a witness, *Ahrens* applies as precedent and can serve as a guide for the court's determination of the question of whether bail must be set.

A case that is precedent is often called "on point." The process and steps to be followed when determining if a court opinion may apply or be relied on as precedent are discussed in detail in Chapter 8.

stare decisis
A basic principle of the common law system that requires a court to follow a previous decision of that court or a higher court when the current decision involves issues and facts similar to those involved in the previous decision. The doctrine that provides that precedent should be followed.

Stare Decisis. The doctrine of stare decisis is a basic principle of the common law system that requires a court to follow a previous decision of *that court or a higher court* when the current decision involves issues and facts similar to those involved in the previous decision. In other words, similar cases will be decided in similar ways. Under the doctrine, when the court has established a principle that governs a particular set of facts or a specific legal question, the court will follow that principle and apply it in all future cases with similar facts and legal questions. In essence, stare decisis is the doctrine that provides that precedent should be followed.

For Example: Suppose a statute of state *X* prohibits employment discrimination on the basis of gender. In the case of *Ellen v. Employer, Inc.,* an employee was fired because the employee was homosexual. The supreme court of state *X* interpreted "discrimination on the basis of gender" as used in the statute to include discrimination based on an individual's sexual preference. The doctrine of stare decisis requires that in subsequent cases, the supreme court of state *X* and all the lower courts of state *X* must follow the interpretation of the statute given in *Ellen v. Employer, Inc.*

The doctrine of stare decisis, however, does not require rigid adherence to the rules or principles established in prior decisions. The doctrine does not apply if there is a good reason not to follow it. Some of these reasons include:

1. The earlier decision has become outdated because of changed conditions or policies.

   For Example: In *Plessy v. Ferguson,* 163 U.S. 537, 16 S. Ct. 1138, 41 L. Ed. 256 (1896), the court adopted the "separate but equal doctrine" that allowed segregation on the basis of race. In *Brown v. Board of Education of Topeka,* 347 U.S. 483, 74 S. Ct. 686, 98 L. Ed. 873 (1954), the Supreme Court refused to follow *Plessy* and overruled it, holding that separate educational facilities were inherently unequal and denied equal protection of the law.

2. The legislature has enacted legislation that has, in effect, overruled the decision of an earlier court.

   For Example: Suppose the state supreme court, in *Stevens v. Soro, Inc.,* ruled that the phrase *on the job* in the Workers' Compensation Act means that an employee is "on the job" from the moment the employee leaves for work until he or she arrives home. After the decision, the state legislature amended the act, defining "on the job" to include only the time the employee is on the premises of the employer. The amendment in effect overrules the prior court decision, and subsequent courts are not required to follow it.

3. The earlier decision was poorly reasoned or has produced undesirable results.

   For Example: Review the gender discrimination example presented in the beginning of this subsection. Suppose the supreme court of state *X,* in a later case, decides that the reasoning in the court's decision in *Ellen v. Employer, Inc.,* was incorrect and that the term *gender discrimination* should not be interpreted to include discrimination on the basis of sexual preference. The court can overrule *Ellen* and is not bound to follow it.

The doctrines of precedent and stare decisis provide stability, predictability, and consistency to court systems by providing the courts, attorneys, and the public with guidance on how matters should and will be decided. A court can be relied on to reach the same decision on an issue as an earlier court when the cases are sufficiently similar. Without these doctrines, a similar case could be decided in an entirely different manner based upon the unique beliefs of the individual judge and jury. The result would be little or no consistency in the common law, and chaos would reign. When a decision of an earlier court may or must be relied on by a subsequent court is discussed later in this chapter in the sections addressing authority.

HIERARCHY OF THE LAW

There is a hierarchy of authority between the two primary sources of law: enacted law and common law. When a question arises concerning which source applies in a case or there is a conflict between sources, a hierarchy governs which source will apply.

In general, within each jurisdiction, the constitution is the highest authority, followed by the other enacted law (legislative and administrative law), then the common or case law. This means that legislative acts and court decisions must not conflict with the provisions of the constitution. A court decision may interpret a legislative act, but it cannot overrule an act unless it is determined that the act violates the constitution.

Between federal and state law, federal law is supreme. If an enacted law or court decision of a state conflicts with a federal law or court decision, the state law or decision is invalid to the extent it conflicts with the federal law or decision.

For Example: A state passes a law declaring that it is illegal to burn the American flag. The state supreme court upholds the statute. Both the state statute and the state supreme court decisions are invalid because they conflict with the Constitution of the United States. The United States Supreme Court has ruled that the freedom of speech provisions of the Constitution include the right to burn the flag. The federal law is supreme, and the state law is invalid to the extent it conflicts with federal law.

AUTHORITY

authority
Anything a court may rely on when deciding an issue. It includes the law, such as constitutions and statutes, and nonlaw sources, such as legal encyclopedias and treatises.

To be able to analyze the law, in addition to knowing the sources of law, you must become familiar with the concept of authority, principles relating to authority, and the various types of authority. *Authority* may be defined as anything a court may rely on when deciding an issue. It includes not only the law but also any other nonlaw source that a court may look to in reaching a decision.

This section discusses the two types of authority and the two roles that authority plays in the decision-making process. The two types of authority are:

1. *Primary authority*—the law itself
2. *Secondary authority*—nonlaw sources a court may rely on

There are two possible roles that authority may play:

1. *Mandatory authority*—the authority a court must rely on and follow when deciding an issue
2. *Persuasive authority*—the authority a court may rely on and follow, but is not bound to rely on or follow

In the following subsections, the two types of authority (primary and secondary) are addressed first. Then the role of authority, that is, the value or weight a court must or may give to authority (mandatory and persuasive authority), is discussed.

Types of Authority

Primary Authority

primary authority
Authority that is composed of the law (e.g., constitutions, statutes, and court opinions).

Primary authority is the law itself. It is composed of the two main categories of law, enacted law and common/case law.

For Example: Primary authority includes constitutions, statutes, ordinances, regulations, court opinions, and so on.

Courts refer to and rely on primary authority first when resolving legal problems.

Secondary Authority

secondary authority
Any source of law a court may rely on that is not the law (e.g., legal treatises, restatements of the law, and legal encyclopedias).

Secondary authority is any source a court may rely on that is not the law, *i.e.*, that is not primary authority. Secondary authority consists of legal resources that summarize, compile, explain, comment on, interpret, or in some other way address the law.

Secondary authority can be used in several ways:

- To obtain a background or overall understanding of a specific area of the law. Legal encyclopedias are useful for this purpose.
- To locate primary authority (the law) on a question being researched. *American Law Reports* (ALR) and treatises can be used for this purpose.

For Example: If the researcher is unfamiliar with a specific area of law, such as defamation, a treatise on tort law will provide an overview of the area. The treatise will also include references to key court cases and enacted law (primary authority) concerning defamation.

- To be relied on by the court when reaching a decision, which usually occurs only when there is no primary authority governing a legal question or it is unclear how the primary authority applies to the question. Treatises, law reviews, and restatements of the law are relied on for this purpose.

There are literally hundreds of secondary sources. An in-depth discussion of all of them is beyond the scope of this text, and therefore, only some of the major secondary sources are summarized here.

Annotations. Annotations are notes and comments on the law. One of the well-known annotations is the *American Law Reports* (ALR). The ALR is a series of books that contains the complete text of selected court opinions, along with scholarly commentaries explaining and discussing issues raised in the case. The commentaries also include an overview of how the issues are treated nationally, focusing on the majority and minority views, and a list of cases from other jurisdictions dealing with the same issues. The ALR is useful for obtaining an in-depth overview of the courts' treatment of specific questions and issues. These annotations are also useful as an aid in locating court decisions dealing with specific issues.

Law Dictionaries. Legal dictionaries include definitions of legal terms (and usually a citation to the authority for the definition) and guides to pronunciation. The two major legal dictionaries are *Black's Law Dictionary,* published by West Publishing, and *Ballentine's Legal Dictionary,* published by Lawyers Cooperative.

Law Reviews. Law reviews are scholarly publications usually published by law schools. They contain articles written by professors, judges, and practitioners and include commentaries written by law students. The articles usually discuss specific topics and legal questions in some depth and include references to key cases on the subjects. These reviews are useful as a source of comprehensive information on very specific topics.

Legal Encyclopedias. A legal encyclopedia is a multivolume set of books that provides a summary of the law. The topics are arranged in alphabetical order, and the set includes an index and cross-references. The two major legal encyclopedias are *Corpus Juris Secundum* (CJS), published by West Publishing, and *American Jurisprudence* (now *American Jurisprudence Second*) (Am. Jur. or Am. Jur. 2d) published by Lawyers Cooperative. An encyclopedia is a valuable source when seeking an overview of a legal topic.

Restatements of the Law. The *Restatements of the Law,* published by the American Law Institute, presents a variety of topics and discusses what the law is on each topic, or what it should be. Following a presentation of the law is a "Comment" that explains the rule of law presented, discusses why the rule was adopted, and gives examples of how the rule applies. The *Restatements* are drafted by authorities and experts in specific areas and are often relied on and adopted by legislatures and courts.

Treatises. A treatise is a single- or multivolume work written by an expert in an area that covers that entire area of law. A treatise is a valuable resource because it provides a comprehensive treatment of a specific area of law, reference to statutes and key cases in the area, and commentaries on the law.

Role of Authority

Once the types of authority have been identified, it is important to understand the role these sources play in the decision-making process. Not all authority referred to or relied on by a court when deciding an issue is given equal weight. Authority is divided into two categories for the purpose of determining its authoritative value, or the extent to which it must be relied on or followed by a court: mandatory authority and persuasive authority.

mandatory authority

Any authority or source of law that a court must rely on or follow when reaching a decision (e.g., a decision of a higher court in the jurisdiction on the same or a similar issue).

Mandatory Authority

Mandatory authority is any source that a court must rely on or follow when reaching a decision. Secondary authority can *never* be mandatory authority. A court is never bound to follow secondary authority because it is not the law. Primary authority can be mandatory authority because courts are required to follow the law itself. As discussed earlier, primary authority is composed of enacted law and common or case law.

Not all primary authority, however, is mandatory authority. Not all law must be followed by a court when reaching a decision. Primary authority becomes mandatory authority only when it governs the legal question or issue being decided by the court. The factors involved in deciding when enacted law and common law may be mandatory authority are briefly discussed here.

Enacted Law. The determination of whether an enacted law applies to govern a legal question or issue before a court is addressed in detail in Chapter 3. The three-step process presented in that chapter is summarized here.

Step 1 Identify all the laws that may govern the question. This requires locating all statutes or laws that possibly govern the legal question.

> ***For Example:*** Some legal questions and fact situations such as gender discrimination are governed by both state and federal law, and on occasion by more than one state or federal law.

Once the laws that may govern the question are identified, a determination of which of these laws applies to the specific legal area involved in the dispute must be made. This requires an analysis of the law.

> ***For Example:*** In the preceding example, an analysis of the law may reveal that even though both federal and state law govern the question of gender discrimination, the federal law requires that the matter be tried in state court before being pursued in federal court. The federal law, therefore, does not apply until the remedies available under state law have been pursued in the state courts.

Step 2 Identify the elements of the law or statute. Once a determination is made of which specific law or laws govern the question, the elements of the law or statute, *i.e.*, the specific requirements that must be met for the law or statute to apply, must be identified. It is necessary to identify the elements before moving on to step 3, determining whether the requirements of the law or statute are met by the facts of the case.

> ***For Example:*** The legal question is whether the client has a claim for breach of implied warranty of merchantability. The transaction involved the sale of goods. After performing the first step, it is determined that article 2 of the state's commercial code is mandatory authority because article 2 applies to the sale of goods, and the transaction involved the sale of goods within the state. A section of article 2 creates an implied warranty of merchantability under specified circumstances. An identification of the elements is necessary to determine what the section requires for the warranty to exist.

These requirements must be identified before it can be determined how the section applies to the client's facts. Assume that an identification of the elements reveals that the implied warranty of merchantability is created only when:

1. the transaction involves the sale of goods, and
2. the seller of the goods is a merchant.

This example is referred to in this chapter as the implied warranty example.

Step 3 Apply the facts of the case to the elements. The final step is to apply the facts of the client's case to the elements to determine how the law or statute applies. If the elements match the facts raised by the legal issue, the law applies and governs the outcome. Even if some of the elements are not met, the law still applies, but the outcome may be different.

For Example: Referring to the implied warranty example in step 2, it was concluded in step 1 that the transaction involved the sale of goods and that article 2 of the state commercial code applies as mandatory authority. Step 2 revealed that an implied warranty exists under article 2 when the transaction involved the sale of goods *and* the seller is a merchant. Step 3 requires the matching of the elements with the facts of the case. The implied warranty exists in the client's case if the seller is a merchant. It does not exist if the seller is not a merchant. If the transaction does not involve the sale of goods, such as the sale of land, article 2 does not apply and is not mandatory authority.

Once it is determined that an enacted law governs a legal question, that law is mandatory authority, and a court must apply the law unless it is determined that the law is unconstitutional.

Common Law/Case Law. For a court opinion to be mandatory authority, binding another court to follow the rule or principle of law established in the opinion, two conditions must be met:

1. The court opinion must be on point.
2. The court opinion must be written by a higher court in that jurisdiction.

For Example: If the highest court in state *A* defines *malice* as used in the state's murder statute, then all the lower courts in state *A* (intermediary and trial courts) are bound to follow the highest court and apply the highest court's interpretation of the term in cases involving the statute.

In regard to this example, is the highest court in state *A*, in later cases, bound to follow the earlier court's definition of malice? No. The highest court is always free to overturn the opinion and change the definition. The court will follow the earlier decision unless it overturns it or in some way amends it. The lower courts do not have this option.

What if the decision of the highest state court is different from the decision of a federal court? If a state court decision conflicts with the Constitution or federal law, the state court must follow the dictates of the federal law. State courts usually have the final say over interpretations of state law. If a federal court is addressing an issue involving state law, the federal court usually follows the interpretation of the state law rendered by the state's highest court.

An in-depth discussion of the process involved in determining whether a case is on point and in case law analysis is presented in Chapter 8.

Persuasive Authority

Persuasive authority is any authority a court is not bound to consider or follow but may consider or follow when reaching a decision. Where there is mandatory

persuasive authority
Any authority a court is not bound to consider or follow but may consider or follow when reaching a decision (e.g., a decision of a court in another state on the same or a similar issue, secondary authority, and so on).

authority, persuasive authority is not necessary, although its use is not prohibited. Persuasive authority consists of both primary authority and secondary authority.

Primary Authority as Persuasive Authority. On occasion, courts look to enacted law as persuasive authority.

> ***For Example:*** A court, when interpreting a term not defined in an act, may apply the definition of the term that is given in another act. Suppose the term *gender discrimination* is not defined in the state's fair housing act but is defined in the state's fair loan act. The fair loan act is not mandatory authority for questions involving the fair housing act because it does not govern housing. It can, however, be persuasive authority. The court may follow or be persuaded to apply the definition given in the fair loan act.

Primary authority represented by common/case law is often used as persuasive authority. Even though common/case law is primary authority, it may not be mandatory authority in a specific situation if it does not apply to govern the situation. A court, however, may be guided by and persuaded to adopt the rule or principle established in another court opinion.

> ***For Example:*** A legal issue has not been addressed by the courts in state *A*. Therefore, there is no mandatory authority that state *A* courts must follow. State *A* courts may consider and adopt the rules and reasoning of other federal or state courts that have addressed the issue. It is not mandatory that state *A* follow the primary authority of the other federal or state courts, but state *A* may be persuaded to adopt the primary authority of these courts.
>
> ***For Example:*** Neither the legislature nor courts of state *A* have adopted strict liability as a cause of action in tort. State *A's* highest court can look to and adopt the common law of another state that has adopted the tort.

> ***For Example:*** A trial court in state *A* has written an opinion on a legal issue. A higher court in state *A* is not bound by the lower court opinion (it is not mandatory authority), but it may consider and adopt the rule and reasoning of the lower court.

When there is no mandatory authority that a court is bound to follow, as in the preceding examples, the court may look to and rely on other primary authority as persuasive authority.

Secondary Authority as Persuasive Authority. As discussed earlier, secondary authority is not the law and, therefore, can never be mandatory authority. Where there is mandatory authority on an issue, it is not necessary to support it with secondary authority, although it is permissible. Secondary authority should not be relied upon when there is mandatory authority. In such situations, the mandatory authority governs. If there is no mandatory authority and there is persuasive primary authority, the secondary authority may be used in support of the primary authority.

> ***For Example:*** An issue has never been addressed by the courts of state *A*. The courts of state *B* have addressed the issue. The rule of law established by the state *B* courts can be persuasive primary authority for state *A* courts. Secondary sources, such as ALR commentaries, law review articles, and so on, may be submitted to a state *A* court in support of the persuasive primary authority from state *B*. Secondary authority also may be submitted to the court for the purpose of opposing the adoption of the persuasive authority from state *B*.

Secondary authority has its greatest value in situations where there is no primary authority, either mandatory or persuasive. This situation is rare, however. There are few matters that have never been addressed by either some legislature or court. As noted earlier, secondary authority is also valuable because it is useful in locating primary authority.

Some secondary authority is given greater weight or considered to have greater authoritative value than other secondary authority.

For Example: A court will more likely rely on and give greater weight to a *Restatement of the Law* drafted by experts in the field than to a law review article written by a local practitioner in the field.

Always locate the available primary authority and exhaust all avenues of research in this direction before turning to the location of secondary authority. There are two reasons for this:

1. Courts will look to and consider primary authority before considering secondary authority.
2. Primary authority will often lead to key secondary authority sources.

For Example: A court opinion addressing an issue may include references to key secondary sources, such as ALR citations.

For Example: State statutes are often annotated, and the annotations include references to ALR and legal encyclopedia citations that address the area of law covered in the statute. The annotations also include references to law review articles that address specific issues related to the statute.

KEY POINTS CHECKLIST: *Analyzing the Law*

- ❑ When analyzing a legal question or issue, always identify the primary authority (the law) that governs the question. Secondary authority should be considered after primary authority. As a general rule, courts will rely on primary authority before considering secondary authority.
- ❑ When you are searching for the law that governs a topic, always consider all the possible sources of law:
  1. Enacted law—constitutions, statutes, ordinances, regulations, and so on
  2. Common/case law
- ❑ Remember that there are two court systems operating in every jurisdiction, state and federal. A legal problem may be governed by either federal law or state law or both. Both sources of law and both court systems must be considered when analyzing a problem.
- ❑ Remember the hierarchy of primary authority. Constitutions are the highest authority, followed by other enacted law, then by common/case law. When there is a conflict between federal and state law, federal law governs.
- ❑ The doctrines of stare decisis and precedent provide that doctrines, rules, or principles established in earlier court decisions should be followed by later courts in the same court system when addressing similar issues and facts. Therefore, when researching a question, always look for and consider earlier cases that are on point. Chapter 8 presents in-depth coverage of case law analysis.
- ❑ Courts are required to follow mandatory authority, so therefore, always attempt to locate mandatory authority before searching for persuasive authority.
- ❑ Do not rely on persuasive authority if there is mandatory authority. No matter how strong the persuasive authority, the court will apply mandatory authority before persuasive authority. Secondary authority is never mandatory authority.

APPLICATION

Some of the principles discussed in this chapter are illustrated in the following example, which addresses the questions raised in the hypothetical presented at the beginning of the chapter.

Renee's research on the subject of gender discrimination identified the following authority that might apply to the issues raised in the client's case:

1. Title VII of the Civil Rights Act of 1964, which prohibits employment discrimination on the basis of gender
2. Section 59-9-4 of the state statutes, which prohibits employment discrimination on the basis of gender
3. *Erik v. Coll, Inc.,* a federal court case with facts almost identical to Ms. Stone's, which held that the conduct of the employer constituted gender discrimination in violation of Title VII
4. *Albert v. Conrad Supplies,* a state supreme court case with facts almost identical to those presented in Ms. Stone's case, which held that the employer's conduct violated the state statute
5. Two law review articles addressing gender discrimination that concluded that the type of conduct encountered by Ms. Stone constituted gender discrimination. One article addressed the question in the context of Title VII, and one article focused on the question in the context of the state statute.

Renee's assignment is to prepare a memo that includes a summary of her research and an analysis of how the law applies to the client's case. She realizes that she must organize and analyze her research before she can draft the memo. After reviewing the principles and concepts presented in this chapter, she proceeds with the following steps:

Step 1 Identify and separate primary authority and secondary authority. This is important because the court will rely on and consider primary authority before referring to secondary authority.

1. Primary authority:
   - Enacted law—title VII and section 59-9-4 of the state statutes
   - Common/case law—*Erik v. Coll, Inc.* and *Albert v. Conrad Supplies*
2. Secondary authority: the two law review articles

Step 2 Organize the presentation of the primary authority. Since the highest authority in the hierarchy of primary authority is the enacted law, followed by the case law, Renee organizes her summary of the law with a presentation of the enacted law first. (She did not locate applicable constitutional law.)

1. *Enacted Law.* In regard to the enacted law, Renee determines which law applies to govern the situation. It is possible that both the state and federal laws apply and that a potential cause of action exists in both federal and state court. It is also possible that the federal law requires that the state remedies be exhausted before a claim in federal court can be pursued. This means that the federal law requires that any remedy available under state law must be completely pursued before a claim can be brought under federal law. It is possible that the federal act does not apply to the specific legal question raised by the facts of the dispute, or the federal act may apply exclusively and there may be no possible cause of action under the state law. All of these possibilities must be considered when she analyzes the enacted law.

Once Renee concludes this part of the analysis, she must identify the elements or requirements of the law or laws that do apply. She then applies the elements to the facts of the client's case to determine how the laws apply and what remedies are available. In her memo, she will include a summary of the law and her analysis. Chapter 3 provides guidelines to follow when analyzing enacted law.

2. *Case Law.* Renee next addresses the relevant case law. She first determines whether the cases are on point. A case is on point if there is a sufficient similarity between the key facts and legal issue addressed in the court opinion and the client's case for the court opinion to apply as precedent. If a case is on point, it provides the court guidance when resolving a legal question or issue.

   If the enacted law is clear and there is no question about how the enacted law applies to the facts of the client's case, there is usually no need to refer to case law.

   For Example: A client is ticketed for driving 90 mph in a 60 mph zone. The statute establishing the speed limit at 60 mph is clear, and there is no need for case law to interpret the statute. A speed of 90 mph is clearly in violation of the statute.

   Even if there appears to be no question about how the statute applies, be sure to check the case law for possible interpretations of the statute.

   If Renee concludes that federal law exclusively governs the area, the state case, *Albert v. Conrad Supplies,* does not apply. If she concludes that only state law applies, the federal case does not apply.

   Once Renee has analyzed the case law, she includes in the memo a summary of her case analysis, discussing whether each case applies and how. Chapter 8 presents the steps involved in determining if a case is on point and the case analysis process.

Step 3 Organize the presentation of the secondary authority. The secondary authority is summarized last in the memo because it has the least authoritative value. In the client's case, there is primary authority, so the secondary authority will be used, if at all, in support or opposition to arguments based on the primary authority. Renee includes a summary of each law review article, emphasizing those aspects of the articles that focus on questions and issues similar to those in the client's case. Even if the articles are not going to be used in court as secondary authority, a summary is included in the memo because it may provide Renee's supervising attorney with information that proves helpful in the case.

Renee's understanding of the primary and secondary sources of law, and the hierarchy of the sources, serves as an essential aid in her organization of the research, analysis of the issues, and preparation of the memo. Chapters 10, 11, 12, and 13 provide useful information concerning the actual preparation of legal memoranda.

SUMMARY

The process of legal analysis and legal writing requires a determination of what law applies to a legal question and how it applies. In order to engage in the process, a paralegal must have an understanding of the law and the basic doctrines and principles that govern and guide the analysis of the law.

There are primarily two sources of law in the United States:

1. Enacted law
2. Common/case law

Enacted law, as used in this text, consists of constitutions, laws passed by legislative bodies, and regulations adopted by administrative bodies to aid in the enforcement and application of legislative mandates. Common/case law is composed of the law created by the courts in two situations:

1. When there is no law governing a topic
2. Through interpretation of enacted law where the meaning or application of the enacted law is unclear

There are two court systems in the United States: the federal court system and the state court system. Although there are differences in each system, they have basic similarities. Both systems have trial courts where matters are initially heard, trials held, and judgments rendered, and both have courts of appeals where the judgments of trial courts are reviewed and possible errors corrected.

In order to provide consistency and stability to the common/case law, two doctrines have evolved:

1. Precedent
2. Stare decisis

Precedent is an earlier court decision on an issue that applies to govern or guide a subsequent court in its determination of identical or similar issues based on identical or similar facts. The doctrine of stare decisis provides that a court must follow a previous decision of a higher court in the jurisdiction when the current decision involves issues and facts similar to those involved in the previous decision.

The two sources of law, enacted and common/case law, are called primary authority. Primary authority is the law itself. Any other authoritative source a court may rely on in reaching a decision is called secondary authority. Secondary authority is not the law but consists of authoritative sources that interpret, analyze, or compile the law, such as legal encyclopedias, treatises, annotations, and so on. Courts always rely on and look to primary authority first when resolving legal issues.

If primary authority governs the resolution of a legal question, it must be followed by the court. This type of primary authority is called mandatory authority. Secondary authority can never be mandatory authority. Any authority the court is not bound to follow but that it may follow or consider when reaching a decision is called persuasive authority. Both primary authority and secondary authority can be persuasive authority.

The application of the basic concepts and principles presented in this chapter are addressed in detail throughout the remaining chapters of this text. Each concept and principle plays a critical role in legal analysis and writing.

EXERCISES

ASSIGNMENT 1

Facts: The paralegal is analyzing a problem involving the sale of goods on credit in state *A*.

Authority: The following authority has been located concerning the problem:

1. State *A's* Uniform Commercial Code Act
2. State *A's* Consumer Credit Act
3. State *B's* Uniform Commercial Code Act
4. A federal statute—Consumer Credit Act
5. *Iron v. Supply Co.*—a decision of the highest court in state *A*
6. *Milk v. Best Buy, Inc.*—a decision of the highest court in state *B*
7. *Control Co. v. Martin*—a decision of an intermediary court of appeals in state *A*
8. *Lesley v. Karl Co.*—a decision of a trial court in state *A*
9. *Irene v. City Co.*—a federal case involving the federal Consumer Credit Act
10. Regulations adopted by state A's Corporation Commission that apply to consumer credit and the sale of goods
11. *Restatements of the Law* defining sales, consumer credit, and other terms related to the problem
12. An ALR reference that directly addresses the issues in the case

Assume that all the cases are on point, *i.e.,* they are sufficiently similar to the facts and issues involved in the problem to apply as precedent.

Questions:

A. Which authority is primary authority, and which is secondary authority?
B. Which authority can be mandatory authority, and why? What would be required for any of the sources to be mandatory authority?
C. Which authority can be persuasive authority? Why?
D. Assuming that all the primary authority applies to the issues raised by the facts of the client's case, list the authority in the hierarchial order of its value as precedent, *i.e.,* authority with greatest authoritative value will be listed first, followed by other authority in the order it will be looked to by the court.

ASSIGNMENT 2

Facts: Your client is the plaintiff in a workers' compensation case. She was injured in 1993 in state *A*. In 1995, her employer destroyed all the business records relating to the client. The destruction of the records was apparently accidental, not intentional. They were destroyed, however, while the client's workers' compensation claim was pending.

Authority: You have located the following authority, all of which is directly related to the issues raised by the facts of the client's case:

1. *Idle v. City Co.*—a 1980 decision by the highest court of state *A* where the court created a cause of action in tort for the wrongful destruction of business records. The court ruled that a cause of action exists if the records were destroyed in anticipation of or while a workers' compensation claim was pending. The court also held that a cause of action exists if the destruction was intentional or negligent.
2. A 1989 state *A* statute—a law passed by the legislature of state *A* that created a cause of action in tort for the intentional destruction of business records. The statute provides that a cause of action exists if the destruction occurs in anticipation of or while a workers' compensation claim is pending.
3. *Merrick v. Taylor*—a 1990 decision of the court of appeals of state *A*. The court of appeals is a lower court than the state's highest court. The court held that *intentional,* within the meaning of the 1989 statute, includes either the intentional destruction of records or the destruction of records as a result of gross negligence.
4. *Davees v. Contractor*—a decision of the highest court of state *B* interpreting a state *B* statute identical to the 1989 state *A* statute. The court held that *intentional,* as used in the statute, includes gross negligence only when the gross negligence is accompanied by a "reckless and wanton" disregard for the preservation of the business records.
5. A 1991 federal statute—the statute is identical to the 1989 state statute but applies only to contractors with federal contracts.
6. An ALR reference—that addresses specific questions similar to those raised in the client's case.

Questions:

A. Which authority is primary authority, and which is secondary authority? Why?
B. Which authority can be mandatory authority, and why? What would be required for any of the sources to be mandatory authority?
C. Which authority can be persuasive authority? Why?
D. Can *Idle v. City Co*. be authority at all? Why or why not?
E. If *Idle v. City Co*. is authority, to what extent?
F. Discuss the impact of *Merrick v. Taylor* in regard to the 1989 state *A* statute.
G. Discuss the authoritative value of *Davees v. Contractor.*
H. Assuming that all the primary authority applies to the issues raised by the facts of the client's case, list the authority in the hierarchial order of its value as precedent, *i.e.,* authority with greatest authoritative value will be listed first, followed by other authority in the order it will be looked to and relied on by the court.

CHAPTER 2

Introduction to Legal Analysis

Marian has worked as Robert Walker's paralegal for the past two years. She conducts initial client interviews, manages the case files, and performs basic research. Robert, a solo practitioner, always determines the merits of a case and performs the substantive research.

Robert called Marian into his office one morning. "Marian," he said, "I'm going to hire another paralegal to do your assignments." Marian wondered, "What have I done wrong?" Robert continued, "I want you to take over some of the more substantive legal work. I want you to start performing the legal analysis of some of the new cases and determine what, if any, possible causes of action exist. Your new responsibilities will be to study the cases and provide me with memoranda of law identifying the legal issues and analyzing how the law applies to the issues. This will free me to concentrate more on trial work. Start with Mr. Lietel's case."

Marian remembered the initial interview with Mr. Lietel. Jerry Lietel has a hot temper. He got into an argument with his neighbor, Tom Spear. Mr. Leitel's temper got the best of him. He punched Tom, and a fight ensued. Steve Spear, the father of Tom and a retired deputy sheriff, came out of the house and announced that he was placing Mr. Lietel under citizen's arrest. After a short struggle, Mr. Lietel was subdued and handcuffed. After Mr. Lietel was handcuffed and had ceased resisting, Steve Spear kicked him about six times, cracking one of his ribs. Mr. Leitel incurred medical bills and lost two days of work. Since the incident, Mr. Lietel has had a lot of trouble sleeping, and he is taking sleeping pills on his doctor's advice. He is fearful of Steve Spear whenever he sees him.

Jerry admits that he punched Tom without provocation and that the citizen's arrest was probably justified, but he wants to sue for his medical bills and the loss of work.

Marian realizes that this is her first analysis assignment, and whether she continues to be assigned this type of substantive legal work will depend on the quality of her product. She asks herself, "What's the best way to approach a legal problem? What is a systematic way to analyze a client's problem that will produce the best result in the least amount of time?" The analysis of Mr. Lietel's case and the answers to Marian's questions are presented in the Application section of this chapter.

INTRODUCTION

As discussed in the preface, the focus of this text is on the process of analyzing the legal questions raised by the facts of a client's case, the process of communicating that analysis in written form, and legal writing in general. This chapter presents an overview of the process of legal analysis and some concepts and considerations involved in that process.

Most cases begin like the Lietel case. A client relays a set of factual events that the client perceives entitle the client to legal relief. The client seeks a solution to what the client believes is a legal problem. The problem may be as simple as the need for a power of attorney or as complex as a question involving multiple parties and several legal issues. The problem may be one for which there is no legal remedy, or it may not be a legal problem at all.

For Example: An individual is fired in retaliation for disclosing a defect in the employer's product. The state where this occurs does not have a statute prohibiting retaliatory discharge, nor have the state courts adopted a cause of action in tort for retaliatory discharge. Therefore, it may be that no legal remedy for this type of discharge is available under state law. It is possible that the client's only recourse is political, that is, the client may be required to attempt to get legislation passed prohibiting retaliatory discharge or to exert social pressure through the media.

The object of legal analysis and legal research is to analyze the factual event presented by the client and determine:

1. What is the legal issue (question) or issues raised by the factual event
2. What law governs the legal issue
3. How the law that governs the legal issue applies to the factual event, including what, if any, legal remedy is available.

Once this is accomplished, the client can be advised of the various rights, duties, and options available.

LEGAL ANALYSIS DEFINED

Before addressing the steps involved in the legal analysis process, it is necessary to understand what is meant by *legal analysis.* The term has different meanings, depending on the context of its usage—*i.e.,* the type of legal analysis being performed.

For Example: The term *legal analysis* can refer to statutory analysis (discussed in Chapter 3), case law analysis (Chapter 8), counteranalysis (Chapter 9), and so on.

legal analysis
The process of identifying the issue or issues presented by a client's facts and determining what law applies and how it applies. The process of applying the law to the facts of a case. It is an exploration of how and why a specific law does or does not apply.

In this chapter, *legal analysis* is used in a broad sense to refer to the process of identifying the issue or issues presented by a client's facts and determining what law applies and how it applies. Simply put, legal analysis is the process of applying the law to the facts of the client's case. It is an exploration of how and why a specific law does or does not apply.

LEGAL ANALYSIS PROCESS

The approach to legal analysis that is commonly used involves a four-step process:

Step 1 *Issue.* The identification of the issue (legal question) or issues raised by the facts of the client's case
Step 2 *Rule.* The identification of the law that governs the issue

Step 3 *Analysis/Application.* A determination of how the rule of law applies to the issue
Step 4 *Conclusion.* A summary of the results of the legal analysis

An acronym commonly used in reference to the analytical process is **IRAC.** It is composed of the first letter of the descriptive term for each step of the legal analysis process. The use of the acronym is an easy way to remember the four-step legal analysis process—issue, rule, analysis/application, and conclusion.

IRAC

An acronym commonly used in reference to the legal analysis process. It is composed of the first letter of the descriptive term for each step of the process--Issue, Rule, Analysis/Application, Conclusion. The standard legal analysis process is the identification of the issue, followed by the presentation of the governing rule of law, the analysis/application of the rule of law, and the conclusion.

Each of these steps is addressed in detail in subsequent sections of this chapter. But before the legal analysis of a case can properly begin, some preliminary preparation must take place:

1. All the facts and information relevant to the case should be gathered, and
2. Preliminary legal research should be conducted to gain a basic familiarity with the area of law involved in the case.

Facts

It is important to keep in mind the crucial role the facts play in the analytical process. The four steps of the analysis process involve the facts of the client's case, and the facts play a major role in each step:

1. *Issue.* Included in the issue are the key facts. The issue is the precise question raised by the *specific facts* of the client's case. A properly stated issue requires inclusion of the key facts. This is discussed in detail in Chapters 6 and 7.

   For Example: Under the provisions of the state battery law is a battery committed by an individual, *present at the scene of a battery, who encourages others to commit the battery but does not actively participate in the actual battering of the victim.* The key facts of this issue are italicized.

2. *Rule.* The determination of which law governs the issue is based on the applicability of the law to the facts of the client's case.

   For Example: If the issue involves oppressive acts by a majority shareholder against the interests of minority shareholders in a closely held corporation, a determination of which corporation statutes apply is governed by the facts. Only those statutes that address acts by majority shareholders can apply. In most states, this is limited to a few statutes.

3. *Analysis/Application.* The analysis/application step is the process of *applying the rule of law to the facts.* It obviously cannot take place without the facts. Without the facts, the law stands in a vacuum.

   For Example: Assume a very simple problem where the client was ticketed for driving 65 mph in a 55 mph zone. The client believes that the speed limit was actually 65 mph and that the officer made a mistake. A determination of whether the client violated the law requires the application of the rule of law to the facts of the client's case. Was the speed limit where the ticket was given 65 mph or 55 mph? *The facts are essential* to the process. Without the facts, a determination of how the law applies cannot be made.

4. *Conclusion.* The conclusion is a summation of how the law applies to the facts, a recap of the first three steps. It requires the facts.

In every case, the analytical process involves a determination of how the law applies to the facts. In court opinions, courts determine how the law applies to the facts presented to the court. Very often students pay too little attention to the facts, focusing on what the law is and what it requires. They ignore the important role the facts play.

In a sense, cases are fact driven—the outcome of the case is determined by the facts. Often, if a single fact is changed, the outcome is different. The application of the law results in a different conclusion.

For Example: In a murder case, the degree of the offense can depend upon a single fact. First-degree murder requires specific intent. It requires not only that the defendant intended to shoot the victim but also that the defendant intended the shooting to kill the victim. If the facts of the case show that the defendant intended to shoot but not kill the victim, the offense is not first-degree murder. The defendant's intent is a fact, and changing this single fact changes the outcome of the case. The application of the law results in a different conclusion. The offense is not first-degree murder but a lesser offense.

With this in mind, the analysis process should begin with a consideration of the facts of the client's case. The facts should be identified and reviewed at the outset. This preliminary step should include the following:

1. Be sure you have all the facts. Ask yourself if you have all the interviews, files, statements, and other information that have been gathered concerning the case. Are the files complete? Are facts or information missing? As discussed in the murder case example, a single fact can determine the outcome of a case. If key facts are missing, your analysis may result in an erroneous legal conclusion.
2. Study the available facts to see if additional information should be gathered before legal analysis can properly begin.
3. Organize the facts. Group all related facts. Place the facts in a logical order, such as chronological order.
4. Weigh the facts. The value of some factual information, such as hearsay, may be questionable.
5. Identify the key facts. Determine which facts appear to be critical to the outcome of the case. Chapter 5 discusses the importance of key facts and the process for identifying key facts.

Preliminary Research

Before the analysis process can begin, it may be necessary to conduct some basic research in the area(s) of law that govern the issue or issues in the case. You may be unfamiliar with the area of law in general or with the specific aspect of the area that applies in the client's case. Unless you have recently worked on a case involving the same or a similar issue, it is best to obtain a basic familiarity with the area of law involved in the case. A general overview may be obtained from reference to a legal encyclopedia or a single-volume treatise. If the specific question or area is known at the outset, an ALR reference or a multivolume treatise may be appropriate.

IRAC Analysis

Once the facts have been gathered and reviewed, the four steps of the IRAC legal analysis process should be followed (see Figure 2–1). The following are important considerations to keep in mind when performing these steps.

Step 1 Issue

Identify the issue (legal question) or issues raised by the facts of the client's case. The issue is the precise legal question raised by the facts of the dispute. The identification of the issue is the first and probably most important step in the analytical process. You must

Step 1	*Issue.* Identify the issue (legal question) or issues raised by the facts of the client's case.
Step 2	*Rule.* Identify the law that governs the issue.
Step 2	*Analysis/Application.* Determine how the rule of law applies to the issue.
Step 4	*Conclusion.* Summarize the results of the legal analysis.

Figure 2-1

Steps in the IRAC Legal Analysis Process

identify the problem before you can solve it. The issue is the starting point. If it is misidentified, each subsequent step in the process is a step in the wrong direction. Time is wasted, and malpractice may result.

For Example: A client complains that the individual who sold and installed the tile in his bathroom installed it in a defective manner. After a few months, the tile began to fall off the wall. The person who installed the tile gave no oral warranty covering the quality of the installation, and there were no written warranties provided concerning the quality of the installation or the quality of the tile.

The paralegal assumes, without conducting research, that the entire transaction is a sale of goods covered by state statutes governing the sale of goods. The paralegal makes this assumption because the transaction involved the sale of goods, the tiles. Under the sale of goods statutes, there is a section that creates an implied warranty that goods are merchantable when sold, which in this case means the tiles will not fall apart.

The statute as interpreted by the state courts, however, does not apply to the service portion of such transactions, which, in the client's case, is the installation of the tile. Based on an incorrect assumption, the paralegal identifies the issue as a question of whether the implied warranty of merchantability was breached. The identification of the issue is incorrect because of the erroneous assumption. The question is not about the quality of the tile but about the quality of the installation. Research on the existence of an implied warranty of merchantability is misdirected.

The case may be lost because the issue is incorrectly identified. The laws governing the sale of a service are different from those governing the sale of goods. A lawsuit claiming breach of an implied warranty of merchantability will probably not prevail because the implied warranty of merchantability statute does not apply.

The client does not pay to have the wrong question answered. The subjects of issue identification and presentation are of such importance that Chapters 6 and 7 are devoted to them. Although in-depth coverage of these topics is presented in Chapters 6 and 7, some important considerations involving issues are discussed briefly here.

1. *Multiple Issues.* The client's fact situation may raise multiple legal issues and involve many avenues of relief. The implied warranty example presented above involves one issue, but there may be several issues in a case.

 For Example: Suppose Mr. Elvan rear-ended the client's car at a stoplight. After the impact, Mr. Elvan exited his car, approached the client's car, and started yelling at the client, threatening to hit the client. He grabbed the client's arm but never struck him. As a result of the incident, the client's car is damaged. The client suffered whiplash from the collision and a bruise on his arm from being grabbed, and since the wreck, he has been upset and had trouble sleeping.

 The client may have several causes of action against Mr. Elvan: a claim of negligence arising from the rear-end collision, civil assault for his conduct of approaching the client in a threatening manner, battery for grabbing the client, and intentional infliction of emotional distress for his conduct after the collision. Each of these potential causes of action may raise legal issues or questions that must be addressed. This example is referred to in this chapter as the rear-end collision example.

 You should be aware of and keep in mind that one set of facts may raise multiple issues and include multiple causes of action.

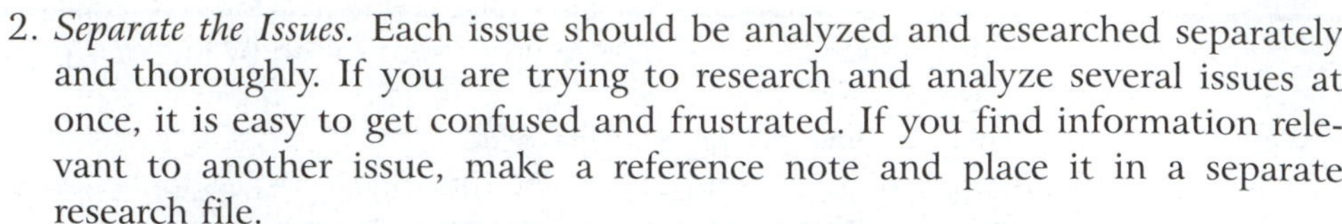

2. *Separate the Issues.* Each issue should be analyzed and researched separately and thoroughly. If you are trying to research and analyze several issues at once, it is easy to get confused and frustrated. If you find information relevant to another issue, make a reference note and place it in a separate research file.
3. *Focus on the Issues of the Case.* Keep your focus on the issues raised by the facts of the client's case or on those issues that you have been assigned to research.

   For Example: In the rear-end collision example, assume that there was a passenger in the vehicle with the client and that the passenger is represented by another law firm. Although there may be many interesting issues involving potential legal claims available to the passenger, the passenger is not the client. The focus should be on the issues in the client's case. The issues involving the passenger are outside the scope of the problem and should not be allowed to become a distraction.

   For Example: Suppose in the rear-end collision example, you are assigned to research the assault issue. Do not research the other issues or clutter your analysis with issues you were not assigned to address. Stick to the assignment. If you come across useful information that is relevant to another issue, note it and give it to the person assigned to address that issue.

   Avoid getting sidetracked and wasting time on interesting aspects or issues of a case you were not assigned to address.

Step 2 Rule

Identify the law that governs the issue. The next step in the IRAC analytical process is the identification of the rule of law that governs the issue. Ask yourself, "What rule of law applies to the question raised by the facts of the case?" This may be enacted law or common/case law.

1. *Enacted Law.* The legal issue may be governed by enacted law. As defined in Chapter 1, enacted law encompasses constitutions, statutes, ordinances, and regulations.

   For Example: Most of the criminal law is governed by enacted law—laws passed by legislative bodies. In the rear-end collision example, the driver of the car who rear-ended the car at the light may be cited for following too closely and careless driving. These may be criminal offenses established by the state legislature when it passed the state's motor vehicle code. Chapter 3 addresses the analysis of issues governed by enacted law.

2. *Common/Case Law.* The issue may be governed by rules or principles established by the courts.

   For Example: In the rear-end collision example, the possible civil causes of action for negligence, battery, assault, and intentional infliction of emotional distress are tort claims. Most tort claims are based upon the common law, which is composed of rules and principles developed over a period of time by the courts.

   Case law and case briefing are discussed in detail in Chapters 4 and 8.
3. *Combination of Enacted Law and Common/Case Law.* In many instances, the rule of law governing a situation requires both enacted law and common/case law.

   For Example: Although freedom of speech is guaranteed by the First Amendment of the United States Constitution, you may have to refer to court decisions to determine which types of speech are protected under the amendment. The provisions of the First Amendment do not indicate whether symbolic acts, such as burning the American flag, are protected as free speech. The decisions of the United States Supreme Court have addressed this question, and the law governing the question of flag-burning includes both the First Amendment and the rules and principles adopted by the courts interpreting the amendment.

This step should also include the identification of all additional case law that may be required to interpret the terms of the statute or act, including the case law that may assist or act as guidance in determining how the law applies to the issue being addressed. Be sure your research is complete. Always conduct thorough research, and be sure to search for other court decisions that address the rule of law that governs the question.

Step 3 Analysis/Application

Determine how the rule of law applies to the issue. Once the rule of law is located, it must be analyzed to determine how it applies to the facts of the client's case. In other words, apply the law to the legal issue. This is a three-part process (see Figure 2–2).

An in-depth discussion of this step in regard to statutory law and case law is presented in Chapters 3 and 8, respectively. The role of the key facts is addressed in Chapter 5. Counteranalysis is discussed in Chapter 9. Therefore, only a brief summary of this step is included here.

Part 1 Identify the component parts (elements) of the rule of law. To determine how a rule of law applies to a fact situation, certain conditions established by the rule must be met. These conditions or component parts are called the elements. The requirements of the rule of law must be identified before the rule can be applied to the issue raised by the facts of the client's case.

For Example: Section 93-85A of the state statute governing the execution of a will provides: "The execution of a will must be by the signature of the testator and of at least two witnesses as follows:

1. The testator, in the presence of two or more witnesses:
   a. signifies to the witnesses that the instrument is the testator's will, and
   b. signs the will or has someone else sign the testator's name at the testator's specific direction.
2. The attesting witnesses must sign in the presence of the testator and each other."

In order to determine how the statute applies to a client's facts, the elements of the statute must first be identified. The elements of the statute are:

1. The testator must indicate to two or more witnesses that the instrument is the testator's will,
2. The testator must sign the will or have someone sign it at the testator's specific direction,
3. The witnesses must sign, and
4. Steps 1 through 3 must be done in the presence of the witnesses and the testator.

This example is referred to in this chapter as the wills example.

Part 2 Apply the facts of the client's case to the component parts. Once the elements of the rule of law have been identified, the facts of the client's case must be matched or applied to the elements and a determination made how the rule applies.

Part 1	Identify the component parts (elements) of the rule of law.
Part 2	Apply the facts of the client's case to the component parts.
Part 3	Consider the possible counterarguments to the analysis of the issue, i.e., conduct a counteranalysis of the analysis.

Figure 2-2
Three Parts of Step 3—Analysis/Application

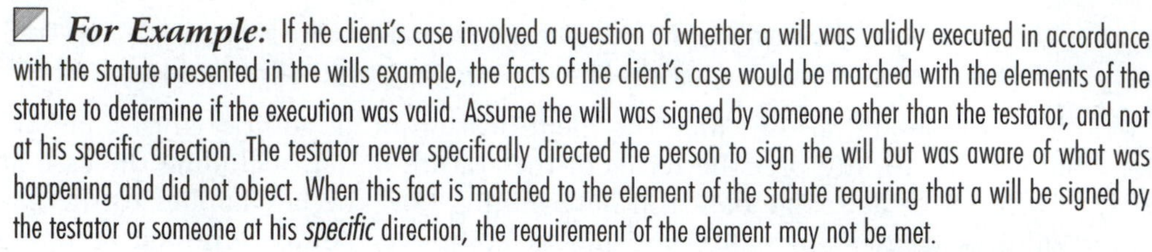

For Example: If the client's case involved a question of whether a will was validly executed in accordance with the statute presented in the wills example, the facts of the client's case would be matched with the elements of the statute to determine if the execution was valid. Assume the will was signed by someone other than the testator, and not at his specific direction. The testator never specifically directed the person to sign the will but was aware of what was happening and did not object. When this fact is matched to the element of the statute requiring that a will be signed by the testator or someone at his *specific* direction, the requirement of the element may not be met.

Once facts of the client's case have been matched to the elements of the rule of law, a determination may be reached regarding how the rule applies in the client's case.

For Example: In the preceding example, a conclusion could be reached that the element allowing a signature by "someone else" at the testator's specific direction was not met. Although the testator was present, he did not specifically direct the other person to sign the will. It could also be concluded that additional research is necessary to determine how the courts have interpreted "specific direction" as used in the statute.

In some cases, the manner in which the rule applies is clear from the face of the rule, and there is no question how the rule applies. All that is required is the application of the facts to the elements of the rule of law to determine how the law applies in the case.

For Example: An eighteen-year-old client wants to know if she is eligible to run for the position of probate judge. Section 34-214 of the election code provides that the minimum age for candidates for the position of probate judge is twenty-one years. It is clear from section 34-214 that the client is not eligible to run.

In many cases, it is not clear from the rule of law how an element applies in a specific fact situation. In such instances, it may be necessary to refer to court opinion where the court, in a similar fact situation, interpreted how the law applies.

For Example: Suppose the rule of law defines slander as the "publication of a false statement of fact concerning the plaintiff that causes damages." In the client's case, the client's neighbor orally communicated to another neighbor a false statement of fact concerning the client. While visiting her neighbor's house, she falsely stated that the client was a thief. The statement damaged the client.

The answer to the question of whether an oral communication to one person constitutes "publication" within the meaning of the statute is not clear from a mere reading of the statute. Reference must be made to case law to determine how the courts have interpreted the term *publication*. The courts' interpretation of the term must then be applied to the client's case. If the courts have defined *publication* as communication to any third person, the communication to the neighbor is slander.

This example is referred to in this chapter as the slander example.

Part 3 Consider the possible counterarguments to the analysis of the issue, i.e., conduct a counteranalysis of the analysis. Once the analysis and application of the rule of law has been completed, any potential counterarguments to the analysis or application should be considered. This involves the anticipation and consideration of any argument an opponent is likely to raise in response to the analysis.

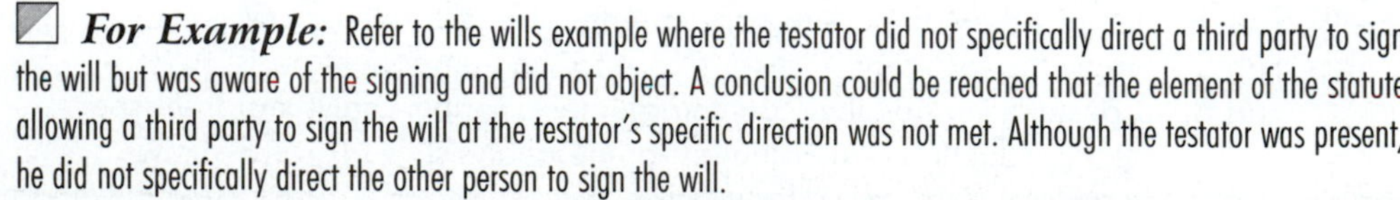

For Example: Refer to the wills example where the testator did not specifically direct a third party to sign the will but was aware of the signing and did not object. A conclusion could be reached that the element of the statute allowing a third party to sign the will at the testator's specific direction was not met. Although the testator was present, he did not specifically direct the other person to sign the will.

A counterargument could be made that this element of the statute is met because the equivalent of "specific direction" took place. The testator was aware that the third person was signing on his behalf and did not object. The failure to object is evidence that the signing took place at his specific direction.

Research should be undertaken to determine if this counterargument has support in the case law. The counterargument should be considered and addressed in this step of the analysis process.

Counteranalysis is addressed in detail in Chapter 9.

Step 4 Conclusion

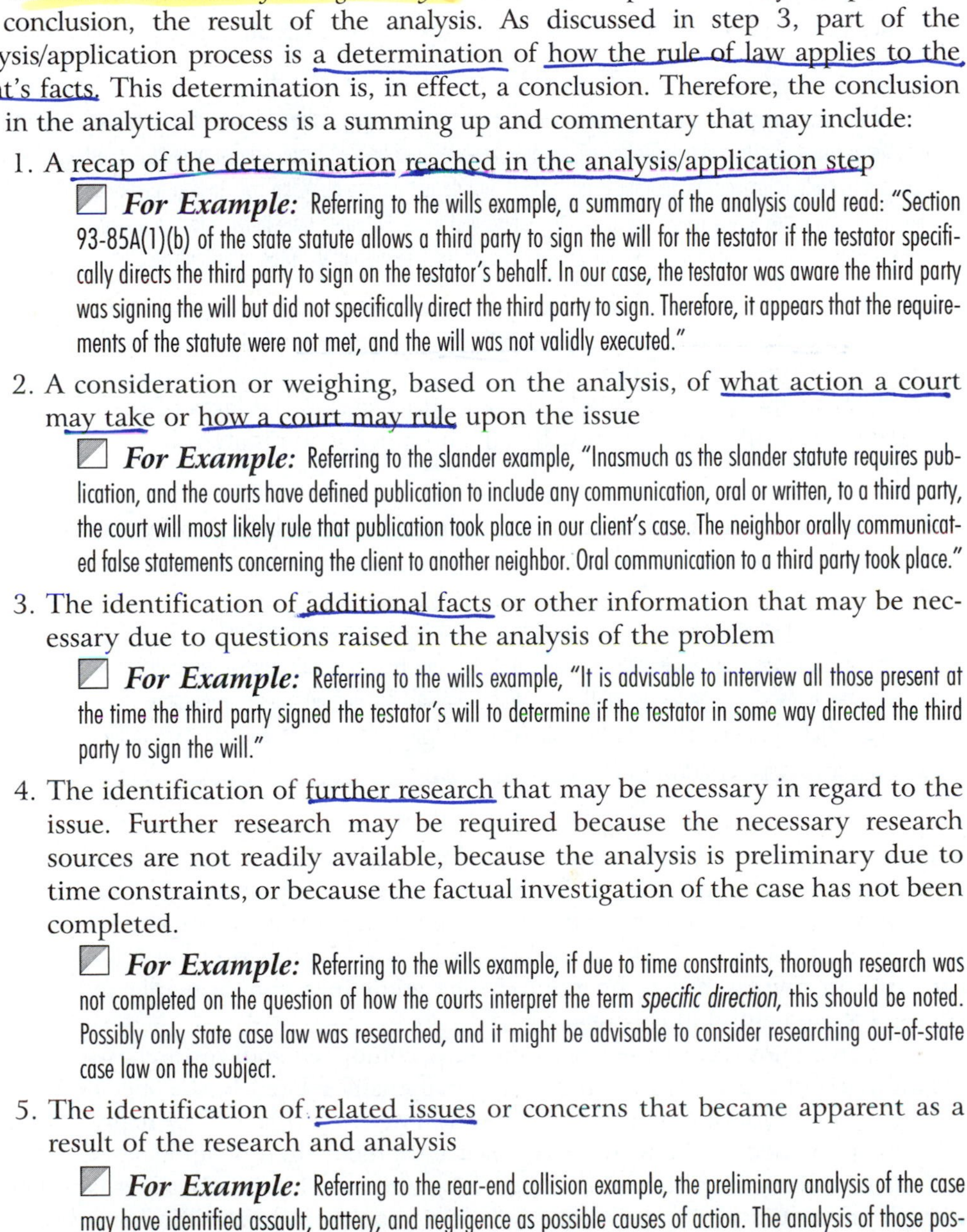

Summarize the results of the legal analysis. The final step in the analytical process is the conclusion, the result of the analysis. As discussed in step 3, part of the analysis/application process is a determination of how the rule of law applies to the client's facts. This determination is, in effect, a conclusion. Therefore, the conclusion step in the analytical process is a summing up and commentary that may include:

1. A recap of the determination reached in the analysis/application step

   For Example: Referring to the wills example, a summary of the analysis could read: "Section 93-85A(1)(b) of the state statute allows a third party to sign the will for the testator if the testator specifically directs the third party to sign on the testator's behalf. In our case, the testator was aware the third party was signing the will but did not specifically direct the third party to sign. Therefore, it appears that the requirements of the statute were not met, and the will was not validly executed."

2. A consideration or weighing, based on the analysis, of what action a court may take or how a court may rule upon the issue

   For Example: Referring to the slander example, "Inasmuch as the slander statute requires publication, and the courts have defined publication to include any communication, oral or written, to a third party, the court will most likely rule that publication took place in our client's case. The neighbor orally communicated false statements concerning the client to another neighbor. Oral communication to a third party took place."

3. The identification of additional facts or other information that may be necessary due to questions raised in the analysis of the problem

   For Example: Referring to the wills example, "It is advisable to interview all those present at the time the third party signed the testator's will to determine if the testator in some way directed the third party to sign the will."

4. The identification of further research that may be necessary in regard to the issue. Further research may be required because the necessary research sources are not readily available, because the analysis is preliminary due to time constraints, or because the factual investigation of the case has not been completed.

   For Example: Referring to the wills example, if due to time constraints, thorough research was not completed on the question of how the courts interpret the term *specific direction*, this should be noted. Possibly only state case law was researched, and it might be advisable to consider researching out-of-state case law on the subject.

5. The identification of related issues or concerns that became apparent as a result of the research and analysis

   For Example: Referring to the rear-end collision example, the preliminary analysis of the case may have identified assault, battery, and negligence as possible causes of action. The analysis of those possible causes of action may reveal the possibility of an additional cause of action for intentional infliction of emotional distress. This should be noted in the conclusion.

GENERAL CONSIDERATIONS

The process of analyzing a legal problem can at times be difficult, especially for a beginner. In addition to the steps addressed in the previous section, the following general considerations and guidelines will prove helpful when analyzing a legal issue.

Focus

Keeping focused is critical when performing the steps of the analytical process. Keeping focused has several meanings, depending on what part of the process is being performed.

At the broadest level, it means to keep focused on the specific task assigned. Analyze only the issue or issues assigned.

For Example: Referring to the rear-end collision example, if the assignment is to analyze the question of whether a cause of action is present for civil assault, keep focused on that issue. Answer only that question. If you come across information relevant to another issue, note it, but do not pursue it. When you have a break or at the end of the day, give your notes to the person assigned to analyze that issue. Valuable time may be lost in researching and analyzing the other issue or in interrupting your work to discuss the information with the other person.

When identifying the issue, keep focused on the facts of the client's case. Ask yourself, what must be decided about which of the facts of the client's case? Chapter 6 addresses issue identification and focus.

When identifying the rule of law, keep focused on the facts of the case and the elements of the rule of law. This will help you quickly eliminate rules of law that may not apply.

For Example: Assume the fact situation involves a credit purchase by the client. There may be several rules of law that govern the transaction, such as the state's usury laws, the state sale of goods statutes, and the federal truth-in-lending laws.

Assume the interest charged in the transaction in question was one percent and the usury statute provides that interest rates in excess of twenty percent are void. If this fact is kept in mind when locating the possible laws that apply to the transaction, the usury statute can be immediately eliminated from consideration. The interest charged does not violate the usury statute, and the statute clearly does not apply. It does not have to be considered when analyzing the problem in step 3.

When analyzing and applying the rule of law in step 3, keep focused on the client's facts and the issue or question being analyzed. It is easy to get sidetracked, especially when reading case law. There may be interesting issues addressed in a court opinion that are close but not directly related to the issues in the client's case. Stay focused. Ask yourself, "Is the issue being addressed in this opinion really related to the issue in my case? Is it on point?" The guidelines and principles addressed in Chapter 8 are helpful in this regard.

If you do not stay focused, after you have completed your research, you may have several cases in front of you that are only marginally related to the specific issue you are analyzing. A lot of time can be wasted reading cases that are not really on point.

Keep focused on the work. Avoidance and procrastination are deadly. When you are stuck or having a difficult time analyzing or researching an issue, it is sometimes easy to procrastinate, to avoid working on the problem. You may find excuses for not working on the problem, such as working on an easier project. The way to overcome this is to *start.* Do not put it off. If you are at the research stage, *start researching*. If you are at the writing stage, *start writing*. Do not be discouraged if the results seem poor at first. Focus on the problem and begin. Often the barrier is beginning.

Intellectual Honesty

In the context of legal analysis, intellectual honesty means to research and analyze a problem objectively. Do not let emotions, preconceived notions, personal views, or stubbornness interfere with an objective analysis of the client's case. Do not assume you know the law. Check your resources. Because you "feel" a certain outcome should occur, do not let that feeling prevent you from objectively researching and analyzing the issue.

intellectual honesty
In the context of legal analysis, intellectual honesty means to research and analyze a problem objectively. This includes analyzing all aspects of a problem free of preconceived notions, personal views, and emotions.

For Example: Suppose the paralegal has a personal history of domestic violence. When he was a child, there was domestic violence in the home. He has a strong aversion to domestic violence and harbors a prejudice against perpetrators of domestic violence. The paralegal interviews a client who complains that, the night before the interview, her husband hit her in the face with his fist. She states that he has beaten her frequently and savagely throughout their ten-year marriage. The client appears to have been severely beaten. She has two black eyes, and her face is swollen around the eyes.

The paralegal is outraged and upset by what happened to the client. As a result of his outrage, he fails to conduct a thorough and objective interview. He does not ask questions to elicit the details of the events of the previous night. He assumes the battery was unprovoked and does not ask questions concerning the reasons the client's husband hit her. His emotions and personal feelings cause him to focus on punishing the husband.

The paralegal knows that in addition to the remedies available under the criminal law, there is also a civil cause of action for domestic battery available under the state's recently passed domestic violence statute. He recommends to the supervising attorney the filing of a civil complaint for domestic battery under the domestic violence statute. Relying on the paralegal's record for thoroughness, the supervisory attorney directs that a complaint be drafted and filed. A few weeks later, the husband's counsel, a friend of the supervising attorney, calls concerning the case. "Why did you file this complaint?" she asks. "My client was acting in self-defense. He hit his wife after she stabbed him." As it turns out, the client decided to kill her husband rather than face a future of beatings. She took a kitchen knife and stabbed him in the chest. In self-defense, he hit her once, and the blow caught her between the eyes, causing the two black eyes and facial swelling.

Had the paralegal not lost his objectivity, he would have conducted a thorough interview. Probing questions concerning the events of the night in question would have revealed the true facts, and the lawsuit may not have been filed.

This is an extreme example, but it occurs in varying degrees. Personal prejudices, personal beliefs, or sympathy for the client can combine to affect objectivity, which may lead to a failure to conduct an objective, critical analysis of the case, to not vigorously pursue potential opposing arguments, or to discount opposing authority.

Remember, the client may not be telling the whole truth. This may not be intentional. It may be the result of forgetfulness or a personal tendency to discount or downplay the importance of adverse facts. In this example, the client may have been so focused upon the years of abuse, and the desire to escape from further abuse, that she truly considered the stabbing insignificant when weighed against what she had gone through.

The analysis of all legal issues should be pursued with intellectual honesty. All the facts affecting the case must be identified. All legal authority concerning the issues should be pursued, including any authority that may negatively affect the client's position. Ignoring adverse authority will not make it go away. It must be addressed. The importance of counterargument and counteranalysis are discussed in detail in Chapter 9.

KEY POINTS CHECKLIST: *Conducting Analysis*

- ❑ Always pay attention to the facts. Keep them in mind when performing each step of the analytical process. The analysis process involves determining how the law applies to the *facts.* Make sure you have all the facts at the outset.
- ❑ Before beginning the IRAC process, perform preliminary research to obtain a familiarity with the area of law involved in the case.
- ❑ Remember IRAC. An easy way to remember the legal analysis process and what to look for when reading a court opinion is to remember the acronym IRAC.
- ❑ When conducting legal analysis, address one issue at a time. If there are several issues involved in the assignment, consider each issue separately. Complete the analysis of one issue before proceeding to the next issue. In doing so, you will be more efficient and avoid confusion.
- ❑ Remember counteranalysis. Always look for authority or arguments counter to your position.
- ❑ Keep focused. Focus on the specific issue you are assigned to analyze and the facts of the client's case, and keep asking yourself, "What must be decided about the facts of this case?"
- ❑ Maintain intellectual honesty. Do not lose your objectivity. Do not let personal beliefs or feelings interfere with a thorough legal analysis.

APPLICATION

The steps of the analytical process are illustrated here through their application to the hypothetical presented at the beginning of the chapter.

Marian's new assignment requires her to analyze the Lietel case, identify the issues, and determine if Mr. Lietel has any cause of action against Steve Spear. Marian realizes that she must first familiarize herself with all the information concerning the facts of the case. She reviews the case file and all interviews that have been conducted. Next, she reviews the notes from the legal research and analysis course she took when she was studying for her degree. She notes a four-step approach for analyzing a case:

- Step 1 *Issue.* Identify the issue (legal question) or issues raised by the facts of the client's case.
- Step 2 *Rule.* Identify the law that governs the issue.
- Step 3 *Analysis/Application.* Determine how the rule of law applies to the issue.
- Step 4 *Conclusion.* Summarize the results of the legal analysis.

Battery Issue

Step 1 Identify the Issue(s). Assume for the purposes of this problem that there is no question concerning the lawfulness of the citizen's arrest by Steve Spear. He had authority to make a citizen's arrest.

Marian, based upon her education and experience as a paralegal, quickly identifies two possible civil causes of action that Mr. Lietel may have against Mr. Spear:

1. Battery
2. Intentional infliction of emotional distress

From her training, Marian knows that the best approach to legal analysis is to address and completely analyze one issue before proceeding to the next one. She decides to begin with the battery issue.

Marian knows that the issue is the legal question raised by the facts of the client's case, and therefore, the statement of the issue must include reference to the law and the facts. The steps of the process Marian follows when identifying and stating the issue are presented in detail in Chapters 6 and 7. She identifies the issue as follows:

> Under the state's tort law, does a civil battery occur when an individual encounters resistance while making a lawful arrest, uses force to overcome the resistance, and kicks the person being arrested several times after the resistance ceases?

Step 2 Identify the Rule of Law. The next step is to identify the rule of law governing battery. Marian first looks for any state statute that defines civil battery. Based upon her familiarity with tort law, she is fairly certain that civil battery is defined in the common law, and there is no applicable statutory law. She researches the statutes, however, to be sure that the state legislature has not enacted any legislation concerning civil battery. Her research reveals that there is no statute. She finds that the common law definition of battery adopted by the state's highest court is: "A civil battery is the unprivileged, intentional, and harmful or offensive contact with the person of another."

Step 3 Analysis Application. The third step is a determination of how the rule of law applies to the facts of the client's case. This is a three-part process:

- Part 1 Identify the component parts (elements) of the rule of law.
- Part 2 Apply the facts of the client's case to the component parts.
- Part 3 Consider the possible counterarguments to the analysis of an issue, *i.e.*, conduct a counteranalysis of the analysis.

Part 1 Identify the components (elements) of the rule of law. After reviewing the definition of battery, Marian identifies the following elements that are required to be present for a battery to occur:

1. unprivileged
2. intentional
3. harmful or offensive
4. contact

Part 2 Apply the elements to the facts of the client's case. If the elements of the common law are met or established by the facts of the case, a cause of action exists. Elements 2, 3, and 4 appear to be clearly established by the facts of the case. Mr. Spear's actions of kicking Mr. Lietel were clearly intentional and harmful and did contact Mr. Lietel's body. Admittedly, Mr. Spear was making a lawful citizen's arrest, and he did encounter resistance. But did the continued use of force after resistance ceased constitute a battery? Was the continued use of force unprivileged?

The common law definition of battery does not provide sufficient guidance for a determination of whether the conduct was unprivileged. Marian must, therefore, refer to additional case law to determine what constitutes "unprivileged" contact. She looks for a court opinion that is on point—*i.e.*, an opinion with facts similar to the client's facts where the court addressed the question of the use of force in making a lawful arrest.

Assume she finds the case of *Art v. Kelly.* In this case, an off-duty police officer, while making a citizen's arrest, continued to use force after the arrest had occurred and resistance had ceased. The court held that whenever a lawful arrest is made, either by a citizen or a law enforcement officer, the privilege to use force in conducting the arrest ceases when resistance ceases. Any continued use of force is a civil battery.

Applying the rule from *Art v. Kelly* to the facts of the case, Marian concludes that the requirements of the first element are met. Although Mr. Spear may have been privileged to use force to overcome resistance when making the citizen's arrest, the continued use of force after resistance ceased constituted a battery under the rule announced in *Art v. Kelly.* Marian concludes that a cause of action exists for civil battery. Mr. Spear's actions of kicking Mr. Lietel after Mr. Lietel had ceased resisting constituted unprivileged, intentional, harmful contact with Mr. Lietel.

Part 3 Counteranalysis. Before proceeding, Marian should conduct a counteranalysis. She should identify and address any counterarguments to the analysis.

For Example: Suppose Marian found a court decision involving an arrest by law enforcement officers that held that some continued use of force after resistance ceases is permissible if the situation is extremely heated. The court reasoned that law enforcement officers are not perfect, and if the situation is extremely heated, the brief continued use of force is privileged. In Marian's analysis, she would have to include the case in her memorandum and discuss how it does or does not apply to the facts of the client's case.

Step 4 Conclusion. The final step in the analysis of the battery issue is a conclusion. When applying the rule of law to the facts of the case in step 3, Marian reached a conclusion that there is a cause of action for civil battery in Mr. Lietel's case. Law firms vary in regard to what should be included in the conclusion. Marian's conclusion could include, among other things, any or all of the following:

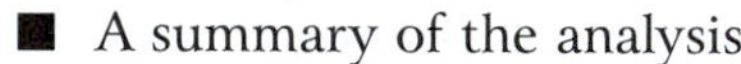

- A summary of the analysis

    For Example: "The common law defines battery as the nonprivileged, intentional, harmful, or offensive contact with the person of another. In the court opinion of *Art v. Kelly,* the court stated that when a lawful arrest is being made, the continued use of force after resistance ceases is unprivileged. Mr. Spear's actions of kicking Mr. Lietel after Mr. Lietel had ceased resisting constituted unprivileged, intentional, harmful contact with Mr. Lietel. Therefore, a cause of action for civil battery is available in this case."

- A weighing or consideration, based on the analysis, of the merits of the cause of action

    For Example: "There is strong support for a battery claim in this case. The testimony of the witnesses supports Mr. Lietel's statements that Mr. Spear kicked him after he was subdued. All the elements of the cause of action are established by the facts of the case. Under the rule of *Art v. Kelly,* Mr. Spear's continued use of force was clearly unprivileged."

- An identification of additional facts or information that may be necessary. In this case, the statements of additional witnesses or other information may be required.
- The identification of further research that may be required. Further research may be necessary because part of the research could not be performed due to time constraints (the memo was due) or the research sources were not readily available.
- The identification of other issues or causes of action that became apparent during the analysis of the case, which is not necessary in this case, since Marian's assignment is to identify all possible causes of action and issues.

Suppose Marian's supervisory attorney believed that only a battery claim was present in this case and Marian's assignment was to address that issue. If her analysis of the battery issue revealed other possible causes of action, she should mention those possibilities in her conclusion.

Intentional Infliction of Emotional Distress Issue

When performing step 1, Marian identified intentional infliction of emotional distress as a possible cause of action. After concluding her analysis of the battery claim, she follows the same steps in analyzing the possibility of an intentional infliction of emotional distress claim.

Step 1 Identify the Issue. Just as with the battery issue, Marian knows that the issue is the legal question raised by the facts of the client's case, and therefore, the statement of the issue must include reference to the law and the facts. She identifies the issue as follows:

> Under the state's tort law, does intentional infliction of emotional distress occur when an individual, who encounters resistance while making a lawful arrest, kicks the party being arrested six times after the resistance has ceased, causing the party to have trouble sleeping and be fearful whenever he sees the individual?

Step 2 Rule of Law. Marian's research reveals that there is no statutory cause of action for intentional infliction of emotional distress. The state common law does establish a cause of action for intentional infliction of emotional distress. There is no cause of action for negligent infliction of emotional distress. Intentional infliction of emotional distress is defined in the common law as intentionally causing severe emotional distress by an act of extreme or outrageous conduct.

Step 3 Analysis/Application. *Part 1 Identify the components (elements) of the rule of law.* Marian's review of the common law reveals four elements:

1. Extreme or outrageous conduct
2. Intent to cause severe emotional distress
3. Severe emotional distress is suffered
4. The conduct causes the distress

Part 2 Apply the elements to the facts of the client's case. Marian's application of the facts of Mr. Lietel's case to the elements raises several questions about whether the requirements of intentional infliction of emotional distress are met in this case:

1. Was Mr. Spear's conduct "extreme or outrageous?"
2. Mr. Spear obviously intended to kick Mr. Lietel, but did he intend to cause severe emotional distress?
3. Was the harm suffered by Mr. Lietel "severe emotional distress"?

The answers to these questions are not apparent from a reading of the definition of intentional infliction of emotional distress. Marian turns to additional case law for guidance and locates the case of *Addik v. Garay,* which appears to answer her questions. In the case, Mr. Garay and Mr. Addik got into a fight at a party. Garay knocked Addik down and, while Addik was down, kicked him multiple times yelling, "I'm not gonna kill you, but you'll remember me in your dreams. You'll never forget this." Addik was so affected by the incident that he had a nervous breakdown and was out of work for two months.

The court, addressing Addik's claim for intentional infliction of emotional distress, ruled that public humiliation, such as that suffered by Addik, constitutes "extreme and outrageous conduct." Ruling that the requisite intent was present, the court held that there must be some *specific conduct* indicating an intent to cause emotional distress. The mere intentional act of kicking was not sufficient to evidence an intent to cause emotional distress, but Mr. Garay's statements while kicking Mr. Addik were specific conduct indicating an intent to cause emotional distress. The court went on to rule that the emotional distress suffered must be severe: the mere loss of sleep is not sufficient. Instead, severe harm, such as loss of work or medical expenses, must result.

Applying the guidelines presented in *Addik v. Garay*, Marian concludes that there is probably not a cause of action for intentional infliction of emotional distress in Mr. Lietel's case. Mr. Spear's conduct of kicking Mr. Lietel in public is sufficiently extreme and outrageous. But it is questionable whether the requirements of elements 2 and 3, intent and severe emotional distress, are met by the facts of the case. There was no conduct by Mr. Spear evidencing a specific intent to cause emotional distress. The act of kicking alone was not sufficient evidence of intent according to *Addik v. Garay.* If Mr. Lietel's loss of work and medical expenses resulted from the battery and were not related to the emotional distress, there is no evidence that Mr. Lietel suffered severe harm as required by *Addik v. Garay.* Fearfulness and loss of sleep are probably not sufficiently severe to meet the *Garay* standards.

Part 3 Counteranalysis. In this part, Marian would identify and address any authority or counterarguments to her analysis. We will assume that she did not identify any counterargument to her analysis of the emotional distress issue.

Step 4 Conclusion. Just as with the battery issue, Marian begins her conclusion with a summary of the analysis.

For Example: The common law definition of intentional infliction of emotional distress is the intentional causing of severe emotional distress by an act of extreme or outrageous conduct. In the case of *Addik v. Garay,* the court ruled that:

1. Public humiliation by kicking constitutes outrageous conduct,
2. The act of kicking alone is not sufficient evidence of intent—there must be additional conduct evidencing an intent to cause severe emotional distress, and
3. Severe harm must result from the severe emotional distress.

In Mr. Lietel's case, there is no evidence of the required intent, and it is questionable whether there was severe harm. Therefore, a cause of action for intentional infliction of emotional distress does not appear to be present.

Marian may include some other items in her conclusion similar to those presented in the conclusion to the battery issue.

For Example: She may identify additional information that is needed. She may note that the client and witnesses need to be reinterviewed to determine whether Mr. Spear said anything while he was kicking Mr Lietel.

SUMMARY

Most clients enter the law office with a problem that must be analyzed and solved. Legal analysis of the problem involves the identification of the legal issues in the client's case and a determination of what law applies and how it applies. The commonly used legal analysis format involves four steps:

1. Identification of the legal issue or issues
2. Identification of the rule of law that governs the issue
3. Analysis and application of the rule of law to the facts of the case. This step is composed of three parts:
   a. A determination of the elements or requirements of the rule of law
   b. A matching of the facts of the client's case to the elements and a determination of how the rule of law applies to the facts
   c. A counteranalysis that addresses any counterarguments to the analysis
4. A conclusion that summarizes the previous steps. The conclusion may also include a weighing of the merits of the case and an identification of other information or avenues of research that should be pursued.

The four steps of the analysis process can be easily referred to and remembered by the acronym IRAC. It is composed of the first letter of the descriptive term for each step: **I**ssue, **R**ule, **A**nalysis/Application, and **C**onclusion.

It is important to keep two general considerations in mind when engaging in legal analysis:

1. Focus
2. Intellectual honesty

Keep focused on the task. Expend energy in the direction of addressing the issues assigned. Focus on the facts of the client's case, and analyze only the issue or issues raised by those facts. Avoid being distracted by interesting or related issues that do not need to be addressed.

Perform analysis with intellectual honesty. Always look for the correct answer, even though that answer may not be in the client's favor or in accordance with your beliefs. Do not let preferences, prejudices, or politics interfere with your duty to objectively and honestly analyze the legal question. The conclusion should be based on an objective analysis of all the facts and law and include both the supporting and opposing positions.

EXERCISES

ASSIGNMENT 1

Client's Facts: The client is the president of an extremist group that believes that the followers of Islam should be deported to Islamic countries. The organization at its ceremonies burns a large replica of the Koran while singing anti-Islamic songs. The organization's letterhead and literature is embossed with a picture of a burning Koran being stepped on by a spiked boot. The local library has books by members of the American Nazi Party, the American Communist Party, and the Ku Klux Klan. The library refuses to include the organization's literature among its materials. The client claims this violates the organization's constitutional rights.

The law firm handles cases involving the violation of constitutional rights.

Assignment: The paralegal is assigned the task of identifying and analyzing the possible causes of action that the client may have against the city library.

A. Discuss and describe in detail the steps the paralegal should follow when conducting the legal analysis.
B. Assume there are possible causes of action based on freedom of speech under the First Amendment and equal protection under the Fourteenth Amendment. For each issue, describe in detail each step of the analytical process.
C. Discuss possible factors that may affect the paralegal's objectivity and how those factors could affect the legal analysis of the problem.

ASSIGNMENT 2

Client's Facts: The client was cited for passing in a no passing zone. Frustrated by a slow-moving vehicle on a two-lane highway, the client admits that he passed the vehicle entirely in a no passing zone—that he began and ended the passing maneuver in an area where the center of the road was marked with two solid stripes. There was no oncoming traffic, and the maneuver was safely made.

Rule of Law: The state's motor vehicle code, section 293-301, provides that it is a violation of state law to pass a vehicle in a no passing zone. In the statute, a no passing zone is defined as that portion of the road marked by two solid lines painted in the center of the road. Passing zones are indicated by single, eight-foot stripes down the center of the road.

Case Law: The only relevant case on the subject is *State v. Roth.* In the case, Mr. Roth was cited for improper passing. He began the passing maneuver in the last thirty feet of a no passing zone and completed it in a passing zone. There were no oncoming vehicles. Evidence presented to the trial court established that the last thirty feet of the no passing zone should have been marked as part of the passing zone. Mr. Roth appealed his conviction in the trial court. On appeal, the state's highest court held that the purpose of the state motor vehicle code is to ensure safety on the public highways. The court ruled that Mr. Roth's passing maneuver was clearly made safely, and in light of the evidence that the no passing zone was improperly marked, a strict reading of the statute was not appropriate. Mr. Roth's conviction was set aside.

Assignment: The paralegal is assigned the task of analyzing the likelihood that the client's ticket can be set aside.

A. Based upon the information presented in the problem, conduct an analysis of the client's case and prepare a complete and detailed analysis of the problem.
B. Repeat Assignment A, assuming the following facts: The client began the passing maneuver approximately twenty feet from the end of the no passing zone and completed it in a passing zone. There was no oncoming traffic, and the maneuver was safely completed.
C. Repeat Assignment A, assuming the following facts: The client began the passing maneuver in a passing zone, but completed it in a no passing zone.
D. What additional information, if any, may be necessary for a complete analysis of the preceding problems?

PART II

The Specifics of Legal Analysis

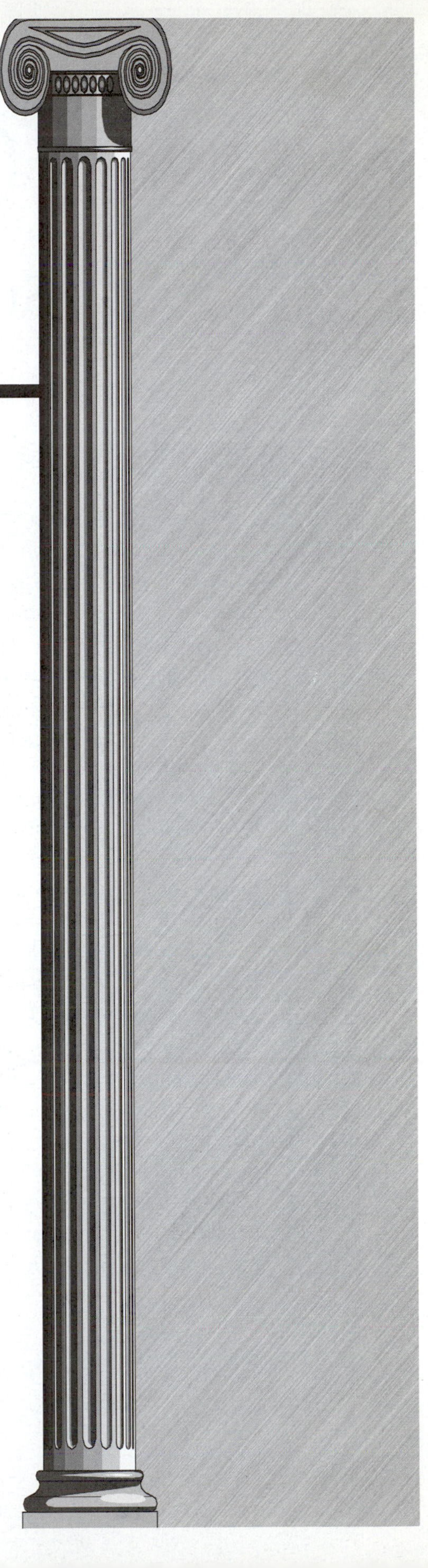

CHAPTER 3

Statutory Analysis

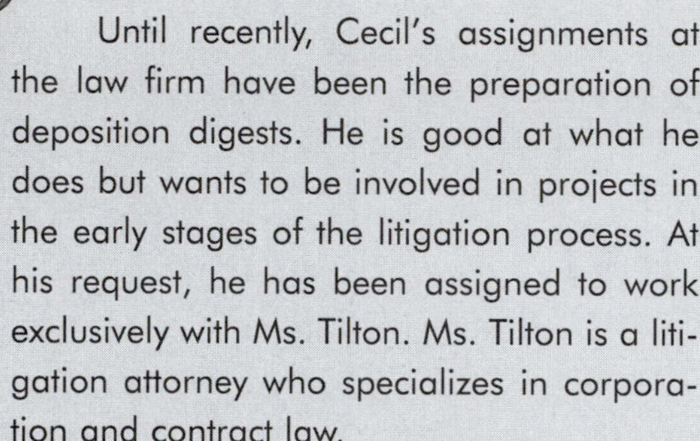

Until recently, Cecil's assignments at the law firm have been the preparation of deposition digests. He is good at what he does but wants to be involved in projects in the early stages of the litigation process. At his request, he has been assigned to work exclusively with Ms. Tilton. Ms. Tilton is a litigation attorney who specializes in corporation and contract law.

His first assignment from Ms. Tilton is to determine if Mrs. Jackson has a cause of action against Beauty Care Beauty Salon for breach of warranty under the sales provisions of the state's commercial code. Mrs. Jackson went to her hair dresser, Beauty Care Beauty Salon, to get their "special long-term-hold" permanent. Once a year for the past three years she has asked for the "special" permanent. Beauty Care made no warranties about the permanent. It did not provide Mrs. Jackson, either in writing or orally, any statements concerning the quality of the permanent. The receipt she received for the permanent listed a twenty dollar charge for the permanent kit and other products and a sixty dollar charge for the services of the beautician.

Three days after Mrs. Jackson was given the permanent, her hair, which had been blond, turned a light green. Five days later, it broke off approximately one inch from the scalp—not a good result.

Cecil, based on his experience as a paralegal, is aware that Mrs. Jackson has a possible tort negligence claim and other possible causes of action against Beauty Care. But his assignment is to determine if there is also a possible breach of warranty claim under the state's commercial code.

Cecil's research indicates that the Commercial Code Sales Act applies only to the sale of goods and includes three warranties that may apply in Mrs. Jackson's case. Cecil has not worked with statutes since he obtained his associate's degree in Paralegal Studies. Several questions occur to him: Does the act apply? Is this a sale of goods within the meaning of the act? If this is a sale of goods, which warranty applies? How do you analyze a statute?

INTRODUCTION

The term *statutory law* usually refers to enacted law—laws or acts passed by a legislative body or adopted by the people that declare, command, or prohibit something. As used in this chapter, the term includes any law or ordinance passed by any legislative body, regulations adopted by administrative agencies, and state and federal constitutions. Laws passed by Congress or state legislatures are generally called acts or statutes. Ordinances are usually passed by local governing bodies, such as city councils. For the sake of clarity, throughout this chapter, the discussion and examples focus on laws passed by legislative bodies, that is, statutes and acts. Note, however, that the principles presented in the chapter apply to the analysis of all enacted law.

statutory law
The body of law composed of laws passed by legislative bodies. The term includes laws or ordinances passed by any legislative body.

Statutory law is a major source of law with which a paralegal must become familiar when researching and analyzing the law. Statutory law has assumed an ever-increasing role in the United States. With the passage of time, the body of law represented by statutory law has expanded greatly. Many matters once governed by common law (court-made law) are now governed by statutory law.

For Example: Criminal law was once exclusively established and regulated by the common law. Today, however, most criminal law is governed by statutory law.

Consequently, with the growth of statutory law, more and more legal problems and issues are governed by it. Since an increasing number of legal problems and issues require the interpretation and application of statutory law, paralegals are more frequently called upon to engage in statutory analysis. Statutory analysis is the process of determining if a statute applies, how it applies, and the effect of that application.

statutory analysis
The interpretation and application of statutory law. The process of determining if a statute applies to a specific fact situation, how it applies, and the effect of that application.

Since most statutes are designed to cover a broad range of present and future situations, they are written in general terms. As a result, a paralegal is required to engage in statutory analysis to determine whether and how a statute applies in a specific fact situation.

The focus of this chapter is the process of statutory analysis. It begins with a presentation of the anatomy of a statute, follows with a discussion of the process of statutory analysis, and ends with general considerations involving statutory construction and analysis.

ANATOMY OF A STATUTE

Before you can analyze a statute, you must be familiar with the basic structure of statutory law, the component parts. Assume, for the purposes of illustration, that you are interested in whether a contract for the sale of goods must be in writing, and the governing law is the Indiana Code. Figure 3–1 shows selected portions of the Indiana Code concerning commercial law. To the left of the sections of the code are terms that describe the components of the code. The following text discusses each descriptive term and that portion of the statute referred to by the term.

Not all of the statutory components included in the discussion of the Indiana Code in Figure 3–1 are included in every statute. It is important, however, to discuss them here so you will be familiar with them if you encounter them in other statutes.

Title article chapter (Part) Section
26-1-2-101

NUMBER OF TITLE

TITLE 26
COMMERCIAL LAW

NUMBER OF ARTICLE

ARTICLE.
1. UNIFORM COMMERCIAL CODE, chs. 1-10.
2. COMMERCIAL TRANSACTIONS, chs. 1-6.
3. WAREHOUSES, chs. 1-7.

ARTICLE 1
UNIFORM COMMERCIAL CODE

NUMBER OF CHAPTER

CHAPTER.
1. GENERAL PROVISIONS, 26-1-1-101 — 26-1-1-208.
2. SALES, 26-1-2-101 — 26-1-2-725.
2.1. LEASES, 26-1-2.1-101 — 26-1-2.1-532.
3. COMMERCIAL PAPER, 26-1-3-101 — 26-1-3-805.
4. BANK DEPOSITS AND COLLECTIONS, 26-1-4-101 — 26-1-4-504.
4.1. FUND TRANSFERS, 26-1-4.1-101 — 26-1-4.1-507.
5. LETTERS OF CREDIT, 26-1-5-101 — 26-1-5-117.
6. BULK TRANSFERS, 26-1-6-101 — 26-1-6-110.
7. [WAREHOUSE RECEIPTS, BILLS OF LADING AND OTHER] DOCUMENTS OF TITLE, 26-1-7-101 — 26-1-7-603.
8. INVESTMENT SECURITIES, 26-1-8-101 — 26-1-8-408.
9. SECURED TRANSACTIONS, 26-1-9-101 — 26-1-9-507.
10. EFFECTIVE DATE, REPEAL, SAVING PROVISION, 26-1-10-101 — 26-1-10-106.

CHAPTER 1
GENERAL PROVISIONS

PART 1. SHORT TITLE, CONSTRUCTION, APPLICATION AND SUBJECT-MATTER OF THE ACT

NUMBER OF SECTION

SECTION.
26-1-1-101. Short title.
26-1-1-102. Purposes — Rules of construction — Variation by agreement.
26-1-1-103. Supplementary general principles of law applicable.
26-1-1-104. Construction against implicit repeal.
26-1-1-105. Territorial application of the act — Parties' power to choose applicable law.
26-1-1-106. Remedies to be liberally administered.
26-1-1-107. Waiver or renunciation of claim or right after breach.
26-1-1-108. Severability.

SECTION.
26-1-1-109. [Repealed.]

PART 2. GENERAL DEFINITIONS AND PRINCIPLES OF INTERPRETATION

26-1-1-201. General definitions.
26-1-1-202. Prima facie evidence by third party documents.
26-1-1-203. Obligation of good faith.
26-1-1-204. Time — Reasonable time — "Seasonably."
26-1-1-205. Course of dealing and usage of trade.
26-1-1-206. Statute of frauds for kinds of personal property not otherwise covered.
26-1-1-207. Performance or acceptance under reservation of rights.
26-1-1-208. Option to accelerate at will.

NUMBER OF SECTION

PART 1. SHORT TITLE, CONSTRUCTION, APPLICATION AND SUBJECT MATTER OF THE ACT

SHORT TITLE

26-1-1-101. Short title. — IC 26-1 shall be known and may be cited as Uniform Commercial Code. [Acts 1963, ch. 317, § 1-101, p. 539; P.L.152-1986, § 110.]

Figure 3–1
Indiana Code—Commercial Law

The statutes reprinted or quoted verbatim in the following pages are taken from the *Burns Indiana Statutes Annotated* Copyright 1990, 1992, by Michie, and are reprinted with the permission of Michie.

PURPOSE CLAUSE

26-1-1-102. Purposes — Rules of construction — Variation by agreement. — (1) IC 26-1 shall be liberally construed and applied to promote its underlying purposes and policies.

(2) Underlying purposes and policies of IC 26-1 are:

(a) To simplify, clarify, and modernize the law governing commercial transactions;

(b) To permit the continued expansion of commercial practices through custom, usage, and agreement of the parties;

(c) To make uniform the law among the various jurisdictions.

. . .

CHAPTER 2

SALES

NUMBER OF SECTION

PART 1. SHORT TITLE, GENERAL CONSTRUCTION AND SUBJECT MATTER

SHORT TITLE

26-1-2-101. Short title. — IC 26-1-2 shall be known and may be cited as Uniform Commercial Code—Sales. [Acts 1963, ch. 317, § 2-101, p. 539; P.L.152-1986, § 119.]

Cross References. Construction against implicit repeal, IC 26-1-1-104.

Rules of construction, IC 26-1-1-102.

Supplementary general principles of law applicable, IC 26-1-1-103.

Indiana Law Journal. The Uniform Commercial Code and Real Estate Law: Problems for Both the Real Estate Lawyer and the Chattel Security Lawyer, 38 Ind. L.J. 535.

Negligence, Economic Loss, and the U.C.C., 61 Ind. L.J. 593 (1986).

Indiana Law Review. The Flammable Fabrics Act and Strict Liability in Tort, 9 Ind. L. Rev. 395.

Survey of Recent Developments in Business and Commercial Law—Vertical Privity and Damages for Breach of Implied Warranty under the U.C.C.: It's Time for Indiana to

SCOPE

26-1-2-102. Scope — Certain security and other transactions excluded from this chapter. — Unless the context otherwise requires, IC 26-1-2 applies to transactions in goods. It does not apply to any transaction which although in the form of an unconditional contract to sell or present sale is intended to operate only as a security transaction, nor does IC 26-1-2 impair or repeal any statute regulating sales to consumers, farmers, or other specified classes of buyers. IC 26-1-2 does not impair or repeal IC 9-14, IC 9-17, or IC 9-22-5. [Acts 1963, ch. 317, § 2-102, p. 539; P.L.152-1986, § 120; P.L.2-1991, § 86.]

Figure 3–1 (Cont.)

Indiana Code—Commercial Law

26-1-1-201. General definitions. — Subject to additional definitions contained in IC 26-1-2 through IC 26-1-10 which are applicable to specific provisions, and unless the context otherwise requires, in IC 26-1:

DEFINITIONS

(1) "Action" in the sense of a judicial proceeding includes recoupment, counterclaim, setoff, suit in equity, and any other proceedings in which rights are determined.

(2) "Aggrieved party" means a party entitled to resort to a remedy.

(3) "Agreement" means the bargain of the parties in fact as found in their language or by implication from other circumstances including course of dealing or usage of trade or course of performance as provided in IC 26-1-1-205 and IC 26-1-2-208. Whether an agreement has legal

SUBSTANTIVE PROVISIONS

PART 2. FORM, FORMATION AND READJUSTMENT OF CONTRACT

26-1-2-201. Formal requirements — Statute of frauds. — (1) Except as otherwise provided in this section, a contract for the sale of goods for the price of five hundred dollars ($500) or more is not enforceable by way of action or defense unless there is some writing sufficient to indicate that a contract for sale has been made between the parties and signed by the party against whom enforcement is sought or by his authorized agent or broker. A writing is not insufficient because it omits or incorrectly states a term agreed upon, but the contract is not enforceable under this paragraph beyond the quantity of goods shown in such writing.

(2) Between merchants, if within a reasonable time a writing in confirmation of the contract and sufficiently against the sender is received and the party receiving it has reason to know its contents, it satisfies the requirements of subsection (1) against such party unless written notice of objection to its contents is given within ten (10) days after it is received.

(3) A contract which does not satisfy the requirements of subsection (1) but which is valid in other respects is enforceable:

(a) If the goods are to be specially manufactured for the buyer and are not suitable for sale to others in the ordinary course of the seller's business and the seller, before notice of repudiation is received and under circumstances which reasonably indicate that the goods are for the buyer, has made either a substantial beginning of their manufacture or commitments for their procurement; or

(b) If the party against whom enforcement is sought admits in his pleading, testimony, or otherwise in court that a contract for sale was made, but the contract is not enforceable under this provision beyond the quantity of goods admitted; or

(c) With respect to goods for which payment has been made and accepted or which have been received and accepted (IC 26-1-2-606). [Acts 1963, ch. 317, § 2-201, p. 539; P.L.152-1986, § 125.]

REFERENCE INFORMATION

Cross References. Action, definition, IC 26-1-1-201.

Additional terms in acceptance or confirmation, IC 26-1-2-207.

Between merchants, definition, IC 26-1-2-104.

Buyer and seller, definition, IC 26-1-2-103.

Contract, definition, IC 26-1-1-201.

Figure 3–1 (Cont.)

Indiana Code—Commercial Law

SUBSTANTIVE PROVISIONS

26-1-2-315. Implied warranty — Fitness for particular purpose. — Where the seller at the time of contracting has reason to know any particular purpose of which the goods are required and that the buyer is relying on the seller's skill or judgment to select or furnish suitable goods, there is, unless excluded or modified under IC 26-1-2-316, an implied warranty that the good shall be fit for such purpose. [Acts 1963, ch. 317, § 2-315, p. 539; P.L.152-1986, § 136.]

REFERENCE INFORMATION

Cross References. Buyer and seller, definition, IC 26-1-2-103.

Cumulation and conflict of warranties, IC 26-1-2-317.

Exclusion or modification of warranties, IC 26-1-2-316.

Goods, definition, IC 26-1-2-105.

Implied warranty of merchantability, IC 26-1-2-314.

Product liability actions, IC 33-1-1.5-1 — 33-1-1.5-8.

Indiana Law Journal. Implied and Express Warranties and Disclaimers Under the Uniform Commercial Code, 38 Ind. L.J. 648.

The Private Law Treatment of Defective Products in Sales Situations, 49 Ind. L.J. 8.

Consumer Warranty or Insurance Contract? A View Towards a Rational State Regulatory Policy, 51 Ind. L.J. 1103.

Indiana's Implied Warranty of Fitness for Habitation: Limited Protection for Used Home Buyers, 57 Ind. L.J. 479.

Negligence, Economic Loss, and the U.C.C., 61 Ind. L.J. 593 (1986).

Indiana Law Review. Landlord-Tenant Law: Indiana at the Crossroads, 10 Ind. L. Rev. 591.

and Damages for Breach of Implied Warranty under the U.C.C.: It's Time for Indiana to Abandon the Citadel, 21 Ind. L. Rev. 23 (1988).

Notre Dame Law Review. Economic Institutions and Value Survey — Warranty Representation and Disclaimers, 8 Notre Dame Law. 602.

Merchantability and the Statute of Limitations, 50 Notre Dame Law. 321.

Utility "Services" under the Uniform Commercial Code: Are Public Utilities in for a Shock?, 56 Notre Dame Law. 89.

Lions & Lionesses, Tigers & Tigresses, Bears & ... Other Animals: Sellers' Liability for Dangerous Animals, 58 Notre Dame L. Rev. 537.

Valparaiso University Law Review. An Emerging Concept: Consumer Protection in Statutory Regulation, Products Liability and the Sale of New Homes, 11 Val. U.L. Rev. 335.

Risk of Economic Loss and Implied Warranty Liability in Tripartite Finance Leases, 22 Val. U.L. Rev. 593 (1988).

NOTES TO DECISIONS

ANALYSIS

In general.
Basis for acceleration.
—Encumbrance.
Evidence.
Good faith.
—Erroneous determination of insecurity.

In General.

Acceleration provisions are valid and enforceable in Indiana. Smith v. Union State Bank, 452 N.E.2d 1059 (Ind. App. 1983).

Basis for Acceleration.

—Encumbrance.

The attachment of a superior lien against property subject to security agreement amounted to an encumbrance and was a basis for acceleration under security agreement which provided for acceleration in case of encumbrance. Van Bibber v. Norris, 419 N.E.2d 115 (Ind. 1981).

Evidence.

Where the maker of the note had incurred other financial obligations, had transferred collateral, and secured equipment in which the holder of the note had no superior security interest, the holder could honestly have believed that its chances of payment had been diminished. Holmes v. Rushville Prod. Credit Ass'n, 170 Ind. App. 509, 353 N.E.2d 509, 54 Ind. Dec. 395 (1976), vacated, 170 Ind. App. 517, 355 N.E.2d 417, reinstated, 170 Ind. App. 509, 357 N.E.2d 734, 55 Ind. Dec. 468 (1977), transfer denied, 267 Ind. 454, 371 N.E.2d 379, 60 Ind. Dec. 413 (1978).

Good Faith.

Where bank had continuing problem of collecting from purchaser of mobile home and such purchaser was delinquent on current payment due and had been arrested and placed in jail and mobile home park had lien on mobile home for rent due, it could not be said that bank did not act in good faith in accelerating payment. Van Bibber v. Norris, 419 N.E.2d 115 (Ind. 1981).

A good faith belief under this section means at least honesty in fact in the conduct or transaction concerned. Smith v. Union State Bank, 452 N.E.2d 1059 (Ind. App. 1983).

—Erroneous Determination of Insecurity.

Assuming a bank was not insecure, even an erroneous determination of insecurity was not necessarily unreasonable or in bad faith. Smith v. Union State Bank, 452 N.E.2d 1059 (Ind. App. 1983).

Figure 3–1 (Cont.)

Indiana Code—Commercial Law

Number

Each statute has numbers assigned for each section of the statute. Every legislative authority—local, state, and federal—follows a different numbering system. Therefore, it is not practical to discuss separately each numbering system. There are some general similarities, however, that can be addressed.

Most laws are divided into broad categories, each of which is assigned a number. Those broad categories are divided into topics or smaller categories that are also assigned numbers. The topics are further divided into subtopics, each of which is assigned a number, and so on. The number of categories and divisions depends on the statutory scheme of the particular legislative authority.

For Example: The laws of Indiana are divided into broad categories called titles. Commercial law is assigned the number 26. (See NUMBER OF TITLE at the top of the first page of Figure 3–1.) Each title is divided into areas called articles. Commercial law in the Indiana Code is divided into three articles numbered 1, 2, and 3. The Uniform Commercial Code article, which governs commercial transactions, is assigned the number 1. The three articles are listed under COMMERCIAL LAW. (See NUMBER OF ARTICLE at the top of the first page of Figure 3–1.) Article 1, the Uniform Commercial Code, is divided into ten chapters. They are listed under UNIFORM COMMERCIAL CODE. (See NUMBER OF CHAPTER on the first page of Figure 3–1.) The chapter governing the sale of goods is chapter 2 (Sales). Each chapter is divided into sections, and each section is assigned a number (see NUMBER OF SECTION in Figure 3–1). Each section contains the actual law that governs a subject. The section of chapter 2 (Sales) that establishes when a contract must be in writing is assigned the number 201. This section is called Formal requirements—Statute of frauds (see § 26-1-2-201 on the second page of Figure 3–1).

Therefore, if you want to read the law in the Indiana Code governing when a contract must be written, you refer to title 26 (Commercial Law), article 1 (Uniform Commercial Code), chapter 2 (Sales), section 201 (Statute of Frauds). This is usually referred to numerically as § 26-1-2-201, Statute of Frauds.

short title

The name by which a statute is known (e.g., Uniform Commercial Code--Sales).

Short Title

The short title is the name by which the statute is known. It is a name that is easy to use when referring to the statute. Included in Figure 3–1 are examples of two short titles in the Indiana Code: the short title of article 1, Uniform Commercial Code (§ 26-1-1-101), and the short title of chapter 2, Uniform Commercial Code—Sales (§ 26-1-2-101). (See SHORT TITLE on the first and second pages of Figure 3–1.)

Purpose Clause

The purpose clause includes the purpose the legislative body intended to accomplish when drafting the statute. It is helpful in determining the legislative intent. (See PURPOSE CLAUSE in Figure 3–1, § 26-1-1-102.)

scope

A statutory section that states what is specifically covered and not covered by the statute.

Scope

Some statutes have sections that state specifically what is and is not covered by the statute. These are called scope sections. A paralegal should first review the scope section when analyzing a statute, as a review of this section may lead to a determination at the outset whether the statute applies. (See SCOPE in Figure 3–1.)

For Example: Assume you are researching a question under Indiana law involving a contract that grants a security interest in goods that are being sold. The scope section of the Uniform Commercial Code, § 26-1-2-102, provides that the section does not apply to such transactions. You know at the outset that the state Uniform Commercial Code does not apply and need not be considered further.

Definitions

Some statutes have definitions sections that define terms used in the statute. The definitions are helpful in determining the parties and situations covered by the provisions of the statute. (See DEFINITIONS in Figure 3–1, § 26-1-1-301.)

Substantive Provisions

The substantive sections set forth the substance of the law. (See SUBSTANTIVE PROVISIONS in Figure 3–1.) They establish the rights and duties of those governed by the statute: that which is required, prohibited, or allowed. A substantive section of the Indiana Code addresses the question posed at the beginning of this chapter, "When must a contract for the sale of goods be in writing?" (See § 26-1-2-201 in Figure 3–1.)

The substantive sections may include sections that provide remedies, such as fines or imprisonment in criminal cases. There may be sections governing procedure, such as which court has jurisdiction over the matters covered by the statute. The substantive provisions are what you usually refer to when addressing the client's legal problem.

Other Provisions

Not included in the example in Figure 3–1 are other types of statutory sections you may encounter.

For Example: There may be statutory provisions that:

- State which administrative agency is responsible for administering the act
- Incorporate by reference sections of other statutes
- Limit the application of the statute through exceptions
- Establish when the statute takes effect
- Repeal other statutes
- State that the statute is cumulative to the common law and other remedies still exist

Reference Information

Following each section of a statute, in small print, are references to various sources of information relative to the section. Some of these are:

- The history of the section, including dates of amendment
- Official comments on the section
- Cross-references to other statutes
- Research guides—references to law reviews and other articles, for example, ALR citations
- Legal encyclopedia citations to discussions of the statute in encyclopedias, such as *Corpus Juris Secundum, American Jurisprudence Second,* and so on)
- Notes to decisions—annotations of key court decisions that have discussed, analyzed, or interpreted the statute

These references are sources of information and are not part of the statute. They are not the law and do not have legal authority. (See REFERENCE INFORMATION in Figure 3–1.)

It is easier to work with statutes after establishing a familiarity with the component parts. The material presented here will help you gain some familiarity, but the greatest familiarity comes with practice. Chose a subject in which you are interested and read the statute in your jurisdiction that governs the area.

STATUTORY ANALYSIS—THE PROCESS

When solving a legal problem or addressing an issue that is governed by a statute, it is helpful to have an approach, a process for analyzing the statute. This process should allow you to approach the matter in a way that efficiently solves the problem in the least amount of time with the least confusion and greatest accuracy.

It is recommended that the three-step approach presented in Figure 3–2 be followed when addressing a legal problem or issue governed by statutory law. These steps are a helpful approach to statutory analysis, although in some instances, a step may be unnecessary—for example, step 1 is unnecessary if you already know that the statute applies—and in other instances, a different approach may be required. Each step in this recommended approach is discussed separately in the following sections.

Step 1 Determine If the Statute Applies

The first step in the process is to determine if the statute covers the legal problem or issue raised by the client's fact situation. Statutes govern certain people and situations. The first task is to determine which statute or statutes govern the question.

This step involves two parts:

- Part 1 Locate all applicable statutes.
- Part 2 Determine which statutes apply.

Part 1 Locate All Applicable Statutes

Before you can determine if a particular statute applies, you first must locate all statutes that possibly apply. The location of one applicable statute does not mean you should stop your search. Make sure your research is thorough and complete. Continue researching until you are confident that all areas of law that may govern the problem have been explored and all potential applicable statutes located. Some matters are covered by more than one statute.

For Example: The client's case may involve the validity and enforceability of a small loan contract. There may be several statutes that govern the enforcement of such contracts: the federal Truth-in-Lending Act, the state Small Loan Act, and the state Usury Act.

Part 2 Determine Which Statutes Apply

Determine whether each statute applies by asking yourself, "Does the general area of law covered by this statute apply to the issue or question raised by the facts

Figure 3–2

Statutory Analysis: A Three-Step Approach

Step 1	Determine if the statute applies.
Step 2	Analyze the statute.
Step 3	Apply the statute to the legal problem or issue.

of my client's case?" This question usually can be answered by referring to the scope section of the statute, the definitions section, or case law.

Reference to the scope section of the statute will often answer the question of whether the statute applies.

For Example: Suppose the problem involves the validity of a contract for the sale of a security interest in a car. The scope section of the Commercial Code—Sales statute provides, "This chapter does not apply to any transaction which . . . is a sale of a security interest or intended to operate only as a security transaction. . . ." Reference to this section clearly indicates that such transactions are not covered by this statute. If the facts involved the sale of the car, rather than the sale of a security interest in the car, the statute might apply.

Often reference to the definitions section of a statute will guide the determination of whether a statute applies.

For Example: Suppose the legal problem involves the sale of a farm. The question of whether this sale is governed by the provisions of the Commercial Code—Sales statute is answered by reference to the definitions section of the statute. In that section, goods are defined as "all things which are movable at the time of the contract for sale. . . ." The statute clearly does not apply to the sale of a farm.

In some instances, reference to case law may be necessary to determine if a statute governs a situation.

For Example: Suppose the client's case involves the lease of goods, and neither the scope nor definitions sections of the Commercial Code—Sales statute indicates whether the term sale includes a lease of goods. Reference to case law may be necessary. Court decisions often define terms not defined in a statute. Often the relevant case law may be located by looking to the reference information following the section of the statute.

It may be that two laws apply and govern a legal question. In this event, two causes of action may be available.

For Example: A small loan may violate provisions of both the federal Truth-in-Lending Act and the state usury law. In this case, there may be a cause of action under the federal law and a cause of action under the state law. If this occurs, steps 2 and 3 would be followed in regard to each statute.

When determining if a statute applies, always check the effective date of the statute to be sure that the statute is in effect. This is usually found in the statute itself or in the historical notes or comments in the reference sections following the statute. Also, always check the supplements of the statute to make sure that the statute you are researching is the latest version. Supplementary material published after the publication of the main text is often located immediately following the statute or in a separate section or pamphlet. The supplements include any changes in the statute or reference material that have occurred since the publication of the book containing the statute.

Step 2 Analyze the Statute

Once you determine that a statute applies, you must carefully read and analyze the statute to determine how it applies. Some statutes are lengthy and difficult to understand. They must be read carefully. It may be necessary to make a chart to assist you in understanding the specific provisions and operation of a statute. Step 2 involves two parts that are addressed in the text that follows:

- Part 1 General concerns when reading statutory law
- Part 2 Statutory elements—what does the statute specifically declare, require, or prohibit?

Part 1 General Concerns

Several general concerns should be kept in mind when reading statutory law:

1. The statute should be read carefully several times.
2. Does the statute set a standard or merely provide factors that must be considered?
3. Does the statute provide more than one rule or test? Are other rules or tests available? Are there exceptions to the rule or test?
4. All the words and punctuation have meaning. Always check the definitions section for the meaning of a term. If there is no definition, consult case law, a legal dictionary, or *Words and Phrases.* Do not assume you know what a term means. Your assumption may be wrong. A legal term may have several meanings, some of which may be unknown to you.

   For Example: Publication in tort law means more than presentation in the print or visual media. It means communication to a third party by any means. Under this definition, two neighbors gossiping over a backyard fence can constitute publication.

   All punctuation counts. If you cannot understand how to read a statute, consult a secondary source, such as a treatise or legal encyclopedia.
5. The entire statute should be reviewed. Look at the entire statute (all sections) to determine if other sections in some way affect or relate to the section you are researching.

   For Example: Section 611-9 of a statute provides:

   > (a) A will that does not comply with Section 611-8 is valid as a holographic will if the signature and the material provisions are in the handwriting of the testator.
   > (b) If a holographic will does not contain a statement as to the date of its execution and it is established that the testator lacked testamentary capacity at any time during which the will might have been executed, the will is invalid unless it is established that it was executed at a time when the testator had testamentary capacity.
   > (c) Any statement of testamentary intent contained in a holographic will may be set forth either in the testator's own handwriting or as part of a commercially printed form will.

   Note that a holographic will is a will written entirely by the testator in his or her own handwriting and not witnessed. Subsection (a) sets the standard for when a holographic will is valid. Subsection (b), however, addresses a situation that affects the validity of a holographic will even if the requirements of subsection (a) are met. Subsection (c) establishes how testamentary intent may be set forth.

   The preceding example illustrates a point that cannot be overemphasized: *Read and consider all parts of a statute.* Suppose the legal question is, "What is required for a holographic will to be valid?" If you stopped reading the statute at subsection (a) because it appeared to answer your question, you would miss the other provisions that also affect the answer to the question. Always read the entire statute.
6. Certain common terminology must be understood. Be aware of the meaning of commonly used terms such as *shall, may, and,* and *or.*

   Shall makes the duty imposed mandatory. It must be done. *May* leaves the duty optional. If *and* is used, all the conditions or listed items are required. If the term *or* is used, only one of the conditions or listed items is required.

> **For Example:** Section 24-6-7-9 of a statute provides, "A person is concerned in the commission of a crime if he:
>
> a. directly commits the crime;
> b. intentionally causes some other person to commit the crime; or
> c. intentionally aids or abets in the commission of the crime."

The use of *or* in this example means that a person is covered by the statute if he or she does *any* one of the listed acts.

> **For Example:** Section 50-9-1 of a statute provides that holographic wills are valid if they are:
>
> "a. entirely in the handwriting of the testator, and,
> b. signed by the testator."

The use of *and* in this statute means that both conditions must be met for the will to be valid.

7. The canons of construction should be kept in mind when statutes are being read. These are presented in the General Considerations section of this chapter.

Part 2 Statutory Elements

What does the statute specifically declare, require, or prohibit? Once the statute has been carefully read, the next part of step 2 is to analyze the section of the statute in question. How does the statute apply? Ask yourself, *"What specific requirements must be met for the statute to apply? What are the elements?"* For a statute to apply, certain conditions established by the statute must be met. These conditions or components of the statute are called elements. Once the elements are identified, you can determine how the statute applies.

statutory elements
The specific conditions or components of a statute that must be met for the statute to apply.

Once you have a sufficient understanding of the statute, begin this part of step 2 by breaking the statute down into its elements. Identify and list the conditions or elements that must be met for the statute to apply. This is necessary because you must know what the elements are before you can proceed to step 3 and apply them to the legal problem or issue raised by the client's facts.

The elements or requirements of the statute are identified by reading the entire statute, analyzing each sentence word by word, and listing everything that is required. This includes listing all the various conditions and exceptions contained in the subsections of the statute in question and the conditions and exceptions included in other statutes that may affect the statute in question.

> **For Example:** Consider section 2-2-315 of the Commercial Code— Sales Act of state *X*:
>
> Where the seller at the time of contracting has reason to know any particular purpose for which the goods are required and that the buyer is relying on the seller's skill or judgment to select or furnish suitable goods, there is an implied warranty that the goods shall be fit for such purpose.

Read the statute in the preceding example sentence by sentence and determine the elements. For the implied warranty of section 2-2-315 to apply, the following requirements must be met.

1. *The person must be a seller of goods.* How do you know "of goods" is required? Section 2-2-315 quoted in the preceding example does not read "seller of goods" but refers only to "the seller." You know "of goods" is required because in step 1, in order to determine if the statute applied to the issue in the client's case, you reviewed the scope section of the act. It provides that the act applies only to the sale of goods.

How is the term *goods* defined? Assume the term is defined in the definitions section of the Commercial Code—Sales Act as "All things movable at the time of sale." The statute also requires the individual to be a "seller." How is seller defined in the definitions section of the act? Assume the term is defined as "anyone who sells goods."

2. *The seller has reason to know the purpose for which the goods are required.* The seller must have reason to know of the purpose for which the buyer wants the goods. The statute does not require actual knowledge on the part of the seller. It provides only that the seller must have "reason to know." You may need to refer to case law to determine what "reason to know" means or requires.

3. *The seller has reason to know the buyer is relying on the seller's skill or judgment.* This is usually established by the words or actions of the buyer which indicate to the seller the buyer's reliance on the seller's skill or judgment.

4. *The buyer must actually rely on the seller's skill or judgment in furnishing suitable goods.* This is required because the statute provides "the seller . . . has reason to know . . . that the buyer *is relying* . . ."

5. *The seller must have known of the purpose for which the goods were required and the buyer's reliance on the seller's skill or judgment in furnishing the goods at the time the sale was taking place, not later.*

Be sure to complete both parts of step 2 before proceeding to step 3.

Step 3 Apply the Statute to the Legal Problem or Issue

Once you have identified the elements, the conditions necessary for the statute to apply, apply the elements to the legal problem or issue raised by the client's fact situation. This entails applying or matching the facts of the client's case to the elements of the statute.

This step may be accomplished in several ways. One way is to prepare a chart that lists the elements of the statute. Next to this, list the facts from the client's case that match or establish each of the elements or requirements of the statute. Another way is to prepare a narrative summary of the elements and how the facts of the case match or establish the elements. The following sections use examples to illustrate the performance of step 3 in both chart and narrative summary format.

Chart Format

In the following example, a chart format is used.

For Example: Tom goes to the local hardware store and informs the salesperson that he needs to grind metal with a power metal grinder. He tells the salesperson that he needs goggles to protect his eyes. The salesperson, after looking through his stock, hands Tom a pair of goggles and tells him, "These are what you need." Tom purchases the goggles, and when he uses them, a piece of metal pierces the lens of the goggle and damages Tom's eye.

Can Tom state a claim under the provisions of the implied warranty statute, section 2-2-315, presented in the previous example? How does the statute apply?

Statutory Elements	Facts of Client's Case
1. Seller of goods	The seller was a salesperson at the local hardware, a seller within the meaning of the statute. The item sold, goggles, meets the definition of goods. (The goggles are "things movable at the time of sale.")

2. Has reason to know the buyer's purpose in purchasing the goods	The seller was directly told Tom's purpose for buying the goggles.
3. Has reason to know of buyer's reliance on seller's judgment	This is implied from Tom's conduct of allowing the seller to select the goods without any input from Tom.
4. Reliance by buyer on seller's skill or	Tom relied on the salesperson's judgment. He indicated the purpose and accepted, without independent judgment or act, what the seller selected.
5. At the time of contracting	The seller knew at the time of the sale, not later, of Tom's purpose and reliance.

After the elements of the statute have been identified and the facts of the client's case compared and matched with the required elements of the statute, a determination may be reached about how the statute applies. In this example, it can be concluded that the conduct of the salesperson is covered by the statute and that an implied warranty was created. All the required elements of the statute are established by the facts in Tom's case:

1. The salesperson was a seller within the meaning of the statute, and the items sold were goods.
2. At the time of the sale, the seller was informed by the buyer of the specific purpose for which the goods were being purchased.
3. The seller knew of the buyer's reliance on his skill and judgment.
4. The buyer relied on the expertise and judgment of the seller.
5. The seller knew at the time of the sale, not later.

Narrative Summary

In the following example, a narrative summary is used rather than a chart.

For Example: Assume section 56-6-1 of the Open Meetings Act provides that "all meetings of two or more members of any board . . . at which any public business is discussed or at which any action may be taken or is taken are declared to be public meetings open to the public." The section further provides:

> "a. Such meetings shall be held only after full and timely public notice.
> b. This section does not apply to chance meetings or social gatherings at which discussion of public business is not the central purpose."

Ida and Dan are members of a three-person state board. They run into each other at a Christmas party and discuss board business.

Is this meeting an open meeting governed by section 56-6-1? The application of step 2 reveals an open meeting is required by the statute when the following elements are present:

1. Two or more board members
2. Meet at other than a chance or social gathering where discussion of public business is not the central purpose and
3. Public business is discussed or action may be or is taken.

A narrative summary of the elements and the application of the statute to the facts illustrates step 3:

1. Two or more board members. This element is met. Both Dan and Ida are board members.
2. Meet at other than a chance or social gathering where discussion of public business is not the central purpose. It appears that this element is not met by the facts. This was a social gathering and also possibly a chance meeting. The gathering was a Christmas party. It does not appear that the discussion of public business was the central purpose. If it is discovered that the sole reason they went to the party was to discuss public business, the exclusion in subsection b of the statute probably does not apply and the meeting may be covered by the act.
3. Public business is discussed or action may be or is taken. This element is met. Public business was discussed.

After performing step 3, it appears that this was not public meeting within the meaning of the act. Although the requirements of the first and third element are met (two or more board members met and discussed public business), the requirements of the second element are not.

When performing step 3, remember to match the client's facts with the required elements of a statute. When this is accomplished, you can determine how the statute applies. In the example concerning the purchase of goggles and the sale of goods, all the required statutory elements were met by the facts of the client's case, and an implied warranty was created. In the public-meetings example, the facts did not meet the requirements of the second element of the statute, and therefore, the meeting was not a public meeting within the meaning of the statute.

Summary of the Statutory Analysis Process

The three steps presented in this section are a useful approach to statutory analysis. These steps may be summarized as follows:

- Step 1 Determine if the statute applies in any way to the legal problem or issue.
- Step 2 Carefully read the statute and identify the required elements.
- Step 3 Compare or match the required elements to the facts of the problem and determine how the statute applies.

In addition to this three-step approach, there are other general considerations that must be kept in mind when analyzing statutory law. These considerations are presented in the following section.

GENERAL CONSIDERATIONS

There are two major considerations and guidelines that *always* must be kept in mind when you are engaged in statutory analysis:

1. Legislative history
2. Canons of construction

These considerations come into play, and are of the greatest importance, when the meaning of the statute is unclear and the meaning has not been determined by a court.

When required to interpret a statute, a court will first look to the plain meaning of the language of the statute. This is called the Plain Meaning Rule. The rule mandates that a statute will be interpreted according to its plain meaning. Words will be interpreted according to their common meanings. The court will render an interpretation that reflects the plain meaning of the language and is consistent with the meaning of all other sections of the act. If the meaning is clear on its face, no additional inquiries concerning the meaning of the statute are allowed. If there is ambiguity in the meaning of a statutory section, the court will look to the legislative history of the statute and apply canons of construction.

plain meaning rule
A canon of construction that provides that if the meaning of a statute is clear on its face, it will be interpreted according to its plain meaning and the other canons of construction will not be applied by the court.

When engaging in statutory analysis, you should be aware of and keep in mind the considerations that the court applies when interpreting the meaning of a statute. The reason for this is obvious: You want your interpretation of the meaning of the statute and how it will be applied to coincide with that of the court. Each of these considerations is addressed in this section.

Legislative History

To determine the meaning of a statute, a court may look to the legislative history of the statute to discover what the legislature intended it to mean. Legislative history is the record of the legislation during the enactment process before it became law. The history is composed of committee reports, transcripts of hearings, statements of legislators concerning the legislation, and any other material published for legislative use in regard to the legislation.

legislative history
The record of legislation during the enactment process. It is composed of committee reports, transcripts of hearings, statements of legislators concerning the legislation, and any other material published for legislative use in regard to the legislation.

Legislative history may be of assistance in several ways when interpreting a statute. The history may identify why an ambiguous term was used and what meaning the legislature intended, what the legislature intended the statute to accomplish, the general purpose of the legislation and so on.

For Example: Suppose section A(9) of the Housing Discrimination Act provides that no person shall deny an individual housing on the basis of gender preference. The court is called upon to interpret the term person. Does it include corporations and businesses such as partnerships?

In the case before the court, a closely held corporation that owned an apartment complex refused to rent an apartment to a couple because of their gender preference. The corporation argued that a corporation is not a person within the meaning of the statute. Included in the legislative history of the statute is a committee report recommending the passage of the legislation. The report contains the following: "The intent of the legislation is to eliminate any and all forms of gender discrimination in housing. The term 'person' is intended to include all individuals and business entities, including corporations." The legislative history in this example provides the court guidance in interpreting the statute.

Note that for federal statutes there is usually a great deal of legislative history. This may be reviewed by consulting the congressional record. Legislative history for state statutes may be very limited or nonexistent, depending on the state. The appropriate state legislative records or service office should be consulted for the availability of legislative history.

Remember, legislative history is considered only if the plain meaning of a statute is not clear or sections of a statute are internally inconsistent. If the meaning is clear, that meaning will be applied by the court even if the legislative history indicates the legislature intended a different meaning.

Canons of Construction

canons of construction
The rules and guidelines courts use when interpreting statutes.

Canons of construction are rules and guidelines the courts use when interpreting statutes. A fundamental rule of construction that determines when canons of construction are applied by a court is the Plain Meaning Rule. If the meaning is clear on its face, the other canons of constructions will not be applied by a court.

The canons of construction are too numerous to be addressed individually in this text, but some of the more well-known canons are presented here.

1. *Expressio Unius*. The entire Latin phrase is *expressio unius est exclusio alterius*, which translates as "the expression of one excludes all others." If the statute contains a list of what is covered, everything else is excluded.

   For Example: If a statute governing artists lists potters, glassblowers, painters, poets, writers, and sculptors but does not list weavers, weavers are not covered by the statute. Only the occupations listed are covered. All other occupations are not covered.

   Note, however, that statutes are often written to state that a list is not exclusive. When so written, this canon of construction does not apply, and the statute is not limited to the items listed.

   For Example: "A 'Building' as used in this statute means a structure on private or commercial property and includes *but is not limited* to a dwelling, an office of fixed location, . . ."

2. *Ejusdem Generis*. This term means of the same genus or class. As a canon of construction, it means that whenever a statute contains a specific list followed by a general term, the general term is interpreted to be limited to other things of the same class or kind as those in the list.

   For Example: A statute regulating self-propelled vehicles lists "bicycles, tricycles, unicycles, and other devices." "Other devices" is limited to mean devices of the same class or kind as bicycles, tricycles, and unicycles. Motorized vehicles are not "other devices" within the meaning of the statute.

3. *Pari Materia*. This Latin phrase translates as "on the same subject matter." As a canon, it means that statutes dealing with the same subject should be interpreted consistently.

   For Example: Assume a state's Fair Housing Act prohibits discrimination against an individual on the basis of "gender preference." The state's Fair Employment Act also uses the term *gender preference*. The term should be interpreted consistently in both statutes unless each statute has a definitions section that gives a clearly different meaning.

4. *Intended Remedy*. Statutes are to be interpreted in a manner that furthers the intended legislative remedy.
5. *Entire Context*. The words, phrases, and subsections of a statute are to be interpreted in the context of the entire statute.
6. *Constitutionality*. Statutes are assumed to be constitutional and should be construed in a manner that preserves their constitutionality, if possible.
7. *Criminal Statutes*. Criminal statutes are to be narrowly interpreted.

The most important consideration to keep in mind when interpreting the meaning of a statute is that courts refer to legislative history and canons of construction only when the meaning of the statute is not clear. If the meaning is clear on its face, there is no room for interpretation. The plain meaning governs.

It is also important to remember that, as with all matters involving common law, when a court interprets a statute, the principle of stare decisis applies. A court will follow the interpretation previously adopted unless the previous interpretation is overruled and a new interpretation is adopted. Stare decisis and precedent are covered in Chapters 1 and 8.

KEY POINTS CHECKLIST: *Working with Statutes*

- ❑ When reviewing a statute, do not limit your focus to a specific section. Remember, a section is one part of an entire act that usually contains several statutory sections. A section must be read in the context of the entire act. Be sure you are familiar with all the sections of the act, as there may be another section, such as a definitions section, that affects the interpretation of the statute you are reading.
- ❑ When you find a statute that appears to apply, do not stop your research. In many instances, more than one statute or legislative act governs or applies to a specific question or fact situation.
- ❑ Read statutes carefully and slowly. Several readings may be necessary. You may have to make a chart or diagram of the various sections and subsections of a statute to gain an understanding of the operation of the statute.
- ❑ All the words of a statute have meaning. If a word does not seem necessary or appears repetitive, you may have misread the statute. Read it again. Consult a secondary source that contains a discussion or interpretation of the statute.
- ❑ Do not assume a word means what you think it does. Many statutory words are terms of art, loaded with meaning. Check the definitions section of the statute, case law, or a legal dictionary to ensure you give the correct meaning to a term.
- ❑ The plain meaning of a statute governs its statutory interpretation. If the meaning is clear, it is not subject to interpretation.
- ❑ If the statute is unclear or ambiguous, look to other sources for guidance, such as legislative history or applicable canons of constructions. Are there court opinions that interpret the statute? Are there secondary sources, such as law review articles, encyclopedia sections, and so on, that discuss the statute?

APPLICATION

The application of the principles of statutory analysis is illustrated in the following examples.

Chapter Hypothetical

In the hypothetical situation presented at the beginning of the chapter, Cecil's research turns up five sections of the state's Commercial Code Sales Act that may apply:

- Section 29-2-102 provides that the act applies to the sale of goods only. Services are specifically excluded in the act.
- Section 29-2-105 defines goods as "all things which are movable at the time of the contract for sale."
- Section 29-2-313 provides that an express warranty is created by a seller's affirmation of fact or promise that relates to the quality of the goods.

- Section 29-2-314 states that "a warranty that the goods shall be merchantable is implied in a contract for their sale if the seller is a merchant with respect to goods of that kind."
- Section 29-2-315 provides, "Where the seller at the time of contracting has reason to know any particular purpose of which the goods are required and that the buyer is relying on the seller's skill or judgment to select or furnish suitable goods there is a warranty that the goods shall be fit for such purpose."

After conducting research on how to analyze statutory law, Cecil applies the steps recommended in this chapter.

Step 1 Determine if the statute applies. When reviewing the statutes, Cecil notes that section 29-2-102 provides that the Commercial Code Sales Act only applies to the sale of goods. If this transaction is not a sale of goods, the statute does not apply and the warranty provisions of the act do not apply.

Section 29-2-105 defines goods as "all things which are movable. . . ." This definition is of no help. Is a permanent hair treatment movable within the meaning of the act? In this case, both goods and services are involved. The service portion, the beautician applying the permanent, does not appear to be goods within the meaning of the statute but is clearly a service. The invoice, however, shows that Mrs. Jackson paid twenty dollars for a perm kit. The perm kit is clearly goods under the act. The transaction is a mixed transaction involving both services and goods. Cecil's review of the statute indicates that there is no section that addresses mixed transactions.

Since the statute does not give guidance concerning mixed transactions, Cecil must refer to case law. In the case of *Elie v. American Saloon,* the court provides guidance for determining when a mixed transaction is a sale of goods covered by the Commercial Code Sales Act.

The court adopted what it called the predominant factor test. Under this test, the nature of the contract will be determined by what predominates. If the transaction involves primarily a service, it is a service contract and is not covered by the act. If the transaction involves primarily the sale of goods, it is a sale of goods and is covered by the act. In its discussion of the application of the test, the court stated that the bill or receipt should be examined. If the largest portion of the bill applies to the cost of the goods sold, the transaction is predominately a sale of goods and the act applies. If the majority of the bill applies to the services provided, the transaction is a service transaction, not covered by the act.

Applying this test to Mrs. Jackson's facts, the bill clearly indicates that the largest portion of the transaction applied to the service of giving the permanent. Twenty dollars was charged for the perm kit (goods) and sixty dollars for giving the permanent (services). Cecil concludes that under the predominant factor test, the service predominates the transaction, and it appears to be a service contract not covered by the act. After performing step 1, Cecil concludes that there is no warranty relief available against Beauty Care Beauty Salon because the Commercial Code Sales Act does not apply to the transaction.

Cecil's conclusion is based on his interpretation of the law. Since he is new at statutory analysis, he knows his analysis could be wrong. To be on the safe side, he continues his analysis in order to provide his supervisory attorney a complete review of the law. He proceeds to steps 2 and 3.

Step 2 Analyze the statute. If the act did apply, that is, if it were concluded that the transaction was a sale of goods rather than a service, which of the warranty remedies, if any, would be available to Mrs. Jackson? Cecil carefully reads the statute and determines that the three warranties included in sections 29-2-313, 29-2-314, and 29-2-315 are the only possible warranties available in the act. Which of these would apply?

Clearly, sections 29-2-313 and 29-2-315 would not apply. Section 29-2-313 requires some affirmation or promise by the seller relating to the quality of the goods. In Mrs. Jackson's case, there was no statement by the beautician, either oral or written, concerning the quality of the permanent. Section 29-2-315 also would not apply, as Mrs. Thomas did not communicate any particular purpose for which the goods were required. Also, there are no facts to indicate that she in any way relied on the beautician's expertise in selecting the permanent, although it could be argued that this is implicit in getting a permanent. To be on the safe side, Cecil reviews the courts' interpretation of the term *particular purpose.* The case law indicates that the term refers to a unique and specific purpose for which the goods are required that is clearly and specifically communicated by the buyer to the seller. The facts in Mrs. Jackson's case show there was no specific communication.

Cecil's last hope is section 29-2-314. He reads the statute and identifies the following as the elements of an implied warranty of merchantability:

1. The transaction must be a contract for the sale of goods.
2. The seller must be a merchant of those goods.

On the face of it, it appears that this statute would apply. Cecil proceeds to step 3.

Step 3 Apply the statute to the legal problem or issue. Cecil applies the statute to the problem through the use of a chart.

Statutory Elements	**Facts of Client's Case**
1. Contract for sale of goods	Assuming that the predominant factor test did lead to the conclusion that this transaction is a sale of goods, not services, then this is a sale-of-goods transaction.
2. Seller is a merchant of those goods	The act defines *merchant* as a person who deals in goods of the kind sold. If the beauty salon and the beautician routinely sell perm kits, then the seller is a "merchant." Here, the salon routinely sells perm kits when it charges for them as a part of a permanent. Therefore, the seller is a "merchant."

After performing this step, Cecil can reach a conclusion on whether the statute would apply and whether Mrs. Jackson would have a cause of action for breach of warranty under section 29-2-314. Assuming that the transaction were a sale of goods, which is doubtful in light of the conclusion reached in step 1, it appears that the statute would apply: there would be contract for the sale of goods by a merchant of those goods.

Under section 29-2-314, the seller warrants that the goods are merchantable, which is defined in case law as meaning "fit for the ordinary purposes for which such goods are used." In Mrs. Jackson's case, the goods obviously were not fit for their ordinary purpose. Her hair broke off and changed color. If section 29-2-314 applies, Mrs. Jackson clearly has a claim for breach of warranty. Remember, however, the conclusion in step 1 was that section 29-2-314 does not apply because the transaction is probably a sale of a service, not goods.

Will Revocation Statute

Section 50-5 of a state statute is the applicable statute in this example. It provides as follows:

> No will in writing, nor any part thereof, shall be revoked unless, with the intent to revoke, the testator:
> a. executes a subsequent will or codicil,
> b. prepares a writing declaring an intention to revoke the same which is executed in a manner in which a will is required to be executed, or
> c. the testator or some person in the testator's presence and by the testator's direction . . . cancels, or destroys the same, with the intent to revoke.

The following facts apply in this example. Before Mary Glenn died, she directed her brother, Tom Glenn, to cancel her will. Because she was too weak to write, she directed her brother to cancel the will by writing across the first page, "I hereby revoke this will. It is my intent that this will be no longer valid. I direct my brother to do this because I can no longer write." Tom took the will to Mary's kitchen, a room adjacent to her bedroom, and wrote what Mary had requested on the first page of the will and added, "This was done at the request of Mary Glenn by me, Tom Glenn."

Was the will validly revoked under the terms of the statute?

Step 1 Determine if the statute applies. The statute appears on its face to apply to this fact situation. The statute governs will revocations and this is an attempted revocation.

Step 2 Analyze the statute. After a careful reading, the statute can be analyzed and the required elements identified. The statute provides three ways in which a written will can be revoked:

1. By a subsequent will or codicil executed by the testator, with the intent to revoke
2. By a writing intended to revoke the will, executed in the same manner as a will is required to be executed
3. By the testator or some person in the testator's presence and by the testator's direction, canceling or destroying the will with the intent to revoke

Step 3 Apply the statute to the legal problem or issue. When the statute is applied to the fact situation, it appears that subsections (a) and (b) clearly do not apply. Subsection (a) requires a subsequent will or codicil, neither of which are present in Mary Glenn's case. Subsection (b) requires a writing revoking the will, executed in a manner in which a will must be executed. Assume that research reveals that the state statutes require a will to be witnessed by two witnesses. There were no witnesses in this case. The requirements of this subsection are not met because the writing by Tom was not executed in the required Manner.

If there is a valid revocation under the statute, it can only have occurred under the cancellation provisions of subsection (c). For a revocation to occur under subsection (c), the following elements must be met:

1. The testator or some person
   a. in the presence of the testator, and
   b. by the testator's direction

2. Cancels or destroys the will
3. With the intent to revoke.

In this example, the required elements of the statute will be applied to the facts of the case in a different way than in the previous example. In the previous example, a chart was used. Here, a narrative summary is used:

1. Testator or some person. The requirements of this element are met. The testator did not cancel the will but "some person," her brother, did.
   a. In the presence of the testator. It is questionable whether this element is met. Does "in the testator's presence" mean actual physical presence in the same room? If the person canceling the will is in an adjacent room, is that "in the testator's presence?" If the statute does not define the term *presence,* case law must be consulted. If the courts have not interpreted the term, the legislative history of the act may shed some light.
   b. By the direction of the testator. This element is met. Mary Glenn directed her brother to revoke the will.
2. Cancels or destroys the will. This element appears to be met. The language clearly revokes the will and appears on the will itself. The statute does not require that the revocation language appear on a specific page of the will such as the signature page. Case law should be consulted to see if the courts have established where the revocation language must be placed.
3. With the intent to revoke. This element is met. The intent to revoke is clearly indicated in the language Mary Glenn chose.

The conclusion is that the statute applies and the will has been revoked if the presence requirement is met and if cancellation language is effective when placed on the first page of a will. By following the three recommended steps, subsections (a) and (b) of the statute were eliminated from consideration, and the subsection that could apply was identified (subsection (c)). The application analysis helps focus the attention on what research is needed to reach a final conclusion. Note that the final conclusion cannot be reached in step 3 until research is conducted to determine what "in the testator's presence" requires under the statute.

SUMMARY

An increasingly expanding source of law in the United States is the law passed by legislative bodies. This body of law, commonly called statutory law, assumes a greater role because many matters once covered by the common law are now addressed by state and federal legislative bodies. As a result of this growth, paralegals are more frequently engaged in analyzing legal problems and issues governed by statutory law, which means they must have the ability to conduct statutory analysis.

Statutory analysis is the process of determining if a statute applies, how it applies, and the effect of that application. A prerequisite to analyzing a statute is a familiarity with the parts or components of a statute. While these may vary in different jurisdictions, it is helpful to have an understanding of the basic framework commonly used.

The most efficient way to address a problem involving a statute is to have a process for or an approach to statutory analysis. This chapter presents a three-step approach.

The first step is the determination of whether the statute governs the situation in any way. This step involves locating all the possible statutes that may apply, then deciding which ones apply to the facts raised by the legal problem. If the problem involves the sale of land, for example, statutes governing the sale of goods do not apply.

The second step is to carefully read the statute and identify what is required for the statute to apply. These requirements are usually referred to as the elements of the statute. A careful analysis may require several readings of the statute and reference to interpretative sources, such as court opinions, or secondary sources, such as treatises, law review articles, and so on.

The third step is the application of the elements to the facts of the legal problem. This step involves matching the elements of the statute to the facts of the case and determining how the statute applies.

When engaging in statutory analysis, there are considerations and guidelines that should be kept in mind. Most of these come into play when the meaning of a statute is unclear or ambiguous. In addition to court opinions, which give guidance to the interpretation of a statute, legislative history and canons of construction may be consulted. Legislative history is composed of all the legislative material and records concerning a statute before it became law. Canons of construction are guidelines developed by courts for use in interpreting ambiguous statutes. These sources should not be used if the meaning of the statute is clear on its face.

The ease with which you are able to analyze a statute increases with practice. The more you read and analyze statutes, the easier it becomes. The exercises at the end of this chapter may prove helpful in this regard.

EXERCISES

In the following exercises, a statute is presented, followed by questions concerning the statute.

ASSIGNMENT 1

Statute: Section 30-1-6, Nuncupative Wills.

A. A nuncupative will may be made only by a person in imminent peril of death and shall be valid only if the testator died as a result of the impending peril, and must be:
   1. Declared to be his last will by the testator before two disinterested witnesses;
   2. Reduced to writing by or under the direction of one of the witnesses within thirty days after such declaration; and
   3. Submitted for probate within six months after the death of the testator.

B. The nuncupative will may dispose of personal property only and to an aggregate value not exceeding one thousand dollars.

C. A nuncupative will does not revoke an existing written will. Such written will is changed only to the extent necessary to give effect to the nuncupative will.

Note, a nuncupative is an oral will, a will that is not written.

Questions:

A. What type of wills does this statute apply to?
B. What requirements must be met for a nuncupative will to be valid—that is, what are the elements?
C. Mr. Lang, on his deathbed, writes his will on a piece of notepaper, signs it, and delivers it to his sister for safekeeping. Does the statute govern the validity of this will?
D. Larry, on his deathbed, declares that it is his will and that all his property should go to his girlfriend, Beth. There are three witnesses present—Beth, Larry's sister Mary, and the next-door neighbor, Tom. Tom is in an adjoining room. The door to the adjoining room is open. Tom hears what Larry is saying. Assume for this example that the will is reduced to writing within thirty days and submitted for probate within six months.
   1. Is this a valid will under this statute? What additional information may be necessary?

2. Assume this is a valid will, and Tom had a previous valid written will. What impact does the nuncupative will have on the written will? What is disposed of by the nuncupative will?

ASSIGNMENT 2

Statute: The following statute is a section of the Commercial Code Sales Act adopted by the state legislature—Section 2-201, Statute of Frauds:

> A contract for the sale of goods for the price of five hundred dollars or more is not enforceable by way of action or defense unless there is some writing sufficient to indicate that a contract for sale has been made between the parties and signed by the party against whom enforcement is sought or by the party's authorized agent or broker. A writing is not insufficient because it omits or incorrectly states a term agreed upon, but the contract is not enforceable under this paragraph beyond the quantity of goods shown in such writing.

Assume that the act applies to the sales of goods. Goods are defined in section 2-100 as "those things movable" and do not include real property.

Questions:

A. Does the statute apply to the lease of goods?
B. What are the required elements of the statute? In other words, for a contract for the sale of goods of five hundred dollars or more to be enforceable, what is required?
C. Mary orally contracts to buy ten car tires at seventy dollars each. The seller prepares a contract and gives it to Mary. Neither party signs the contract.
   1. Who can enforce the contract under the provisions of the statute?
   2. Assume the contract is signed by Mary only. Who can enforce the contract?
   3. Assume that both parties sign the contract and the written contract incorrectly provides for nine tires at seventy dollars each. Is the contract enforceable under the statute? If so, to what extent?
   4. Assume both parties sign the contract and it reads fifteen tires at seventy dollars each. Is the contract enforceable under the statute? If so, to what extent?
   5. Assume there is no written contract. The seller hands Mary a slip of paper upon which he has written "this is to confirm our oral agreement." He and Mary both sign the paper. Is there an enforceable contract under the provisions of the statute? If so, to what extent?

ASSIGNMENT 3

Statute: Section 35-1-4, Privileged Communications—Husband and Wife:

> In all actions, husband and wife may testify for or against each other, provided that neither may testify as to any communication or admission made by either of them to the other during the marriage, except in actions:
>
> a. between such husband and wife, and,
> b. where the custody, support, health or welfare of their children or children in either spouse's custody or control is directly in issue.

Questions:

A. Prepare an outline of the statutory elements.
B. When can a husband or wife testify against each other? When are they prohibited from testifying against each other?
C. Husband, while driving under the influence of alcohol, ran a stop sign and his vehicle collided with a vehicle driven by Mr. Smith. Husband's spouse (Wife) and two children were passengers in the car. The day after the wreck, Husband told Wife that he knew he ran the stop sign because he was drunk. Mr. Smith sues Husband for negligence. When answering the following questions, identify any additional information that may be necessary to answer the question.
   1. Can Wife be compelled to testify concerning her conversation with Husband? Why or why not?
   2. Can Wife voluntarily testify concerning the conversation? Why or why not?
   3. If Husband and Wife are legally separated, can Wife voluntarily testify concerning the conversation? Why or why not?
   4. Is the conversation admissible if they are divorced at the time of the lawsuit? Why or why not?
   5. Husband and Wife have lived together as husband and wife for the past twenty years. They have never been formally married. Can Wife testify against Husband concerning the conversation? Why or why not?
   6. Is the conversation admissible in a divorce action between Husband and Wife? Why or why not?

CHAPTER 4

Case Law and Case Briefing

After obtaining an associate's degree in Paralegal Studies, Carolyn took time off to be with Josh, the newest addition to her family. Josh was born three days after Carolyn's last final examination. She was glad he waited until finals were over.

Carolyn decided it was important to give Josh her full attention for as long as she could. She was financially in a position to take a year off from work.

After the year had passed, she was hired by a large law firm and assigned to the torts section of the paralegal department. Her first assignment was to brief several cases that another assistant had located for possible use in a response to a motion to dismiss. The first case she was given was *Rael v. Cadena.* (This case is presented in the Court Opinion—Elements section of this chapter. See Figure 4–1.)

Carolyn knew it was important to do a good job on her first assignment. After reading *Rael v. Cadena,* she realized she needed to refresh her memory on case briefing. It had been a long time since she had briefed a case. She thought to herself, "How do I brief a case? What should a good case brief look like? Why is it important?"

INTRODUCTION

The focus of this chapter is on court opinions and the briefing of them. The chapter addresses the same questions Carolyn faced when undertaking her assignment—that is, what is a case brief, and what are the elements of a court opinion and a case brief? Throughout this chapter, a brief of a court opinion will be referred to as a case brief.

COURT OPINIONS—IN GENERAL

As discussed in Chapter 1, the two major sources of law are enacted law (constitutions, laws enacted by legislative bodies, including ordinances, and so on) and the common law. Common law consists of the law made by courts when they interpret existing law or create new law. It is often called case law. The terms *case law* and *common law* are used interchangeably in this chapter.

The common law is found in the written opinions of the courts. Courts often announce rules of law when interpreting statutory or constitutional provisions or create new law when there is no statutory or constitutional law governing the legal dispute.

For Example—Statutory Interpretation: Suppose a statute uses the term *publication* but fails to define it. The court, addressing the issue of what constitutes publication, announces a rule of law that the term *publication* as used in the statute means communication to a third party.

For Example—Creating Law: Assume a state has not enacted legislation recognizing strict liability as a cause of action in tort. The highest court in the state, in a case before it, announces a rule of law adopting strict liability as a cause of action in the state.

common law/case law

The body of law created by courts. It is composed of the general legal rules, doctrines, and principles adopted by courts when interpreting existing law or when creating law in the absence of controlling enacted law.

Rules of law announced by the courts in court opinions are commonly referred to as common law, case law, or judge-made law. Case law or common law is the body of law on a particular subject created by the court opinions on that subject.

According to *Black's Law Dictionary,* a court opinion is a statement "by a judge or court of the decision reached in regard to a cause tried or argued before them, expounding the law as applied to the case, and detailing the reasons upon which the judgment is based." It is the court's decision and the reasons for the decision. In other words, it is the court's resolution of the legal dispute that is before the court and the reasons in support of its resolution.

court opinion

The statement of a court of its decision reached in a case, the rule that applies, and the reasons for the court's decision.

Often the terms *court opinion, case,* and *decision* are used interchangeably to refer to a court's resolution of an issue or a decision in a dispute. In this chapter, the terms *court opinion* and *case* are used to refer to the written opinion of a court.

For Example: "The case stands for the principle that. . . ." "The court opinion holds that flag-burning is protected under the Freedom of Speech provisions of the First Amendment."

COURT OPINIONS—IMPORTANCE

Of the two major sources of law, enacted law and case (common) law, case law constitutes the largest body of law, far larger in volume than constitutional or statutory law. In the broadest sense, it is essential to acquire a general familiarity with this body of law, since it represents such a large portion of the law. In a narrower sense, you must study case law because so many areas of law are governed by case law.

There are numerous additional reasons why reading and analyzing court opinions and studying case law are important. Overall, the major reasons are the following:

1. *To Learn the Common Law.* Much of the law is court-made. In order to determine the elements of a cause of action for a court-made law, you must refer to case law. Your client's fact situation may be governed by case law, and to determine what law applies and the probable outcome, case law must be analyzed.

   For Example: In most states, the cause of action for civil battery is a creation of case law, not statutory law. To identify the elements necessary to state a battery claim, the case law must be researched.

2. *To Interpret Constitutional or Statutory Law.* Court opinions often announce rules of law that govern how a statutory or constitutional term or provision is to be interpreted or applied. Therefore, case law must be consulted to understand how to interpret and apply statutes and constitutional provisions.

   For Example: The United States Supreme Court has issued many opinions on the types of speech protected by the First Amendment. To determine if an individual who burns a state flag in front of the state capital is protected by the First Amendment's freedom of speech provisions, Supreme Court opinions interpreting freedom of speech must be consulted.

3. *To Understand the Litigation Process.* Court opinions often address legal questions that arise in the context of the litigation process—either before, during, or after trial. Court opinions give insight into the process by explaining what conduct is appropriate, which arguments are successful, where errors are made, how procedural rules apply, how trials and motion hearings should proceed, and so on.
4. *To Gain Insight into Legal Analysis.* In a court opinion, the court often analyzes the law. The court discusses what law applies, how it applies, the reasons for its application, and how the reasons operate to govern the application of the law to the facts of the case. By studying court opinions, you learn how to assemble a legal argument, how to determine if a law applies, and how to support a legal argument.
5. *To Develop Legal Writing Skills.* Judges are usually experienced in legal writing, and most opinions are well written. You may read opinions with an eye to how sentences and paragraphs are structured, how case law and statutory law are referred to and incorporated into legal writing, and how transitions are accomplished. If you have a problem putting some aspect of your research into writing, look at an opinion to see how a court handled a similar matter.

For Example: Suppose you are preparing a research memorandum. There is no case law in your jurisdiction governing the issue; however, there is strong persuasive precedent from another jurisdiction. You are unsure about how to introduce the persuasive precedent in your memorandum. By reading a court opinion where the court relied on persuasive precedent, you can study the language the court used to introduce the persuasive precedent and use the court's language as a guide after which to model your introduction.

For Example: In *Smith v. Jones*, the court stated, "There is no case law in this jurisdiction interpreting the term 'publication' as used in § 55-5-67A. The state of Texas, however, has an identical statute, and the Supreme Court of Texas, in the case of *Frank v. Inex*, interpreted 'publication' to mean communication to a third party."

For the above reasons and many others, the study of case law is important. The skill of being able to correctly analyze and apply case law is essential to legal analysis.

COURT OPINIONS—SOURCES

Where are court opinions printed, and how do you locate them? This text does not address the fundamentals of legal research. That subject by itself requires an entire text and, hopefully, is addressed by a separate course in your studies. Therefore, only a brief summary of where and how case law is found is provided here.

Court opinions are generally found in the law library. They are printed in reporters, advance sheets, and slip opinions (recent opinions). They are also available through various computerized sources, such as WESTLAW, LEXIS, Law on Disc (for those states that have law on CD-ROM), and on the Internet.

For Example: A California supreme court opinion may be found in the *California Reporter, Pacific Reporter,* or through WESTLAW or LEXIS.

A United States Supreme Court opinion may be found in the *United States Reports, Supreme Court Reporter, Supreme Court Reports—Lawyer's Edition,* WESTLAW, LEXIS, and so on.

Some of the sources that may be consulted to help you locate a court opinion are digests, ALRs *(American Law Reports),* legal encyclopedias, treatises, looseleaf sources, legal periodicals, *Shepard's, Words and Phrases,* WESTLAW, LEXIS, and

CD-ROM and Internet databases. Many of these sources that are helpful in locating a case also may be consulted to help you gain an understanding of the case.

For Example: ALRs, legal encyclopedias, treatises, legal periodicals, and so on often include a discussion of an opinion along with the opinion and address the areas of law that are considered in the opinion.

COURT OPINIONS—ELEMENTS

In General

The first requirement in properly analyzing a court opinion is to be familiar with the elements of an opinion. A court opinion usually includes some or all of the following components:

1. The facts that gave rise to the legal dispute before the court
2. The procedural history and posture of the case—that is, what happened in the lower court or courts, who appealed what decision and why
3. The issue or issues that are addressed and resolved by the court
4. The rule of law that governs the dispute
5. The application of the rule of law to the facts—in other words, the holding
6. The reason or reasons supporting the court's application of the rule of law to the facts, that is, why the court decided as it did
7. The relief granted or denied. For example, "The judgment of the trial court is upheld."

Elements of a Reported Case

West Publishing Company, the publisher of the regional reporters and most of the federal reporters, follows a uniform format when publishing court opinions. A similar format is followed by Lawyers Cooperative Publishing in its publication of *Supreme Court Reports—Lawyer's Edition.* Since the majority of court opinions are published by West Publishing, an example of an opinion published by West Publishing is presented in Figure 4–1. The case, *Rael v. Cadena,* is published in the *New Mexico Reports* and the *Pacific Reporter.* Note that the components of the case are identified in the left margin next to each section of the opinion. These components are summarized in the following text.

Citation

The citation refers to the volume number, page number, and the name of the reporter where the case may be found. The citation for *Rael v. Cadena* is 93 N.M. 684, 604 P.2d 822. That means the printed opinion of this case is published and may be found in two reporters: volume 93 of the *New Mexico Reports* at page 684, and volume 604 of the *Pacific Reporter,* second series, at page 822. (See CITATION in Figure 4–1.)

citation
Information that allows the reader to locate where a reference can be found. In case law, the term refers to the volume number, page number, and name of the reporter where a case may be found.

Caption

The caption includes the names of the parties to the lawsuit and their court status. Eddie Rael was the plaintiff at the trial court level, and he is the appellee on appeal. (The appellee is the person against whom the appeal is filed, the person who

party
A plaintiff or defendant in a lawsuit.

won at the trial court level.) Emilio Cadena was the defendant at the trial court level and is the appellant on appeal. (The appellant is the person who lost at the trial court level and the person who filed the appeal.) Manuel Cadena is listed as a defendant-appellant, but he is not involved in the appeal. The caption of the case used on appeal is usually the same as the caption used in the trial court. The caption of the case in the trial court includes both Cadenas as defendants, and therefore, the caption on appeal is the same. Note that the plaintiff and defendant's last names are printed in all capitals. (See CAPTION in Figure 4–1.) When referring to or citing the case, only the names in all capitals are used.

For Example: When citing this case, the citation should read: *Rael v. Cadena,* 93 N.M. 684, 604 P.2d 822 (Ct. App. 1979).

Note that below the caption is "No. 3921." This is the docket number of the case assigned by the court of appeals. Below the docket number is the name of the court that decided the case and the date of the decision. This is indicated in the citation as: (Ct. App. 1979). If the decision had been rendered by the highest court in the jurisdiction, such as the supreme court of New Mexico, only the year of the decision would appear in the parentheses: (1979). If the citation does not include a state reporter citation, a reference to the state is included in the parentheses.

For Example: *Smith v. Jones,* 292 S.W.2d 425 (Tex. 1980).

Syllabus

The syllabus is a brief summary of the opinion. It is written by West Publishing Company, not the court, and cannot be relied upon as the holding of the court. It is presented as a useful aid in providing the reader with a brief overview of the opinion. (See SYLLABUS in Figure 4–1.)

Headnotes

headnotes
Summaries of the points of law discussed in a court opinion prepared by the publisher of the opinion.

key numbers
West Publishing Company has divided all areas of American law into various topics and subtopics. Each area is identified by a topic name, and each specific topic or subtopic is assigned a number called a key number.

The headnotes are summaries of the points of law discussed in the case. Headnotes follow in sequential order the relevant paragraphs of the opinion. The number to the left of the headnote corresponds to the bracketed number in the body of the opinion. (See HEADNOTES in Figure 4–1.)

For Example: In *Rael v. Cadena,* headnote 1 contains a summary of the point of law discussed in the body of the opinion between [1] and [2]. Headnote 2 is a summary of the point of law discussed in the opinion between [2] and [3]. Headnote 3 is a summary of the law discussed in the opinion between [3] and the end of the opinion.

Note: Headnotes are prepared by West Publishing Company. They are prepared for the convenience of individuals researching the case and are useful in providing a quick overview of the law and legal principles addressed in the opinion. They are not the opinion of the court and have no authority of law. *Any reference to or quote from an opinion must be taken from the opinion itself, not from the headnotes.*

Key Numbers

In bold print next to the headnote number are a few words indicating the area of law addressed in the headnote. Next to this bold print description of the area of law is a small key symbol and a number. (See KEY NUMBERS in Figure 4–1.) West

Publishing Company has divided all areas of American law into various topics and subtopics. Each area is identified by a topic name (the bold print), and each specific topic or subtopic is assigned a key number. West Publishing publishes separate volumes called *digests* that contain summaries of court opinions organized by topic and subtopic.

For Example: Next to headnote 1 in *Rael v. Cadena* is "Assault and Battery," followed by a key symbol and the number 18. The key symbol and the number 18 refer to a specific subtopic of assault and battery. The subject of this subtopic can be determined by consulting the index to "Assault and Battery" in the digest. In the body of the opinion between [1] and [2], the area of law covered is assault and battery in general. A reference to the digest reveals that key number 18 is the specific subtopic of assault and battery concerning the liability of persons who aid or encourage an assault or battery. If you want to read other court opinions in which liability for battery was based upon the conduct of aiding or encouraging a batterer at the scene of a battery, refer to the volume of the digest containing the topic "Assault and Battery." Look to the subtopic key number 18. Under that key number is a summary of all court opinions that have addressed this subtopic and the citations of those opinions.

Through this system you have easy access to all court opinions dealing with the question you are considering. The key number system is an invaluable research tool.

Attorneys

This section provides the names and cities of the attorneys in the case and who they represent. (See ATTORNEYS in Figure 4–1.)

Judge

The name of the judge who wrote the opinion is given at the beginning of the opinion itself. (See JUDGE in Figure 4–1.)

Body of the Opinion

The body of the opinion usually includes the facts of the case, the prior proceedings, the issue or issues addressed by the court, the rule of law governing the dispute, the holding, the reasoning in support of the holding, and the relief granted. (See BODY OF THE OPINION in Figure 4–1.) There are no hard-and-fast rules dictating what must be contained in a court opinion, and often one or more of the listed elements may be missing. Each of the elements of the body are discussed separately in the following:

1. *Facts.* Opinions usually include the facts that gave rise to the legal dispute. Often the opinion may include very few facts or more facts than appear relevant to the matter decided.
2. *Prior Proceedings.* In this part of the opinion, the court presents a summary of what happened in the lower court and who appealed. This may be a very brief summary, as in *Rael v. Cadena,* or it may be extensive and detailed.
3. *Issue or Issues.* The issue is the legal question addressed by the court in the opinion. The court may present the issue narrowly in the context of the facts.

   For Example: Under New Mexico tort law, does a battery occur when an individual, present at a battery, verbally encourages the assailant by yelling "Kill him!" and "Hit him more!" but does not in any other way participate in the battery?

prior proceedings
The events that occurred in the litigation in a lower court or administrative hearing.

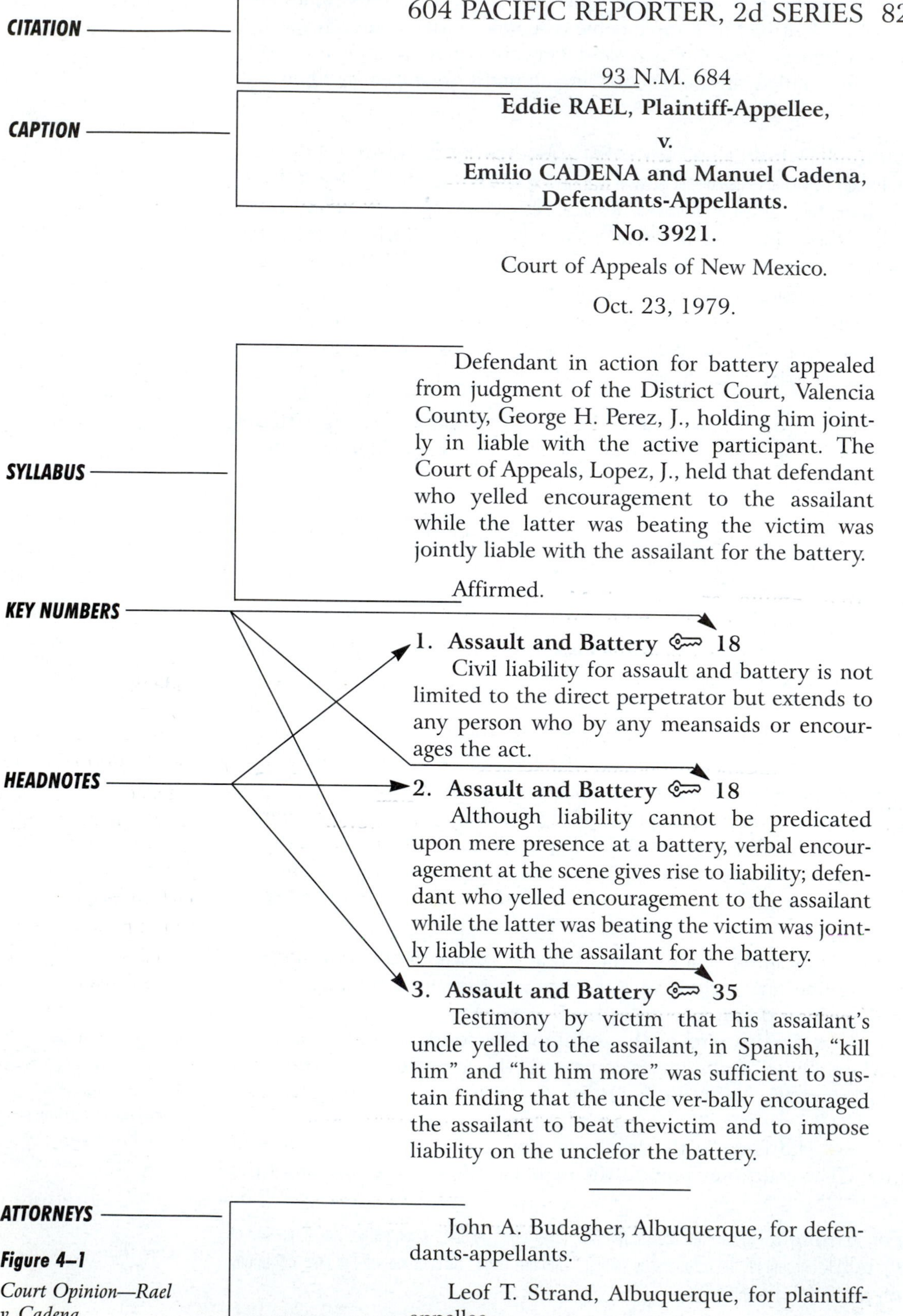

604 PACIFIC REPORTER, 2d SERIES 822

93 N.M. 684

Eddie RAEL, Plaintiff-Appellee,

v.

Emilio CADENA and Manuel Cadena, Defendants-Appellants.

No. 3921.

Court of Appeals of New Mexico.

Oct. 23, 1979.

Defendant in action for battery appealed from judgment of the District Court, Valencia County, George H. Perez, J., holding him jointly in liable with the active participant. The Court of Appeals, Lopez, J., held that defendant who yelled encouragement to the assailant while the latter was beating the victim was jointly liable with the assailant for the battery.

Affirmed.

1. **Assault and Battery** 🔑 18

Civil liability for assault and battery is not limited to the direct perpetrator but extends to any person who by any meansaids or encourages the act.

2. **Assault and Battery** 🔑 18

Although liability cannot be predicated upon mere presence at a battery, verbal encouragement at the scene gives rise to liability; defendant who yelled encouragement to the assailant while the latter was beating the victim was jointly liable with the assailant for the battery.

3. **Assault and Battery** 🔑 35

Testimony by victim that his assailant's uncle yelled to the assailant, in Spanish, "kill him" and "hit him more" was sufficient to sustain finding that the uncle ver-bally encouraged the assailant to beat thevictim and to impose liability on the unclefor the battery.

John A. Budagher, Albuquerque, for defendants-appellants.

Leof T. Strand, Albuquerque, for plaintiff-appellee.

Figure 4–1

Court Opinion—Rael v. Cadena

JUDGE

BODY OF THE OPINION

OPINION

LOPEZ, Judge.

Defendant Emilio Cadena, a non-active participant in the battery of plaintiff Eddie Rael, appeals the judgment of the trial court finding him, along with the active participant, jointly and severally liable for the battery. We affirm.

The issue on appeal is whether a person present at a battery who verbally encourages the assailant, but does not physically assist him, is civilly liable for the battery.

On a visit in Emilio Cadena's home, Eddie Rael was severely beaten on the head and torso by Emilio's nephew, Manual Cadena. As a result of the beating, he suffered a fractured rib and was hospitalized. Eddie Rael testified that once the attack had started, Emilio yelled to Manuel in Spanish, "Kill him!" and "Hit him more!" The trial court sitting without a jury found that Emilio encouraged Manuel while Manuel was beating Eddie. Based on this finding, the court held the Cadenas jointly and severally liable for the battery.

Emilio urges that in order for the trial court to have held him jointly liable for the battery, it had to find either that he and Manuel acted in concert, or that Manuel beat and injured Eddie as a result of Emilio's encouragement. This is a misstatement of the law.

[1] This is an issue of first impression in New Mexico. It is clear, however, that in the United States, civil liability for assault and battery is not limited to the direct perpetrator, but extends to any person who by any means aids or encourages the act. *Hargis v. Herrine,* 230 Ark. 502, 323 S.W.2d 917 (1959); *Ayer v. Robinson,* 163 Cal. App.2d 424, 329 P.2d 546 (1958); *Guilbeau v. Guilbeau,* 326 So.2d 654 (La.App.1976); *Duke v. Feldman,* 245 Md. 454, 226 A.2d 345 (1967); *Brink v. Purnell,* 162 Mich. 147, 127 N.W. 322 (1910); 6 Am.Jur.2d *Assault and Battery* § 128 (1963); 6A C.J.S. *Assault and Battery* § 11 (1975); Annot., 72 A.L.R.2d 1229 (1960). According to the Restatement:

> [f]or harm resulting to a third person from the tortious conduct of another, one is subject to liability if he
>
> * * * * * *
>
> (b) knows that the other's conduct constitutes a breach of duty and gives substantial assistance or encouragement to the other so to conduct himself. * * *

Restatement (Second) of Torts § 876 (1979).

[2] Although liability cannot be predicated upon mere presence at a battery, *Duke, supra;* 6 Am.Jur., *supra,* verbal encouragement at the scene gives rise to liability. *Hargis, supra; Ayer, supra, Brink, supra.*

> [A] person may be held liable for the tort of assault and battery if he *encouraged* or incited *by words* the act of the direct perpetrator. * * * (Emphasis added.)

6 Am.Jur., *supra* at 108. Because he yelled encouragement to his nephew while the latter was beating Eddie Rael, Emilio Cadena is jointly liable with his nephew for the battery.

[3] Contradictory evidence was offered as to whether Emilio Cadena did yell anything during the beating. Eddie Rael claimed that Emilio urged Manuel to beat him; Emilio denied that he said anything; and Manuel testified that he never heard Emilio. However, the trial court found that Emilio did verbally encourage Manuel to beat Eddie. Although the evidence was in conflict, the court could conclude from the testimony of Eddie Rael that Emilio Cardena verbally encouraged his nephew to attack. This testimony, if believed, is substantial evidence to support the trial court's finding. It is not the function of the appellate court to weigh the evidence or its credibility, or to substitute its judgment for that of the trial court. So long as the findings are supported by substantial evidence, they will stand. *Getz v. Equitable Life Assur. Soc. of U.S.,* 90 N.M. 195, 561 P.2d 468, *cert. denied,* 434 U.S. 834, 98 S.Ct. 121, 54 L.Ed.2d 95 (1977).

The judgment of the trial court is affirmed.

IT IS SO ORDERED.

SUTIN and ANDREWS, JJ., concur.

holding
The court's application of the rule of law to the legal question raised by the facts of a case. The court's answer to the legal issue in a case.

Or the court may state the issue broadly, merely phrasing the issue in the context of the area of law.

> **For Example:** Did the defendant commit a civil battery?

In many instances, more than one legal issue is addressed in a case. Also, the court may not present a statement of the issue or issues at all, and it may be difficult to determine what they are. The process of issue identification is discussed in Chapter 6.

Identifying and understanding the issue is the most important task of reading an opinion. If the issue is not understood, the rule of law applied by the court may not be understood, and the opinion consequently may be misanalyzed and misapplied.

4. *Rule of Law.* The rule of law is the law that governs the issue. It may be a statutory or constitutional provision or a common law doctrine, rule, principle, and so on. In *Rael v. Cadena,* common law governs the law of civil assault and battery.
5. *Holding.* The holding is the court's application of the rule of law to the facts of the case. The holding is usually presented immediately after the rule of law in the opinion or after the reasoning at the end of the opinion.
6. *Reasoning.* The reasoning is the court's explanation of how or why the rule of law applies to the dispute. On occasion the reasoning is difficult to follow. Often it is helpful to read the holding first and determine how the court ruled, then read the reasoning. By first understanding what decision was reached, you may be better able to understand the reasoning in support of the decision.
7. *Disposition/Relief Granted.* The relief granted is usually a one-sentence statement by the court that includes the order of the court as a result of the holding.

> **For Example:** In *Rael v. Cadena,* the relief granted is presented in the next to the last sentence where the court states, "The judgment of the trial court is affirmed."

A court has several options when granting relief:

- It may agree with the trial court and *affirm* the trial court's decision.
- It may disagree with the trial court and *reverse* the trial court's decision. If it reverses the decision, it will *remand,* that is, send the case back to the trial court. When a case is remanded, the appellate court may order the trial court to:
  1. Enter a judgment or order in accordance with the appellate court decision
  2. Retry the case (conduct a new trial)
  3. Conduct further proceedings in accordance with the appellate court decision
- If there are several issues, it may affirm the trial court on some of the issues and reverse the trial court on other issues.

8. *Concurring Opinion.* In some instances, a judge may agree with the majority holding but for different or additional reasons than those presented by the majority. The judge may then set out his or her reasons in support of the majority in

what is called a concurring opinion. There may be more than one concurring opinion if other judges also agree with the majority conclusion but for different or additional reasons.

9. *Dissenting Opinion.* If a judge disagrees with the majority decision, the judge may present his or her reasons in what is called a dissenting opinion. Since a dissenting opinion does not agree with the majority view, it does not have the force of law. It is valuable, however, because it may help a reader understand the majority opinion.

   For Example: The dissent may summarize what the court stated in the majority opinion. Note, however, that since the dissent disagrees with the majority view, it may mischaracterize the majority opinion.

   The dissenting opinion is also important because it may become the majority view in the future when the composition of the court changes or there is a shift in the court's position. The dissent may provide the basis for future arguments in support of overruling outdated precedent. Remember, at one time the United States Supreme Court ruled that segregation on the basis of race was legal, *Plessey v. Ferguson,* 163 U.S. 537, 16 S. Ct. 1138, 41 L. Ed. 256 (1896). Now, segregation on the basis of race is illegal, *Brown v. Board of Education of Topeka,* 347 U.S. 483, 74 S. Ct. 686, 98 L. Ed. 873 (1954).

COURT OPINION—BRIEFING (CASE BRIEF)

case brief
A written summary identifying the essential components of a court opinion.

Introduction

As a paralegal, you may be assigned the task of reading and briefing court opinions. A court opinion is usually called a case, and a brief of a court opinion is usually called a case brief or a case abstract. A case brief is a written summary identifying the essential components of a court opinion.

Importance of Briefing

The process of briefing a case serves several useful purposes and functions:

1. *Analysis/Learning.* Writing a summary of the essential elements of an opinion in an organized format leads to better understanding of the case and the reasoning of the court. Opinions are often complex, and the reasoning is hard to identify, difficult to follow, or spread throughout the opinion. The preparation of a case brief requires study of the opinion, identification of what is essential, and elimination of the nonessential. This process of studying a case and analyzing it piecemeal helps the reader gain a better understanding of it. The analytical process of focusing on the heart of the structure of the case helps you gain an understanding of the reasoning, thereby assisting your analysis of the law.
2. *Research/Reference.* A case brief is a time-saving research tool. It provides a summary of the essentials of a case that can be quickly referred to when reviewing the case. This saves the time that would be involved in having to reread and reanalyze the entire case in order to remember what the court decided and why. When working on a complex legal problem involving

several court opinions or when time has passed since a case was read, the availability of case briefs can result in a considerable savings of time because it is often difficult to remember which opinion said what.

A case brief is a valuable tool for the attorney assigned to the case. The attorney may not need to read all the cases related to an issue. The attorney can read the case briefs prepared by the paralegal and save time by quickly weeding out those cases that are not key and identifying and focusing on the cases that should be read.

3. *Writing.* The process of briefing a case serves as a valuable writing tool. It provides you with an exercise in which you learn to sift through a court opinion, identify the essential elements, and assemble your analysis into a concise written summary.

How to Read a Case

Before you can brief a case, you must first read it *carefully.* Sometimes it is necessary to read the entire opinion or parts of it several times to gain an understanding of the decision and the reasoning. You cannot expect to skim or quickly read an opinion and hope to understand it. It cannot be read like a newspaper or novel. There are several reasons for this:

Why to go slow:

1. Opinions are written by judges with the assumption that the reader has an understanding of the law, legal terminology, and the legal system. If you are a beginner, you are slowed by having to look up the meaning of legal terms and become familiar with the style of legal writing.

   For Example: In the first sentence of *Rael v. Cadena,* the court uses the phrase *jointly and severally liable.* Without a legal background, a novice would have to stop reading and look up these terms before continuing to read the case.

   Do not get discouraged if at first it takes a long time to read and understand case law. It is normal to "crawl through" court opinions when you are a novice at reading them. As you become familiar with the terminology and style of legal opinions, you will read them faster and with greater understanding. The process, however, is gradual and usually takes months rather than days to learn. No matter how skilled you are, cases *always* must be read carefully to be fully understood.

2. Some opinions are difficult to read and take time because they involve complex, abstract, or unfamiliar subjects involving multiple issues. In such instances, you may have to read the entire case or portions of it several times. You may have to prepare outlines or charts as you read to help you follow and understand the court's reasoning. You may have to refer to a treatise, encyclopedia, or other research tool to obtain an understanding of the area of law involved in the case.
3. Some opinions are difficult to read because they are poorly written. Not all judges are great writers. The reasoning may be scattered throughout the case or not completely presented.
4. Some opinions are difficult to read and understand because the court may have incorrectly interpreted or applied the law. You may be surprised when you read the holding that the court reached a conclusion that is the opposite of the outcome you expected. Remember, some decisions have been overruled because a higher or subsequent court has determined that the earlier

opinion was incorrect. Therefore, it is important to read each case with a critical eye.

In regard to the reasons presented in 3 and 4 above, the difficulty in reading and understanding an opinion may have nothing to do with your ability to read the case. Yet, in all instances, the opinion must be read carefully to be understood.

The purpose of reading a court opinion is to obtain an understanding of the law or principle addressed by the court. To gain this understanding, cases must be read and analyzed *carefully* and with *close scrutiny*. This is a must. The ability to read cases with greater understanding and speed comes with experience.

Several chapters in this text present specific guidelines to assist the reader in reading, interpreting, and analyzing court opinions:

1. Identifying the key facts of a court opinion is discussed in the Key Facts Identification—Case Law section of Chapter 5.
2. Identifying the issue in a court opinion is addressed in the Issue Identification—Case Law section of Chapter 6.
3. How to determine if a court opinion is on point and may be used as precedent is covered in the Determining If a Case Is on Point section of Chapter 8.
4. Counteranalysis and case law is discussed in the Case Law section of Chapter 9.

Case Brief—Elements

There is no standard form for a brief of a court opinion, nor are there any hard-and-fast rules governing format. Some texts recommend that case briefs contain as few as five parts, some as many as sixteen. The style of a case brief may vary from individual to individual and office to office. Be prepared to adapt to different styles.

The goal of a good case brief is to prepare a concise summary of the essentials of the court opinion that may be used as a quick reference in the future. Therefore, the brief should be concise. It certainly should not be as long or longer than the case. Do not fill the brief with excessive quotes from the case or long summaries. Spend more time thinking than writing. Reduce the opinion to its essence.

A recommended outline for a case brief format is presented in Figure 4–2. This format should be viewed as a basic outline of the essential parts of a case brief. It can be adapted as necessary to meet your needs. A discussion of each section of the outline follows.

Case Brief Format

Citation:
Parties:
Facts:
Prior Proceedings:
Issue:
Holding:
Reasoning:
Disposition:
Comments:

Figure 4–2
Case Brief Format

Citation

The citation includes the name of the parties, where the case can be found, the court that issued the opinion, and the year of the opinion.

For Example: In *Rael v. Cadena,* the citation is *Rael v. Cadena,* 93 N.M. 684, 604 P.2d 822 (Ct. App. 1979).

- *Rael v. Cadena*—name of the case
- 93 N.M. 684, 604 P.2d 822—the volume and page numbers of the books where the case can be found. This case can be found in volume 93 of the *New Mexico Reports* at page 684, and in volume 604 of the *Pacific Reporter,* second series, at page 822.
- (Ct. App. 1979)—The court that rendered the opinion and the year of the opinion. The New Mexico Court of Appeals rendered the opinion in 1979. If the date alone appears in parentheses—(1979)—the opinion was written by the highest court of the state. If there is no reference to a state reporter, a reference to the state would also be included with the date: (N.M. Ct. App. 1979).

Parties

The caption at the beginning of the opinion gives the full name and legal status of each party.

For Example:

- Eddie Rael, Plaintiff-Appellee
- Emilio Cadena, Defendant-Appellant
- Manuel Cadena, Defendant-Appellant

The legal status refers to the litigation status of the parties. This includes the status at the trial and appellate level. The status is usually indicated in the caption. The plaintiff is the person who filed the lawsuit, and the defendant is the party against whom the suit is brought. Often terminology other than *plaintiff* and *defendant* is used.

For Example: *Petitioner* and *respondent* are often used in divorce cases. The petitioner is the party who filed the divorce, and the respondent is the person against whom the divorce petition is filed.

The appeal status of the parties immediately follows the trial court status in the caption.

For Example: In *Rael v. Cadena,* Eddie Rael was the plaintiff at trial (he filed the lawsuit), and he is the party against whom the appeal was filed (he won at the trial level).

Facts

The fact section of a case brief includes a summary of those facts that describe the history of the events giving rise to the litigation. The fact section should include key and background facts.

Key Facts. The key facts are those facts in the opinion to which the law applies and that are essential to the decision reached by the court. They are those facts upon which the outcome of the case is determined. If the key facts were different, the outcome of the case would probably be different. How to identify key facts in a court opinion is discussed in Chapter 5.

Background Facts. Background facts are those facts that put the key facts in context. They are facts necessary to make sense of the story and thereby provide the reader with an overall context within which the key facts occur, an overall picture of the events of the case.

For Example: In an automobile collision case, where the impact took place on a country road, the fact that the collision took place on a country road may not be a key fact, but its inclusion in the fact section of the brief helps provide the reader with an overview of the context and scene of the collision.

In some texts, the case brief format presents the Prior Proceedings before the Facts. It is recommended that the Facts section precede the Prior Proceedings section of the brief. Since the facts of the case are the events that led to the litigation and, therefore, occurred prior to the litigation, it is logical that in the case brief format they should precede the court events (the prior proceedings). Also, it is easier, from a briefing standpoint, to identify what happened before the matter went to the trial court, then identify what happened in court. Try it both ways and choose the sequence that is most comfortable for you.

Prior Proceedings/Procedural History

Prior proceedings are those events that occurred in each court before the case reached the court whose opinion you are briefing. Most opinions are not written by trial courts. They are written by courts of appeals—either:

- An intermediary court of appeals, such as the United States Court of Appeals, or
- The highest court of the jurisdiction, such as the United States Supreme Court.

Therefore, there are usually prior proceedings. If you are briefing an opinion of a trial court, there may be no prior proceedings because the trial court was the first court to hear the case.

The prior proceedings should include:

1. The party initiating the proceeding and the cause of action
2. The court before which the proceeding was brought
3. The result of the proceeding
4. The party appealing and what is being appealed

For Example: "The plaintiff sued the defendant claiming medical malpractice. The trial court granted the defendant's motion to dismiss, ruling that the statute of limitations had run. The plaintiff appealed the trial court's ruling that the statute had run."

Issue or Issues

The issue is the legal question addressed and answered by the court. It is the precise legal question raised by the specific facts of the case. The issue should be stated as narrowly and concisely as possible in the context of the facts of the case. A court opinion may contain several issues. Each issue should be separately identified in the case brief unless you are instructed to brief only one or fewer than all of the issues.

For Example: In an opinion involving an automobile collision case, the court may address several issues, some involving insurance, some involving evidence, some involving negligence, and some involving battery. The attorney working on a client's case may be interested only in the court's resolution of an evidentiary question raised by the facts in the court case. The client's case may involve an evidentiary question and fact situation similar to that addressed in the court opinion. Therefore, the paralegal may be instructed to provide a case brief of only that portion of the opinion that addresses the evidentiary question. Although the opinion involves several issues, the case brief will address only one issue.

Refer to Chapter 6 for a discussion of how to identify an issue in a court opinion. Refer to Chapter 7 for information on how to state (write) an issue.

Holding

The holding is the court's resolution of the issue. It is the decision of the court, the answer to the issue. There should be a separate holding for each issue identified in the issue section of the case brief. Some texts prefer that the holding be a simple, one-word, "yes" or "no" response to the issue. It is recommended that the holding be presented as a complete response to the issue, which means that the presentation of the holding should include all the elements of the issue and should be in the form of a statement.

For Example: The issue in the case is "Under Indiana's probate code, Ind. Code § 29-1-5-2, is a will valid if the witnesses are brothers of the testator?" If the court ruled that the will was valid, the holding should be presented as follows: "Under Indiana's probate code, Ind. Code § 29-1-5-2, a will is valid if the witnesses are brothers of the testator as long as there is no evidence of undue influence."

Reasoning

Usually the largest part of an opinion is the court's presentation of the reasons in support of the holding. Just as for each issue there is a holding, for each holding there should be reasons explaining why the holding was reached.

The reasoning portion of an opinion usually consists of two parts:

1. The rule of law that governs and applies to the facts of the dispute. It may be constitutional, legislative, or case law, and it may consist of any legal principle, doctrine, or rule of law that applies to the issue in the case.
2. The court's application of the rule to the facts of the case

For Example: Suppose the issue in the case is, "Under state tort law, does a battery occur when law enforcement officers, while making a lawful arrest, encounter resistance, use force to overcome that resistance, and continue to use force after the resistance ceases?"

The reasoning presented in the opinion is as follows:

- Rule of law—"In *Smith v. Jones,* the supreme court ruled that a civil battery occurs whenever unauthorized harmful contact occurs."
- Application of this rule to the facts of the case—"The defendants argue that inasmuch as they were making a lawful arrest, they were authorized to use force; and therefore, their conduct was not unauthorized within the meaning of *Smith v. Jones.* In this case, however, although the officers were making a lawful arrest, their conduct ceased to be lawful when they continued to use force against plaintiff after plaintiff ceased resisting. Law enforcement officers are authorized to use the amount of force necessary to overcome resistance. Once resistance ceases, any continued use of force is unauthorized within the meaning of *Smith v. Jones* and constitutes a civil battery."

In some instances, it is difficult to identify the reasoning in a court opinion, as it may be scattered throughout the opinion. A helpful approach may be to work backward from the holding. Look to the holding first, and keep it in mind while reading the case. It may be easier to see how the court assembled the reasons in support of the holding if you know the holding or outcome while reading the case.

Also, the rule of law or legal principle governing the issue is usually clearly stated by the court and is easy to identify. The reasons for the application of the rule or principle to the facts of the case usually follow the presentation of the governing law. Therefore, identification of the governing law also may help you locate the reasoning.

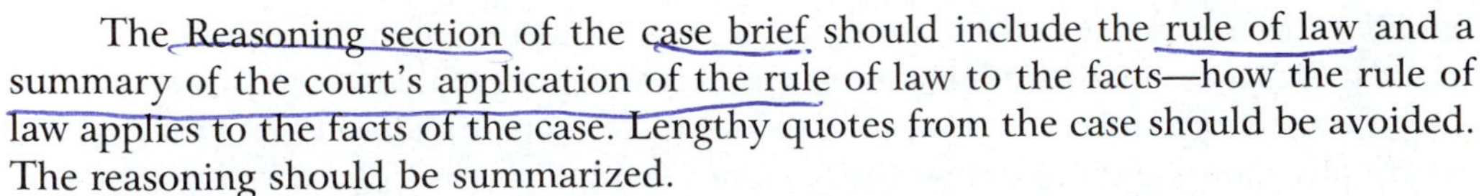

The Reasoning section of the case brief should include the rule of law and a summary of the court's application of the rule of law to the facts—how the rule of law applies to the facts of the case. Lengthy quotes from the case should be avoided. The reasoning should be summarized.

> ***For Example:*** In the excessive force example presented in the preceding text, the reasoning section of the case brief would appear as follows: "A civil battery occurs whenever unauthorized harmful contact occurs. *Smith v. Jones.* Law enforcement officers are authorized to overcome resistance. Once resistance ceases, any continued use of force is unauthorized and constitutes a civil battery."

Included in the reasoning section should be a summary of the reasoning of any concurring opinion.

Disposition

In this section, include the relief granted by the court, which is the order entered by the court. This is usually located at the very end of the opinion.

> ***For Example:*** The judgment of the trial court was affirmed.

Comments

Include in this section of the case brief any observations you may have concerning the court opinion. This could include any of the following:

1. Why you agree or disagree with the decision
2. A summary of any dissenting opinions. Does the dissenting opinion contain information that is useful in understanding the majority opinion? Does the dissenting opinion contain valuable legal arguments that may be useful in arguing against the use of the case as precedent? This is especially helpful if the holding of the court goes against your client's position. Note: Some case brief formats have a separate section for dissenting opinions.
3. Why the case may or may not be on point. The subject of when a case is on point and may act as precedent is discussed in detail in Chapter 8.

   > ***For Example:*** Referring to the excessive force example, assume that in the client's case there is evidence that the client never ceased resisting. You might include the following comment in the comment section of the brief: "It is questionable whether this case can be relied on as precedent due to the factual differences between the facts of the case and our client's facts. In the court case, force continued after resistance ceased, and the court held that the continued use of force constituted a battery. Inasmuch as in our case there is evidence that resistance never ceased, the court opinion may not be applicable."

4. References to the opinion in subsequent cases or secondary sources, such as a law review article
5. Any information updating the case, that is, concerning whether the case is still good law. This is discussed in the next section.

Case Brief—Updating

Whenever an assignment requires you to brief a case, it is necessary to determine if the case is still good law, which means you must check to determine if the opinion has been reversed, modified, or in any way affected by a later court decision. The primary method of accomplishing this is through the use of the appropriate *Shepard's* citator. *Shepard's* citators are published by Shepard's/McGraw-Hill, Inc. A paralegal must be familiar with *Shepard's Citations* in order to update a court opinion. Instructions on how to use a *Shepard's* citator are included in the beginning of each volume.

In addition, there are computerized services that provide on-line citators that are usually more up-to-date than the *Shepard's* printed citators. Some of these on-line services are the following:

- *LexCite*—includes a list of the recent cases citing a case (available through LEXIS)
- *Insta-Cite*—provides a summary of the prior and subsequent history of a case and includes references to the case in *Corpus Juris Secundum* (available through WESTLAW)
- *QuickCite*—includes a list of all cases citing a case (available through WESTLAW)
- *Shepard's Citator Services*—presents information not yet included in the *Shepard's* printed volumes (available through both WESTLAW and LEXIS)

KEY POINTS CHECKLIST: *Reading and Briefing Court Opinions*

❑ Read opinions carefully and slowly. You cannot speed-read case law. Often you may have to take notes as you read a case.

❑ If you have a problem identifying the key facts, refer to Chapter 5.

❑ Watch for the court's statement of the issue. The court may state the issue in a broad or procedural context. If you have a problem identifying or stating the issue, refer to Chapters 6 and 7.

❑ If you have trouble understanding the majority opinion, often the concurring or dissenting opinion will summarize and clarify the arguments and reasoning adopted by the majority. Be aware that the dissenting opinion may mischaracterize the majority opinion in support of its position.

❑ If you have trouble understanding the opinion, shepardize the case to determine if there are any law review articles, ALR citations, or other secondary sources of information concerning the case. Consult a treatise that discusses the area of law involved in the opinion. Refer to the digest for other cases addressing the same area of law.

❑ Do not be discouraged if you have trouble reading and understanding opinions. It takes time and experience. The more you read opinions, the easier it becomes. Your skill improves only through doing. Therefore, read as many cases as possible.

❑ Read opinions with a critical eye. Court opinions are just that—opinions. On occasion, courts are wrong. Do not read with unquestioning blind faith. Read critically. Question! Ask yourself, "Does the reasoning support the conclusion?"

APPLICATION

The principles presented in the case briefing section of this chapter are applied here to two cases: *Rael v. Cadena,* the case assigned to Carolyn in the hypothetical presented at the beginning of this chapter (see Figure 4–1), and *Sterling Computer Systems of Texas, Inc. v. Texas Pipe Bending Company,* which is reprinted in the following text.

Brief of *Rael v. Cadena*

The sample brief is presented first, followed by comments on the brief.

Citation: Rael v. Cadena, 93 N.M. 684, 604 P.2d 822 (Ct. App. 1979)

Parties: Eddie Rael, Plaintiff-Appellee
Emilio Cadena and Manuel Cadena, Defendants-Appellants

Facts: While visiting Emilio Cadena's home, Eddie Rael was beaten by Emilio's nephew, Manuel Cadena. After the attack began, Emilio yelled to Manuel "Kill him!" and "Hit him more!" Emilio never actually struck Rael nor physically participated in the battery. Rael was hospitalized as a result of the beating.

Prior Proceeding: Eddie Rael sued Emilio and Manuel Cadena for battery. The trial court, sitting without a jury, found Emilio jointly liable with Manuel for the battery. Emilio appealed the judgment of the trial court.

Issue: Under New Mexico tort law, does a battery occur when an individual, present at a battery, encourages the perpetrator of the battery by yelling "Kill him!' and "Hit him more!" but does not in any other way participate in the battery?

Holding: Yes. An individual may be liable for battery by encouraging or inciting the perpetrator by words or acts.

Reasoning: The rule of law in the United States is that civil liability for assault and battery is not limited to the direct perpetrator but extends to any person who by any means aids or encourages the act. The act of verbal encouragement at the scene may give rise to liability. The trial court found that Emilio Cadena yelled encouragement to his nephew while the nephew was beating Rael and, therefore, under the rule of law, is jointly liable for the battery.

Disposition: The judgment of the trial court was affirmed.

Comments: If, in the client's case, less aggressive language was used, it may be valuable to review other cases to determine the type of encouragement necessary to constitute a battery. Here, Emilio's comments were very aggressive. Would he have been liable for battery had he merely said, "Go ahead, Manuel"?

Comments on the Case Brief

Note that the brief includes the essential information of the case:

1. The name of the case and where it can be found
2. The names of the parties and their status before the court
3. The facts that gave rise to the dispute

4. What the trial court did
5. The issue, or legal question
6. The holding
7. The law governing the issue and the application of that law to the facts of the dispute
8. The disposition
9. Relevant comments

You may want to include in the Comments section a notation that the issue in the case was a matter of first impression in New Mexico—that is, the issue addressed in the case had never been decided by New Mexico courts. That is why the reasoning refers to non–New Mexico law and secondary authority rather than to New Mexico law. See the Reasoning section of the brief.

Brief of *Sterling Computer Systems of Texas, Inc. v. Texas Pipe Bending Company*

A second example of the application of the principles presented in this chapter is illustrated with the brief of the *Sterling Computer Systems* case. The case is presented in the following text. Comments concerning the case brief follow the brief.

CASE

STERLING COMPUTER SYSTEMS OF TEXAS, INC., Appellant,
v.
TEXAS PIPE BENDING COMPANY, Appellee.
No. 965.
Court of Civil Appeals of Texas.
Houston (14th Dist.).
March 20, 1974.
Rehearing Denied April 10, 1974.
507 S.W.2d 282 (Tex. Ct. App. 1974)

Action for breach of contract for data-processing service. The District Court, Harris County, Paul Pressler, J., granted summary judgment for defendant, and plaintiff appealed. The Court of Civil Appeals, Tunks, C. J., held that contract, which contained an express provision that plaintiff would not be liable for an outright refusal to perform data-processing services for defendant, and which contained no requirements that plaintiff make a reasonable effort to perform, failed for want of mutuality and was unenforceable.

Affirmed.

Contracts 🔑 10(2)

Contract, which contained an express provision that plaintiff would not be liable for an outright refusal to perform data-processing services for defendant, and which contained no requirement that plaintiff make a reasonable effort to perform, failed for want of mutuality and was unenforceable.

Alvin L. Zimmerman, Houston, for appellant.

Robert H. Singleton, Percy D. Williams, Houston, for appellee.

TUNKS, Chief Justice.

The issue in this case is the propriety of a summary judgment for the defendant in a breach of contract suit, which was granted on the theory that the contract lacked mutuality.

The appellant, Sterling Computer Systems of Texas, Inc., brought suit for breach of contract against the appellee, Texas Pipe Bending Company. In essence, the contract in question provided that Texas Pipe Bending was to provide Sterling with digitized cards and computer programs each month, with which Sterling was to perform data processing services for Texas Pipe Bending. Certain prices were quoted in the agreement, which were "based on a minimum of 20,000 digitized cards per month." The term of the agreement was to have been for one year, but after providing cards and paying in full for eight months, Texas Pipe Bending refused to further provide Sterling with digitized cards. The trial court granted Texas Pipe Bending's motion for summary judgment. Although the judgment does not so recite, it was apparently based on the argument proposed by Texas Pipe Bending that the contract was unenforcible because of the lack of mutuality. Sterling has appealed.

The relevant portion of the contract is found in a clause denominated as "LIMITATION OF LIABILITY." This clause provides in part as follows:

> SCS [Sterling] shall not be liable for its failure to profide [sic] the services herein and shall not be liable for any losses resulting to the client [Texas Pipe Bending] or anyone else by reason of such failure.

The general rule as stated in Texas Farm Bureau Cotton Ass'n v. Stovall, 113 Tex. 273, 253 S.W. 1101, 1105 (1923), is:

> [A] contract must be based upon a valid consideration, and . . . a contract in which there is no consideration moving from one party, or no obligation upon him, lacks mutuality, is unilateral, and unenforcible.

Under the express terms of the contract in question Sterling would not be liable for an outright refusal to perform the data processing services. This fact renders its obligation a nullity.

Sterling cites various cases which purportedly support its position that the trial court erred in granting summary judgment for Texas Pipe Bending. The gist of these cases is that although a contract may not expressly obligate a party to perform, such an obligation may be implied by its terms. In Texas Gas Utilities Company v. Barrett, 460 S.W.2d 409 (Tex.Sup.1970), the Texas Supreme Court held, under a similar contention, that there was a mutuality of obligation. In that case the contract provided that the Gas Company would not be liable for failure to deliver when such failure was "caused by conditions beyond its reasonable control," and then enumerated certain situations which exemplified the above phrase (over none of which would the Gas Company have control). The Court noted, "It [Gas Company] was bound, however, to supply *available* natural gas to respondents. . . ." Texas Gas Utilities Company v. Barrett, *supra* 460 S.W.2d at 413. In the present case there existed no requirement that Sterling make a reasonable effort to perform. The exculpatory clause allowed Sterling to refuse to perform with impunity.

Clement v. Producers' Refining Co., 277 S.W. 634 (Tex.Comm'n App. 1925, jdgmt adopted), was another case in which mutuality was found. That case involved a contract for an agent's commission. By the terms of the agreement the principal was to pay the agent a commission on goods which "may be supplied" by the principal. Notwithstanding this provision the Commission of Appeals held that the contract impliedly obligated the principal to supply goods to the agent. However, the Court stated:

> [A]s there is no language used which would clearly indicate that the company was not obligated to furnish goods and products, the courts are not warranted in holding that no such obligation was imposed . . . by its terms. Clement v. Producers' Refining Co., *supra* at 635.

The case at bar is distinguishable because the contract contained an express provision that Sterling would not be liable if it did not perform. Various other cases cited by appellant are similarly distinguishable because in those cases contracts were involved which did not expressly provide that one of the contracting parties could fail to perform without incurring liability.

As a matter of law the contract in question fails for want of mutuality. The trial court correctly granted summary judgment for the defendant, Texas Pipe Bending Company.

Affirmed.

Citation:	Sterling Computer Systems of Texas, Inc. v. Texas Pipe Bending Company, 507 S.W.2d 282 (Tex. Ct. App. 1974).
Parties:	Sterling Computer Systems of Texas, Inc., Plaintiff-Appellant Texas Pipe Bending Company, Defendant-Appellee
Facts:	Sterling Computer Systems (Sterling) entered into a contract with Texas Pipe Bending (Texas Pipe) under

which Texas Pipe was to provide Sterling with digitized cards and computer programs each month with which Sterling was to perform data-processing services for Texas Pipe. After complying for eight months, Texas Pipe refused to provide Sterling with the cards. The contract contained the following provision, "SCS [Sterling] shall not be liable for its failure to profide [sic] the services herein and shall not be liable for any losses resulting to the client [Texas Pipe] or anyone else by reason of such failure."

Prior Proceedings: Sterling sued Texas Pipe for breach of contract. Texas Pipe moved for summary judgment, arguing that the contract was unenforceable because it lacked mutuality. The trial court granted the motion. Sterling appealed.

Issue: Under Texas contract law, does a contract lack consideration and is, therefore, unenforceable if it contains a limitation of liability clause that provides that a party "shall not be liable for its failure to provide the services herein and shall not be liable for any losses resulting . . . by reason of such failure?"

Holding: Yes. Under Texas contract law, a contract lacks consideration and is unenforceable if it contains a limitation of liability clause that provides that a party "shall not be liable for its failure to provide the services herein and shall not be liable for any losses resulting . . . by reason of such failure."

Reasoning: The rule of law presented in *Texas Farm Bureau Cotton Association v. Stovall,* 113 Tex. 273, 253 S.W. 1101 (1923), is that where there is no obligation upon a party to a contract, the contract lacks mutuality, is unilateral, and is unenforceable. Under the limitation clause, Sterling is not liable for its refusal to perform. Therefore, as a matter of law, the contract fails for want of mutuality.

Disposition: The trial court's granting of the motion for summary judgment was affirmed.

Comments: The court did not address any potential avenues of relief that may be available to Sterling in equity, such as equitable restitution or reliance. Such avenues may be available in our case and should be explored. Also, does Sterling have a claim against the drafters of the contract for legal malpractice?

Comments on the Case Brief

Note that the court identifies the issue as: "The issue in this case is the propriety of a summary judgment for the defendant in a breach of contract suit, . . ." The actual issue in the case, however, is whether a contract is enforceable when it contains a clause that allows a party to escape liability when it fails to perform. Often a court will state the issue in the procedural context of how the matter came before the court.

For Example: "The issue in this case is whether the motion for summary judgment was properly granted by the trial court." This is how the matter came before the court procedurally: an appeal was taken from the trial court's ruling on the motion for summary judgment.

The real issue involves a question of whether, in light of the facts and the applicable law, there was a sufficient basis for the court to rule as it did. In answering the procedural question, the court actually addresses the substantive question raised by the facts of the case. The substantive question is what the case is actually about. In this case, summary judgment was granted because, as a matter of law, the contract failed for want of mutuality (lack of consideration) due to the limitation of liability clause. Therefore, Sterling could not enforce the contract because it was not valid. The substantive issue addressed by the court was whether the clause rendered the contract unenforceable due to the lack of consideration. *Always* look for the substantive issue when the court states the issue in a procedural context.

SUMMARY

A court opinion, often referred to as a case, is the court's resolution of a legal dispute and the reasons in support of its resolution. When resolving disputes, courts often interpret constitutional or statutory provisions or create law when there is no governing law. The body of law that emerges from court opinions is called the common or case law. It constitutes the largest body of law in the United States, far larger than constitutional, legislative, or other sources of law.

Since you must read court opinions to learn the common law, it is necessary to become familiar with and proficient at reading and analyzing case law. There are several additional reasons, however, for reading opinions. A court opinion:

1. Helps you understand and interpret constitutional provisions and statutory law
2. Helps you understand the litigation process
3. Helps you gain insight into the structure of legal analysis and legal argument
4. Provides a guide to proper legal writing

Most court opinions are composed of the facts of the case, the procedural history of the case (what happened in the lower court), the questions (issues) that are addressed by the court, the decision or holding of the court, the reasons for the decision reached, and the disposition (the relief granted).

A case brief is a written summary of a court opinion that presents, in an organized format, all the essential information of the opinion. A paralegal may be assigned the task of briefing a case. A case brief is valuable because it:

1. Saves an attorney the time of reading the case. The brief may so sufficiently inform the attorney of the contents of the opinion that he or she will not need to read the case.
2. Serves as a valuable learning tool. The process of briefing a case forces the reader to study the case and analyze it piecemeal. A better understanding of the opinion is usually gained as a result of this process.
3. Is a reference tool. A case brief serves as a valuable reference guide, allowing the paralegal to avoid having to reread an entire case in order to remember what the court decided and why.

4. Is a writing tool. It provides an exercise in assembling a written summary of a court decision.

The first and possibly most important step in briefing a case is to read it carefully and slowly. Reading case law is often a difficult process, especially for the beginner. It becomes easier as more opinions are read.

The elements of a case brief are as follows:

Citation:
Parties:
Facts:
Prior Proceedings:
Issue:
Holding:
Reasoning:
Disposition:
Comments:

Chapters 5, 6, 7, and 8 provide guidelines that are helpful in identifying many of these elements of a case brief.

The importance of case law cannot be overemphasized. The difficulties you encounter in reading and briefing court opinions can be lessened through the use of the guidelines presented in this chapter.

EXERCISES

ASSIGNMENT 1
List and describe the elements of a case brief.

ASSIGNMENT 2
Why are court opinions important?

ASSIGNMENT 3
Following the format presented in this chapter, read and brief the following court opinions.

A. *United States v. Leon* (see Appendix A)
B. *Acacia Mutual v. American General* (see Chapter 6)
C. *Commonwealth v. Shea* (see Appendix A). Brief only the issue of whether the ocean can be considered a deadly weapon.
D. *Atlantic Beach Casino, Inc. v. Morenzoni* (see Chapter 13). Brief only the issue concerning the constitutionality of the municipal ordinances.
E. *Cardwell v. Gwaltney* (see Appendix A)
F. *State v. Benner* (see Appendix A). Brief only the issue of the sufficiency of the evidence to support the conviction.
G. *McClain v. Adams* (see Appendix A)
H. *Cooper v. Austin* (see Appendix A). Brief only the issue of the validity of the codicil.

CHAPTER 5

Key Facts

When Alice was recently hired by the Kinsey law firm, she was placed under the guidance and supervision of Karen, a fifteen-year veteran paralegal. They just finished the initial interview with Mr. Aper. Alice sat in on the interview to observe the process and gain experience. After the interview, Karen told Alice, "I'm going to prepare a summary of the interview, then prepare a list of the potential issues. I want you to identify the key facts that should be included in the statement of the issues."

Alice's notes of the interview indicate that Mr. Aper owns a one-thousand-acre farm on the outskirts of town. He has lived on the farm for the past twenty years. About two hundred acres of the property are forested, and deer are often seen in the forest. Mr. Aper refuses to allow hunting on the property and, to discourage hunting, has fenced and posted the property.

One day, two weeks ago, Mr. Aper noticed a new path entering the forested portion of the farm. Someone had removed part of the wood fence surrounding the forest and had apparently entered the property several times. He followed the trail and found that several small pine trees had been cut down and a crude lean-to had been constructed from the trees. In front of the lean-to was a small fire pit where recently there had been a fire; the coals were still warm. Some of the wood removed from the fence was still smoldering in the fire. Mr. Aper got up early the next morning, before dawn, and watched the lean-to from a hidden spot in the bushes. Shortly after sunrise, he saw his neighbor, Eric Rascon, an avid bow hunter, come down the trail carrying a hatchet and loaded down with bow hunting gear.

Eric proceeded to set up camp. He started a fire with wood from the fence and some old tree branches, and he cut down a small tree and added it to the lean-to. Mr. Aper stepped out from behind the bushes and confronted Eric. "What are you doing here? You know you can't hunt here. Who told you, you could cut down these trees? Get off my property!" Eric angrily replied, "You stingy old man. These deer should be hunted; it's nature's way. I'll leave, but I'll be back and start again; you can't watch this forest every hour of every day." Eric then left.

Mr. Aper wants to take whatever legal action he can against Eric. Alice's assignment is to identify the key facts in the case. How Alice performs her assignment is discussed in the Application section of this chapter. The chapter addresses facts in general and emphasizes the critical role of the key facts in a case.

INTRODUCTION

Most, if not all, attorney-client relationships begin with the initial interview with the client. During the interview, the client presents information concerning a situation the client perceives requires a legal solution. If a lawsuit is ultimately filed, the process begins here. The role of the attorney, often performed by the paralegal, is to sift through the facts and determine what relief, if any, the law may provide for the problem raised by the facts. Any legal solution to a client's problem involves the application of the law to the facts of the client's case.

Usually some of the factual information the client provides in an interview is not relevant to the outcome of the case. Sometimes important factual information is left out. Before a legal solution to the client's problem can be identified or a determination made whether a lawsuit should be filed, it is necessary to identify the facts that are critical to the outcome of the case—the key facts. To ensure that all the key facts are identified, to make sure none are missed, all the factual information concerning the problem must be identified at the outset. This is accomplished by a thorough and comprehensive initial interview.

Often the importance of certain facts may not be determined until the legal issues and the governing law are identified.

For Example: In regard to the hypothetical at the beginning of the chapter, assume the paralegal, based on her experience, concludes that the burning of the fence may give rise to a cause of action for conversion (an improper act that deprives an individual of the rightful possession of the individual's property). Upon conducting subsequent research, she learns that conversion requires that the person suing must be in possession of the property.

It is an important fact, therefore, that Mr. Aper not only owns the land but that he was in possession of the land when the events took place. If the land was rented out to a tenant, the tenant would be in possession of the land. The tenant, being the person in possession of the land, would have the right to sue for conversion. The landlord, Mr. Aper, would not be in possession of the land and, therefore, would not have a right to sue Eric Rascon for conversion. The importance of the fact that Mr. Aper not only owned the land but that he was also in possession of it may not become apparent until the legal question and governing law are identified.

This example illustrates another important point concerning facts. When a lawsuit proceeds to trial, the facts presented at trial are those facts identified and considered important prior to trial. The identification and gathering of these facts depends entirely on the thoroughness and quality of the pretrial preparation. If a sloppy job is done, that is, the facts are not thoroughly gathered and researched, a poor outcome may be the result. The case may be lost.

For Example: Referring to the previous example, assume the land was leased. Mr. Aper did not reveal this fact during the interview because, being the owner of the land, he did not think it mattered who was in possession. The interview was not thorough because Mr. Aper was not asked who was in possession of the land. Assume, also, that the paralegal believed that the "possession" requirement of conversion was met if the party suing owned the property. The paralegal did a sloppy job of research and did not thoroughly research what constitutes "possession" under the law.

If a lawsuit alleging conversion against Mr. Rascon went to trial and this key fact was not identified, Mr. Aper would lose because he was not in possession of the land and did not have a right to sue. The key fact of who was in possession of the land was not identified prior to trial and, therefore, was not presented at trial. The poor quality of the interview and subsequent research resulted in a poor outcome.

This may appear to be an extreme example, but it illustrates an important point: the facts presented at trial and the quality of the trial are entirely dependent on the quality of work prior to trial.

The focus of this chapter, and the task assigned to many paralegals, is the identification of those facts that give rise to the legal dispute in either a client's case or a court opinion. The facts that give rise to the legal dispute are often referred to as significant, material, or key facts. In this chapter, and throughout the text, these facts will be referred to as key facts.

Many of the concepts and principles introduced in this chapter are also addressed in Chapter 6, Issue Identification, and Chapter 7, Stating the Issue. As noted in those chapters, key facts and issues are integrally related. The key facts are an essential element of the issue. They are essential in the identification and statement of the issue because they give rise to the legal dispute. Disputes arise and take place in the context of facts.

FACTS IN GENERAL—DEFINITION

What are facts? *Black's Law Dictionary* defines a fact as "A thing done; an action performed or an incident transpiring; an event or circumstance; an actual occurrence." In other words, a fact is the information present in a case concerning some thing, action, event, or circumstance.

fact
Information concerning some thing, action, event, or circumstance.

For Example: In the hypothetical at the beginning of the chapter, the presence of the lean-to, Mr. Rascon's actions of entering the property, and Mr. Rascon's statements are all facts.

Facts should not be confused with a rule of law. A rule of law is a standard, established by a governing authority, that prescribes or directs action or forbearance. It may be a constitutional provision, statute, ordinance, regulation, or common law doctrine. Its application determines the outcome of the question raised by the facts of a dispute.

For Example: Title 23, section 1991, of the state statutes provides that the maximum speed limit in a school zone is 10 mph while school is in session. When an individual proceeds through a school zone at 12 mph, this statute governs the question of whether the individual is speeding, that is, the outcome of the question raised by the facts.

Before defining and discussing key facts, it is helpful to consider the importance of facts in general and to identify and distinguish the various types of facts present in a client's case and a court opinion.

IMPORTANCE OF FACTS

The importance of giving due consideration to the facts of a dispute cannot be overemphasized. Often minimal attention is given to the facts. This is surprising, since our legal system revolves around resolving disputes by applying the rules of law to the facts of a case. Notice the two major factors here—*rules of law* and *facts of the case.* Both are equally important. Students, however, often focus primarily on the rules of law.

Rules of law are general principles designed to apply to multiple fact situations. Key facts are an essential element of the issue. Consequently, the role they play in the determination of what is in dispute in a case is of primary importance. Clients often have little knowledge or concern about general legal principles, but they are very concerned with how the law applies to the facts of their case.

Facts are also important because the determination of how or if a law applies to the client's case often depends on the presence or absence of certain facts.

For Example: Tom is stopped at a light at a four-way intersection in the city, waiting for the light to change. Mary, stopped behind him, accidentally lets her foot slip off the brake, and her vehicle bumps into Tom's vehicle. After exiting their vehicles and examining them, they discover that there is no visible damage to either vehicle. Tom, however, complains of neck pain from whiplash. This hypothetical is referred to as the minor impact example throughout this chapter.

Tom sues Mary for negligence. The paralegal working for Mary's attorney knows that the elements of negligence are duty, breach of duty, proximate cause, and damages. Based on her research and education, she also knows that in order to state a claim, Tom must present facts that establish each of the elements of negligence. While there are facts to support the first two elements, since there was no damage to the vehicle, it is questionable whether the impact was severe enough to cause neck injuries due to whiplash. Therefore, it is possible that Tom may not be able to establish the element of proximate cause. Also, if the impact did not cause whiplash injuries and there is no damage to Tom's vehicle, there are no facts that establish the element of damages.

In the preceding example, as in every case, there are two equally important factors—the law and the facts. The law establishes the conditions that must be met in order to state a claim for negligence, *i.e.*, the elements of negligence. The outcome of the application of the law depends on the existence of facts, and on one fact in particular in the case—was Tom's injury caused by the impact? Like this example, all legal problems are fact-sensitive, that is, the outcome depends on the existence or nonexistence of a particular fact or facts.

Another reason facts are important is that the determination of whether a court opinion is on point is largely governed by the similarity between the facts of the court opinion and the facts of the client's case. There must be a sufficient similarity between the key facts of the court opinion and those of the client's case before the court opinion can be considered on point and apply as precedent in the client's case. Chapter 8 presents an in-depth discussion of key facts in the context of determining whether a case is on point.

TYPES OF FACTS IN GENERAL

In either a client's case or a court opinion, there may be hundreds of facts, some of which are critically important, some of which are not. To identify the legal issue, the paralegal must sort through the facts and determine which facts give rise to the legal question and are essential to its resolution. Helpful to this process is an understanding of the basic categories of facts present in a case. The facts of a case may be placed within the three broad categories presented in Figure 5–1.

Irrelevant Facts

Irrelevant facts are those facts that are coincidental to the event but are not of significant legal importance in the case.

For Example: In the minor impact example, the race or gender of the parties, the day of the week, and whether Mary's car was insured are all irrelevant facts. They are irrelevant because they are facts that are not necessary to establish or satisfy the elements of the cause of action in the case. They are not necessary to prove or disprove the

Figure 5–1
Types of Facts

- Irrelevant Facts
- Background Facts
- Key Facts

claim. The race or gender of the parties is irrelevant to the question of whether Mary was negligent. Whether it was Sunday or Wednesday when the accident occurred does not affect the outcome of the case. Mary's insurance status will not affect a determination of whether she is liable.

Beware, certain facts may be relevant in one situation and not relevant in another.

For Example: In the minor impact example, whether it was snowing is probably not a relevant fact. Both vehicles were stopped at a light, and the existence of snow should not affect Mary's duty to keep her foot from slipping off the brake pedal. If the facts, however, were that she was approaching the stoplight and failed to apply the brakes in a timely fashion, the existence of snow conditions becomes a relevant fact. The nature of her duty to exercise care while driving varies with the weather conditions, and the existence of snow conditions requires her to exercise greater care when braking.

Background Facts

Background facts are those irrelevant facts that put the key facts in context. They give an overview of the factual event and provide the reader with the overall context within which the key facts occurred. They are not key facts because they are not essential to a determination of the issues in the case, but they are usually necessary and often helpful because they provide information that helps the reader have an overall picture of the environment within which the key facts occurred.

background facts
Facts presented in a court opinion, case brief, or legal memorandum that put the key facts in context. They give an overview of a factual event and provide the reader with the overall context within which the key facts occurred.

For Example: In the minor impact example, the location and type of intersection are background facts that provide the reader with an overview of the context and scene of the collision. The reader is aware that the impact took place at an intersection in the city, rather than in the country. This information is not essential, but it may be helpful for many reasons. The reader, for example, may want to visit the scene at a later date to investigate and determine if individuals working in the area witnessed the accident.

Key Facts

Key facts are often referred to as significant, material, or ultimate facts. They are facts that are critical to the outcome of the case.

For Example: In the minor impact example, some of the key facts are:

- Mary's foot slipped
- The cars impacted
- The lack of damage to the vehicles

These are key facts because they are critical in the determination of whether Mary was negligent. If Mary's foot never slipped, she would not have breached her duty to operate her vehicle in a safe manner. Even if her foot did slip, if the cars never impacted, there clearly would be no claim for negligence. If there had been damage to Tom's vehicle as a result of the impact, there would be facts establishing the element of damages, and Tom would most likely be able to support a negligence claim.

The next section presents a discussion of the definition and types of key facts.

KEY FACTS—DEFINITION AND TYPES

Definition

Key facts are the legally significant facts of a case that raise the legal question of how or whether the law governing the dispute applies. They are those facts upon which the outcome of the case is determined: the facts that establish or satisfy the elements of a cause of action and are necessary to prove or disprove a claim. A key fact is a fact that is so essential that, if it were changed, the outcome of the case would probably change. In fact, a useful test in determining whether a fact is key is to ask the question, *"If this fact is changed, would the outcome of the application of the law be affected or changed?"*

key fact(s)
The legally significant facts of a case that raise the legal question of how or whether the law governing the dispute applies. The facts upon which the outcome of the case is determined. They are the facts that establish or satisfy the elements of a cause of action and are necessary to prove or disprove a claim. A key fact is a fact that is so essential that, if it were changed, the outcome of the case would probably change.

For Example: Consider a fact situation where law enforcement officers are sued for battery based on the following facts. Law enforcement officers pursued a suspect on foot for five blocks after observing him snatch a woman's purse. While making the arrest, the officers encountered resistance, used force to overcome that resistance, and continued to use force for over a minute after the resistance ceased. Assume the law provides that law enforcement officers may use the amount of force necessary to overcome resistance when making a legal arrest. This hypothetical is referred to in this chapter as the resisting arrest example.

What are the key facts in the preceding example? *Which of the facts, if changed, would change the outcome in this case?* If the suspect had never resisted, the use of force would have been clearly improper. If the suspect had never ceased resisting, the officers' continued use of force would have been proper. If the officers had ceased using force when the resistance ceased, the use of force probably would have been proper. If the arrest had been illegal, the use of force would have been improper. The key facts are the following:

- A lawful arrest was being made
- There was resistance to the arrest
- Force was used to overcome the resistance
- The resistance ceased
- The use of force continued for over a minute after the resistance ceased

Each of these facts are key facts. Each fact, if changed, would affect the outcome of the case.

Other facts, however, are not key facts. How far the officers pursued the suspect or the fact that the pursuit was on foot are not key facts. These facts, if changed, would not change the outcome of the case.

For Example: In the minor impact example discussed earlier, the lack of damage to Tom's automobile is a key fact. It is a fact that, if changed, would affect the outcome of the case. If there had been damage to Tom's vehicle, he clearly would have a claim. Damage is an element of negligence, and the existence of damage is a fact that is essential to stating a negligence claim.

Types of Key Facts

There are basically two categories of key facts:

- Individual key facts
- Facts considered as a group—groups of facts

Individual Key Facts

It is often the case that an individual or several individual facts are key facts in a case. A key fact is an individual key fact if it meets the following test: *if the fact is changed, the outcome of the case is affected or changed.*

individual key facts
A key fact that, if it were changed, the outcome of the case would be affected or changed.

For Example: In the resisting arrest example, all the facts identified as key facts are individual key facts: a lawful arrest was being made, there was resistance to the arrest, force was used to overcome the resistance, resistance ceased, and the use of force continued after the resistance ceased. Each of these facts, if changed, would change or affect the outcome of the case.

For Example: Consider a breach of contract case where the claim of breach is that payment was received nine days late, and the contract specifically provided that late payments constituted a breach of contract. The lateness of the payment is a key fact. This individual fact, if changed, would change the outcome of the case.

Groups of Facts

There are fact situations in which no individual fact standing alone is a key fact—that is, no single fact is so significant that, if changed, it would change the outcome.

key facts—groups
Individual facts that when considered as a group, are key facts. Individual facts that when treated as a group may determine the outcome of a case.

For Example: An inmate is challenging the conditions of his confinement as cruel and unusual punishment. He alleges the following: there are cockroaches in his jail cell, the recreational periods are too short, his mail is improperly censored, his visitation rights are too restricted, and the temperature in his cell is too low in the winter and too high in the summer. It may be that no single fact by itself meets the test of a key fact, that is, no single fact is so critical that, if changed, the outcome of the case would change. The fact that there are cockroaches in his cell may not be sufficient, by itself, to constitute cruel and unusual punishment; the fact that the recreational periods are too short, by itself, may not constitute cruel and unusual punishment, and so on.

All the individual facts, however, when considered as a group, may determine the outcome of the case and, if changed as a group, would change the outcome. This may be observed in a court opinion when the court states, "No single fact of plaintiff's allegations constitutes cruel and unusual punishment. When taken as a whole, however, the individual allegations combine to establish a violation of the Eighth Amendment's prohibition against cruel and unusual punishment."

Recognizing groups of facts is important because, when analyzing a case, you must be aware that individual facts that seem to be insignificant may be key facts when considered and weighed as a group. When addressing a problem that involves key facts as a group, first review the facts individually to determine whether any individual fact, standing alone, is a key fact. If there is no individual fact that, if changed, would change the outcome of the case, look to the facts as a group.

There is no magic formula for determining how many or what types of facts are required for facts to be considered as a group, or what is necessary for a group of facts to be considered a "key fact." Usually it is necessary to consult case law and locate a case where the court addressed a similar legal problem involving a group of facts.

The next step, after defining and categorizing key facts, is to determine how to locate them in both a client's case and a court opinion. Since the key facts are an element of the issue, the steps involved in identifying and stating the issue necessarily include, in part, some of the steps necessary for locating key facts. Therefore, there is some overlap between Chapters 5, 6, and 7 regarding the discussion of key facts.

KEY FACTS IDENTIFICATION—CLIENT'S CASE

A client's fact situation usually includes a mix of facts—some irrelevant, some background, and some key. A paralegal's assignment may be to identify the key facts in the case. The four-step process presented in Figure 5–2 is recommended for determining which of the client's facts are key facts.

The following example is referred to in this section when discussing the operation of this four-step process.

Figure 5–2

Steps in Key Fact Identification—Client's Case

Step 1	Identify each cause of action possibly raised by the facts
Step 2	Determine the elements of each cause of action identified in step 1
Step 3	List all the facts possibly related to the elements of the causes of action identified in step 2
Step 4	Determine which of the client's facts apply to establish or satisfy the elements of each cause of action—the key facts

Example: The paralegal is assigned the task of identifying the key facts in a case. A review of the file reveals the following facts. Jerry and Ann are neighbors. They have lived on adjoining one-half acre lots in a rural subdivision for the past fifteen years. Their children are close friends and ride the school bus together. Four years ago, Jerry put in a hedge and planted several trees along his property line with Ann. Every year since then, Jerry rakes the leaves from the hedge and trees into a big pile close to the shared property line and burns it. The prevailing wind carries the smoke and soot across Ann's property, preventing her from working in her garden and usually soiling the clothes that are drying on Ann's clothesline. Every year she asks him to not burn the leaves, and every year he ignores her request and burns the leaves.

Ann wants Jerry to stop burning the leaves and pay her for the clothes that have been "ruined" by the smoke. When used in this chapter, this hypothetical is referred to as the trespass example.

Step 1 Identify Each Cause of Action

Identify each cause of action possibly raised by the facts. This step involves determining the possible cause or causes of action raised by the facts. Depending on the education and legal experience of the paralegal, this initial step may not require any research.

In the trespass example, upon reviewing the facts, the paralegal may come to a preliminary conclusion that the possible causes of action include trespass to land, private nuisance, and negligence.

Step 2 Determine the Elements

Determine the elements of each cause of action identified in step 1. This step usually requires some research. Research may be necessary either to determine the elements of the possible cause of action or to ensure that the law has not changed since the last time research was conducted. This step is necessary because, to state a claim and thereby obtain relief, the plaintiff must present facts that establish or prove the existence of each element of the cause of action. These facts are the key facts of the case.

For Example: The assistant's research reveals that the elements of trespass to land are as follows:

1. An act
2. Intrusion on land
3. In possession of another
4. Intent to intrude
5. Causation of the intrusion

The paralegal also would identify the elements of each of the other potential causes of action identified in step one.

Step 3 List All Facts Related to the Elements

List all the facts possibly related to the elements of the causes of action identified in step 2. This includes gathering the facts from the client interview, and any interviews that have been conducted with witnesses, and reviewing any documents in the case file that may contain factual information. As discussed in Chapter 2, the client files must be checked to ensure they are complete. At the initial stages of a case, the client interview may be the only available source of information.

When listing the facts, include all facts that may possibly be related to any of the causes of action. Err on the side of listing too many facts. You want to have all possibly related facts at hand when you proceed to step 4, in which the irrelevant facts are eliminated and the key facts are identified.

For Example: The fact that the children ride the school bus probably is not related to any of the potential causes of action. The nature of what is being burned may be related. The number of years Jerry has burned the leaves may be related. The weather conditions when the leaves are burned may be related.

Consider the elements of each cause of action individually when performing this task.

For Example: Using trespass to land as a cause of action, take each element and determine what facts from the client's case possibly establish or are related to that element. Which of the facts relate to intrusion? Which of the facts relate to "in possession of another"? Which of the facts relate to the intent to intrude? Which of the facts relate to causation of the intrusion? After completing this process for the elements of trespass, do the same for each potential cause of action identified in the previous steps.

Note that some facts may establish or relate to more than one cause of action. Some causes of action overlap. Therefore, all the facts must be reviewed when considering the elements of each cause of action.

For Example: The fact that the smoke from the burning leaves crosses on to Ann's property may establish or relate to both trespass to land and private nuisance. The smoke crossing to Ann's land may be the act of trespass, and the crossing coupled with the interference to Ann's enjoyment of her gardening may relate to nuisance. The fact that smoke crosses the property relates to elements of both of these causes of action.

Step 4 Determine Which Facts Apply

Determine which of the client's facts apply to establish or satisfy the elements of each cause of action—the key facts. The facts identified in this step are the key facts. Be sure to consider each fact listed in step 3 and determine if it is essential to establish or satisfy an element of any potential cause of action. It is important to consider all the facts identified in step 3. Step 4 primarily is the process of eliminating those facts listed in step 3 that are not essential or key facts. This is accomplished by taking each element of each cause of action and determining which facts are essential in establishing or satisfying that element.

For Example: Referring to the trespass to land cause of action, the key facts are as follows:

1. Act—the burning of the leaves produces smoke
2. Intrusion on land—the smoke crossing over Ann's land
3. In possession of another—Ann owns and lives on the land
4. Intent—Jerry built the fires (they were not caused by lightening or the acts of another), and he continued to build fires after he was notified of the problem
5. Causation of the intrusion—the fire produced the smoke that passed over Ann's property, and there is no evidence that it came from another source

When determining which facts identified in step 3 establish or satisfy an element, apply the following test:

- *"Which of these facts, if changed, would change the outcome of the application of that element?"* Or, in other words,
- *"Which of these facts, if changed, would affect the determination of whether there is present a fact or facts which establishes or satisfies that element?"*

For Example: Referring to the trespass to land cause of action, if the smoke did not pass over Ann's land, there would be no facts to support the element of intrusion. If the smoke crossing her land came from a source other than Jerry's land, Jerry would not be responsible for the causation of the trespass.

Other facts that were identified in step 3 as related to the elements may not establish or satisfy an element and, therefore, are not key facts.

For Example: In step 3, the facts of what was being burned, the weather conditions when the burning took place, and the number of years Jerry had burned the leaves were considered as possibly related to the trespass cause of action. If it is determined that these facts, if changed, would not tend to establish or satisfy an element of trespass, they are not key facts and are eliminated from further consideration.

All the facts identified in step 4 are the key facts. They are essential to the outcome of the case. Note that steps 2 and 3 are steps that are followed, in part, in the identification of the issue, which is discussed in Chapter 6.

Multiple Issues

Steps 2 through 4 should be applied to each potential cause of action identified in step 1. Some causes of action may be eliminated because there are no facts present that support the existence of an element.

For Example: If the smoke harmlessly passes over Ann's land and does not interfere with her use or enjoyment of the land, there may be no cause of action for private nuisance.

It may be that additional potential causes of action are identified as research and investigation take place. Each step should be applied to each cause of action identified. Be sure to address each element of each possible cause of action and determine if there is any fact in the case that tends to establish or satisfy the element.

Caveat: These steps are useful tools and helpful guides when identifying key facts. They will usually help you quickly identify the key facts. Nothing, however, is foolproof. You may not be certain that a fact meets the required standard necessary to support the existence of an element. That determination may not take place until trial.

For Example: The court may rule that the smoke crossing Ann's land is not a sufficient intrusion to constitute trespass.

Just make sure that there is some fact that *arguably* meets the requirements of each element of the cause of action.

KEY FACTS IDENTIFICATION—CASE LAW

Every court opinion involves the court's application of the law to the facts of the case. The key facts are those facts in the case to which the law is applied and that are essential to the decision reached by the court. If the key facts had been different, the outcome of the case probably would have been different.

Those situations where the court clearly points out the key facts are not addressed in this chapter.

For Example: The court states, "The critical facts in the resolution of this dispute are . . ."

The focus here is on those situations where the key facts are not so easily determined, such as in cases where the court opinion intersperses many irrelevant and background facts with the key facts.

The steps recommended in Chapter 6 for identifying the issue in a court decision are similar, in part, to the steps for identifying the key facts presented here. As with determining the key facts in a client's case, there is no magic formula for identifying key facts in a court opinion. The three-step process presented in Figure 5–3 is recommended, however, and may prove helpful.

In this section, the following example is referred to when discussing the application of these steps. Notice that the example is factually similar to the case of *Rael v. Cadena,* presented in Figure 4–1 in the last chapter.

For Example: In the case of *Joins v. Stevens,* the court summarized the facts as follows: Jason Stevens and his nephew Allen Stevens had known Mark Joins for several years. The three occasionally engaged in recreational activities, such as attending baseball games and going on fishing trips. On these outings, they usually drank alcoholic beverages, often to excess. On some occasions, their spouses joined in the activities.

On one of the fishing trips, on a Sunday afternoon in July, they were standing under a tree, drinking beer, and waiting for the rain to stop so they could resume fishing. They had been drinking since morning and were a little drunk. Earlier in the day Mark had been the only one who had caught any fish. Mark had an annoying habit of bragging, especially when he drank. Jason and Allen became increasingly angry as Mark claimed that he was the only "real fisherman" of the group. He continued bragging for an irritatingly long period. When he claimed that he was actually the "only real man" of the three, Allen lost control and beat him up. While the beating was going on, Jason yelled to Allen, "Hit him harder! Kick him! Kick him!"

Mark suffered two broken ribs and was hospitalized. He sued Jason and Allen for the tort of battery. In deciding that Jason had committed a battery, the court stated, "Although liability cannot be based upon one's mere presence at a battery, a person may be held liable for the tort of battery if he encourages or incites by words the act of the direct perpetrator. Because he yelled encouragement to his nephew while the latter was beating Mark Joins, Jason Stevens is jointly liable with his nephew for the battery."

Step 1 Read the Entire Case

Read the entire case with the following general question in mind: "What was decided about which facts?" Since the key facts in a court opinion are those facts necessary to the resolution of the legal question (the decision) reached by the court, you must have a general overview of the case before you can focus on determining which of the facts are key facts. You must read the entire case in order to determine the legal

Step 1	Read the entire case with the following general question in mind: "What was decided about which facts?"
Step 2	Look to the holding.
Step 3	Identify the facts necessary to the holding—the key facts.

Figure 5–3
Steps in Key Fact Identification—Case Law

question addressed and the decision reached by the court, keeping in mind the question: *"What was decided about which facts in this case?"*

- *"What was decided . . ."* keeps the mind focused on the holding or decision reached.
- *"About which facts . . ."* keeps the mind focused on specific facts, those specific facts necessary to the resolution of the legal question—the key facts.

By the time you finish reading the entire case, you usually realize that the decision rests on only some of the facts presented early in the opinion. If at this point you have not clearly identified which of the facts are the key facts, proceed to step 2.

Step 2 Look to the Holding

The holding is the court's application of the rule of law to the legal question raised by the facts of the case. It is the court's answer to the legal question. Ask the following questions to help identify the holding:

- *"What is the court's answer to the legal question?"*
- *"How does the court apply the rule of law to the legal question raised?"*

Refer to Chapter 4 for a discussion of how to locate the holding in a court opinion. In this example, the last two sentences are the court's presentation of the rule of law and the holding—the application of the rule of law to the facts:

- Rule of law—"Although liability cannot be based upon one's mere presence at a battery, a person may be held liable for the tort of battery if he encourages or incites by words the act of the direct perpetrator."
- Holding—"Because he yelled encouragement to his nephew while the latter was beating Mark Joins, Jason Stevens is jointly liable with his nephew for the battery."

Step 3 Identify the Key Facts

Identify the facts necessary to the holding—the key facts. This step is composed of two parts:

- Part 1 List all facts in any way related to the holding.
- Part 2 Identify which of the listed facts are key facts.

Part 1 List All Facts Related to the Holding

List all the facts presented in the case related to the holding. This may require going through the case and listing all the facts presented by the court. The court may present a multitude of background and irrelevant facts that in no way affect the outcome of the case. If that is the situation, identify and list only the facts that are possibly related or necessary to the decision reached.

In the preceding example, it is not necessary to list all the facts presented by the court. Some facts, such as the fact that the spouses sometimes accompanied the men, clearly are not relevant. Some facts—for example, it was a Sunday in July—are merely background facts that provide the reader with the time context of the event. All the facts relating to the argument should be included, such as the location of the argument, the fact they had been drinking, what was said, and so on.

Part 2 Determine the Key Facts

From the facts listed, determine the key facts by identifying those facts necessary or essential to the decision reached. Which facts determine the outcome of the case? There are several ways to identify these facts.

1. One test is to ask yourself whether the decision would have been the same if a fact had not occurred, or if the fact had occurred differently. If Jason had merely stood by and watched, would he be liable for battery? In the resisting arrest example discussed in the Facts in General—Definition section earlier in this chapter, if the individual had never ceased active resistance, would the police be liable for battery? Apply this test to each fact listed.
2. If this test is applied to each fact and no single fact, when changed or omitted, would affect or change the decision, ask whether the decision was governed by the court's consideration of the facts as a group.

   For Example: The court may state, "No single act of the defendant is sufficient to constitute breach of contract. The defendant's various acts, however, when taken as a whole are sufficient to establish breach of contract."

3. Where the court lists in its reasoning the elements of a cause of action, ask yourself which of the facts apply to establish the elements. In the battery example, the court stated that an individual may be liable if that individual "incites by words" the acts of the perpetrator. Jason's inciting words are the facts that relate to this element.
4. Ask yourself whether the court indicates that a certain fact is a key fact:
   a. Does the court describe a fact as "essential," "key," or "important"?
   b. Is a fact repeated throughout the opinion, especially in the reasoning supporting the decision?
   c. Does the court agree with a party's description of a fact as critical or key?

   For Example: The court may state, "We agree with plaintiff's position that the failure to make timely payment is a key fact in the determination of whether a breach of contract occurred."

5. Ask yourself if the key facts are identified in concurring or dissenting opinions. Be aware, however, that the concurring or dissenting judge may have a different view of which facts are key facts, and may identify as key facts, facts which the majority did not consider key.

Multiple Issues

The foregoing discussion has focused upon locating the key facts related to a single issue and holding in a case. Often there are several issues and holdings in a court opinion. The steps presented should be applied to determine the key facts related to each issue and holding. Follow each step *completely* for each issue and holding.

Caveat: The steps presented in this section are useful tools and guidelines. Following them will help you identify the key facts of a case. There are instances where the court may omit key facts. Also, as you read more cases and become more familiar with case law, you may automatically focus in on the key facts without using any of the steps presented here.

KEY POINTS CHECKLIST: *Identifying Key Facts*

- ❑ Do not overlook the importance of the facts. Facts give rise to the legal dispute and, therefore, are an integral part of it. Disputes have little meaning outside the context of the facts. How many court opinions have you read that did not have any facts?
- ❑ Key facts are those facts that establish or satisfy the elements of a cause of action and are necessary to prove or disprove a claim. Therefore, the nature and presence or absence of certain facts determine the outcome of a case.
- ❑ A useful test to use when determining if a fact is a key fact is to ask the question, "If this fact is changed or omitted, would the outcome of the application of the law be changed?"
- ❑ Follow the steps recommended for the determination of key facts in a client's case. Be aware that the importance of certain facts may not become apparent until legal research is conducted and the elements of a cause of action are determined.
- ❑ When identifying key facts in a court opinion, keep in mind the question, "What was decided about which facts in this case?"
- ❑ Do not get discouraged. The process of identifying key facts becomes easier with practice, and parts of the process become intuitive.

APPLICATION

In this section, examples of key fact identification in a client's case and in a court opinion are presented. Each example illustrates the application of the principles discussed in this chapter.

Client's Fact Situation

The following example illustrates the application of the principles to the hypothetical presented at the beginning of the chapter.

Step 1 Identify Each Cause of Action. *Identify each cause of action possibly raised by the facts.* Based on Alice's recently completed education and limited job experience, she identifies three potential causes of action Mr. Aper may have against Mr. Rascon: trespass to land, trespass to chattels, and conversion. This preliminary identification may be expanded or reduced as additional research is conducted.

For Example: Case law may reveal that Mr. Rascon's conduct also constitutes a private nuisance.

Step 1 provides a starting point for the identification of the key facts in the case.

Step 2 Determine the Elements. *Determine the elements of each cause of action identified in step 1.* For each potential cause of action, identify the elements necessary to state a claim. Research is usually required to determine the elements. Facts must be present that establish or satisfy each element of each cause of action. These facts are the key facts of the case. For illustration purposes, we will apply step 2 to the conversion cause of action.

Alice's research reveals that the elements of conversion are as follows:

- Personal property
- Plaintiff is in possession of the property or is entitled to immediate possession

- Intent to exercise dominion or control over the property by the defendant
- Serious interference with plaintiff's possession
- Causation of the serious interference

Step 3 List All Facts Related to the Elements. *List all the facts possibly related to the elements of the causes of action identified in step 2.* All facts potentially related to each of the elements of each cause of action should be listed. In this fact situation, these facts include:

1. Mr. Aper owns a farm with a two-hundred-acre area that is forested and inhabited by deer.
2. The property is fenced and posted.
3. He discovered a newly traveled path through the property.
4. Part of the fence had been removed, several small trees had been cut down, and a lean-to had been constructed from the trees.
5. A fire had been built, and some of the wood from the fence was still smoldering in the fire.
6. Eric Rascon, a neighbor, was observed by Mr. Aper entering the property with his hunting gear, building a fire, and cutting a tree.
7. Mr. Aper saw Mr. Rascon add a tree to the lean-to.

Note that some of the facts included may not be related to any element, such as the fact that deer inhabit the forest or that Mr. Rascon is a neighbor. In this step, however, it is better to include all potentially related facts rather than omit them. Later, research may demonstrate the importance of a fact thought to be insignificant.

Step 4 Determine Which Facts Apply. *Determine which of the client's facts apply to establish or satisfy the elements of each cause of action—the key facts.* The facts identified in this step are the key facts. Using the conversion cause of action as an illustration, the key facts are as follows:

- Personal property—the wood from the fence and the trees that were cut are Mr. Aper's personal property. Research may reveal that things growing on the land are real property and, therefore, are not covered by this tort. It may be that once cut down, a tree becomes personal property. This fact should be included until research determines the status of this property.
- Plaintiff is in possession of the property or entitled to immediate possession—Mr. Aper owns and occupies the land
- Intent to exercise dominion and control over the property—Mr. Rascon's actions of adding the fence wood and trees to the fire and cutting down the trees for the lean-to
- Serious interference with plaintiff's possession—the cutting of trees and burning of wood seriously interferes with Mr. Aper's rights of possession
- Causation of serious interference—Mr. Rascon's actions of cutting and burning are clearly the cause of the interference. There is no other factual cause present.

Notice that this step results in the identification of those facts related to the elements of the cause of action and the elimination of all facts that are not necessary to establish a claim. This step must be applied to identify the key facts for each potential cause of action identified in step 1. Once this is done, all the key facts for each claim are identified. Note that the relationship between key facts, issue identification, and stating the issue is discussed in the next two chapters.

Court Opinion

This example illustrates the operation of the principles when identifying the key facts in a court opinion. Read the *Flowers v. Campbell* case presented in the following text and apply the steps presented in this chapter to determine the key facts of the collateral estoppel issue.

Note that the doctrine of collateral estoppel is discussed in the case. The doctrine of collateral estoppel prevents a party in a lawsuit from relitigating an issue that was decided in a previous lawsuit. In *Flowers v. Campbell,* the trial court ruled that the question of whether the defendant, Campbell, used excessive force in resisting the assault of Flowers was already litigated in an earlier criminal case. Based upon this ruling, the trial court determined that the doctrine of collateral estoppel applied and dismissed Flowers's claim that Campbell used excessive force.

CASE

FLOWERS v. CAMPBELL

725 P.2d 1295 (Or. Ct. App. 1986)

ROSSMAN, Judge.

Plaintiff brought this assault and battery action to recover damages for injuries allegedly sustained in a skirmish with defendant Campbell (defendant), who was, at the time, an employee of defendant Montgomery Ward & Company. Plaintiff alleges that defendant used excessive force to repel his own aggressive behavior, for which plaintiff was convicted of assault in the fourth degree and harassment. The trial court dismissed the action after ruling, on defendant's motion for a directed verdict, that all material issues of fact were decided against plaintiff at his criminal trial and that he was precluded from relitigating those issues. We reverse.

The violence erupted after plaintiff accused defendant of charging him $12.99 for a lock that had been advertised for $9.97.[1] Plaintiff admits that he became involved in a verbal exchange with defendant immediately before the fight and that he "threw the first punch." He also concedes both that the jury at his criminal trial necessarily found that his use of force was not justified and that he is collaterally estopped from relitigating that issue. *See Roshak v. Leathers,* 277 Or. 207, 560 P.2d 275 (1977). He contends, however, that the dispositive issue in this civil action is whether defendant responded to his own admitted aggression with excessive force. He contends that that issue was not litigated at his criminal trial.

Under the doctrine of collateral estoppel, a party to an action may be prevented from relitigating issues that were actually decided and necessary to the judgment in a previous action. *State Farm v. Century Home,* 275 Or. 97, 550 P.2d 1185 (1976); *Bahler v. Fletcher,* 257 Or. 1, 474 P.2d 329 (1970). Plaintiff was convicted in the criminal action of assault and harassment. The victim's use of more force than was justified to repel the attacker's criminal acts is not a defense to either of those crimes. It follows that defendant's response to plaintiff's actions could not have been an issue that was necessarily decided in plaintiff's criminal trial. Accordingly, because an aggressor may recover in an action for battery if he proves that the defendant used more force than was justified in repelling the aggression, *Linkhart v. Savely,* 190 Or. 484, 497, 227 P.2d 187 (1951), the trial court erred in holding that plaintiff was precluded from litigating all issues "essential" to his recovery by reason of the judgment entered in his criminal trial.

Reversed and remanded.

1. Plaintiff was 62 years old at fight time; defendant was 33. Plaintiff allegedly sustained a broken arm and a detached retina. Defendant's jaw was broken.

Step 1 Read the Entire Case. *Read the entire case with the following general question in mind: "What was decided about which facts?"* This step helps you keep the facts in mind while obtaining an overview of what legal questions were addressed and answered.

Step 2 Look to the Holding. The holding is the application of the rule of law to the legal question raised by the facts of the case. *"What is the court's answer to the legal question? How did the court apply the rule of law to the legal question(s) raised?"* These are questions to ask when looking to the holding.

In this case, the court stated that the doctrine of collateral estoppel prevents a party from relitigating issues that were actually decided in a previous action. The court noted that the victim's use of more force than was justified to repel the attacker's criminal acts is not a defense to assault or harassment. Therefore, the issue of the victim's use of excessive force to repel the plaintiff's attack was not litigated in the plaintiff's criminal trial. The court concluded that the trial court erred in applying the doctrine of collateral estoppel to preclude the plaintiff from litigating the question of the victim's use of excessive force to repeal the plaintiff's aggression.

Step 3 Identify the Key Facts. *Identify the facts necessary to the holding—the key facts.*

Part 1 List All Facts Related to the Holding. What facts are possibly related to the holding? Plaintiff filed an assault and battery civil action against defendant to recover damages for injuries sustained in a skirmish with defendant. Plaintiff and defendant became involved in a fight as a result of a dispute over an amount plaintiff was charged for an item. Plaintiff threw the first punch. He claims that defendant responded with excessive force to plaintiff's aggression. Plaintiff was tried in a separate criminal action and convicted of assaulting and harassing defendant. All of these facts are possibly related to the holding. Some of the facts of the case, such as what they were fighting about, are clearly not related and are eliminated in this part of step 3.

The trial court in this action ruled that the plaintiff was precluded from relitigating his claim in this action because the issues of fact regarding the fight were decided in the criminal action. The trial court, therefore, dismissed his claim.

Part 2 Determine the Key Facts. Which of the facts listed in part 1 are necessary or essential to the decision reached? Which of the facts, if changed, would change the outcome of the case?

- The trial court's ruling that the issue of the victim's response was litigated in the criminal case is clearly a key fact. Had the trial court ruled otherwise, the case would not have been dismissed and the appeal filed. Note that a "fact" in this case is how the trial court ruled.
- The fact that plaintiff was convicted of assault and harassment in an earlier criminal case is clearly a key fact. Had there been no criminal trial, the civil trial court could not have applied the doctrine of collateral estoppel.
- The fact that defendant (victim) used force in response to plaintiff's aggression is a key fact. Plaintiff's lawsuit rests upon the nature of defendant's response.
- The fact that the victim's alleged use of excessive force to repel an attacker's acts of assault or harassment is not a defense to those acts in a

criminal case is also key. Had this been a defense to those acts, the question of the victim's use of excessive force would have been litigated in the criminal case and the trial court's ruling would have been correct. Note that in this case, a key fact is a rule of law—the victim's use of force in response to assault and harassment is not a defense to either crime.

- The fact that plaintiff threw the first punch in his fight with defendant is probably not a key fact. It is not necessary to establish or satisfy any element of the collateral estoppel issue.

This case is somewhat different from some other cases because the key facts on appeal involve the facts of what occurred between the plaintiff and the defendant, the actions of the trial court, and the law governing defenses to assault and harassment.

SUMMARY

All lawsuits arise as a result of disputes involving facts. Our legal system revolves around resolving disputes through the application of rules of law to the facts of a case. Therefore, the two major components of the dispute resolution process are the applicable law and the facts of the dispute. Each component deserves appropriate attention.

Some facts are more important than others, and the most important facts are the key facts—those facts upon which the outcome of the case depends. Key facts are those facts necessary to prove or disprove a claim. A key fact is so essential that if it were changed, the outcome of the case would be different. Key facts are an element of a legal issue, and that role is discussed in Chapters 6 and 7.

There are four recommended steps to follow when determining the key facts of a client's case:

- Step 1 Identify each cause of action possibly raised by the facts.
- Step 2 Determine the elements of each cause of action identified in step 1.
- Step 3 List all the facts possibly related to the elements of the causes of action identified in step 2.
- Step 4 Determine which of the client's facts apply to establish or satisfy the elements of each cause of action—the key facts.

There are three recommended steps for identifying the key facts in a court opinion:

- Step 1 Read the entire case with the following general question in mind: "What was decided about which facts?"
- Step 2 Look to the holding.
- Step 3 Identify the facts necessary to the holding—the key facts.

These recommended steps are usually helpful in identifying the key facts. You may develop shortcuts or different methods as you become more proficient in analyzing a client's case or a court opinion.

EXERCISES

ASSIGNMENT 1

Identify the key facts in Assignments 1 and 2 in the Exercises section of Chapter 6.

ASSIGNMENT 2

Identify the key facts in each of the hypotheticals presented at the beginning of Chapters 6, 7, and 8.

ASSIGNMENT 3

Identify the key facts in the cases listed in A, B, C, and E of Assignment 3 in the Exercises section of Chapter 4.

ASSIGNMENT 4

Identify the key facts in the first three assignments in the Exercises section of Chapter 13.

ASSIGNMENT 5

Facts: Terry, a bill collector, has been attempting to collect a bill from Client. Every other evening for the past two weeks, he has called Client at home after 8:30 P.M. and threatened to call her employer and inform him that she refuses to pay her bills. On every Monday, Wednesday, and Friday during the two-week period, he has called Client at work. She has repeatedly requested that he quit calling her at work. On the past two Saturdays, he has come by her home and threatened to sue her and throw her in jail.

Rule of Law: Infliction of emotional eistress—extreme or outrageous conduct that causes severe emotional distress.

Assignment: The paralegal's assignment is to determine if the actions of the bill collector constitute "extreme or outrageous conduct." Discuss the assignment from the perspective of individual key facts and from the perspective of a group of facts.

CHAPTER 6

Issue Identification

It was the late afternoon of an already long day when Kevin realized he still had a lot of work to finish before he could go home. Kevin has been Randi McGuire's paralegal for the past five years. He admires her for her tenacity and appreciates the responsibility and independence she gives him in the performance of his assignments. Kevin's primary role is to conduct the initial interview with the client, prepare a summary of the interview, and assemble a legal memorandum containing an identification of the legal issues and an analysis of the applicable law.

Identifying the legal issue is often the trickiest part of Kevin's job. It did not seem, however, that it would be too much of a problem in Ida Carry's case. He had just finished his interview with Ms. Carry, whose home is across the street from Roosevelt Elementary School. Ms. Carry's best friend, Karen, lives a block away. Karen's seven-year-old son attends school at Roosevelt.

Last month, on April 14, Ida was in her front yard planting tulips. It was lunchtime, and children were playing in the playground. She heard the crossing guard's whistle blow and tires squealing. She looked up and saw a car approaching a curve in the school zone at a very high rate of speed. It jumped the curb, crashed through the chain-link fence surrounding the playground, and hit the seesaw. The first thing she recognized was the car—it was Bob Barton's hot-rod Camaro. It looked like he was going too fast, lost control on the curve in the school zone, and crashed through the fence.

Bob, a local teen, continually raced in the neighborhood. Several teachers had complained to his parents, who had done nothing. Bob had received several speeding tickets.

The second thing Ida noticed was that two children playing on the seesaw were injured. One of them was Karen's son, Tim. When she realized it was Tim, she became extremely upset.

Since the wreck, Ida has had severe insomnia and extreme anxiety. When she can sleep, she has nightmares. Her doctor has prescribed medication for her nerves and to help her sleep, and he recently referred her to a psychologist. Ida has come to Ms. McGuire's office seeking to recover the expenses she has incurred.

After summarizing the interview, Kevin's attention focused on the next task, identifying the legal question in this case. He asked himself, "What is the legal issue?" The process of identifying the issue, commonly referred to as "spotting the issue," is the subject of this chapter. The answer to Kevin's question is discussed in the Application section of this chapter.

INTRODUCTION

The most important task a paralegal faces when engaging in legal analysis is to correctly identify the legal issue. The identification of the issue is the first step of the legal analysis process. The identification of the legal issue(s) presented by the fact situation is the foundation and key to effective legal analysis. It guides the researcher to the specific legal problem raised by the unique facts of the client's case. You must know what the precise legal problem is before you can begin to solve it. The identification of the issue determines which direction the research will take. It is like selecting a road—if you select the wrong road, you will waste a lot of time before you get to your destination, or you may get lost and never get there. Half the battle of legal research and analysis is knowing what you are looking for, that is, what is the issue?

If you misidentify the issue (ask the wrong legal question), you waste time and commit legal error. If you ask the wrong question, you will get the wrong answer to the client's problem.

For Example: If you incorrectly identify the issue as a contract law issue when it is really a corporation law issue, time will be wasted researching contract law, and the answer you find will not apply to the client's case.

The client does not retain counsel to find the answer to the wrong question. The client pays to have a problem solved. If the issue is misidentified, the problem remains unsolved, time is wasted, and you are no better off than when you started. If the error is not caught, you may have committed malpractice because the client is billed for a service not requested.

Not only is identification of the issue the most important step in the analytical process, it is often the most difficult. When you ask a professional how to spot an issue, the response often is, "I just know" or "After a while it becomes intuitive." And indeed it does become intuitive after reading and working on hundreds of cases. This, however, does not help the beginner. There is no simple rule or magic formula, but there are techniques and steps that are helpful and useful when identifying the issue in a client's fact situation or a court opinion. The starting point is to know what an issue is—how it is defined.

DEFINITION AND TYPES

issue
The precise legal question raised by the specific facts of a dispute.

In the broadest sense, the issue is a question—the legal question raised by the dispute. It is the legal question that must be answered before a case can be resolved. It occurs whenever there is disagreement or uncertainty about whether or how a rule of law applies to a client's facts. In a narrower sense, it is the precise legal question raised by the specific facts of a dispute.

Issues may be broken in to three broad categories:

1. A question of which law applies

   For Example: Do the traffic code provisions of Municipal Code § 2254 or state statute § 35-6-7-28 apply when an individual is stopped in a municipality for driving under the influence of intoxicants?

2. A question of how a law applies

   For Example: Under the provisions of Colorado battery law, is a battery committed by an individual, present at the scene of a battery, who encourages others to commit the battery but does not actively participate in the actual battering of the victim?

3. A question of whether a law applies at all

For Example: Does Municipal Code § 2100, Public Sales/Auctions, govern garage sales held on private property?

Regardless of the type of legal questions raised by a dispute, the definition is the same. *The issue is the precise legal question raised by the specific facts of the dispute.*

Now that you know what an issue is, the next step is to determine what it is composed of—the elements. Every issue is composed of elements, and these elements must be determined to identify the issue. Knowing what the issue is composed of is the key to the process of identifying the issue. The issue is identified by finding its parts, and the parts of the issue are the elements. Therefore, it is necessary to identify those elements in order to identify the issue. In fact, once you have determined the elements, the issue can be easily identified.

ELEMENTS

A client enters the law office with a unique fact situation that may or may not have a legal remedy. The role of the attorney is to identify the precise question raised by the facts and determine if a legal remedy is available and, if so, what legal remedy is available. Since the issue is defined as the precise legal question raised by the specific facts of the client's case, a correctly identified issue is composed of the three elements presented in Figure 6–1.

Applicable Law

Applicable law is the specific law that governs the dispute. This may be a constitutional provision, statute, ordinance, regulation, or common law doctrine, principle, rule, test, or guide.

For Example: Under Indiana Code § 35-42-3-2, kidnapping . . .
According to Florida's law governing breach of contract, . . .

Legal Question

This refers to the legal question concerning the law governing the dispute, raised by the facts of the dispute.

For Example: Does kidnapping occur when . . .
Is a contract breached when . . .

Key Facts

Key facts are the key or legally significant facts that raise the legal question of how or whether the law governing the dispute applies.

For Example: . . . when the individual is held against her will but is not held for ransom?
. . . when the product delivered is grade A- and the contract calls for grade A?

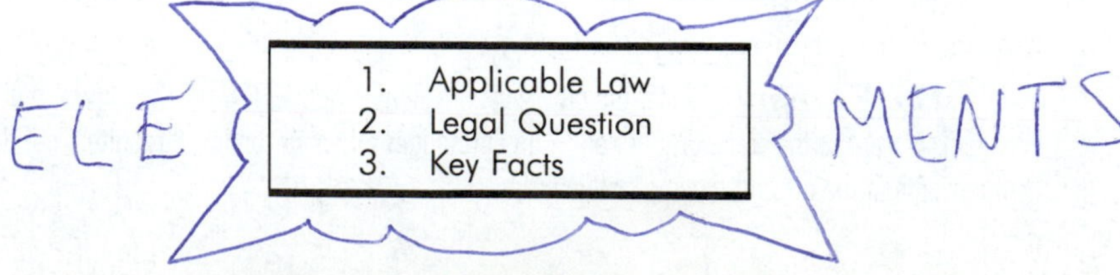

Figure 6-1
Elements of an Issue

Examples

These three elements of the issue—*the applicable law, the legal question concerning the law, and the key facts that raise the legal question*—are referred to in this text as a narrow or specific statement of the issue. Each element should be identified as precisely and completely as possible. The following are examples of statements of issues containing the three elements:

■ Under the holographic will statute, Colo. Rev. Stat. § 15-11-503,	***(Applicable Law)***
is a holographic will valid if	***(Legal Question)***
it is handwritten by a neighbor at the direction of the testator, but not written in the testator's handwriting?	***(Key Facts)***
■ Under Arizona tort law,	***(Applicable Law)***
does a battery occur when	***(Legal Question)***
law enforcement officers, while making a lawful arrest, encounter resistance, use force to overcome that resistance, and continue to use force after resistance ceases?	***(Key Facts)***
■ Does Municipal Code § 3362	***(Applicable Law)***
permit the installation	***(Legal Question)***
of a sign that is twenty feet high by forty feet wide, more than fifteen feet from the property line, and does not block the view of traffic?	***(Key Facts)***

Each of these examples contain the precise law, legal question, and the key facts essential to the resolution of the dispute. Note that the issue is narrowly focused upon the law and specific facts of the client's case.

Failure to include these elements results in an abstract question, a broad statement of the issue that is missing the legal (applicable law) and factual context.

For Example: If the three previous examples were stated broadly, and did not include the specific elements discussed in this section, they would appear respectively as follows:

- Was the will valid?
- Did the police commit a battery?
- Is the sign in violation of the municipal ordinance?

Each broad statement of the issue in this example could apply to a multitude of cases involving wills, batteries, or sign ordinance violations. Each issue fails to inform the researcher of the specific factual context of the dispute, the precise law involved, and the question that must be resolved in order to determine if, and what, remedy is available to the client. In short, an issue broadly identified is an issue not truly identified at all.

The importance of focusing on the elements of the issue and identifying the issue in terms of the elements is critical. It reduces the chance of misidentifying the question presented by the facts and helps guide the researcher, thereby saving time and effort.

The task is to identify these elements as precisely and completely as possible. Chapters 5 and 7 are useful when identifying the elements. Refer to Chapter 5 for a discussion of what key facts are and how they are identified. There is some overlap between the discussion of key facts in Chapter 5 and this chapter because the identification of key facts is an integral part of issue identification. Refer to Chapter 7 for an in-depth discussion of how to present the issue, that is, how to draft the issue.

A paralegal or an attorney becomes involved in issue identification in two different but related situations:

1. Identifying the issue(s) in a client's case
2. Identifying the issue(s) in a court opinion

In each situation, it is necessary to determine the three elements of the issue to correctly identify the issue. The next two sections contain recommended steps in identifying the issue in a client's case and in a court opinion.

ISSUE IDENTIFICATION—CLIENT'S CASE

The client's fact situation presents a legal question (issue) or set of questions that must be identified before the case can be resolved. Time spent in correctly identifying the specific issue or issues at the outset of the case saves time lost in misdirected research later. A helpful tool is to keep in mind, from the outset of the case, this question: "*What must be decided about which facts?*," or phrased another way, "*What question* concerning *which law* is raised by *these facts?*" This keeps you focused on the elements of the issue—the law, question, and key facts of the case. It helps you avoid being sidetracked by related or interesting questions raised by the facts that are not necessary to resolve the legal question(s) of the case. The value of keeping these questions in mind will be illustrated throughout this section.

The identification of the legal question(s) or issue(s) in a client's case is primarily a four-step process (see Figure 6–2).

Step 1 Identify Each Type of Cause of Action

Identify each type of cause of action and area of law possibly involved. The first step is the identification of the potential cause(s) of action and area(s) of law raised by the client's fact situation. This includes a broad identification of potential issues, the general areas of law, and the client's facts related to each area of law. This preliminary identification is based upon education and experience and usually does not require any research.

Figure 6–2

Issue Identification—Client's Case—Four Steps

Step 1	Identify each type of cause of action and area of law possibly involved.
Step 2	Determine the elements of each cause of action identified in step 1.
Step 3	Determine which of the facts of the client's case apply to establish or satisfy the elements of each cause of action—the key facts.
Step 4	Assemble the issue from the law and key facts identified in steps 2 and 3.

For Example: Mary is stopped at a stoplight waiting for the light to change. She is drinking a soft drink. She has been stopped for about ten seconds when a pickup, driven by Sam, slams into the back of her vehicle. Her automobile is knocked into the intersection and narrowly misses being struck by a vehicle passing through the intersection. Sam jumps out of his pickup, runs to Mary's vehicle, and screams at her that she should not have been stopped and she caused the wreck. Mary thinks he is either crazy or drugged. She is afraid he might hit her. He yanks open her vehicle door and pulls her out of the automobile screaming, "It's all your fault, it's all your fault." He pulls out a knife and waves it around. A couple of pedestrians approach, and Sam runs back to his pickup.

As a result of the incident, Mary suffered whiplash injuries and bruises on her arm, and she experiences anxiety whenever she is stopped at a light and severe insomnia. This hypothetical is referred to as the rear-end collision example throughout this chapter.

Based upon experience and tort classes, the paralegal identifies four possible causes of action involving four broad areas of law: Was Sam's failure to stop negligence? Did he commit an assault? Did he commit a battery? Did his actions constitute intentional infliction of emotional distress?

This initial identification of the broad issues and areas of law requires no research and may be expanded or reduced after subsequent research is conducted. The purpose is twofold:

- To identify in general terms the issues involved
- To provide a starting point for the identification and clarification of each specific issue that must be resolved in the case

Step 2 Determine the Elements of Each Cause of Action

Determine the elements of each cause of action identified in step 1. Steps 2, 3, and 4 should be applied separately to each potential issue or cause of action identified in step 1. In other words:

- One potential issue identified in step 1 should be chosen.
- Steps 2, 3, and 4 are applied to that issue.
- The identification of that issue should be completed before addressing the next potential issue.

For Example: In the rear-end collision example, there are four broad issues and areas of law involved: negligence, assault, battery, and emotional distress. Choose one area, such as negligence, and complete steps 2 through 4. Be careful to identify and finish with that issue before addressing the next issue.

Focusing on one issue at a time avoids the confusion that may occur when dealing with multiple causes of action that often have overlapping elements. In this example, some of Sam's conduct may constitute elements of both assault and intentional infliction of emotional distress. Researching both issues at the same time could cause confusion.

Step 2 requires researching the area of law to determine the elements necessary to establish a cause of action. To know whether the law provides relief for the client, it is necessary to determine what the law requires to be established in order to obtain that relief—the elements.

For Example: Using the rear-end collision example, suppose the paralegal begins with the issue involving intentional infliction of emotional distress. Research reveals that the following elements must be established to prevail:

1. The defendant's conduct must be intentional.
2. The conduct must be extreme and outrageous.

3. There must be a causal connection between the defendant's conduct and the plaintiff's mental distress.
4. The plaintiff's mental distress must be extreme or severe.

Once the elements are identified, proceed to step 3.

Step 3 Determine the Key Facts

Determine which of the facts of the client's case apply to establish or satisfy the elements of each cause of action—the key facts. Every issue is a question of how the law applies to the facts of the client's case. Steps 1 and 2 identify the law that must be included in the issue, and step 3 allows the identification of the facts that must be included in the issue. These facts are called the key facts.

The key facts are identified by determining which facts of the client's case apply to establish or satisfy the requirements of each element of the cause of action. This step is necessary because, in order to state a claim, and thereby obtain relief, facts must be presented that establish or satisfy the requirements of each element. These facts are the key facts.

For Example: Using the rear-end collision example, apply the client's facts to the elements:

1. Defendant's conduct must be intentional. In this case, the defendant's running toward the client screaming, opening her car, pulling her out, and waving his knife are the facts showing intentional conduct that satisfy or apply to establish this element. This conduct is clearly intentional.
2. The conduct must be extreme and outrageous. The acts identified in number 1 are the facts showing extreme and outrageous conduct that establish this element.
3. There must be a causal connection between the defendant's conduct and the plaintiff's mental distress. Since the accident, the client has been unable to sleep and is anxious when stopped at a light. These facts satisfy the third element.
4. Plaintiff's distress must be extreme or severe. Anxiety whenever stopped at a light and severe insomnia are facts showing extreme or severe distress and are the facts that establish the fourth element.

By matching the facts with the required elements, the key facts of the emotional distress issue are identified. Since the question is how the law applies to the facts, these facts become part of the issue and must be included. Once step 3 is completed, all the elements necessary to identify the issue are in place. All that is left is to proceed to step 4 and assemble the issue.

Note: You may not be certain whether a fact meets the standard established for an element. Often that determination does not take place until trial. Just make sure there is some fact that *arguably* meets the requirements of each of the elements of the cause of action.

For Example: A determination of whether Mary's insomnia and anxiety are extreme or severe enough to warrant relief may not be decided until trial. But her symptoms are sufficient to arguably meet the requirement of the fourth element. If research, however, reveals that this harm is not sufficiently extreme for the requirements of emotional distress, then there is no emotional distress issue.

If there are no facts that satisfy or establish an element, there probably is no cause of action or issue. In this example, if Mary did not suffer anxiety or insomnia, there would be no facts that would meet the requirements of the fourth element, and there most likely would be no emotional distress issue.

Step 4 Assemble the Issue

The last step is the easiest. *Gather and assemble the elements of the issue from the law and key facts identified in steps 2 and 3.* The law is emotional distress, the legal question is whether emotional distress occurred, and the key facts are the facts identified in step 3. Putting it all together, the issue is as follows:

> Under (name of state) law of emotional distress, does emotional distress occur when the driver of the rear vehicle in a rear-end collision runs screaming toward the other driver, opens her car door, pulls her out, and waves a knife, and the other driver suffers anxiety and insomnia as a result of the conduct?

Chapter 7 focuses on how to assemble the elements of an issue once they are identified.

The four steps presented here simplify the issue identification process by breaking it down into workable steps. It may not be necessary to follow all the steps. The issue may be apparent in step 1 or at some other point. This process, however, takes some of the mystery out of issue identification and provides a useful tool when the issues are not clear or easy to identify. It allows you to answer the question of "What question concerning which law is raised by the client's facts?"

The answer to the emotional distress issue identified in the preceding example may be determined by reference to case law. The important thing to remember is that by concisely identifying the issue in the context of the key facts, the key facts are less likely to be overlooked. By including the key facts in the issue, the researcher's focus is narrowed, and the researcher is less likely to omit a critical fact and thereby ignore a crucial line of inquiry, or misidentify the issue entirely. In the rear-end collision example, it may be that Sam's actions are not sufficiently outrageous to constitute emotional distress—maybe there is not sufficient evidence to connect the anxiety and insomnia to the acts, or maybe the harm is not the type of harm for which relief is granted in emotional distress cases.

As mentioned in step 2, steps 2 through 4 are applied to each of the issues broadly identified in step 1. Identify and address each issue separately and completely before proceeding to the next issue. It may be that certain issues are eliminated as the other steps are followed, such as when research reveals that there are not sufficient facts present to support a cause of action. It may be that additional issues are identified as research takes place.

For Example: In the above example, it may be that emotional distress was not considered until research on another issue, such as assault, revealed a case with similar facts that included a discussion of emotional distress.

Multiple Issues

Often there are multiple issues in a case. In the rear-end collision example, there were four possible causes of action, each one involving a separate issue. Be sure to list all the facts in the client's case and examine each one to determine if it relates to any identified issue or in any way gives rise to a new issue. In the rear-end collision example, the fact that Mary was drinking a soda may not be important. The fact that Sam ran from his car rather than walked may be critical. It is important to ensure that all the facts are considered and nothing is overlooked. All potential issues should be identified, and the four-step process helps ensure nothing is missed.

Also, note that a single issue may have multiple parts or subissues.

For Example: In the rear-end collision example, the intentional infliction of emotional distress issue may have separate subissues:

- Was Sam's conduct sufficiently extreme and outrageous?
- Are anxiety and severe insomnia "extreme or severe distress" within the meaning of the law?

Each part or subissue should be separately considered and addressed.

Caveat: The steps presented in this section are useful tools and guides. There is no magic formula for identifying the issues present in a client's case. These steps will usually help you quickly identify the issue. Remember that the process gets easier with experience.

ISSUE IDENTIFICATION—CASE LAW

Case briefing and case law analysis are discussed in Chapters 4 and 8, respectively. Key fact identification is discussed in-depth in Chapter 5. This section focuses on the identification or spotting of the issue or issues in a court opinion. The issue is the legal question addressed and answered by the court. It is what the case is about. If you do not know what question was addressed by the court, it is possible to misunderstand the rule of law applied or adopted in the opinion. As a result, it is likely that you will misunderstand how or if the rule of law applies in your client's case.

This section does not address those situations where the issue is easily identified because somewhere in the opinion the court clearly states the issue.

For Example: "In this case we decide whether an individual's Fourth Amendment right to be free from unreasonable searches is violated when officers executing a search warrant for a stolen television search the individual's pockets and discover drugs."

This section is concerned with those situations where the identification of the issue is difficult because the court does not identify the issue, states the issue in such broad terms that it is not helpful, or states the issue in terms of the procedural context in which the case was brought before the court:

- *Issue not stated*—In some opinions, the court never clearly discusses what the issue is in the case.
- *Broad statement of the issue*—"The issue in this case is whether the defendant breached the contract."

  Comment: This is a broad statement of the issue. It fails to inform the reader what the case is about. In the ultimate sense, the court decided whether the defendant breached the contract; but in reality, it reached that conclusion by making a substantive decision concerning the specific facts of the defendant's conduct.

  For Example: The court may have concluded that the defendant's delivery of the order on time, ninety-five percent of the time, was substantial compliance with the contract and, therefore, not a breach.

- *Issue stated in the procedural context*—"The issue in this case is whether the trial court erred when it granted the motion to suppress the evidence."

  Comment: The court stated the issue in the context of how the case came before the court procedurally—an appeal of a trial court order granting a motion to suppress. To answer this question, the court actually addressed a substantive question raised by the facts of the case, and the substantive issue is what the case is actually about.

For Example: The substantive issue decided was, "Under the provisions of the exclusionary rule, should evidence be suppressed when law enforcement officers obtained the evidence as a result of requiring the defendant to allow them to inspect the glove box when they were making a routine stop for speeding?"

Beginning students often make the mistake of identifying the issue in the procedural context stated by the court when, in reality, the issue involves a substantive determination of the application of the law to the facts of the case.

The goal when reading a case should be the identification of the substantive issue(s) in the case. Ask yourself when reading the case, *"What was decided about which facts in this case?"* or *"What question concerning which law and key facts was decided by the court?"* Like a client's case, a court case is about a dispute concerning how the law applies to the facts. Had there been no dispute involving how the law applied to the facts, the case would not have gone to trial. If your identification of the issue in a court opinion fails to include the rule of law applied and the key facts, you have failed to identify the issue correctly.

How, then, is issue identification in a court opinion accomplished? Again, there is no magic formula. The three-step process presented in Figure 6–3 is suggested as a useful tool.

Step 1 General Question

The first part of this step is to *read the entire court opinion before attempting to identify the issue.* Important information concerning an issue may be scattered throughout the opinion. An initial reading of the entire case provides the researcher with an awareness of where information is located in the opinion and an overview of the case. This is helpful when you begin to analyze specific portions of the opinion. *The entire opinion should be read at the outset, even if the court clearly identifies the issue.*

While reading the case, keep in mind the question, *"What was decided about which facts in this case?"* This general question is valuable because it helps keep your mind focused on what you need to look for while reading the case in order to identify the elements of the issue:

- *"What was decided?"* helps keep the mind focused on searching for the legal issue that was resolved and the law necessary for its resolution.
- *"About which facts?"* helps keep the mind focused on looking for the facts essential to the resolution of the legal question.

If you keep this question in mind as you read the case, you will stay focused on the essence of the case: the court's application of a rule of law to the legal question raised by the facts. The facts are usually introduced early in the opinion. You will not know what was decided about them until you reach the holding, usually at the end. Asking this question forces you to keep the facts in mind as you read because you are aware that you must decide which of the facts relate to the holding. When you get

Step 1	General question
Step 2	Look to the holding
Step 3	Assemble the issue

Figure 6–3

Issue Identification—Case Law—Three Steps

to the end of the opinion, you may realize that the holding relates to only a few of the facts presented.

Do not attempt to identify the issue(s) from the Syllabus or Headnotes of the opinion. As noted in Chapter 4, these are prepared by the publisher of the opinion. They are not part of the court opinion and are not intended to be used to identify the issue(s) addressed in the opinion.

If you have not identified the issue by the time you have finished reading the case, proceed to step 2.

Step 2 Look to the Holding

As noted in Chapter 4, the holding is the court's application of the rule of law to the legal question raised by the facts of the case. It is the court's answer to the legal question. In a court opinion, the key facts, legal question, and holding are all related. Finding one will help you find the others. Therefore, often the fastest way to track down the issue is to focus on the holding and ask the following questions:

1. *"What was decided in the holding?"* In other words, "What legal question or issue was addressed and answered by the holding?" This identifies the second element of the issue, the legal question addressed by the court.
2. *"What statute, rule of law, principle, and so on, was applied by the court to reach this holding?"* This question helps identify the relevant rule of law, the first element of the issue.
3. *"Which of the facts presented in this case are related and necessary to the determination of the question identified as addressed in the holding?"* or *"Which of the facts, if changed, would change the outcome of the holding?"* These questions help identify the third element of the issue, the key facts. An in-depth discussion of identifying key facts is presented in Chapter 5.

By answering these questions, the elements of the issue are identified: the rule of law, question, and key facts. The issue can then be stated by adding the rule of law and key facts to the holding and stating the holding in question form. It sounds complicated, but it is not.

For Example: In a workers' compensation case, the court presents several facts concerning the plaintiff before and after she joined a monastery, including the following:

1. Her duties as a monastic
2. Her written application for admission as a volunteer to the service of God
3. The written invitation from the monastery, which included an offer of spiritual guidance and room and board in exchange for volunteer service
4. Information concerning her previous career
5. The fact that she did not receive a paycheck
6. Her spiritual motivation
7. Her daily duties
8. The fact that she was injured while mopping the floor
9. Her family relationships
10. The fact that there was no contract of employment

The case was on appeal from a decision of the trial court granting the defendant's motion to dismiss for failure to state a claim. The issue is not stated in the opinion. The holding in the case was: "Plaintiff rendered services out of religious devotion as indicated by her application as a volunteer, lack of employment agreement, and lack of a paycheck, therefore, she was not an employee within the meaning of the law, and the trial court's dismissal of the complaint is affirmed." This example is referred to in this chapter as the monastery example.

A quick way to identify the issue in the case in the preceding example is to focus on the holding and keep in mind the question, "What was decided about which facts to reach this holding?" Then, identify the elements of the issue by asking:

1. *"What question was decided in this holding?"* The question decided is whether the plaintiff was an employee. The answer to this question provides the legal question element of the issue.
2. *"What rule of law or principle was applied by the court to reach this holding?"* The answer to this question provides the rule of law element of the issue. It may be a statute, common law principle, doctrine, and so on. Assume here it is the Workers' Compensation Act § 36-9-7.
3. *"Which facts mentioned in the opinion are related and necessary to the determination of the question of whether the plaintiff is an employee?"* The answer to this question provides the key facts element of the issue. In this case, the court focused on the written application as a volunteer, the absence of an employment agreement, and the lack of a paycheck. These facts, if changed, would probably change the outcome. If treated as a group, the changing of all these facts would change the outcome.

Step 3 Assemble the Issue

Assemble the identified elements in the question format presented in Chapter 7. The rule of law is the Workers' Compensation Act § 36-9-7. The question is whether the plaintiff was an employee. The key facts are the written application for admission to the monastery as a volunteer, the absence of an employment agreement, and the lack of a paycheck. The issue, when assembled, is: "Under the provisions of Workers' Compensation Act § 36-9-7, is an individual an employee when the individual is admitted to a monastery upon a written application as a volunteer, does not receive a paycheck, and does not have an agreement of employment?"

Other Aides—Case Law Issue Identification

Concurring or Dissenting Opinion

In a concurring or dissenting opinion, the issue may be set out more clearly than in the majority opinion. Therefore, these opinions should not be overlooked when identifying the issue. Be aware, however, that the concurring or dissenting judge may have a different view of what the issue is, especially in the case of a dissent. Even if the formulation is different, the discussion of the issue by the concurring or dissenting judge may be helpful in determining the issue in the majority opinion.

Other Opinions

Reading other opinions cited in the case may provide guidance concerning the issue in the case you are researching. Also, reading a later court's discussion of the case may prove helpful, as it may summarize and clarify the issue in the case you are reading. *Shepard's Citator* will guide you to subsequent cases.

Multiple Issues

The foregoing discussion is focused on locating a single issue. Often there are multiple issues in a court opinion. The steps discussed above should be applied to all the issues in the case. Be sure to follow all the steps presented in this section completely when identifying an issue before proceeding to identify the next issue. Remember, for each issue, you must identify the rule of law, specific question, and relevant facts.

You may be reading a case in order to find the answer to a single question relevant to your client's fact situation, or you may be looking for a specific legal principle, doctrine, or rule of law addressed by the court.

For Example: The court opinion you are researching involves several torts, and you are only interested in the court's discussion of the emotional distress issue. The steps mentioned above should be followed to identify the emotional distress issue, but make sure that the court's resolution of the other issues does not in some way impact the emotional distress issue. This can be accomplished by reading the entire opinion and checking for any overlap of the issues or interconnectedness of the reasoning.

Caveat: As in the Issue Identification—Client's Case section, the steps presented in this section are to be considered useful tools and helpful guidelines. Remember, there is no magic formula for correctly identifying the issue in a court opinion. When followed, these steps will usually, but not always, help you quickly identify the issue in a court opinion. There are instances when the opinion is so obscure that you may not be able to identify the issue. Also, as you read more and more cases, a sort of intuition develops, and you may immediately spot the issue without the use of any of the steps.

KEY POINTS CHECKLIST: *Identifying the Issue*

- ❑ When determining the issue(s) in a *client's case,* it is helpful to keep in mind the question, "What must be decided about which facts in this case?" This question helps keep the mind focused on the rule of law in conjunction with the facts.
- ❑ When identifying the issue(s) in a *court opinion,* as you read, keep asking the question, "What was decided about which facts in this case?" All cases are about how the law applies to facts. By keeping focused on the law and facts of the case, you are less likely to be sidetracked by issues and questions that do not need to be addressed.
- ❑ Address one issue at a time. For each issue under consideration, follow each of the steps presented in this chapter before proceeding to the next issue. In multiple issue cases, separate the issues and identify one completely before addressing the next one.
- ❑ When reading a court opinion or working on a client's case, keep in mind the three elements of the issue: *rule of law, question,* and *key facts.* This helps you stay focused on what you need to determine in order to identify the issue.
- ❑ Do not be concerned if you cannot immediately identify the issue or issues in a client's case. The complete identification of the issue may not take place until research is conducted, laws and cases read, and the required elements of the cause of action identified. The existence of additional issues likewise may not be known until research reveals their presence.
- ❑ Do not stop when you have identified one issue. Most cases have more than one legal question. Separate areas of law, such as torts and contracts, may occur in one fact situation. Always look for all possible causes of action that may arise from a fact situation.
- ❑ Use any technique that works for you. The steps suggested here are designed as guidelíness to assist you. They are not magic formulas cast in stone. Use any or all of them and anything else that works.

APPLICATION

In this section, two examples of issue identification or issue spotting are presented. Each example illustrates the principles discussed throughout this chapter and includes a discussion of the application of those principles.

Client's Fact Situation

The following example involves the application of the principles to the hypothetical presented at the beginning of the chapter.

Step 1 Identify each possible cause of action and area of law involved. The first step is to identify each type of cause of action and area of law that may be raised by the client's fact situation. Kevin, based upon his training, realizes that this is a civil, not a criminal, matter. No crime has been committed against Ms. Carry. He also knows that the applicable area of civil law is tort. By a process of elimination, based upon experience, he focuses on infliction of emotional distress. There is no assault or battery because there is no act directly or indirectly aimed at the client. Step 1 may require no research. Kevin may arrive at this point based solely on his education and experience, although he may realize, as he conducts research into the cause of action identified, that other causes of action also are present. If more than one claim is identified, steps 2 through 4 are to be followed separately for each.

For Example: If a part from the car flew off and hit Ms. Carry, there is a potential battery issue, and steps 2 through 4 would be followed for that issue.

Step 2 Determine the elements of each cause of action identified in step 1. Kevin's research reveals that emotional distress is a common law doctrine developed in case law. The legislature has not adopted a statute concerning emotional distress. The state's highest court has recognized the tort of intentional infliction of emotional distress. The court requires that the following elements be established to state a claim:

- Element 1 The defendant's conduct must be either intentional or grossly or recklessly negligent.
- Element 2 The conduct must be extreme and outrageous.
- Element 3 There must be a causal connection between the defendant's conduct and the plaintiff's mental distress.
- Element 4 The plaintiff's mental distress must be extreme or severe.

Step 3 Determine which of the facts of the client's case apply to establish or satisfy the elements of each cause of action—the key facts. In other words, decide which of the facts are key facts.

- Element 1 Defendant's conduct of driving at a very high rate of speed, crashing through the fence, hitting the seesaw and injuring plaintiff's friend's son are the facts that apply to satisfy the first element of intentional or grossly negligent conduct.
- Element 2 Driving through a school zone at an extremely high rate of speed is the fact that satisfies the second element of extreme or outrageous conduct.
- Element 3 Ms. Carry's insomnia and anxiety immediately after the event are facts that apply to the third element of causation.
- Element 4 Ms. Carry's anxiety and insomnia are extreme and apply to establish the fourth element.

If Kevin could not find a fact that would arguably apply to each element, there would be no issue involving that area of law, and that cause of action would have to be abandoned as a potential avenue of redress for Ms. Carry.

For Example: If Ms. Carry did not suffer any anxiety or insomnia, there probably would be no cause of action for emotional distress.

Note: As discussed in the Issue Identification—Client's Case section of this chapter, you may not be certain whether a fact meets the established standard for an element. Often that determination may not take place until trial. Just make sure there is some fact that *arguably* meets the requirements of each of the elements of the cause of action.

For Example: A determination of whether Ms. Carry's insomnia and anxiety are extreme enough to warrant relief may not be decided until trial. But her symptoms are sufficient to arguably meet the requirements of the fourth element. If research reveals that this harm is not sufficiently extreme to meet the requirements of emotional distress, there is no emotional distress issue.

Step 4 Assemble the issue. Assemble the elements and state the issue. Kevin now has all the elements necessary to identify and state the issue: the area of law, the legal question, and the key facts. Following the format presented in the next chapter, he identifies the issue as: "Under (name of state) tort law, does intentional infliction of emotional distress occur when a person suffers severe insomnia and anxiety as a result of witnessing a friend's child being injured by a vehicle that is out of control due to being driven at a high rate of speed through a school zone?"

By following the four steps, moving from a broad identification of the possible causes of action to the specific elements and facts involved under each cause of action, Kevin has identified an issue. He knows what must be decided about which facts for this cause of action. His research is focused on cases in which the conduct involved accidents in school zones where witnesses suffered harm similar to that of Ms. Carry.

If there were other possible causes of action identified in step 1, steps 2 through 4 would be followed for each potential cause.

Court Opinion

The following example illustrates the application of the principles to the identification of the issues in a court opinion. There are three steps to follow:

- Step 1 *General Question*—While reading the case, keep in mind the general question, "What was decided about which facts in the case?"
- Step 2 *Look to the Holding*—Identify the rule of law and key facts relevant to the holding.
- Step 3 *Assemble the Issue.*

Read *Acacia Mutual Life Insurance Company v. American General Life Insurance Company* in the following text.

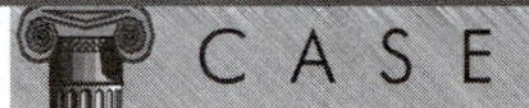

ACACIA MUTUAL LIFE INSURANCE COMPANY, et al., Plaintiffs,

v.

AMERICAN GENERAL LIFE INSURANCE COMPANY, et al., Involuntary Plaintiff,

111 N.M. 106, 802 P.2d 11 (1990)

OPINION

BACA, Justice.

Appellant David Silver was the general partner of the Santa Fe Private Equity Fund II, L.P. (SFPEF II), a limited partnership. He appeals from a court order that affirms a settlement agreement arrived upon by the limited partners through their receiver, John Clark, appellee. The order distributes the assets of the limited partnership in order of priority mandated by the legislature in Section 54-2-23 of the Uniform Limited Partnership Act. *See* NMSA 1978, §§ 54-2-1 to -30 (Repl.Pamp. 1988). Silver claims that this order unjustly bars his contractual indemnification claim as set out in the partnership agreement. The right to contract is jealously guarded by this court, but if a contractual clause clearly contravenes a positive rule of law, it cannot be enforced, *General Electric Credit Corp. v. Tidenberg,* 78 N.M. 59, 428 P.2d 33 (1967). The indemnification clause clearly contravenes the order of priority in the distribution of assets of a dissolved limited partnership as set out by the legislature. We, therefore, affirm.

FACTS

In February 1987 the limited partners unanimously voted to terminate their failing partnership, which had shown a loss from the outset, and filed in district court for a confirmation of the dissolution of SFPEF II. They also voted to remove Silver as general partner, but allowed him to resign. Clark was named as receiver and published a notice of dissolution of the partnership in *The Santa Fe New Mexican* on March 23, 1987. This notice requested creditors to respond with claims against the partnership within fourteen days. Silver wrote a letter within this time, asserting his claim under the partnership agreement for indemnification and reimbursement from the partnership for any partnership debts he paid.

After the notification of dissolution, Clark began negotiations with known creditors of the limited partnership and a determination of the status of the SFPEF II. In analyzing the assets and liabilities of SFPEF II, Clark determined that the limited partners had contributed in excess of $7 million, but he could document only $2.4 million in investments. The estimated value of SFPEF II was eventually determined to be negative $1.4 million, equaling a loss to the limited partners of $8.4 million. Aside from checks written to the general partners in excess of $1 million, the balance of the limited partners' contributions remains unaccounted for.

Clark determined the amount necessary to settle all creditors' claims and on that basis made a third, partial capital call to limited partners to wind up affairs and terminate the partnership. At this point some of the limited partners refused to pay a third partial capital call, claiming other limited partners had not yet paid on the second call.

Approximately a year after the request for confirmation of dissolution was filed, the dispute finally was settled. Clark arrived upon a global settlement agreement that allowed creditors to be paid and the receivership to be terminated. Under the settlement the limited partners were to contribute a final $1.3 million. The settlement agreement also provided for payment of creditors, distribution of any remaining liquid assets to the limited partners, and assignment of all of the partnership's claims against the general partners to one limited partner. Approval of the settlement by the court would bar all claims of creditors who had not asserted a claim. The motion for confirmation was served on Silver, who objected and asserted his indemnification claim from SFPEF II. This was over a year after notification of dissolution and the letter written by Silver to the receiver in March of 1987—the only notice of Silver's indemnification claim. The district court held that Silver's claim was untimely and approved the settlement that foreclosed Silver's indemnification claim. This appeal is taken from that order.

ISSUES—AND NON-ISSUES

Silver phrases the six points of his appeal in terms of his timely notice of a claim against the partnership and of an improper "bar" to this claim for indemnification, along with related claims of procedural due process, equal protection violations, and laches. We identify the issues differently.

We are dealing here with the time-worn principles underlying limited partnerships that restrict the potential liability of a "limited" partner and hold a "general" partner to general, personal liability. "[L]imited partners * * * take no part in management, share profits and *do not share* *losses beyond their capital contributions to the firm."* A. Bromberg, *Crane & Bromberg on Partnership,* § 26 at 143 (1968) (emphasis added).

Indemnifying a general partner for partnership debts by essentially forcing limited partners to pay for them violates the general public policy of limited partnership law. However, it is not necessary to decide this case on general policy grounds alone because such grounds are incorporated into specific statutory provisions that control the order of priority of distribution of assets in these circumstances, and the general partner is statutorily the last in priority. A court cannot depart from the express language of an act, but can only say what the legislature intended. *Security Escrow Corp. v. Taxation & Revenue Dep't,* 107 N.M. 540, 760 P.2d 1306 (Ct.App.1988); *State v. Michael R.,* 107 N.M. 794, 765 P.2d 767 (Ct.App.1988).

The partnership agreement itself supports our interpretation. Silver argues that in the partnership agreement a clause existed, 13(b), which provides that the "Partnership * * * shall indemnify * * * the General Partner [and] its partners * * * against all claims * * * incurred by them in connection with their activities on behalf of the Partnership * * *." This clause, however, is subject to paragraph 6(f) of the partnership agreement, which deals with liability of limited partners and states in pertinent part: "No limited Partner shall be liable for any debts or obligations of the Partnership, including obligations in respect of indemnification provided in paragraph 13, in excess of its unpaid Capital Contribution * * *."

The partnership was terminated, pursuant to its requirements, when the limited partners unanimously voted to terminate. At this point the partnership, along with potential remaining capital calls, went into receivership and dissolution, and this dissolution came under the New Mexico Limited Partnership Act. NMSA 1978, Section 54-2-23 (Repl.Pamp.1988) sets out the order of priority for the distribution of assets:

> A. In settling accounts after dissolution the liabilities of the partnership shall be entitled to payment in the following order:
>
> (1) those to creditors, in the order of priority as provided by law, except those to limited partners on account of their contributions, and to general partners;
>
> (2) those to *limited partners* in respect to their share of the profits and other compensation by way of income on their contributions;
>
> (3) those to *limited partners* in respect to the capital of their contributions;
>
> (4) those to *general partners* other than for capital and profits;
>
> (5) those to general partners in respect to profits;
>
> (6) those to general partners in respect to capital.
>
> (Emphasis added.)

The law of New Mexico mandates that in a dissolution of a limited partnership, the limited partners are to be paid off before the general partners. The interpretation of the indemnification clause in the contract urged by Silver would have the general partners paid off *by* the limited partners. Since there are no assets left in this terminated partnership, to indemnify the general partner would require the limited partners to contribute even more funds to a dead entity. The clear language of a statute must be given its full meaning. *Schoonover v. Caudill,* 65 N.M. 335, 337 P.2d 402 (1959); *Weiser v. Albuquerque Oil & Gasoline Co.,* 64 N.M. 137, 325 P.2d 720 (1958). To indemnify the general partners would contravene this statute and is therefore unenforceable. We AFFIRM.

IT IS SO ORDERED.

Step 1 General Question. Read the entire case. While reading the case, ask yourself, "What did the court decide about which facts?" To answer this question, it is necessary to keep in mind the elements of the issue—the rule of law, legal question, and key facts. Keeping this question in mind helps you focus on these elements.

Step 2 Look to the Holding. You probably cannot identify the issue after completing step 1. The court did not specifically state the issue, nor is the issue clear from a simple reading of the case. Follow step 2 and find the holding. Here, the holding is presented in the next to the last sentence: "To indemnify the general partners would contravene this statute and is therefore unenforceable." Once identified, locate the elements of the issue relevant to this holding. Ask the following questions:

1. *"What was decided in the holding?"* In other words, "What legal question or issue was addressed and answered by the court?" The answer to this question is determined by looking to the holding and deciding what question was answered by the holding.

   Here, Silver, a general partner and an appellant in the case, argued that section 13(b) of the partnership agreement allowed him to be reimbursed, by additional contributions from the limited partners, for partnership debts he paid. In other words, section 13(b) would require limited partners to share losses beyond their capital contributions to the partnership and require limited partners to pay off general partners. The court held that the section, so interpreted, would clearly contravene the provisions of the statute. The legal question, then, is whether an interpretation of the section of the agreement that would require such payments by limited partners is enforceable.

   In this case, it is difficult to identify the issue without this step because there is information included in the opinion that tends to mislead the reader.

   For Example: The last two sentences in the "Facts" section of the opinion indicate that the appeal was taken from a trial court ruling that Silver's claim was untimely. Based upon those statements, the reader is led to believe the case involves a timeliness issue and looks for the court's discussion of that question. The court, however, never mentions timeliness in the rest of the opinion. By looking to the holding and following this step, the reader is directed to the issue actually decided by the court.

2. *"What statute, rule of law, principle, and so on was applied by the court when it reached this holding?"* In this case, the court looked to section 54-2-23 of the New Mexico Limited Partnership Act.
3. *"Which facts mentioned in the opinion are related and necessary to the determination of the question addressed in the holding?"* "Which of the facts, if changed, would change the holding?" In other words, "What are the key facts?" In this case, as in many cases, the court presents several facts that have nothing to do with the holding. Usually these facts are presented to give the reader the background and context of the holding. The presentation of too many background facts, however, may mislead the reader and make it difficult to determine what the case is actually about.

   This is especially true in this case. The opinion contains several paragraphs discussing the financial status of the partnership and the details of the global settlement agreement arranged by the receiver. So much is presented concerning these facts that the reader tends to focus on them, and not on the key facts that involve the provisions of the partnership agreement.

   When the holding, however, is referred to and the question is asked, "Which facts are necessary or related to this holding?," it is clear that the facts relevant to the holding are the facts concerning section 13(b) of the partnership agreement, and Silver's interpretation of that section. The key facts are the section of the partnership agreement that provides that the partnership shall indemnify the general partner against all claims, and Silver's interpretation of that section to require limited partners, upon dissolution of the partnership, to reimburse general partners with contributions beyond their capital contributions.

Step 3 Assemble the Issue. The final step is to assemble the issue. All the elements have been identified in step 2:

- The rule of law is section 54-2-23 of the New Mexico Limited Partnership Act.
- The question is whether an indemnification provision of the partnership agreement is enforceable.
- The key fact is an interpretation of the indemnification provision that requires limited partners, upon dissolution of the partnership, to reimburse general partners with additional contributions beyond their capital contributions.

Referring to the format presented in Chapter 7, the issue is: "Under the provisions of § 54-2-23 of the New Mexico Limited Partnership Act, is an indemnification provision of a partnership agreement enforceable when it is interpreted to require limited partners, upon dissolution of the partnership, to reimburse general partners with additional contributions beyond their capital contributions?"

SUMMARY

The most important task in either analyzing a client's case or reading a court opinion is the correct identification of the issue or issues. The problem must be identified before it can be solved. A misidentified issue can result not only in wasted time but also in malpractice.

The issue is the precise legal question raised by the facts of the dispute. Therefore, each issue is unique because the facts of each case are different, and each issue must be narrowly stated within the context of the facts of that case. The issue is composed of the applicable law, the legal question relevant to the law, and the facts that raise the question. These elements must be precisely identified to determine the issue.

There is no magic formula. This chapter includes steps that help in issue identification. When working on a client's case there are four recommended steps:

1. Identify each area of law possibly involved.
2. Identify the elements necessary for a cause of action under each law identified in the first step.
3. Apply the elements of the law to the client's facts to determine the key facts.
4. Assemble the issue from the law, elements, and key facts identified in the first three steps.

When locating the issue in a court opinion, there are three steps:

1. General question—while reading the case, keep in mind the question, "What was decided about which facts?"
2. Look to the holding to identify the rule of law, legal question, and key facts of the case.
3. Assemble the issue.

These are the recommended steps. They usually work when followed and are always helpful in focusing the practitioner's attention on that which is essential—the rule of law, legal question, and facts.

EXERCISES

ASSIGNMENT 1
Identify the issue in the following two fact situations.

Part A

Beth loaned Allen $5,000. The agreement was oral. Allen commutes to a nearby city to work. Beth needs to go to the city three times in May. Allen told her he would give her three free rides to the city to help repay the loan. On one of the trips, Allen was not paying attention, lost control of the car, and wrecked. Beth suffered severe injuries and wants to sue Allen to recover damages.

The state automobile guest statute bars suits against drivers by automobile guests. The statute does not apply if the passenger confers a substantial benefit on the driver and that is the reason the driver provided the ride.

Part B

Tom and Alex are next-door neighbors. While arguing with Tom, Alex breaks Tom's lawn chair, and as Alex begins to break more lawn furniture, Tom makes a citizen's arrest of Alex. Tom's sons help Tom, and after Alex is subdued, they continue to hit and kick him for a few moments. Alex wants to sue Tom.

The state's common law defines battery as unauthorized harmful contact; it also allows a citizen's arrest when the purpose is to prevent the destruction of property.

ASSIGNMENT 2

Part A

Read *Dean v. Dickey* in Appendix A. Identify the validity of the will issue.

Part B

Read *United States v. Martinez-Jimenez* in Appendix A. Identify the issue concerning whether the weapon was a dangerous weapon.

Part C

Read *Wolcott v. Wolcott* in Appendix A. Identify the issue concerning the modification of child support due to change of circumstances.

Part D

Read *People v. Sanders* in Appendix A. Identify the issue concerning the existence of spousal privilege for communications made in the presence of the children.

ASSIGNMENT 3
Read *Paur v. Rose City Dodge, Inc.* presented in the following text. Identify the battery issue involving defendants Green and Devon.

PAUR v. ROSE CITY DODGE, INC.
438 P.2d 994 (Or. 1968)

HOLMAN, Justice.

Defendants in this action for damages for an alleged battery appeal from a judgment entered upon a jury verdict for plaintiff, assessing damages as $5,000 general, $499.50 special, and $15,000 punitive.

Plaintiff, Louis Paur, was employed as a salesman at defendant Rose City Dodge (Rose City), a car dealership. Defendant Anthony ("Tony") Moss was employed as a lot boy as Rose City. Defendant Robert Green was general manager, and defendant James DeVon was sales manager.

Plaintiff testified that as he was leaving the Rose City premises, he was attacked from behind, knocked down, and beaten by defendant Moss. Plaintiff claims that defendants Green and DeVon directed Moss to commit the alleged battery. Prior to the attack, Green and DeVon had been informed that plaintiff had interfered with a deal between Rose City and a Mrs. Betty Tuttle, a friend of plaintiff. Plaintiff told Mrs. Tuttle not to sign a contract for the sale of an automobile which was tendered her, and he marked changes on it which would have resulted in a substantial price reduction. As a result he had been discharged.

We first consider the assignments of error which challenge the denial of the motion of defendants Rose City, Green and DeVon for a directed verdict. The question presented is whether there was any substantial evidence to show that the individual defendants participated in the battery, and that defendant Rose City was liable vicariously.

There was testimony that Green, after learning of plaintiff's action, told plaintiff he was fired, and then told Moss in the presence of DeVon and plaintiff: "If Mr. Paur comes back throw him out." Later, according to plaintiff, Green told the plaintiff, who had come back to Rose City to return the keys of a car: "Get out of here, if you ever come back I will have you thrown out." According to plaintiff, he left the premises and then returned after noticing that Green had gone home. Plaintiff asked DeVon to assist plaintiff in collecting outstanding commissions. At the conclusion of their conversation, DeVon, according to plaintiff, made the following statements in the presence of Moss and plaintiff:

> "* * * If you think I'm going to see that you get any of your commissions, you have coming after you screwed us out of a start of a deal you are crazy. * * *"
>
> * * * * * *
>
> "* * * Get out of here. * * * I will have you thrown out. * * * Well, you can't lose an $800 deal for us and want me to still be your friend. * * * Tony, throw him out. * * *"

The battery immediately followed.

To be liable for battery, each defendant must have participated in, aided, or procured the battery. Tauscher v. Doernbecher Mfg. Co., 153 Or. 152, 160, 56 P.2d 318 (1936). The evidence that Green and DeVon told Moss to "throw out" plaintiff was sufficient to raise a jury question whether Moss's battery upon plaintiff was pursuant to the directions of Green and DeVon.

Also, it was a jury question whether Green, as general manager, and DeVon, as sales manager, had authority to direct removal by force of unauthorized persons from Rose City's premises. If either of them did, and such one as had authority ordered plaintiff's removal pursuant to such authority, and excessive force was used in carrying out the order, the corporate principal is responsible for the resultant injury. 10 Fletcher, Corporations 463, § 4883.

> "* * * where the use of force at times is part of the duty of the servant, the master is not excused from liability when the servant uses excessive, and even unjustifiable, force in the performance of his duty, and even though in so doing the servant disobeys positive instructions of the master. * * *" Barry v. Oregon Trunk Railway, 197 Or. 246, 261, 253 P.2d 260, 266, 267 (1953).

We next consider the assignments which challenge the trial court's refusal to withdraw the issue of punitive damages from the jury.

Defendants contend that there was no evidence of malice on the part of Green and DeVon, and therefore punitive damages should have been withdrawn as to all in accord with the rule in this state that plaintiff waives punitive damages if he joins as defendant one who is not liable therefor. Gill v. Selling et al., 125 Or. 587, 594–595, 267 P. 812 (1928).

Both Green and DeVon knew that plaintiff had interfered with a profitable deal Rose City had proposed to Mrs. Tuttle. The purported statements of both is evidence indicating that individually they resented plaintiff's interference. From these statements the jury could infer malice.

Since Green and DeVon were entrusted with executive management of Rose City, the corporation could be found liable vicariously for their malicious acts. Pelton v. Gen. Motors Accept. Corp., 139 Or. 198, 204–205, 7 P.2d 263, 9 P.2d 128 (1932); Barry v. Oregon Trunk Railway, supra, at 257; 10 Fletcher, Corporations 452, § 4882.

****

It is only fair to remark that, on both sides, the trial of this case was a bare-knuckled affair with more emphasis on the prejudicial than on the relevant. There is no necessity to consider the charges of error relating to instructions. The judgment is reversed and the case is remanded for a new trial.

ASSIGNMENT 4

Read *In re Maltby* presented in the following text and identify the issue concerning the representation of antagonistic clients.

IN RE MALTBY

202 P.2d 908 (Ariz. 1949)

PER CURIAM.

Several complaints of improper and unethical practice were filed with the Local Administrative Committee for Maricopa County of the State Bar of Arizona, hereafter referred to as the State Bar, against A. L. Maltby, a duly licensed and practicing attorney in Phoenix, Arizona, hereafter referred to as respondent.

On March 29, 1947, a hearing was had by said committee at which time one of the complainants dropped his charges. The committee heard the case wherein respondent was charged with not properly accounting for his client's funds. The committee itself lodged a charge against respondent for using and distributing book matches with his name thereon as a form of advertising.

While the committee had the matter under advisement, two written complaints were filed against the respondent with the secretary of the State Bar on June 20 and July 8, 1947, by Mrs. Dell Adair. Mrs. Adair alleged that respondent represented her in a divorce suit and was not representing her former husband, Mr. Isaacs, in the same action.

Altogether the committee held three hearings. Respondent was present at two of them but did not appear at one hearing, although invited. Testimony and other evidence were duly introduced. The committee reported a summary of its proceedings to the Board of Governors of the State Bar with findings of fact. Respondent argued the matter before the board on October 22, 1948. The board then instructed its secretary to certify the entire record to this court for appropriate action. A formal hearing was had here January 10, 1949.

The most serious matter is respondent's action in representing Mr. Isaacs, husband of his former client. On February 12, 1946, respondent, as attorney for Mrs. Isaacs, now Mrs. Dell Adair, filed a divorce complaint in cause No. 17107, Superior Court, Maricopa County, styled Isaacs v. Isaacs. He secured a divorce judgment for his client which gave her the custody of the minor children of the parties. His services were completed in September, 1946. In the spring or summer of 1947 he undertook to represent Mr. Isaacs in the same cause, asking for a change in the custody of the children. He persisted in that course over objections of his former client made both to him and to the court below. His defense was that facts and circumstances had changed; that he had at no time gained any evidence while he was her attorney to use against her. Nonetheless Mrs. Adair complained that he betrayed her confidence and wanted him out of the case. The court below denied the change in the custody of the children so her rights were not affected. Evidently respondent misconceived his duty in the matter.

It should go without saying that a lawyer must not represent clients antagonistic to one another in the same case. Even though Mrs. Isaacs was not damaged she might well have been. A lawyer must not only avoid evil, he must also avoid the appearance of evil when placed in a position of trust and confidence by a client.

It is the opinion of this court that respondent has been guilty of indiscretions and unethical practice by:

1. Not keeping the accounts of his client in a manner respecting the confidence and trust placed in him.
2. Advertising by means of book matches with his name, as an attorney, printed on them.
3. Representing a client against a former client in the same cause of action.

Respondent's actions and attitude in this matter are wholly unbecoming to a member of the legal profession. While his actions are not deserving of suspension or disbarment, yet he has been guilty of infractions of the Canons of Ethics. Respondent's own conscience, in the absence of any objection by Mrs. Adair, should have dictated to him the utter impropriety of representing any interest in the Isaac's divorce case adverse to her.

This court owes a duty both to the public and to the profession to the extent at least that such things shall not go unnoticed. We cannot, and will not, countenance such practice without censure. We adopt in substance the language employed by this court in the case of In re Myrland, 43 Ariz. 126, 29 P.2d 483, and are of the opinion that in view of all the circumstances a disbarment or even a suspension of respondent would be too severe a penalty for the offenses of which he has been guilty. Therefore, we confine our action to a statement of our opinion of the character of his conduct and a formal reprimand of respondent therefor. Further infraction of the Canons of Ethics by the respondent will result in suspension or disbarment.

LA PRADE, C. J., and UDALL, STANFORD, PHELPS, and DE CONCINI, JJ., concur.

CHAPTER 7

Stating the Issue

"Mary, I want you to determine if we can get the evidence suppressed in this case. I need a memo on this by the day after tomorrow, if possible." Jan handed Mary the case file as she gave these instructions. Mary Strate is a legal assistant working in an Oregon law firm that specializes in criminal defense. Jan Brite is her supervising attorney, and according to Jan, Mary is her "right hand."

After reviewing the case and conducting some research, Mary's focus turns to the significant facts relevant to the suppression of the evidence issue. She determines that there are several key facts. The evidence was seized by the state police during the execution of a search warrant. The warrant was improperly issued by a state court judge. The warrant was improperly issued, and therefore, defective because sufficient probable cause to justify the search was not presented to the court by the state police. The opposing side, the state, concedes that the warrant was improperly issued. The officers did not know the warrant was defective and executed it in the good faith belief that it was valid.

Mary's research indicates that the resolution of the issue is governed by Oregon's exclusionary rule which provides that evidence illegally seized may not be admitted at trial. The rule was adopted by the state supreme court and is not statutory. As Mary begins the assignment, her first question is how to phrase the issue. What is the proper format? What is the best way to effectively communicate precisely what is in dispute in this case? The answer to the latter question is presented in the Application section of this chapter. The material discussed in this chapter prior to the Application section addresses the other questions posed by Mary.

INTRODUCTION

Chapter 6 points out that the most important step in the case analysis process is the correct identification of the issue. If the issue is misidentified, time is wasted researching and writing about the wrong question. If you call a cat a dog, you will never find a cat while looking for a dog. Once the issue is identified, it is equally important to correctly state it. Of what value is it to correctly identify the question, then fail to accurately formulate and communicate what you have identified? Therefore, how Mary states the issue is of critical importance because the issue governs the direction of the research and communicates the nature of the dispute.

A well-crafted issue informs the reader of the scope of the memo by identifying in a sentence the precise legal question raised by the key facts of the case. It informs the reader of the relevant law, the key facts of the case, and the legal question raised by the law. The exactness and degree of specificity with which the question is posed determines its usefulness to the reader and researcher.

The goal is to inform the reader of what you have identified as the legal question raised by the dispute. This goal is achieved by focusing your attention on drafting the issue clearly, concisely, and completely. Because so much hinges on the correct presentation of the issue, several drafts may be required. Do not get discouraged. The final draft may not emerge until well into the process, and often not until after extensive research and writing.

Chapter 6 identifies the issue as being composed of the law, the question, and the key facts. The focus of that chapter was on how to identify these elements in a client's situation and a court opinion. Here the focus is on how these elements are presented when framing the issue—how the issue should be written to ensure that the reader knows the precise legal question at the core of the dispute and how the law, question, and key facts are integrated and presented to clearly and completely communicate the question in dispute.

Ultimately, the issue is the legal question raised by the dispute. Since it is a question, it should be drafted as a question rather than a statement.

The issue may involve a question of which law applies, how it applies in a specific situation, or whether a law applies at all. Regardless of the nature of the question, an effective issue should include:

- The applicable law
- The legal question
- The key facts

While there are no established rules governing what the issue must contain or how it should be assembled, these elements should be included to achieve the goal of clearly, concisely, and completely communicating the nature of the dispute. A simple test to determine if the statement of the issue is complete (whether it does its job) is the following: *If the issue alone were read—if the rest of the memorandum or brief were lost or not referred to—would the reader know what specific legal question, concerning what law, and involving what facts is in dispute in **this** case?* With this in mind, there are two ways to state the issue, one effective and one not:

- A shorthand, or broad, statement.
- A comprehensive, or narrow, statement.

SHORTHAND/BROAD STATEMENT OF THE ISSUE

A shorthand statement is a very broad formulation of the issue that usually does not include the specific facts or law.

issue--short/broad statement

A broad formulation of the issue that usually does not include reference to the specific facts of the case or the applicable law.

For Example:

- Did Mr. Smith commit a battery?
- Can Mr. Jones recover damages for negligence?
- Did the court err when it granted the motion to dismiss?
- Did the chair of the board violate his fiduciary duty?

A broadly framed issue is often used in conversation or oral communications when the participants are familiar with the facts and know the law that applies to the case. It is appropriate in this informal context. It may also be appropriate initially in the analytical process by helping to focus attention on the general area of the law that needs to be researched—for example, in the preceding list, the first two illustrations focus the researcher's attention on the general areas of battery and negligence. A broadly stated issue may be proper in such situations, but it is not appropriate in legal research and writing for several reasons:

1. It is not helpful or useful for the reader who is not familiar with the facts of the case. This may be a judge in the case of a brief in support of a motion, or an attorney in the office referring to an old memorandum in the office files. The reader may wonder who Mr. Smith is and what he did that may or may not be a battery.
2. It does not guide the reader to the specific law in question. What specific fiduciary duty did the chair of the board violate? What statute did he violate? What is the precise legal context of this dispute?
3. It is not useful to the individual drafting and researching the issue.

For Example: "Did Mr. Smith commit a battery?" is such a broad formulation of the issue that it is of little value.

Stated this way the issue applies to all battery cases. So stated, it is useless. It fails to focus the researcher's inquiry or guide the researcher to the specific area of battery law in dispute.

In West Publishing's widely used key number system, there are over one hundred battery subtopics under the topic "Assault and Battery." A broad statement of the issue forces the researcher to scan all the subtopics looking for the one that applies. If the issue is stated comprehensively, or narrowly, the inquiry is narrowed.

For Example: "Under California's tort law, is a battery committed when an individual encourages and convinces his brother to beat another individual, and that individual is beaten as a result of the encouragement?" This narrow statement of the issue focuses the researcher's attention to that specific area of the digest involving individuals liable for battery, *i.e.,* Assault and Battery—Key Number 18, Persons Liable.

As the preceding example illustrates, a comprehensive statement directs the researcher's inquiry to a specific subtopic in the digest, and research time is saved. Also, the question is not abstract. The reader does not have to refer to the facts in order to understand what is in dispute.

In summary, a shorthand/broad statement of the issue fails to inform. It results in an abstract question that forces the reader to engage in further inquiry to determine what specifically is in dispute in the case. In short, it is useless except in casual conversation or conversations where the participants are familiar with the case.

COMPREHENSIVE/NARROW STATEMENT OF THE ISSUE

The most effective formulation of the issue is a comprehensive, or "narrow," statement. In one sentence, the specific law, legal question, and key facts are presented. This form communicates the specific law that may have been violated in a specific fact situation, or whether and how that law applies in a specific situation. It conveys, in the terms and circumstances of the case, the precise law and question in dispute.

issue--comprehensive/narrow statement
A complete statement of the issue that includes the specific law, legal question, and key facts.

For Example:

- Under the requirements of Florida tort law, can a claim for negligent infliction of emotional distress be made by a witness, not related to the victim, who witnesses a severe beating of the victim?
- According to New Washington's probate code, N. Wash. Code § 29-1-5, is a will valid if the witnesses are brothers of the testator?

Note that the specific law and question involved in the dispute are presented in the context of the facts of the dispute.

The value and importance of phrasing the issue comprehensively cannot be overemphasized.

1. For a researcher, it directs the research to the specific area of the law that controls the question raised by the facts involved in the dispute. This narrowing of focus saves research time because the researcher is immediately directed to the specific area of the law, and only cases with similar key facts need to be read. (See number 3 in the previous section, Shorthand/Broad Statement of the Issue.)
2. In an interoffice memorandum or a court brief, a comprehensive, or narrow, formulation of the issue sets the scope of the memo by informing the reader at the outset what precisely is in dispute. It does not force the reader to try to determine what the question is from the analysis section. It thereby makes it less likely that the reader will misunderstand what is in dispute.
3. In a law office setting, a narrowly framed issue saves time. Future researchers, by merely reading the issue, know precisely what law and facts are discussed in the memorandum. They are not forced to read the analysis section to determine if the memo is related or may apply to the case on which they are working.

With the above in mind, the issue, then, should include the three elements presented in Figure 7–1. The three elements are:

1. The specific *law or rule* that controls the dispute
2. The *legal question* regarding the law raised by the facts
3. The *key or legally significant facts* that determine whether or how the law or principle applies

The challenge is to include all three elements completely, concisely, and clearly in one sentence. The key is to keep your focus on:

1. *Completeness*—Include the precise law, question, and key facts.
2. *Conciseness*—Include no more than is absolutely necessary to guarantee completeness.
3. *Clarity*—Craft the complete and concisely assembled material in the most effective manner (discussed in the following).

There are several ways to meet this challenge:

1. The facts can be presented first, followed by the legal question and the law.

1. Applicable Law
2. Legal Question
3. Key Facts

Figure 7–1
Elements of an Issue

For Example: "Can a witness, not related to the victim, who witnesses a severe beating of the victim state a cause of action for negligent infliction of emotional distress under Florida tort law?"

"If the brothers of the testator witness the will, is the will valid under the provisions of the California wills attestation statute?"

2. The law can be presented first, followed by the facts, and then the legal question.

   For Example: "Under Florida's tort law, can a witness, not related to the victim, who witnesses a severe beating of the victim state a cause of action for negligent infliction of emotional distress?"

   "Under the California wills attestation statute, if the brothers of the testator witness the will, is the will valid?"

3. The legal question can be presented first, followed by the law and the facts.

   For Example: "Can a claim for negligent infliction of emotional distress be made under Florida tort law when a witness, not related to the victim, witnesses a severe beating of the victim?"

   "Is a will valid under the California wills attestation statute if the brothers of the testator witness the will?"

4. The rule of law can be presented first, followed by the legal question and the facts.

   For Example: "Under Florida's tort law, can a claim for negligent infliction of emotional distress be made by a witness, not related to the victim, who witnesses a severe beating of the victim?"

   "Under the California wills attestation statute, is a will valid if the brothers of the testator witness the will?"

Any of these structures may be used. There are no hard-and-fast rules that mandate the selection of one form over another. However, the format presented in number 4 in the preceding paragraph is recommended. The formula for this format is presented in Figure 7–2.

In sentence form, the formula in Figure 7–2 is: *"Under this law, what legal question is raised by these facts?"* There are several reasons for recommending this format:

1. It follows the standard legal analysis format, which proceeds from the general to the specific—the general law followed by the application of the law to the specific facts.

   For Example: In a court brief or an interoffice legal research memorandum, the applicable law is presented first, followed by the application of the law to the specific facts.

   The suggested format for the formulation of the issue presented in Figure 7–2 follows the same format: the general legal context is presented first, followed by the specific facts of the dispute.

2. The rule should be presented first for readability purposes. A reader understands the importance of the facts in a dispute in the context of the law. If the facts are presented first and the law last, the reader must reread the facts in order to put them in the proper legal context because the legal context (the law that applies) is not known until the end of the issue.

Figure 7–2

Formula Format for the Issue

Relevant Law + Legal Question + Key Facts

3. There are often multiple key facts, and multiple facts are generally easier to write and read when placed at the end of a sentence.
4. The last and probably most important reason is that it is usually *easier to write the issue* following this format. It is a most effective tool when confronting the complex challenges presented by multiple fact issues. Try it. Once the specific law and significant or key facts are identified, it is much easier to craft the issue in the sequence of law + question + key facts.

For these reasons, the examples used throughout this chapter and the text follow the Relevant Law + Legal Question + Key Facts format.

ISSUE—LAW COMPONENT

The relevant law obviously must be included in the statement of the issue because every case involves whether or how a law applies in a specific fact situation. If it is not included, you are asking the reader to either guess or infer what law applies or conduct research to find the applicable law. To avoid possible confusion and save extra work, the relevant legal context should be established at the beginning of the issue.

The law may be presented in a broad context, such as "corporations," or a narrow one, such as a specific section of a statute. It should include the specific jurisdiction and the area of law.

For Example:

	(jurisdiction)	*(area)*
■ Under	New Washington	contract law
■ Under	N. Wash.Code § 35-42-7	kidnapping law

The law component of the issue is composed of either enacted law or common law. As defined in Chapter 1, the term *enacted law* includes any constitutional law or rule or enactment of a legislative body, such as a statute, ordinance, or regulation. Common law refers to any court-made doctrine, law, rule, principle, test, or guide.

Issue Based on Common Law

When an issue is based on common law, no single case citation should be referred to because the common law is usually based on a group or body of cases, and generally no single case encompasses the relevant law. It is sufficient to present the law with a short introductory phrase that includes the jurisdiction and the area of the law. The easiest format is as follows:

	(jurisdiction)	***(area)***
Under	New Mexico	corporation law
Applying	Utah's	emotional distress law
According to	Indiana's	doctrine of res ipsa loquitur
In light of	California's	definition of confinement in false imprisonment actions

However it is stated, the description should be as focused and specific as possible. The goal is to inform the reader, as precisely as possible, of the area of law involved in the dispute. Therefore, such broad statements as "According to the Colorado case law . . ." or "Under the common law . . ." are generally not acceptable.

Such statements are so broad as to be meaningless. The reader is given no direction about which area of the law is involved in the dispute.

Along these same lines, a specific description is preferable to a broad one.

For Example:

- "Under Wyoming's definition of oppressive conduct by majority shareholders . . ." is preferable to "Under Wyoming corporation law . . ."
- "Applying Georgia's definition of consideration . . ." is preferable to "Applying Georgia contract law . . ."
- "Under California's law of trespass to chattels . . ." is preferable to "Under California tort law . . ."

Again, the key is to be as specific and focused as possible when describing the area of the law. The greater the specificity of the legal description, the greater the reader's understanding of what precisely is at issue in the dispute. If you are using a broad description, such as torts, reexamine the issue to determine if a narrower focus, such as false imprisonment, battery, and so on, can be applied.

Issue Based on Enacted Law

An issue based on enacted law, such as a constitutional provision or statute, may be presented in several ways. The various ways may include a specific citation, a title, and/or a description.

For Example:

(citation) (title)

- "According to N. Wash. Code § 20-40-1, kidnapping . . ."

(title paraphrased) (description)

- "Under the New Washington kidnapping statute, which includes intent to confine as an element of kidnapping, . . ."

(title paraphrased) (citation)

- "In light of the provisions of the involuntary dissolution of corporations statute, N. Wash. Corp. Code § 56-7-14, . . ."

The choice or combination of choices selected is governed by the goal of clearly, completely, and concisely communicating the issue. This, in turn, is governed by the complexity of the issue and the degree to which the description conveys the necessary information.

Enacted Law—Citations

Is it necessary or advisable to include the citation in the statement of the issue? Some believe the inclusion of the citation clutters the issue, arguing that it is not necessary because the citation can be determined by referring to the analysis section of the memorandum. Others believe the inclusion of the citation is, if not required, at least advisable. It focuses the reader on the exact section of the law in dispute, allowing the reader to immediately refer to that section if necessary. In a law office, a subsequent researcher reviewing a memo from the memo files, by referring to the issue, can tell what specific law is discussed in the memo. By merely referring to the issue, the researcher knows if the memo involves the same law as the law being researched.

For Example: A researcher is checking the office memorandum files to determine if any research has been conducted on section 956.05(b) of the corporation statutes. If the citation is included in the issue, a mere glance at the issue tells the researcher if the memo involves the same statute. The researcher's time is saved by not having to read the body of the memo to determine if it is on point.

In some instances, the firm may require or prefer the inclusion or exclusion of the citation in the issue. In the case of a court brief, the court rules may determine the question. If the choice is yours, do what works. If the length or complexity of the issue precludes the use of the citation, leave it out.

There are a couple of rules to keep in mind when a citation is being used:

1. Use the proper citation form. A brief summary of citation form is presented in Appendix C.
2. Do not use a citation alone. In addition to a citation, a title or description is necessary to adequately inform the reader of the legal context of the issue.

For Example: *Incorrect:* "Under Ind. Code § 29-1-5-5, does . . ." Without a description or title, one does not know which area of the law is being considered. The reader will be forced to stop and look up the citation unless he or she is familiar with that particular section.

Correct: "Under Ind. Code § 29-1-5-5, legal execution of a will, . . ." The specific area of law covered in the citation is provided.

Enacted Law—Titles and Descriptions

Whereas citations should not be used without a title or description, a title or description can be used without a citation when describing enacted law. Titles and descriptions provide the amount of information sufficient to inform the reader of the legal context of the issue. Although the citation is not required, its inclusion may be advisable for the reasons discussed in the preceding subsection.

A title of a constitutional section, statute, and so on, is a heading that provides the name by which an act or section is individually known. A description is a brief summary of the relevant portions of the act and may include part of the title.

For Example: *Examples of titles:*

- Ind. Code § 29-1-5-2. Writing required—Witnesses, competency, interest.
- Cal. Corp. Code § 1800. Verified complaint; plaintiffs; grounds; intervention by shareholder or creditor; exempt corporations.

Examples of descriptions:

- "Under the Indiana statute that governs the writing and witnessing of wills, . . ."
- "In light of the provisions of the California corporation statute that applies to lawsuits against corporations and intervention by shareholders, . . ."

When using a title or description of enacted law, the guiding principle is whether it provides the reader with enough information to know the legal context of the issue.

The title alone may provide sufficient information. The terms from the titles in the following example are in italic:

For Example:

- "Applying the provisions of the Maryland's *kidnapping* statute, . . ."
- "Under California's *holographic wills* statute, . . ."

Occasionally the title may require modification. Words may need to be added or deleted to enhance clarity and readability. In the following examples, the title is presented followed by the modified statement of the issue containing additional language.

For Example:

- Limitation of actions. (Title of N.M. Stat. Ann. § 41-1-2.) "Under the limitation of action provisions of New Mexico's wrongful death statute, . . ."
- Holographic wills; requirements. (Title of Cal. Prob. Code § 6111.) "According to the requirements of the holographic wills section of the California statutes, . . ."

Sometimes it is necessary to delete language from the title because it is not relevant to the issue or needed to enhance clarity. In the following examples, the title is presented first, followed by the modification containing less language.

For Example:

- Verified complaint; plaintiffs; grounds; intervention by shareholder or creditor; exempt corporations. (Title of Cal. Corp. Code § 1800.) "Under the California corporation statute that allows the intervention by shareholders in dissolution actions, . . ."
- Writing required—Witnesses, competency, interest. (Title of Ind. Code § 29-1-5-2.) "In light of the requirements of the Indiana wills statute that governs witness competency, . . ."

Comment: In these examples, "exempt corporations, interest" and other language was deleted because these terms, although included in the title, are not relevant to the issue in the case.

If the title of a statute or law does not provide the required information or it is necessary to emphasize an aspect or element of the statute or law, the use of a description may be appropriate. In the following examples, the title is presented first, followed by an example.

For Example:

- Nuncupative wills. (Title of Ind. Code § 29-1-5-4.) "Under the provisions of the Indiana statute that provides that an oral will does not revoke an existing written will, . . ."
- Limitations of actions. (Title of N. M. Stat. Ann. § 41-1-2.) "Under the wrongful death statute of New Mexico, which requires that an action be brought within three years of the date of death, . . ."
- Ski area sign requirements. (Title of Wash. Rev. Code § 70.117.010.) "Under the Washington statute that requires a resort to post a notice at the top of closed trails, . . ."

As mentioned, there are no rules mandating a particular format you must follow when composing the legal component of the issue. The unwritten rule, however, is to keep focused on the goal:

- *Is the information included sufficient to provide the reader with the specific legal context of the issue?*
- *Is the legal component of the issue stated so broadly that the reader will have to look elsewhere (in the analysis portion of the memorandum or in the statutes) to determine what precise area of the law is in dispute?*

Format of the Law Component

There are two basic formats that may be followed when presenting the legal component of the issue:

1. The jurisdiction or citation followed by the title or description
2. The title or description followed by the jurisdiction or citation

For Example: Jurisdiction or citation followed by title or description:

- *(jurisdiction) (title)*
  "Under the New Mexico wrongful death statutes, . . ."
- *(jurisdiction) (description)*
  "Under the Washington statute that requires a resort to post a notice at the top of closed trails, . . ."
- *(citation) (title)*
  "According to Ind. Code § 35-42-3-3, kidnapping, . . ."
- *(citation) (description)*
  "Under Cal. Civ. Proc. Code § 340, which establishes a one-year statute of limitations in slander cases, . . ."

For Example: Title or description followed by jurisdiction or citation:

- *(title) (jurisdiction)*
  "According to the wrongful death provisions of the Colorado statues, . . ."
- *(description) (jurisdiction)*
  "In light of the requirement that drivers carry proof of insurance under California law, . . ."
- *(title) (citation)*
  "Under the kidnapping statute, Ind. Code § 35-42-3-3, . . ."
- *(description) (citation)*
  "Under the statute that requires skiers to ski within the range of their ability, Wash. Rev. Code § 70.117.020, . . ."

ISSUE—QUESTION COMPONENT

The question component is really what the issue is about. What legal question is being raised by the facts? In the formula adopted in this chapter, the question follows the law component. It must:

1. relate to or concern the specific law included in the law component,
2. present the specific legal question raised by the facts, and
3. link the law with the facts.

In the following examples, the question component is italicized. The linking verbs are boldfaced.

For Example:

- Under New York landlord-tenant law, ***does** a landlord **breach** his duty to provide a habitable residence* when he fails to provide air conditioning?
- Under Cal. Civ. Proc. Code § 340, which establishes a one-year statute of limitations in slander cases, ***did** the statute of limitations **begin** to run* when the newsletter was printed or when the newsletter was distributed to the customers?
- According to the statute governing oppressive conduct, Cal. Corp. Code § 1800, ***does** a majority shareholder **engage** in oppressive conduct* when he refuses to issue dividends while providing himself with bonuses equal to twice his salary?
- Under the Colorado law governing ski resorts, ***is** a resort **responsible** for warning* skiers of hazardous areas between ski runs?

Note that in all the preceding examples, the question specifically relates to the law included in the issue. Note, also, that the question links the law to the facts. This linkage may be accomplished through the use of linking verbs. There are many possible linking verbs, such as *constitute, establish,* and various forms of *to be*—for example *is, was,* and so on. In drafting this component of the issue, the main focus should be to ensure that the legal question raised by the facts is included. In other words, under the law included in the issue, is the precise legal question raised by the facts clearly presented?

ISSUE—SIGNIFICANT/KEY FACTS COMPONENT

The last section of the formula for writing an issue is the presentation of the significant or key facts. What significant or key facts are, and how they are identified, are discussed in Chapters 5 and 6. It is especially important to keep in mind the goals of clarity, completeness, and conciseness because cases with multiple or complex facts often make these goals difficult to achieve. The fact component must:

1. be readable,
2. include key facts legally relevant to the law component, and
3. set the factual scope of the legal question.

It should not be so complex that the reader has trouble understanding the issue.

It is always preferable to include all key facts. Where, however, there are multiple key facts, it may be necessary for the sake of clarity to take other steps, such as categorizing, condensing, or listing the facts. Examples of the key fact component follow:

For Example: All key facts included:

- According to the provisions of New Mexico's ski safety act, does a resort have a duty to warn skiers of ice hazards on expert runs?
- Under the holographic will statute, Colo. Rev. Stat. § 15-11-503, is a holographic will valid if it is handwritten by a neighbor at the direction of the testator, but not written in the testator's handwriting?

Comment: Note that the facts are presented clearly and in a logical sequence.

For Example: Key facts condensed; some included, and some referred to:

- Under Ohio's corporation law governing oppressive conduct, does oppressive conduct occur when a majority shareholder of a closely held corporation engages in several acts that may be harmful to a minority shareholder, such as refusing to issue dividends and firing the minority shareholder from her position in the corporation without a stated cause?
- Under Texas's constitutional provision prohibiting cruel and unusual punishment, are conditions of confinement cruel and unusual when the confinement may be unhealthy in several ways, such as the total calories served each inmate daily are less than the recommended minimum and the jail cells are kept at under sixty degrees in the winter?

For Example: Key facts are presented in general categories:

- Under Indiana corporation law, does oppressive conduct occur when a majority shareholder engages in several actions that are beneficial solely to the majority shareholder and detrimental to the interests of the minority shareholders?
- Under Arizona's constitutional provision prohibiting cruel and unusual punishment, are conditions of confinement cruel and unusual when they are unsanitary, unsafe, and in violation of various health codes?

Comment: Note that care must be taken to avoid distorting or misstating the issue when condensing or categorizing the key facts. In the previous two examples, there are assumptions contained in the categorizations. It is assumed the actions of the majority shareholder are solely beneficial to the majority shareholder, and it is assumed the conditions of confinement are unsanitary. To avoid these problems, it may be necessary to present multiple or complex facts in the form of a list.

For Example: Key facts are listed:

- According to the provisions of California corporation law, Cal. Corp. Code § 1800, does oppressive conduct occur when a majority shareholder:
  1. fires a minority shareholder from her job without stating a reason;
  2. refuses to issue dividends when the corporation has a cash surplus of over $1,000,000 and there are no plans for use of the money by the business;
  3. triples his salary three times within one year and his salary was twice the amount of similarly situated employees when the raises were given; and
  4. gives himself a $100,000 cash bonus without a stated reason for the bonus?
- Under the United States Constitution's prohibitions against cruel and unusual punishment, are conditions of confinement cruel and unusual when:
  1. the food is nutritionally deficient in that the total calories per meal are less than the recommended minimum;
  2. jail cells designed for one inmate currently house three inmates;
  3. jail cell temperatures are routinely kept below sixty degrees in the winter; and
  4. jail cells are roach- and ant-infested?

Remember, it is always best to include all key or significant facts in the fact component of the issue. If to do so would make the issue unreadable or lacking in clarity, however, one of the options presented in the preceding examples may be employed.

OBJECTIVELY STATING THE ISSUE

The preceding sections discuss the structure of the issue—that is, what information must be included and the best sequence for presenting that information. An additional matter to consider when composing the issue is that it should be stated objectively. "Stated objectively" means the issue is written in a manner that fairly and completely presents all the key facts and is not constructed in a manner that favors an outcome.

When writing for the client, the supervising attorney, and often for the court, the issue should be stated objectively so that a conclusion is not suggested, nor is the reader misled. The purpose and goal of a communication with the client or an office legal memorandum is to inform the reader how the law applies to a particular legal problem. The goal is usually not to persuade someone to adopt a position but rather merely to inform.

There are several reasons why the issue should be stated objectively.

1. A one-sided presentation of the facts or an elimination of some unfavorable key facts can mislead the reader and may result in disaster. Either the opposing side or the court will discover and point out the misrepresentation.
2. Ultimately the law will govern the issue, and usually no amount of creative phrasing will change the outcome. Provide the reader with an objective presentation of the facts, and let your legal argument do the persuading.
3. If the issue is presented in a biased or slanted manner, the reader may question the ability and credibility of the author and discount the legal argument that follows.

For Example: "Applying Colorado's law of conversion, does conversion occur when an individual, with a known reputation as a thief and a burglary conviction, takes and uses his neighbor's electric saw without permission?"

Comment: The statement is not objective. The facts relating to the individual's reputation and conviction are prejudicial and not relevant. Readers will conclude either that you do not know what relevant facts are or that you are trying to influence them.

For Example: "Under the Colorado ski act, does a resort have a duty to warn of an obviously dangerous ice hazard?"

Comment: In this example, assume these additional facts are left out: the skier was a novice skier skiing on an expert ski run, and the nature and degree of the ice hazard has not been determined. The issue is not stated objectively for two reasons:

1. The ice condition is described in such a way as to lead the reader to a conclusion that it was dangerous.
2. A key fact is omitted: the skier is not an expert. This fact could very well govern the outcome of the case. It may be that the ice condition is hazardous only to novice skiers, and since the run is an expert run, the resort does not have a duty to warn. This fact will come to light as the case progresses, and its omission only serves to mislead. The reader will conclude that you are misstating the question with the intent to mislead or that you do not understand the law.

For Example: "Under the United States Constitution's prohibitions against cruel and unusual punishment, are conditions of confinement cruel and unusual when the conditions are unsanitary and unhealthy?"

Comment: The issue is stated prejudicially and too broadly. It is prejudicial because it assumes that conditions are unsanitary and unhealthy. Whether the conditions are unsanitary and unhealthy is what is in dispute and has yet to be decided. It is too broad because the facts concerning the conditions are not included, just conclusions about the facts. What are the factual conditions that are allegedly unsanitary and unhealthy? Are the jail cells unclean? Is the water unsafe to drink?

Always state the issue objectively. When in doubt, err on the side of completeness. If condensing or categorizing key facts results in a biased or distorted statement of the question, do not condense or categorize. It is better to have a long or complicated issue than a loss of credibility.

In many instances, when the question is to be presented to a court in a court brief, it may be desirable to state the issue in a persuasive manner. This may be necessary when you are trying to persuade the court to adopt a legal position or concept that is favorable to the client. Great care must be taken when constructing an issue persuasively in order to avoid misleading the court or misrepresenting the issue. The examples presented in this section point out some of the hazards.

Persuasive issue writing is generally applicable in the courtroom in oral argument or in trial and appellate briefs. It usually is not applicable in research and writing projects assigned to legal assistants, such as the preparation of an interoffice legal memorandum. The considerations involved in persuasive issue writing and persuasive writing in general are addressed in Chapter 14.

GENERAL CONSIDERATIONS

There are several general considerations to keep in mind when drafting an issue.

Name

Do not identify people or events specifically by name. Specific names have no meaning to the reader unless they are familiar with the case or unless they have read the body of the memorandum. When a research memo is retrieved from the office memo files, the reader probably will not be familiar with the names of the people or events.

For Example: *Incorrect:* Under . . ., did oppressive conduct occur when Tom Hardin refused to issue a three dollar dividend and gave himself a $20,000 bonus?

Correct: Under . . ., does oppressive conduct occur when a majority shareholder, who is also the sole director of a closely held corporation, refuses to issue dividends and grants himself a $20,000 bonus?

Approach

Write the issue several times. Have an issue page in your research outline or material, and keep that page nearby. Whenever it comes to you how the issue should be stated (regardless of how broadly or poorly phrased), write it down on the issue page. This way your ideas are not lost.

Even your poorly drafted constructions of the issue may contain something valuable. You may ultimately have a page full of various formulations of the issue. The final draft may require a combination of the various initial drafts, and having them all in one place may help you put together that combination. See Chapter 10 for a discussion of the use of an outline when drafting the issue.

The following is a *basic approach:*

1. State the question in the context of the general area of law. For example: Was there false imprisonment?
2. Identify the specific law that applies.
3. List all the key facts.
4. Put the elements in the sequence presented in the text.

Law	***Question***		***Facts***
Under	.is	. . . .	.when
In light of	.did	. .exist	.when
According to . . .	.does	.constitute . . .	.when
Applying	.was	.required	.when
Under	.does	.establish . . .	.when

Multiple Issues

Separate the issues. If the research involves several related questions or complex questions, break the questions into individual issues. Address them one at a time, applying the principles presented in this chapter.

KEY POINTS CHECKLIST: *Drafting an Issue*

- ❑ Do not expect to accurately state the issue on the first draft or early in the research and analysis process. A broad statement may be all you can come up with until you research and study statutory and case law. The key facts may not emerge until you have studied the case in depth.
- ❑ Always prepare a comprehensive/narrow pre sentation of the issue. Include in the statement of the issue: the specific law, the legal question and the key facts.
- ❑ Remember the format recommended in this chapter for presenting the issue: Relevant Law + Legal Question + Key Facts. It is easier to draft the issue in this format.
- ❑ If you get stuck, *start.* If you cannot seem to get started writing, just write anything

about the issue on the issue page, that is, *start.*

- ❑ Sometimes when you are stuck, it may be that you need to *stop.* Often the brain needs time to assimilate information. Take a break. Sleep on it. The brain will continue to work while you rest, and after you wake, it may all fall into place.
- ❑ Remember, the issue is the legal question in dispute in the case and should be phrased as a question, not a statement.

APPLICATION

Presented below are two examples that illustrate the principles discussed in this chapter. Each example includes a discussion of the application of those principles.

Chapter Hypothetical

This example is based on the memorandum assignment introduced at the beginning of the chapter. In the assignment, Mary Strate, the legal assistant, has determined that the key facts are:

1. The state police were acting in good faith when they relied on the validity of the search warrant.
2. The evidence was seized pursuant to the execution of the warrant.
3. The warrant was improperly issued due to judicial error.

Mary's research reveals that the law governing the issue is the state court's adoption of the exclusionary rule.

There are several ways the issue can be framed:

A. "Should the evidence be suppressed?"

B. "Does Oregon's exclusionary rule require the suppression of the evidence?"

Comment: Both issues A and B are too broad. They are examples of a shorthand statement of the issue. Issue A is so broadly phrased that it is of little value to the reader. What law is involved? What facts? This statement of the issue could apply to any case involving the suppression of evidence. Issue B informs the reader of the applicable law but omits the facts necessary for the resolution of the question. Both of the issues require additional reading and research in order to determine the law and facts involved in the dispute in the case.

C. "Does Oregon's exclusionary rule require the suppression of evidence seized by officials acting upon a warrant improperly issued due to judicial error?"

Comment: This construction of the issue is neither objective nor complete. It leaves out a key fact: the officers were acting in good faith when they relied on the validity of the warrant. This key fact is critical if the state's exclusionary rule has an exception that allows the admission of evidence when officers execute a warrant in the good faith belief that it is valid. Failure to include this key fact misleads the reader and slants the question in favor of suppression.

D. "Under Oregon's exclusionary rule, must evidence be suppressed when it is seized by law enforcement officers acting in the good faith belief in the validity of a warrant that was invalid due to judicial error?"

Comment: This statement of the issue is complete. It identifies the law in question, includes all the significant or key facts that are necessary for the resolution of the issue, and informs the reader of what legal question must be resolved. It meets the test presented at the beginning of the chapter: *Does the reader, by reading the issue alone, know what specific factual dispute concerning what law is involved in this case?*

False Imprisonment

The client, Steve, has a history of respiratory problems. Tom is an acquaintance of Steve who is secretly jealous of him. Both Steve and Tom vie for the affections of Karen. One cold winter evening, before leaving for a party at Tom's house, Steve took some cough medicine for a cold he had been fighting. After a few drinks at the party, he told Tom he did not feel well and wanted to lie down for a minute. Tom directed him to a back bedroom. Steve went to the room and promptly fell into a deep sleep.

The bedroom had recently been converted from a storage room. It had no windows, and Tom shut the heat off when he did not have guests. The door to the room was usually kept open, and the room stayed reasonably warm. It quickly became very cold, however, when the door was shut. Tom, knowing Karen was coming to the party, checked on Steve. When he saw Steve was asleep, he locked the bedroom door and did not turn on the heat.

Three hours later, after Karen left, he unlocked the bedroom door. Steve woke up shortly thereafter and left. He was not aware that he had been locked in the room until Tom told him several days later. As a result of being in the cold room, Steve's cold got worse and he incurred medical expenses. Steve wants to know if he can sue Tom for false imprisonment. Assume this takes place in Montana. Some of the ways the issue can be framed are as follows:

A. "Can Steve recover his medical expenses?"
B. "Under Montana law, did false imprisonment occur?"

Comment: These issues are incomplete and too broadly framed. Issue A is of little value, as it provides the reader with no information, no guidance as to the facts of the case. Stated this way, the issue could apply to a thousand cases. Issue B provides the law but no facts. It could apply to any false imprisonment case. Neither issue communicates the specific law or facts in dispute in this case.

C. "Under Montana law, does false imprisonment occur when an individual maliciously locks another in a room and turns off the heat, intending to cause the person harm?"

Comment: This issue is incomplete, inaccurate, and not objective. It leaves out the critical key facts that Steve was unaware of the confinement and was harmed. It is inaccurate because it states that Tom intended to cause Steve harm, and there are no facts to support this. It is not objective because it characterizes Tom as malicious and intending to cause harm. It is a prejudicial formulation of the issue that misleads the reader and is slanted against Tom.

D. "Under Montana tort law does false imprisonment occur when an individual, suffering from a cold, is locked in a room while asleep and is unaware of the confinement, but suffers physical harm as a result of a worsening of the cold due to the confinement?"

Comment: Issue D is complete. The reader is provided with the question, the law, and all the key facts necessary to determine what must be decided under the law. Without any additional reading or research, the reader is informed of the specific legal and factual context of the dispute.

SUMMARY

Writing the issue is one of the most critical tasks in the legal research and writing process. It should communicate what is in dispute. In order to accomplish this task, it is necessary to completely, concisely, and clearly identify the question to be resolved. A poorly crafted issue either fails to inform because it is too broad, or misleads because it adds improper information or omits critical information.

There are two ways to state an issue:

1. A shorthand/broad statement that presents the question in the context of the general area of the law
2. A comprehensive/narrow statement that presents the specific question in the context of the relevant law and specific facts

A broad statement may be appropriate in a situation where the participants are thoroughly familiar with the case. A comprehensive, or narrow, statement is the appropriate form for use in research and writing. It specifically identifies all the essential information necessary to understand and resolve the dispute.

There are several formats that may be followed when crafting the issue, but the recommended format is as follows:

Law + Question + Key Facts

There are several reasons for this recommendation. First, it follows the standard legal analysis format of the presentation of the law followed by the application of the law to the specific facts. Second, it is easier to draft an issue when the facts are inserted at the end.

When drafting the issue, the law component should always include the jurisdiction and area of the law. The question portion must introduce the specific law presented in the law component. The fact section should present all key facts if possible, although it may be necessary to categorize or condense the key facts.

The issue should be objectively presented and not phrased so as to mislead the reader or misrepresent the nature of the dispute. A well-crafted issue meets the following test: *Does the reader, by reading the issue alone, know what specific legal question, concerning what law, involving what facts, is in dispute in the case?*

EXERCISES

ASSIGNMENT 1

Distinguish between a broad and narrow formulation of an issue. Describe the elements of a narrow statement of an issue. Why is it important to phrase an issue narrowly when engaged in legal writing?

ASSIGNMENT 2

The statute is Cal. Corp. Code § 1800. The title of the statute is: Verified complaint; plaintiff; grounds; intervention by shareholder or creditor; exempt corporations. The statute applies in dissolution cases and includes the grounds for dissolving a corporation. The dispute involving this corporation statute is whether there are grounds for dissolution of the corporation.

Part A

Draft the law component of the issue, including the relevant portion of the title.

Part B

Draft the law component of the issue and include the relevant portion of the title and the citation.

Part C

Draft the law component of the issue using a description that focuses on an element of the statute. The element in question is the requirement of shareholder deadlock. Assume the statute provides that a court may dissolve a corporation in the event of a dispute among the shareholders only if there is shareholder deadlock.

Part D

To the answer in part C above, add the statutory citation.

ASSIGNMENT 3
In the following problems:

- Draft a shorthand/broad statement of the issue.
- Draft a comprehensive/narrow statement of the issue in the Law + Question + Key Facts format. For the law component in problems A through C, use either the relevant section of your state's probate code or New Wash. Prob. Code § 60, Exception Pertaining to Holographic Wills. Assume this statute applies to all the fact situations presented in problems A through C. For each problem, draft the issue twice. One draft should contain the title or a description of the title. One draft should contain the title or description and the citation.

Part A

Key Facts: A will is handwritten. One-half is in the testator's handwriting, and the other half is in the handwriting of a witness. The will is properly witnessed.

Question: Is the will valid?

Part B

Key Facts: A will is handwritten. One-half is in the testator's handwriting, and the other half is in the handwriting of a witness. It is witnessed by three witnesses, two of whom will inherit under the will.

Question: Is the will valid?

Part C

Key Facts: A will is handwritten. One-half is in the testator's handwriting, and the other half is in the handwriting of a witness. The testator's name was signed by a witness at the direction of the testator. The will was properly witnessed.

Question: Is the will valid?

ASSIGNMENT 4
In the following problems:

- Draft a shorthand/broad statement of the issue.
- Draft a comprehensive/narrow statement of the issue in the Law + Question + Key Facts format.

Part A

Key Facts: An individual on a radio talk show states that all the town's psychiatrists are frauds.

Question: Is the statement "concerning" the plaintiff?

Law: Assume the law of slander in your jurisdiction is common law (court-made) and one of the elements is that the statement must concern the plaintiff.

Part B

Key Facts: Use the same facts as in the preceding problem, with the additional fact that the plaintiff is the only psychiatrist in the town.

Question: Same as in A.

Law: Same as A.

ASSIGNMENT 5
Redraft the following issues in the format presented in this chapter.

Part A

Can a bystander who witnesses the death of a victim from three blocks away recover for negligent infliction of emotional distress under Ohio law?

Part B

Does oppressive conduct occur, according to the provisions of the Texas Corporation Code, when a majority shareholder refuses to issue dividends, triples his salary, and grants himself excessive bonuses?

Part C

The issue is whether a newspaper that publishes an article indicating that Tom Smith has criminal connections has committed libel according to Florida tort law.

Part D

Do law enforcement officers commit a battery when, while making a lawful arrest, they encounter resistance, use force to overcome that resistance, and continue to use force after the resistance ceases?

FOR FURTHER READING

Ray, Mary Barnard, and Barbara J. Cox. *Beyond the Basics.* St. Paul: West Publishing Co., 1991. This text presents an excellent and expanded discussion of the Law + Question + Key Fact format recommended in this chapter.

CHAPTER 8

Case Law Application

"That bum has cheated us for the last time," David Simms said as he walked out the office door. David Simms and his brother, Don, had just finished their initial interview with Ms. Booth, the attorney who would handle their case. Their tale was one of financial abuse by their older brother, Steve.

Their father, Dilbert Simms, died in December 1993 and left his plumbing business, Happy Flush, Inc., to his three sons—Steve, Don, and David. Steve, who had been running the business since 1990, was left 52% of the stock. David and Don, who never worked at Happy Flush and were employed in other occupations, were each left 24%.

As the majority shareholder, Steve completely controls the business. To date, he has refused to issue stock dividends even though the corporation has an accumulated cash surplus of $500,000. He has given himself three very large salary increases and several cash bonuses since his father's death. When questioned by David and Don about stock dividends, he tells them, "You don't work in the business. You don't deserve any money out of it. If you want any money, you're going to have to get your hands in the poop every day just like I do."

After this conversation, David and Don consulted the supervising attorney, Ms. Booth. They seek redress for the wrong they feel their brother has committed in refusing to issue dividends.

The paralegal's task, assigned by Ms. Booth, is to find the applicable statute and the leading case on point in the jurisdiction. The statute, section 96-25-16 of the Business Corporation Act, provides that a court may order the liquidation of a corporation when a majority shareholder has engaged in oppressive conduct. The statute, however, does not define what constitutes oppressive conduct.

The hard part of the assignment is locating a case on point in the jurisdiction that defines or provides the elements of oppressive conduct. After an extensive search, only one case dealing with oppressive conduct is located, *Karl v. Herald*. In this case, a husband and wife owned a small corporation in which the husband owned 75% of the stock and the wife owned 25%. When they divorced, he fired her from her salaried position of bookkeeper, took away her company car, and refused to issue stock dividends. The company was very profitable, had a large cash surplus, and was clearly in a financial position to issue dividends. After the divorce, the husband gave himself a hefty salary increase. The court held that he had engaged in oppressive conduct in freezing his wife out of the corporation. It defined oppressive conduct as "any unfair or fraudulent act by a majority shareholder that inures to the benefit of the majority and to the detriment of the minority."

Upon finding this case, several questions run through the paralegal's mind. Is this case on point? How do you determine if a case is on point? Why does it matter?

INTRODUCTION

Legal research, analysis, and writing are all related and are often part of a single process. The law is found through research, a determination of whether the law applies is made through analysis, and the results are assembled and integrated into useable form in legal writing. Chapter 4 provides an introduction to case law. It covers the elements of a court opinion and how opinions are briefed. Chapters 5 and 6 discuss how to find the key facts and legal issues in a case.

This chapter primarily focuses on the application of case law to a legal question. It covers the analytical process you engage in to determine if the decision reached by the court either governs or affects the outcome of a client's case. A case that governs or affects the outcome of a client's case is commonly referred to as being "on point."

Throughout the chapter, reference is made to single issues and single rules of law or legal principles when discussing court opinions and clients' cases. The focus is on how to determine if a single issue, addressed in a court opinion, is on point and, therefore, may affect or govern an issue in a client's case. Always be aware that there are often multiple issues and legal rules/principles involved in court opinions, some of which may be on point, and therefore govern the outcome of an issue in the client's case, and some of which may not be on point. The steps discussed in this chapter should be followed separately for each issue in a client's case when determining if an opinion is on point.

The chapter opens with a definition of the term *on point,* followed by a discussion of the importance of locating a case on point and the process of determining if a case is on point.

DEFINITION

on point

A case is on point if the similarity between the key facts and rule of law or legal principle of the court opinion and those of the client's case is sufficient for the court opinion to govern or provide guidance to a later court in deciding the outcome of the client's case.

Throughout the chapter, the term *on point* is used to describe a court opinion that applies to the client's case. What does "on point" and "applies to the client's case" mean? A case is on point if the similarity between the key facts and rule of law or legal principle of the court opinion and those of the client's case is sufficient for the court opinion to govern or provide guidance to a later court in deciding the outcome of the client's case. In other words, does the court opinion govern or guide the resolution of an issue in the client's case? Is the court opinion precedent? If a case is on point, it is precedent. The terms *on point* and *precedent* are often used interchangeably.

IMPORTANCE

Before discussing the process involved in determining if a case is on point, it is helpful to understand why you must engage in the process of finding past court decisions that affect the client's case. Why is it important?

As discussed in Chapter 1, case law is a major source of law in the legal system. Through case law, courts create law and interpret the language of constitutions, legislative acts, and regulations. The determination of whether a case is on point is important because of two doctrines covered in Chapter 1—precedent and stare decisis. The doctrines of precedent and stare decisis govern and guide the application of case law, and thereby provide uniformity and consistency in the common law (case law) system. They help make the law more predictable. A brief revisiting of these doctrines is helpful in obtaining an understanding of the process involved in determining whether a case is on point.

Precedent

Precedent is an earlier court decision on an issue that governs or guides a subsequent court in its determination of an identical or similar issue based on identical or similar key facts. This chapter identifies the steps involved in determining when a case may be either mandatory or persuasive precedent. A case is precedent (on point) if there is a sufficient similarity between the key facts and rule of law or legal principle of the court opinion and the matter before the subsequent court.

For Example: Suppose the state collections statute provides that efforts to collect payment for a debt must be made in a reasonable manner. The statute does not define "reasonable." In the case of *Mark v. Collections, Inc.*, the supreme court of the state held that it is not reasonable, within the meaning of the collection statute, for a bill collector to make more than one telephone call a day to a debtor's residence, nor is it reasonable to make calls before sunrise or after sunset. The facts of the case are that the collector was making seven calls a day, some of which were after sunset.

The facts of the client's case are that a bill collector is calling the client six times a day between the hours of 9 A.M. and 5 P.M.. The ruling in *Mark v. Collections, Inc.*, applies as precedent to the issue of whether the frequency of the calls by the collector is unreasonable and, therefore, in violation of the act. The *Mark* case is sufficiently similar to the current case to apply as precedent. Both cases involve:

- The same law—the collections statute
- The same question—a determination of when the frequency of the telephone calls constitutes unreasonable conduct within the meaning of the act
- Similar key facts—six telephone calls per day and seven calls per day

The application of *Mark* as precedent guides the court in its resolution of the question presented in the client's case of whether six calls a day are a violation of the act. The court in *Mark* held that more than one call a day is unreasonable. Therefore, the six calls a day in the client's case are unreasonable in light of the holding in the *Mark* case. This example is referred to as the collections example in this chapter.

Mandatory Precedent

Mandatory precedent is precedent from a higher court in a jurisdiction. If a court opinion is on point, that is, if it is precedent, the doctrine of stare decisis mandates that it be followed by the lower courts in that jurisdiction. In the above example, if the decision in *Mark v. Collections, Inc.*, is the ruling of the highest court in the jurisdiction, it must be followed by the lower courts in the jurisdiction.

Persuasive Precedent

Persuasive precedent is precedent that a court may look to for guidance when reaching a decision but is not bound to follow. In the collections example, courts in other jurisdictions are not bound to follow the *Mark* decision. Also, if the decision was by a lower court in the jurisdiction, such as a trial court, then a higher court, such as a court of appeals, is not bound to follow the decision. A higher court, however, may choose to refer to and use a lower court decision as guidance when deciding a similar case before it.

Stare Decisis

The doctrine of stare decisis is a basic principle of the common law system that requires a court to follow a previous decision of that court or a higher court in the jurisdiction when the decision involves issues and key facts similar to those involved in the previous decision. In other words, the doctrine of stare decisis requires that similar cases be decided in the same way—that cases that are precedent should be followed. The doctrine applies unless there is good reason not to follow it.

For Example: In regard to the *Mark* case discussed above, stare decisis is the doctrine that holds that once it is determined that the case is precedent, it must be followed by the lower courts in the jurisdiction unless good cause is shown. It is mandatory precedent.

Without the doctrines of stare decisis and precedent, there would most likely be chaos in the court decision-making process. Judges and attorneys would not have guidance about how matters should be decided. Similar cases could be decided differently based upon the whims and diverse beliefs of judges and juries. These doctrines provide stability, predictability, and guidance for courts and attorneys. An individual can rely on a future court to reach the same decision on an issue as an earlier court when the cases are sufficiently similar.

With the above in mind, it becomes clear why the determination of whether a case is on point is important and why a researcher needs to find a case that is on point:

1. The determination of whether a case is on point must be made before the case may apply as precedent and be used and relied on by a court in its determination of how an issue will be decided. Note that the court may be unaware of the case, and it may be necessary to bring it to the court's attention.
2. Inasmuch as the court will consider precedent in reaching its decision, cases that are on point need to be found to provide guidance to the attorney in regard to how the issue in the client's case may be decided. Cases that are on point must be located and analyzed to determine what impact they may have on the decision in the client's case. If a case that is on point indicates that the decision will most likely be against the client, it may be appropriate to pursue settlement or other options.

DETERMINING IF A CASE IS ON POINT

case law analysis
The analytical process engaged in to determine if and how a decision in a court opinion either governs or affects the outcome of a client's case.

The process of deciding if a court opinion is on point involves determining how similar the opinion is to the client's case. The more similar the court opinion is to the client's case, the more likely it will be considered precedent—that is, the more likely the rule/principle applied in the opinion will govern or apply to the client's case.

In the Definition section of this chapter, a case is defined as being on point if there is a sufficient similarity between the key facts and rule of law or legal principle of the court opinion and those of the client's case. Therefore, in order for a case to be on point and apply as precedent, there are *two requirements:*

1. The significant or key facts of the court opinion must be sufficiently similar to the key facts of the client's case; or if the facts are not similar, the rule of law or legal principle applied in the court opinion must be so broad that it applies to many diverse fact situations, *and*
2. The rule of law or legal principle applied in the court opinion must be the same or sufficiently similar to the rule of law or legal principle that applies in the client's case. *Rule of law* and *legal principle,* as used here, include any constitutional, legislative, or common law provision, act, doctrine, principle, or test relied on by the court in reaching its decision.

If these two criteria are not fulfilled, the court opinion is not on point and may not be used as precedent for the client's case. The two-step process presented in Figure 8–1 is recommended for determining if the two requirements are met.

Step 1 Are the Key Facts Sufficiently Similar?

The first step in the analysis process is to determine if the significant or key facts in the court opinion are sufficiently similar to the key facts in the client's case so that the court opinion may apply as precedent. This is accomplished by comparing the key facts of the court opinion with those of the client's case. As defined in Chapter 5, a key fact is a fact that, if it were changed, the court's decision would most likely change. It is so essential that it affects the outcome of the case. Refer to Chapter 5 for guidance in identifying the key facts. They must be identified before you can determine if a case is on point. If there is not a sufficient similarity between the key facts of the client's case and the court opinion, the opinion *usually* cannot be used as precedent—that is, it is not on point.

Two situations may be encountered when comparing the key facts of a client's case and a court opinion:

1. The key facts are directly on point—that is, they are identical or nearly identical.
2. The key facts are different.

Identical or Nearly Identical Key Facts

When the key facts in the court opinion are identical or nearly identical with those of the client's case, the opinion is on point factually and can be a precedent that applies to the client's case if the requirements of step 2 are met. The phrase *on all fours* is often used to describe such opinions: opinions where the facts of the opinion and those of the client's case and the rule of law that applies are identical or so similar that the court opinion is clearly on point. When such an opinion is the opinion of a higher court in a jurisdiction, it is mandatory precedent that the lower courts in the jurisdiction must follow.

on all fours

A prior court opinion in which the key facts and applicable rule of law are identical or nearly identical with those of the client's case or the case before a court.

For Example: In the case of *Davis v. Davis,* Ms. Davis had sole custody of her two daughters, ages eight and ten years old. Ms. Davis had a boyfriend who occasionally stayed overnight at her home. The children were aware of the overnight visits. Mr. Davis, her former husband, filed a motion with the court asking for a change of custody. He based his claim solely upon his ex-wife's alleged "immoral conduct." No evidence was presented indicating how the overnight visits impacted the children. The trial court granted a change of custody.

The court of appeals overturned the trial court, ruling that "mere allegations of immoral conduct are not sufficient grounds to award a change of custody." The court required the presentation of evidence showing that the alleged immoral conduct harmed the children.

Assume, in this example, that the client was divorced one year ago and granted sole custody of his two minor daughters, ages eight and twelve. On occasion, his girlfriend stays overnight, and the children are aware of the overnight visits. The client's former spouse has filed a motion for change of custody alleging that his immoral conduct is grounds for a change of custody. She does not have evidence that the children have been harmed or negatively impacted.

Step 1	Are the key facts sufficiently similar for the case to apply as precedent?
Step 2	Are the rules/principles of law sufficiently similar for the case to apply as precedent?

Figure 8–1

Steps in Determining If a Case Is on Point

Clearly, *Davis v. Davis* is factually "on point" and, therefore, is precedent that applies to the client's case. Note that the requirements of step 2 are met. The same legal principle is being applied in the court opinion and the client's case: mere allegations of immorality are not sufficient grounds for granting a change of custody. Step 2 addresses the requirement that the legal principles must be sufficiently similar.

Although some of the facts are different—in the client's case, it is the father who has custody and his girlfriend stays overnight, while in *Davis v. Davis* it is the mother who has custody and her boyfriend who stays overnight—these facts are not key facts. The sex of the custodial parent and the sex of the person staying overnight are not key facts. (Refer to the discussion in Chapter 5 of key facts.) The key facts are identical: occasional overnight visits, the children are aware of the visits, the children are preteen (the age of the children is always an important consideration), and there is no evidence presented that the children are harmed. This example is referred to as the custody example throughout the remainder of this chapter.

It is rare to find instances where the key facts are identical. Usually there is some difference in the key facts. When you find a case with identical facts that you determine is mandatory precedent, be thankful if the holding supports your client's position. It is difficult for a lower court not to follow the higher court's decision when it is so clearly on point.

Different Key Facts

When the key facts of the court opinion and the key facts of the client's case are not identical, the opinion *may* be on point and *may* apply as precedent. It depends on the degree of the difference. If some of the key facts are different, it must be determined whether the differences are of such a nature or degree that they render the court opinion unusable as precedent. The three-part process presented in Figure 8–2 is recommended for use when making this determination. Throughout this discussion of different key facts, assume that the requirements of step 2 are met—that is, the rule of law applied in the court opinion is the same or sufficiently similar to the rule of law that applies in the client's case.

For Example: The client's case is the same as the custody example except that instead of occasional overnight visits by the girlfriend, the girlfriend has moved in with the client. Is the case of *Davis v. Davis* on point?

To answer the question at the end of the example, perform the following steps:

Part 1 Identify the similarities between the key facts. In both the client's case and the *Davis* case:

- The minor children are under the age of twelve.
- Someone of the opposite sex is staying overnight with the custodial parent.
- There is no showing that the children have been harmed by the conduct.

Part 2 Identify the differences between the key facts. The difference in the *key* facts is that in *Davis v. Davis,* the overnight visits are occasional. In the client's case, there is cohabitation rather than occasional overnight visits.

Part 3 Determine if the differences are of such a significant degree that the opinion cannot apply as precedent. To determine the significance of the differences, substitute the

Figure 8–2

Three-Part Process for Addressing Different Key Facts

Part 1	Identify the similarities between the key facts.
Part 2	Identify the differences between the key facts.
Part 3	Determine if the differences are of such a significant degree that the opinion cannot apply as precedent.

client's key facts for those of the court opinion. If the substitution of the key facts would result in changing the outcome of the case, the court opinion cannot be used as precedent.

In this example, would the court in *Davis v. Davis* have reached the same conclusion if Ms. Davis's boyfriend had moved in with her? Probably. The same legal principle applies—*i.e.,* allegations of immoral conduct alone are not sufficient grounds to award a change of custody; there must be a showing that the conduct harmed the children.

As indicated in *Davis v. Davis,* an essential element necessary before a change of custody is granted is the showing of harm to the children. A key fact in the *Davis* decision was the lack of showing of harm to the children. In both the court opinion and the client's case, there is a lack of showing of harm to the children, and therefore, the principle applied in *Davis* should apply to the client's case even though the *Davis* opinion involved overnight visits and the client's case involves cohabitation.

You must be careful, however. There may be another statute or common law doctrine providing that cohabitation is per se harmful to children—that is, in cohabitation cases such as the client's case, the law presumes that cohabitation is harmful to the children. If this were the situation, harm would not need to be separately established by the plaintiff in cohabitation cases such as the client's, evidence of harm would not need to be presented, and the *Davis* opinion would not be on point and could not be used as precedent. The difference in the key facts would be so significant that the substitution of the client's cohabitation fact with the court's occasional overnight visits fact would change the decision reached by the court because a different statute would apply.

There are four variations that may be encountered when dealing with different key facts. These variations are presented in Figure 8–3.

Minor Differences in Key Facts. Some key facts are so insignificantly different that they clearly do not affect the use of a court decision as precedent.

For Example: If, in the custody example, the client's children were nine and eleven years old as opposed to eight and ten, *Davis v. Davis* would clearly apply as precedent. Although the age of the children is a key fact, a minor difference of one year in the ages of the children is not a significant difference in the key facts. If the client's children were several years older than the children in *Davis v. Davis,* such as ages seventeen and eighteen, the age difference could be a major difference in the key facts because a different standard might apply if the children were in their late teens.

Major Difference in Key Facts—Case Not on Point. The following example presents a situation where the key facts of the court opinion and the key facts of the client's case are different, and the opinion is not on point and does not apply as precedent. This example is referred to in this chapter as the arrest example.

For Example: In the court case of *State v. Thomas,* Mr. Thomas was handcuffed and taken to the police station after officers broke up a fistfight. Thomas was not read his rights at the scene of the fight. He was read his rights

1. Minor Differences in Key Facts
2. Major Difference in Key Facts—Case Not on Point
3. Major Difference in Key Facts—Case on Point
4. Major Difference in Key Facts—Case on Point, Broad Legal Principle

Figure 8–3
Different Key Fact Variations

and formally arrested at the police station thirty minutes later. The court, ruling that he was under arrest when handcuffed at the scene, stated, "an arrest takes place when a reasonable person does not believe he is free to leave."

In the client's case, the client explains that he was handcuffed and told to stay in the hallway of the house while the officers executed a search warrant. He was not allowed to leave. It appears that the key facts regarding whether an arrest has taken place are nearly the same. In both the court opinion and the client's case, the individual was handcuffed and not free to leave. The critical difference in the facts is the context of the seizure of the individual. In *Thomas,* the seizure took place at the scene of a fight. There were no warrants involved. In the client's case, the seizure took place during the execution of a search warrant.

In regard to the question of whether the client was under arrest when handcuffed and detained in the hallway, is *State v. Thomas* on point? The answer is no. Although the facts of the detention are similar, the difference in the context of the seizure is a critical key fact difference. There is other case law that holds that a seizure during the execution of a search warrant is an exception to the rule stated in *Thomas,* and such seizures do not constitute an arrest.

The other case law provides that a search warrant implicitly carries with it the authority to detain an individual for the purposes of the officer's safety and to determine if there is cause to make an arrest. Therefore, such detentions do not constitute an arrest within the meaning of the law. Because of this authority, the difference between the key facts of *Thomas* and the client's case is critical, and the case is not on point.

Major Difference in Key Facts—Case on Point. A major difference in the key facts does not necessarily result in a determination that the case is not on point. The opinion may still be on point, but the outcome may be different. The legal principle applied by the court may still apply. Its application may just lead to a different result.

For Example: In the custody example, if there was an additional key fact in the client's case that the spouse seeking custody had evidence showing that the children were being harmed by exposure to the cohabitation, *Davis v. Davis* could still be on point. This could occur even though there was no evidence of harm to the children presented in the *Davis* case. Although there is now a major difference between the key facts of the court opinion and the client's case, the court opinion may still apply as precedent and govern the outcome of the change of custody question.

The court in the *Davis* case concluded that there were not sufficient grounds to award a change of custody because there was *no evidence* presented showing harm to the children. The same principle governing *Davis* governs the facts here—that is, allegations of immorality, *standing alone,* are not sufficient for an award of a change of custody; there must be a showing of harm to the children.

A corollary of the rule, however, is that if there *is a showing of harm* to the children, there may be sufficient grounds for a change of custody. It can be argued that when the key fact of evidence of harm is present, the corollary of the rule applies. Even though the facts of the court opinion and the client's case are different, the corollary applies to support a change of custody award—a result different from the result reached in the court opinion.

Major Difference in Key Facts—Case on Point, Broad Legal Principle. Generally, if key facts are significantly different, it is highly probable that a different rule or principle applies and a court case will not apply as precedent. There are, however, instances where the key facts are different, but the court opinion is on point because the rule of law or legal principle is so broad that it applies to many different fact situations. This situation is addressed in greater detail in *step 2* in the next section.

For Example: The client was detained with a group of exotic dancers in a bar. The officers who detained the client were not executing a search or arrest warrant. Before informing the dancers they were under arrest, or in any way informing them what was taking place, the officers moved them to a separate room where they were detained for over an hour. They were clearly not free to leave. They were formally arrested two hours later, then taken to jail.

In regard to the question of whether the client was under arrest when detained in the room prior to arrest, *State v. Thomas* is probably on point. The definition of arrest presented in *Thomas* applies to the client's case even though the factual context of the seizures are different. Applying that definition to the client's case results in the conclusion that an arrest occurred when the client was moved to a separate room and detained for over an hour. A reasonable person in the client's situation would not believe he was free to leave. The definition of arrest presented in *Thomas* is so broad that it applies to a wide range of detention situations.

Note: Be careful. It is always preferable to locate an opinion that is as factually similar to the client's case as possible. The more dissimilar the key facts, the easier it is for the other side to argue that the differences are critical, the opinion is not on point, and it does not apply as precedent to the case at hand.

A difference in key facts should alert you to be careful and cause you to explore all potential legal avenues that may arise due to the fact differences. Focus on the differences. Ask yourself, "Are they important?" Engage in counteranalysis (see Chapter 9). Conduct further research and *shepardize* the case to determine if there are other cases more on point.

In summary, if the key facts are the same and the same rule of law applies (step 2), the court opinion is usually on point and can be considered as a precedent that applies to your client's case. If the key facts are different, either in part or totally, careful analysis must be performed to ensure that the factual differences are not so significant that they are fatal to the use of the court opinion as precedent.

Step 2 Are the Rules/Principles of Law Sufficiently Similar?

Through the application of the principles presented in step 1, it is determined whether the key facts of the court opinion are sufficiently similar to the key facts of the client's case for the opinion to apply as precedent factually. Once this is accomplished, half of the task is completed. It is important to note that this is a *two-step* process; both steps *must* be completed before it can be determined whether a case is on point and apply as precedent.

The second step is to determine whether the rule of law or legal principle applied in the court opinion is the same rule of law or legal principle that applies in the client's case. If it is not the same rule of law, is it sufficiently similar to the rule that applies in the client's case for the opinion to still apply as precedent? As mentioned at the beginning of the Determining If a Case Is on Point section, the rule of law or legal principle includes any constitutional, legislative, or common law provision, act, doctrine, principle, or test relied on by the court in reaching its decision. There are two situations that may be encountered when performing step 2:

1. *The rule or principle applied in the court opinion is the same rule or principle that applies in the client's case.*
2. *The rule or principle applied in the court opinion is different from the rule or principle that applies in the client's case.*

Same Rule or Principle

If you have determined that the key facts are sufficiently similar so that the court opinion can apply as precedent and the same rule of law is involved in both the opinion and the client's case, the requirements of step 2 are met, and the case is on point. The rule of law comparison is simple. The rule of law applies in the client's case in the same way as it was applied in the court opinion.

For Example: In the custody example, if the client's case involves the situation of the client having occasional overnight visits by his girlfriend, the same rule of law governs the court opinion and the client's facts—that is, allegations of immorality without evidence of harm to the children are not sufficient grounds to support a change of custody. The rule applies in the same way in the client's case as in the court opinion—a change of custody will not be granted where there is no showing of harm to the children.

For Example: The client is charged with erecting a sign too close to the street in violation of section 19-b of the Municipal Code, which prohibits the erection of a sign "unreasonably close" to any property line abutting a street. In your research, you come across the case of *City v. Guess,* which interprets "unreasonably close" as within ten feet of the property line. If the key facts of the court opinion are sufficiently similar to the client's key facts, the rule of law analytical process is simple. The same rule of law applied in the opinion applies to the client's case, in the same way: if the client's sign is within ten feet of the property line abutting the street, it is in violation of the statute.

Different Rule or Principle

Problems occur when the rule of law applied in the opinion is different from the rule of law that applies in the client's case. In other words, what if there is no court decision in your jurisdiction applying or interpreting the rule or legal principle that applies to your client's case? What if the rule or principle applied in the closest court opinion you can find is different from the rule or principle that applies in the client's case? Can the court opinion apply as precedent? The general rule is *no.* Usually this is obvious. For example, a child custody opinion rarely can be precedent for a murder case.

Again, there are exceptions. The court's interpretation of a provision of a legislative act or common law rule or principle may be so broad in scope that it applies to the different law or rule that governs the client's case. Keep in mind, though, that since the law or rule applied in the court opinion is different from that which applies to the client's case, the court opinion is *persuasive* precedent. The court hearing the client's case does not have to follow it—it is not *mandatory* precedent. The court has discretion and must be persuaded.

There are two areas that should be explored when considering these exceptions: legislative acts and common law rules or principles. In regard to these two areas, it is important to remember that the discussion involves *only* those situations where there is *no court opinion* in the jurisdiction that directly interprets the same legislative act or common law rule that applies to the client's case.

Legislative Acts. A court opinion interpreting one legislative act may be used as precedent for a client's case that involves the application of a different legislative act when the two requirements presented in Figure 8–4 are met.

For Example: Assume there are three statutes adopted in the jurisdiction:

- Section 56 provides that an individual must be a resident of the county to be eligible to run for the position of county animal control officer.
- Section 3105 provides that an individual must be a resident of the county in order to run for a seat on the county school board.
- Section 4175 provides that an individual must be a resident of the state to be eligible to run for the office of governor.

Figure 8–4

Requirements When Different Legislative Acts Apply

1. There is a similarity in language between the legislative acts, and
2. There is a similarity in function between the legislative acts.

The term *resident* is not defined in any of the statutes, and none of the statutes establishes a length of residency requirement. The only case in the jurisdiction that defines the term is *Frank v. Teague,* a case involving section 3105. In this case, the court ruled that in order to be eligible to run for a seat on the school board, the candidate must be a resident of the county of the school board district for a minimum of three months immediately prior to the election. This example is referred to in this chapter as the residence example.

Suppose the client, a resident of the county for three and one-half months, wants to run for the office of governor. Does the *Frank* opinion apply as precedent and support the client's claim of eligibility to run for the office of governor? Probably not.

Although there is a similarity in the language of the statutes in that both use the term *resident,* there is not a similarity in function. The considerations involved in determining the length of residence required as a prerequisite for eligibility to run for each office are quite different. The court's decision in *Frank,* imposing a three-month residency requirement for the school board position, may be based upon the court's determination that this is the amount of time an individual needs to become sufficiently familiar with the county to perform the duties of a school board member. The position of governor, however, involves different considerations. The office is statewide, and the court could conclude that a longer residency period is necessary for an individual to become sufficiently familiar with the state to adequately perform the duties of governor.

For Example: The client wants to run for the position of animal control officer. He has been a resident of the county for four months. In this situation, it is more likely that *Frank* will apply as precedent, that it is on point and supports the position that the client is eligible to run for animal control officer.

Again, both statutes use the same language, *resident.* They are more closely related in function, however, than the school board and governor statutes. Both involve countywide positions wherein the duties are focused on county concerns. It can be argued that no more time is required to become familiar with the county to perform the duties of animal control officer than is required to perform the duties of a school board member.

The court, following this line of reasoning, could conclude that the residency requirement for the position of animal control officer should not exceed the minimum residency set for a seat on the school board. It could, therefore, adopt the three-month standard established in the *Frank* case as the standard for the animal control officer statute.

Since the statutes are different, you are always open to a counterargument pointing out some critical difference in function between the statutes.

> ***For Example:*** In this example, it could be argued that the duties of animal control officer are much different than those of a school board member, that the duties of the animal control officer require a great degree of familiarity with the geography of the county, and that a longer period of residency should therefore be required to ensure that a candidate has sufficient time to become familiar with the county.

In every situation where the statutes are different in function, even if they have some similarities, an argument can be made that the difference, no matter how slight, dictates that a court's interpretation of one statute in one case cannot apply to another statute in a different case.

The above examples involve statutes from the same state. All the statutes were passed by the same state legislature, and the court opinion came from a court in that state. What if, in the residency example, there is no case law in the state interpreting the term *resident,* and the *Frank v. Teague* opinion is a decision from another state interpreting a statute of that state that is identical or very similar to section 3105. Can *Frank* apply as precedent?

The answer is the same as the answer discussed in the above examples. If there is sufficient similarity in language and function of the statutes, the opinion can apply as precedent. If there is not sufficient similarity, it cannot apply as precedent. As long as the court is convinced that the similarity is sufficient, it can apply.

Bear in mind that a decision from another jurisdiction is only persuasive precedent, and a court is more likely to adopt persuasive precedent from a court within the jurisdiction than from a court without. It is best to locate authority within your jurisdiction. Look out of state only if there is no opinion that could apply as persuasive precedent within the jurisdiction.

Realistically, it is always risky arguing that a court's interpretation of a provision of one statute applies as precedent for the interpretation of a provision of a different statute. You are always open to, and will probably have to fend off, arguments that the statutes are functionally different and that reliance on a particular court opinion is misplaced. Your position is never solid. Always try to find another opinion or pursue another avenue of research.

Common Law Rule or Principle. The same principles mentioned in the preceding section apply when attempting to use as precedent a court opinion interpreting a common law rule or principle. Can a court opinion interpreting a common law rule or principle apply as precedent for a client's case that requires the application of a different common law rule or principle? The requirements are similar to those mentioned in the preceding section. Are the common law rules or principles similar in language and function? The requirements are presented in Figure 8–5.

For Example: Suppose the jurisdiction recognizes the torts of intrusion and public disclosure of a private fact. Both of these torts have been established by the highest court in the jurisdiction. There is no statutory law defining or governing the torts. One of the elements of the tort of *intrusion* is an act of intrusion into the *private affairs* of the plaintiff. One of the elements of the tort of *public disclosure of a private fact* is the public disclosure of a fact concerning the *private affairs* of the plaintiff.

In the client's case, the client was having an affair with the wife of a city council member. A campaign rival of the client disclosed the existence of the relationship at a campaign rally. The campaign rival acquired the information from a campaign aide who obtained the information by peeking through the client's bedroom window. The client wants to sue for public disclosure of a private fact. The question is whether the affair is a private fact.

The only case in the jurisdiction is *Claron v. Clark,* an intrusion case where a private investigator, through the means of a wiretap, discovered that the plaintiff was engaged in an affair. The court ruled that the term *private affairs* includes any sexual activity that takes place within the confines of an individual's residence.

Is the *Clark* opinion, an intrusion case, on point? Can it be precedent in the client's case, which involves a different tort—public disclosure of a private fact? May it be used as precedent in the client's case to guide the court in its interpretation of the meaning of the term *private affairs?* There is a similarity in the elements of the torts; both use the term *private affairs.* Both torts are similar in function. They are designed to protect the private affairs and lives of individuals. Intrusion protects against the act of prying or probing into the private affairs of an individual and public disclosure of a private fact protects against the act of publishing information concerning the private affairs of an individual.

If the court is convinced that the similarities are sufficient, the case can apply as precedent. It can always be argued, however, that since the torts are different, there is a difference in function, no matter how slight, that dictates that a court's interpretation of the one tort cannot apply to a different tort. In this case, it can be argued that prying is different from publication, and therefore, the difference in the interest being protected in the torts is sufficient to prevent an interpretation of a term in intrusion from being used to interpret the same term in public disclosure of a private fact.

Figure 8–5

Requirements When Different Common Law Rules/Principles Apply

1. There is a similarity in language between the common law rules or principles, and
2. There is a similarity in function between the common law rules or principles.

Again, be careful. The same pitfalls exist here as when different legislative acts apply. A court opinion within the jurisdiction interpreting a different rule of law is only persuasive precedent. It is not mandatory precedent that must be followed. It is very easy to present a counterargument that the functions of the two doctrines are clearly different, so the court opinion cannot apply as precedent. Also, keep in mind that when the decision is from another jurisdiction, it is still only persuasive precedent, and a court is more likely to adopt persuasive precedent from a court within the jurisdiction than from a court without.

Note: Be careful. It is always preferable to locate an opinion that applies a rule or legal principle that is the same as the rule or principle that applies in the client's case. If different rules or principles are involved, it is easier for the other side to argue that the opinion is not on point and, therefore, does not apply as precedent for the case at hand.

Where different rules or principles are involved, you should conduct further research and *shepardize* the case to determine if there are other cases more on point.

KEY POINTS CHECKLIST: *Determining If a Case Is on Point*

- ❑ Focus on the key facts and the rule of law/legal principle of both the court opinion and client's case.
- ❑ Where there are differences between the key facts of the court opinion and the client's case, carefully determine whether the differences are significant. Beware! Different key facts may lead to the application of an entirely different law or principle despite other key fact similarities. The rule of law or legal principle, however, may be so broad that it applies to many different fact situations.
- ❑ Clearly identify the rule of law/legal principle that applies in the court opinion and in the client's case.
- ❑ Where the rule of law applied in the court opinion is different from the rule that applies in the client's case, consider using the court opinion as precedent *only when there is no authority* interpreting or applying the rule/principle that applies in the client's case.
- ❑ Consider authority from another jurisdiction *only* when there is no authority in the jurisdiction.
- ❑ If in doubt about whether a fact is a key fact, continue your analysis until you are certain.
- ❑ Follow your instincts. If an opinion does not appear to be on point but your intuition tells you it is on point, continue your analysis until you are certain. If you never reach the point of feeling certain, search elsewhere.

APPLICATION

In this section, two examples are given that illustrate the application of the principles presented in this chapter for determining if a case is on point.

Chapter Hypothetical

This example is based on the fact pattern presented at the beginning of this chapter. Returning to that problem, is the case of *Karl v. Herald* on point so that it applies as precedent for the client's case?

Step 1 Are the key facts sufficiently similar? The first step is a determination of whether the key facts of *Karl v. Herald* are sufficiently similar to the client's case for

Herald to apply as precedent—to be on point. Although the facts in *Herald* are somewhat different, they are sufficiently similar. In both cases, the corporation was in a position to pay dividends. In both cases, while refusing to pay dividends, the majority shareholder allegedly enriched himself through excessive raises and/or bonuses. In both cases, the minority shareholders were effectively frozen out from benefiting in the corporation.

A difference in *Herald* is the plaintiff worked in the business. In the client's case, the brothers did not work in the business. This difference in the cases is not a key fact difference. The fact that the plaintiff in *Herald* worked in the business relates to her status as an employee, but it is not related to her status as a shareholder. In *Herald,* the court defined oppressive conduct as conduct against shareholders, not employees. The plaintiff's status as an employee may give rise to employee rights, but it is not related to rights as a shareholder and, therefore, is not a key fact.

Step 2 Are the rules/principles sufficiently similar? Is there a sufficient similarity between the law that applies in *Karl v. Herald* and that which applies in the client's case for the case to be considered on point and apply as precedent? The same statute, section 96-25-16 of the Business Corporation Act, applies to both the court opinion and the client's case. Both cases involve allegations of oppressive conduct by a minority shareholder against a majority shareholder and are governed by the same section of the statute.

In the *Herald* opinion, oppressive conduct was defined as "any unfair or fraudulent act by a majority shareholder that inures to the benefit of the majority and to the detriment of the minority." The client's case also involves questions of oppressive conduct by the majority shareholder and is governed by the same definition. Just as in *Herald,* there is alleged unfair conduct by the majority shareholder that inures to the benefit of the majority and to the detriment of the minority. There are no major differences between *Herald* and the client's case that restrict the application of *Herald* as precedent.

Note: What if you determined that *Herald* was not on point, but it was the only case in the jurisdiction that discusses oppressive conduct? You would need to be sure you analyzed the case in the memorandum to your supervisor and point out why the case is not on point.

Libel Case

The following fact situation and court opinion illustrate another example of the use of the steps discussed in this chapter.

For Example: Jerry lives in an apartment building. He often sees couples, and sometimes individuals, entering and leaving Eve's apartment in the late evening and early morning. Convinced that Eve is engaged in immoral behavior, he prepares a petition requesting that Eve be kicked out of the building. He intends to present copies of the petition to the other tenants of the building and submit the signed petitions to the landlord. In the petition, he refers to Eve as a prostitute.

Early one evening he decides to confront Eve. In the ensuing conversation, he discovers that Eve is a marriage counselor employed by a local business. The couples he has seen visiting her apartment are workers at the business who, due to their schedule, can come to counseling only during the late evening. She has an agreement with her employer that allows her to counsel couples and individuals in her apartment.

Jerry, realizing he is mistaken about Eve, decides to destroy the petitions. On the way to the incinerator, he unknowingly drops a copy of the petition. It is found by another tenant and ultimately is circulated among the tenants of the building. Eve hears about the petition and decides to sue Jerry for libel.

The state has a libel statute in which libel is defined as "the intentional publication, in writing, of false statements about a person." A leading libel case in the jurisdiction is *Cox v. Redd.* In this case, Redd wrote a letter he intended to mail to Cox wherein he called Cox a crook and a thief. The statements were not true. Redd intended for Cox, and no one else, to read the letter. The day before he planned to mail the letter, he invited several friends over to spend the evening. He forgot to put the letter away. He left it opened on the dining room table, and some of the guests read it. Redd was not aware that his guests had read the letter. Cox heard about it and sued Redd for libel.

The court, interpreting the libel statute, ruled that "intentional publication" means either the actual intent to publish or, where there is no intent to publish, reckless or grossly negligent conduct that results in publication." The court held that Redd's conduct of leaving the letter opened where he knew his guests could see it was grossly negligent conduct, and that, therefore, he had intentionally published the letter and had committed libel. The court commented that Redd knew company was coming to his house, and his failure to exercise care in securing the letter in light of that knowledge was gross negligence.

In this example, is *Cox v. Redd* on point so that it applies as precedent in Jerry's case?

Step 1 Are the key facts sufficiently similar? Both cases involve false written statements that were published. In both cases, there is the question of whether there was intentional publication. In the *Cox* case, even though he may not have intended to publish the letter, Redd's carelessness in leaving it out resulted in its publication.

Are the facts concerning intentional publication in Eve's case sufficiently similar? It is questionable. In the *Cox* case, Redd was careless and took no steps to secure the letter. In Eve's case, Jerry was taking steps to avoid publication and accidentally dropped a copy of the petition. It could be argued that some key facts are clearly different, that his conduct was simple negligence and not gross negligence, and that, therefore, the case is not on point. It could also be argued that due to the extreme sensitivity of the contents of the petition, Jerry should have taken great care to ensure that all the copies of the petition were burned, and the failure to exercise that care constitutes gross negligence. Under this argument, the case can apply as precedent.

It is important to note that there is a difference in the key facts that makes it questionable whether the case is on point. To remove doubt, additional research must be conducted to determine what constitutes gross negligence and whether Jerry's conduct rises to the level of gross negligence.

Step 2 Are the rules/principles sufficiently similar? If it is decided that there is a sufficient similarity in the facts, is there a sufficient similarity between the law that applies in the *Cox* opinion and that which applies in the client's case for the opinion to be considered on point and apply as precedent? Both cases are libel cases that apply the same libel statute. Both cases involve the element of intent to publish. Both cases are concerned with an aspect of that element—whether there is "intentional publication" when the conduct that results in publication is unintentional.

Therefore, there is little question that *Cox* is on point in regard to step 2. If it is determined that Jerry's conduct is gross negligence, under the rule of law applied in *Cox,* Jerry's conduct is intentional publication.

SUMMARY

Court opinions are important because under the doctrines of precedent and stare decisis, judges reach decisions according to principles laid down in similar cases. Therefore, a researcher needs to find a case that is precedent (on point) because it guides the attorney in regard to how the issue in the client's case may be decided. An opinion is on point, and may be considered as precedent, if there is a sufficient similarity between the key facts and the rule of law/legal principle that governs both the court opinion and the client's case.

When considering the key facts, the heart of the process is the identification of the similarities and differences between them. The more pronounced the differences between the facts of the court opinion and those of the client's case, the greater the likelihood that the opinion is not on point. Be very critical in your analysis when there are differences. Always check other avenues of research when the key facts are different.

Where the key facts are sufficiently similar for the opinion to be considered on point, look to the rule of law that governs the court opinion and the client's case. Where the same rule applies in the same way, the opinion is usually on point. Where a different rule applies, a court opinion usually cannot apply as precedent. Where the language and function of the applicable rules/principles are sufficiently similar, however, it can be argued that an opinion is on point and can be used as precedent.

Reliance on a court opinion that applies a different rule/principle than that which applies in the client's case is risky and should occur only when there is no case that interprets the rule or principle governing the client's case.

EXERCISES

ASSIGNMENT 1
What does it mean when a case is "on point"? When is a case "on point"?

ASSIGNMENT 2
Describe the two-step process for determining when a case is "on point."

ASSIGNMENT 3
Describe the three-part process for determining if a case is on point when there are different key facts.

ASSIGNMENT 4
Describe the two steps to follow when the doctrine/rule applied by the court is different from the doctrine that applies in the client's case.

ASSIGNMENT 5
In each of the following examples, a brief summary of the court opinion is presented, followed by a client's fact situation. For each client fact situation, Parts A–G, determine:

A. What are the fact similarities and differences between the court opinion and the client's situation?

B. Is the court opinion on point? Why or why not?

C. If the opinion is on point, what will the probable decision be in regard to the question raised by the client's facts?

Example 1

Court Opinion: *State v. Jones.* Mr. Jones, a first-time applicant for general relief funds, was denied relief without a hearing. The denial was based on information in Mr. Jones's application which indicated that his income was above the threshold maximum set out in the agency regulations. The regulation provides that when an applicant's income, or the financial support provided to an applicant plus income, exceeds twelve thousand dollars a year, the individual may be denied general relief funds. The regulation is silent about the right to a hearing.

Mr. Jones's application reflected that the gross income from his two part-time jobs exceeded by two thousand dollars the maximum allowable income for eligibility. He believed there were special circumstances that would allow him to be eligible for general relief. His demand for an appeal hearing to explain his special circumstances was denied.

The court held that the due process clause of the state constitution entitles a first-time applicant for general relief funds to a hearing when special circumstances are alleged. The question in the following three fact situations is whether the client is entitled to a hearing.

Part A

Client's Facts: Tom lives at home with his parents. He has a part-time job. He does not pay rent and utilities. He uses the money from his job to attend school. He has very little left over. His application for general relief was denied. The written denial stated that the combination of the support provided by his parents and his part-time income exceeded the maximum allowable income. His application for an appeal hearing was denied.

Part B

Client's Facts: In the last session of the state legislature, the legislature passed legislation which provided that when applicants for general relief were denied relief based on information provided in the application, they were not entitled to an appeal hearing. The purpose of the legislation was to cut costs.

Mr. Taylor, a first-time applicant for general relief funds, was denied benefits based solely on his application. He believes that he has special circumstances that entitle him to benefits. His request for an appeal hearing was denied.

Part C

Client's Facts: Client has been receiving general relief funds for the past year. Last week he received notice that his relief is being terminated due to information received from his employer indicating that he had received a raise, and his income is now over the statutory maximum. His request for an appeal hearing on the termination of relief was denied.

Example 2

Court Opinion: *Rex v. Ireland.* Mr. Rex, the landlord, filed an eviction suit against his tenant, Mr. Ireland. Mr. Rex served notice of default upon Mr. Ireland by rolling up the notice of default and placing it in Mr. Ireland's mailbox. The mailbox was situated next to the street. Mr. Ireland retrieved the notice the next day. Mr. Ireland, in his defense to the eviction suit, stated that he was not given proper notice of default under the provisions of section 55-67-9 of the Landlord/Tenant Act; therefore, the case should be dismissed. The statute provides that notice of default may be accomplished by:

1. delivery by certified mail,
2. hand delivery to the individual to be evicted, or
3. posting at the most public part of the residence.

The statute further provides that the court may enter an order of eviction if the notice of default is not responded to within thirty days.

The court, denying the request for dismissal, ruled that the intent of the statute was to ensure that tenants receive notice of default, and although the method of delivery by Mr. Rex did not comply with the statute, the intent of the act was accomplished inasmuch as Mr. Ireland had actual notice of default and was not prejudiced by the improper notice. The question in the following four fact situations is whether the notice of default is effective.

Part D

Client's Facts: The client is a tenant. The landlord told the client's daughter to inform the tenant that he was in default and, under the terms of the lease, would be evicted if he did not pay or otherwise respond within thirty days. The daughter informed the tenant the next day. Would it make any difference if the daughter informed the tenant after thirty days but before the eviction suit was filed?

Part E

Client's Facts: Client, the tenant, was on vacation when the landlord posted the notice of default on the front door. Client did not return from vacation and learn of the default until after the thirty-day default period had passed.

Part F

Client's Facts: Landlord sent the notice of default by regular mail, and it was received by the tenant.

Part G

Client's Facts: The landlord sent the notice by certified mail, but the client refused to accept it.

CHAPTER 9

Counteranalysis

On a frigid Saturday in December, Mr. Henry "Hot Dog" Thomas, an inexperienced skier, was skiing an expert run at a local resort. As he came over a hill, he encountered a patch of ice, lost control, crashed into a tree, and was severely injured. The ski resort had not posted a warning sign indicating the presence of the ice patch. Mr. Thomas consulted with Ms. Booth, a local attorney, and retained her to represent him. Shortly thereafter Ms. Booth filed a negligence suit against the resort. She sent her paralegal a memo indicating that the resort's attorney had filed a rule 12(b)(6) motion to dismiss for failure to state a claim. The paralegal was asked to prepare a legal research memo assessing the likelihood that the motion would be granted.

The Ski Safety Act, which governs the rights and liabilities of skiers and ski resorts, provides that:

- The resort has a duty to warn of hazardous conditions.
- The skier has the duty to be aware of and the responsibility for snow and ice conditions.

The act also provides that skiers have a duty to refrain from skiing beyond the range of their ability. One of the questions to be addressed by the paralegal is which of the duties apply in the client's case.

The memo prepared by the paralegal focused on the resort's duty to warn and the skier's duty in regard to snow and ice conditions. Based on this focus and the relevant case law, the paralegal concluded that the resort had the duty to warn of the ice patch that the client encountered. Therefore, the 12(b)(6) motion would probably not be granted.

At the motion hearing, the resort's counsel did not focus on the issue of the resort's duty to warn, but rather argued the issue in the context of probable cause. The resort's counsel contended that the cause of the accident was the skier's admitted violation of his statutory duty to refrain from skiing beyond the range of his ability. As an admitted inexperienced skier, his skiing an expert run was a violation of the statute and, therefore, the cause of the accident as a matter of law. The skier's attorney, relying on the paralegal's memo, which did not address the proximate cause issue, was unprepared to counter this argument. Consequently, the motion was granted and the case dismissed.

INTRODUCTION

What went wrong in the preceding hypothetical? Of course, the supervising attorney should have more carefully reviewed the paralegal's memo, noticed that the assistant had not addressed the proximate cause issue, and engaged in additional research. But often an attorney is too busy and, based on past excellent and reliable performance by a paralegal, may rely fully on the paralegal's work product and not sufficiently review what has been submitted.

counteranalysis
The process of discovering and considering the counterargument to a legal position or argument; the process of anticipating the argument the opponent is likely to raise in response to the analysis of an issue. It is the identification and objective evaluation of the strengths and weaknesses of a legal argument.

What went wrong with the paralegal's research? The paralegal failed to anticipate the legal argument the opposing side was likely to make. He failed to analyze the position from the other side's point of view. In other words, he failed to provide a complete counteranalysis in the memo. A paralegal's role in conducting legal research, or in any situation where legal analysis is required, includes determining the potential weaknesses of a legal argument and the counterarguments the other side may present.

The purpose of legal research is not only to discover how the law applies to the client's case but also to determine the strength of that case. To accomplish this, the strength of the opponent's case must be analyzed as well. The case must be looked at in its entirety to determine its strengths and weaknesses.

The focus of this chapter is the process of determining the strengths and weaknesses of a client's case through an analysis of the case from the perspective of the opposition. That is, the focus is on counteranalysis. It is assumed that thorough research has been conducted and all applicable law has been identified prior to the beginning of the process.

COUNTERANALYSIS—DEFINITION

If analysis is the application of the law to the facts of a case, what is counteranalysis? At one level, it is an exploration of how and why a specific law does or does not apply to the facts of a case. In essence, it is the process of discovering and considering the counterargument to a legal position or argument. It is the process of anticipating the argument the opponent is likely to raise in response to your analysis of an issue. It involves an identification and objective evaluation of the strengths and weaknesses of each legal argument you intend to raise.

COUNTERANALYSIS—WHY?

The role of the attorney and paralegal is to represent the client to the best of their ability and to pursue a course of action that is in the best interest of the client. This can be accomplished by engaging in research and analysis that thoroughly examines all the aspects of the case. One of those aspects, counteranalysis, is important for several reasons:

counterargument
The argument in opposition to a legal argument or position. The argument the opponent is likely to raise in response to the analysis of an issue.

1. An attorney has an ethical duty as an officer of the court to disclose legal authority adverse to the position of the client that is not disclosed by the opposing counsel. See Model Rules of Professional Conduct Rule 3.3(a)(3). The American Bar Association's Code of Professional Responsibility Disciplinary Rule 7-106(b) requires disclosure of authority that goes against your client's position.

   The goal of the adversary system is that justice be served. The ends of justice require the discovery and presentation of all relevant authority in order that a just resolution of the issues may be achieved. Therefore, a paralegal, to properly inform the attorney, must locate and provide the attorney with all relevant authority, including that which is adverse to the client.

2. Both the attorney and paralegal have an ethical duty to do a complete and competent job. Research and analysis are not complete unless all sides of an issue and all legal arguments have been considered. Failure to completely analyze a problem can constitute malpractice.

   In order to represent the client competently, you must be prepared to respond to any legal argument raised by the other side. The identification of opposing arguments allows you to consider what the other side's position is likely to be. It allows you to answer the questions:

   - "What will they do?"
   - "How can we counter their arguments?"
   - "What preparation is necessary to respond?"

   In essence, counteranalysis allows you to anticipate opposing arguments and prepare to counter them. The last thing a paralegal wants is to be responsible for the supervisory attorney being unprepared to respond to an argument.

3. Counteranalysis aids in the proper evaluation of the merits of a case and can assist in the selection of the appropriate course of action to follow.

   For Example: Counteranalysis may reveal a weakness in the client's case that leads to the conclusion that settlement should be pursued. Without conducting a thorough counteranalysis, an improper course of action could be followed, such as taking the matter to trial rather than pursuing settlement options.

4. It is important to locate and disclose adverse authority in order to maintain credibility with your supervisor. You may not be considered reliable and the credibility of your research may be questioned if you ignore or fail to identify and disclose adverse authority. The opposition or the court, if the issue comes before the court, most likely will discover the opposing authority. Your failure to do so indicates lack of ability, sloppiness, or intentional concealment. Your credibility and trustworthiness will be enhanced if you candidly reveal and meet head on unfavorable authority.

5. When a legal brief is submitted to a court, if you identify and address adverse authority in the brief, you have an opportunity to soften its impact by discrediting or distinguishing it. You have an opportunity to provide reasons why the adverse authority does not apply, and your credibility is enhanced. The reader is allowed to consider the adverse authority in the context of your response to it. This opportunity is missed if you fail to include the adverse authority.

Weaknesses in your position or analysis will not go away if you ignore them. No matter how strongly you feel you are right, you can count on the other side raising some counterargument, and if you have not considered and prepared for the counterarguments, you may very well lose in court.

COUNTERANALYSIS—WHEN

Counteranalysis should be employed whenever legal research is conducted or the strengths and weaknesses of a case are considered, in other words, *always.* When a legal problem is being addressed, look for all potential counterarguments to any position taken. Counteranalysis is required when preparing an interoffice legal memorandum or conducting any research on an issue in a case. It is certainly necessary when you are assisting in the preparation of a response to a brief filed by the opposing party. Also, you should engage in the process even when you are just thinking about the legal issues in the client's case. Counteranalysis may be required even in the initial stages of a case.

For Example: Some paralegals conduct the initial interview with a client and provide the supervisory attorney with a summary of the interview and the applicable statutory and case law. The summary of the applicable law should include a counteranalysis section that introduces any apparent weaknesses in the client's case.

COUNTERANALYSIS—TECHNIQUES

In General

Before counteranalysis can begin, a prerequisite is that the issue or legal position being analyzed must be thoroughly researched. You must know the law before you can respond to it. Because of its importance, this point is emphasized and repeated throughout the chapter. Thorough research may reveal the weaknesses of a legal position and the counterarguments to it.

For Example: Mary Kay, a door-to-door sales representative for Ace Brush, sold Ella Smith a set of brushes at Ms. Smith's residence. Ms. Smith signed a contract to purchase the brushes. The contract provided for three monthly payments. Ms. Smith called two days later and canceled the contract. When Ace Brush attempted to deliver the goods, Ms. Smith refused to accept the delivery. Ace Brush sued Ms. Smith for breach of contract.

Tom, a paralegal with the firm representing Ace Brush, was assigned the task of determining whether Ms. Smith could legally cancel the contract after it was signed. He determined that article II of the state Commercial Code governed the transaction. His research indicated that the code had no provision allowing a cooling-off period for door-to-door sales, and therefore, he concluded that Ms. Smith's rejection of the goods was a breach of the contract.

Tom, however, committed a major error. He failed to thoroughly research the question. The state had another statute, called the Consumer Sales Act, that provided that in the event of a credit transaction involving a home solicitation sale, the buyer had a right to cancel the sale within three days of the transaction.

Had Tom's research been thorough, he would have located the weakness in his legal position based upon the Commercial Code and identified the counterargument to the conclusion that the contract was breached. Remember, the first step is to conduct thorough research.

When embarking on counteranalysis, always assume that there is a counterargument to the position you have taken. Put yourself in the opponent's place and ask yourself:

- "How do I respond to this argument?"
- "What is the argument in response to this position?"

Remember, counteranalysis consists of the challenges to your position that the opponent likely will make.

The purpose of legal research is to identify the law supporting the client's case and the strengths of the case. Part of exploring the strength of the case is determining any challenge or counterargument the opponent may use to challenge the authorities on which you rely. You *must* identify all possible arguments attacking your position.

In order to determine what the counterarguments to an argument or position are likely to be, it is necessary and helpful to consider the ways a legal argument is attacked. Once you are familiar with the techniques used to challenge an argument, use those techniques to seek out the weaknesses in your argument and to anticipate the likely counterarguments.

A legal argument or legal position is usually based on enacted law or court opinion or both. The various approaches that may be used to attack or challenge an argument based on an enacted law or court opinion are explored separately in the following two sections.

Enacted Law

Ways to challenge or attack a legal position or argument based on an enacted law are discussed here. *Enacted law,* as defined in Chapter 1, includes any law passed or adopted by the people through a representative body, such as Congress or a state legislature, city council, and so on. The term includes constitutional provisions, statutes, codes, ordinances, regulations, rules, and so on. Throughout this section and the remainder of the chapter, the term *statute* will be used when discussing legal arguments or positions based on enacted law.

There are several approaches to consider when attacking a legal position based on a statute. Some of these approaches are listed in Figure 9–1. Consider all of them when analyzing an argument based on a statute to ensure that all possible weaknesses are identified and counterarguments determined.

Elements of the Statute Are Not Met

Every statute is composed of components (parts) that must be met before the statute can apply. As discussed in Chapter 3, these components are called elements. When a client's case is based on a statute, there must be present in the case facts that establish or satisfy each of the elements of the statute.

For Example: Criminal Code § 1000 defines burglary as the breaking and entering of the residence of another with the intent to commit a crime. The elements are:

1. Breaking and entering
2. The residence
3. Of another
4. With the intent to commit a crime

There must be facts present that establish or satisfy *each* of these elements before an individual can be convicted of burglary.

1. The elements of the statute are not met.
2. The statute is sufficiently broad to permit a construction or application different from that urged by the opposition.
3. The statute has been misconstrued or does not apply.
4. The statute relied upon as a guide to interpret another statute does not apply and, therefore, cannot be used as a guide in interpreting the other statute.
5. The statute relied on has not been adopted in your jurisdiction.
6. The interpretation of the statute urged by the opposition is unconstitutional or violates another legislative act.
7. The statute relied on is unconstitutional.

Figure 9–1
Counteranalysis Approaches to a Legal Position Based on a Statute

One way to attack a legal position based on a statute is to argue that the elements of the statute have not been met—that is, there are not facts present in the case to establish or satisfy each element (one or more elements) of the statute.

For Example: Mary is charged under Criminal Code § 1000 with burglary of Steve's house. Steve is a friend of Mary, and Mary often stays at Steve's house. On the date of the alleged burglary, Steve's house was unlocked. Mary came over to see Steve, entered the house, saw money on the kitchen table, took it, and left.

The counterargument to the prosecution's reliance on the statute is that there are no facts present in the case to satisfy two elements of the law:

1. Mary did not break into the house, as it was unlocked.
2. Mary did not enter with the intent to commit a crime. She entered with the intent to visit Steve. The intent to commit a crime did not occur until after entry had taken place.

When conducting counteranalysis of an argument based on a statute, closely examine the facts relied on to establish or satisfy *each* of the required elements. Ask yourself, *"Have the elements of the statute been met?"* Look for any argument that can be raised that the facts do not establish or satisfy an element or elements.

Statute Is Sufficiently Broad—Different Construction

In many situations, a statute may be sufficiently broad to allow an interpretation or application different from that relied on by the opposing side.

For Example: Section 54-9-91 of the state domestic relations statute provides that custody shall be determined in the best interest of the children. Gerald contends that he should be granted custody of the children because he lives in a small town, and his former spouse lives in a large city. He argues that a small town is a better environment because it is safer and free from the pressures of gang violence and drug use.

A counterargument can be made that the benefits of the city, such as greater access to the arts, museums, and universities, offset the alleged disadvantages of a large city. The term *best interest of the children* can be interpreted in a manner different from that urged by the opposing side.

Where the language relied on in a statute is broadly crafted, such as in this example, always be aware of and look for the counterargument that a different interpretation is permissible because of the broadness of the language. Ask the question, *"Is the statute sufficiently broad to permit a construction or application different from that urged by the opposition?"*

Statute Misconstrued or Does Not Apply

This approach is related to that discussed in the preceding subsection. Explore the possibility that a counterargument may be raised that the statute is being misconstrued or misapplied.

For Example: Section 9(A) of the Deceptive Trade Practices Act provides a remedy in tort for "deceptive practices in negotiation or performance" of a contract for the sale of goods. Tom and Larry have a contract for the delivery of goods. Under the contract, Tom is to deliver the goods on the fifth of each month. Every month Tom comes up with some excuse for not delivering the goods on the fifth, and the goods are always delivered between the seventh and fifteenth of the month. Finally, Larry gets fed up and sues Tom for violation of the Deceptive Trade Practices Act, claiming that Tom is engaging in deceptive practices in violation of §(9)A of the act.

Assume a review of the legislative history and case law clearly indicates that the act is not designed to apply to simple breach of contract cases. The Sale of Goods provisions of the Commercial Code statutes govern breach of contract situations. The courts have consistently held that when there is an adequate remedy in contract law, the tort remedy available under the act does not apply. Therefore, a counterargument can be raised that the statute has been misconstrued and does not apply in a simple contract case such as that of Tom and Larry.

When a legal position or argument is based on a statute, always engage in counteranalysis to ensure that the statute is not being misconstrued or applied in a situation to which it clearly does not apply. *Always consult case law to determine if the courts have interpreted or applied the statute in a manner different from that relied on.* Ask the following questions: *Has the statute been misconstrued or does not apply? Does another statute apply?"*

Statute Relied on as a Guide Does Not apply

In some situations, the statute that governs does not have a provision that addresses a specific question raised by the facts of a client's case. In such instances, there may be an argument that a different statute, which has a section that governs a similar fact situation, may be used as guidance in interpreting the applicable statute. It is usually argued that the different statute can be used as guidance because the language and functions of the statutes are similar.

When this occurs, a counterargument can *always* be made that the statute relied on to interpret another statute is not intended to govern or apply to the type of situation presented by the client's case and, therefore, cannot be used as a guide. The argument usually is that the statute governs or applies only to those limited fact situations covered by the language of the statute and cannot be used as a guide for the interpretation of another statute.

For Example: Assume the jurisdiction has adopted the following statutes:

- § 59-1 provides that an individual must be a resident of the county to be eligible to run for the position of animal control officer.
- § 200-1 provides that an individual must be a resident of the county for three months to run for a position on the county school board.

Aaron, a resident of the city for three months, wants to run for the position of animal control officer. She argues that since § 59-1 is silent on the length of residency necessary to be eligible to run for the position of animal control officer, the three-month residency requirement established in § 200-1 should be used as a guide to determine the length of residency required under § 59-1. She reasons that since both statutes are similar in language (both use the word *resident)* and since both involve county elective offices, they are sufficiently similar for the residency requirement of § 200-1 to be used as the standard for § 59-1.

Since the statutes are different, however, a counterargument can be made that the duties of animal control officer are much different from those of a school board member. The duties of the animal control officer require a degree of familiarity with the geography of the county that cannot be acquired in three months. Therefore, the differences in the requirements of the positions represent a factual difference that renders § 200-1 inappropriate for use as a guide to interpret § 59-1.

In every situation where it is argued that a provision of one statute may apply or be used to interpret a provision of a different statute, a counterargument can *always* be made that no matter how similar in language and function, the statutes differ functionally in some way. Therefore, the provisions of one statute cannot be relied on or applied to interpret or govern the other statute.

When your legal position or argument is based on the use of one statute as a guide to interpret another statute, *always* consider the counterargument that focuses on the differences in the statutes. Keep in mind the question, *"Is it possible that the statute relied on as a guide is so functionally different that it cannot be used as a guide to interpret the statute being analyzed?*

Statute Relied on Has Not Been Adopted in Jurisdiction

It may occur that the jurisdiction has no law or statute governing a fact situation, and your legal position is based upon an argument that advocates the adoption of the language of, or principles embodied in, a statute from another jurisdiction. In such situations, you are attempting to persuade the court to adopt the law, or the principles embodied in the law, of another jurisdiction.

A counterargument can always be made that a statute, or principles that apply to facts in another jurisdiction, should not be adopted to apply to similar facts in your jurisdiction. It is usually possible to point out some difference between the jurisdictions or difference in the public policy of the jurisdictions and argue that the difference precludes the adoption of the language or principles of the statute.

For Example: Ida, a resident of state *A*, borrows her next-door neighbor's lawn mower. Due to a defect in the mower, Ida is injured. Ida sues the manufacturer, a local company, for breach of warranty. The manufacturer moves for dismissal, claiming that the warranty does not extend to nonpurchasers. The commercial code adopted in state *A* does not address the question, nor is there any case law on point. Ida argues that the language of the law of state *B*, a neighboring state, should be adopted by the court. Section 2-389 of state *B*'s commercial code provides that warranties extend to the buyer and any person who may be reasonably expected to use the goods, which includes a neighbor.

The manufacturer's counterargument could be that the law of state *B* should not be looked to because of policy differences between the states. State *A*, in order to encourage and protect the growth of local industry, has traditionally adopted a policy that narrowly limits manufacturer liability. State *B*'s position represents an expansive view that broadly extends manufacturer liability, a position contrary to state *A*'s traditional view.

When conducting counteranalysis, be alert for an argument that the statute relied on has not been adopted and should not apply. Ask the question, "*Where a legal position is based upon an argument that advocates the adoption of the language or principles embodied in a statute of another jurisdiction, are there differences in the jurisdictions that preclude the adoption of the language or principles of the statute?*" Note that there is always the additional counterargument that such matters are of legislative concern and should be addressed by the legislature, not the courts.

Interpretation of Statute Is Unconstitutional or Violates Another Legislative Act

Be alert for an argument that the *application* or *interpretation* of the statute advocated is unconstitutional or violates another statute.

For Example: Section 22 of the state's Secured Transaction Code allows a creditor to repossess collateral after providing the debtor with notice of default and allowing the debtor sixty days to cure the default. A car dealer, after providing notice of default and waiting over sixty days for the customer to cure the default, repossessed the customer's car from the customer's residence while the customer was at work. The car dealer interpreted the statute to not require prior court approval and, therefore, did not seek a court order authorizing the repossession.

The customer sued the car dealer, claiming the dealer illegally seized the car because the due process clause of the state constitution requires a court order before property can be seized. The dealer claimed that the seizure was legal because he complied with the statute—that is, he provided notice of default and waited sixty days.

The counterargument is that the interpretation of the statute urged by the dealer is unconstitutional because it allows for prejudgment seizure—that is, it allows the seizure of property without prior court approval.

Always counteranalyze a legal position or argument based on an *interpretation of a law* for the possibility that the interpretation violates a constitutional or statutory provision. Ask yourself, *"Is the interpretation of the statute urged by the opposition unconstitutional or does it violate another legislative act?"*

Statute Relied on Is Unconstitutional

Although statutes are not usually unconstitutional and, therefore, are not likely to be vulnerable to constitutional attack, you should always consider the constitutionality of the statute on which a legal position is based. Has the constitutionality of the statute been questioned in scholarly journals, law reviews, and so on? Try to anticipate any argument based on a constitutional challenge.

For Example: Ellen is prosecuted under a local ordinance that prohibits the sale of any material that "shows genitalia or excites a prurient interest." Such a statute may be subject to challenge as being unconstitutional because the term *prurient interest* is too vague.

When working with statutes always consider a counterargument based on a challenge to the constitutionality of the statute. Always consider the question, *"Is the statute unconstitutional?"*

Caveat: When a legal position or argument is based on a statute, always be sure that thorough research is conducted to ensure that some other law, provision, or court decision does not apply that affects your reliance on the statute.

Case Law

Chapter 8 presents an extensive discussion of the process of determining if a court opinion is on point and, therefore, can be used as precedent in support of a client's legal position. In order to understand how to counteranalyze a legal position or argument based upon reliance on a court opinion, it is necessary to understand the process involved in determining if a court opinion is on point. Therefore, it is helpful to review Chapter 8 before beginning this section. When used in this section, the terms *rule of law* and *legal principle* include any constitutional, legislative, or common law provision, act, doctrine, principle, or test relied on by the court in reaching its decision.

There are several approaches for challenging a legal position based on a court opinion. Some of these approaches are listed in Figure 9–2. Each of them should be considered when conducting counteranalysis.

Reliance on Court Opinion Is Misplaced—Key Fact Difference

Techniques for identifying key facts are presented in Chapter 5. Techniques for determining whether the key facts of a court opinion and a case are sufficiently similar for the court opinion to apply as precedent are presented in Chapter 8. Apply the test from the Determining If a Case Is on Point section of Chapter 8: "Substitute the client's key facts for those of the court opinion. If the substitution of the key facts would result in changing the outcome of the case, the court opinion cannot be used as precedent."

For Example: Assume that the plaintiff requests that a psychologist's records be admitted into evidence. Plaintiff bases his argument on the holding in the case of *Smith v. Jones,* which allowed the admission of a psychologist's records into evidence. In that case, the evidence was admitted because no claim was raised that the evidence was privileged. The decision turned on the key fact that privilege was not claimed.

1. Reliance on the court opinion is misplaced because the key facts in the opinion and the key facts of the client's case are different to such a nature or degree that they render the court opinion unusable as precedent.
2. Reliance on the court opinion is misplaced because the rule of law or legal principle applied in the court opinion does not apply.
3. The court opinion is subject to an interpretation different from that relied on in support of a legal position.
4. The rule or principle adopted in the opinion relied on is not universally followed.
5. The opinion relied on presents several possible solutions to the problem, and the one urged by the opposition is not mandatory and is not the best choice.
6. The position relied on no longer represents sound public policy and should not be followed.
7. There are other equally relevant cases that do not support the position adopted in the case relied on.

Figure 9–2

Counteranalysis Approaches to a Legal Position Based on Case Law

In the plaintiff's case, privilege is vigorously claimed. Therefore, *Jones* cannot be relied on as precedent to support the argument for the admission of the records because it is not on point. There is such a significant difference in the key facts that the case cannot be relied upon as precedent. In *Jones,* privilege was not claimed, but in the plaintiff's case, it is claimed.

Be cautious when your legal argument relies on a court opinion that has key facts that are different from your case. Refer to Chapter 8 and conduct counteranalysis to identify a possible counterargument that the court opinion relied on does not apply because of differences in the key facts. Always consider the question, *"Is the opinion relied on not on point because of key fact differences?"*

Reliance on Court Opinion Is Misplaced—Rule of Law or Legal Principle Does Not Apply

When conducting counteranalysis, always look for the counterargument that the legal principle applied in the court opinion does not apply in the case at hand. Refer to the Determining If a Case Is on Point section of Chapter 8 when considering this approach.

For Example: This example refers to the custody example presented in the Determining If a Case Is on Point section of Chapter 8. In the case of *Davis v. Davis,* Ms. Davis had sole custody of her two daughters. Ms. Davis's boyfriend occasionally stayed overnight at her home, and the daughters were aware of the overnight visits. Mr. Davis, her former husband, filed a motion with the court asking for a change of custody. He based his claim solely upon his wife's alleged "immoral conduct." No evidence was presented indicating how the overnight visits impacted the children.

The trial court granted a change of custody. In overturning the trial court, the court of appeals ruled that "mere allegations of immoral conduct are not sufficient grounds to award a change of custody." The court stated that there must be evidence presented showing that the alleged immoral conduct harmed the children.

Assume that in the client's case, the facts are the same as those in *Davis v. Davis* except that instead of occasional overnight visits, the custodial spouse is cohabiting with another person. Also assume there is a statute in the jurisdiction which provides that cohabitation is per se harmful to the children—that is, in cohabitation cases, evidence of harm to the children need not be presented because cohabitation is presumed to be harmful to them.

If the custodial spouse relies on *Davis* for the proposition that the noncustodial spouse's request for change of custody must be denied because he has failed to present evidence of harm to the children, the reliance is misplaced.

The reliance is misplaced because the cohabitation statute does not require the presentation of evidence of harm to the children. Therefore, the rule of law presented in *Davis* is not applicable in the client's case, and the case is not on point.

When a court opinion is used to support a legal position, always ask the question, *"Is reliance on the opinion misplaced because the principle applied does not apply to the case at hand?"*

Court Opinion Is Subject to a Different Interpretation

The court may have interpreted a term in a manner that is subject to an interpretation different from that relied on in support of a legal position.

For Example: Mr. Johns is charged with violating Municipal Code § 982, which prohibits nude dancing. Mr. Johns was dancing in see-through bikini briefs. In prosecuting Mr. Johns, the city relied on the court opinion of *City v. Dew.* In that case, the court, in interpreting the term *nude dancing,* ruled that a dancer is nude when the breast or genitalia are exposed. In Dew, the dancer was completely nude.

In Mr. Johns's case, the city contends that Mr. Johns was nude dancing because his genitalia were exposed when he wore see-through bikini briefs. A counterargument could be made that the term *exposed,* as used in the opinion, should be interpreted to mean uncovered. Therefore, a dancer is not nude under the definition adopted in *Dew* when he is covered by any fabric, no matter how sheer. The counterargument is that the language of the opinion is subject to an interpretation different from that relied on by the opposition.

Always closely scrutinize the language of the court opinion to determine if it is subject to another interpretation. Be aware that the interpretation you adopt may not be the only possible interpretation. Always ask the question, *"Is the court opinion subject to a different interpretation from that relied upon?"*

Rule or Principle Adopted in Opinion Relied on Is Not Universally Followed

This should be a consideration when the opinion relied on is not mandatory precedent—that is, when there is no court opinion directly on point, and a party is urging the court to follow a rule or principle adopted by another court ruling in a similar case in either the same or a different jurisdiction.

For Example: The counterargument could be, "Although the plaintiff relies on and urges the adoption of the principle presented in *Smith v. Jones,* and that opinion is followed by the Ninth, Fifth, and Seventh circuits, several other circuits have chosen not to follow it. The better position, presented in the case of *Grape v. Vine,* is followed by the Fourth, Sixth, and Eleventh circuits. The principle adopted in *Vine* more accurately reflects the policies of this jurisdiction."

Identify the other rules or legal principles that may apply by reading the opinions of courts that have adopted other positions in similar cases. Keep in mind the question, *"Is the rule or principle of the case relied on universally followed?"*

Opinion Presents Several Possible Solutions; One Urged by Opposition Is Not Mandatory and Is Not Best Choice

Always check the court opinion relied on in support of a legal position to determine if the opinion includes other solutions in addition to the one relied on. Also, check other court opinions to identify different solutions that may have been adopted in other cases. If it is not mandatory to follow a single solution or position, conduct counteranalysis to identify the other possible solutions and anticipate counterarguments that may be based on one of the other solutions. Ask yourself, *"If the opinion relied on is not mandatory precedent, does the opinion or another court opinion allow for other possible positions?"*

For Example: A counterargument could be, "In the case of *Smith v. Harris,* the court stated that the plaintiff could pursue several avenues of relief, including injunction and damages. The defendant argues that *Harris* mandates the pursuit of injunctive relief when, in fact, the court allowed the pursuit of several avenues of relief in addition to injunction."

Position Relied on No Longer Represents Sound Public Policy and Should Not Be Followed

If the court opinion is mandatory precedent and, therefore, must be followed, explore the possibility that it no longer represents sound public policy and should be overruled. This approach is available only if the court considering the question has the authority to overrule the precedent. A trial court does not have the power to overrule a higher court decision. If an intermediary court of appeal set the precedent, that court has the power to overturn it. If the highest court in the jurisdiction set the precedent, only that court has the power to overturn it.

This approach is always risky because a court will not lightly choose to ignore precedent. A court usually requires a strong argument to support a decision to abandon or not follow precedent. When a position, however, is based on a court opinion, always consider the possibility that the rule or principle adopted in the opinion should no longer be followed due to some policy or other change. In such situations, it can always be argued that fairness demands that the court reexamine the law.

For Example: Mr. Clark wishes to move into an apartment complex that has restrictions based on parental status. The restrictions provide that no individual or couple may rent an apartment if they have children. The restrictions also provide that if tenants have children after they rent an apartment, they must vacate the premises within three months of the birth of a child. The only case on point is the 1935 case of *Edwards v. Frank.* In that case, the court ruled that restrictions based on parental status did not violate the Constitution and, therefore, were enforceable.

An argument can be presented that current public policy strongly favors families with children, that current policy dictates that rental restrictions based on parental status are no longer acceptable or desirable, and that, therefore, *Frank* should no longer be followed.

Always consider the possibility that the court opinion should no longer be followed. Always consider the question, *"Does the court opinion relied on no longer represent sound public policy and, therefore, should not be followed?"*

Other Equally Relevant Cases Do Not Support Position Adopted in Case Relied on

In some instances, a matter has not been clearly settled by the highest court in the jurisdiction, or the opinions of the highest court appear to conflict. Always look for other opinions that may take a position different from the one taken in the court opinion relied on to support a legal position or argument. Ask yourself, *"Are there equally relevant cases that do not support the position adopted in the case relied on?"*

For Example: The client is seeking punitive damages in a negligence case. There are three court opinions from the highest court in the jurisdiction. In the case of *Yaws v. Allen,* it was held that punitive damages may be recovered in a negligence case when there is a showing of gross negligence on the part of the tortfeasor. In the case of *X-ray v. Carrie,* the court ruled that before punitive damages can be awarded in a negligence case, there must be some demonstration that the tortfeasor had a culpable state of mind. In the case of *Casy v. Cox,* the court held that the establishment of gross negligence by itself does not indicate the existence of a culpable state of mind; it is also necessary to demonstrate willful and wanton misconduct by the tortfeasor.

Reliance on *Yaws v. Allen,* in support of a legal position that the establishment of gross negligence on the part of the tortfeasor is sufficient to obtain punitive damages, is subject to challenge. A counterargument can be presented that the *Carrie* and *Cox* cases, also from the highest court in the jurisdiction, require more than gross negligence.

Caveat: When a legal position or argument is based on a court opinion, always be sure that thorough research is conducted to find any other law, provision, or court decision that may affect your reliance on the opinion. The research should identify all court opinions that present possible solutions and approaches to the problem being analyzed.

COUNTERANALYSIS TECHNIQUES—COMMENTS

When engaging in legal research or analysis, review all the approaches presented in the preceding sections and determine if the legal position or argument may be challenged through any of them. Be aware, however, that the techniques and considerations presented here are not inclusive of all the available ways to attack or challenge a legal position or argument based on a legislative act or court opinion. In addition to using the techniques listed, use any other approach that comes to mind. Also, combinations of methods may be utilized. The particular circumstances of the case will determine which, if any, of the suggested approaches are applicable. It is important to remember that when your position or argument is based on a legislative act or court opinion, you must engage in thorough counteranalysis to locate any weaknesses, anticipate any counterarguments, and prepare a response.

COUNTERANALYSIS—WHERE?

Now that the process has been discussed, the next question is where does counteranalysis fit in an interoffice research memorandum or court brief? Since counteranalysis involves analysis, it obviously fits in the analysis section. But where in the analysis section does it belong? There are no established guidelines or formal rules for the placement of counteranalysis. The following are recommendations and considerations.

Court Brief

In a court brief, inasmuch as counteranalysis involves discussing potential counterarguments to or weaknesses in your analysis, it is recommended that counteranalysis be presented in the middle of the analysis, *i.e.,* immediately after the analysis but before the conclusion. Present your argument and analysis first. Then present the other side's position after your argument, in the middle of the analysis.

Presenting counteranalysis in the middle of the analysis keeps the focus on your position rather than on your opponent's position. A reader tends to remember the beginning and end of a presentation more than the middle. Since you believe your analysis or legal argument is correct and should prevail, you want the memory of your analysis to be foremost in the reader's mind. Therefore, you do not want to place the counterargument in a location where it is more likely to be remembered or emphasized, such as at the beginning or end—hence, its placement after the analysis and prior to the conclusion, *i.e.,* in the middle.

For Example: "It is appropriate for the court to allow the admission of DNA test results based on the IMAK test. In this state, in the case of *State v. Diago,* the supreme court ruled that the results of scientific tests are admissible when the test's reliability and scientific basis are recognized by competent authorities. The IMAK test, developed in 1992, is universally accepted by all competent authorities as scientifically valid.

Defendant's reliance on the state case of *Arc v. Arc* is misplaced. In that case, the court's refusal to allow the admission of DNA evidence was based on the disagreement among experts about the reliability of the test being administered at the time, the ITAK test. The ITAK test was not universally accepted and was not as accurate as the current IMAK test. Indeed, IMAK test results have been admitted into evidence in all cases where they have been submitted. For the reasons of universal scientific acceptance, reliability, and court acceptance, the results of IMAK DNA testing should be admitted in this case."

Interoffice Research Memorandum

In an interoffice research memorandum, it is recommended that counteranalysis be placed after the analysis of each issue. It logically follows the analysis, and this placement ensures that it will be reviewed by the supervisory attorney before he or she proceeds to the next issue(s). It may be useful, for the purpose of making certain that it is not overlooked, to include a separate counteranalysis subsection for each issue addressed in the memo. One possible outline of the analysis portion of a legal research memorandum is as follows:

Analysis Section—The legal analysis of the issue(s)
Issue I

A. *Introductory sentence.*
B. *Rule of law.* State the rule of law that governs the issue. This may be a constitutional provision, statutory provision, court doctrine, principle, and so on.
C. *Case(s).* Present the case or cases that are on point and illustrate the application of the rule of law to the facts.
D. ***Counteranalysis***
E. *Conclusion*

Assume the information included in the previous example is being presented in an interoffice memorandum. A portion of the analysis and counteranalysis section of the memo may appear as follows:

Analysis

It is likely the court will allow the admission of DNA test results based on the IMAK test. The state supreme court, in the case of *State v. Diago,* ruled that the results of scientific tests are admissible when the test's reliability and scientific basis are recognized by competent authorities. The IMAK test, developed in 1992, is universally accepted by all competent authorities as scientifically valid.

Although the courts of this state have not addressed the question of the admission of DNA evidence based on the IMAK test, the United States Court of Appeals for the Fifth Circuit has considered the matter. In *Eric v. Eric,* the court of appeals stated, "The time has arrived to admit the results of DNA testing into evidence. The IMAK test meets the requirements established by this court for the admission of scientific evidence." IMAK test results have been admitted into evidence in all cases where they have been submitted. For the reasons of universal scientific acceptance, reliability, and court acceptance, the results of IMAK DNA testing should be admitted in this case.

Counteranalysis

Defendant may rely on the state case of *Arc v. Arc* and argue that the results of the test should not be admitted. In *Arc,* the court refused to allow the admission of

DNA test results from the ITAK test. The court's refusal was based on the disagreement among experts about the reliability of the test. The ITAK test was not universally accepted and was not as accurate as the current IMAK test. Since the *Arc* opinion involved a different test that was neither as universally accepted nor as accurate as the IMAK test, the opinion is not on point and cannot be relied on as precedent in this case.

For an in-depth discussion of the analysis section of an interoffice legal research memorandum, see Chapter 13.

KEY POINTS CHECKLIST: *Conducting Counteranalysis*

- ❑ Remember, for every issue presented in a legal research memorandum, consider how the other side is likely to respond.
- ❑ Put yourself in your opponent's position. Assume you are the opponent and consider all possible counterarguments, no matter how ridiculous—be ruthless.
- ❑ The more strongly you believe in the correctness of your analysis, the greater the likelihood that you will miss or overlook the counteranalysis to that analysis. Beware, when you feel extremely confident or sure, take extra precautions. Overconfidence can seriously mislead you.
- ❑ A weakness in an argument will not go away if you ignore it. You can count on either the other side or the court to bring it to light. It is much better for you to raise the counterargument and diffuse it.
- ❑ Do not let your emotions, preconceived notions, or stubbornness interfere with an objective counteranalysis of your position.
- ❑ When analyzing court opinions, a counteranalysis of the majority opinion may be found in the dissenting opinion or other opinions that criticize or distinguish the majority opinion.
- ❑ When conducting counteranalysis, always consider *each* of the approaches listed in this chapter. Remember, more than one approach may apply, and approaches other than those listed may be available.
- ❑ Always research thoroughly. Look for other laws or court opinions that may apply.

APPLICATION

This section explores the application of the principles discussed in this chapter. Three situations are explored in the following examples.

Chapter Hypothetical

Review the example presented at the beginning of the chapter. In the hypothetical, the paralegal failed to conduct a thorough counteranalysis. The assignment was to assess the likelihood that a rule 12(b)(6) motion to dismiss for failure to state a claim would be granted. In a 12(b)(6) motion, the movant is basically claiming that under the facts of the case, the plaintiff cannot state a claim. In order to state a claim in a negligence case, there must be facts present that establish or satisfy each of the elements of negligence: duty, breach of duty, proximate cause, and damages. In the example, the paralegal's attention was focused on duty, that is, on which duty applied. In light of the provisions of the applicable statute, the Ski Safety Act, and the facts of the case, there appeared to be a conflict of duties. The paralegal focused on which duty applied:

- the resort's duty to warn of hazards, or
- the skier's duty to know of and be responsible for snow and ice conditions.

The paralegal's mistake was the failure to conduct a complete counteranalysis. A proper counteranalysis would have led the paralegal to consider the opponent's possible challenge involving the other areas of negligence—breach of duty, proximate cause, and damages. Had this been done, the paralegal would have recognized that the opposing side could raise a proximate cause argument: the cause of the accident was the skier's breach of duty by skiing beyond the range of his ability, not the resort's failure to warn. Had this argument been considered, a response could have been prepared, and the motion may not have been granted.

This example illustrates one of the most important considerations in counteranalysis: *when analyzing a legal position, always conduct thorough and complete research that considers every possible attack, no matter how remote.*

Counteranalysis—Reliance on Legislative Act

Section 35-6-6A of the Construction Industries Licensing Act provides that contractors must be licensed. The section requires all licensed general contractors to take reasonable steps to ensure that the subcontractors they hire are licensed. The section also provides that licensed general contractors who hire unlicensed subcontractors are vicariously liable in breach of contract suits filed against the unlicensed subcontractors.

In the client's case, the client (Plaintiff) is acting as the general contractor; the subcontractor (SC) is unlicensed. Tom's, Inc. (TI), a licensed general contractor, has used SC on projects in the past and has acted as an agent for SC, often helping SC obtain jobs with other general contractors. Plaintiff, a private individual building his own home, contacted TI seeking assistance in locating a subcontractor. TI arranged the contract between SC and Plaintiff. TI recommended that SC be hired and fully disclosed to Plaintiff that TI was merely an agent for SC. TI was not party to the contract. SC breached its contract with Plaintiff, and Plaintiff sued both SC and TI.

In the lawsuit, Plaintiff argues that § 35-6-6A allows a cause of action for breach of contract against a general contractor who *is not* a party to the contract. This cause of action exists when the general contractor is acting as an agent for an unlicensed contractor who *is* a party to the contract. Plaintiff also contends that § 35-6-6A imposes an implied duty on licensed general contractors to protect third parties against all unlicensed contractors, not just unlicensed subcontractors. Plaintiff reasons that the implied duty arises because the intent of the statute is to place a duty on licensed general contractors to assist in the elimination of use of unlicensed contractors on construction projects.

The counterargument is that the statute is being too broadly interpreted. The statute, by its language, applies only to subcontractors hired by general contractors. In the case at hand, TI was merely a disclosed agent. TI did not hire SC, SC was not a subcontractor of TI, and TI was not a party to the contract. Therefore, the statute does not apply.

Further counteranalysis may reveal an additional counterargument: the law of agency governs the case rather than the contractor statute. Agency law provides that disclosed agents who are not parties to a contract are not liable for breach of contract. In this case, TI fully disclosed that it was acting only as an agent for SC and, therefore, under the law of agency, is not liable.

This example illustrates the application of two counteranalysis approaches:

- The legal position is based on a misinterpretation of the legislative act.
- Another legal principle governs rather than the act relied on.

Counteranalysis—Reliance on Court Opinion

Customer is suing Bank, claiming that Bank's debt collection calls to his place of employment constitute intentional infliction of emotional distress. The calls were placed daily for a two-week period between 11:00 A.M. and noon. Assume the issue is whether Bank's conduct is "outrageous conduct"—an essential element of intentional infliction of emotional distress.

There are no cases in the jurisdiction addressing the question of whether contact with a debtor at the debtor's place of employment constitutes outrageous conduct. The case of *Tyron v. Bell,* however, involved a case where a bill collector made daily telephone calls for three weeks to a debtor's residence. In that case, the highest court in the jurisdiction ruled that daily calls to a debtor's residence do not constitute outrageous conduct as long as only one telephone call per day is made and the call is placed at a reasonable time—between 8:00 A.M. and 7:00 P.M.

Bank argues that *Bell* is analogous and on point because both cases involve daily telephone calls to a debtor, made at a reasonable time. Relying on this reasoning, Bank contends that its conduct, like the conduct in *Bell,* cannot be considered outrageous.

The counterargument is that the court opinion is clearly distinguishable and, therefore, cannot apply as precedent. Telephone calls to an individual's place of employment are much more threatening than telephone calls to the individual's residence. Telephone calls to the place of employment disrupt the individual's work, interfere with job performance, and disrupt the work of others who have to answer the calls. Such persistent work interruptions can cause the employer to fire the employee. Calls to the workplace are outrageous because they pose a threat to the individual's livelihood. No such threat exists when the calls are to a residence. Therefore, calls to the workplace are clearly distinguishable, and the court opinion is not analogous, is not on point, and does not apply as precedent.

In this example, the counteranalysis challenges reliance on a court opinion by focusing on differences in the key facts of the opinion and the case. The counterargument is based on a commonsense comparison of the facts of *Bell* and the facts of the client's case. This comparison leads to the conclusion that the key facts are so different that *Bell* cannot apply as precedent. Whenever your legal position or argument is based on a court opinion, be sure to conduct a counteranalysis of the position using all the approaches presented in this chapter as well as any other approach that comes to mind. It is also helpful to refer to Chapters 5 and 8 when dealing with key facts and determining if a case is on point.

SUMMARY

Counteranalysis is the process of discovering and presenting the counterarguments to a legal position or argument. It is important because to be able to adequately address a legal problem, all aspects of the problem must be considered. This includes identifying all the potential weaknesses in a legal position and being prepared to respond to all challenges to the position.

Counteranalysis should be employed whenever you are researching a legal issue or addressing a legal problem. You should always be alert and look for counterarguments.

A prerequisite to engaging in counteranalysis is thorough research of the question or legal argument. This may help you identify some counterarguments and give credence to or dismiss those already identified. Once the research is complete, there are many approaches that may be employed to assist you in counteranalysis.

Since most legal arguments are based on enacted law or court opinions, this chapter focuses on various counterarguments that may be raised when attacking reliance on an enacted law or court opinion. The list of approaches presented in this chapter is by no means inclusive of all the available ways to challenge a legal argument or position. It is important to make sure that you engage in counteranalysis using *all* the avenues listed (and any other approach) when looking for potential weaknesses in or counterarguments to a legal position. You can count on the opposing side to discover weaknesses in your position and use them against you. Remember, whenever you are reviewing your client's case in regard to addressing a legal issue, you are negligent if you fail to engage in counteranalysis.

EXERCISES

ASSIGNMENT 1
List seven ways to challenge an argument based on an enacted law.

ASSIGNMENT 2
List seven ways to challenge an argument based on a court opinion.

ASSIGNMENT 3

Counteranalysis—Legal Position or Argument Based on a Statute

Legislative Act: Section 40-3-6-9A of the state criminal code provides that a noncustodial parent can be convicted of custodial interference when the noncustodial parent "maliciously takes, detains, conceals, entices away, or fails to return the child, without good cause, for a protracted period of time."

Assume there is no case law on point in the jurisdiction relevant to the following fact situation.

Facts: Mary has primary custody of her son. The father, Tom, has legal custody for two months in the summer. Tom takes the son for two months in the summer but fails to tell Mary where the son is and does not allow her to communicate with him. Before he leaves with the son, Tom tells Mary, "I'm going to punish you for the way you've treated me."

Assignment: The following are arguments presented by Mary in support of her claim that Tom is in violation of the statute. What are the counterarguments to each argument?

Part A

Tom's actions constitute concealment within the meaning of the statute.

Part B

Same facts as above, but when Tom is leaving, he says, "Since you wouldn't allow me to communicate with him when you had custody, I'm going to do the same." Mary argues that Tom's actions constitute concealment.

Part C

Same facts except that Tom says nothing when he picks up the son.

Part D

Tom allows the son to communicate with Mary, but he returns the son one day late. Mary argues that this constitutes failing to return the child without good cause for a protracted period of time.

Part E

Same facts as in part D except that Tom returns the son two weeks late.

Part F

Same facts as in part E except that Tom explains that he was unable to return the son on time because his car engine blew up, and it took two weeks to fix it.

ASSIGNMENT 4

Counteranalysis—Legal Position or Argument Based on a Court Opinion

In the following example, assume that the only court opinion that is on point is *United States v. Leon* (see Appendix A).

Facts: Officer Jones submits to Judge Bean a request for a search warrant for the search of Steve's apartment. Officer Jones knows that there is not sufficient probable cause for the issuance of the warrant, but he also knows that Judge Bean is very pro–law enforcement and will most likely issue the warrant anyway. Judge Bean issues the warrant. Officer Jones gives the warrant to other officers and instructs them to execute it. He does not tell them that he knows it is defective because of the lack of probable cause for its issuance. The other officers execute the warrant in the good faith belief that it is valid. Drugs are found, and Steve is charged with possession.

Steve moves for suppression of the evidence, claiming that the search was illegal and the evidence must be excluded under the exclusionary rule. What is the counterargument to the prosecution's position in each of the following situations?

Part A

The prosecution argues that since the officers executing the warrant were acting in the good faith belief that the warrant was valid, *United States v. Leon* governs the case. The good faith exception to the exclusionary rule applies and, therefore, the evidence should not be suppressed.

Part B

Same facts as above except that officer Jones delivers the warrant to members of the Citizens Protection Association, a private group of citizens trained by the police to assist in the performance of minor police functions. The group volunteers its services and is not employed by the police. They execute the warrant and make a citizen's arrest of Steve. The prosecution argues that *United States v. Leon* governs, and the case holds that the exclusionary rule is designed only to protect against police misconduct, not misconduct by private citizens.

ASSIGNMENT 5

Legislative Act: Section 41-1-6-9 of the state statutes defines defamation as the intentional publication of a false statement about a person. The statute defines publication as communication to a third person.

Case Law: *Ender v. Gault* is an opinion of the highest court in the state. In the case, Gault wrote a letter to Ender accusing Ender of defrauding his clients. Gault intended to hand-deliver the letter to Ender at a party at Ender's house. Gault became intoxicated at the party and left the letter on Ender's kitchen table. The letter was in an unsealed envelope with Ender's name on it. A business competitor of Ender who was at the party opened and read the letter.

Ender sued Gault for defamation. In its ruling in favor of Ender, the court stated that *"intentional publication"* as used in the statute includes publication that occurs as a result of the gross negligence of the defendant." The court held that Gault's act of leaving the envelope unsealed on the kitchen table during a party constituted gross negligence.

Facts: Tom is a business associate of Allen. He believes Allen is stealing from their clients. Tom writes a letter to Allen stating that he knows Allen is stealing and that he intends to file criminal charges.

Tom, intending to hand-deliver the letter to Allen, goes to a restaurant where Allen usually has lunch. After waiting an hour for Allen, one of Allen's friends enters the restaurant. Tom folds the letter and seals it with scotch tape. He gives the letter to the friend and asks him to deliver it to Allen. He does not tell the friend not to open the letter. The friend peels back the tape, reads the letter, reseals it and delivers it to Allen. Allen finds out that the friend read the letter and sues Tom for defamation under section 41-1-6-9.

Assignment: Take into consideration the statute, the court opinion, and the facts when doing the following.

Part A

Prepare an argument in support of the position that Tom defamed Allen.

Part B

Prepare a counterargument to the argument prepared in part A.

PART III

Legal Writing

CHAPTER 10

Legal Writing Process General Considerations

For the past five years, Rick Strong has been the paralegal for Sara Fletcher, a criminal defense attorney. Rick performs a wide range of paralegal tasks for Sara. He interviews clients and witnesses, conducts legal investigations, arranges and maintains client files, conducts legal research, and occasionally prepares legal memorandums.

Rick enjoys legal research and determining the answers to legal questions. He dreads the actual writing process, the assembly of the research and analysis into a written format.

Sara has just been retained by Carol Beck to represent her in the case of *State v. Carol Beck*. In the case, police officers obtained a search warrant from a magistrate court judge authorizing a search of Ms. Beck's house for drugs. On the bottom of the warrant, the judge wrote, "Unannounced entry is authorized to ensure officer safety." When the officers obtained the warrant, they told the judge that in other drug search cases, if the officers announced their presence prior to entry, the persons occupying the premises being searched often posed a threat to the officers. Based on this statement, the judge authorized the officers to enter Ms. Beck's house unannounced. When the officers executed the warrant, they did not announce their presence and purpose prior to entry. Their search recovered a plastic bag containing an ounce of cocaine. Carol Beck was charged with possession with intent to distribute.

Sara and Rick have just begun the preliminary stages of preparing Ms. Beck's defense. Rick's assignment is to prepare a legal memorandum addressing the possibility of obtaining a suppression of the evidence on the basis that the search was illegal. Sara tells Rick that any suppression motion must be filed in thirty days. What is the process Rick should follow when preparing the memorandum? The legal writing process is presented in this chapter. The answer to Rick's question is discussed in the Application section of the chapter.

INTRODUCTION

The focus of Part III of this text is on legal writing and the legal writing process, including:

- General writing considerations
- Legal writing style
- Interoffice legal memorandum
- External memorandum
- Correspondence

This chapter presents a collection of general considerations involved in legal writing, including an approach to the writing process and guidelines to follow when engaging in the process.

The legal issue raised by the facts of a client's case must be researched and analyzed and the results communicated, usually in written form. Legal research, analysis, and writing are all related. Each is a step in a process designed to answer legal questions and lead to the resolution of disputes. Legal writing is the last step: the step where the research and analysis are assembled in a written form designed to concisely record and communicate the answer to a legal question or questions.

For various reasons, many people believe that most legal communication is oral and takes place either in the courtroom or in a law office. This is not the case, however. The bulk of legal communication is written. The vast majority of cases never go to trial. They are settled, and the settlements are reduced to writing. When cases do go to trial, much of the trial work involves writing: written motions, trial briefs, jury instructions, and so on. In many instances, the practice of law engaged in by law firms rarely involves litigation but instead focuses on the preparation of contracts, wills, corporation instruments, and other legal documents. A great deal of time is spent in research and in communicating that research in the form of legal memorandums and legal instruments.

IMPORTANCE OF WRITING SKILLS

There are several reasons why it is critically important for a paralegal to possess good writing skills. The following are some of the major reasons:

In many instances, paralegals spend most of their time engaged in legal writing in one form or another. A paralegal possessing good writing skills can produce a finished product in a shorter time than an individual who does not possess such skills. This results in greater productivity, which enhances the value of the paralegal to the law firm.

The quality of a written product is based on writing skill. The greater the skill, the greater the quality of the product. Part of a paralegal's job evaluation may be based on the quality of the paralegal's written product. In addition, a written product that leaves the firm, such as correspondence to a client, represents the law firm. A shoddy product reflects poorly on the firm's reputation.

Legal research and analysis are meaningless if the results cannot be clearly and concisely communicated. The goal of a legal research memorandum is to inform and record information. A paralegal who does not possess good writing skills may not be able to fulfill this goal.

Poor writing skills also may lead to miscommunication. A paralegal may intend the writing to convey a certain meaning when, in fact, it literally conveys a different meaning. This may lead to disaster if the supervising attorney relies on the literal meaning and commits an error. Correspondence to a client may be so unclear that the client does not understand the communication.

For Example: The written communication reads, "Individuals who file with the court promptly receive consideration." This is ambiguous. Does it mean that individuals who file promptly with the court receive redress, or does it mean that those who file with the court will receive prompt redress?

GOAL OF LEGAL WRITING

Before presenting the considerations involved in the legal writing process, it is important to identify the goal of legal writing. Law offices are busy places, and the reader of a paralegal's work product is usually a busy person who does not have time to wade through flowery prose, extraneous or unclear material, or general rambling. The primary goal of legal writing, therefore, should be to clearly, concisely, and completely convey legal information in a manner that accomplishes both of the following:

- Fully addresses the topic in as few words as possible
- Allows the reader to gain a clear understanding of the information in as little time as possible

You may feel that you do not possess good writing skills or that you do not have the capability of clearly, concisely, and completely conveying information in a written form. Writing may be a struggle for you. Writing skills can be developed and writing made easier through practice and the use of a *writing process.*

LEGAL WRITING PROCESS

legal writing process
A systematic approach to legal writing. An organized approach to legal research, analysis, and writing. It is composed of three stages: prewriting, writing, and postwriting.

A writing process helps you develop writing skills. It makes legal writing easier and is necessary for several additional reasons, which are discussed in the following text.

Legal writing is highly organized and structured. The organized structure helps ensure that complex subject matter is clearly communicated.

For Example: The IRAC (Issue, Rule, Analysis, Conclusion) analytical method discussed in Chapter 2 is a structured approach to problem solving. The IRAC format, when followed in the preparation of a legal memorandum, helps ensure the clear communication of the complex subject matter of legal issue analysis.

The use of a legal writing process helps you conduct research and analysis within the structure and format of the type of legal writing assigned. A writing process saves time by providing the means for the organization of your legal analysis and research material as it is gathered.

If you do not have a writing process and merely gather research material and immediately begin to write, a great deal of time will be wasted. You are not ready to write. If you begin to write without having organized your research and analysis, or without having thought through what you are going to write, you will flounder. If you have gathered a mountain of research that requires a great deal of analysis, time will be wasted in the struggle to determine what goes where and how. A writing process forces you to think before you write. It forces you to follow an organized structure from the beginning. When you sit down to write, you will be ready. The project will have been thought through and organized.

When you are researching or analyzing an assignment or engaging in legal writing, a writing process helps you capture ideas as they come to you. A process provides a framework for capturing ideas and recording them in their proper place as they occur. Without a process, ideas may be lost. This is discussed in the Use of an Outline subsection of this chapter.

A writing process also helps you overcome difficult areas. You may get stuck in a difficult analytical area or encounter writer's block. A writing process helps you avoid these problems by providing a stepped approach. Often you become stuck or blocked because you have missed a step or left something out. A process is a guide that includes all the steps and helps ensure that nothing is left out.

This section presents a general overview of the writing process and discusses matters that should be considered at each stage of the process. There are many different processes and combinations of processes that may be adopted when engaging in legal writing. What works for one person may not work for another. You may ultimately adopt a process that includes steps from various approaches to legal writing, including some of those presented in this chapter. It does not matter what process you ultimately adopt, but it is essential that you adopt some writing process.

The process of legal writing consists of the three basic stages presented in Figure 10–1. Each of these stages is discussed in the following sections. A prerequisite to the first stage, to the beginning of any writing process, is the assembly of all available information concerning the case.

For Example: Suppose the assignment is to prepare an office legal memorandum addressing the question of when the statute of limitations runs in a client's medical malpractice case. All information concerning the case should be gathered before you begin. This includes the client's file, depositions, interrogatories, witness interviews, any other discovery information, and so on.

Prewriting Stage

Novice writers often begin to write without being adequately prepared. One of the most important aspects of the writing process is the performance of the steps necessary to become adequately prepared to begin. Drafting is made much easier if you are fully prepared when you begin to write. This stage of the writing process may be divided into the three sections presented in Figure 10–2.

prewriting stage
The stage in the legal writing process where the assignment is organized, researched, and analyzed.

Assignment

The writing process begins with an identification of the type and purpose of the assignment. There are three questions that must be considered when reviewing the assignment:

- *Is the assignment clearly understood?*
- *What type of legal writing (document) is required?*
- *Who is the audience?*

Is the Assignment Clearly Understood? You may receive the assignment in the form of a written memorandum or through oral instructions from the supervising attorney. An early and important step in the prewriting stage is to be sure that you understand

- Prewriting Stage
- Writing Stage
- Postwriting Stage

Figure 10–1
Stages of the Legal Writing Process

Figure 10–2
Sections of the Prewriting Stage

1. *Assignment.* An identification of the type and purpose of the writing assignment
2. *Constraints.* A consideration of any constraints placed on the assignment
3. *Organization.* The organization of the writing assignment

the task you have been assigned. If you have any questions concerning the general nature or specifics of the assignment, ask.

A misunderstanding of the assignment can result in a great deal of time being wasted in the performance of the wrong task. Most attorneys welcome inquiries and prefer that a paralegal ask questions rather than proceed in a wrong direction. In this regard, if the assignment is unclear in any way, summarize the assignment orally with the attorney. Another approach could be to draft a brief recapitulation of the assignment and submit it for the attorney's review and signature.

What Type of Legal Writing (Document) Is Required? The next step is to determine the type of legal writing the assignment requires. This is important because each type of legal writing has a different function and different requirements. Before you begin, you must know what form of legal writing is required.

There are various types of legal writing and numerous ways to categorize the types. The focus of this text is on legal research and analysis and the types of writing related to legal research and analysis, such as the following.

Law Office Legal Research and Analysis Memorandums. A paralegal may be assigned the task of researching and analyzing the law that applies to a client's case. The law office legal memorandum is designed to inform the reader of the results of the research and analysis. The assignment may be as simple as identification of the statutory or case law that applies to a legal issue or as complex as identification of the issues in a case and analysis of the law that applies. The preparation of a law office legal memorandum is discussed in Chapters 12 and 13.

Correspondence. There are several types of correspondence that a paralegal may be required to draft: demand letters, settlement proposals, notices of events such as hearing dates, and so on. The assignment may require the preparation of the draft of a letter to be sent to the client informing the client of the law that applies in the client's case and how the law applies. A paralegal cannot give legal advice to the client, but the paralegal may prepare the draft of the correspondence that the attorney will send to the client. Legal correspondence is addressed in Chapter 15.

Court Briefs. A court brief is a document filed with a court that contains an attorney's legal argument and the legal authority in support of that argument. There are primarily two categories of court briefs: trial court briefs and appellate court briefs.

1. *Trial Court Briefs.* A court may require an attorney to submit a brief in support of a position taken by an attorney in regard to a legal issue in the case. A trial court brief is usually submitted in support of or in opposition to a motion filed with the court.

For Example: An attorney files a motion to dismiss a complaint, claiming that the statute of limitations has run. In support of the motion, the attorney files a legal brief that contains the legal and factual reasons why the court should grant the motion. The opposing side will also file a brief in opposition to the granting of the motion.

2. *Appellate Court Briefs.* An appellate brief is a formal document filed with an appellate court. It presents the legal arguments and authorities in support of the client's position on appeal. It is designed to persuade the appellate court to rule in the client's favor.

Court briefs are discussed in detail in Chapter 14.

Each of these types of legal writing is structured differently. The organization of and considerations involved in the drafting of these documents vary. The subsequent stages of the writing process are governed by an initial determination of the type of legal writing the assignment requires. Therefore, an early step in the prewriting stage is the identification of the type of writing required.

Other types of legal writing may involve the drafting of legal documents such as contracts, wills, pleadings, and so on. The specific considerations involved in the drafting of these documents are not addressed in this text. The writing process presented in this chapter, however, may be followed when preparing such documents.

Who Is the Audience? An important step when assessing the requirements of an assignment is to identify the intended audience. Inasmuch as the goal of legal writing is to clearly communicate information to the reader, it is necessary to ensure that the writing is crafted in a manner suited to meet the needs of the reader.

Legal writing assignments may be designed to reach a number of different audiences. The intended reader may be a judge, an attorney, a client, or some other person. The ability of the reader to understand the writing will depend on the legal sophistication of the reader and the manner in which the document is written. A legal writing designed to inform a client or other layperson of the legal analysis of an issue is drafted differently than a writing designed to convey the same information to an attorney. The use of fundamental legal terminology may be appropriate when the writing is to be read by a person trained in the law. On the other hand, if the reader has little or no legal training, it may be necessary to use nonlegal terms to clearly convey the same information.

For Example: Communication to the supervising attorney: "The motion to suppress the evidence should be granted. Exigent circumstances that would have justified an unannounced entry were not present at the time the officers executed the warrant, and the judge who issued the search warrant did not authorize unannounced entry."

Communication of the same information to the client: "The court may not allow the prosecution to use at trial the evidence seized when the officers searched your house. The law requires officers to announce their presence before they enter your house to conduct a search. They are required to do this unless a judge gives them permission to enter without first announcing their presence. They may also enter unannounced if, when they arrive at your house, they believe that you are destroying evidence or present a danger to them. In your case, the judge did not authorize the officers to enter unannounced and nothing occurred when they arrived at your house to indicate you were destroying drugs or you were a threat to them."

Another factor to consider is whether the writing is intended solely for internal office use. A writing that will be read only by individuals working in the office may contain information, comments, or assessments that would not be included in a writing intended to be read outside the office.

For Example: "After analyzing the facts of the client's case and the applicable law, it may be necessary to convince the client to reconsider the amount of damages he believes he is entitled to recover and the possibility of settling this case. He needs to be informed about the amount of damages he can realistically expect to receive. He is adamant in his belief that he is entitled to over one million dollars, and he is not willing to consider settling for less. The range of recovery is more likely between ten thousand and one hundred thousand dollars."

The audience must be identified in order to ensure that the legal communication is crafted in a manner commensurate with the ability of the reader to understand the contents.

Constraints

The next step in the prewriting process is to consider any possible constraints that may affect the performance of the assignment. Three major constraints that should be considered are presented in Figure 10–3.

Time. The performance of an assignment may be governed by a time constraint. Most assignments have a deadline. You must determine what the deadline is. Once this is done, allocate a specific amount of time to each stage of the writing process.

For Example: Suppose you have fifteen days to write a legal research memorandum on an issue in a case. You should allocate your time among the prewriting, writing, and postwriting stages of the writing process. A possible allocation could be six days for prewriting, five days for drafting, and four days for postwriting.

If you fail to allocate your time or fail to stick to the allocation, you may become absorbed or stuck in one stage and fail to leave enough time to properly complete the assignment. It does no good to completely research and analyze an issue if you do not have time to translate the research and analysis into a written form.

For Example: You may have fifteen days to prepare an office memorandum. You become absorbed in the intricacies of the research and leave only two days to write the memo. This is not sufficient time to prepare a well-crafted product. The memorandum will either not be turned in on time, or be poorly written. In either event, your professional reputation is negatively affected.

Length. The assignment may have a length constraint. The supervising attorney may require that it not exceed a certain number of pages. If this is the case, the length limitation should be kept in mind from the start. The amount of research material you gather is affected by this limitation. Of course, you must gather all the applicable law. You must, however, screen the research to ensure that you do not gather excessive information. With the space limitation in mind, consider how much of the material that you are gathering can be included in the writing. Also, organize the writing to make sure that each section is allotted sufficient space.

For Example: The assignment is to prepare a legal research memorandum that does not exceed fifteen pages. The organization must allocate sufficient space for each section of the memorandum. If the analysis ends up consisting of fourteen pages, there will not be sufficient space for the statement of the facts, the issue, or the conclusion.

Format. Most law offices have rules or guidelines that govern the organization and format of most types of legal writing, such as case briefs, office memorandums, and correspondence. Courts have formal rules governing the format and style of briefs and other documents submitted for filing.

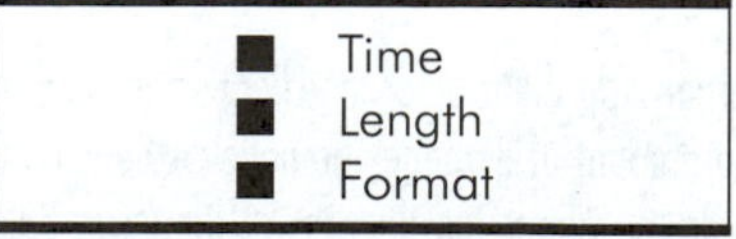

Figure 10–3
Constraints on the Writing Process

For Example: Many courts have rules governing the size of the paper, the size of the margins, the length of briefs, and so on.

Inasmuch as the assignment must be drafted within the constraints of the required format, that format must be identified at the beginning of the prewriting process.

Organization

Organization in the prewriting stage is the key to successful legal writing. You must be organized when conducting research and analysis in the prewriting stage, and the assignment must be organized when it is written. This may be accomplished through the development and use of an outline. An outline is the skeletal structure and organizational framework of the legal writing. Three aspects of outlines are presented here:

- *The value of an outline*
- *The creation of an outline*
- *The use of an outline*

outline
The skeletal structure and organizational framework of a writing.

Value of an Outline. An outline is usually considered useful in the writing stage. It makes writing easier by providing an organized framework for the presentation of research and analysis. An outline, however, is of *greatest value* when properly used in the prewriting stage. There are several reasons for this:

- The act of creating an outline causes you to organize ideas and prepare an approach to the assignment at the beginning of the process. This helps you to think through all the aspects of the assignment and take a global view and thereby avoid gaps and weaknesses in your approach. You focus your attention and organize your thinking before you jump into the assignment.
- An outline provides an organized framework for the structure of the assignment and for conducting research and analysis. It provides a context within which to place research and ideas as they are found. This use will be discussed in detail below in the Use of an Outline subsection.
- An outline breaks complex problems into manageable components. It provides an organized framework from which to approach complex problems.

Creation of an Outline. The goal when creating an outline is to prepare the skeletal framework of the document you are going to draft. The outline should provide an overall picture of how all the pieces of the assignment relate to each other and fit together. The form of the outline is not important. Whether you use roman numerals (I and II), capital letters (A and B), narrative sentences, fragments of sentences, or single words does not matter. Use whatever form or style works for you. It is recommended that you do use indentations to separate main topics from subtopics.

For Example:

I. Introduction
II. Issue
III. Analysis
  A. Rule of law
  B. Case law
    1. Name of case
    2. Facts of case

The outline of the legal writing is governed by the type of writing you are preparing. Locate the standard format used in the office for the type of legal writing you are preparing. In the case of an office legal memorandum or correspondence, the law office may have a special format that must be followed. Use that format as the basis for the outline. If the writing is to be filed in court, such as an appellate brief, follow the format set out in the court rules. Whatever the basic format is, it may be necessary to make additions and expand the outline.

For Example: Assume the firm's format for an office legal memorandum is:

1. Description of assignment
2. Issue
3. Facts
4. Analysis
5. Conclusion

This is a broad format that needs a lot of filling in to be useful. It may be necessary to fill in details for each section.

For Example: An expansion of the analysis section may be as follows:

4. Analysis
   1. Introduction
   2. Rule of law
   3. Case interpreting the rule of law
      a. Name of case/citation
      b. Facts of case
      c. Rule of law or legal principle presented in the case that applies to the client's facts
      d. Application of rule/principle from the case to the client's facts

This outline example is referred to in this chapter as the analysis outline example.

When developing an outline, there are several points to keep in mind. These are discussed in the following text.

Keep the facts and issues of the assignment in mind while developing the outline. It may be necessary to expand the outline to accommodate additional facts and issues.

For Example: The standard office outline may have only one issue. Your assignment may involve more than one issue. Your outline should be expanded to apply the standard office outline to each issue.

Be flexible when creating and working with an outline. Realize that it may be necessary to change the outline as you conduct research.

For Example: Assume the assignment involves the drafting of a simple office legal memorandum that addresses one issue. The outline you decide to follow is the analysis outline example presented above. When research is conducted, it becomes apparent that there are two aspects of the rule of law that apply to the issue and two court opinions that need to be included in the analysis. The memo outline must now be expanded:

4. Analysis
   1. Introduction
   2. Rule of law
   3. Case interpreting the meaning of *publication* as used in the rule of law
      a. Name of case/citation
      b. Facts of case
      c. Interpretation of term
      d. Application of the interpretation to the client's facts

4. Case interpreting the meaning of *written* as used in the rule of law
   a. Name of case/citation
   b. Facts of case
   c. Interpretation of term
   d. Application of the interpretation to the client's facts

Do not be surprised if it is necessary to reorganize the outline as a result of your research. Research may provide a clearer picture of the relationship between issues and necessitate a rethinking of the organization of the outline.

For Example: As a result of your research, you may realize that the sequence in which you plan to address the issues should be changed. The issue you thought should be discussed first should come second.

The basic organizational format for most legal writing is the IRAC format. That is, first state the question or issue, next identify the rule of law that governs the issue, then analyze how and why the rule applies, and end with a conclusion summarizing the analysis. This format may be followed when addressing each issue and subissue. If for some reason you are at a loss for a format to follow, the IRAC format can be used. It is discussed in detail in Chapters 2, 12, and 13.

Include in the outline a reference to or some notation for transition sentences. Transition sentences connect the major sections of the writing and lead the reader smoothly through the legal analysis. They make the document more readable. It is easy to become so focused on the law, cases, and analysis that you forget the transitions.

For Example: "The rule of law that governs this issue is § 36-6-6, which prohibits oppressive conduct by majority shareholders. In the case of *Jones v. Thomas,* the court held. . . ." There should be a transition sentence linking the case to the rule of law: "The rule of law that governs this issue is § 36-6-6, which prohibits oppressive conduct by majority shareholders. *Since the statute does not provide a definition of the term* oppressive conduct, *case law must be referred to. A case on point is* Jones v. Thomas where the court held. . . ."

Outline formats for correspondence, office legal memorandums, and court briefs are presented in Chapters 12 through 14.

Use of an Outline. The value of an outline is determined by its use. If you prepare an outline and then set it aside while you are researching and analyzing the assignment, it is of limited value. Its only value when used in this manner is to help organize your thinking and provide the organizational framework for the writing that follows. An outline is of greatest value when it is actively integrated into the prewriting stage. It can serve as an *invaluable guide* during the research and analysis process.

For Example: Follow the outline format when researching and analyzing: first identify the issue, next locate the rule of law that governs the issue, then identify the case law that interprets the rule of law in a fact situation similar to the client's case, and so on.

When integrated in the research and analysis process, an outline provides an organized context within which to place research and ideas. When so used, it will result in the development of a rough draft while research and analysis are being conducted. The result is a tremendous savings of time and effort. *The integrated use of an outline in the prewriting stage simplifies the writing stage and makes it much easier.*

How, then, is an outline integrated into the research and analysis process—the prewriting stage? There are several ways this may be accomplished. The practical approach suggested here is to use an expanded outline. This approach is composed of the two steps presented in Figure 10–4.

Figure 10–4

Two-Step Approach for Use of an Outline in the Prewriting Stage

Step 1	Convert the outline to a usable form—an expanded outline.
Step 2	Integrate all research, analysis, and ideas into the outline while research and analysis are being conducted.

Assume for discussion purposes that you are assigned the task of preparing an office legal memorandum addressing a single issue in a client's case. The cause of action is a slander tort claim. The broad issue is whether there was publication within the meaning of the law. Section 20-2-2 of the state statutes provides that civil slander is "the oral publication of a false statement of fact concerning an individual. . . ." The statute does not define *publication*. The facts of the case are that neighbor *A*, while visiting neighbor *B's* house, communicated to neighbor *B* a false statement of fact concerning the client. This example is referred to in this chapter as the slander example.

The format for the body of an office legal memorandum adopted in the office is as follows:

I. Issue
II. Statement of facts
III. Analysis/application
  1. Rule of law—the rule of law that governs the issue—enacted/common law
  2. Case(s)—court interpretation of rule if necessary
    A. Name and citation
    B. Brief summary of facts showing case is on point
    C. Rule/principle/reasoning applied by the court that applies to client's case
    D. Application—discussion of how the rule of law presented in the court decision applies in the client's case
  3. Counteranalysis
IV. Conclusion—a summary of the analysis

outline--expanded
An outline that has been expanded so that it may be used in the prewriting stage. The use of an expanded outline allows the integration of all research, analysis, and ideas into an organized outline structure while research and analysis are being conducted. It facilitates the preparation of a rough draft.

Step 1 Convert the outline to a usable form—an expanded outline. The memorandum format used in the office is typed on one page of paper and is not very useful in this form. The first step in the use of the outline is to convert it to a usable form—to expand the outline. This is accomplished by taking several sheets of three-holed or binder paper, or creating separate pages if you are using a computer, and writing the name of each section and subsection of the outline at the top of a separate page.

For Example: At the top of one sheet of paper or computer page, write the word *Issue.* At the top of another page, write *Statement of facts.* At the top of another page, write *Analysis—rule of law.* Continue with a new page for each of the following: *Analysis—case, Analysis—application of case to client's facts, Counteranalysis,* and *Conclusion.*

Some sections of the outline may require more than one page.

For Example: The *Analysis—case* section may require two pages: one page for *Analysis—case—citation and facts of case* and one page for *Analysis—case—rule/principle/reasoning.* Two or more pages may be required for a case because, in many instances, a great deal of information may be taken from a case, such as lengthy quotes from the court's reasoning.

If more than one rule of law applies, there should be a separate page for each rule of law. If several cases apply, there are separate pages for each case. If there are separate issues, each issue should be researched and analyzed separately, and there should be a separate expanded outline for each issue.

When completed, there should be a separate page for each section and subsection of the outline. The pages should be placed in a loose-leaf binder or entered in the computer in the order of the outline. In other words, the first page will be the Issue page, followed by the Statement of facts page, then the Analysis—rule of law, page, and so on. If you are using binder paper, blank sheets of paper should be inserted between each section. This allows for the expansion of each section to accommodate additional notes, comments, ideas, and so on. The end result is a greatly expanded outline that is usable in the prewriting stage.

Step 2 Integrate all research, analysis, and ideas into the outline while research and analysis are being conducted. As research is conducted and ideas occur concerning any aspect of the case, they should be entered on the appropriate page of the expanded outline.

Ideas. When any idea occurs concerning the case, it should be entered on the page of the expanded outline that relates to that idea.

For Example: In the slander example, you may have a broad definition of the issue such as "Was there publication?" As research is conducted and more thought is given to the case, more refined formulations of the issue will become apparent, such as: "Under § 20-2-2, does slander occur when one person orally communicates to a third party false statements of fact concerning an individual?" As soon as this formulation of the issue comes to you, it should be written on the issue page. When it comes time to write the memorandum, there will be multiple versions of the issue listed on the issue page. When all the ideas concerning the issue are in one place, it is easier to assemble the final statement of the issue.

The term *ideas* as used here includes all thoughts relating to the writing of the assignment, such as how transition sentences should be composed.

For Example: While researching a case, an idea may come to you about how the transition sentence linking the case to the rule of law should be written. Write the sentence in the beginning of the case section of the expanded outline or at the end of the rule of law page.

Keep the expanded outline with you at all times, even when you go home. Often the mind will work on an aspect of a case during sleep. You may wake up in the middle of the night or in the morning with an idea concerning the assignment or the answer to a problem. If the expanded outline is handy, you can immediately enter the idea or answer in the appropriate section.

The value of the ability to immediately place ideas where they belong in the structure of the writing cannot be overemphasized. The following are some of the benefits.

- Ideas are not lost. When researching, you often may have an idea and say to yourself, "I'll remember to include this when I write the ______ section." Five minutes later, the idea is lost. If you can immediately write the idea down where it belongs, it will not be lost.
- Confusion is avoided if ideas are recorded in the section where they will appear in the writing.

  For Example: While you are reading a case that interprets the rule of law, an idea may occur that relates to another aspect of the assignment, such as, "This gives me an idea about the counteranalysis of this issue." You may jot the idea down on a separate piece of paper or think you will remember it. You say to yourself, "I'll remember to include this when I write the counteranalysis."

By the time you get down to writing, time has passed, and you cannot remember what the idea was or, if you jotted it down, where the idea fits into the assignment. There are several pieces of paper with notes and ideas, many of which you have forgotten what they relate to or why.

If you keep the binder with the expanded outline with you throughout the prewriting stage, and all ideas are placed where they belong as they come to you, confusion is avoided and time is not lost figuring out what ideas go where.

- Writing is made easier. When you sit down to write, all ideas are there, each in its proper place. Time is not wasted in performing the additional step of organizing ideas. Ideas are automatically organized as they come to you.

  For Example: If the issue page of the expanded outline contains all the ideas concerning the ways the issue may be stated, it is easier to craft the final draft of the issue. Visually before you in one place are all the possible variations. Drafting the issue is just a matter of assembling the issue from the best of the variations.

Research. Just as ideas are placed in the proper place in the expanded outline as they occur, all the relevant research should be entered in the appropriate page as research is conducted.

For Example: Referring to the slander example, when the slander statute, § 20-2-2, is located, it should be placed on the rule of law page. This should include the proper citation and a copy of the statute. All the information concerning the statute that you may need when writing should be included in the outline on this page. This avoids having to look up the statute more than once.

For Example: When the case or cases on point are found, the information concerning the case should be entered on the appropriate case page of the outline. This should include information such as the full citation, pertinent quotes concerning the rule of law or legal principle applied by the court, and the legal reasoning.

When researching case law, retrieve everything you may need from the case and include it in the expanded outline as you read the case. Why waste time looking up the same case twice? Place a copy of the case in the outline if necessary.

For Example: First, read through the entire case. Then, on the second reading, as you come upon a statement of the legal principle or legal reasoning that may apply to the client's case, *stop reading.* Enter the information from the case in the appropriate page of the expanded outline. Indicate the page of the case from which it was taken and, if appropriate, quote the information.

All too often the tendency when reading a case for the second time is to tell yourself that you will come back later and note the pertinent information. If there is any possibility that you will use information from a case, retrieve it as you find it and place on the appropriate case page of the outline. You will save time by not having to reread portions of the case.

Often the reasoning or rule you want to use is not where you remembered, and time is wasted wading through the case trying to relocate it. If it turns out that information retrieved will not be used in the legal writing, it is simply not used. It is much better to have everything concerning the case in your expanded outline when you sit down to write than to have to stop, retrieve, and reread the case.

If you use an expanded outline as suggested here, you are ready to write. All your research and ideas are assembled and organized. In effect, you have prepared a rough draft, and the writing task is made much simpler: the organization is done, the research is assembled in its proper place, and many transition sentences are already crafted and in place. The writing task is reduced to simply converting the outline to paragraph and sentence form.

Writing Stage

The second stage in the writing process is the actual drafting of the legal writing. Many individuals find it difficult to go from the research stage to the drafting stage, from the prewriting stage to the writing stage. This is often called "writer's block." Some of the obstacles that often make it difficult to begin writing are organizing the research and determining what goes where and how it relates and is connected. If you use an expanded outline in the prewriting stage, it is much easier to begin writing. The research and analysis is already organized, the relationship of the material is already established by the outline, and many introductory and transitional sentences have been written.

writing stage
The stage in the legal writing process where research, analysis, and ideas are assembled into a written product.

Rules and guidelines that govern the style and content of legal writing are presented in the next chapter. A detailed discussion of what must be included when writing an office legal memorandum, court brief, or legal correspondence is included in Chapters 12 through 15. Some rules and guidelines that help with the writing process in general are presented here.

Prepare the writing location. Make sure the work environment is pleasant and physically comfortable. Have available all the resources you need, such as paper, computer, research materials, and so on.

Write during the time of day when you do your best work.

For Example: If you are a "morning person," write in the morning and save other tasks for later in the day.

Limit interruptions. Legal writing requires focus and concentration. Therefore, select a writing time and environment that allows you to be as free from interruptions and distractions as possible.

Begin writing; do not procrastinate. Often one of the most difficult steps is beginning. Do not put it off. The longer you put it off, the harder beginning will become. Start writing anything that has to do with the project. Do not expect what you start with to be great, just start. Once you begin writing, it will get easier.

Begin with a part of the assignment you feel most confident about. You do not have to write in the sequence of the outline. Write the easiest material first, especially if you are having trouble starting.

Do not try to make the first draft the final draft. The goal of the first draft should be to translate the research and analysis into organized paragraphs and sentences, not to produce a finished product. Just write the information in rough form. It is much easier to polish a rough draft than to try to make the first draft a finished product.

Do not begin to write until you are prepared. Do all the research and analysis before beginning. It is much easier to write a rough draft if the prewriting stage is thoroughly completed.

If you become stuck, move to another part of the assignment. If you are stuck on a particular section, leave it. The mind continues to work on a problem when you are unaware of it. That is why solutions to problems often seem to appear in the morning. Let the subconscious work on the problem while you move on. The solution to the difficulty may become apparent when you return to the problem.

Establish a timetable. Break the project into logical units and allocate your time accordingly. This helps you avoid spending too much time on one section of the writing and running out of time. Do not become fanatical about the time schedule, however. You created the timetable, and you can break it. It is there as a guide to keep you on track and alert you to the overall time constraints.

Postwriting Stage

postwriting stage
The stage in the legal writing process where an assignment is revised, edited, and assembled in final form.

The postwriting stage involves revising and editing the writing developed in the writing stage.

Revising

The first draft will not be the final draft. All initial drafts should be reviewed with the idea of improving quality and clarity. Do not be surprised if the initial draft requires several redrafts. Do not set a limit on the number of redrafts that may be required. The goal should be that the final product will clearly, concisely, and completely convey the information it is designed to convey. The number of redrafts should be governed by this goal. Develop a checklist for use when reviewing a draft. Some items that you may wish to include in the checklist are the following:

1. Is the writing well organized? Is it organized in a logical manner? Does each section logically follow the previous section?
2. Is it written in a manner the audience will understand? If the writing is addressed to a layperson, is the draft written in plain language the reader will understand?
3. Is the writing clear? Does it make sense? Are the sections connected with transition sentences that clearly link the sections and guide the reader from one section to the next?
4. Is the writing concise? Are there extra words that can be eliminated? Is it repetitive? If multiple examples are included to illustrate a single point, are all the examples necessary?
5. Is the writing complete? Are all the aspects of the assignment covered? If there are multiple issues, is each issue and subissue thoroughly analyzed?
6. Are the legal authorities correctly cited? Are all legal citations in the correct form? All legal research sources must be correctly cited. Unless the local court rules or the supervisory attorney's preferences dictate otherwise, proper citation form is governed by *The Bluebook: A Uniform System of Citation. The Bluebook* is published by The Harvard Law Review Association. A brief summary of citation form is presented in Appendix C.

When reviewing a draft, allow time to elapse between drafting and revising. This allows the mind to clear. You will then be able to approach the revision with a fresh perspective and are more likely to catch errors and inconsistencies.

Editing

Editing is actually part of the revision process. The revision process discussed in the previous section addresses the broad intellectual and structural content of the legal writing, such as overall organization, clarity, and conciseness. Editing focuses on technical writing issues, such as punctuation, spelling, grammar, phrasing, typographical errors, and citation errors. Many of these specific areas are discussed in the next chapter. A few general editing tips to keep in mind, however, are the following:

1. Be prepared to edit a legal writing several times. It may be necessary to edit a revision several times to catch all the errors.
2. Read the document out loud. When you silently read your own draft, the mind may automatically fill in a missing word or correct an error without your knowing it, and you will not catch the error. If possible, have a colleague read it to you.
3. Have another person edit the document. Have a colleague whose writing skill you respect edit the document.

GENERAL RESEARCH SUGGESTIONS

Research is a major part of the prewriting stage of the writing process. Although this is not a research text and does not focus on the steps involved in legal research, some general suggestions and guidelines concerning legal research as it relates to the prewriting stage are included in Figure 10–5.

1. *Prepare and use an expanded outline when conducting research.* This is discussed in detail in the Use of an Outline subsection of this chapter.

2. *Identify the issue first.* The first step should be to identify the issue, as you cannot begin to look for an answer until you know the question. The preliminary identification of the issue may be very broad, such as "Did negligence occur?" or "Was there a breach of contract when the goods were delivered ten days late?" This preliminary identification of the issue will usually identify the general area of law to be researched, such as contracts, negligence, and so on.

3. *Research issues one at a time.* Thoroughly research to its conclusion one issue before proceeding to the next issue. If you find material on another issue, note a reference to it on the page in the expanded outline for that issue. Frustration and confusion can result from an attempt to research several issues at once.

4. *Become familiar with the area of law.* If you are unfamiliar with the area of law that applies to the issue, obtain a general overview. Legal encyclopedias and treatises are examples of sources to consult to obtain an overview of an area of law.

5. *Locate the enacted law that governs the question.* Look first for any enacted law that governs the question, such as a statute or constitutional provision.

6. *Locate the common/case law that may apply.* Locate the relevant common/case law if there is no enacted law that governs or if the enacted law is so broadly drafted that case law is required to interpret the enacted law. Mandatory precedent should be located first, then persuasive precedent and secondary authority. Enacted law is discussed in Chapter 3.

7. *Make sure that the research is current.* Check supplements and shepardize cases to be sure that the authority located is current.

1. Prepare and use an expanded outline when conducting research.
2. Identify the issue first.
3. Research issues one at a time.
4. Become familiar with the area of law.
5. Locate the enacted law that governs the question.
6. Locate the common/case law that may apply.
7. Make sure that the research is current.
8. If you reach a dead end, reanalyze the issue.

Figure 10–5

Suggestions and Guidelines—Legal Research and the Prewriting Stage

8. *If you reach a dead end, reanalyze the issue.* If you cannot find any authority, either primary or secondary, chances are the issue is too broadly or too narrowly stated. Restate the issue. If the issue is too broadly stated, restate it in narrower terms. Return to a basic research source for guidance, such as a legal encyclopedia. If the issue is too narrowly framed, restate it in broader terms. Chapters 6 and 7 provide help in regard to identifying and stating issues.

KEY POINTS CHECKLIST: *The Writing Process*

- ❑ Adopt a writing process. An organized approach is essential for legal writing. Develop a process that works for you. Follow the process recommended in this chapter or create your own.
- ❑ Work from an expanded outline in the prewriting stage. An expanded outline provides a framework for organizing your research and capturing your ideas.
- ❑ Consider the audience. Always identify the audience early in the process. The style, depth, and complexity of the finished product is influenced by the type of audience.
- ❑ Consider time, length, and format constraints. Identify any constraints that affect the assignment, and design the approach to the assignment with these constraints in mind.
- ❑ Do not procrastinate. If you have trouble beginning to write, start with the easiest section. Sit down and begin. Do not worry about quality—just start.
- ❑ Break large assignments into manageable sections. Do not become overwhelmed by the complexity of an assignment.
- ❑ Be prepared to compose several drafts. The goal is a quality product. Let the number of redrafts be determined by this goal.
- ❑ Update your research. Check all authority to ensure that it is current.

APPLICATION

This section presents an overview of the writing process through the application of the process to the hypothetical presented at the beginning of the chapter. After gathering and reviewing all the information available in the office concerning Ms. Beck's case, Rick follows the process recommended in this chapter. An outline of Rick's application of the process is as follows.

Prewriting Stage

I. *Assignment.* Rick first reviews the assignment.

A. *Is the assignment clear?* He reviews the assignment to be sure he understands what is required. Rick has no question in this regard. The assignment is to research and analyze the question of whether the evidence seized in the case can be suppressed.

B. *What type of legal writing is required?* The assignment is to draft an office legal memorandum. Rick retrieves the office memorandum outline form used by the firm. The body of the outline is presented here.

I. Issue
II. Statement of facts
III. Analysis/application
1. Rule of law—the rule of law that governs the issue—enacted/common law

2. Case(s)—court interpretation of the rule of law if necessary
   A. Name and citation
   B. Brief summary of facts showing case is on point
   C. Rule/principle/reasoning applied by the court that applies to client's case
   D. Application—discussion of how the rule of law presented in the court decision applies in the client's case
3. Counteranalysis

IV. Conclusion—a summary of the analysis.

C. *Who is the audience?* The memorandum is for office use. Rick knows it does not have to be written in layperson's terms.

II. *Constraints.* What are the constraints on the assignment? Rick has a time constraint. Any motion to suppress the evidence must be filed in thirty days. He must finish the memorandum sufficiently in advance of the thirty days to allow Ms. Fletcher time to review it and prepare the appropriate motion. Based on past experience, he knows Ms. Fletcher prefers to have ten days to review the memorandum and prepare the motion. This leaves him twenty days to complete the assignment.

Rick also knows that Ms. Fletcher prefers shorter memos. She has told him that a single issue memo should not exceed seven pages. He knows he must budget his time and research to meet these constraints.

III. *Organization.* Rick organizes the assignment around the outline.

A. *Creation of expanded outline.* Rick expands the outline as suggested in the Organization subsection of the Prewriting Stage section of this chapter. The initial expanded outline is composed of eight pages of paper or computer pages. The pages are labeled as follows: Issue; Facts; Analysis—rule of law; Analysis—case name, facts, and citation; Analysis—case rule/principle and reasoning; Analysis—application of case to facts; Counteranalysis; and Conclusion.

B. *Use of expanded outline.* Rick begins his research with the expanded outline at hand. He studies the facts and begins to formulate the issue. Every time he thinks of a way to state the issue, he writes it on the issue page.

For Example: The first formulation of the issue is "Can the evidence be suppressed?" Later formulations are "Can evidence be suppressed when officers execute a warrant unannounced based on the warrant's authorization of unannounced entry?" and "Under the state's exclusionary rule, can evidence be suppressed when officers conduct a search unannounced, pursuant to a warrant authorizing unannounced entry to ensure officer safety, and the authorization is based upon an affidavit that gives no particularized facts regarding threats to officer safety?"

As he researches, Rick finds article II, section 5, of the state constitution which prohibits illegal searches and seizures. He copies article II, section 5, and places it on the *Analysis—rule of law page.* He realizes this provision is so broadly formulated that he must locate case law for an interpretation of how it applies in an unannounced entry situation.

While looking for a case on point, he thinks of a transitional sentence that will connect the rule of law section of the memo to the case law section.

For Example: Article II, section 5, does not provide guidance as to what constitutes an illegal search when law enforcement officers enter into a residence unannounced; therefore, case law must be consulted.

Rick immediately writes this sentence at the end of the *Analysis—rule of law* page of the outline.

Rick locates the court opinion of *State v. Brick.* Addressing a fact situation almost identical to Ms. Beck's, the court held that a warrant may authorize unannounced entry. The court went on to state, however, that the authorization must be based on a "particularized showing that the individuals whose residence is being searched have in the past represented a threat to officer safety. Any authorization based upon a generalized statement, such as 'Drug offenders often present a threat to officers' safety during the execution of search warrants,' violates article II, section 5, and the exclusionary rule requires the suppression of any evidence seized."

Rick enters all the relevant information from the case in the appropriate *Analysis—case* pages of the outline. He includes the full citation, any relevant quotations from the case, and the page number references for the quotations. He does not have to reread the case when he writes the memorandum. All the key information is in the expanded outline.

While analyzing the case, he thinks of a sentence he will use when discussing how the case applies to the client's facts. He enters this sentence in the *Analysis—application of case to facts* page of the outline.

For Example: "In our case, just as in *State v. Brick,* the officers executed a warrant unannounced, based on the authorization contained in the warrant. In our case, as in *Brick,* the authorization was based upon a generalized statement that drug offenders often pose a threat to officer safety when the officers announce their presence prior to entry. In *Brick,* the court ruled that such searches violate the state constitution and the evidence seized must be suppressed. If the trial court follows the rule of law presented in *State v. Brick,* the evidence should be suppressed."

If there are more cases that need to be included in the memo, Rick will add additional pages to the outline for each case and enter the pertinent information on the appropriate page.

Rick will identify any counterargument, such as that contained in conflicting case law, and enter it in the counteranalysis section of the outline. If Rick has any thoughts concerning the conclusion while conducting the research and analysis, he will enter them in the conclusion section of the outline.

While working on the assignment, Rick keeps the outline or a note pad with him. He takes it home after work. He writes any idea concerning the assignment on the appropriate page when the idea occurs. Nothing is lost, and all his ideas and research are organized in the outline. Transitional sentences and other parts of the writing, such as how the issue should be written, are already drafted and in the proper place. If more than one issue needs to be addressed, Rick will prepare a separate section of the outline for that issue and the rule of law and case law that apply to it.

Writing Stage

Once the research and analysis are completed, Rick prepares a rough draft. This task is greatly simplified because of the use of the expanded outline. All the research, analysis, and ideas are already organized, and many of the sentences are written and in place. All Rick has to do is to convert the outline into sentence and paragraph form and fill in the gaps. When drafting, Rick keeps in mind the guidelines presented in the Writing Stage section of this chapter, such as do not procrastinate, prepare a comfortable writing location, and so on.

Postwriting Stage

The final step is to revise and edit the memorandum. Focusing on conciseness, clarity, and completeness, Rick utilizes a checklist similar to the one presented in the Postwriting Stage section of this chapter. Several drafts may be required, and considerable time may be spent redrafting. Rick's work is judged by the finished product; therefore, care is taken in this stage.

Note that a great deal of emphasis is placed in this chapter on the prewriting stage of the writing process. If organization and care are taken at this stage and an expanded outline is utilized, the entire writing process is greatly simplified. It may seem like a lot of work to prepare an expanded outline, but its use will actually save time in the long run.

SUMMARY

Contrary to popular belief, the bulk of the practice of law involves writing in one form or another. Legal writing includes the preparation of documents such as office legal memorandums, legal correspondence to clients and other individuals, litigation documents that will be filed with a court, and transaction documents prepared for clients' use, such as contracts.

Legal writing is often complex, requiring in-depth research and detailed analysis. The complexities of an assignment, time constraints, and heavy workloads dictate the necessity of following a writing process when engaging in legal writing. There is no established standard writing process. Each individual should adopt or create a process that works.

In this text, a recommended process is presented that focuses on the three stages of the writing process:

1. Prewriting stage
2. Writing stage
3. Postwriting stage

The prewriting stage is composed of three sections: the assignment, constraints affecting the assignment, and the organization of the assignment. When approaching an assignment, the paralegal should first review the assignment to be sure the task is clearly understood. Next, the paralegal should identify the type of writing required and the audience the writing is intended to reach. After the assignment is reviewed, the paralegal should then consider any constraints that affect the assignment, such as time, length, and format.

Once these matters are addressed, the writer should prepare an outline of the assignment. It is recommended that the paralegal prepare an *expanded outline* and use it when engaging in the research and analysis of the assignment.

An expanded outline consists of a separate notebook page or computer-generated page for each topic and subtopic of the outline. Research and analysis are entered in the expanded outline throughout the prewriting stage as material is gathered and analysis conducted. The use of this approach results in the capture and organization of ideas and material throughout the prewriting stage. The end result is essentially a rough draft that has developed during the prewriting stage.

The adoption of a prewriting process simplifies and makes easier the writing stage. In the writing stage, the rough draft represented by the expanded outline is converted to the finished product, for example, a legal memorandum. Being overwhelmed by the size of the assignment and putting off starting to write are often major stumbling blocks in the writing stage. The use of an expanded outline helps simplify complex projects. Also, an expanded outline helps overcome the problem of starting because many of the beginning steps in writing, such as organization, are already accomplished.

All drafts must be revised and edited. A revision focuses on ensuring clarity, completeness, and conciseness. Editing focuses on narrower concerns involving accuracy, such as punctuation, grammar, and so on. The number of drafts is not preset but is governed by the goal of producing a quality product. If the steps of the writing process are followed, the goal of producing a well-crafted, quality product will be attained.

This chapter concludes with a list of suggestions concerning legal research as it relates to the prewriting stage of the writing process, such as start with the identification of the issue and be sure to update all research.

EXERCISES

The following exercises may be helpful in developing an understanding of and familiarity with the use of a writing process.

ASSIGNMENT 1
Describe the stages of the legal writing process.

ASSIGNMENT 2
Describe the steps of the prewriting stage.

ASSIGNMENT 3
Describe the types of legal writing discussed in this chapter.

ASSIGNMENT 4
Why is the type of audience important?

ASSIGNMENT 5
What are some of the constraints that may affect your performance of an assignment? How do they affect your performance of an assignment?

ASSIGNMENT 6
What is an expanded outline? Describe the creation and elements of the body of an expanded outline for an office legal memorandum.

ASSIGNMENT 7
Describe the use of an expanded outline in the preparation of an office legal memorandum.

ASSIGNMENT 8
What are some of the rules to keep in mind during the writing stage?

ASSIGNMENT 9
Prepare a checklist for revising and editing.

ASSIGNMENT 10
What are the general factors to keep in mind when engaging in research?

ASSIGNMENT 11
The paralegal is assigned the task of preparing an office legal memorandum. The memorandum is due in ten days, and there is a five-page limit. The facts and law are as follows.

Facts: Mary was Tom's stockbroker and financial advisor. Tom owned five acres of property. Mary advised Tom to sell the property to Ana at a price slightly below the market price. She recommended that Tom buy stock with the proceeds. Tom sold the property to Ana and now wants to have the transaction set aside because he believes Mary unduly and improperly influenced his decision. Mary and Ana are very close friends.

Law: *Statutory law*—section 96-4-4-1 of the state statutes provides that a contract for the sale of land may be set aside if it is entered into under undue influence.

Case law—Lorn v. Bell. In a fact situation similar to Tom's, the court ruled that under § 96-4-4-1, undue influence occurs when:

1. The person influenced is susceptible to undue influence.
2. The person influenced is influenced to enter the contract.

3. The opportunity to influence is present.
4. Undue influence is present.
5. The person exercising the undue influence benefits from the undue influence.

Part A

Describe in detail the application of each step of the prewriting stage to this assignment.

Part B

For the organization step of the prewriting stage, prepare an expanded outline based on the outline presented in the Use of an Outline, Step 2 subsection.

Part C

Based only on the information presented above, fill in the expanded outline. Include a statement of the issue, analysis, counteranalysis, conclusion, and recommendations.

CHAPTER 11

Fundamentals of Writing

Your professional reputation and usually job performance evaluations are determined by the quality of your work. If the job involves legal writing, your reputation as a paralegal is primarily based upon the quality of your writing. The value of the finished product depends not only on the accuracy and thoroughness of legal research and analysis but also on the manner of its presentation. Excellent research and analysis skills are undermined if you cannot present the results of the research and analysis clearly and free of mechanical errors. Therefore, good writing skills are equally as important as good research and analysis skills.

Good writing skills are also important because a poorly written product affects more than the paralegal's reputation. It also affects the reputation of the law firm. A law firm's reputation is affected, either positively or negatively, when a written product is directed to an audience outside the law firm, such as the client. A writing that contains grammatical or other mechanical errors reflects poorly on the firm. The client may wonder if the errors extend to the quality of the research and question the capability of the firm to handle the case. Opposing counsel may conclude that the firm is not capable of mounting an effective opposition and be less inclined to settle a case they otherwise would settle.

The creation of a professionally written product requires knowledge of the fundamentals of writing. This chapter summarizes some of these fundamentals and highlights areas where writing errors commonly occur. In this regard, the chapter presents general information concerning sentences, paragraphs, word selection and usage, grammar, punctuation, and some formal writing conventions. The chapter does not provide a comprehensive, in-depth exploration of these topics. Sources you may refer to for additional guidance are listed at the end of the chapter.

SENTENCES

The sentence is the fundamental building block of writing. It is usually a statement that conveys an idea or ideas. Good writing skills include a knowledge of the basics of proper sentence construction.

Sentence—Structure/Pattern

A sentence is usually a statement in which the actor (the subject) performs some action or describes a state of being (the predicate).

For Example: *Subject* *Predicate*
John wrecked the car.
John is ill.

sentence
The fundamental building block of writing. It is composed of a group of words that convey a single thought. It is usually a statement in which the actor (subject) performs some action or describes a state of being (the predicate).

The predicate is composed of the verb and object of the verb, such as a direct object (if necessary). An object of the verb may be required to receive the action of the verb.

For Example: *Subject* *Predicate*
John wrecked the car.
The car is a direct object that receives the action of the verb *wrecked.*

At a minimum, a sentence must have a subject and a predicate. In its simplest form, a sentence requires a noun and a verb.

For Example: Judges rule.

Make sure your sentences have a subject and a predicate.

Sentence—Basic Rules

The following subsections introduce some basic rules involving sentences and sentence structure. A list of topics covered by these rules is presented in Figure 11–1. This list should be kept in mind when drafting or reviewing sentences.

Subject/Verb Distance

The subject and verb should be kept as close together as possible. A sentence is easier to understand if the subject and verb are close together. Intervening words, clauses, or phrases disrupt the action and make the sentence difficult to understand.

For Example: **Intervening words in italic:** John, *apparently upset and in a bad mood,* hit James.
Revision: Apparently upset and in a bad mood, John hit James.
Intervening clause in italic: The argument that the good faith exception applies *because the officers were acting in good faith and the warrant was defective due to magistrate error* is supported by the facts.
Revision: The argument that the good faith exception applies is supported by the facts. The officers were acting in good faith and the warrant was defective due to magistrate error.

Sentence Length

Although there is no rule governing sentence length, the shorter a sentence, the easier it is to understand. The length of a sentence will vary according to the nature of the information it must convey. A good average for sentence length is twenty to twenty-five words. If you find that your sentences are too long, eliminate extra words or break the sentence into shorter sentences.

Subject/Verb Distance
Sentence Length
Active/Passive Voice
Action Verbs
Transitions

Figure 11–1
Topics to Keep in Mind when Reviewing Sentences

For Example: **Sentence too long:** The evidence should be suppressed because the warrant did not authorize unannounced entry, and there were no exigent circumstances at the scene that provided justification for the officers' actions of entering the residence unannounced.

Revision: The evidence should be suppressed because the warrant did not authorize unannounced entry. In addition, the circumstances at the scene did not provide justification for unannounced entry.

Watch out for run-on sentences. Each sentence should contain one main idea. It is often tempting to pack more than one idea into a sentence. This usually occurs when the ideas being conveyed are related. If the sentence you are reviewing is very long, it may be that it is a run-on sentence, and you are attempting to convey too many ideas in one sentence.

For Example: **Run-on sentence:** "Thomas does not dispute the fact that the court properly resorted to estimating a plant quantity for the 1991 grow, his dispute concerns the basis for the court's estimation." Note that this sentence conveys two related ideas: what he does not dispute and what he does dispute. Each idea should be presented in separate sentences.

Revision: "Thomas does not dispute the fact that the court properly resorted to estimating a plant quantity for the 1991 grow. His dispute concerns the basis for the court's estimation."

Active/Passive Voice

active voice
The subject of the sentence is performing the action in the sentence. (The automobile hit the child.)

Active Voice. The general rule is that you should draft sentences using active voice. When active voice is adopted, the subject of the sentence is the actor. When passive voice is used, the subject of the sentence is acted upon.

For Example: **Active voice:** "The automobile hit the child." "The construction workers built the dam."
Passive voice: "The child was hit by the automobile." "The dam was built by the construction workers."

Active voice is easier to understand and is more powerful. It is easier to understand because the doer of the action is mentioned at the beginning of the sentence prior to the action. Readers do not have to read the entire sentence before they are informed of who is performing the action. Active voice is more powerful because, at the outset, it identifies the actor as the performer of the action. This focuses attention on the actor and emphasizes the actor's actions. When passive voice is used, the actor is removed from the action or not identified at all.

For Example: **Active voice:** The defendant breached the contract when he failed to deliver the goods on time.
Passive voice: The contract was breached when the goods were not delivered on time. (The actor is not identified.)

Passive Voice. There are situations where it is appropriate to use passive voice. You may use passive voice when the actor is unknown or unimportant or when you do not want to emphasize the actor's conduct. See Chapter 14 for a discussion of the appropriate use of passive voice in court briefs.

passive voice
The subject of the sentence is acted upon. (The child was hit by the automobile.)

For Example: **Actor unknown:** A portion of the transcript was lost.
Actor unimportant: The bank deposit was found by a passerby.
Actor de-emphasized: The vase was broken and the plaintiff injured when the vase slipped from the defendant's hand.

Action Verbs

Whenever possible, select verbs that are active rather than verbs that show a state of being or are passive.

For Example: **Passive:** Mary reached the conclusion that Tom was guilty.
Revision: Mary concluded that Tom was guilty.
State of being: The record keeper is Steve Jones.
Revision: Steve Jones keeps the records.

Transitions

Transitional words and phrases connect sentences and serve to establish the relationship between the subjects of the sentences. Transitions are important because they guide the reader and make the writing cohesive.

For Example: **No transition:** The statute requires that fences exceeding five feet in height must be located no closer than ten feet from the property line. Your fence will be six feet high; you must build it ten feet from the property line.

With transition—transition in italic: The statute requires that fences exceeding five feet in height must be located no closer than ten feet from the property line. *Therefore, since* your fence will exceed five feet, you must locate it ten feet from the property line.

The following are some examples of transitional words and phrases:

however	even so	but	still
furthermore	nevertheless	so	and
although	simply put	for	on the other hand
conversely	moreover	that is	in other words
contrary to	above all	clearly	more importantly
initially	meanwhile	finally	all the same
specifically	therefore	thus	consequently
arguably	in contrast	instead	to illustrate
likewise	allegedly	unlike	subsequently
undoubtedly	in addition	likewise	in conclusion
in summary	nonetheless	since	without question

PARAGRAPHS

A paragraph is a group of sentences that address the same topic. Paragraphs are important because they organize the writing according to topic. They make it easier for the reader to understand the material by separating it into manageable units. A reader may encounter difficulty understanding the subject matter when it is not divided into paragraphs. Start a new paragraph when a new idea or topic is being addressed. You should use transitional phrases or sentences to link new paragraphs.

paragraph
A group of sentences that address the same topic.

A paragraph usually consists of the following elements:

- A topic sentence
- The body
- A closing sentence

Each of these elements is not always required in every paragraph. A short paragraph, for example, may not have a closing sentence. The following subsections discuss the elements of a paragraph and other considerations to keep in mind when writing paragraphs.

Paragraph—Topic Sentence

The topic sentence identifies the subject of the paragraph. It introduces the subject and provides the focus of the paragraph for the reader. The topic sentence is usually placed at the beginning of the paragraph.

For Example:

- Topic sentence of a paragraph that discusses why the exclusionary rule is necessary: "The Supreme Court has identified several reasons why the exclusionary rule is necessary."
- Topic sentence of a paragraph that discusses Mr. Smith's actions: "Mr. Smith's actions do not constitute a breach of contract."
- Topic sentence of a paragraph that addresses required conditions: "A warranty of fitness for a particular purpose is created when the following conditions are present."

Paragraph—Body

The body of a paragraph is composed of a sentence or sentences that support or develop the subject introduced by the topic sentence. The sentence(s) should develop the subject clearly and in a logical manner.

For Example: The topic sentence in this example is printed in italic to separate it from the body. *"In order to support a negligence claim against Mrs. Jones, four elements must be proven.* First we must establish that she had a duty to keep the tree on her property trimmed. Next, we must show that she failed to properly trim the tree. Then it is necessary to prove that as a result of her failure to trim the tree, a branch fell and struck Mr. Thompson. Finally, we must establish that Mr. Thompson's injuries resulted from the branch striking him."

Notice in this example that the sentences in the body are presented clearly and in logical order. Remember, when preparing the body of a paragraph, the goal is to draft it clearly, concisely, and logically.

Paragraph—Closing Sentence

A paragraph should end with a closing sentence. The content of the sentence varies according to the subject matter covered in the paragraph. It should summarize the topic addressed in the body or apply the subject discussed to the facts of the case.

For Example: **Summary:** Therefore, to establish a claim for negligence, we must show that Mrs. Jones had a duty, the duty was breached, the breach caused the accident, and the accident caused the harm that resulted.

Application of subject to the facts of the case: The rule of law adopted in the *Craig* case clearly applies in this case because Mr. Smith failed to warn Mr. Jones that the brakes were defective.

Paragraph—Transition Sentence

Transitional words, phrases, or sentences are required to connect the subjects discussed in different paragraphs. They serve as a guide for the reader by linking the paragraphs, thereby providing coherence to the overall writing. The topic or closing sentence of a paragraph may include the transitional language. Transitional words, phrases, and sentences are usually placed at either the beginning or the end of the paragraph.

For Example: **Transitions at the beginning of a paragraph. The transitional language is in italic:**

- "If the *above mentioned* requirements are not met, breach of contract may not be claimed."
- "There are, *however,* exceptions to this rule."

- *"In addition* to a cause of action for negligence, Mr. Smith may allege. . . ." (Where the body of the paragraph addresses the other possible causes of action, and the previous paragraph discusses the negligence cause of action.)
- "The *second* element of the statute requires. . . ." (Where separate paragraphs are used to discuss separate elements.)

Transitions at the end of the paragraph. The transitional language is in italic:

- "The statute, *however,* does not define 'publication'; therefore, case law must be consulted." (Where the next paragraph introduces the case law.)
- *"In addition* to this case, there are other cases that discuss the requirements of the statute." (Where the following paragraph discusses the other cases.)

Paragraph Length

As with sentences, there is no rule that establishes a standard length for paragraphs. Paragraphs usually are three to six sentences in length. Most paragraph topics can be covered comfortably in six to seven sentences, although a paragraph may be as short as one sentence or as long as ten sentences. Determine the length by keeping in mind the goal of clearly and completely covering the topic of the paragraph. The reader may have difficulty understanding or become confused by extremely long paragraphs. A series of extremely short paragraphs may lack transition and distract the reader. Therefore, extremely long and short paragraphs are not recommended. The following are examples of short paragraphs.

For Example: **One-sentence paragraph:** The second element of the rule requires that the witness be present at the signing.

Two-sentence paragraph: Section 2(b) of the statute addresses the requirement of the number and presence of witnesses. It requires that there must be a minimum of two witnesses and both must be present at the signing.

Notice that the examples lack transition language or sentences that connect the paragraphs to the paragraphs that follow.

WORD SELECTION AND USAGE

Not only is it necessary to be skilled in sentence and paragraph construction, you also must be skilled in selecting and using words. This section discusses some guidelines on word selection and usage.

Excessive/Redundant Words

Avoid the use of excessive or redundant words. Check each sentence for words that can be eliminated. Simplify the finished product.

For Example: **Excessive words:** The statute provides individuals protection against the use, at trial, of evidence obtained by warrantless wiretaps.

Revision: The statute prohibits the use of evidence obtained by warrantless wiretaps.

Redundant words: The sole and exclusive remedy provided by the statute is criminal prosecution.

Revision: The exclusive remedy provided by the statute is criminal prosecution.

The following is a list of some commonly used redundant pairs. Any *one* of the terms can be used; the use of both terms is not required or appropriate.

full/complete	merged/together	cease/desist
each/every	few/in number	null/void

true/correct
end/result
and/moreover
join/together
due/owing
alter/change
sole/exclusive
exact/same
descend/down
specific/example

Noun/Verb Strings

A noun/verb string is the use of a group of related words to convey information. It is a form of redundancy that should be avoided when a single descriptive word will accomplish the same end.

For Example: **Noun/verb strings:** "The distributor is not responsible for failures to perform due to *riots, floods, earthquakes, and acts of God.*" "A stockholder may not *grant, give, sell, or assign* her interest in the stock without the consent of the other shareholders."

Revisions: "The distributor is not responsible for failure to perform caused by events beyond the distributor's control." "A stockholder may not transfer her interest in the stock without the consent of the other shareholders."

Nominalizations

A nominalization is a noun created from a verb.

For Example:

Verb	*Noun*
determine	determination
realize	realization
possess	possession
important	importance

Nominalizations weaken a sentence by taking the action away from the actor. They make the sentence passive and less forceful.

For Example: **Nominalizations:** "He came to the *realization* that the assignment required more work." "The *importance* of the opinion is that . . ."

Revisions: "He *realized* that the assignment required more work." "The opinion is *important* because . . ."

Legalese

Legalese as used here refers to terms of art used in the legal profession that are not generally known outside the profession. The goal of legal writing is to effectively communicate information. Writing in plain English usually accomplishes this goal, and plain English should be used when possible.

The extent to which you incorporate legal terminology in legal writing is governed by the audience. Legal terms are appropriate when communicating with others in the field. If the reader is trained in the law, the use of legal terms or phrases, such as *res ipsa loquitur,* is much easier than having to provide a definition or explanation. When the recipient is a nonlawyer, however, the use of legal terms should be avoided. You *must* define legal terms when communicating with nonlawyers if the meaning of the term is not obvious.

For Example: **Legalese in italic:** The constitution requires *probable cause* before the police can conduct a search of your residence.

Revision: The constitution requires the police to have a valid reason before they can search a house. An example of a valid reason would be if a reliable person informed the police that they saw illegal drugs in the house.

Archaic Words

Archaic terms are words or phrases frequently used in the past that are being phased out of legal writing. Do not include such terms in your writing. Some of these terms are *saith, party of the first part, aforesaid, hereinbefore, hereinafter, henceforth,* and *the said party.*

Sexist Language

In any form of writing, the incorporation of gender-specific language is prejudicial and not appropriate unless it refers to a specific person and the gender is known. Sexist language has no place in legal writing. There are several guidelines that help ensure gender-neutral writing.

Words

Change gender-specific terms to gender-neutral terms.

For Example:

Gender-specific	*Gender-neutral*
chairman	chairperson
wife	spouse
draftsman	drafter
forefathers	forbearers
housewife	homemaker

He/She

You can use *he or she* in place of *he* to render a sentence gender-neutral. The result, however, may be awkward.

For Example: The rule requires the plaintiff to file his or her response within fifteen days.

There are several alternatives that you may adopt to avoid the use of *his or her, he/she,* and so on.

1. Restate the sentence so the antecedent is plural.

   For Example: The rule requires the *plaintiff* to file *his* pleadings . . .

   Revision: The rule requires *plaintiffs* to file *their* pleadings . . .

2. Eliminate the use of the pronoun.

   For Example: The officer is responsible for the actions of *his* troops.

   Revision: The officer is responsible for the actions of *the* troops.

3. Repeat the name.

   For Example: Before the client may liquidate the assets of the company, *he* must . . .

   Revision: Before the client may liquidate the assets of the company, the *client* must . . .

4. Use *one, you,* or *your* when possible.

   For Example: "Everyone has a right to *his* personal preferences."

   Revisions: "Everyone has a right to personal preferences." "You have a right to *your* personal preferences."

Appropriate Reference to Gender

Reference to gender is appropriate only when you intend to refer to one sex.

For Example: Each member of the women's basketball team had her name printed on the back of her uniform.

Specific Words—Problem Areas

Some words are commonly misused. You can avoid problems of misuse by following some basic rules.

Shall and May

The word *shall* is used to impose a duty that is mandatory. The performance of the duty is not optional.

For Example: "Mr. Smith *shall* terminate all contact with Mrs. Black." The duty to terminate all communication is mandatory. Mr. Smith has no option.

The word *may* indicates that the performance of an act is not mandatory. The performance of the act is optional.

For Example: "Mr. Smith *may* terminate all communication with Mr. Black." The act of terminating all communication is optional with Mr. Smith. He has a choice whether to terminate the communication.

And/Or

When the word *and* is used in regard to a list of words, all the items listed are included and required.

For Example: "The case law requires the plaintiff to prove duty, breach of duty, proximate cause, *and* damages." The use of *and* means that all four elements must be proved. All the listed items are included in the requirement.

When *or* is used, all the items listed are not required to be included. Any one or all of the items are included.

For Example: "The case law requires the corporate president to provide notice orally, by mail, *or* by facsimile." All the listed items are not required. Only one of the items is required. The president has the choice of giving notice by one or all of the means listed.

The use of *and/or* creates an ambiguity and is not proper.

For Example: "The statute requires that the notice be given orally, by mail, *and/or* by facsimile." What does the statute require? Are all the listed items required? If so, *and* should be used. If only one of the items is required, *or* should be used.

That/Which

You should use *that* to introduce restrictive clauses and *which* to introduce nonrestrictive clauses. A restrictive clause is a clause that is necessary to the meaning of the sentence.

For Example: "You must perform all the steps *that are listed in the statute."* The italicized clause is a restrictive clause. It informs the reader that the required steps are the steps listed in the statute. It is necessary to an understanding of the steps that must be taken.

A nonrestrictive clause is a clause that is not necessary to the meaning of the sentence. It can be set off from the rest of the sentence with commas without changing the meaning of the sentence.

For Example: "I always buy his products, which *usually are high quality."* The italicized clause is a nonrestrictive clause. It is not necessary to the meaning of the sentence.

GRAMMAR

The rules of grammar govern the construction of sentences. This section introduces some of the basic rules of grammar that you should keep in mind when performing a writing assignment.

Subject/Verb Agreement

The subject and verb should agree in person and number. This means that singular subjects require singular verbs and plural subjects require plural verbs.

For Example: **Incorrect:** "The decision in the case *require* the defendant to give notice to the plaintiff." This sentence has a singular subject, *decision,* and a plural verb, *require.*

Correct: "The decision in the case *requires* the defendant to give notice to the plaintiff." The singular subject *decision* agrees with the singular verb *requires.*

The following are some basic rules concerning subject/verb agreement:

1. Two or more subjects joined by *and* usually require a plural verb.

   For Example: Mary and Joan *were* present.

2. Two or more subjects joined by *or* or *nor* require a verb that agrees with the subject closest to the verb.

   For Example: "Tom or his brothers *are* going to attend." "Either the brothers or Tom *is* the responsible party."

3. Most indefinite pronouns require singular verbs. Indefinite pronouns are pronouns that do not refer to a specific person or thing, such as *anyone, everybody, nobody, someone, each,* and *something.*

   For Example: Everybody *is* responsible.

4. Some indefinite pronouns require a verb that matches the noun to which they refer. Some of these pronouns are *all, none, most, some,* and *any.*

   For Example: "All of the property *is* distributed." "All of the items *are* missing."

5. Collective nouns usually require a singular verb. A collective noun is a noun that refers to a group: *jury, family, crowd, majority,* and so on.

   For Example: "The jury *was* deadlocked." "The family *is* present."

6. Nouns that are plural in form but have a singular meaning require a singular verb, for example, *politics, news,* and *tactics.*

   For Example: "The news *is* bad. "The politics of the party *is* corrupt."

7. The title of a work takes a singular verb.

   For Example: *Military Tactics* is wonderful reading.

8. A relative pronoun requires a verb that agrees with its antecedent. A relative pronoun is a pronoun that refers to another noun in the sentence. *Which, who,* and *that* are examples of relative pronouns. The noun the relative pronoun refers to is called the antecedent.

For Example: "Our *client* is one of the persons *who* has been indicted in the case." *Who* is the relative pronoun, and *client* is the antecedent.

If the antecedent is singular, the verb should be singular. If the antecedent is plural, the verb should be plural.

For Example: **Singular:** "Our *client, who* was present at the scene, *has* been indicted." The antecedent *(client)* of the relative pronoun *(who)* is singular; therefore, *who* takes a singular verb *(has)*.

Plural: "The *clients, who* were present at the scene, *have* been indicted." The antecedent *(clients)* of the relative pronoun *(who)* is plural; therefore, *who* takes a plural verb *(have)*.

Verb Tense

Verb tense is the time in which a verb's action occurs. Events happening in the present use the present tense, events that occurred in the past use the past tense, and events that will take place in the future use the future tense. Usually sentences and paragraphs are written in the same tense. You should check to ensure that your writing does not have inappropriate changes in verb tense.

For Example: **Inappropriate change in verb tense:** "The complaint *was* filed on January 1, 1997. The defendants *move* to dismiss the complaint. The motion *was* denied." Notice that the verb tense in this sentence moves from past, to present, then back to past tense.

Revision: "The complaint *was* filed on January 1, 1997. The defendants *moved* to dismiss the complaint. The motion *was* denied." Notice that all the verbs are in past tense.

Guidelines concerning correct verb tense include the following:

1. When presenting your position or legal analysis, use present tense.

   For Example: Plaintiff *contends* that the rule *requires* thirty days' notice.

2. When addressing a court opinion that has already been decided, use past tense.

   For Example: In *Smith v. Jones,* the court *held* that the rule does not require thirty days' notice.

3. When discussing a law or rule still in effect, use present tense.

   For Example: The provisions of section 44-556 *require* a contractor to give thirty days' notice.

Parallel Construction

Parallel construction means that the items listed are similar in grammatical structure. It means that in sentences that include a list, a group of activities, and so on, each of the items must use the same grammatical form, that is, all the items or members of the group should agree in verb tense, number, and so on.

For Example: **Lack parallel construction:**

- The defendant is a trained officer with fifteen years' experience who has won several service medals.
- The goals of the association are the following:

  a. educating the public about crime,
  b. to provide support for the police, and
  c. improvement of local neighborhood watch groups.

Revisions with parallel construction:

- The defendant is a trained officer *who has* fifteen years' experience and *who has* won several service medals.
- The goals of the association are the following:
  a. *to educate* the public about crime,
  b. *to provide* support for the police, and
  c. *to improve* local neighborhood watch groups.

Superfluous Verbs

Avoid the use of verb constructions that are unnecessarily wordy.

For Example: **Superfluous verbs in italic:**

- He decided to *perform an investigation* into the matter.
- The arbitrator decided to *give consideration* to the argument.
- The judge *reached a decision* on the question.
- The contractor *made an attempt* to complete the contract on time.

Revisions without superfluous verbs:

- He decided to *investigate* the matter.
- The arbitrator *considered* the argument.
- The judge *decided* the question.
- "The contractor *attempted* to complete the contract on time.

Modifier and Infinitives

Modifiers are words or phrases that provide descriptions of the subject, verb, or object in a sentence. The four types of problems involving modifiers that frequently occur are presented in Figure 11–2.

Misplaced Modifiers

Misplaced modifiers are words or phrases that are placed in the wrong location in a sentence. You may create an ambiguity or cause a loss of clarity by misplacing a modifier.

For Example: **Misplaced modifiers:**

- "If we contend that the contract applies, it will be attacked by the defense." What will be attacked, our contention or the contract?
- "Present the client's counterargument only in the third section of the brief." Does this mean the counterargument should be presented in the third section and no other section, or does it mean that the third section should consist only of the counterargument?

The solution to misplaced modifiers is to rephrase the sentence or to move the modifier to ensure clarity.

- Misplaced modifiers
- Dangling modifiers
- Squinting modifiers
- Split infinitives

Figure 11–2
Problem Modifiers

For Example: **Revision—sentence rephrased:**

- If we contend that the contract applies, the contention will be attacked by the defense.

Revision—modifier moved:

- In the third section of the brief, present only the client's counterargument.

Dangling Modifiers

Modifiers that do not modify any other part of the sentence are dangling modifiers.

For Example: **Dangling modifier in italic:** *To determine whether the contract was breached,* the provisions of the statute must be referred to.

The italicized modifier does not refer to or modify any part of the sentence. It refers to a contract mentioned in another sentence. Check sentences in your writing to make sure modifiers refer to a noun or nouns in the sentence.

For Example: **Dangling modified eliminated:** To determine whether the terms of the contract violate the statute, the statutory provisions must be referred to.

Squinting Modifiers

A squinting modifier is a modifier located in a position in the sentence that makes it unclear whether it modifies the word that precedes it or the word that follows it. Avoid squinting modifiers when you edit your writing.

For Example: **Squinting modifier in italic:** "The report that was prepared *routinely* indicated that the structure was unsafe." Was the report prepared routinely, or did the report routinely indicate the structure was unsafe?
Revision: The report that was routinely prepared indicated that the structure was unsafe.

Split Infinitives

An infinitive is a verb form that functions as a noun or as an auxiliary verb, such as *to argue, to understand,* and *to consider.* The general rule is that infinitives should not be split, that is, an adverb should not be placed after the *to* and before the verb.

For Example: **Split infinitives:** In each of the following examples, the infinitive is split: "to completely understand," "to rapidly climb," "to thoroughly test." An adverb is placed between the *to* and the verb.
Revisions: "to understand completely" "to climb rapidly" "to test thoroughly"

Noun/Pronoun Agreement

Pronouns must agree in number (singular/plural) and gender (feminine/masculine/neuter) with the nouns to which they refer, their antecedents. A list of pronouns follows: *I, me, mine, my, we, us, our, you, yours, your, he, him, his, she, her, hers, it, its, they, them, their,* and *theirs.*

There are several guidelines to follow to ensure noun/pronoun agreement.

1. Pronouns must agree with their antecedents. The noun the pronoun refers to is the antecedent.

   For Example: "The *workers* put on *their* helmets when they entered the building." The pronoun *their* agrees in number (plural) with its antecedent *workers* (plural).

"*Mary* was required to wear *her* helmet." The pronoun *her* agrees in number and gender with the antecedent *Mary.*

2. Pronouns that do not refer to a definite person or thing are indefinite pronouns. Some examples of indefinite pronouns are *all, anyone, anybody, each, everyone, someone, somebody, everything, something,* and *none.* Indefinite pronouns are usually singular.

   For Example: *Everyone* has the freedom to select *his or her* candidate.

3. Antecedents joined by *and* require a plural pronoun.

   For Example: "Tom and Mary are separating *their* property." "Tom, Jon, and Mary are going *their* separate ways."

4. Antecedents joined by *or* or *nor* require a pronoun that agrees in number and gender with the antecedent closest to the pronoun.

   For Example: "Mary or the other defendants must conduct *their* investigation." "The defendants or Mary must conduct *her* investigation."

   When it appears awkward, as the second sentence does, consider rephrasing the sentence.

   For Example: Mary or the defendants must conduct an investigation.

5. The number of a pronoun that refers to a collective noun is determined by the function of the collective noun. A collective noun is a noun that refers to a group. If the collective noun functions as a unit, the pronoun is singular.

   For Example: "The *committee,* after reviewing the matter, presented *its* conclusion." In this sentence, the collective noun, *committee,* functions as a unit; the report is the act of the committee as a whole; and therefore, the pronoun *its* is singular.

   If the collective noun does not function as a unit, that is, the members of the collective noun are acting separately and not as a unit, a plural pronoun is required.

   For Example: "The *team* have stated *their* various positions on the question of whether *they* should wear the new helmets." In this example, the collective noun, *team,* does not function as a unit. The reference is to the team as individual members; therefore, the sentence takes the plural pronoun *they.*

PUNCTUATION

Punctuation is designed to make writing clear and easy to understand. Poor punctuation may cause the reader to misunderstand the context or be distracted by the errors and not focus on the context. Poor punctuation usually causes the reader to question the competency of the author. A comprehensive discussion of all the rules governing punctuation would require an entire text. This section discusses the major elements of punctuation and summarizes some of the rules that apply to problem situations commonly encountered.

Comma (,)

The function of a comma is to separate the parts of a sentence. It is the most frequently used punctuation mark. Some basic rules that apply to commas are the following:

1. Use a comma before a conjunction that joins two main or independent clauses.

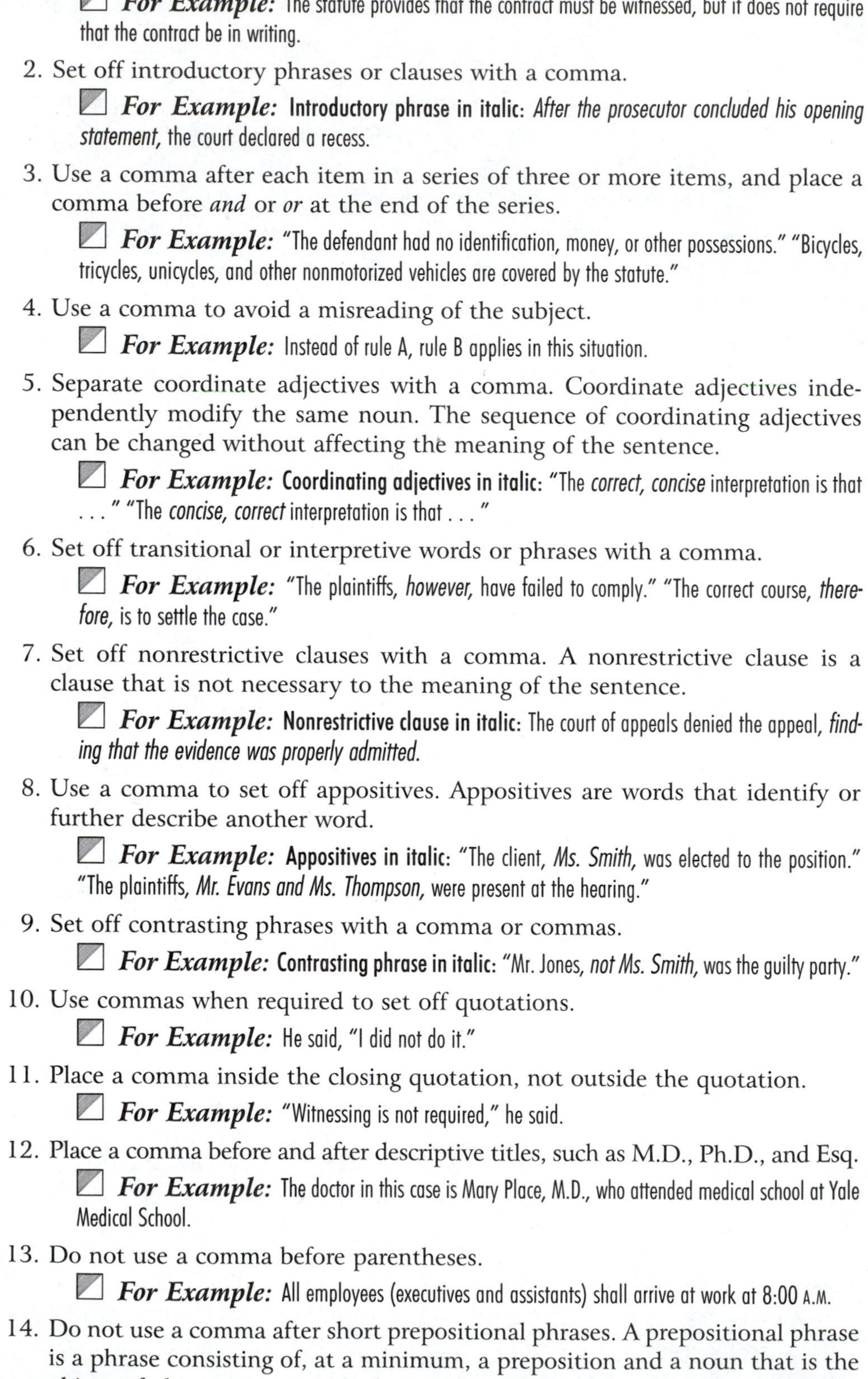

For Example: The statute provides that the contract must be witnessed, but it does not require that the contract be in writing.

2. Set off introductory phrases or clauses with a comma.

   For Example: **Introductory phrase in italic:** *After the prosecutor concluded his opening statement,* the court declared a recess.

3. Use a comma after each item in a series of three or more items, and place a comma before *and* or *or* at the end of the series.

   For Example: "The defendant had no identification, money, or other possessions." "Bicycles, tricycles, unicycles, and other nonmotorized vehicles are covered by the statute."

4. Use a comma to avoid a misreading of the subject.

   For Example: Instead of rule A, rule B applies in this situation.

5. Separate coordinate adjectives with a comma. Coordinate adjectives independently modify the same noun. The sequence of coordinating adjectives can be changed without affecting the meaning of the sentence.

   For Example: **Coordinating adjectives in italic:** "The *correct, concise* interpretation is that . . . " "The *concise, correct* interpretation is that . . . "

6. Set off transitional or interpretive words or phrases with a comma.

   For Example: "The plaintiffs, *however,* have failed to comply." "The correct course, *therefore,* is to settle the case."

7. Set off nonrestrictive clauses with a comma. A nonrestrictive clause is a clause that is not necessary to the meaning of the sentence.

   For Example: **Nonrestrictive clause in italic:** The court of appeals denied the appeal, *finding that the evidence was properly admitted.*

8. Use a comma to set off appositives. Appositives are words that identify or further describe another word.

   For Example: **Appositives in italic:** "The client, *Ms. Smith,* was elected to the position." "The plaintiffs, *Mr. Evans and Ms. Thompson,* were present at the hearing."

9. Set off contrasting phrases with a comma or commas.

   For Example: **Contrasting phrase in italic:** "Mr. Jones, *not Ms. Smith,* was the guilty party."

10. Use commas when required to set off quotations.

    For Example: He said, "I did not do it."

11. Place a comma inside the closing quotation, not outside the quotation.

    For Example: "Witnessing is not required," he said.

12. Place a comma before and after descriptive titles, such as M.D., Ph.D., and Esq.

    For Example: The doctor in this case is Mary Place, M.D., who attended medical school at Yale Medical School.

13. Do not use a comma before parentheses.

    For Example: All employees (executives and assistants) shall arrive at work at 8:00 A.M.

14. Do not use a comma after short prepositional phrases. A prepositional phrase is a phrase consisting of, at a minimum, a preposition and a noun that is the object of the preposition. A short prepositional phrase does not require a comma.

For Example: **Incorrect—the prepositional phrase is in italic:** *In every situation,* you should read the contract.

Correct: *In every situation* you should read the contract.

Semicolon (;)

A semicolon is used primarily in two situations:

- To separate major elements of complex sentences
- To separate items in a series if the items are long or if one of the items has internal commas

In regard to these situations, note the following rules:

1. Use a semicolon to separate main or independent clauses in a sentence that are *not* joined by a coordinating conjunction. Both main and independent clauses have a subject and a verb. Each could be a separate sentence. A conjunction is a word that is used to connect words and phrases. A coordinating conjunction, such as *and, but,* and *or,* is a conjunction that connects like elements.

   For Example: **Incorrect:** "The shareholders held their meeting at noon, the board of directors met immediately thereafter." The use of the comma is incorrect because there is no coordinating conjunction, such as *and,* connecting the two clauses. The coordinating conjunction is in italic in the following sentence.

   Correct—coordinating conjunction used: The shareholders held their meeting at noon, *and* the board of directors met immediately thereafter.

   Correct—semicolon used: The shareholders held their meeting at noon; the board of directors met immediately thereafter.

2. Use a semicolon when independent clauses are joined by a conjunctive adverb. Some examples of conjunctive adverbs are the following: *therefore, however, furthermore, consequently, likewise,* and *nevertheless.*

   For Example: The rule requires that the will must be witnessed in writing; *however,* there are three exceptions.

3. When a series of items is long or commas are already used in some of the items in the series, use a semicolon to separate the items.

   For Example: **Long items:** The plaintiffs must prove the following to establish that the will was validly witnessed:

   a. there were two witnesses to the will;
   b. the witnesses were present in the room when the will was signed; and
   c. the witnesses were not related to the testator or were not bequeathed anything in the will.

   List of items with internal commas: The stockholders present were Mary Hart, the president; Tom Jones, the secretary; and Monica Murton, the treasurer.

Colon (:)

You should use a colon when you want to introduce or call attention to information that follows, such as lists, conclusions, explanations, and quotations. The function of a colon is to introduce what follows. It must be preceded by a main clause that is grammatically complete, that is, a complete sentence.

For Example: **Incorrect:** "The statutory requirements are: the will must be witnessed by two witnesses, the witnesses must be present when the testator signs the will, and the witnesses must sign the will." The sentence

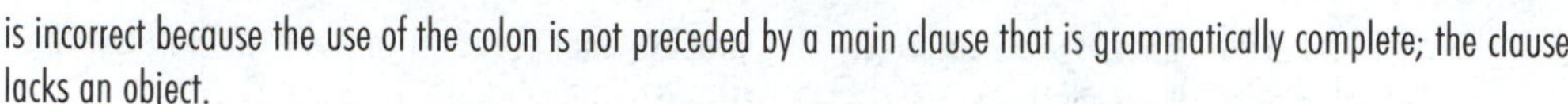

is incorrect because the use of the colon is not preceded by a main clause that is grammatically complete; the clause lacks an object.

Correct: The statutory requirements are the following: the will must be witnessed by two witnesses, . . .

For Example: **Emphasize a quotation:** The Senator concluded his remarks with the following statement: "I do not choose to run for reelection."

Apostrophe (')

An apostrophe serves to indicate possession or to form a contraction. Some of the basic rules governing the use of apostrophes to indicate possession are the following:

1. Make singular nouns possessive by adding an apostrophe and an *s.*

   For Example: "the officer's car" "Mr. Jones's house"

   Singular nouns ending in *s* take an apostrophe and an *s* just like any other singular noun. Note the possessive of Mr. Jones in the preceding example.

2. Make plural nouns possessive by adding an apostrophe after the *s.*

   For Example: "the players' uniforms" "the workers' organization"

3. Use an apostrophe and an *s* after the last word of a compound word or word group.

   For Example: "attorney general's office," "Fred and Tom's car" (where Fred and Tom own the same car), "Fred's and Tom's cars" (where Fred and Tom own separate cars)

4. The possessives of personal pronouns do not require an apostrophe.

   For Example: yours, his, hers, ours, its (possessive of *it*), whose (possessive of *who*)

An apostrophe is also used to form contractions. Contractions are generally not used in formal writing. To make a contraction, use an apostrophe in place of the omitted letter or letters.

For Example: they're (they are), can't (cannot), don't (do not), who's (who is), it's (it is)

Note the difference between *it's* and *its. It's* is the contraction for *it is. Its* is the possessive pronoun form for *it.*

Quotation Marks(" ")

Use quotation marks to identify and set off quoted material. Note the following guidelines when quoting material.

1. Long quotations are not set off by quotation marks. Instead, they are set off from the rest of the text by a five-space indentation from the left and right margins. They are also single-spaced. These quotations are called block quotations and, according to *The Bluebook,* should be used for quotations of fifty words or more.

   For Example: The court made the following statements in regard to the requirement of the presence of the witness:

   > The statute requires the witnesses to be present when the testator signs the will. The witnesses must be in the same room with the testator, not in a separate room from which they can see the testator. The witnesses also must actually see the testator sign the will. Their presence in the room is not sufficient if they do not actually see the testator sign the will.

As readers tend to skip over or skim long quotations, use them sparingly and only when the entire language, verbatim, is essential.

2. Place periods and commas inside the quotation marks.

   For Example: He was described as "a dangerous individual."

   Other punctuation, such as semicolons, colons, question marks, and exclamation marks, are placed outside the quotation marks unless they are a part of the quotation.

   For Example: The court defined publication as "communication to a third party"; therefore . . .
   The victim then shouted, "I've been hit!" (The exclamation mark is part of the quotation; therefore, it belongs within the quotation marks.)

3. You may use quotation marks to indicate that a word is used in a special way or is a special term.

   For Example: The attorney acted as "hired gun" in the case.
   The term "oppressive conduct" has a special meaning in corporation law.

4. When quoting a quote within a quote, use single quotation marks.

   For Example: The court held that "the term 'oppressive conduct' requires that the shareholder engage in some wrongful conduct."

Ellipses (. . .)

The function of an ellipsis is to indicate the omission of part of a quotation.

For Example: The statute provides that skiers are "responsible for . . . snow and ice conditions. . . ."

Note the following rules in regard to the use of ellipses:

1. When an ellipsis occurs at the end of a sentence, add a fourth period for the punctuation to end the sentence.

   For Example: The statute requires that "the majority shareholder must refrain from engaging in oppressive conduct. . . ."

2. When the omission is at the beginning of a quote, do not use an ellipsis.

   For Example: **Incorrect:** In this case, the court stated that ". . . the act does not require specific intent."
   Correct: In this case, the court stated that "the act does not require specific intent."

3. If the quote is a phrase or clause, no ellipsis is required.

   For Example: **Incorrect:** The state must establish ". . . specific intent."
   Correct: The state must establish "specific intent."

Brackets ([ ])

Brackets usually perform two separate functions:

- To show changes in or add information to quotations, usually for the purpose of providing clarification to the quotation
- To indicate an error in the original quotation

For Example: **To show changes in a quotation:** "The privilege [against self-incrimination] allows an individual to remain silent."
To indicate an error in the original quoted material: "The bord [sic] of directors voted against the proposal."

Parentheses "( )"

Use parentheses to add additional information to the sentence that is outside the main idea of the sentence or of lesser importance.

For Example: The cost of the paper (only $2) was not included in the invoice.

When referring the reader to other cases, attached material, or an appendix, or when providing summary information following a case citation, you may use parentheses.

For Example: **Reference to an appendix:** (See Appendix A.)
Reference to other cases: *See also Smith v. Jones,* 981 N.E.2d 441 (N. Wash. 1993) (where the court required specific intent in a similar situation).

Hyphen (-)

A hyphen is required to form compound modifiers and compound nouns. There are numerous words that may or may not require hyphenation.

For Example: ex-judge, well-known personality, self-defense

Consult a dictionary when you are unsure whether a word must be hyphenated. Be sure to consult a recently published dictionary. This is an area of the English language that frequently changes.

Dash (—)

Use a dash in the following situations:

- To emphasize something
- To set off lists or briefly summarize materials containing commas
- To show an abrupt change of thought or direction

For Example: **To emphasize:** The child—only eight years old—was clearly not capable of understanding what he was doing.
To set off a list: The items located at the scene—the knife, the drugs, and the scarf—have disappeared from the evidence room.
To show a sudden break: Basel Corporation—primarily known for its herbs—is involved in the manufacture of glassware.

GENERAL CONSIDERATIONS

Three additional matters that require attention when you are performing a writing assignment are spelling, use of numbers, and formal writing conventions. These matters are addressed in the following subsections.

Spelling

Obviously, all the words you use must be spelled correctly. If you are in doubt about the spelling of a word, use a dictionary. Legal writing requires the use of both a regular and legal dictionary; therefore, you must have both of these dictionaries.

If you use a computer that checks spelling, you still must carefully check for word usage errors. The computer may catch a spelling error, but generally it will not catch the use of the wrong word or typographical errors that result in the use of a wrong word.

For Example: **Use of a wrong word:** You may have used the word "to" when you intended use "too" Spell check on a computer will not catch the use of the wrong word.

Typographical error that results in the use of a wrong word: You may have typed "cast" when you meant to type "case." *Cast* is a word, and spell check will not consider this an error.

Numbers

There are several rules regarding the presentation of numbers. Some of these rules are listed here.

1. Spell out numbers that are composed of one or two words (but, see number 3 below).

   For Example: "one" "twenty-seven"

2. Use numerals for numbers that are composed of three or more digits.

   For Example: "379" "1,300" "145,378"

3. If there is a list of numbers and one of the items on the list should be written with numerals, use numerals for all the items listed.

   For Example: The numbers in the code are 16, 44, 397, and 1,001.

4. Hyphens are used for fractions and numbers from twenty-one to ninety-nine.

   For Example: "Fifty-six of the stockholders were present." "The thirty-seven shareholders represented three-fourths of the outstanding shares."

Formal Writing Conventions

Most legal writing is considered formal, and formal writing conventions apply, especially to legal briefs and memorandums. Two of these conventions are in regard to the use of contractions and personal pronouns.

As mentioned in the subsection addressing the use of apostrophes, the use of contractions is not considered acceptable in formal writing. Do not use contractions unless instructed to do so.

The general rule is that you should draft legal memorandums or briefs in the third person. Also, unless instructed otherwise, use the third person in correspondence to clients.

For Example: **Incorrect:** "It is my position the court should grant the motion." "We feel that the contract has been broken."

Correct: "The court should grant the motion." "It is Mr. Black's position that the contract has been broken."

KEY POINTS CHECKLIST: *Successful Legal Writing*

- ❑ The goal of legal writing is to prepare a professional product. A professional product is free of substantive and mechanical error. Perform the number of edits and redrafts necessary to attain this goal.
- ❑ Use short, clear sentences whenever possible. Twenty to twenty-five words is a good average length for sentences. Excessively long sentences are difficult to understand.
- ❑ A paragraph should address one topic and should usually range from three to six sentences.
- ❑ Keep the reader in mind when drafting. Avoid legalese when possible, especially when the reader is a person not trained in the law.

- ❑ Make sure the writing is grammatically correct. Check for subject/verb agreement, parallel construction, and so on.
- ❑ Check the punctuation. Are the commas and other punctuation devices used correctly?
- ❑ Check the spelling to ensure that all words are spelled correctly.

APPLICATION

Check Sheet

The check sheet presented in Figure 11–3 may be used as a guide to help you proofread and correct your legal writing.

SUMMARY

One of the requirements of a legal writing assignment is the preparation of a final product that is free from mechanical errors. The value of quality research and analysis is undermined if the written presentation is poorly assembled. This chapter presents an overview of some of the fundamental writing skills essential for good writing. The chapter addresses sentence and paragraph structure, word selection and usage, grammar, punctuation, and other general considerations involving the mechanics of good writing.

A sentence is the fundamental building block of writing. It is usually a statement; at a minimum, it must have a subject and a predicate. Sentences are most powerful when they do not exceed twenty-five words in length and are written in active voice. A sentence is written in active voice when the subject performs the action.

The second fundamental component of writing is the paragraph. A paragraph is a group of sentences that addresses the same topic. Paragraphs are usually composed of a topic sentence, a sentence or sentences discussing the topic, and a closing sentence. Transition words, sentences, or phrases are used to link paragraphs and provide coherence to the writing.

The proper selection and use of words are critical elements of good writing. Action verbs enhance and stimulate the writing. The improper use of words or the use of sexist language or legalese detracts from the quality of the writing.

Rules of grammar guide the drafting of legal writing. Subject-verb agreement, parallel construction, proper verb tense, noun-pronoun agreement, and so on are all necessary to good writing.

Spelling and punctuation are the final subjects addressed in the chapter. Proper spelling is always required. In like manner, proper punctuation is a basic requirement of proper writing. The correct uses of commas, semicolons, apostrophes, and other punctuation devices are summarized in the chapter.

All of the rules and guidelines discussed in the chapter are essential to good writing skills. You must learn and employ them when engaged in legal writing. The chapter only briefly addresses the rules and guidelines that apply to legal writing; you should refer to other resources for detailed coverage of each topic.

General Considerations
- ❑ Spelling
- ❑ Numbers
- ❑ Formal Writing Conventions

Sentence Structure/Pattern
- ❑ Subject/Verb Distance
- ❑ Sentence Length
- ❑ Active/Passive Voice
- ❑ Action Verbs
- ❑ Transitions

Punctuation
- ❑ Comma
- ❑ Semicolon
- ❑ Colon
- ❑ Apostrophe
- ❑ Quotation
- ❑ Ellipses
- ❑ Brackets
- ❑ Parentheses
- ❑ Hyphen
- ❑ Dash

Grammar
- ❑ Subject/Verb Agreement
- ❑ Verb Tense
- ❑ Parallel Construction
- ❑ Superfluous Verbs
- ❑ Modifiers and Infinitives
- ❑ Noun/Pronoun Agreement

Paragraphs
- ❑ Topic Sentence
- ❑ Body
- ❑ Closing
- ❑ Transition Sentence
- ❑ Paragraph Length

Word Selection and Usage
- ❑ Excessive/Redundant Words
- ❑ Noun/Verb String
- ❑ Nominalizations
- ❑ Legalese
- ❑ Archaic Words
- ❑ Sexist Language
- ❑ Specific Words—Problem Areas

Figure 11–3
Proofreading Checklist

EXERCISES

ASSIGNMENT 1
Discuss the essential requirements of a well-crafted sentence.

ASSIGNMENT 2
Discuss the elements and requirements of a well-crafted paragraph.

ASSIGNMENT 3
What is the difference between active voice and passive voice?

ASSIGNMENT 4
Draft the following sentences in active voice.

- The defendant was attacked by the plaintiff at the beginning of the argument.
- It is a requirement of good writing skills that active voice be used.
- Payment must be made by Mr. Smith no later than May 15, 1997.

ASSIGNMENT 5
What is a nominalization? What are some examples of nominalizations?

ASSIGNMENT 6
What is legalese? Give three examples of legalese.

ASSIGNMENT 7
Rephrase the following sentences using nonsexist language.

- A paralegal may draft a letter to the client informing him of an upcoming hearing.
- The lawyer must file his response within thirty days.
- The chairman of the committee conducted a private hearing.
- Each person must bring his records to the conference.
- Everyone must bring his records to the hearing.

ASSIGNMENT 8
Discuss the proper use of *shall/may, and/or,* and *that/which.*

ASSIGNMENT 9
What are the basic rules concerning subject-verb agreement, proper verb tense, and noun-pronoun agreement?

ASSIGNMENT 10
What is parallel construction?

ASSIGNMENT 11
What are squinting modifiers? List some examples of squinting modifiers.

ASSIGNMENT 12
What are the rules concerning the proper use of commas, colons, semicolons, and apostrophes?

ASSIGNMENT 13
Correct the following sentences by properly using colons and semicolons.

- The court's instructions to the respondent are: to refrain from contacting the plaintiff in person, by telephone, or by mail; to pay monthly child support, and to perform one hundred hours of community service.
- The following statutes govern the issue, section 29-9-516, section 29-9-517, and section 29-9-544.

ASSIGNMENT 14
Summarize the rules governing the use of quotations, ellipses, brackets, parentheses, hyphens, and dashes.

ASSIGNMENT 15
Correct the paragraphs presented in part A and part B. Use the proofreading checklist presented in Figure 11–3.

Part A

The governments' first witness at Bean's sentencing were the DEA Task Force Officer Tony Silva. He testifies that in his debriefing Luiz had told him about four seperate marijuana "grows" in which Luiz had participated. The first was in 1986 In Tress, Texas: this "grow" produced 700 marijuana plants. The second was in 1987 in the Tonto wilderness; and it produced approximatly 1500 marijuana plants. The third "grow" was in 1988 in Sies Colorado and they produced approximately 900 marijuana plants.

The final "grow was in 1991, also at the Sies site.

Before the plants in this grow had been harveted, a Colorado State Police aircraft was spotted doing a "fly-over" of the property. This prompted Luiz to completely destroy the crop, only fifty two plants were seized. As they were seized the officers noted that two or three plants were in a single grow site. Approximately 1,000 "grow holes", with sprinkler heads connected to an extensive irritation system, were found another one thousand uninstalled sprinkler heads, two water tanks and fertilizer also was found on the property.

Part B

The trial court sentenced Smith well within the statutory limits. Therefore the sentence is legal.

The record thoroughly, clearly and positively shows that Smith and his attorney have ample time to thoroughly review Smiths' sentence report prior to sentencing. They did so and had: "no problems with it." It is shown by the record that Smith never appealed his conviction or sentence. His section 2255 Motion were his first and only attempt to challenge his sentence. Any objections to the sentence report as submitted were clearly waived by Smith. The defendant have the responsibility to advise the Court of any claimed errors in the sentence report. His failure to voice any objections waive any issue not properly presented. It has been long held by this court that "Section 2255 is not available to test the legality of matters which should have been raised on appeal. Unless good cause can be shown why a defendant did not appeal or raise a particular issue on appeal; the defendant is barred from raising that issue in a section 2255 Motion

FOR FURTHER READING

Block, Gertrude. *Effective Legal Writing.* 4th ed. Westbury, NY: Foundation Press, 1992.

Good, Edward. *Mightier Than the Sword.* Charlottesville, VA: Blue Jeans Press, 1989.

Strunk, William, Jr., and E. B. White, The *Elements of Style.* 3rd ed. New York, NY: MacMillan, 1972.

Tepper, Pamela R. *Basic Legal Writing.* Lake Forrest, IL: Glenco, 1992.

CHAPTER 12

Office Legal Memorandum Assignment—Issues and Facts

Jeff Lyons, a paralegal with Berdwin and Associates, received the following memo.

"To: Jeff Lyons, Paralegal
From: Rita Berdwin, Attorney
Date: April 20, 1997
Office File No: Cr. 97-136
Re: State of Illinois v. Meril Findo, Cr. 97-378, privileged communication

We have been retained to represent Meril Findo in the above-referenced case. He is charged with assault with a deadly weapon. Mr. Findo allegedly assaulted his neighbor Joseph Markham with a hammer. Mr. Findo and Mr. Markham were arguing over the location of a fence Mr. Markham was building. According to Mr. Findo, Mr. Markham became angry and attempted to hit him with a brick. A struggle ensued, and the brick fell and hit Mr. Markham on the head. Mr. Markham claims that Mr. Findo became increasingly angry as the argument progressed; Mr. Findo grabbed a hammer and struck him repeatedly on the head and arms. Mr. Markham claims he never assaulted Mr. Findo with a brick. There were no witnesses to the argument. Mrs. Findo is currently separated from Mr. Findo and has agreed to testify against him. Her testimony is that before the confrontation, Mr. Findo stated, "Markham is out there building that damn fence again. I'll put a stop to this once and for all." He grabbed a hammer and went out the door. The Findo's children, Tomas, age sixteen, and Alice, age ten, were present and heard the conversation. Neither Mrs. Findo nor the children saw the confrontation.

Prepare a memorandum addressing the question of whether the conversation between Mr. and Mrs. Findo is a privileged spousal communication and, therefore, not admissible in the trial of Mr. Findo. I need the memo within two weeks. You can probably cover this in three to five pages."

The *process and considerations* involved in preparing an office legal memorandum are addressed in this chapter and Chapter 13. The office legal memorandum is usually composed of some or all of the sections presented in Figure 12–1.

The Application section of this chapter addresses the first half of Jeff's assignment—the heading through the fact sections. The Application section of Chapter 13 covers the remainder of the assignment—the analysis through the recommendations sections.

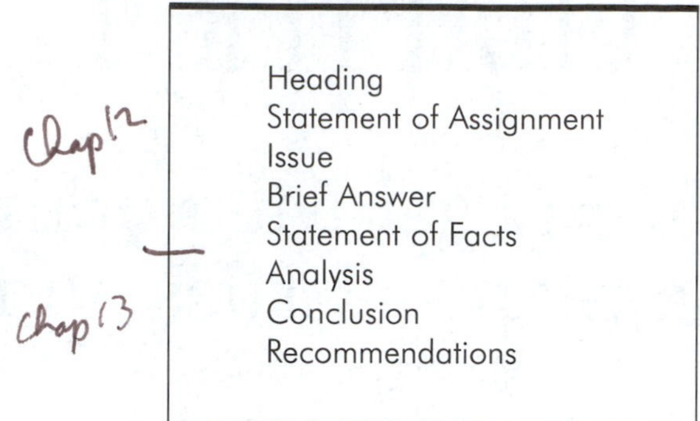

Figure 12–1
Sections of an Office Legal Memorandum

INTRODUCTION

The office legal memorandum is the type of legal writing a paralegal engaged in legal research and analysis most frequently prepares. The role of most paralegals is to provide assistance and support to an attorney. When this support function involves legal research, it usually focuses on research and analysis of the legal issues in a client's case. The results of this research and analysis are communicated to the attorney in the form of an office legal memorandum. It is one of the most effective and valuable ways a paralegal can support an attorney.

Chapters 12 and 13 are devoted to the preparation of office legal memorandums. Two chapters are devoted to this topic for the following reasons:

- Most law office analytical legal writing involves the preparation of office legal memorandums.
- The considerations involved in the preparation of office legal memorandums also apply to the preparation of documents for external use.

Chapter 12 focuses on the basic format for the office legal memorandum and the preparation of the first half of the memorandum: the heading through the statement of facts sections. The focus of Chapter 13 is on the heart of the memo: the legal analysis through the recommendation sections.

The preparation of an office legal memorandum is a multistep process involving the integration of legal research, analysis, and writing. This chapter and Chapter 13 cannot be read in a vacuum. They require the integration of the material presented in Chapters 1 through 10. Although it is assumed you are familiar with those chapters, cross-references to specific chapters are included to help you integrate the material.

For Example: The issue section of this chapter includes cross-references to Chapters 6 and 7. Chapters 6 and 7 present guidelines for identifying and drafting the issue that are helpful when preparing the issue section of an office legal memorandum.

As mentioned above, the majority of the legal research and writing prepared by a paralegal is designed for the use of the supervising attorney and not for external use, *i.e.,* use outside the office. The basic format and analytical process that are followed are fundamentally the same for both an office legal memorandum and a legal analysis document designed for external use. Therefore, the information presented in Chapters 12 and 13 should be kept in mind when reading Chapters 14 and 15. External use documents usually involve:

- Correspondence to clients or other individuals informing them of the analysis of a problem
- Briefs submitted to a trial court or a court of appeals

DEFINITION

An office legal memorandum provides an objective, critical analysis of a legal problem. It is an informative document that summarizes the research and analysis of the legal issue or issues raised by the facts of a client's case. It contains a summary of the law and how the law applies to the facts of the case. It presents an objective legal analysis and includes the arguments in favor and in opposition to the client's position.

A legal memorandum prepared for office use is referred to by many different names: interoffice legal research memorandum, office legal memorandum, office research memorandum, objective memorandum, legal memo, and so on. In this and the next chapter, the term office memo is used when referring to an office legal memorandum.

office legal memorandum

A legal memorandum prepared for office use. It presents an objective legal analysis of the issue(s) raised by the facts of the client's case and usually includes the arguments in favor of and in opposition to the client's position. It is often referred to by other names, such as interoffice legal research memorandum, office research memorandum, and interoffice memorandum of law.

PURPOSES, USES, AND IMPORTANCE

The major purposes and functions of an office memo are to:

1. Identify and record the law that applies to a specific issue or issues raised by the client's facts
2. Analyze and explain how the law applies to the issue
3. Assess the strengths and weaknesses of the client's case
4. Present a conclusion and proposed solution based on the analysis

A well-crafted office memorandum may be put to a variety of uses in a law office.

- It may be used as a guide to determine whether a claim exists.

  For Example: Assume one of the client's potential causes of action involves a breach of the implied warranty of merchantability. In the client's case, the sale took place at a garage sale. The office memo reveals that under the applicable statute, the warranty applies only if the seller is a merchant. The case on point provides that individuals holding a garage sale are not merchants within the meaning of the statute. The office memo reveals that no cause of action exists for a breach of implied warranty of merchantability.

- It may be used as a guide to the course of action to be pursued.

  For Example: Assume that the case involves a question of whether the client had a duty to discover and disclose information in a real estate transaction. The client was unaware that his house had termites, and consequently, the buyer was not informed of this problem. The office memo reveals that the case law requires the seller to inspect for termites and disclose the results of the inspection to the buyer. This information may lead the attorney to recommend that settlement be pursued.

- It may serve to inform subsequent researchers in the law office, working on other cases with similar issues and facts, how the law applies. Future researchers do not have to spend time reinventing the wheel.
- It may serve to refresh the memory of the attorney assigned to the case on how the law applies to an issue. This is especially true in complex cases. It is also true in cases where the memo is prepared early in the case, and the issue is not referred to by the attorney until months later when the matter is addressed by the court.
- It may be used as a guide for the attorney preparing a document to be filed with the court or correspondence for the client. The office memo may contain the statutory law, case law, and legal analysis that serve as the basis for the document being prepared.

  For Example: The office memo may address the question of whether a search warrant was improperly issued due to the insufficiency of the affidavit in support of the warrant. The standards required for a warrant to be sufficient are spelled out in the office memo. The attorney may use the office memo as a basis for the preparation of a brief in support of, or opposition to, a motion to suppress the evidence seized when the warrant was executed.

Office memos are of primary importance because they provide the answer to legal questions. Their importance is evidenced by the fact that office memos are required at every stage of the litigation process:

- Early in the case, they are used to identify the required elements of the cause of action and what is required to state a claim.
- They are used to determine whether the client has a defense or a cause of action.
- They are used throughout the litigation to determine what is required to support or oppose a motion.
- In the discovery process, a legal memo may be required to address discovery issues, such as what constitutes an attorney's work product.
- At the trial stage, an office memo often analyzes evidentiary issues, such as whether evidence is admissible.
- At the posttrial stage, an office memo may address issues raised on appeal, such as whether the court properly ruled on a matter during the trial.

Regardless of the purpose of the memo or at what point in the litigation process it is prepared, the actions of the supervisory attorney and the outcome of the case may largely depend upon the quality of the office memo. It is critical, therefore, that the performance of research, analysis, and drafting of the memo be thorough, careful, and complete.

As discussed in Chapter 10, legal writing is easier if you use a writing process. It is suggested that the writing process recommended in that chapter be followed when preparing an office memo. In this chapter, the writing process discussed in Chapter 10 is used as the framework for the preparation of an office memo. The office memo writing process consists of the three stages listed in Figure 12–2.

Figure 12–2

Stages in the Office Memo Writing Process

- Prewriting Stage
- Writing Stage
- Postwriting Stage

PREWRITING STAGE

The prewriting stage is composed of the three sections presented in Figure 12–3. A prerequisite to beginning the prewriting stage is the assembly of all available files and information concerning the client's case. All the relevant files and information must be complete. Once this is accomplished, the three sections can be addressed.

Nature of the Assignment

The first section of the prewriting stage requires a review of the assignment. This involves a determination of the following:

- Is the assignment clearly understood?
- What type of legal writing is required?
- Who is the audience?

Is the Assignment Clearly Understood?

Ask yourself if there are any questions concerning the nature or specifics of the assignment. The assignment may be vague or you may be unsure of what the attorney wants. If there are any questions, ask. Most attorneys would prefer you seek clarification rather than misunderstand the assignment and waste time addressing the wrong question.

For Example: The assignment is to analyze the client's case. You may need to seek clarification on which aspects of the case the supervisory attorney wants you to analyze or the specific questions or areas of law you should address.

The assignment may appear simple and clear at first, but as research and analysis progress, multiple issues or separate causes of action may become apparent. It may be necessary to have a brief follow-up meeting with the supervising attorney to determine if the focus should be narrowed.

For Example: A case that involves what appears to be a car wreck situation with a simple negligence issue may blossom into a case involving multiple issues, such as negligence, battery, and negligent infliction of emotional distress. It may be necessary to consult with the supervisory attorney to determine if you should pursue each issue or if some of the issues should be assigned to other paralegals. If there are time constraints, it may be necessary for other paralegals to address the newly identified issues.

An additional concern when addressing this question is to consider whether the assignment requires skills that you have not yet acquired.

For Example: Assume you have just begun working as a paralegal for a solo practitioner, and you are assigned the task of analyzing a complex products liability issue. The research and analysis skills required for the assignment may be beyond your current ability. If this occurs, discuss the matter with the attorney. More harm may occur if you try and fail than if you communicate your concerns. The attorney may divide the task into manageable sections and reassign parts of it to other paralegals or assign you to work with others to gain experience.

The Nature of the Assignment
The Constraints on the Assignment
The Organization of the Assignment

Figure 12–3
Three Sections of the Prewriting Stage

What Type of Legal Writing Is Required?

The next step in assessing the assignment is to determine the type of legal writing the assignment requires. This question is easily answered; the assignment usually identifies the type of writing required. In the example at the beginning of the chapter, the assignment calls for the preparation of a law office memorandum. The organization, format, and elements of the office memo are discussed in the organization section of the prewriting stage in the following text.

Who Is the Audience?

An office memo is usually designed for office use only. Therefore, the reader of the memo (the audience) will be familiar with the law, and the use of legal terminology is appropriate. Determine the writing preferences of the person the office memo is being prepared for, such as those regarding style.

For Example: Some attorneys prefer that the paralegal summarize the requirements of the statutory or case law. Some prefer that the law be quoted.

If the memo may be read outside the office, you should be sure to exclude any comments, recommendations, and so on that are intended only for office use, such as, "The client's expectations are unreasonable."

Constraints on the Assignment

The next section of the prewriting stage requires the identification of any constraint that may affect the preparation of the office memo. Ask yourself if there are any time or page limitations. These matters should be taken into consideration at the beginning. The allocation of time for research, analysis, and drafting is governed by time constraints. The depth of research and analysis may be limited by length constraints.

For Example: If you are limited to five pages and one week, you may want to focus your research on the lead case or cases. There may not be sufficient time or space to address additional cases or secondary authority.

Organization of the Assignment

When preparing an office memo, the most important section of the prewriting stage is the organization of the memo. In this section, the format or outline of the office memo is identified and an expanded outline is created and used.

Most law offices have a preferred format to follow when preparing an office memo. This format serves as a basic outline and starting point for the organization of the assignment. The creation and use of an expanded outline from the office format is discussed in the prewriting section of Chapter 10. In this chapter, the focus is on the format and outline of an office memo and the requirements and considerations involved in the preparation of each section of the outline. In this and the next chapter, the use of an expanded outline is included in the discussion of the preparation of each section of the office memorandum.

There is no standard format for an office memo. Formats vary from office to office, and attorneys within an office may have different preferences. Follow the format preferred by your supervisor. The format presented in Figure 12–4 is a recommended format that includes all the basic sections of an office memo that you may encounter.

Certain sections, such as the "Statement of Assignment" and "Brief Answer" sections, are not included in all formats and may not be included in the format adopted

Heading
Statement of Assignment
Issue
Brief Answer
Statement of Facts
Analysis
  Rule of law
  Case law (if necessary)—interpretation of rule of law
  Application of law to facts of case
  Counteranalysis
Conclusion
Recommendations

Figure 12–4
Basic Office Legal Memorandum Format

by your supervisory attorney. They are included here so that you will be familiar with them in the event they are included in the format used in your workplace. Other sections, such as the "Issue" and "Analysis" sections, are required in all office memos. In addition, note that the organization of the format may vary from office to office.

For Example: Some offices may prefer that the "Fact" section precede the "Issue" section. Usually the "Issue" section follows the "Statement of Assignment" and precedes the "Fact" section.

The recommended formats for a basic office memo and a complex office memo are presented in Figures 12–4 and 12–5. Following the presentation of the formats, the requirements and considerations involved in the preparation of each section are addressed in detail.

There is no definition of what constitutes a complex office legal memorandum. Generally a complex office memo consists of more than one issue and is relatively long (over ten pages). The formal outline of a complex office memo is merely an expansion of the basic office memo format. The components and considerations involved in the preparation of a complex office memo are the same as those involved in the preparation of a basic office memo. The sections are the same in basic content, although the number of sections is expanded.

For Example: A complex memo may consist of three issues. The procedures recommended for identifying, stating, and analyzing each issue are the same as those involved in the preparation of a basic single issue memo. Each issue is addressed separately, and the process for addressing each issue is the same as that followed when addressing the single issue in a basic office memo.

A complex office legal memorandum format is presented in Figure 12–5.

The office memo format may require the inclusion of a table of authority or a table of contents. These usually follow the statement of the assignment.

For Example:

TABLE OF CONTENTS

		Page
I.	Issues	2
II.	Facts	3
III.	Analysis Issue I	5
IV.	Analysis Issue II	10
V.	Recommendations	18

TABLE OF AUTHORITIES

CASES	Page
Smith v. Jones, 354 F.2d 786 (9th Cir. 1970)	7
Tod v. Doe, 559 N.E.2d 31 (Ind. App. 1988)	13
CONSTITUTIONAL PROVISIONS	
Art. 3 Ind. Constitution	6
STATUTES	
Ind. Code § 35-42-3-2	6
Ind. Code § 35-42-3-8	13

SECTIONS OF THE OFFICE MEMORANDUM

The heading, statement of assignment, issue, brief answer, and fact sections of the office memo are discussed in this section. The analysis, conclusion, and recommendation sections are addressed in Chapter 13. The preparation of the office memo requires the use of information presented in all of the preceding chapters of the text. As mentioned in the beginning of this chapter, reference to those chapters is included

Figure 12–5
Complex Office Legal Memorandum Format

Heading
Statement of Assignment
Issue I
Issue II
Issue III
Brief Answer Issue I
Brief Answer Issue II
Brief Answer Issue III
Statement of Facts
Analysis Issue I
- Rule of law
- Case law (if necessary)—interpretation of rule of law
- Application of law to facts of case
- Counteranalysis
- Conclusion Issue I

Analysis Issue II
- Rule of law
- Case law (if necessary)—interpretation of rule of law
- Application of law to facts of case
- Counteranalysis
- Conclusion Issue II

Analysis Issue III
- Rule of law
- Case law (if necessary)—interpretation of rule of law
- Application of law to facts of case
- Counteranalysis
- Conclusion Issue III

Recommendations (Separate recommendation sections may follow conclusion of each issue.)

as a guide to help you integrate the material presented in the chapters in the writing process.

Heading

Most office memos begin with a heading. The heading is usually brief and at a minimum contains:

- A heading in all capitals indicating the type of document, *i.e.*, MEMORANDUM OF LAW
- The name of the person to whom the memo is addressed
- The name of the person who prepared the memo
- The date
- Information identifying the subject of the memo. This may include the case name, the client's name, the case number, the office file number, and the subject matter of the memo. It usually follows "Re:"

There are various styles for the heading. Some of these are as follows:

For Example:

MEMORANDUM OF LAW

To: Susan Day, Attorney
From: Tom Clug, Paralegal
Date: December 1, 1997
Case: Smith v. Garage Doors, Inc.
Office File No.: Civ. 97-1136
Docket No.: Civ. 97-378
Re: Whether a contract for the sale and installation of a garage door is a sale of goods covered by the commercial code or is a sale of a service.

OFFICE LEGAL MEMORANDUM—CONTRACTS

Title: Smith v. Garage Doors, Inc., Civ. 97-378
Office File Civ. 97-1136
Requested by: Susan Day, Attorney
Submitted by: Tom Clug, Paralegal
Date Submitted: 12/1/97
Re: Contract law, Commercial Code § 42-2-205
Sale of goods/sale of service

OFFICE RESEARCH MEMORANDUM

To: Susan Day, Attorney
From: Tom Clug, Paralegal
Date: Dec. 1, 1997
Re: Smith v. Garage Doors, Inc., Civ. 97-378.
Whether a contract for the sale and installation of a garage door is a sale of goods or a sale of a service; Commercial Code § 42-2-205.

Statement of Assignment

This section may also be referred to as a "Background" or "Purpose" section. Some offices require a section that presents a discussion of what the writer has been assigned to do. This section usually follows the heading and may include some background information. The purpose of this section is to provide the reader with a description of the topic covered and the parameters of the assignment.

For Example: STATEMENT OF ASSIGNMENT. You have asked me to prepare a legal memorandum on the question of whether the sale and installation of a garage door by Garage Doors, Inc., is a sale of a service or a sale of goods covered by Commercial Code § 42-2-205.

For Example: STATEMENT OF ASSIGNMENT. You have asked me to research the question of whether the search of our client's automobile was an illegal search when she was stopped for a minor traffic offense and did not consent to the officer's request for permission to search the back seat of her vehicle. Pursuant to your request, this memo includes an analysis of the relevant state and federal law.

Issue

In a office memorandum, present the issue or issues at the beginning of the memo following the heading and the statement of assignment. Doing so establishes the focus of the memo. A well-crafted memo informs the reader at the outset of the following:

- The law that applies
- The precise legal question
- The significant facts of the case

In other words, it identifies the specific question to be addressed and places it in the context of the applicable law and the facts of the case. It sets the scope of the memo, thereby saving the reader from having to determine the issue from a reading of the analysis section.

There are several matters to keep in mind when preparing the issue section of the memo:

- The issue should be correctly identified.
- The issue should be completely and correctly stated.
- An expanded outline should be used when preparing the section.
- Issues are addressed separately when preparing complex office memos.

Identify the Issue

The issue is the precise legal question raised by the facts of the client's case. One of the most important tasks in the legal analysis process is the correct identification of the legal issue. You cannot solve the client's legal problem until it is correctly identified. If the issue is misidentified, everything that follows—time spent researching, analyzing, and writing—is wasted. Chapter 6 presents the analytical process that will help you identify the issue when preparing a memo.

Correctly State the Issue

The issue should be completely and correctly presented. When stated correctly, the reader is informed of the focus of the memo at the outset and saved from the distraction of having to identify the precise question while reading the analysis section.

For Example: Assume the issue involves a question of whether a will is valid if one of the witnesses does not actually see the testator sign the will. If the issue were stated, "Was the will validly executed?," the reader would have to read the analysis section of the memo to determine why it may not have been validly executed. There could be several reasons why the will may not have been validly executed: it may not have been witnessed correctly, there may not have been enough witnesses, it may have been signed improperly, and so on. If the issue is stated, "Under Probate Code § 29-5-7, is the execution of a will valid if one of the witnesses is present in the room when the testator signs but does not actually see the testator sign?," the issue is correctly and completely stated. The reader knows the precise question being addressed, the key facts, and the applicable law. The reader is not forced to obtain this information from the analysis section of the memo.

Chapter 7 presents guidelines to help you draft a comprehensive and precise statement of the issue. Refer to that chapter when preparing the issue section of the memo.

Use the Expanded Outline

The use of an expanded outline can greatly simplify the identification and drafting of the issue. On the issue page of the expanded outline, write every formulation of the issue as it comes to mind. The initial draft may be as simple as, "Was the will valid?" As you conduct research and gain a greater understanding of the applicable law, more complete formulations will become apparent.

For Example: "Under the state probate code, is a will validly executed if a witness is merely present in the room when the testator signs?" "Under the probate code, is the execution of a will valid if one of the witnesses is present in the room when the testator signs but does not actually see the testator sign?"

When you begin to write the issue section of the memo, all your ideas concerning the issue and drafts of the possible ways it may be stated are before you in one place. The crafting of the final statement of the issue is merely a matter of selecting and combining the necessary elements from the various drafts. The use of the expanded outline is discussed in detail in Chapter 10. Its use in regard to the preparation of an office memo is illustrated in the Application section of this chapter.

Address Issues Separately

Office memoranda assignments, such as a complex memorandum, often involve more than one issue. When addressing such assignments, it is preferable that each issue be listed sequentially in the issue section of the memo. In the analysis section of the format, each issue is addressed separately and completely (this is discussed in the next chapter). An outline of the format is presented in Figure 12–6.

Analysis Issue I
- Rule of law
- Case law (if necessary)—interpretation of rule of law
- Application of law to facts of case
- Counteranalysis
- Conclusion Issue I

Analysis Issue II
- Rule of law
- Case law (if necessary)—interpretation of rule of law
- Application of law to facts of case
- Counteranalysis
- Conclusion Issue II

Analysis Issue III, and so on.

Figure 12–6

Complex Memorandum—Analysis Section Format

When there are multiple issues, they should be listed in the issue section in the order in which they are discussed in the analysis section. The issue listed as Issue I in the issue section should be the first issue addressed in the analysis section. Issue II in the issue section should be the second issue addressed in the analysis section, and so on. The issues also should be listed in logical order. If the analysis of one issue is dependant on or affected by the analysis of another issue, the issue that affects the other issue should be presented first. For example, if the analysis of issue *B* is in some way affected by the analysis of issue *A*, issue *A* should be addressed first in the memo.

For Example: Assume that the client alleges that she entered into a contract to purchase dresses from a dressmaker, and the dressmaker installed defective zippers in the dresses. The dressmaker claims that the contract between them was not a valid contract, and even if there was a valid contract, the zippers were not defective. There are two separate issues. The issue of whether there is a valid contract should be presented and discussed first because if there is no contract, there can be no breach. The issue section would appear as follows:

Issue I Existence of contract
Issue II Breach of contract

If the issues are not dependent on or affected by other issues, they should be presented in chronological order.

For Example: Assume the client was involved in an automobile accident. The defendant ran a red light and hit the client's car. After the wreck, the defendant approached the client's car screaming and threatening the client. The defendant then pushed the client. At least four possible causes of action are present. They should be presented in the order in which they occurred:

Issue I Negligence—the car wreck
Issue II Assault—approaching client's car threatening and screaming
Issue III Battery—pushing the client
Issue IV Infliction of emotional distress—arising from the combined acts of assault and battery

A checklist for the issue section is presented in Figure 12–7.

Brief Answer

brief answer
A section of a memorandum of law that presents a brief, precise answer to the issue(s) addressed in the memo.

The brief answer section of the office memo is composed of a brief, precise answer to the issue(s). It informs the attorney of the answer to the question and should include a brief summary of the reasons in support of the answer. Its purpose is to provide a quick answer to the issue. It should not include information that is not discussed in the analysis section of the memo.

Usually this section begins with a one or two word answer, such as "Yes," "No," "Maybe," or "Probably not." The brief answer is followed by a brief statement of the grounds in support of the answer.

- ❑ Is the issue correctly identified?
- ❑ Is the applicable rule of law included in the issue?
- ❑ Is the citation of the rule correct?
- ❑ Is the legal question clearly stated in the issue?
- ❑ Are the key facts included in the issue?
- ❑ If there are multiple issues, are they presented in the proper order, such as logical or chronological?

Figure 12–7
Checklist—Issue Section

For Example:

Issue: According to the provisions of the Ski Safety Act § 679-33, does a resort have a duty to warn skiers of ice hazards on expert runs?

Brief Answer: No. The act provides that resorts have the duty to warn of hazards, and skiers are responsible for snow and ice conditions. The state supreme court has ruled that resorts have a duty to warn of snow and ice hazards only on intermediary and novice ski runs. The court specifically held that there is no duty to warn of any ice hazard on an expert run.

For Example:

Issue I Under the holographic will statute, Colo. Rev. Stat. § 15-11-503, is a holographic will valid if it is handwritten by a neighbor at the direction of the testator, but not written in the testator's handwriting?

Issue II Under the holographic will statute, Colo. Rev. Stat. § 15-11-503, is a holographic will valid if one of the witnesses to the testator's signature is a beneficiary of the will?

Brief Answer Issue I: Yes. The statute requires a holographic will to be handwritten by the testator. The state court of appeals has held that the statute should be interpreted liberally to effect the intent of the testator. If there is clear and convincing evidence that the writing took place at the direction of the testator, the will is valid even if it is not written in the testator's handwriting.

Brief Answer Issue II: No. The statute requires that the testator's signature be witnessed by two disinterested witnesses.

A checklist for the brief answer section is presented in Figure 12–8.

Statement of Facts

Following the brief answer section is the presentation of the facts of the case. The purpose of the fact section is to inform the attorney of the factual context of the issue. There are four considerations to keep in mind when preparing the fact section (see Figure 12–9).

statement of facts
The section of a memorandum of law that presents the factual context of the issue(s) addressed in the memorandum.

Fact Section—Importance

Some paralegals underemphasize the fact section of an office memorandum because they fail to understand the importance of the facts. The facts and, therefore, the fact section of the memo are important for several reasons:

- Every legal dispute involves a question of how the law applies to the facts of the case. Legal questions are not decided in a vacuum. The law is always applied in the context of a dispute raised by the facts of the case. The rule of law selected is determined by identification of the law that applies to the facts.
- The fact section may serve to refresh the memory of the attorney. The attorney may be working on other issues in the case or on several other cases and may not recollect the specific factual context of the issues addressed in the assignment. The fact section saves the supervisory attorney from having to review the file to determine the facts.

- ❑ Does the brief answer follow the office format, e.g., a one- or two-word answer followed by a short statement of the reasons?
- ❑ Is it brief? Does it summarize the reasons in one or two clear sentences?
- ❑ Is there a separate answer for each issue?

Figure 12–8
Checklist—Brief Answer Section

Figure 12–9
Considerations—Fact Section

The importance of the facts The contents of the section The organization of the section The manner of the presentation of the facts

- In many law offices, office memorandums are kept in research files, categorized by areas of law. They are available for reference and use in other cases involving similar issues. Subsequent researchers may not be familiar with the facts of the case. The memo, therefore, should be self-contained. A subsequent reader should be able to obtain all the facts necessary to understand the analysis from the fact section. It should not be necessary to review the case file.
- The fact section protects you from possible criticism. If additional facts come to light after the preparation of the memo that affect the analysis of the issue and lead to a different conclusion, a well-drafted fact section provides a record of the factual basis of your conclusion. It protects you from the criticism that you misanalyzed or misapplied the law.

Fact Section—Content

The fact section of the office memorandum should not simply repeat the facts included in the memo assignment; it should include only a brief statement of the background and key facts. The preparation of this section requires the identification of those facts necessary to provide the reader with a complete understanding of the factual context of the issues analyzed in the memo. It may require fewer facts than those included in the memo assignment, or it may require additional facts.

All facts referenced or included in the analysis section of the memo should be included in the fact section. The goal should be to provide, as briefly as possible, enough facts so the memo is a self-contained document; that is, it should be sufficiently complete so that any reader who is not familiar with the facts of the case does not have to refer to the case file. To accomplish this end, the fact section should include background and key facts.

- *Background facts:* Background facts are necessary because they put the key facts in context. That is, they provide the reader with information necessary for an overall understanding of the context within which the key facts occurred.
- *Key facts:* Key facts are those facts upon which the outcome of the case is determined. A key fact is a fact that is so essential that if it were changed the outcome of the case would probably be different.

An in-depth discussion of key facts is presented in Chapter 5. When preparing the fact section of the office memo, refer to that chapter for assistance in identifying key and background facts.

Fact Section—Organization

The fact section should be organized in a manner that enables the reader to clearly understand the events that relate to the issue(s) addressed in the memo. There are basically three organizational formats for presenting the facts:

- Chronological
- Topical
- A combination of chronological and topical

The format selected is usually governed by the nature of the facts.

Chronological Order. A chronological organization of the facts usually is adopted when the facts are a series of events related by time or date.

For Example: Assume the memo involves the following fact situation: On December 1, the client, Mr. Smith, was driving in the 600 block of First Street when the defendant, Mr. Doe, ran a red light at the intersection of First and Rose Street. As a result, Mr. Doe's vehicle collided with Mr. Smith's vehicle. Mr. Smith suffered a broken leg, and his wallet was stolen at the scene. On the way to the hospital, the ambulance was involved in a collision when it yielded at a stop sign. Mr. Smith suffered additional injuries, including a separated shoulder, in this collision. At the emergency room, his back was sprained when he was being helped onto the examining table by the hospital staff. Mr. Smith wants to know who he can sue for his various injuries and whether he can recover from Mr. Doe for the loss of his wallet. This example is referred to as the auto collision example in the remainder of this chapter.

The best way to present the facts of the case in the preceding example is chronologically. The facts that give rise to the various causes of action occurred in a linear sequence, and they are most clearly understood when narrated chronologically.

When facts occur in a linear sequence of events, such as in the auto collision example, the best form of presentation is chronological.

Topical Order. Some fact situations do not lend themselves to a chronological presentation. In such situations, the facts are related more by topic than by time sequence.

For Example: The memo involves the following divorce situation. The client, Mrs. Jones, is the petitioner in a divorce action. Mr. and Mrs. Jones disagree on the property distribution. They own three pieces of real property, parcels A, B, and C. All three parcels are held in both their names as joint tenants.

Parcel A includes the family home. The property is paid for. Forty percent of the mortgage was paid from an inheritance Mrs. Jones received from her father. The remainder was paid by both Mr. and Mrs. Jones from income from their respective employments. The assessed value is $150,000.

Parcel B is a rental property. They purchased the property shortly after the marriage. The mortgage on the property is being paid from the rent payment and contributions from the income of both Mr. and Mrs. Jones. Their current equity is $100,000. Ten thousand dollars of the equity is a contribution by Mr. Jones from his separate property.

Parcel C is recreational property. It was purchased five years after the marriage. It includes a small cabin and a storage shed. Their equity in the cabin and shed is $75,000. Mrs. Jones contributed $12,000 of the equity from lottery ticket winnings. The balance of the equity represents equal contributions from Mr. and Mrs. Jones.

In this example, a presentation of the facts by topic is most appropriate. The dates of purchase and the dates payments were made on the various parcels may be available, but a presentation of these facts by date would not lead to the clearest presentation of the facts. In the fact section, all the facts relating to each parcel should be presented separately, by parcel, regardless of the time sequence. All the facts relating to parcel A should be presented together; all the facts relating to parcel B should be presented together; and all the facts relating to parcel C should be presented together. The facts are more clearly understood when all the facts relating to each parcel are presented together; therefore, each parcel should be addressed separately in the analysis section of the memo.

Combination of Chronological and Topical Order. It may be appropriate to present the facts both chronologically and topically.

For Example: In the previous example, assume that parcel B was purchased by the husband three years prior to the marriage, parcel A immediately after the marriage, and parcel C five years later. Assume, also, that there is personal property: an automobile purchased two years after the marriage and a boat purchased three years after the marriage.

In addition to the issues concerning the three parcels, there are other issues in the divorce involving the other property. The appropriate presentation of the facts is a combination of the chronological and topical schemes.

In this situation, the real and personal property may be presented in the fact section in a chronological sequence according to the order of purchase, such as parcel B first, then parcel A, followed by the automobile, the boat, and finally parcel C. Note that all the information concerning each parcel of property is included when the parcel is discussed even though some factual events concerning the parcel may have occurred after the purchase of another parcel.

For Example: All the information concerning parcel B is included in the discussion of parcel B even though some of that information may have occurred after the purchase of parcel A. Mr. Jones's $10,000 contribution of separate property may have taken place after parcel A, the automobile, and the boat were purchased.

It would be confusing in this example to present all the facts in chronological order only. It is much clearer to present the property in chronological order and, in the discussion of each piece of property, present all the facts relating to that piece of property regardless of when they occurred.

The goal in the organization of the fact section is the clear presentation of the facts. Select the organizational format that best meets this goal.

Fact Section—Presentation

When drafting the fact section, you should present the facts accurately and objectively and avoid legal conclusions.

Accuracy. Accuracy in presenting the facts means that all the facts are presented, including those unfavorable to the client.

For Example: If, in the auto collision example, Mr. Smith was speeding when the defendant ran the red light, this fact should be included. Although it may not be a key fact that affects the outcome of the negligence claim, it is at minimum a background fact that should be included.

Accuracy also means not adding or changing facts. It is not proper to add a fact even if the existence of the fact seems obvious.

For Example: In the auto collision example, it is not proper to state that the defendant knew she was running a red light if there are no facts indicating her actual awareness of that fact. It is improper to add such a fact even if it seems obvious.

Objectivity. The facts should be stated objectively, which means you should present the facts in a neutral, not slanted, manner.

For Example: *Slanted presentation:* "Mr. Banker obviously knew what he was doing when he advised Mrs. Widow to buy a risky stock when the market was at its peak. Mrs. Widow unfortunately relied on his bad advice to her detriment."

The use of *obviously, unfortunately, detriment, bad,* and *risky* slant the presentation of the facts in favor of Mrs. Widow. The facts should be stated neutrally.

For Example: *Neutral presentation:* "The stock was at a two-year high when Mr. Banker advised Mrs. Widow to buy the stock. Mrs. Widow relied on his advice and purchased the stock. The value of the stock subsequently fell, and Mrs. Widow suffered a loss of $1,000."

Legal Conclusions. When composing the fact section, avoid legal conclusions.

For Example: "Mrs. Roe was driving negligently through the school zone." The phrase *driving negligently* is a legal conclusion.

State the facts without legal conclusions.

For Example: "Mrs. Roe was driving thirty-five miles per hour through the school zone. The posted speed is fifteen miles per hour."

A checklist for the fact section of an office memo is presented in Figure 12–10.

- ❑ Are sufficient background facts presented to inform the reader of the factual context of the assignment? Will the reader be required to refer to the case file to understand the analysis of the issues?
- ❑ Are all the key facts included? Will the reader have to refer to the case file to obtain key facts?
- ❑ Are the facts organized chronologically, topically, or chronologically and topically combined?
- ❑ Are the facts presented accurately and objectively?
- ❑ Are legal conclusions excluded from the fact presentation?
- ❑ Is the fact section complete?

Figure 12–10
Checklist—Fact Section

KEY POINTS CHECKLIST: *Preparing an Interoffice Memorandum*

- ❑ An office memorandum should be a self-contained document. All the information necessary to understand the context of the legal analysis should be included in the memo. Subsequent readers should not be required to refer to the case file to understand the issue, facts, or analysis.
- ❑ To achieve the goal of properly presenting the issue, the issue should include the rule of law, legal question, and key facts. Refer to Chapters 7 and 8 when identifying and stating the issue.
- ❑ The fact situation should be presented objectively and include both background and key facts.
- ❑ Follow the format adopted where you work when preparing the office memo. You may be familiar with or prefer a different format; if appropriate, recommend changes to the office format. If your suggestions are not adopted, be sure to follow the format used in the office.
- ❑ Be sure you understand the assignment. If you are unclear about any aspect of the assignment, ask the supervisory attorney. Do not waste time pursuing answers to the wrong question or performing the wrong task.
- ❑ If the complexity of the task requires skills beyond your ability, communicate your concerns.

APPLICATION

In this section, the principles and guidelines discussed in the previous sections are illustrated through their application to the assignment presented in the hypothetical at the beginning of the chapter. Jeff Lyons's assignment is to research a question involving privileged spousal communications. He performs the assignment by adopting and following the writing process presented in Chapter 10. A brief summary of the steps Jeff follows when applying the writing process is included in this section.

The first step of the prewriting stage of the writing process is to review the assignment. After reviewing the assignment, Jeff has no questions concerning the nature of the task ahead and the constraints on the performance of the task. The assignment is to prepare an office memorandum for Rita Berdwin, his supervisory attorney; the memo should not exceed five pages; and the memo should be completed within two weeks.

The next step of the prewriting stage is to organize the approach to the research, analysis, and writing of the assignment. To accomplish this, Jeff retrieves the office memorandum format preferred by Ms. Berdwin. Assume the format preferred by Ms. Berdwin is the recommended office memorandum format presented in Figure 12–1. From this format, Jeff prepares an expanded outline. Using three-holed, binder paper (or computer files if he has access to a computer), he creates a separate page for each section of the outline. One page is titled Statement of Assignment, one page is titled Issue, one page is titled Brief Answer, one page is titled Statement of Facts, and so on. He continues in this manner until there is a separate page for each section and subsection of the outline.

Once the expanded outline is completed, Jeff begins the prewriting process. As any idea comes to him concerning the assignment, he enters the idea on the appropriate page of the outline.

For Example: Assume that, at the outset, he has an idea about how the issue should be stated. "Is the conversation between Mr. and Mrs. Findo a privileged interspousal communication that cannot be admitted at trial?" He immediately enters this possible formulation of the issue on the Issue page of the expanded outline.

Jeff locates the statute governing privileged spousal communications, 735 ILCS 5/8-801 (West 1992). The relevant portion of this statute provides, "In all actions, husband and wife may testify for or against each other, provided that neither may testify as to any communication or admission made by either of them to the other or as to any conversation between them during marriage. . . ." He places a copy of this statute in the Rule of Law section of the outline.

Jeff's research locates the lead case on point, *People v. Sanders,* 99 Ill. 2d 262, 457 N.E.2d 1241 (1983). He places the relevant portions of the case in the Case Law section of the expanded outline. These portions are as follows:

- The defendant's murder conviction was based in part upon the testimony of his wife.
- She was allowed to testify about two conversations she had with the defendant that took place in the presence of their three children, thirteen, ten, and eight years old.
- The conversations implicated the husband in the murder.

- The defendant appealed the conviction, claiming the trial court erred when it allowed the testimony.
- The defendant argued that under the statute the conversations were privileged spousal communications and, therefore, were not admissible.
- The state supreme court, upholding the court of appeals, stated, "The appellate court appears to have exhaustively researched the subject and concluded, as we do, that the great weight of authority is that the presence of children of the spouses destroys confidentiality unless they are too young to understand what is being said. (citations omitted). Nothing in the record indicates that Robert, then 13 years old, was not old enough or sufficiently bright to understand the conversation which he heard, particularly inasmuch as the wife's testimony indicates that some of it was directed to him. In these circumstances, under the rule followed in this State, his presence rendered the conversation ineligible for the protection of the statutory privilege."

Jeff may place the entire case in the outline or include only the relevant parts. If only the relevant quotations are included in the outline, he notes the page numbers of the quotations.

Upon reviewing the information at hand, Jeff concludes that he has sufficient information to complete the assignment. He continues researching, however, to make sure he has thoroughly explored the question, and he updates his research to ensure that it represents the current law.

While researching and thinking about the case, whenever Jeff has an idea about how something should be written or where something should be placed in the memo, he enters the information in the expanded outline.

For Example: A reading of the statute reveals that the privilege applies only to conversations between spouses during the marriage; therefore, a key fact is that the conversation took place during the marriage. While reading the case, he discovers that the presence of children of the spouses destroys confidentiality unless the children are too young to understand. Therefore, the fact that the children in the client's case, present during the conversation, were sixteen and ten years old is also a key fact. As he becomes aware of this information, Jeff notes these key facts on the fact and issue pages of the expanded outline.

When Jeff has completed the prewriting stage of the writing process, the expanded outline contains all the information necessary to write the memo. Each section of the expanded outline contains:

- The research relevant to the section
- Any draft sentences, sentence fragments, and ideas relevant to the section, such as transition sentences
- Notes concerning the drafting of each section, such as order of presentation and what must be included

A brief summary of each section of the expanded outline is as follows:

- On the statement of assignment page, Jeff has noted all of his thoughts regarding how this section should be written.
- The issue page includes a reference to the statute, key facts, and every formulation of the issue that has occurred to Jeff as he worked on the assignment.

- The brief answer page includes draft sentences on how the brief answer should be phrased. Ideas for this section may have come to him while he was preparing the analysis or conclusion sections of the memo.
- Included on the facts page is a list of all the key and background facts he has identified as he conducted research. Jeff also has noted any drafts of sentences he may use regarding the composition of the section.
- On the rule of law page of the analysis section, he has included the applicable statute with the correct citation. He has listed here any ideas he had on drafting this section, such as transition sentences.

> ***For Example:*** "The statute does not provide guidance concerning what effect the presence of children during the communication has on the privilege. Therefore, case law must be consulted."

- The case law page of the analysis section contains the case citation and a copy of the case or relevant sections of the case. Also included here are any notes Jeff has made concerning the discussion or presentation of the case in the memo.
- On the application page of the analysis section, Jeff has included any information, ideas, or sentences regarding how the rule of law from the case and statute will be applied to the facts.
- The counteranalysis page of the analysis section includes any information concerning the counteranalysis, such as opposing case law.
- On the conclusion and recommendation pages of the outline, just as on the other pages of the expanded outline, Jeff has included notes, ideas, draft sentences, and so on that may be used when drafting these sections.

Once the research and analysis are finished and the expanded outline is completed, the writing process can begin. The use of the expanded outline greatly simplifies the writing process.

> ***For Example:*** Included on the issue page of the expanded outline are all the various ways the issue may be stated: "Is the communication between Mr. and Mrs. Findo privileged?" "Is the conversation between Mr. and Mrs. Findo a privileged interspousal communication that cannot be admitted at trial?" "Does the presence of children of the spouses during a conversation render the communication nonprivileged?" "Is the interspousal communication privilege destroyed if the communication takes place in the presence of children of the spouse?" "Under Illinois law, is the interspousal communication privilege destroyed when the conversation takes place in the presence of sixteen- and ten-year-old children of the spouses?"
>
> When Jeff begins to draft the issue section of the memo, the task is made easier because all the various formulations of the issue are in one place. All Jeff has to do is compose the issue by selecting and combining the best language from the various formulations on the issue page of the expanded outline.

Using the writing process presented in Chapter 10, the writing tips presented in Chapter 11, and the guidelines presented in the other chapters of this text, Jeff completes the assignment. The completed portions of Jeff's assignment that involve the sections of the office memorandum discussed in this chapter, the heading through the facts sections, are presented below. Since the remaining portions of an office memorandum, the analysis through recommendations sections, are discussed in the next chapter, those sections of Jeff's completed office memorandum are presented in the Application section of that chapter.

OFFICE MEMORANDUM OF LAW

To:	Rita Berdwin, Attorney
From:	Jeff Lyons, Paralegal
Date:	April 30, 1997
Case:	State v. Findo
Office File No.:	Cr. 97-136
Docket No.:	Cr. 97-378
Re:	Privileged spousal communications

Statement of Assignment

You have asked me to prepare a memorandum of law addressing the question of whether the conversation between Mr. Findo (our client) and Mrs. Findo, which took place in the presence of their children, ages sixteen and ten years old, is a privileged spousal communication and, therefore, is not admissible in the criminal trial of Mr. Findo.

Issue

Under the Illinois privileged spousal communication statute, 735 ILCS 5/8-801 (West 1992), is a spousal conversation privileged and not admissible into evidence if it takes place in the presence of the spouses' children, ages sixteen and ten years old?

Brief Answer

No. The communication is not a privileged communication protected by the provisions of the statute. The state supreme court has ruled that the privilege is destroyed when the conversation takes place in the presence of children of the spouses who are old enough to understand the content of the communication.

Statement of Facts

Mr. Findo is charged with assaulting his neighbor, Mr. Markham, with a deadly weapon, a hammer. Mr. Markham claims that Mr. Findo attacked him and struck him several times with a hammer. Mr. Findo claims he did not attack Mr. Markham with a hammer; he claims that Mr. Markham attacked him with a brick and during the struggle the brick fell and hit Mr. Markham on the head. Mrs. Findo, currently separated from her husband, has agreed to testify that before the confrontation, Mr. Findo stated, "Markham is out there building that damn fence again. I'll put a stop to this once and for all." This conversation took place in the presence of the Findo's children, Tomas, age sixteen, and Alice, age ten. There were no witnesses to the argument. Neither Mrs. Findo nor the children saw the confrontation.

SUMMARY

The drafting of an office legal memorandum is one of the most important and often difficult types of legal writing assignments a paralegal is required to perform. It requires the integration of the research, analysis, and writing skills discussed throughout this text.

An office memorandum is designed for office use and is usually drafted for the supervisory attorney. It involves the legal analysis of issues raised by the facts of a client's case. It is designed to identify the law that applies to the legal issue, analyze how the law applies to the issue, and present a proposed solution or conclusion based on the analysis.

It is recommended that you follow the writing process presented in Chapter 10 when preparing an office memorandum. The recommended format for the organization of the office memorandum is as follows:

Heading
Statement of Assignment
Issue
Brief Answer
Statement of Facts
Analysis
  Rule of law
  Case law (if necessary)—interpretation of rule of law
  Application of law to facts of case
  Counteranalysis
Conclusion
Recommendations

This chapter presents the considerations involved in the preparation of the heading, statement of assignment, issue, brief answer, and statement of facts sections of the office memorandum. The considerations involved in the preparation of the analysis through recommendations sections are discussed in Chapter 13.

The heading section contains information describing who the memo is from and to, the name of the case, and the nature of the issue. The statement of assignment section provides a description of the topic covered and the parameters of the assignment.

The issue section follows the statement of assignment. It is one of the most important parts of the memo. It informs the reader of the precise legal question addressed in the analysis section of the memo. It should include the applicable rule of law, the exact legal question, and the key facts that are necessary for the resolution of the issue. The brief answer section provides a brief and precise answer to the issue and a brief summary of the reasons in support of the answer.

The statement of facts section provides the facts of the client's case that gave rise to the issue addressed in the memo. It includes the background and key facts of the dispute and should provide sufficient factual information to allow the reader to understand the analysis without having to refer to the case file or any other source outside the memo.

Many of the procedures and steps involved in preparing an office memorandum apply to the preparation of legal writing designed for external use, such as correspondence to clients and documents to be filed with a court, including trial court and appellate court briefs. In order to thoroughly cover this topic, the analysis, conclusion, and recommendations sections of the office memorandum are covered in the next chapter.

EXERCISES

ASSIGNMENT

For each of the assignments presented at the end of Chapter 13, prepare the heading, statement of assignment, issue, brief answer, and statement of facts sections of an office memo. Use the format and guidelines presented in this chapter when performing this assignment.

CHAPTER 13

Office Legal Memorandum Analysis to Conclusion

Ellen Taylor is a paralegal intern working in a district attorney's office in the hypothetical state of New Washington. Ms. Taylor recently received the following assignment.

To:	Ellen Taylor, Intern
From:	Carl Pine, Assistant District Attorney
Re:	State v. Kent. Arrest during execution of search warrant and constructive possession
Case:	Cr. 97-404

On January 7, 1997, police officers executed a search warrant that authorized the search of the apartment of David Kent for narcotics. Mr. Kent's apartment is located on the third floor of a four-story apartment complex. Upon entering the apartment, the officers found Mr. Kent lying on the bed in the bedroom. The officers secured the apartment and, after frisking Mr. Kent for weapons, handcuffed him and moved him into the kitchen for the stated purpose of "his and our safety." They did not read him his rights or officially place him under arrest at this time.

The search of the apartment did not reveal any narcotics. The police, however, discovered an "eight-inch hole" in the only window in the bedroom, and the window screen was pushed out. The police went downstairs and searched the area below the window. The bedroom window faces the rear of the apartment complex, and below the window is a parking lot. In the parking lot, three stories below Mr. Kent's bedroom window, the officers found a plastic bag containing one ounce of rock cocaine. The parking lot is a common area of the complex, accessible to the public and all apartment dwellers. No witnesses have been located who saw the defendant throw the cocaine out the window. There were no fingerprints on the bag or other evidence linking Mr. Kent to the cocaine. After the bag was located, the defendant was read his rights and placed under arrest. He was charged with possession of a controlled substance.

Please research and prepare an office legal memorandum addressing the following questions:

1. Was the defendant under arrest when he was handcuffed and moved into the kitchen?
2. Is the connection between the defendant and the cocaine sufficient to support charges of possession of a controlled substance?

The office legal memorandum prepared by Ms. Taylor is presented in the Application section of this chapter.

INTRODUCTION

Chapter 12 focuses on the process involved in preparing the first half of an office legal memorandum: the heading, statement of assignment, issue, brief answer, and statement of facts sections. This chapter addresses the preparation of the second half of the office legal memorandum: the analysis, conclusion, and recommendations sections. In this chapter, as in Chapter 12, an office legal research memorandum is referred to as an office memo.

The discussion in Chapter 12 addressing the adoption of a writing process and the use of an expanded outline also applies to the preparation of the second half of an office memo. The guidelines presented in that chapter in regard to the writing process and the use of an expanded outline should be followed when preparing the analysis, conclusion, and recommendations sections of the office memo. The use of an expanded outline when preparing these sections is briefly covered in this chapter. Refer to Chapter 10 for a comprehensive discussion of the use of an expanded outline in the prewriting stage. The examples in this chapter refer to the enacted and case law of the hypothetical state of New Washington.

ANALYSIS SECTION

The purpose of an office memo is to provide a legal analysis of the issue(s) in a case. The memo informs the reader of the law that governs the issue(s) and how it applies in the client's case. The analysis section is the part of the memo where the law is presented, analyzed, and applied to the issue(s). It connects the issue with the conclusion. It is the heart of an office memo assignment.

The analysis section is often referred to as the discussion section. The conventional analytical format, and the most efficient way through which to approach a legal question, is the IRAC format, that is, Issue, Rule, Analysis, Conclusion. The IRAC approach is discussed in detail in Chapter 2. Under the IRAC approach and the office memo format introduced in Chapter 12, the issue is presented at the beginning of the memo; the rule of law, analysis, and application of the rule of law to the facts are covered in the analysis section; and the conclusion summarizes the analysis. The reasons for following this approach are obvious:

- The reader must know the question in order to know the context in which the rule is analyzed.
- The rule that applies to the question must be identified before the rule can be analyzed and applied to the facts of the case.
- The application of the rule to the facts must take place before a conclusion can be reached.

Although IRAC is the basic format for addressing legal issues, it is only a broad outline of the format. It is necessary to have a more detailed outline of the analysis section to effectively approach an office memo assignment and prepare an office memo.

Analysis—Format

The recommended format of the analysis section is presented in Figure 13–1.

In the prewriting stage of the writing process, each of the subsections of the analysis section should be assigned at least one page in the expanded outline: a page for the rule of law, a page for each case, at least one page for the application of the law to the facts, and at least one page for the counteranalysis.

Part A. Rule of law
Part B. Case law (if necessary)—interpretation of rule of law
  1. Name of case
  2. Facts of case—sufficient to demonstrate case is on point
  3. Rule or legal principle from case that applies to the client's case
Part C. Application of the law to the facts of the client's case
Part D. Counteranalysis

Figure 13–1
Basic Four-Part Format—Analysis Section

If the memo is a complex memo involving multiple issues, the same basic format is followed for each issue (see Figure 13–2).

If more than one rule of law applies to a specific issue, the outline should include a reference to each rule.

For Example:

Issue I—Analysis
  Part A. Rule of law
    1. Section 59-703 of the commercial code
    2. Section 45-211 of the usury statute

If more than one case is required to interpret the rule of law, such as when more than one element of the rule requires case law interpretation, the outline should include a reference to each case.

For Example:

Issue I—Analysis
  Part A. Rule of law—section 59-703 of the commercial code
  Part B. Case law
    1. Case 1. *Smith v. Jones*—interpreting the term *sale* as used in § 59-703
      A. Facts of case—sufficient to demonstrate case is on point
      B. Rule or legal principle from case that applies to the client's case
    Part C. Application of the law to the facts of the client's case
    Part D. Counteranalysis
    2. Case 2. *Row v. Downs*—interpreting the term *merchant* as used in § 59-703
      A. Facts of case—sufficient to demonstrate case is on point
      B. Rule or legal principle from case that applies to the client's case
    Part C. Application of the law to the facts of the client's case
    Part D. Counteranalysis
  Part A. Rule of law—section 45-211 of the usury statute
  Part B. Case law
    1. *Doe v. Dean*—interpreting the term *loan* as used in § 45-211.
      A. Facts of case—sufficient to demonstrate case is on point
      B. Rule or legal principle from case that applies to the client's case
    Part C. Application of the law to the facts of the client's case
    Part D. Counteranalysis

The elements of the basic format for the analysis section of an office memo are discussed in the remainder of this section. Once the considerations involved in preparing the analysis of a single issue are mastered, complex memo assignments that address multiple issues or separate subissues are approached by applying the basic process to the analysis of each issue or subissue.

Issue I—Analysis
- Part A. Rule of law
- Part B. Case law (if necessary)—interpretation of rule of law
  1. Name of case
  2. Facts of case—sufficient to demonstrate case is on point
  3. Rule or legal principle from case that applies to the client's case
- Part C. Application of the law to the facts of the client's case
- Part D. Counteranalysis

Issue II—Analysis
- Part A. Rule of law
- Part B. Case law (if necessary)—interpretation of rule of law
  1. Name of case
  2. Facts of case—sufficient to demonstrate case is on point
  3. Rule or legal principle from case that applies to the client's case
- Part C. Application of the law to the facts of the client's case
- Part D. Counteranalysis

Issue III—Analysis (same format as Issues I and II)

Figure 13–2

Complex Memo—Analysis Section Format

Analysis—Part A Rule of Law

Inasmuch as the analysis section of an office memo addresses how the law applies to the issue(s) and facts of the client's case, the starting point is a presentation of the rule of law or legal principle that applies. This is necessary because the law must be presented before it can be applied.

The governing law may be enacted law, such as a constitutional provision or a legislative act, or common law, such as a court-adopted rule of law. Comprehensive coverage of enacted and case law analysis is presented in Chapters 3, 4, and 8.

Some considerations to keep in mind when preparing the rule of law portion of the analysis section are listed in Figure 13–3.

Rule of Law—Introduction

The analysis section begins with the presentation of the rule of law. Do not start immediately with a presentation of the rule; use introductory language. The introductory language is italicized in the following examples.

For Example: "*The rule of law governing the sale of securities* is section 59-903 of the New Washington Commercial Code. The section provides . . ."

"*In New Washington, the doctrine of strict liability was established in the case of Elton v. All Faiths Hospital*, 931 N. Wash. 395, 396 (1976), where the court stated . . ."

- Introducing the rule of law
- What to include
- Multiple rules of law
- Citation

Figure 13–3

Part A—Rule of Law—Considerations

Rule of Law—What to Include

When presenting the rule of law, paraphrase or quote only the relevant portions of the law. In some instances, the rule of law is very lengthy, and only portions of the law apply to the issue being addressed. This is often true when the applicable law is statutory law and the statute is composed of many subsections and only one subsection applies. If this is the case, include only the relevant portion of the law.

For Example—*Statutory Law:* "The rule of law governing oppressive conduct is § 50-14-5, which provides:

A. The district courts may liquidate the assets and business of a corporation:

1. in an action by a shareholder when it is established that: . . .

(b) the acts of the directors . . . are illegal, oppressive, or fraudulent. . . ."

Note: Subsection (a) is omitted because the provisions of subsection (a) do not apply to the issue being discussed.

For Example—*Common Law:* "The rule of law governing a ski resort's duty to warn of snow and ice conditions was established in the case of *Jones v. Mountain Ski Resort,* 943 N. Wash. 857, 877 (1988), where the court stated, 'Resorts have a duty to warn of snow and ice conditions in the following situations: . . . when the snow or ice condition is a latent hazard. . . .'"

Note: Portions of the opinion are omitted because they do not apply to the issue being discussed.

Rule of Law—Multiple Rules

The analysis may require consideration of more than one rule of law. If this is the case, the format is similar to that discussed in the preceding text. Use introductory language, and present the relevant portions of each rule.

For Example: "The New Washington Commercial Code section 50-101 establishes which contracts must be in writing. In our case, two subsections of that section apply: section 50-101B, which requires that 'An agreement which is not to be performed within one year from the making . . .' must be in writing, and section 50-101C, which provides that 'Contracts for the sale of goods in the amount of $500 or more . . .' must be in writing."

When the rule of law involves both general and specific sections of a statute, the relevant general portion of the statute should be presented first, followed by the specific portion of the statute.

For Example: "Section 50-501 creates an implied warranty of merchantability if the seller is a merchant with respect to goods of that kind. The term *merchant* is defined in section 50-401 as 'A person who deals in goods of that kind. . . .'"

Rule of Law—Citation

Whenever the reference is to a rule of law or legal principle, you must present the authority in support of your statement of the rule. If the source for the rule is enacted law, cite the enacted law; if it is case law, cite the case. Note that in the previous four examples, the reference includes the source for the rule of law—either statutory or case law. Without a reference to the authority, it is merely your word that the rule of law presented in the memo is actually what the law provides. The reader needs to know the source in order to check for accuracy and answer any questions concerning the law.

Analysis—Part B Rule of Law Interpretation—Case Law

Three considerations you should keep in mind when addressing the interpretation of the rule of law discussed in the memo are presented in Figure 13–4.

case interp of law

Figure 13–4
Rule of Law Interpretation—Considerations

- Is interpretation required?
- What is the role of case law?
- What is the process for presenting case law?

Rule of Law Interpretation—No Interpretation Required

In some instances, the rule of law, whether it is statutory or case law, can be applied directly to the facts of the client's case. Further case law is not required to determine how the rule applies.

For Example: The rule of law establishes a 15 mph speed limit in school zones, and the client was ticketed for driving 30 mph in a school zone. In this situation, case law is not needed to determine how the law applies. The law can be applied directly to the facts: driving 30 mph in the school zone is a violation of the law.

In such instances, proceed to the Analysis—Part C Application of Rule of Law to Client's Case section of this chapter for guidance.

Note, however, you should *always* perform at least a cursory check of the case law. This is necessary to ensure that there is not some special interpretation of the rule or a term used in the rule that is not apparent from a plain reading of it.

Rule of Law Interpretation—Role of Case Law

Usually the rule of law that governs the issue being analyzed has some unexpected, unobvious quirk or is so broadly stated that case law must be referred to determine how it applies. Case law, in effect, provides the link between the rule of law and the issue raised by the facts of the client's case. Court opinions determine and explain how the law is interpreted and applied in specific fact situations.

For Example: The First Amendment protects freedom of speech. The amendment does not define what constitutes speech. If the client's case involves the question of whether a symbolic act such as burning a state flag is protected under the First Amendment's freedom of speech provisions, case law must be consulted. The Supreme Court has interpreted how the First Amendment applies in this specific fact situation. Acts such as burning a state flag are considered symbolic speech and are protected under the First Amendment.

For Example: Suppose a statute prohibits oppressive conduct by majority shareholders against minority shareholders, and *oppressive conduct* is not defined in the statute. Court decisions may define what constitutes oppressive conduct in specific fact situations, and reference to court decisions is necessary to determine how the law applies.

Rule of Law Interpretation—Process for Presenting Case Law

When presenting the case law that interprets how the law applies to a fact situation such as the client's, the format presented in Figure 13–5 is recommended.

Name and Citation of Court Opinion. When presenting the case, first identify the case name and citation. The reader should know the name of the case at the beginning of

Figure 13–5
Format for Presenting Case Law

- Name and Citation of Court Opinion
- Facts of the Case—Those facts sufficient to demonstrate that the case is on point
- Rule of Law—The rule of law or legal principle presented in the case that applies to the issue being addressed in the office memo

the discussion. This eliminates any possible confusion that may arise about which case is being discussed.

For Example: "The case that defines the term *publication* as used in the statute is *Smith v. Jones,* 956 N. Wash. 441, 881 N.E.2d 897 (1995)."

Facts of the Case. The next step is to provide sufficient information concerning the facts and rule of law applied in the case to demonstrate that the case is on point. To accomplish this, you must include enough information about the court opinion to demonstrate that the similarity between the key facts and rule of law of the opinion and those of the client's case is sufficient for the court opinion to govern or provide guidance in deciding how the law applies.

For Example: Assume the client's case involves the question of whether a majority shareholder in a closely held corporation engaged in oppressive conduct when he refused to issue dividends while granting himself, as CEO of the corporation, semiannual bonuses in an amount triple his annual salary. Section 90-9-4 of the state corporation statutes prohibits oppressive conduct by majority shareholders against minority shareholders. The statute does not define *oppressive.* The case on point is *Cedrik v. Ely,* 956 N. Wash. 776, 881 N.E.2d 451 (1995).

The introduction of the case may read as follows: "The case that defines what constitutes 'oppressive' conduct in a fact situation such as that presented in our case is *Cedrik v. Ely,* 956 N. Wash. 776, 881 N.E.2d 451 (1995). In that case, just as in our case, a majority shareholder of a closely held corporation granted himself bonuses in excess of triple his salary. In *Cedrik,* the majority shareholder also refused to issue dividends. In defining what constitutes 'oppressive conduct' under § 90-9-4, the court stated. . . . *Id.* at 778."

Chapter 8 presents a comprehensive discussion of the steps and considerations involved in determining if a case is on point. Refer to that chapter for assistance in deciding what must be included in the presentation of a case to demonstrate that the case is on point.

Rule of Law. The last step when discussing a case that is on point is to identify the rule of law or legal principle adopted by the court that applies to the issue being addressed in the office memo.

For Example: The state collections statute provides that efforts to collect payment for a debt must be made in a "reasonable manner." *Reasonable manner* is not defined in the statute. In the client's case, the collector called the client three times a day, often after 9 P.M. The case on point is *Cerro v. Collectors,* Inc., 955 N. Wash. 641, 880 N.E.2d 401 (1994). The presentation of the *rule of law* applied by the court would read as follows: "In the *Cerro* case, the court stated that 'reasonable contact' as used in the collections statute means no more than one telephone call a day to the debtor's residence. The court went on to state that no calls should be placed before 6 A.M. or after 7 P.M. *Id.* at 645."

Two considerations should be kept in mind when presenting the rule of law from the case:

1. Quote the language of the court whenever practical. Quotations are stronger than paraphrases. Sometimes the language does not lend itself to quotation, such as in situations where the rule is composed of several parts or steps that are presented in more than one paragraph of the opinion.

   Do not use too many quotations. Quotations should be used to quote the law or legal principle presented by the court and key portions of the court's reasoning. They should not be used in place of your analysis. You have failed to properly analyze the case law if your analysis consists almost entirely of quotations of a court's presentation of the law and its reasoning.

2. When presenting the law, always cite the page of the court opinion where the rule is presented.

For Example: "In defining what constitutes 'oppressive conduct' under § 90-9-4, the court stated, 'Oppressive conduct occurs when a majority shareholder engages in wrongful conduct which inures to the benefit of the majority and the detriment of the minority.' *Id.* at 778."

In summary, the sequence when presenting a case is as follows:

- Case name and case citation
- Relevant facts from the case that demonstrate the case is on point
- The rule of law or principle adopted by the court that applies to the issue in the client's case

This sequence is recommended because it is logical to discuss a case using this format for the following reasons:

- It is more readable if the reader knows first the name of the case; then what happened, the facts; then the rule of law applied by the court.
- It is logical to discuss the rule of law last because the next step is the application of the rule to the issue(s) and facts of the client's case. The memo flows more smoothly if the *application* of the rule immediately follows the *presentation* of the rule.

This is only a recommended sequence, however, not a hard-and-fast rule. In some instances, it may be better to address the rule of law from the opinion first, then present the name and facts from the case. Follow a sequence that works best for the memo you are drafting.

Analysis—Part C Application of Rule of Law to Client's Case

The purpose of the office memo is to determine how the law applies. A critical element, therefore, of the analysis section is the application of the law to the issue(s) raised by the facts of the client's case. There are two situations you will encounter when applying the rule of law to the facts of the case.

- The rule does not require interpretation through the use of case law.
- The rule requires interpretation through the use of case law.

Application of Rule That Does Not Require Case Law Interpretation

As discussed in the Analysis—Part B Rule of Law Interpretation—Case Law section, there are some instances where case law is not required to determine how the rule of law applies to the issue being analyzed. It is clear from the face of the rule how it applies. In such instances, the rule is simply applied directly to the issue being addressed in the office memo.

For Example: "Municipal ordinance 91-1 establishes 25 mph as the maximum speed in residential areas of the municipality. The client was ticketed for driving 55 mph in a residential neighborhood. The application of the ordinance is clear. The client violated the ordinance."

Application of Rule That Requires Case Law Interpretation

In most instances, there is a question of how the rule of law or an element of the rule applies to the issue(s) being analyzed. In such cases, it is necessary to refer to case law for guidance as to how the law applies. Once the case on point is discussed, as addressed in the previous section, *the rule of law or legal principle adopted by the court must be applied to the facts of the client's case.* This is the next step of the analysis process. It immediately follows the presentation of the rule of law from the case on point.

For Example: "In this case, the court defined *oppressive conduct* as 'wrongful conduct that inures to the benefit of the majority and the detriment of the minority.' *Id.* at 675. The court ruled that the majority shareholder's act of granting himself a bonus triple his annual salary while refusing to allow dividends was wrongful, inured to his benefit and the detriment of the minority shareholders, and was, therefore, 'oppressive conduct' within the meaning of the statute.

"In our case, just as in the *Cedrik* case, the defendant (the majority shareholder) gave himself bonuses in excess of triple his salary while refusing to allow the issuance of dividends. If the court follows the definition of 'oppressive conduct' established in the *Cedrik* case, the defendant engaged in oppressive conduct."

For Example: "In the *Cerro* case, the court held that 'reasonable contact' as used in the collections statute means no more than one telephone call a day to the debtor's residence, and no call should be placed before 6 A.M. or after 7 P.M. *Id.* at 645."

"The collection agency contacted our client more than three times a day for seven straight days, and several of the calls were made after 9 P.M. If the trial court follows the rule adopted in *Cerro,* the outcome should be in our favor. The collections statute has clearly been violated."

Remember, you must include in the analysis a discussion of how the law applies to the issue(s) and facts of the client's case. It is useless to introduce the rule of law and discuss how the rule is interpreted through the presentation of a case on point, then fail to apply the law to the facts of the client's case. The purpose of the office memo is to demonstrate how the rule of law and the case law apply to guide or govern the determination of the issue being addressed in the memo.

Analysis—Part D Counteranalysis

The next part of the analysis section is the counteranalysis. The analysis of a legal issue is not complete unless counterarguments to the analysis are explored. The process of addressing the counterarguments is called counteranalysis. Chapter 9 is devoted to the subject of counteranalysis. Refer to that chapter when conducting counteranalysis and drafting the counteranalysis portion of the analysis. Note the following when preparing the counteranalysis:

- In the analysis section, the counteranalysis should follow part C, the application of the law to the issue and facts of the client's case. The reader, therefore, is immediately apprised of any counterargument and can easily compare and contrast the arguments and counterarguments and evaluate the merits of each.
- If rebuttal is necessary, it should follow the counteranalysis. Rebuttal may be required if you believe it is necessary to explain why the counterargument does not apply, or if you want to evaluate the merits of the counterargument.

  For Example: "The opposing side may argue that oppressive conduct did not occur, and the *Cedrik* case does not apply, because the majority shareholder in our case earned the triple bonuses by working long hours and weekends. In *Cedrik,* just as in our case, the majority shareholder worked long hours, and the court noted 'Even though the majority shareholder is entitled to receive extra compensation, he is not entitled to receive an amount of compensation that results in the total denial of benefits to the minority shareholders.' *Id.* at 778."

A checklist for the analysis section is presented in Figure 13–6.

Figure 13–6
Checklist—Analysis Section

- ❑ Does the analysis section follow the proper format? The format is Rule of Law + Case Interpreting the Rule of Law (if necessary) + Application + Counteranalysis.
- ❑ If the application of the rule of law is not clear, is case law presented that is on point and interprets how the rule of law applies?
- ❑ Is the proper citation presented for each rule of law and authority included in the analysis?
- ❑ Is there a separate analysis section for each issue addressed in the memo?
- ❑ Is the rule of law, presented in the analysis, applied to the issue raised by the facts of the client's case?
- ❑ Is there a counteranalysis and rebuttal to the counteranalysis if necessary?

CONCLUSION

Part C of the analysis section, the application of the rule of law to the client's case, is a discussion of how the rule of law or legal principle applies to the issue. This application of the law to the issue is really a mini-conclusion: it concludes how the law applies. In effect, a conclusion is presented in the analysis section. The conclusion section of the memo, therefore, should be composed of a general summary of the entire office memo.

The conclusion section should not introduce new information or authorities, nor should it merely repeat the brief answer. It should summarize the conclusions reached in the analysis section. It is recommended that the conclusion be crafted to include a reference to and summary of all the law discussed in the analysis section, both the enacted and case law. In addition, it requires fewer introductory and transitional sentences. Ideally, the conclusion should briefly inform the reader of all the law that applies and how it applies. The reader should be able to obtain from the conclusion a general understanding of the law and its application without having to read the entire memo.

The advantage of this type of conclusion is that researchers working on similar cases can determine from the conclusion if a memo from the office memo files applies to their case. They should be able to obtain all the essential information by merely reading the conclusion. The researcher saves time by not having to read the entire memo if all that is needed is a summary of the law and analysis.

For Example: "Section 30-3-9 of the criminal code prohibits the possession of proscribed drugs. The case of *Smith v. Jones* provides that when an individual does not have actual possession, he may be in constructive possession if there is either direct or circumstantial evidence establishing that the defendant had both knowledge and control of the drugs. In our case, there is no evidence, either direct or circumstantial, that the client had either knowledge or control of the drugs he was charged with possessing. If *Smith v. Jones* is followed, there is not sufficient evidence to support charges of possession under § 30-3-9."

For Example: "Article II, section 7, of the state constitution prohibits illegal searches and seizures. In the case of *State v. Idle,* the court held that an individual is seized within the meaning of the law when the actions of the law enforcement officers are such that a reasonable person would not believe that he was free to leave. In our case, the client was handcuffed and ordered to sit in the back seat of a police car. He was not placed under arrest. A reasonable person would not believe he was free to leave in this situation; therefore, if the test adopted in *State v. Idle* is followed in our case, our client was under arrest."

Note that in these examples, *introductory sentences* are not used to introduce the law, and *transitional sentences* are not utilized to connect the statutory and case law.

The importance and use of introductory and transitional sentences in the other sections of an office memo are discussed in the General Considerations section of this chapter (following the Recommendations section).

When there are multiple issues, the conclusion is usually presented immediately after the analysis of each issue. When there are only two issues and the analysis is not complex, one conclusion that summarizes the analysis of both issues may be presented at the end of the memo.

A checklist for the conclusion section is presented in Figure 13–7.

RECOMMENDATIONS

Not all law firms require the inclusion of a recommendations section as part of the basic format of an office memo. In some formats, recommendations are included in the conclusion section. Generally a separate section for any comments or recommendations should follow the conclusion section. Recommendations are not really part of the analysis or conclusion sections; they frequently address matters to be considered and steps to be taken as a result of conclusions reached in the analysis section. The recommendations section should include any comments or recommendations you have concerning the client's case or matters discussed in the memo.

Some areas that may be addressed in the recommendations section are the following.

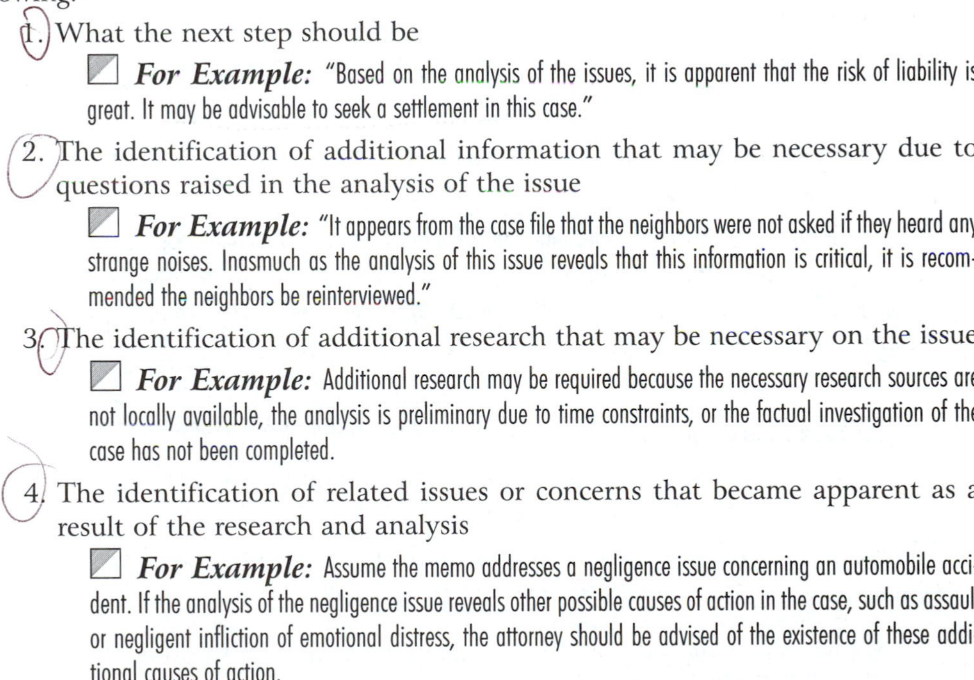

1. What the next step should be

   For Example: "Based on the analysis of the issues, it is apparent that the risk of liability is great. It may be advisable to seek a settlement in this case."

2. The identification of additional information that may be necessary due to questions raised in the analysis of the issue

   For Example: "It appears from the case file that the neighbors were not asked if they heard any strange noises. Inasmuch as the analysis of this issue reveals that this information is critical, it is recommended the neighbors be reinterviewed."

3. The identification of additional research that may be necessary on the issue

   For Example: Additional research may be required because the necessary research sources are not locally available, the analysis is preliminary due to time constraints, or the factual investigation of the case has not been completed.

4. The identification of related issues or concerns that became apparent as a result of the research and analysis

   For Example: Assume the memo addresses a negligence issue concerning an automobile accident. If the analysis of the negligence issue reveals other possible causes of action in the case, such as assault or negligent infliction of emotional distress, the attorney should be advised of the existence of these additional causes of action.

- ❑ Does the conclusion include a brief summary of the analysis of each issue?
- ❑ Is all the law discussed in the analysis section summarized in the conclusion, both enacted and case law?
- ❑ Is new information or authority excluded from the conclusion?

Figure 13–7
Checklist—Conclusion Section

GENERAL CONSIDERATIONS

The following are some general considerations to keep in mind when preparing an office research memorandum. A separate section is devoted to these matters because they often apply to more than one section of a memo and should be kept in mind when approaching a memo assignment in general.

Heading

Although an office memo is written in paragraph form, use headings for each section. Headings provide the overall structure of the assignment, guide the reader, and apprise the reader of what is covered in each section. The reader may desire to read a specific section, such as the analysis, in which case a heading allows the reader to quickly locate that section. Headings also serve as a guide for the preparation of the table of contents if a table is needed. Use the format presented in Chapter 12 as a guide for the appropriate headings. Refer to the Application sections of this chapter and Chapter 12 for examples.

Introductory Sentences

Introductory or topic sentences should be used to inform the reader of what is to follow. Avoid immediately jumping into the discussion of a topic, such as the presentation of the law.

For Example: **No introduction:** "Section 59-3-2 of the criminal code provides that possession of cocaine is illegal. In *Smith v. Jones,* the defendant. . . ."

Provide an introduction when discussing a topic. The introductions are italicized in the example.

For Example: **Includes an introduction:** *"The rule of law prohibiting the possession of cocaine* is criminal code § 59-3-2 which states that possession of cocaine is illegal. The statute does not define possession; therefore, case law must be referred to. *The case that provides guidance as to what constitutes possession in a fact situation such as ours* is *Smith v. Jones.* In this case, . . ."

Transition Sentences

Use transition sentences to connect sections, subsections, and related topics. The following example lacks a transition.

For Example: "The rule of law governing possession of drugs is § 59-3-2. Section 59-3-2c makes it illegal to possess cocaine. *Smith v. Jones* provides that possession occurs when. . . ."

A transition should be used in this example to connect the statutory law with the case law. The reader should be informed why case law is being presented.

The following example uses a transition sentence. The transition sentence is italicized in the example.

For Example: "The rule of law governing possession of drugs is § 59-3-2. Section 59-3-2c makes it illegal to possess cocaine. *The statute does not define what constitutes possession; therefore, it is necessary to refer to case law for guidance.*

"A case that defines what constitutes possession in a fact situation such as ours is *Smith v. Jones.* In this case, . . ."

Paragraphs

Paragraphs add coherence and make the memo more readable. Each area or topic should be addressed in a separate paragraph.

> ***For Example:*** In the analysis section of the memo, the discussion of the rule of law, the case that serves as a guide to the interpretation of the rule of law, the application of the rule to the issue, the counteranalysis, and the rebuttal to the counteranalysis should each be addressed in a separate paragraph or paragraphs.

Persuasive Precedent

When presenting persuasive authority, you must indicate the reason you are relying on this type of authority and lay a proper foundation for its use.

> ***For Example:*** "Section 90-9-6 prohibits oppressive conduct by a majority shareholder. The statute does not define what constitutes oppressive conduct, and the courts of this state have not addressed the question.
>
> "The state of New Washington, however, has a statute identical to our statute, and the New Washington courts have addressed the question of what constitutes oppressive conduct under the statute. In the case of *Darren v. Darren*, . . ."

In the preceding example, the reader is *informed why the out-of-state law (persuasive precedent) is referred to:* the statute does not define the term, and the state courts have not addressed the question. A *foundation for the presentation of the persuasive precedent is laid:* the statute of the state referred to is identical to our state statute, and the other state's courts have addressed the question. In the following example, a foundation is laid for the use of a court interpretation of one statute to interpret another statute.

> ***For Example:*** "Our courts have not defined the term oppressive conduct as used in § 90-9-6. Section 45-5-6C of the Small Loan Act prohibits 'oppressive conduct' in small loan transactions. The state court of appeals, in the case of *Irons v. Fast Loans, Inc.*, has defined what constitutes oppressive conduct under the Small Loan Act, and we can look to that definition for guidance in interpreting § 90-9-6."

The use of persuasive precedent is discussed in Chapters 2 and 8. Refer to those chapters when relying on persuasive precedent.

Conclusions

In many instances, after researching and analyzing a legal problem, you may not be able to provide a definite yes or no answer as to how it may be resolved.

> ***For Example:*** If there is no mandatory precedent and persuasive precedent or secondary authority is relied on, you may not be able to provide an answer as to how the court is likely to resolve the issue. If the case law that applies is very old and policies have changed, it may be questionable if the case law will be followed.

In such instances, you should present your conclusions and explain your reservations.

> ***For Example:*** "In conclusion, the courts of this state have not addressed this question. The majority of states that have addressed this issue follow the rule adopted by the New Washington supreme court in the case of *Tyler v. Tyler*. As stated in the analysis of this issue, the progressive approach of the New Washington court reflects the approach our supreme court has taken in resolving similar issues and will likely be adopted by the court."

Revisions/Redrafts

When preparing an office memo, it is essential to produce a professional product. This demands thorough research and analysis of all issues assigned and all aspects of each issue. It also requires assembly of the research and analysis into an organized, error-free final product. Be prepared to compose a number of redrafts.

Additional Authority

If there are several cases on point, it is not necessary to thoroughly discuss each case. Present and discuss thoroughly the most recent case on point, and refer to the other cases.

For Example: "The case that defines what constitutes 'oppressive' conduct in a fact situation such as that presented in our case is *Cedrik v. Ely,* 956 N. Wash. 776, 881 N.E.2d 451 (1995). In this case, the majority shareholder gave himself three bonuses that were triple his salary. At the same time, he refused to allow dividends to be issued. In defining what constitutes "oppressive conduct" under § 90-9-4, the court stated, 'Oppressive conduct occurs when a majority shareholder engages in wrongful conduct which inures to the benefit of the majority and the detriment of the minority.' *Id.* at 778. *See also Tyre v. Casey,* 953 N. Wash. 431, 878 N.E.2d 49 (1993) (oppressive conduct found when no dividends were issued and majority shareholder received several bonuses and was provided an extravagant expense account); *Ireland v. Ireland,* 952 N. Wash. 288, 873 N.E.2d 553 (1992) (oppressive conduct found when no dividends were issued and majority shareholder was given a house as a bonus)."

KEY POINTS CHECKLIST: *The Interoffice Memorandum—Analysis to Conclusion*

- ❑ Follow the standard format for the analysis section of a memo: Rule + Case Law (interpretation of the rule) + Application of Rule + Counteranalysis. This format is based on the standard IRAC model.
- ❑ The presentation of a case in a case brief is different from the presentation of a case in an office memo. When introducing a case in the analysis section of a memo, it is not necessary to include all the information you would include in a case brief.
- ❑ In the analysis section, *always* discuss how the rule of law applies to the issue and facts of the client's case.
- ❑ *Always* conduct a counteranalysis. If there is no counterargument, mention the fact that there is no counterargument or different position supported by the case law.
- ❑ Provide enough information in the conclusion to inform the reader of all the applicable enacted and case law.
- ❑ Use introductory and transition sentences. Do not jump from one topic to another. Provide a smooth transition between subjects.
- ❑ Before presenting persuasive precedent or secondary authority, indicate why you are not relying on mandatory authority.
- ❑ Do not be disturbed if you do not reach a definite conclusion as to how the law applies. There are many gray areas and issues that have not been ruled upon. Your job is to inform the reader of the existing law and provide a well-reasoned analysis of its application. Predicting the legal outcome always involves some measure of uncertainty.

APPLICATION

The first example in this section illustrates the application of the principles to the analysis, conclusion, and recommendations sections of the office memo assignment introduced at the beginning of Chapter 12. Recall that the Application section of that chapter only addressed the first half of the memo assignment presented at the beginning of that chapter, that is, the heading, assignment, issue, brief answer, and fact sections of the memo. The second example in this section illustrates the application of the principles discussed in this chapter and the previous chapter to the office memorandum assignment presented at the beginning of this chapter.

Both Chapters 10 and 12 discuss the use of an expanded outline and present examples that illustrate the use of an expanded outline when drafting an office memo. Inasmuch as the use of an expanded outline is illustrated in those chapters, a detailed discussion of its use is not included in the two examples explored in this section. The examples in this section present the completed office memoranda.

Example 1

This example illustrates the completion of the memorandum assignment introduced at the beginning of Chapter 12. The heading through fact sections of the assignment are included in the Application section of that chapter. The remainder of the memorandum is presented below.

Analysis

The rule of law governing privileged communications between spouses is 735 ILCS 5/8-801 which provides, "In all actions, husband and wife may testify for or against each other, provided that neither may testify as to any communication or admission made by either of them to the other or as to any conversation between them during marriage. . . ." The statute does not include any sections that address waiver of the privilege. There is, however, Illinois case law that discusses the question of when the privilege is waived.

A state supreme court case that addresses the question of waiver of the privilege when children are present during the spousal communication is *People v. Sanders,* 99 Ill. 2d 262, 457 N.E.2d 1241 (1983). In this case, the trial court admitted into evidence conversations between the defendant and his spouse. The conversations took place in front of their children, ages eight through thirteen years old; the conversations implicated the defendant in a murder. When addressing the question of whether the communications were privileged, the supreme court stated that the rule followed in the state is that the presence of children of the spouses destroys confidentiality unless the children are too young to understand what is being said.

In our case, just as in *People v. Sanders,* the conversation between the spouses involved incriminating statements made in the presence of children. In our case, just as in *Sanders,* the children were old enough to understand the conversation. If the rule of law presented in *Sanders* is followed by the trial court, the conversation between Mr. Findo and Mrs. Findo is not a privileged communication under the statute and is admissible into evidence in the trial of Mr. Findo.

There is no case law in this jurisdiction that establishes an exception to the rule presented in *Sanders.* The only possible counterargument is that the children, although present, did not hear the conversation. The *Sanders* opinion does not directly state that the children must actually hear the conversation, but this is implied by the requirement that the children must be old enough to understand what is being said. See the Recommendations section in regard to taking steps to determine if the children heard and understood the conversation.

Conclusion

The rule of law governing privileged spousal communications is 735 ILCS 5/8-801 which provides that communications between spouses during the marriage are privileged. In *People v. Sanders,* the court held that the privilege is waived if it takes place in front of children old enough to understand what is being said. In our case, since the conversation took place in the presence of children old enough to understand, it appears that the privilege does not apply, and the conversation is admissible into evidence.

Recommendations

1. We should conduct further investigation to determine if the children heard and understood the conversation.
2. Additional research should be conducted to determine if there are any cases that address the question of whether, in addition to being present, the children must actually hear the conversation.

Example 2

This example illustrates the completion of the office memo assignment presented in the hypothetical at the beginning of this chapter. Assume that Ellen Taylor's expanded outline includes the following law from the state of New Washington that applies to the assignment.

- **Article II, section 4,** of the state constitution. "The right of the people to be secure in their persons, houses, papers and effects against unreasonable searches and seizures shall not be violated. . . ."
- **Section 95-21-14** of the state criminal code provides that "It is unlawful for any person intentionally to possess a controlled substance. . . ." Cocaine is listed as a controlled substance under the act.
- ***State v. Ikard,* 945 N. Wash. 745, 853 N.E.2d 652 (1989).** In this case, law enforcement officers were looking for a suspect in an armed robbery. The officers recognized a friend of the suspect walking down a street. They stopped him, handcuffed him, and asked him where the suspect was. When he refused to answer the question, the officers searched him and found marijuana in his shirt pocket. The officers then arrested him for possession of narcotics.

  In regard to the initial stop and handcuffing of the defendant, the court held that a person is seized (arrested) within the meaning of article II, section 4, of the state constitution when a reasonable person would believe he was not free to leave. The court held that a reasonable person in the defendant's position would not believe he was free to leave; therefore, the defendant was under arrest when the officers stopped and handcuffed him.
- ***State v. Wilson,* 953 N. Wash. 111, 878 N.E.2d 431 (1993).** In this case, law enforcement officers were executing a search warrant. Upon entering the premises, an officer held the defendant by the arm and refused to allow him to leave. In addressing the question of whether the defendant was under arrest when the officer held him by the arm and refused to allow him to leave, the court held that "Not all detentions constitute a seizure within the meaning of [a]rticle II, [s]ection 4 of the constitution. A warrant to search for contraband founded on probable cause implicitly carries with it the limited authority to detain the occupants of the premises while a proper search is conducted. Such a detention does not constitute a seizure within the meaning of the constitution." *Id.* at 121.

- ***State v. Bragg*, 955 N.Wash. 221, 880 N.E.2d 998 (1994).** In this case, the police searched an apartment where Bragg and several other people resided. Narcotics were found in a drawer in the kitchen. There was no evidence linking Bragg to the drugs. Only Bragg was charged with possession. The court noted that possession may be either actual or constructive.

  In overturning his conviction, the court ruled that in a situation where several individuals have access to the location where the drugs are found, and there is no evidence indicating that the defendant has actual possession of the drugs, a conviction can still take place if there is evidence that the defendant is in constructive possession of the drugs. The court stated that in order to convict the defendant of constructive possession, there must be either direct or circumstantial evidence presented that he had knowledge of the presence of the drugs and control over the drugs. In this case, there was no such evidence.

The following is the memorandum prepared by Ellen Taylor.

OFFICE RESEARCH MEMORANDUM

To: Carl Pine, Assistant District Attorney
From: Ellen Taylor, Intern
Re: State v. Kent
Case: Cr. 97-404
Re: Arrest during the execution of a search warrant and constructive possession of drugs

Statement of Assignment

You have asked me to prepare a memorandum addressing the following questions: Was Mr. Kent under arrest when he was handcuffed and held in the kitchen while his apartment was searched? Is there sufficient evidence to support charges of possession in this case?

Issues

Issue I: Under article II, section 4, of the state constitution, is an individual seized (under arrest) when police officers handcuff and detain him in the kitchen during the execution of a search warrant?

Issue II: Under § 95-21-14 of the criminal code, is there sufficient evidence to support charges of possession when the defendant is located in the bedroom of a third-story apartment and the drugs are located below a broken window of the bedroom in a parking lot?

Brief Answer

Issue I: No. The state supreme court has held that detentions during the execution of a search warrant do not constitute seizures within the meaning of article II, section 4, of the state constitution.

Issue II: No. When drugs are found in a common area accessible to multiple individuals and there is no evidence that the defendant has actual possession, the defendant may constructively possess the drugs. The state supreme court has ruled that constructive possession requires evidence that the defendant has knowledge and control of the drugs. In our case, there is no evidence that the defendant had knowledge and control of the drugs found in the parking lot.

Facts

On January 7, police officers executed a search warrant for the apartment of the defendant, David Kent. The apartment is located on the third floor of an apartment complex. When the police entered the apartment, Mr. Kent was lying on the bed in the bedroom. He was frisked for weapons, handcuffed, moved to the kitchen, and detained while the search was conducted. He was not placed under arrest or read his rights. The police found a broken window in the bedroom, and the window screen was pushed out. In the parking lot three stories below the bedroom window, the officers found a bag containing cocaine. There were no witnesses who saw the defendant throw anything out of the apartment window. There were no fingerprints found on the bag or any other evidence linking Mr. Kent to the cocaine. Mr. Kent has been charged with possession of a controlled substance.

Analysis

Issue I

The rule of law governing arrest in New Washington is article II, section 4, of the state constitution which provides, in part, "The right of the people to be secure in their person, . . . against unreasonable searches and seizures shall not be violated. . . ." Neither the constitution nor the state statutes define the term *seizure.* There is, however, New Washington case law that defines the term.

The New Washington case that establishes the standard for what constitutes a seizure is *State v. Ikard,* 945 N. Wash. 745, 853 N.E.2d 652 (1989). In this case law enforcement officers were looking for a suspect in an armed robbery. The officers recognized a friend of the suspect walking down a street. They stopped him, handcuffed him, and asked him where the suspect was. When he refused to answer the question, the officers searched him and found marijuana in his shirt pocket. The officers then arrested him for possession of narcotics. In ruling that the defendant was under arrest when he was stopped and handcuffed, the court held that a person is seized (arrested) within the meaning of article II, section 4, of the state constitution when a reasonable person would believe he was not free to leave. *Id.* at 750.

The rule of law defining seizure adopted in *State v. Ikard* is so broadly stated that it can apply to a number of seizure situations, including the situation presented in our case. In our case, a reasonable person would not believe he was free to leave when handcuffed and moved to the kitchen during the execution of a warrant. It appears, therefore, that Mr. Kent was seized (under arrest) within the meaning of *Ikard.*

Not all detentions, however, constitute a seizure. There are exceptions. One exception is when the detention takes place while officers are executing a search warrant. This exception was announced by the court in the case of *State v. Wilson,* 953 N. Wash. 111, 878 N.E.2d 431 (1993). In this case, after entering the premises during the execution of a search warrant, an officer held the defendant by the arm and refused to allow him to leave. In regard to whether the seizure constituted an arrest, the court held, "Not all detentions constitute a seizure within the meaning of Article II, Section 4 of the constitution. A warrant to search for contraband founded on probable cause implicitly carries with it the limited authority to detain the occupants of the premises while a proper search is conducted. Such a detention does not constitute a seizure within the meaning of the constitution." *Id.* at 121.

In our case, just as in *Wilson,* the police were executing a search warrant and the defendant was detained while the search was being conducted. None of our facts indicates the warrant was issued without probable cause. If it was based on probable cause, under *Wilson,* the police had the authority to detain the defendant, and the detention was not a seizure within the meaning of the constitution.

There is no case or statutory law in New Washington that contradicts or limits the *Wilson* ruling in regard to detention during the execution of a warrant. The only counterargument possible is that the warrant was issued without probable cause, and therefore, the police did not have authority to detain Mr. Kent. There is no evidence in the case file that indicates a problem in this regard. See the Recommendations section below.

Issue II

The rule of law governing the possession of cocaine is section 95-21-14 of the state criminal code which provides that "It is unlawful for any person intentionally to possess a controlled substance. . . ." Cocaine is listed as a controlled substance under the statute. The statute does not define what constitutes possession; therefore, it is necessary to refer to case law for guidance.

A case in which the supreme court has defined possession is *State v. Bragg,* 955 N. Wash. 221, 880 N.E.2d 998 (1994). In this case, the police searched an apartment where Bragg and several other individuals resided. Narcotics were found in a drawer in the kitchen. There was no evidence linking Bragg to the drugs. Only Bragg was charged with possession. The court noted that possession may be either actual or constructive. In overturning Bragg's conviction, the court ruled that in a situation where several individuals have access to the location where the drugs are found, and there is no evidence indicating that the defendant has actual possession of the drugs, a conviction can still take place if there is evidence that the defendant is in constructive possession of the drugs. The court stated that in order to convict for constructive possession, "there must be either direct or circumstantial evidence presented that the defendant had knowledge of the presence of the drugs and control over them." *Id.* at 225.

In our case, just as in *Bragg,* there is no evidence indicating that the defendant actually possessed the drugs. Also, there is no evidence, either direct or circumstantial, of constructive possession. There is no evidence that the defendant had knowledge of the presence of the drugs in the parking lot. Also, there is no evidence that he had control of the drugs. The drugs were found three stories below his apartment in a parking lot. There is no evidence linking the defendant to the drugs. If the rule of law presented in *Bragg* is followed, it appears that there is not sufficient evidence to support charges of possession.

There is no New Washington case law that contradicts *Bragg* or establishes a different definition of constructive possession. A possible counterargument is that the fact the drugs were found below the defendant's broken apartment window is sufficient to link him to the drugs. There is no case law to support this position. It may be necessary to look for additional evidence that links the defendant to the drugs. See the Recommendations section below.

Conclusion

Article II, section 4, of the state constitution prohibits the unreasonable seizure (arrest) of individuals. The case of *State v. Ikard* states that an arrest takes place if a reasonable person would not believe he was free to leave. The case of *State v. Wilson* provides that a detention that takes place during the execution of a search warrant does not constitute a seizure within the meaning of the constitution. In our case, the defendant was detained during the execution of a search warrant. Therefore, under the ruling in *Wilson,* it appears the detention of the defendant was not a seizure (arrest).

Section 95-21-14 of the state criminal code provides that it is illegal to possess cocaine. In *State v. Bragg,* the court held that to establish constructive possession, evidence must be presented that shows that the defendant had knowledge of the presence of the drugs and control over them. In our case, the defendant did not actually possess the drugs, and there is no evidence that indicates he had knowledge or control of them. Therefore, it appears that there is not sufficient evidence to support charges of possession.

Recommendations

1. We should determine whether the issuance of the search warrant was supported by probable cause or if there is any other matter that affects the legality of the search. If the issuance of the warrant or the execution of the search was in some way defective, the detention exception established in *State v. Wilson* may not apply.

2. We need to conduct further investigation to determine if there is any evidence that links the defendant to the drugs found in the parking lot. For example, was glass from the window embedded in the bag? Were there any individuals in the apartment complex who heard a window being broken?

Comments on Examples

Note that the analysis section of both memos follows the same analytical format: Rule of law + Case law interpreting the rule of law + Application of the law to the issue and facts of the client's case + Counteranalysis. There are transition sentences linking the presentation of the rule of law to the case law. No extra or superfluous material is presented; the reader is not required to wade through related but not necessary case law or analysis. The applicable law is introduced, explained, and applied. The reader is clearly and concisely informed of the law and how it applies.

Note that, in both examples, there is one conclusion that includes a reference to the applicable law and summarizes the analysis of the issues. The conclusion summarizes all the applicable enacted and case law. If the reader desires a detailed analysis and discussion of the law, the analysis section can be referred to. When the memo is more complex and involves multiple issues, it may be appropriate to provide a conclusion section at the end of the analysis of each issue.

SUMMARY

This chapter addresses considerations involved in preparing the second half of an office memorandum: the analysis, conclusion, and recommendations sections. The focus of the chapter is on the analysis section.

The heart of an office memorandum is the analysis section. The purpose of a memorandum is to inform the reader of the law that governs the issue and how the law applies in the client's case. This information is conveyed in the analysis section of the office memo. In this section, the reader is informed through:

- A presentation of the law that governs the issue
- An explanation of how the law applies through reference to court opinions that applied the law in similar situations
- A discussion of how the law applies to the issue(s) in the client's case

Included in the analysis is a discussion of any counterargument the opposing side may raise.

The recommended basic format for the analysis section is as follows:

Part A. Rule of law
Part B. Case law (if necessary)—interpretation of rule of law
1. Name of case
2. Facts of case—sufficient to demonstrate case is on point
3. Rule or legal principle from case that applies to the client's case
Part C. Application of the law to the facts of the client's case
Part D. Counteranalysis

Following the analysis section is the conclusion. Since the application of the law to the issue is discussed in the analysis section, the conclusion should contain a summary of the law and analysis already presented. It should inform the reader of all the applicable law and how it applies.

The recommendations section is the last section of the office memo. It includes any recommendations concerning the next steps to be taken or further research or investigation that should be conducted. In some law firms, the recommendations section is included in the conclusion or not required at all.

The format discussed in this chapter is a recommended format. There is no standard office memorandum format. Different law offices have different preferences. Use the format presented in this chapter if appropriate; modify it according to your needs.

EXERCISES

In each of the following exercises, the assignment is to prepare an office memorandum. Each assignment contains the assignment memo from the supervisory attorney that includes all the available facts of the case. Complete the memo based on these facts. If additional facts need to be identified, note this in the recommendations section of the memo. When preparing the heading of each assignment, use your name for the "To" line, and put "Supervisory Attorney" after the "From."

Following each assignment is a reference to the applicable enacted and case law. In some assignments, the case citation includes a reference only to the regional reporter citation; the state reporter citation is not included. Use only the citation presented in the assignment. The cases are presented in Appendix A.

The first time you cite the opinion, use the citation format you are given for the opinion in the assignment.

> ***For Example:*** *Britton v. Britton* is cited in Assignment 5 as 100 N.M. 424, 671 P.2d 1135 (1983).

This is how you should cite this opinion the first time it is used in the memorandum. When you need to quote from an opinion in the memo, use a blank line to indicate the page number from which the quotation is taken.

> ***For Example:*** *Britton,* 100 N.M. at _____, 671 P.2d at _____, or *Id.* at _____, 671 P.2d at _____.

Do not conduct additional research. Complete the assignment using the facts, enacted law, and case law contained in each assignment.

ASSIGNMENT 1

To: (Your name)
From: Supervisory Attorney
Re: Dixon v. Cary
Probate of holographic will

We represent Holly Dixon, the widow of Thomas Dixon, in the case of Dixon v. Cary. She wishes to challenge the probate of the holographic will of Thomas Dixon. Mary Cary, the sister of Thomas Dixon and personal representative of his estate, has submitted for probate a holographic will prepared by Mr. Dixon.

The first half of the will is in the handwriting of Mr. Dixon. The second half is typewritten. It was typed by the next-door neighbor, Edgar Mae. Mr. Mae states that Mr. Dixon asked him to finish the will because Mr. Dixon was too weak to continue. The will is signed by Mr. Dixon. There are no subscribing witnesses to the will, but it includes a self-proving affidavit that meets the requirements of the statute.

Is the will admissible to probate under Texas law?

Statutory Law: Tex. Prob. Code. Ann. § 59, Requisites of a Will (Vernon 1980), provides: "Every last will and testament . . . shall be in writing . . ., and shall, if not wholly in the handwriting of the testator, be attested by two (2) or more credible witnesses. . . ."

Tex. Prob. Code. Ann. § 60, Exception Pertaining to Holographic Wills (Vernon 1980), provides: "Where the will is written wholly in the handwriting of the testator, the attestation of the subscribing witnesses may be dispensed with. Such a will may be made self-proved at any time during the testator's lifetime by the attachment or annexation thereto of an affidavit by the testator to the effect that the instrument is his last will; that he was at least eighteen years of age when he executed it . . .; that he was of sound mind; and that he has not revoked such instrument."

Case Law: *Dean v. Dickey,* 225 S.W.2d 999 (Tex. Civ. App. 1949) (see Appendix A).

ASSIGNMENT 2

To: (Your name)
From: Supervisory Attorney
Re: Eldridge v. Eldridge
Modification of child support

We represent Gwen Eldridge in the case of Eldridge v. Eldridge. The Eldridges were divorced in

1992. Mrs. Eldridge was awarded custody of their two minor children. Mr. Eldridge was ordered to make child support payments in the amount of $700 per month. He lost his job in January of 1993 and was unemployed from that date through October of 1993. He then obtained employment as an electrician.

Mr. Eldridge did not make child support payments for the months he was unemployed. In January of 1994, Mrs. Eldridge filed a motion with the court that entered the divorce decree, seeking an order forcing Mr. Eldridge to pay the child support payments due for the months he did not make payments; the amount totaled $7,000. Mr. Eldridge countered with a petition to modify his child support obligation. The petition requested that he be excused from having to pay the obligations that accrued during the ten months he was unemployed. The court ordered Mr. Eldridge to pay one-half of the amount due, $3,500, and excused him from paying the remaining $3,500. The court stated that Mr. Eldridge did not have to pay the full amount because he was unemployed during the months the child support accrued. The attorney that represented Mrs. Eldridge in the trial court told her that there is no basis for an appeal of the court order.

Please check the statutory and case law to determine if the trial court acted properly when it excused Mr. Eldridge from paying $3,500 of the back child support.

Statutory Law: Ind. Code § 31-2-11-12, Modification of delinquent support payment, provides:

(a) Except as provided in subsection (b) . . . , a court may not retroactively modify an obligor's duty to pay a delinquent support payment.

(b) A court with jurisdiction over a support order may modify an obligor's duty to pay a support payment that becomes due:

(1) After notice of a petition to modify the support order has been given . . . to the obligee . . . and

(2) Before a final order concerning the petition for modification is entered.

Case Law: *Cardwell v. Gwaltney,* 556 N.E.2d 953 (Ind. Ct. App. 1990) (see Appendix A).

ASSIGNMENT 3

To: (Your name)
From: Supervisory Attorney
Re: Commonwealth v. Jones
Assault by means of a dangerous weapon—lightning

This is a bizarre case to say the least. We have been appointed by the court to represent Sedrick Jones in the case of Commonwealth v. Jones. Mr. Jones is charged with attempted murder, battery, false imprisonment, and assault with a dangerous weapon. Mr. Jones has had a stormy ten-year relationship with Elizabeth Steward. The relationship has been marked by multiple instances of domestic violence. They live in a cottage located on a bluff overlooking the Atlantic Ocean. On April 5 of this year, after an extended bout of drinking and arguing, Mr. Jones dragged Ms. Steward outside and tied her to the lightning rod attached to the cottage. This took place during a violent electrical storm. When he tied her to the pole, he said, "I'll fix you, you're gonna fry." Lightning did not strike the pole. This act is the basis of the assault by means of a dangerous weapon charge. The state claims that the dangerous weapon is lightning.

Please prepare a memo addressing the question of whether there is a sufficient basis to support the assault by means of a dangerous weapons charge.

Statutory Law: G.L. c. 265, § 15A, Assault and Battery with Dangerous Weapon (state of Massachusetts), provides: "(b) Whoever, by means of a dangerous weapon, commits assault and battery upon another shall be punished by imprisonment in the state prison for not more than five years. . . ."

Case Law: *Commonwealth v. Shea,* 38 Mass. App. Ct. 7, 644 N.W.2d 244 (1995) (see Appendix A).

ASSIGNMENT 4

To: (Your name)
From: Supervisory Attorney
Re: United States v. Canter
Armed bank robbery with a dangerous weapon

We have been appointed to represent Eldon Canter in the case of United States v. Canter. Mr. Canter is charged with one count of armed bank robbery, in violation of 18 U.S.C. § 2113(a) and (d).

On January 5 of this year, Mr. Canter robbed the First State Bank. After he entered the bank, he approached a teller and pulled from his pocket a crudely carved wooden replica of a 9mm Barretta handgun. He had carved the replica from a block of pine wood and stained it with dark walnut wood stain to make it look black. He drilled a hole in the barrel end in an attempt to make it look like a real Barretta.

The teller was so frightened that he only glanced at the wooden gun. He believed it was real. The teller at the next window looked at the replica and afterward stated that she was fairly certain at the time that it was fake. No one else noticed whether the wooden replica was real.

Please determine whether in light of the facts of this case there is sufficient evidence to support the charge that Mr. Canter committed bank robbery by use of a "dangerous weapon."

Statutory Law: 18 U.S.C. § 2113(a) & (d), Bank robbery and incidental crimes, provides:

> (a) Whoever, by force and violence, or by intimidation, takes, or attempts to take, from the person or presence of another . . . any property or money or any other thing of value belonging to, or in the care, custody, control, management, or possession of, a bank. . . .
>
> Shall be fined under this title or imprisoned not more than twenty years, or both.
>
> (d) Whoever, in committing, or in attempting to commit, any offense defined in subsections (a) and (b) of this section, assaults any person, or puts in jeopardy the life of any person by use of a dangerous weapon or device, shall be fined under this title or imprisoned not more than twenty-five years, or both.

Case Law: *United States v. Martinez-Jimenez,* 864 F.2d 664 (9th Cir. 1989) (see Appendix A).

ASSIGNMENT 5

To: (Your name)
From: Supervisory Attorney
Re: Mr. Arturo Garcia
Child support modification

After fifteen years of marriage, Arturo Garcia and Mary Chavez were granted a divorce in May 1987. There are three children from the marriage. Mr. Garcia was awarded primary custody of the children. Ms. Chavez, a brain surgeon at the time of the divorce, was ordered to pay monthly child support in the amount of $3,000 per month. The terms of the divorce order were undivided in that it did not specify a "per child" amount.

Ms. Chavez always resented the amount of child support she was ordered to pay; her frustration over this led her recently to quit her medical practice and enroll in the paralegal program at the community college. This career change resulted in a substantial reduction in her income. She told several individuals that she quit her practice because she "can't stand to pay that much money to my ex-husband."

Four months ago, the oldest child turned eighteen and moved out of Mr. Garcia's house. As soon as the oldest child moved out, Ms. Chavez reduced by one-third the amount of child support she was paying. She did not seek nor obtain a court order granting a modification of her support obligation. She told Mr. Garcia that she did not have to pay the full amount because the oldest child had turned eighteen. Two months ago, she unilaterally reduced her child support payments to $500 per month. She told Mr. Garcia, "That's all I can afford to pay now that I'm going to school."

Mr. Garcia has come to us seeking legal advice. With the above facts in mind, prepare a memo addressing the following questions:

1. Was it permissible for Ms. Chavez to unilaterally reduce support when the oldest child reached the age of majority?
2. What is the likelihood of the court granting a modification of child support due to Ms. Chavez's change of occupation?

Statutory Law: NMSA § 28-6-1 (Repl. Pamp. 1991) (state of New Mexico) provides that the age of majority is reached when an individual turns eighteen years old.

NMSA § 40-4-7 (Repl. Pamp. 1994)—Proceedings; spousal support; support of children; division of property—(state of New Mexico), section F, provides: "The court may modify and change any order in respect to . . . care, custody, maintenance . . . of the children whenever circumstances render such change proper. The district court shall have exclusive jurisdiction of all matters pertaining to the . . . care, custody, maintenance . . . of the children so long as the children remain minors."

NMSA § 40-4-11.4(A) (Repl. Pamp. 1994)—Modification of child support orders; exchange of financial information—the relevant portion of section A provides: "A court may modify a child support obligation upon a showing of material and substantial changes in circumstances subsequent to the adjudication of the pre-existing order."

Case Law: *Britton v. Britton,* 100 N.M. 424, 671 P.2d 1135 (1983) (see Appendix A).

Wolcott v. Wolcott, 105 N.M. 608, 735 P.2d 326 (Ct. App. 1987) (see Appendix A).

ASSIGNMENT 6

To: (Your name)
From: Supervisory Attorney
Re: Kells v. Simns
Implied warranty—fitness for a particular purpose.

Our client, Mr. Merril Simns, is being sued by Tom Kells for breach on an implied warranty of fitness for a particular purpose in the case of Kells v. Simns. Mr. Simns placed an ad in the *Daily Post* offering to sell a Ryder 1000 riding lawn mower for $400. Mr. Kells responded to the ad and came to Mr. Simns' house to purchase the mower. Mr. Kells told Mr.

Simns that he needed a good riding mower because he had two and one-half acres that had to be mowed once a week. Mr. Simns responded that, although he had never needed to mow more than an acre, the mower had always done a good job for him. After discussing the terms, Mr. Kells purchased the mower for $300.

One week later, Mr. Kells called Mr. Simns and informed him that the mower was too small and underpowered for his needs, and he wanted his money back. Mr. Simns refused, and Mr. Kells has filed suit in small claims court, claiming breach of an implied warranty of fitness for a particular purpose. Mr. Simns's only experience with riding mowers is based on his use of the Ryder 1000. He does not have any special expertise concerning riding mowers.

Please assess the likelihood of Mr. Kells prevailing on an implied warranty of fitness for a particular purpose claim.

Statutory Law: ORS 72.3150, Implied warranty: fitness for particular purpose (state of Oregon), provides: "Where the seller at the time of contracting has reason to know any particular purpose for which the goods are required and that the buyer is relying on the seller's skill or judgment to select or furnish suitable goods, there is unless excluded or modified under ORS 72.3610 an implied warranty that the goods shall be fit for such purpose."

Case Law: *Beam v. Cullett,* 48 Or. App. 47, 615 P.2d 1196 (1980) (see Appendix A).

ASSIGNMENT 7

To: (Your name)
From: Supervisory Attorney
Re: Commonwealth v. Clavel
Execution of search warrant—unannounced entry

We represent Darren Clavel in the case of Commonwealth v. Clavel. In this case, police officers executed a search warrant that authorized the search of the client's home for drugs. When the police arrived at Mr. Clavel's house, they knocked on the door, shouted "police, open up," waited fifteen seconds, kicked the door open, and searched the premises. Mr. Clavel, who is hard of hearing, heard some noise and was approaching the door to open it when it was kicked open. Upon searching the house, the police found a pound of marijuana in the bedroom closet. Mr. Clavel was charged with intent to distribute narcotics.

Please prepare a memo assessing the likelihood of having the evidence suppressed because of the manner in which the officers executed the warrant.

Statutory Law: The Fourth Amendment of the United States Constitution (U.S. Const. amend. IV).

Case Law: *Commonwealth v. DeMichel,* 442 Pa. 553, 277 A.2d 159 (1971) (see Appendix A).

ASSIGNMENT 8

To: (Your name)
From: Supervisory Attorney
Re: Mrs. Joyce Helger
Probate of copy of lost original will

We represent Mrs. Helger in the probate of her husband's estate. Mr. Helger died four weeks ago after a sudden heart attack. Mrs. Helger has been unable to locate the original of Mr. Helger's will. She knows that he had prepared a will, and she has a conformed copy of the will executed December 1, 1991. She also has a conformed copy of a codicil executed on May 6, 1996. She does not have the original of the codicil. Mrs. Helger thought the law firm who prepared the will kept the original, but she was informed that the firm could not locate the original. The senior partner at the firm told her that they do not keep the original of wills or codicils.

Please assess the likelihood of the probate court granting a petition for administration of the conformed copy of the will and codicil.

Rule of Law: The rule of law governing this question is case law rather than statutory law—*In the Estate of Parson,* 416 So. 2d 513, 515 (Fla. Dist. Ct. App. 1982): The court held that there is a "presumption that a will which was in the possession of the testator prior to death and which cannot be located subsequent to death was destroyed by the testator with the intention of revoking it."

Case Law: The court opinion that interprets the application of the rule stated in the above case is the following case: *In re Estate of Kuszmaul,* 491 So. 2d 287 (Fla. Dist. Ct. App. 1986) (see Appendix A).

ASSIGNMENT 9

To: (Your name)
From: Supervisory Attorney
Re: Mad Dog Review v. Jonesville
First Amendment—freedom of expression

We represent Mad Dog Review, a local rap band. As you know, this is a controversial group. The lyrics of one of their songs, "Mad Dog City Council," describes our city council in explicit terms using "dirty" words and language generally considered obscene. Based upon the language in their songs, and specifically that in "Mad Dog City Council," the city council of Jonesville (a neighboring municipality) has banned the group from performing in their community.

The Jonesville city council based their authority to enact the ban on Municipal Ordinance section 355-20. The ordinance provides: "The City Council, upon majority vote, may prohibit the public performance of any type of entertainment that does not comport with local standards of decency or acceptability." The ordinance does not define "local standards of decency or acceptability" or provide any standards or guidelines that the city council must follow.

Mad Dog Review wants to challenge the authority of the Jonesville city council to ban their performance. Please prepare an office memorandum addressing the question of whether the municipal ordinance violates the group's right to freedom of expression.

Rule of Law: First Amendment of the United States Constitution (U.S. Const. amend. I).

Case Law: Assume that the only case law governing this question is *Atlantic Beach Casino, Inc. v. Morenzoni,* 749 F. Supp. 38 (D. R.I. 1990). The relevant portions of the case are presented in the following text.

ATLANTIC BEACH CASINO, INC.
d/b/a the Windjammer, et al., Plaintiffs,

v.

Edward T. MARENZONI, et al., Defendants.
Civ. A. No. 90-0471.

United States District Court,
D. Rhode Island.

Sept. 28, 1990.
749 F. Supp. 38 (D. R.I. 1990)

OPINION AND ORDER

PETTINE, Senior District Judge.

In the last few years legislators and citizens have paid increasing attention to the lyrical content of popular music. The interest if not entirely new, for "rulers have long known [music's] capacity to appeal to the intellect and to the emotions and have censored musical compositions to serve the needs of the state." *Ward v. Rock Against Racism,* ___ U.S. ___, 109 S.Ct. 2746, 2753, 105 L.Ed.2d 661 (1989). The controversy some groups have ignited is not, in itself, any reason to take such speech outside the First Amendment. Indeed, expression may "best serve its high purpose when it induces a condition of unrest, creates dissatisfaction with conditions as they are, or even stirs people to anger." *Terminiello v. Chicago,* 337 U.S. 1, 4, 69 S.Ct. 894, 96, 893 L.Ed. 1131 (1949). The message and reputation of the rap music group 2 Live Crew evidently came to the attention of the Westerly Town Council, for they have taken steps toward possibly preventing the group from playing a scheduled concert. It is in this way that 2 Live Crew became the subject of, though not a party to, the present litigation.

On September 19, 1990, plaintiffs, who have contracted to present the 2 Live Crew concert, moved for a temporary restraining order prohibiting the defendants, members of the Westerly Town Council, from holding a show cause hearing on September 24, 1990, concerning the revocation of plaintiffs' entertainment license; from revoking the plaintiffs' entertainment license; from prohibiting the 2 Live Crew concert scheduled for October 6, 1990; and from imposing any special requirements on plaintiffs relative to the October 6 presentation. On September 21, 1990, the parties and this Court agreed that the matter would be considered as an application for a preliminary injunction and that the show cause hearing would be continued until October 1, 1990, subject to and dependent upon this Court's ruling. Based on the September 21 conference and my review of the parties' briefs, this Court has determined that the central issue in this case is plaintiffs' facial challenge to the town of Westerly's licensing ordinances on First Amendment grounds. Because I find, for the reasons set out below, that the ordinances as written are unconstitutional under the First and Fourteenth Amendments, defendants are enjoined from conducting a show cause hearing and from revoking plaintiff's entertainment license. I also enjoin the defendants from prohibiting the concert for failing to allege sufficient harm to overcome plaintiffs' First Amendment rights.

* * * *

III. INJUNCTIVE RELIEF

In order for plaintiffs to prevail in their request for a preliminary injunction, they must meet the following standards: the plaintiff must demonstrate a likelihood of success on the merits, immediate and irreparable harm, that the injury outweighs any harm engendered by the grant of injunctive relief and that the public interest will not be adversely affected by such grant. *LeBeau v. Spirito,* 703 F.2d 639, 642 (1st Cir. 1983). I shall address each of these standards in turn.

A. Likelihood of Success on the Merits

Rather than allow 2 Live Crew to perform and then prosecute for any illegal activity that could occur, the Town Council wishes to review and decide in advance whether to allow the performance to go forward. This is a prior restraint. *See Southeastern Promotions, Ltd. v. Conrad,* 420 U.S. 546, 554–55, 95 S.Ct. 1239, 1244–45, 43 L.Ed.2d 448 (1975). "Any system of prior restraints of expression comes to this Court bearing a heavy presumption against its constitutional validity." *Bantam Books, Inc. v. Sullivan,* 372 U.S. 58, 70, 83 S.Ct. 631, 639, 9 L.Ed.2d 584 (1963). A licensing scheme involving such prior restraint survives constitutional scrutiny only when the law contains "narrow, objective and definite standards to guide the licensing authority." *Shuttlesworth v. Birmingham,* 394 U.S. 147, 150–51, 89 S.Ct. 935, 938–39, 22 L.Ed.2d 162 (1969), *see Lakewood,* 486 U.S. 760, *Southeastern Promotions,* 420 U.S. at 553, 95 S.Ct. at 1243–44, *Cox v. State of Louisiana,* 379 U.S. 536, 557–58, 85 S.Ct. 453, 465–66, 13 L.Ed.2d 471 (1965), *Irish Subcommittee v. R.I. Heritage Commission,* 646 F.Supp. 347, 359 (D.R.I.1986).

The Westerly Ordinance, see *supra* note 3, provides even less guidance than the law struck down in *Shuttlesworth. Id.* 394 U.S. at 149, 89 S.Ct. at 937–38 (permit could be denied if demanded by the "public welfare, peace, safety, health, decency, good order, morals or convenience"). For example, Section 17-87 merely states, "Any license granted under Section 17-84 and 17-88 may be revoked by the Town Council after public hearing for cause shown." As in *Venuti,* the Westerly ordinance is utterly devoid of standards. See 521 F.Supp. at 1030–31 (striking down entertainment license ordinance). It leave the issuance and revocation of licenses to the unbridled discretion of the Town Council. Our cases have long noted that "the danger of censorship and of abridgement of our precious First Amendment freedoms is too great where officials have unbridled discretion over a forum's use." *Toward a Gayer Bicentennial Committee v. Rhode Island Bicentennial Foundation,* 417 F.Supp. 632, 641 (D.R.I.1976) (quoting *Southeastern Promotions,* 420 U.S. at 553, 95 S.Ct. at 1242–44).

The defendants assert that they are guided by specific concerns for public safety, as outlined in their notice to plaintiffs, and not by the message of 2 Live Crew's lyrics. When dealing with the First Amendment, however, the law does not allow us to presume good intentions on the part of the reviewing body. *Lakewood,* 486 U.S. at 770, 108 S.Ct. at 1243–44. The standards must be explicitly set out in the ordinance itself, a judicial construction or a well-established practice. *Id.* Without standards there is a grave danger that a licensing scheme "will serve only as a mask behind which the government hides as it excludes speakers from the . . . forum solely because of what they intend to say." *Irish Subcommittee,* 646 F.Supp. at 357. Such exclusion is repugnant to the First Amendment.

This Court recognizes that the Westerly Town Council has a valid interest in regulating entertainment establishments. It is well established that time, place and manner restrictions on expressive activity are permissible, but even then the regulations must be "narrowly and precisely tailored to their legitimate objectives." *Toward a Gayer Bicentennial,* 427 F.Supp. at 638, *see Shuttlesworth,* 394 U.S. at 153, 89 S.Ct. at 940, *Cox,* 379 U.S. at 558, 85 S.Ct. at 466. The Westerly licensing ordinances do not even approach the necessary level of specificity constitutionally mandated.

Given the complete lack of standards in the ordinances and the long and clear line of precedent, plaintiffs' likelihood of success is overwhelming.

* * * *

ORDER

Because Westerly Code of Ordinances, Sections 17-84 and 17-87 are facially unconstitutional, because the plaintiffs have met the other requirements for a preliminary injunction, and because defendants have failed to allege sufficient harm. IT IS ORDERED that defendants are enjoined from conducting a show cause hearing, revoking plaintiffs' license pursuant to these ordinances or from otherwise prohibiting the scheduled concert.

CHAPTER 14

External Memoranda—Court Briefs

Pam Hayes, a paralegal living in the hypothetical state of New Washington, received the following assignment from her supervisor.

To: Pam Hayes, Paralegal
From: Alice Black, Attorney
Case: Civil 97-601, Nick Shine v. Blue Sky Ski Resort
Re: Motion to dismiss for failure to state a claim

On December 5, 1996, Nick Shine, an expert skier, was skiing Bright Light, an intermediate ski run, at Blue Sky Ski Resort. At the midway point, the run takes a sharp, slightly uphill turn to the south, then plunges steeply downhill. When Mr. Shine encountered the turn, the sun was shining directly in his eyes; he did not see that the run was completely covered with ice. Due to the sun's glare, he could not see the ice hazard until it was too late to avoid it. He immediately lost control and hit a tree, breaking his left arm and leg. There was no warning sign posted to indicate the presence of the ice hazard.

We filed Mr. Shine's complaint against the resort on April 6, 1997. In the complaint, we allege that the resort was negligent in failing to post a warning indicating the presence of the unavoidable and latent ice hazard.

On April 20, Blue Sky Ski Resort filed a motion to dismiss under Rule 12(b)(6) of the Rules of Civil Procedure for failure to state a claim. In the motion, Resort argues that under the Ski Safety Act, the resort does not have a duty to warn of ice hazards. They argue that ice conditions are the responsibility of the skier under the act; therefore, we cannot, as a matter of law, state a claim in regard to duty.

Please prepare a response to their motion for my review.

Note that this assignment is a variation of the assignment presented at the beginning of Chapter 9. The following sections of this chapter introduce the guidelines that Ms. Hayes will follow when performing her assignment. The completed assignment is presented in the Application section.

INTRODUCTION

The focus of this text is on legal analysis and the main type of writing related to legal analysis: the legal research memorandum. The text does not address some of the other types of legal writing, such as the preparation of complaints and motions or transactional documents (contracts, deeds, and so on). Chapters 12 and 13 address the type of legal writing most frequently performed by a paralegal engaged in legal analysis: the office legal memorandum.

As discussed in Chapters 12 and 13, the office legal memorandum is designed for use within the law office and is drafted primarily as an objective research and analysis tool. This chapter and Chapter 15 discuss the preparation of documents using legal analysis that are designed for use outside the law office:

- Documents submitted to a court, such as briefs in support of motions
- Documents designed for other external use, such as correspondence to clients and opposing attorneys.

A paralegal is less frequently involved in the preparation of external use documents than those designed for use within the law office; however, a paralegal may be called upon to prepare the initial drafts of documents intended for external use.

This chapter focuses on the considerations involved in the preparation of legal analysis documents designed for submission to a court: trial court and appellate court legal memorandum briefs. In this chapter, a legal memorandum brief submitted to a trial court is referred to as a trial brief, and a brief submitted to a court of appeals is referred to as an appellate court brief. An example of a trial court brief is provided in the Application section of this chapter; an example of an appellate court brief is included in Appendix B of this text.

GENERAL CONSIDERATIONS

Both trial and appellate court briefs are similar in many respects to office legal memorandums, and the fundamental principles that apply to the preparation of office memorandums also apply to the preparation of court briefs. The similarities are outlined here.

Similarities—Court Briefs and Office Memoranda

Legal Writing Process

Just as it is necessary when preparing an office memorandum to adopt and use a legal writing process, it is also necessary to do so when preparing a court brief. The basic writing process is the same for both court briefs and office memoranda:

- Prewriting Stage
  - Assignment—type of brief, audience, and so on
  - Constraints—time, length, format (court rules)
  - Organization—creation of an expanded outline
    - Use of an expanded outline
- Writing Stage
- Postwriting Stage
  - Revising
  - Editing

Refer to Chapter 10 for instructions and information concerning the use of a writing process.

Basic Format

Court briefs follow the same basic format as office memoranda. Both include a presentation of the issue(s), the relevant facts, a legal analysis, and a conclusion. Refer to Chapters 12 and 13 for information and guidelines concerning the preparation of these components of a brief.

Analysis Approach

Court briefs follow the same basic organizational approach to the legal analysis of an issue as office memoranda: the rule of law is presented first, then the interpretation of the rule of law through the case law (if interpretation is necessary), the application of the law to the issues presented by the facts of the case, followed by the conclusion. The basic format of this approach is presented in Figure 14–1.

Refer to Chapter 13 when preparing the analysis and conclusion sections of a court brief.

Dissimilarities—Court Briefs and Office Memoranda

As noted above, court briefs, both trial and appellate, are similar in many respects to office legal memoranda. They are similar primarily in basic format and content. The major difference is in the presentation of the format and content. An office memorandum is designed to present an objective analysis of the law. The goal is to provide a neutral analysis that thoroughly addresses all sides of an issue and provides the attorney with guidance on how the court may resolve the issue.

Whereas an office memorandum is designed to objectively inform, a court brief is designed to convince. A court brief is an advocacy document designed to persuade the court to adopt a position or take an action that is favorable to the client. Therefore, although the elements of an office memorandum and court brief are basically the same, court briefs are different in that they are designed to advocate a position and persuade the reader.

The following discussion addresses the guidelines, factors, and considerations involved in the preparation of persuasive court briefs. In order to avoid repetition, this section addresses the factors involved in the persuasive presentation of both trial and appellate court briefs. Therefore, the detailed discussion of court briefs presented in the Trial Court Briefs and Appellate Court Briefs sections of this chapter does not include information on persuasive presentation factors. The information

Rule of law
Case law (if necessary)—interpretation of rule of law
1. Name of case
2. Facts of case—sufficient to demonstrate case is on point
3. Rule or legal principle from case that applies to the issue being addressed
Application of law to the issue being addressed
Discussion of opposing position (similar to counteranalysis in office legal memorandum)
Conclusion

Figure 14–1
Legal Analysis—Court Brief Organizational Approach

presented here applies to the preparation of both trial and appellate court briefs and should be kept in mind when preparing those briefs.

Both an office memorandum and a court brief must present the issue(s), fact statement, and analysis accurately, clearly, and concisely. A court brief should present this information in a persuasive manner. The guidelines for how this is accomplished are presented in the following subsections. When preparing a persuasive presentation of a legal position or argument, you must keep in mind the importance of intellectual honesty as discussed in Chapter 2. Although designed to persuade, a court brief must present the argument honestly. It should not mislead, distort, or hide the truth.

Issues—Persuasive Presentation

Once you have identified the issue, you should introduce each of its elements—the law, the question, and the key facts—in a persuasive manner.

Law Component of the Issue. You should state the law component of the issue persuasively.

For Example: Assume a case involving oppressive conduct by a majority shareholder against the minority shareholders in the hypothetical state of New Washington. The corporation consists of three shareholders. The majority shareholder holds 60% of the stock and is employed as president of the corporation. The minority shareholders are not employed by the corporation.

In the case, the defendant, the majority shareholder, controls the board of directors and has refused to allow the issuance of dividends for a ten-year period. During this period, he has given himself an annual 40% raise each year and an annual bonus equal to 50% of his salary. The minority shareholders have filed a suit claiming that the majority shareholder's actions constitute oppressive conduct.

Section 53-6 of the New Washington statutes authorizes the court to dissolve the corporation when the majority shareholder engages in oppressive conduct. This example is referred to in this chapter as the corporation example.

In an office memorandum, the law component of the issue in this example is stated objectively: "Under the New Washington corporation statute, NWSA § 53-6, did oppressive conduct occur when . . .?" In a court brief, however, the law is presented persuasively. The persuasive language is italicized: "Under the New Washington corporation statute, NWSA § 53-6, *which prohibits oppressive conduct,* did . . .?"

Note that the persuasive presentation of the law component emphasizes the prohibitory nature of the statute.

For Example: If your position is that the statute has limited application, the law should be presented in a manner that focuses on that limitation: "Under NWSA § 51-7, which *limits the requirement of a written contract to. . . .*"

If you want to emphasize the applicability of the statute, the law should be presented in a manner that focuses on applicability: "Under NWSA § 51-7, *which requires that a contract be in writing when. . . .*"

Question Component of the Issue. You should present the question component of the issue in a persuasive manner that suggests a result.

For Example: *Objective presentation:* ". . . did oppressive conduct occur when . . .?"

Persuasive presentation: ". . . was the majority shareholder's conduct oppressive when . . .?" or ". . . did the majority shareholder engage in oppressive conduct when . . .?" Note that in the objective presentation, the focus is on the conduct. In the persuasive presentation, the statement links the conduct immediately to the majority shareholder.

The language used should focus on the result desired.

For Example: The key language is italicized: ". . . does the statute *allow* oral contracts for . . .?" ". . . does the statute *require* oral contracts for . . .?" ". . . does the statute *prohibit* oral contracts for . . .?"

Fact Component of the Issue. You should state the key facts of the issue in a manner designed to focus the reader on the facts favorable to the client and persuade the reader to favor the client's position.

For Example: *Objective presentation:* ". . . did oppressive conduct occur when dividends were not issued for a ten-year period and the majority shareholder received annual salary increases and bonuses?"

Persuasive presentation: ". . . did the majority shareholder engage in oppressive conduct when he refused to issue dividends for a ten-year period while giving himself large annual salary increases and bonuses?"

For Example: *Objective presentation:* ". . . when the defendant entered the property after being advised not to enter?"

Persuasive presentation: ". . . when the defendant intentionally entered the property even though he was warned not to enter?"

Note that in both examples, the persuasive presentation focuses on the defendant and links the defendant directly to the improper conduct.

Refer to Chapters 6 and 7 for guidance when identifying and stating issues. A checklist for use in the persuasive presentation of the issue(s) is presented in Figure 14–2.

Statement of Facts—Persuasive Presentation

The statement of facts section of a court brief presents the facts of the case. This section is often called the "statement of the case." In a court brief, just as in an office memorandum, the statement of facts should include both the background and the key facts. In a court brief, you should introduce the facts credibly, persuasively, and in a light most favorable to the client's position. This is accomplished by emphasizing favorable facts and de-emphasizing or neutralizing unfavorable facts.

There are several techniques you may use to emphasize favorable facts and neutralize unfavorable facts. Some of these are discussed in the following subsections.

Placement. Readers tend to remember information presented at the beginning and end of a section, and usually the most attention is given to opening and closing sentences. Therefore, introduce the facts favorable to the client's position at the beginning and the end of the factual statement. Present the facts unfavorable to the client's position that you wish to de-emphasize in the middle of the section.

For Example: Referring to the corporation example, "The defendant is the majority shareholder and controlling member of the board of directors of XYZ corporation. He has refused to authorize the issuance of dividends for ten years. During this time, the defendant has been the president of the corporation. As president, he has granted himself a 40% raise each year. In addition, he has given himself an annual bonus equal to 50% of his salary. It is claimed by the defendant that he is entitled to the salary increases and bonuses because he works long hours, is underpaid, and is the

- ❏ Law Component of the Issue
- ❏ Question Component of the Issue
- ❏ Fact Component of the Issue

Figure 14–2
Issues—Persuasive Presentation—Checklist

person in charge. The defendant has rebuffed the plaintiff's repeated requests to discuss the defendant's grants to himself of salary increases and bonuses and failure to issue dividends. The defendant has informed the plaintiff that he does not intend to issue dividends."

In this example, the facts least favorable to the defendant, his failure to issue dividends and receipt of salary increases and bonuses, are presented at the beginning. His conduct immediately captures the reader's attention. His conduct is also mentioned again at the end of the presentation. The reader's first and last impressions are focused on the acts least favorable to the defendant. The facts favorable to the defendant, that he is entitled to the salary increases and bonuses, are de-emphasized by their placement in the middle of the fact statement.

If the fact statement is composed of several paragraphs, place the favorable material at the beginning of the presentation and close with a summary or rephrasing of the favorable key facts. Place the unfavorable facts in the middle of the presentation and mention them only once or as few times as possible.

Note that the goal is a persuasive presentation of the facts. This goal should not be so rigidly pursued that clarity is lost.

For Example: It may not be practical to state the favorable facts immediately at the beginning of a paragraph. To ensure clarity, you may need to present transitional or introductory sentences first, then follow them with the presentation of the favorable facts.

Sentence Length. Use short sentences to emphasize favorable information and long sentences to de-emphasize unfavorable information. Shorter sentences generally draw the attention of the reader, are easier to understand, and therefore are more powerful.

For Example: "The defendant is the majority shareholder and controlling member of the board of directors of XYZ corporation. He has refused to authorize the issuance of dividends for ten years. During this time, the defendant has been the president of the corporation. As president, he has granted himself a 40% raise each year."

The sentences in this example are short, clear, and draw the reader's attention. Longer sentences that string together several facts tend to downplay and reduce the impact of each fact.

For Example: "It is claimed by the defendant that he is entitled to the salary increases and bonuses because he works long hours, is underpaid, and is the person in charge."

In this example, if each of the defendant's actions were presented in separate sentences, they would stand out and be clearer.

Active Voice. Use active voice to emphasize favorable information and passive voice to de-emphasize unfavorable information. When active voice is used, the subject of the sentence is the actor. When passive voice is used, the subject is acted upon. Active voice draws the attention to and emphasizes the actor. Passive voice draws attention away from and de-emphasizes the actor.

For Example: *Passive voice:* "It is claimed by the defendant that he is entitled to the bonuses. . . ." The use of passive voice draws attention away from the actor, the defendant.

Active voice: "The defendant claims he is entitled . . ." is less wordy and focuses the attention on the actor.

The use of active and passive voice is discussed in Chapter 11.

Word Choice. Ideally the words you choose should introduce the client's facts in the most favorable light and the opponent's facts in the least favorable light. You should present the client's position in the most affirmative manner and the opponent's position in the most questionable manner.

For Example: "The plaintiff states that. . . ." "The defendant alleges. . . ."

In this example, notice that the plaintiff's presentation sounds stronger, since it is presented as a statement. The defendant's position is presented as a charge—an "allegation" rather than a statement of fact. There are numerous ways in which positions can be presented in a strong or weak manner. Be sure to check your word choice.

It is easy, however, to get carried away and state the facts in such a slanted way that your bias is painfully obvious.

For Example: "The defendant stubbornly and unreasonably refuses to issue dividends."

In this example, the presentation of the facts is clearly biased and heavy-handed. It is better to just note that the defendant has refused to issue dividends. When in doubt, exercise restraint.

Refer to the techniques presented in the preceding text when preparing a persuasive presentation of the facts. A checklist for use in conjunction with the guidelines for the persuasive presentation of the statement of facts is in Figure 14–3.

Chapter 5 is helpful when identifying key and background facts. Many of the considerations involved in preparing the statement of facts section of an office memorandum are the same as those involved in preparing the statement of facts section of a court brief. The Statement of Facts section of Chapter 12, therefore, also will prove helpful when preparing this section.

Argument—Persuasive Presentation

The persuasive tone and orientation of the court brief is initially established in the presentation of the issue and fact statements. The persuasive techniques discussed in the previous sections of this text, such as word choice, sentence length, active and passive voice, and so on, also apply and should be employed when crafting the argument section of a court brief.

The argument section is the heart of the court brief. It is the equivalent of the analysis section of an office legal memorandum. Unlike the analysis section of an office memo, however, the argument section of a court brief is not an objective presentation of the law. It should be crafted in a persuasive manner. The goal of the argument section is to persuade the court that your position is valid. This is accomplished by a persuasive presentation of the following:

- The law in support of your position
- The analysis of the law
- The argument that your analysis is valid and the opposition's analysis is invalid

The following text presents a summary of the techniques you may use to ensure that the argument component of a court brief is presented in a persuasive manner.

- ❑ Placement—Favorable and Unfavorable Facts
- ❑ Sentence Length
- ❑ Active/Passive Voice
- ❑ Word Choice

Figure 14–3
Statement of Facts—Persuasive Presentation—Checklist

There are several helpful guidelines that apply to both trial and appellate court briefs. The Trial Court Briefs and Appellate Court Briefs sections of this chapter introduce additional information concerning the format and content of the argument section. Those sections focus on the differences between trial and appellate court briefs.

Organization. The organization of the argument section is similar to that of the analysis section of the office memorandum: *the rule of law is introduced, followed by an interpretation of the law (usually through case law), then an application of the law to the issue raised by the facts of the case.* Rather than a separate counteranalysis section, the opposing position is addressed in the presentation of the argument.

Issue Presentation. Where there is more than one issue or where there are issues and subissues, discuss the issue supported by the strongest argument first. There are several reasons for this:

- First impressions are lasting. The tone of the argument is set at the beginning. By presenting the strongest argument first, you set a tone of strength and credibility.
- If you introduce the strongest argument first, the court is more likely to be persuaded that your position is correct and look more favorably on your weaker arguments.
- Judges are often very busy. On some occasions, a judge may not read the entire brief, especially if the brief is a long one. In such instances, the judge may not read your strongest argument if you do not present it first or near the beginning of the brief. For this reason, if there are several arguments in support of a position, omit the weak arguments. Arguments or positions that are weak or have little supporting authority detract and divert attention from the stronger arguments.

Rule of Law Presentation. Present the rule of law, whether it is enacted or case law, in a manner that supports your argument.

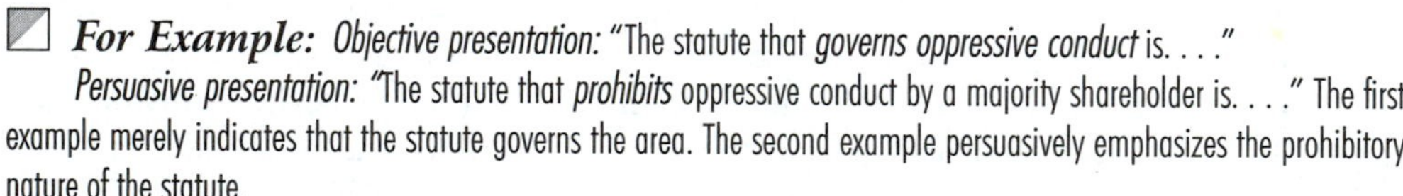

For Example: *Objective presentation:* "The statute that *governs oppressive conduct* is. . . ."

Persuasive presentation: "The statute that *prohibits* oppressive conduct by a majority shareholder is. . . ." The first example merely indicates that the statute governs the area. The second example persuasively emphasizes the prohibitory nature of the statute.

For Example: *Objective presentation:* "The courts of other states are split on what constitutes oppressive conduct. Most courts follow *Smith v. Jones,* which provides. . . . A minority of courts follow *Dave v. Roe.* . . . The majority view is based on the premise that the conduct need be either wrongful or improper. . . ."

Persuasive presentation: "The majority of courts follow the definition of oppressive conduct presented in *Smith v. Jones.* In this case, the court defined oppressive conduct as. . . . This definition is based on the well-reasoned view that the conduct need only be wrongful or improper. A minority of courts follow. . . ."

In this example, the persuasive presentation is more forceful and introduces the majority view in a manner that indicates it is preferable. The objective view is passive and treats both the majority and minority views equally. It does not emphasize one view as favorable. Refer to the discussion in the Issues—Persuasive Presentation section of this chapter when drafting the rule of law component of the argument section of a brief.

Case Presentation. When introducing case law, discuss the favorable case law first, followed by the unfavorable or opposing case law, then a response or rebuttal that emphasizes why the favorable case law should be followed. This is similar to the format followed in the fact statement: *the placement of the unfavorable material in the middle of the presentation following the favorable material tends to minimize its importance.*

The discussion of the case law should emphasize the similarities and applicability of the case you rely on and the dissimilarities and inapplicability of the case relied on by the opposition.

For Example: "The term 'oppressive conduct' is defined in the case of *Tyrone v. Blatt*. In *Tyrone,* the majority shareholder refused to authorize the issuance of dividends. The defendant granted himself four major pay increases, quadrupling his salary during the period dividends were not issued. In the holding, the court noted that there was no justification for the salary increases and ruled that his conduct was oppressive. The court stated that 'oppressive conduct' occurs when there is wrongful conduct that inures to the benefit of the majority shareholder and to the detriment of the minority shareholders.

"In our case, just as in *Tyrone,* the majority shareholder refused to issue dividends. In our case, like *Tyrone,* the majority shareholder gave himself large salary increases. In both cases, there was no justification for the increases. Therefore, the court should apply the standard established in *Tyrone* and find that the defendant engaged in oppressive conduct.

"It is argued by the defendant that the court should apply the holding reached in *Wise v. Wind* and find that the defendant's conduct was not oppressive. The defendant's reliance on *Wise* is misplaced. In *Wise,* there was evidence that the salary increases were justified.

"Our situation is distinguishable. There is no evidence that the salary increases the defendant awarded himself and the refusal to issue dividends were justified. Therefore, the *Wise* opinion is not on point and is not applicable. The *Tyrone* opinion is on point and should be followed."

When preparing the case law section of the argument, refer to Chapter 8 for guidance in case law analysis and determining if a case is on point.

Argument Order. When interpreting and applying a rule of law, always introduce your arguments first, address the counterargument, then present your response. In addition, spend more time affirmatively stating your position than responding to the opponent's counterargument. There are several reasons for this:

- Just as with the presentation of the fact statement and organization of the argument, the reader tends to remember and emphasize information presented at the beginning and end of a section or paragraph. You want to draw attention to and emphasize your argument; therefore, address it first.
- By introducing your argument first, you have the opportunity to soften the impact of the opposing argument through the strong presentation of your position.
- In a busy court, if you discuss your position or argument after the opponent's, you run the risk of it not being read by the court.
- By following the counterargument with a response or rebuttal that sums up your position, you remove the counterargument further from the reader's attention. It is buried in the middle of the argument where its significance is downplayed and it is de-emphasized. The defendant's position is italicized in the following example.

  For Example: "It is appropriate for the court to allow the admission of the INDM test results. The court of appeals in *State v. Digo* ruled that scientific tests are admissible when the reliability and scientific basis of the test are recognized by competent authorities. The INDM test, developed in 1985, is universally accepted by all competent authorities as scientifically valid. *It is argued by the defendant that the test results should not be relied on by the court. Defendant relies on the case of* Ard v. State *to support this argument. Defendant's reliance on* Ard v. State *is misplaced. In this 1985 case, the court of appeals did not allow the* *admission of the INDM test results because the INDM was a new test not universally accepted.* The ruling in *Ard* is no longer applicable. The INDM test is no longer a new test and is universally used and accepted."

Word Choice. Careful word selection is an invaluable aid in the crafting of a persuasive argument. The argument can be significantly enhanced by the use of forceful, positive, and confident language.

For Example: *Ineffective:* "We believe that the defendant engaged in oppressive conduct."
Effective: "The defendant engaged in oppressive conduct."
Ineffective: "It is the defendant's position that the search was illegal. . . ."
Effective: "The search was illegal. . . ."

Present the opposing position in a manner that de-emphasizes its importance or credibility.

For Example: *Ineffective:* "The defendant *states*. . . ."
Effective: "The defendant *alleges*. . . ."
Ineffective: "The defendant's *position is*. . . ."
Effective: "The defendant *claims*. . . ."

point heading

A summary of the position advocated in the argument section of a trial or appellate brief.

Point Headings. Point headings are a summary of the position advocated in the argument. They are presented at the beginning of the argument. The Trial Court Briefs section of this chapter addresses the details of format, content, and presentation of point headings. This section discusses the persuasive nature and presentation of point headings.

The persuasive role of a point heading is to focus the reader on the position advocated in the argument. Therefore, you should draft a point heading in a manner that provides a positive presentation of that position.

For Example: *Not persuasive:* "The court should not grant the motion to suppress. . . ." "The photos of the victim were inflammatory and should not have been admitted into evidence by the trial court."

Persuasive: "The court should deny the motion to suppress. . . ." "The inflammatory nature of the photographs of the victim outweigh their probative value, and their admission was highly prejudicial to the defendant and was improper."

The difference in the two presentations in this example is that the persuasive presentation more affirmatively and positively characterizes the position argued. The discussions in the previous section concerning word choice and active voice apply to point headings.

A checklist for use in the persuasive presentation of the argument in a court brief is presented in Figure 14–4.

Figure 14–4

Argument—Persuasive Presentation—Checklist

- ❑ Argument Organization
  - ❑ Issue Presentation
  - ❑ Rule of Law Presentation
  - ❑ Case Presentation
- ❑ Argument Order
- ❑ Argument—Word Choice
- ❑ Argument—Point Headings

TRIAL COURT BRIEFS

In many instances, when a trial court is in the process of ruling on a motion or an issue in a case, the judge requires the attorneys to submit a memorandum of law. This memorandum of law is often referred to as a memorandum of points and authorities. The memorandum of law presents the legal authority and argument in support of the position advocated by the attorney. In this chapter, a memorandum of law submitted to a trial court is referred to as a trial brief.

trial court brief
An external memorandum of law submitted to a trial court. It presents the legal authority and argument in support of a position advocated by an attorney, usually in regard to a motion or issue being addressed by the court.

A trial brief is similar to an office memorandum in many respects. Both are designed to inform the reader how the law applies to the issues raised by the facts of the case. Most of the considerations involved in the preparation of an office memorandum also apply to the preparation of a trial brief. Therefore, when preparing a trial brief, in addition to this chapter, refer to Chapters 12 and 13 for guidance. As discussed in the Dissimilarities—Court Briefs and Office Memoranda section of this chapter, the major difference between an office memorandum and a trial brief is that a trial brief is designed to persuade the reader to adopt the position advocated in the brief, whereas an office memorandum is designed to present an objective analysis of the law.

The guidelines for preparing a persuasive trial brief are discussed in the previous section. This section addresses other considerations involved in the preparation of a trial brief, such as the application of the writing process.

Audience

The audience for the trial brief is the judge assigned to the case. Trial court judges are usually busy with heavy case loads and may rule on several motions a day. They may not have time to carefully read lengthy drawn-out briefs. Therefore, a judge usually appreciates a trial brief that consists of a short, well-organized, and concise presentation of the law.

Constraints

The major constraints on a trial brief are usually imposed by the local court rules. Many trial courts have local rules that govern various aspects of a trial brief.

court rules
Procedural rules adopted by a court that govern the litigation process. Court rules often govern the format and style of documents submitted to the court.

For Example: A local rule may establish a maximum length of a trial brief and require the permission of the court before that length can be exceeded.

The local rules must always be consulted when preparing a trial brief.

Usually there is a time constraint. The court or the local rules often require the submission of the brief within a certain number of days. Become aware of the time deadline and allocate your time accordingly. Usually, but not always, extensions of time may be granted by the court upon request.

Format/Content

The format of a trial brief varies from court to court and jurisdiction to jurisdiction. In many instances, the local court rules establish a required format. Generally, a trial court brief includes some or all of the components presented in Figure 14–5.

Figure 14–5

Components of Trial Court Brief

Caption
Table of Contents
Table of Authorities
Preliminary Statement
Question(s) Presented—Issue(s)
Statement of the Case (Fact Statement)
Argument
Conclusion

If the brief is short, such as in the case of a single issue brief, a table of contents, table of authorities, or preliminary statement may not be required. Each of the components in Figure 14–5 is briefly discussed in the following subsections. For examples of these components, refer to the Application section of this chapter and Appendix B.

Caption

Every brief submitted to a trial court requires a caption. The format varies from court to court, but the caption usually includes:

- The name of the court
- The names and status of the parties
- The file number and type of case—civil or criminal
- The title of the document, such as BRIEF IN SUPPORT OF MOTION TO DISMISS

Refer to the Application section of this chapter for an example of a caption.

Table of Contents

If a table of contents is required, it follows the caption page. The table of contents lists each component of the brief and the page number. If point headings are used in the argument section, they are stated in full in the table of contents. The table allows the reader to locate the various components of the brief. For an example of a table of contents, see the appellate brief presented in Appendix B.

Table of Authorities

If a table of authorities is required, it is presented after the table of contents page. A table of authorities lists all the law used in the brief and the page on which the law is cited in the brief. This allows the reader to quickly locate where the authority is discussed in the brief. Present the case law and enacted law in separate sections. List the case law in alphabetical order by case name. For an example of a table of contents, see the appellate brief presented in Appendix B.

Preliminary Statement

The preliminary statement introduces the procedural posture of the case. It usually includes:

- An identification of the parties
- The procedural events in the case relevant to the matter the court is addressing
- A description of the matter being addressed by the court, such as "This matter is before the court on a motion to dismiss the complaint."

- The relief sought, such as "This memorandum is submitted in support of the motion to suppress the evidence seized during the search."

For Example:

PRELIMINARY STATEMENT

Edna and Ida Tule, the plaintiffs, are minority shareholders in Tule, Inc. Their brother, Thomas Tule, is the defendant in this action, the majority shareholder, and president of Tule, Inc. On January 9 of this year, a request for the production of company records relating to salary increases and bonuses granted to Mr. Tule was delivered to him. Mr. Tule has refused to produce the company records. This memorandum is submitted in support of a motion to compel the production of those documents.

Question(s) Presented

This section of a brief discusses the legal issue(s) addressed in the brief. The issue should include the rule of law, legal question, and the key facts. When there is more than one issue, list the issues in the order in which they are discussed in the argument section of the brief. An office memorandum identifies the issue(s) objectively. In a trial brief, you should draft the issue(s) in a persuasive manner. The Issues—Persuasive Presentation section of this chapter discusses the techniques involved in the persuasive drafting of the issue. Chapters 6 and 7 address issue identification and presentation, and Chapter 12 addresses the presentation of the issue(s) in an office memorandum. Refer to these chapters when preparing the issue.

Statement of the Case

This section is often referred to as the statement of facts. It corresponds to the statement of facts section of an office memorandum. Its purpose is to explain the facts of the case. This section in a trial brief is different from that in an office memorandum because it is drafted in a persuasive manner designed to introduce the facts in a light that most favors the client's position. The persuasive nature of the fact section is discussed in the Statement of Facts—Persuasive Presentation section of this chapter. That section and the Application section of this chapter introduce examples of persuasive statements of facts. The fact section should be accurate and complete and should include background and key facts. For additional guidance when drafting the fact section, refer to Chapter 5, Key Facts, and the Statement of Facts section of Chapter 12.

Argument Section

The argument section of a trial brief, like the analysis section of an office memorandum, is the heart of the document. It is unlike the analysis section of an office memorandum in that it is not an objective legal analysis. Rather, it is designed to persuade the court to adopt your interpretation of the law. The Argument—Persuasive Presentation section of this chapter discusses the considerations involved in crafting the argument in a persuasive manner. This section addresses the basic organization of the argument and the components. The organization and components are presented in Figure 14–6.

The format in Figure 14–6 is a recommended one and is not necessarily followed in every office, and a different format may be required by local court rule. In some instances, a summary of the argument may not be required, and some local court rules and office formats do not require point headings. This is often the case when the brief is short and involves a single issue. All of the components of the

Figure 14–6

Organization and Components of Argument Section of Trial Brief

1. Summary of argument
2. Point headings
3. Argument
   Rule of law
   Case law (if necessary)—interpretation of rule of law
   Application of law to the issue being addressed
      Discussion of opposing position (similar to counteranalysis in office legal memorandum)

argument section are presented here so that you will be familiar with them when they are required.

Summary of Argument. The argument section of a trial brief should begin with an introductory paragraph that summarizes the argument. It presents the context of the argument, the issues in the order in which they will be discussed, a summary of the conclusions on each issue, and the major reasons that support each conclusion.

> ***For Example:*** On December 12, 1995, John Jones, the defendant, was arrested for possession of cocaine. On January 1, 1996, he was indicted for possession of four ounces of cocaine. The trial commenced on October 25, 1996. On November 11, 1996, he was found guilty by a jury and convicted of possession of four ounces of cocaine. This matter is before the court on Mr. Jones's motion for a new trial, filed March 7, 1997. Mr. Jones's motion is based on the claim that new evidence has been uncovered that shows the drugs belonged to a Mr. Tom Smith, a visitor in Mr. Jones's home. In order for a new trial to be granted on the basis of newly discovered evidence, the defendant must demonstrate that the newly discovered evidence was not available or discoverable at the time of trial. The information concerning Mr. Smith was available at the time of trial. The defense made no effort to interview Mr. Smith or in any way discover whether the drugs belonged to him. The evidence regarding Mr. Smith is not newly discovered evidence, and the motion should be denied.

The use of an argument summary is valuable when you believe the judge may not have time to read the entire brief. It may not be necessary if the brief is short or when a single issue is involved. It should be a complete summary; the reader should not have to refer to the body of the argument to understand the summary.

Point Headings. Point headings are a summary of the position you are asking the court to adopt. They should be drafted persuasively. The guidelines for drafting persuasive point headings are addressed in the Argument—Persuasive Presentation section of this chapter.

Point headings are designed to:

- Organize, define, and emphasize the structure of the argument
- Act as locators—they allow the reader to quickly find specific sections of the argument
- Focus the court's attention on the outcome you advocate and provide an outline of your theory

Point headings may not be required in a trial brief, especially when the brief is short or addresses a single issue. In such instances, they are not needed as an organizational tool, nor are they needed to guide the reader. Check the court rules and office format to determine when they are required.

In regard to point headings, note the following guidelines:

1. Place the point headings at the beginning of each section of the argument and include them in the table of contents.
2. Divide the point headings into major and minor point headings. There should be a major point heading for each issue presented. Use minor headings to introduce significant points supporting the major heading.

   For Example:

   ARGUMENT

   I. THE TRIAL COURT ERRED WHEN IT RULED THAT MR. SMITH'S CONDUCT DID NOT CONSTITUTE BREACH OF CONTRACT BECAUSE THE GOODS WERE DEFECTIVE AND DELIVERED LATE.

   A. Mr. Smith's delivery of the widgets ten days late constituted a breach of the contract. (Text of argument.)

   B. The delivery of the widgets with a five-pound spring instead of a ten-pound spring constituted a breach of the contract. (Text of argument.)

3. Each heading and subheading should be a complete sentence.
4. Each heading should identify the legal conclusion you want the court to adopt and the basic reasons for the conclusion.

   For Example: "THE TESTIMONY OF DR. SMITH IS PROBATIVE OF THE DEFENDANT'S INTENT AND THEREFORE IS ADMISSIBLE."

   "THE DISTRICT COURT'S SUPPRESSION OF THE EVIDENCE WAS IMPROPER BECAUSE THE SEARCH WARRANT WAS SUPPORTED BY PROBABLE CAUSE."

5. Use minor headings only if there are two or more. The rules of outlining require more than one subheading when subheadings are used. Minor headings present aspects of a major point heading in the context of the specific facts of the case. Note that the minor point headings in the example in number 2 above present two aspects of the major point heading. The minor point headings are stated in the specific context of the facts of the case:

   A. Mr. Smith's delivery of the widgets ten days late constituted a breach of the contract.

   B. The delivery of the widgets with a five-pound spring instead of a ten-pound spring constituted a breach of the contract.

6. Type major headings in all capitals and minor headings in regular type. Minor headings may be underlined. Check the court rules for the proper format. The example in number 2 above illustrates the format for major and minor point headings.

Argument Format. The argument section of the trial brief is similar to the analysis section of an office memorandum, and the Analysis Section of Chapter 13 should be referred to when preparing a trial brief. The same basic IRAC format is followed:

Rule of law
Case law (if necessary)—interpretation of rule of law
  1. Name of case
  2. Facts of case—sufficient to demonstrate case is on point
  3. Rule or legal principle from case that applies to the issue being addressed
Application of law to the issue being addressed
  Discussion of opposing position (similar to counteranalysis in office legal memorandum)

The major difference between the argument component of an office memorandum and that of a trial brief is that the trial brief introduces the argument in a persuasive rather than an objective manner. A trial brief is designed to persuade, and you should draft the argument in a persuasive manner. Refer to the Argument—Persuasive Presentation section of this chapter for guidance in organizing and preparing a persuasive argument.

Conclusion

The conclusion section of a trial brief requests the specific relief desired. Depending on the complexity of the brief, it may be a single sentence stating the requested relief or a summary of the entire argument.

For Example: *Single sentence:* "For the foregoing reasons, the defendant requests that the motion to dismiss be granted."

A single sentence conclusion is appropriate when the trial brief is a simple, one- or two-issue brief, and the argument section concludes with a summary of the analysis. When the trial brief is longer and more complicated, the conclusion may include an overall summary of the law presented in the argument section and end with a request for relief. This type of conclusion is similar to the conclusion section of an office memorandum discussed in the Conclusion section of Chapter 13. Refer to that section of Chapter 13 when preparing this type of conclusion. Note that the conclusion should summarize the argument section and should reflect the persuasive nature of the argument.

APPELLATE COURT BRIEFS

appellate court brief
An external memorandum of law submitted to a court of appeals. It presents the legal analysis, authority, and argument in support of a position that the lower court's decision or ruling was either correct or incorrect. It is often referred to as an appellate brief.

An individual who disagrees with the decision of a trial or lower court may appeal the decision to a court of appeals. The individual who appeals is called the *appellant,* and the individual who opposes the appeal is called the *appellee.* On appeal, the appellant argues that the lower court made an error, the error affected the outcome of the case, and the appellant is entitled to relief. The appellee argues that the lower court did not commit an error that entitles the appellant to relief.

Appellate court briefs are the written legal analysis and arguments submitted to the appellate court by the parties on appeal. The format and style of the appellate brief is strictly governed by appellate court rules, and these rules *must* be consulted when preparing an appellate brief.

The preparation of an appellate brief is a complex undertaking, and a detailed discussion of this subject is beyond the scope of this chapter. Entire texts are available at the local law library that address the detailed considerations involved in preparing an appellate brief, and you should refer to those texts when assigned the task of preparing an appellate brief.

A paralegal is not usually required to draft appellate briefs. A paralegal, however, may be called upon to assist in the preparation of the brief and, therefore, should be familiar with its components. This section presents a summary of the format and basic components of an appellate brief.

An appellate brief, like a trial brief, is designed to advocate a legal position and to persuade the court to adopt the position argued in the brief. Therefore, you should draft the brief in a persuasive manner. The discussion of the persuasive nature of court briefs, presented in the Dissimilarities—Court Briefs and Office Memoranda section of this chapter, applies to the preparation of appellate briefs: an appellate brief should be crafted in a persuasive manner.

An appellate brief, like a trial brief, is similar to an office memorandum in many respects. For example, a writing process should be used when preparing both briefs. Therefore, in addition to this chapter, refer to Chapters 10, 12, and 13 when performing an appellate brief assignment.

Audience

A trial court brief is submitted to a single judge, the trial judge assigned to the case. The audience for the appellate brief is usually a panel of three or more judges. In addition, the judge's law clerk usually reads the brief; on many occasions the law clerk is the first to read the brief. Although you are writing to a wider audience, the same basic considerations are involved in the preparation of trial court and appellate court briefs. Appellate court judges, like trial court judges, are usually busy with substantial case loads and appreciate an appellate brief that is a short, well-organized, and concise presentation of the law.

Constraints

The major constraints on appellate briefs are similar to those on trial court briefs in that they are imposed by the court's rules. The appellate court rules differ from trial court rules in that they are usually much more detailed than trial court rules: the appellate court rules may establish the sections that must be included, the format of the sections, the type of paper, the citation form, a maximum length for the briefs and a requirement that permission of the court be obtained before the length can be exceeded, and so on. Always consult the appellate court rules when preparing an appellate brief.

Format/Content

The format of an appellate brief varies from jurisdiction to jurisdiction. Generally, the basic appellate court brief includes some or all of the components presented in Figure 14–7.

The following subsections briefly discuss each of the components of the appellate brief presented in Figure 14–7.

Cover Page/Title Page
Table of Contents/Index
Table of Authorities
Opinions Below/Related Appeals
Jurisdictional Statement
Question(s) Presented—Issue(s)
Statement of the Case/Statement of Facts
Summary of Argument
Argument
Conclusion

Figure 14–7

Components of a Basic Appellate Court Brief

Cover Page/Title Page

The court rules govern the format of the cover page, often called the title page. The cover page usually includes the:

- Name of the appellate court
- Number assigned to the appeal
- Parties' names and appellate status (appellant and appellee or petitioner and respondent)
- Name of the lower court from which the appeal is taken
- Names and addresses of the attorney(s) submitting the brief

Refer to the appellate brief presented in Appendix B for an example of a cover page.

Table of Contents/Index

Sometimes referred to as an index, the table of contents lists the major sections of the brief and the page number of each section. The table of contents provides the reader with a reference tool for the location of specific information within the brief. The table includes the point headings and subheadings. The point headings, when included in the table of contents, serve to provide the reader with an overview of the legal arguments and allow the reader to easily locate the discussion of the arguments in the brief. The appellate brief in Appendix B includes an example of a table of contents.

Table of Authorities

The table of authorities lists all the law cited in the brief. The authorities are listed by category, such as constitutional law, statutory law, regulations, case law, and so on. The table includes the full citation of the authority and the page number or numbers on which it appears.

See Appendix B for an example of a table of authorities in an appellate brief.

Opinions Below/Related Appeals

The brief *may* include a section that references any prior opinions on the case or related appeals.

For Example: *From a Supreme Court brief:* "The opinion of the Court of Appeals is reported at 580 F.2d 501. The order of the District Court is not reported."

Jurisdictional Statement

The brief usually includes a separate section that introduces, in a short statement, the subject matter jurisdiction of the appellate court.

For Example: "This court has jurisdiction under 42 U.S.C. 1983."

Some appellate rules do not require a jurisdictional statement. Some appellate rules require, in addition to the jurisdictional statement, a history of the case and how the matter came before the court.

For Example: "The judgment of the trial court was entered on October 5, 1994. The notice of appeal was filed on October 26, 1994. The jurisdiction of the court is invoked under 42 U.S.C. 1983."

Question(s) Presented

This section may also be referred to as legal issues or assignment of error. The section lists the legal issues the party requests the court to consider. List the issues in the order in which they are addressed in the argument section, and write them in a persuasive manner as discussed earlier in this chapter in the Issues—Persuasive Presentation section. Also, refer to Chapters 6, 7, and 12 when preparing the issue section of the brief.

Statement of the Case/Statement of Facts

The statement of the case section, often referred to as the statement of facts, is generally similar to the statement of facts section of the trial brief, and the same considerations apply when preparing both.

The statement of the case in an appellate brief, however, differs from the statement of facts in a trial brief in that the statement of the case should also include a summary of the prior proceedings (what happened in the lower court) and appropriate references to the record. In the following example, "Tr." refers to the pages in the transcript of the trial record, and "Doc." refers to documents included in the record on appeal.

For Example: After the presentation of the key and background facts of the case, the information concerning the prior proceedings might read:

"At the motion to suppress hearing, held on December 12, 1995, the trial court denied the motion to suppress. (Tr. at 37). At the hearing, Officer Smith, the officer conducting the search, testified. . . . (Tr. at 33). The trial court stated that there were sufficient exigent circumstances present at the scene to support the unannounced entry by the officers. (Tr. at 38).

"Trial was held on January 15, 1996. (Tr. at 201). On January 18, 1996, the jury found the defendant guilty of possession of an ounce of cocaine. (Tr. at 291). On January 28, 1996, the defendant filed a notice of appeal. (Doc. 44). On March 7, 1996, the defendant was sentenced to a term of imprisonment of five years. (Doc. 49)."

Summary of Argument

This section may be optional under the appellate court rule. Rule 28 of the Federal Rules of Appellate Procedure states that the argument *may* be preceded by a summary. The content of an argument summary is discussed in the Trial Brief—Argument Section subsection of this chapter.

Argument Section

Point Headings. The considerations involved in preparing point headings are the same for appellate and trial court briefs. Refer to the discussion of point headings in the Trial Brief—Argument Section subsection of this chapter when preparing point headings for appellate briefs. See the appellate brief in Appendix B for examples.

Body. The argument section of an appellate brief is similar to the argument section of a trial brief. The format is the same as in a trial brief. Refer to the Trial Brief—Argument Section subsection of this chapter when preparing the argument section of an appellate brief. Remember to present the argument section of an appellate brief in a persuasive manner as discussed in the Argument—Persuasive Presentation subsection of this chapter. Review that subsection when preparing the argument. For an example of an argument section of an appellate brief, see Appendix B.

Conclusion

Prepare the conclusion section of an appellate brief in the same way as the conclusion of a trial brief. The content, structure, and considerations involved are the same for both. Refer to the Trial Brief—Conclusion subsection of this chapter when preparing the conclusion. Refer to the appellate brief in Appendix B for an example.

KEY POINTS CHECKLIST: *Preparing a Court Brief*

- ❑ Trial and appellate briefs are similar to office memoranda in many fundamental respects. Chapters 10, 12, and 13 should be referred to when preparing them.
- ❑ The drafting guidelines presented in Chapter 11 apply to all legal writing and should be kept in mind when preparing court briefs.
- ❑ Remember to craft the brief persuasively. Court briefs are designed to persuade the reader to adopt the position taken or recommended in the analysis. They are not supposed to present a purely objective analysis.
- ❑ De-emphasize the position taken by the opposition. Part of the persuasive nature of a court brief is to downplay and discredit the opponent's position. This is accomplished through the use of passive voice, long sentences, the placement of the opposing argument in the middle of the analysis, and so on.
- ❑ *Always* check the court rules. The format, length, and so on of court briefs are often governed by the rules of the court. The appellate court rules extensively govern most aspects of appellate briefs.
- ❑ The required components of trial and appellate court briefs may vary from jurisdiction to jurisdiction. Some of the components discussed in this chapter may not be required or necessary, such as a table of contents, table of authorities, and argument summary. This is often the case when the analysis is brief.

APPLICATION

This section illustrates the guidelines and principles discussed in this chapter by applying them to the hypothetical presented at the beginning of the chapter. The paralegal, Pam Hayes, approaches this assignment through the use of an expanded outline as discussed in Chapter 10. She also follows the guidelines and principles discussed in Chapters 12 and 13 to the extent they apply to the preparation of a trial brief. The Similarities—Court Briefs and Office Memoranda subsection of this chapter addresses the similarities between the office memorandum and the trial brief. Inasmuch as that material is covered in the chapters on office memoranda, a detailed discussion of the application of the guidelines is not included here. What follows is a presentation of the trial brief prepared by Ms. Hayes and comments on the brief.

In regard to the assignment, Ms. Hayes found the following New Washington law on point.

Statutory Law. Chapter 70 of the New Washington Statutes, the Ski Safety Act, governs ski resorts and the sport of skiing. New Washington Statutes Annotated (NWSA) § 70-11-7A provides, "The ski area operator shall have the duty to mark conspicuously with the appropriate symbol or sign those slopes, trails, or areas which are closed or which present an unusual obstacle or hazard." Furthermore, NWSA § 70-11-8B provides, "A person who takes part in the sport of skiing accepts as a matter of law the dangers inherent in that sport, and each skier expressly assumes the risk and legal responsibility for any injury to a person or property which results from . . . surface or subsurface snow or ice conditions. . . ."

Case Law. In *Karen v. High Mountain Pass,* 55 N. Wash. 462, 866 N.E. 995 (Ct. App. 1994), a skier broke his leg after failing to negotiate a series of moguls that were present in the middle of a sharp turn of a ski run. The moguls were unavoidable. The trial court granted the resort's motion to dismiss for failure to state a claim. On appeal, the court of appeals stated that skiers are responsible for snow and ice hazards, and moguls, even though unavoidable, are snow hazards easily observable and routinely present on most ski runs. The court went on to state that under the statute, the skier assumes the risk of snow and ice hazards that are easily observable and routinely encountered on ski runs, and resorts have no duty to warn of such hazards under NWSA § 70-11-7A.

In *Aster v. White Mountain Resort,* 55 N. Wash. 756, 866 N.E. 421 (Ct. App. 1994), a skier was skiing a newly opened intermediate run. Several fairly large rocks had not been removed from the run. Normally the rocks would be removed before the run was opened. The rocks were covered by approximately two and one-half feet of new snow and were not visible. The resort did not post a warning that the large rocks were present on the run. Mr. Aster hit a rock with the tip of his ski, lost control, and injured his knee and back. The trial court, in granting the resort's motion to dismiss for failure to state a claim, held that the hazard was a snow hazard for which the skier was responsible under NWSA § 70-11-8B. On appeal, the court of appeals noted that the snow condition was an unavoidable latent hazard. The court ruled that under NWSA § 70-11-7A, a resort has a duty to warn of hazardous snow conditions if they are unavoidable and latent. The court stated, "The statute will not be interpreted to reach an absurd result, and requiring a skier to be responsible for unavoidable latent hazards would lead to an absurd result. Skiers are only responsible for those unavoidable snow or ice conditions which are not latent or unobservable."

Myron v. Cox Inc., 40 N. Wash. 210, 740 N.E. 309 (1989), sets the standard for the granting of a rule 12(b)(6) motion to dismiss. The court stated, "A Rule 12(b)(6) motion to dismiss is properly granted only if it appears that there is no provable set of facts which entitles the plaintiff to relief."

Trial Brief

The following is the trial brief prepared by Ms. Hayes.

LINCOLN COUNTY DISTRICT COURT
STATE OF NEW WASHINGTON
NO. CIV. 97-601

NICK SHINE
Plaintiff,

vs.

BLUE SKY SKI RESORT
Defendant.

BRIEF IN OPPOSITION TO MOTION TO DISMISS

PRELIMINARY STATEMENT

On December 5, 1996, Nick Shine, the plaintiff, was injured while skiing on a ski run at Blue Sky Ski Resort. He was injured skiing on an ice hazard that the resort admits was not marked with any type of warning sign. Mr. Shine filed a complaint against the resort for negligence in failing to warn of the hazard. The resort has filed a Rule 12(b)(6) motion to dismiss for failure to state a claim, alleging that they do not have a duty to warn of ice hazards. This memorandum is submitted in opposition to that motion.

QUESTION PRESENTED

Under the New Washington Ski Safety Act, sections 70-11-1 *et seq.,* can a negligence claim be stated when a skier is injured on an unmarked ice hazard that is unavoidable and unobservable by the skier due to the sun glare?

STATEMENT OF THE CASE

On December 5, 1996, Mr. Shine, an expert skier, was skiing on an intermediate ski run at Blue Sky Ski Resort. Midway through the run there is a slightly uphill turn to the south. When Mr. Shine encountered the turn, the sun was directly in his eyes, and the glare prevented him from seeing that the trail was entirely covered with ice. Due to the glare, he was unable to avoid the dangerous ice hazard. He immediately hit the ice and lost control. As a result, he slid into a tree and broke his left arm and leg. No signs warning of the ice hazard were present.

On April 6, 1997, Mr. Shine filed a negligence complaint against Blue Sky Ski Resort for the resort's negligent failure to warn of the unavoidable ice hazard. On April 20, 1997, the resort filed a motion to dismiss under Rule 12(b)(6), alleging that they do not have a duty to warn of ice hazards, and therefore, as a matter of law, a claim for negligence cannot be stated.

ARGUMENT

MR. SHINE'S ARGUMENT THAT THE ICE HAZARD IS UNAVOIDABLE AND LATENT IS A SET OF FACTS WHICH, IF PROVEN, WOULD ESTABLISH THE DEFENDANT'S DUTY TO WARN AND, THEREFORE, A CLAIM CAN BE STATED AS TO DUTY.

This matter is before the court on a Rule 12(b)(6) motion to dismiss for failure to state a claim. In the case of *Myron v. Cox,* Inc., 40 N. Wash. 210, 215, 740 N.E. 309, 314 (1989), the New Washington Supreme Court established the standard for the granting of a 12(b)(6) motion. The court stated, "A Rule 12(b)(6) motion to dismiss is properly granted only if it appears that there is no provable set of facts which entitles the plaintiff to relief." Blue Sky Ski Resort's motion specifically alleges that a claim cannot be stated in this case in regard to duty. In order to survive this motion, Mr. Shine must demonstrate that there is a provable set of facts that would establish the duty of Blue Sky to warn of the ice hazard in this case.

The Ski Safety Act establishes the duties of ski resorts and skiers. Section 70-11-7A sets out the duties of the resort; it provides, "The ski area operator shall have the duty to mark conspicuously with the appropriate symbol or sign those slopes, trails, or areas which are closed or which present an unusual obstacle or hazard."

Section 70-11-8B sets out the duties and responsibilities of the skier:

> A person who takes part in the sport of skiing accepts as a matter of law the dangers inherent in that sport, and each skier expressly assumes the risk and legal responsibility for any injury to a person or property which results from . . . surface or subsurface snow or ice conditions. . . .

The act does not define the terms "hazard" or "snow and ice conditions." The statute also does not provide guidance as to which duty applies in a fact situation such as the one presented in this case. New Washington case law, however, does provide guidance.

The controlling case is *Aster v. White Mountain Resort,* 55 N. Wash. 756, 866 N.E. 421 (Ct. App. 1994). In the *Aster* case, Mr. Aster was skiing on a newly opened run from which several fairly large rocks had not been removed. Normally the rocks would be removed before the run was opened. The rocks were covered by approximately two and one-half feet of new snow and were not visible. The resort did not post a warning that the large rocks were present on the run. Mr. Aster hit a rock with the tip of his ski, lost control, and was injured. The court ruled that under NWSA § 70-11-7A, a resort has a duty to warn of hazardous snow conditions if they are unavoidable and latent. The court stated, "The statute will not be interpreted to reach an absurd result, and requiring a skier to be responsible for unavoidable latent hazards would lead to an absurd result. Skiers are only responsible for those unavoidable snow or ice conditions which are not latent or unobservable." *Id.* at 759.

Mr. Shine's complaint, like the complaint in the *Aster* case, states that the ice condition encountered was an unavoidable latent hazard. Under *Aster,* the resort has the duty under § 70-11-7A to warn of such hazards. Under the rule adopted in *Aster,* Mr. Shine's complaint does present a provable set of facts that establishes a claim as to duty and entitles him to relief. Therefore, the motion to dismiss should be denied.

It is contended by Blue Sky that they do not have a duty to warn of the ice hazard, and in support of this contention, they rely on *Karen v. High Mountain Pass,* 55 N. Wash. 462, 866 N.E. 995 (Ct. App. 1994). In this case, a skier broke his leg after failing to negotiate a series of moguls that were present in the middle of a sharp turn of a ski run. The moguls were obvious to the skier but unavoidable. The trial court granted the resort's motion to dismiss for failure to state a claim. On appeal, the court of appeals, in upholding the trial court, held that under the statute, the skier assumes the risk of snow and ice hazards that are easily observable and routinely present on ski runs.

Blue Sky's reliance on *Karen* is misplaced. The case is clearly distinguishable. The snow condition in *Karen,* though unavoidable, was clearly observable, and moguls are routinely present on ski runs. Skiers are aware that they will encounter moguls and know they must be able to navigate them. Ice conditions also may be encountered on ski runs. The ice condition Mr. Shine encountered, however, was not a routine ice condition. It was unobservable, unavoidable, and extremely dangerous due to the glare of the sun. The *Karen* case involves observable, routine snow hazards. The present case involves unobservable ice hazards that are not routinely encountered. *Karen* is obviously not on point and is not controlling in this case.

The hazard encountered by Mr. Shine was identical in nature to the hazard in the *Aster* case: the ice condition was an unavoidable, latent hazard. Under the holding in *Aster,* the resort has a duty under § 70-11-7A to warn of this type of hazard. Mr. Shine's complaint argues that the hazard is an unavoidable and latent hazard. The complaint presents a provable set of facts in regard to duty upon which relief can be granted, and, therefore, a claim for duty can be stated and the motion to dismiss should be denied.

CONCLUSION

Blue Sky Ski Resort's motion to dismiss for failure to state a claim should be denied. Mr. Shine's argument that the ice condition constitutes a latent hazard is a provable set of facts that entitles him to relief.

Comments

1. Note that the preceding example of a trial brief does not have a table of contents or a table of authorities. When a trial brief is short or involves a single issue and few authorities, these tables may not be required. Be sure to check the local court rule.
2. The preliminary statement presented at the beginning of the brief is often called an introduction.
3. A summary of the argument section is not included in this brief. A summary of the argument is usually included in an appellate brief, but not always in a trial brief. It is useful in a trial brief, and may be necessary, when there are several issues or the analysis is complex, but it is not necessary when the analysis involves a single issue or is not complex.

4. Note the persuasive tone of the brief:

   - The statement of the case introduces the facts with language that favors the client: *dangerous hazard, he immediately lost control.*
   - The statement of the case and argument sections state the client's position in short, clear sentences using active voice. The opponent's position is presented in a long sentence using the passive voice: "It is contended by Blue Sky that they do not have a duty to warn of the ice hazard. . . ."
   - The argument section downplays the opposition's position. It is placed in the middle of the argument and is immediately discounted after it is presented.
   - The conclusion is very short. In a brief that is short or does not involve a complex analysis, an abbreviated conclusion is appropriate.

SUMMARY

The preparation of documents involving legal analysis that are designed to be submitted to a court is the focus of this chapter. Such a document, usually called a court brief, is often formally referred to as a "memorandum of law" or a "memorandum of points and authorities." The chapter presents an overview of the major considerations, key points, and guidelines involved in the preparation of court briefs that may prove helpful to the paralegal.

At the trial court level, these documents are legal memorandum briefs submitted in support of a legal position advocated by an attorney. They are usually submitted in conjunction with a motion that requests some action or relief by the trial court. At the appellate court level, the documents submitted to an appellate court that involve legal analysis are the appellate court briefs.

Office legal memoranda and court briefs are similar in many respects. When preparing both office memoranda and court briefs, it is helpful to use a writing process such as that suggested in Chapter 10. Office memoranda and court briefs follow a similar format: presentation of the issue, facts, analysis, and conclusion.

The major difference between an office memorandum and a court brief is the orientation of the presentation. An office memorandum is designed to inform and is written in an objective manner. A court brief is designed to advocate a position and persuade the court; therefore, the issue(s), facts, and legal argument are crafted in a persuasive manner designed to convince the court to adopt the position advocated. The Dissimilarities—Court Briefs and Office Memoranda section of this chapter discusses the techniques for drafting a persuasive court brief.

A trial court brief is a memorandum of law submitted by an attorney to a trial court. In the memorandum, the attorney introduces the legal authority and analysis that supports a position advocated by the attorney. An appellate court brief is the written legal argument submitted to a court of appeals. In the appellate brief, an attorney presents the legal authority and analysis in support or opposition to an argument that a lower court committed reversible error.

Trial and appellate court briefs are similar in many respects. A major difference is that appellate court briefs are usually more formal: the style and format are more strictly governed by the appellate court rules. Both trial and appellate court briefs, however, are governed to some degree by court rules, and these rules must be carefully reviewed when preparing a court brief.

A legal assistant's role in preparing a court brief usually involves conducting legal research and analysis and preparing a rough draft. The final document requires the attorney's signature and is usually prepared by the attorney assigned to the case.

EXERCISES

ASSIGNMENT 1

Describe how to draft each of the following components of a brief in a persuasive manner. Include the considerations involving organization, word choice, sentence structure, and so on.

A. Issue
B. Fact Statement
C. Point Heading
D. Argument

ASSIGNMENT 2

Describe in detail the components and format of a trial and appellate court brief.

ASSIGNMENT 3

Restate the following question component of the issue in a persuasive manner.

A. ". . . should the evidence be suppressed when . . .?" In the case, the police failed to obtain a search warrant prior to searching a vehicle.

B. ". . . did the court err when . . .?" In the case, the trial court admitted hearsay evidence.

C. "Under the statute of frauds . . ., is an oral contract valid when . . .?" Rewrite this portion of the issue using language that focuses on a desired result.

D. "Under the sale of goods statutes, . . . is a statute enforceable when . . .?" Rewrite this portion of the issue using language that focuses on a desired result.

ASSIGNMENT 4

Restate persuasively each of the following issues. Each issue should be redrafted twice—persuasively from the view of the opposing sides.

A. Under the provisions of the exclusionary rule, should evidence be suppressed when law enforcement officers executed a search warrant by unannounced entry because they saw the defendant run into the apartment upon their arrival at the scene?

B. Did the district court improperly exercise its discretion when it admitted into evidence photographs of the murder victim?

C. In light of the provisions of the hearsay rule, did the trial court improperly admit into evidence the defendant's statements to his neighbor that he would kill his wife?

D. Does the privileged communications statute allow the admission into evidence of the defendant's threats of physical harm to his spouse?

ASSIGNMENT 5

Restate the following point headings in a more persuasive manner.

A. THE EVIDENCE WAS INCORRECTLY SUPPRESSED BY THE TRIAL COURT SINCE THERE WERE SUFFICIENT EXIGENT CIRCUMSTANCES AT THE SCENE.

B. THE DENIAL OF THE DEFENDANT'S MOTION FOR MISTRIAL WAS NOT ERROR BY THE TRIAL COURT BECAUSE THE PROSECUTOR'S COMMENT ON THE DEFENDANT'S PRIOR CONVICTION WAS ADMISSIBLE.

C. THE TRIAL COURT'S ALLOWANCE OF THE PEREMPTORY CHALLENGE WAS PROPER. THE CHALLENGE WAS NOT RACIALLY MOTIVATED.

D. THE COURT SHOULD NOT GRANT THE DEFENDANT'S MOTION TO DISMISS. . . .

ASSIGNMENT 6

Restate the following rule of law presentations in a more persuasive manner.

A. In determining whether an individual has constructive possession, the court decides whether the defendant had knowledge and control of the drugs.

B. Under the first part of the test, it must be shown that the defendant had knowledge of the presence of the drugs.

C. The court has stated that an arrest has taken place when a reasonable person would not feel free to leave.

CHAPTER 15

Correspondence

In the hypothetical introduced at the beginning of the last chapter, Alice Black, the supervisory attorney, assigned Pam Hayes, the paralegal, the task of preparing a response to a motion to dismiss for failure to state a claim. Assume that after Ms. Hayes completed the assignment, she received the following memo.

To: Pam Hayes, Paralegal
From: Alice Black, Attorney
Case: Civil 97-601, Nick Shine v. Blue Sky Ski Resort
Re: Correspondence to client

Please prepare a letter to Mr. Shine advising him of the status of the case. Include in the letter the following:

- Inform Mr. Shine that a motion to dismiss has been filed. Explain to him what a motion is, and tell him how the court will proceed in regard to the motion.
- Summarize the analysis of the law contained in the memorandum brief you prepared in response to the motion.

The correspondence prepared by Ms. Hayes and other sample correspondence is included in the Application section of this chapter.

INTRODUCTION

This chapter and Chapter 14 focus primarily on the preparation of documents that contain legal research and analysis and are designed for an audience outside the law office. Chapter 14 focuses on documents designed for submission to a court, *i.e.*, court briefs. This chapter examines the preparation of documents designed for an external audience other than a court. These documents are usually correspondence addressed to a client. A paralegal, however, may be called on to draft correspondence to a variety of external audiences, such as witnesses, court personnel, and opposing counsel.

Correspondence is a major form of written communication between the law firm and the outside world. Other than documents submitted to courts and transaction documents, such as contracts, correspondence is the *primary form* of writing designed for an audience outside the law office.

It is essential, therefore, that correspondence be well-crafted because it helps establish and maintain the image and reputation of the law firm. Correspondence that contains grammatical or substantive errors or is difficult to understand reflects poorly on the law firm:

- A client may question the capability of the firm to handle the client's case.
- The court may question the competence of the individual who signs the document.
- Opposing counsel may conclude that if the law firm is incapable of preparing quality correspondence, it is not capable of successfully representing its client.

Since most legal correspondence is in letter rather then memo form, the term *letter* is used in this chapter when referring to legal correspondence. A paralegal may prepare letters for a variety of purposes. The three main categories of letters that include legal research and analysis to some degree are the following:

1. Letters that provide information—*informational letters*
2. Letters that provide answers or legal opinions—*opinion letters*
3. Letters that demand action—*demand letters*

Although the focus in this chapter is on letters that contain legal research and analysis, other types of letters are briefly mentioned. Following a discussion of the components common to all of the three categories mentioned above, each category is addressed in a separate section of this chapter.

BASIC COMPONENTS

There are basic conventions that apply to the various types of letters prepared in a law office and basic components that are usually present in all types of letters. Each of these components may not be necessary or required in every letter you draft. This section, however, introduces all of the possible components so that you will be familiar with them.

The content and manner of presentation of each of the components discussed in the following text may vary from office to office. Compose your letters according to the guidelines adopted in your office. Refer to the Application section of this chapter for examples of the components discussed in the following subsections.

The basic format and components of letters prepared in a law office are presented in Figure 15–1.

- Letterhead/Heading
- Date
- Method of Delivery
- Recipient's Address Block
- Reference (Re:) Line
- Salutation
- Body
- Closing
- Signature and Title
- Initials of Drafter
- Enclosure Notation
- Others Receiving Copies

Figure 15–1

Basic Format and Components of Letters

Letterhead

The letterhead usually contains the full name, address, telephone number, and facsimile number of the law firm. It is usually preprinted on the firm's stationery and centered at the top of the page. An example of the information in a letterhead is as follows:

Thomas, Belter and Ryan
751 Main Street
Friendly, New Washington 00065
(200) 444-7778 • FAX 444-7678

Subsequent pages contain an identification of the letter, which is usually called a *header.* These pages do not contain the letterhead. The header includes the name of the addressee, the date, and the page number. It is placed at the top left or right margin of the page. An example of a header is as follows:

Jon Jones
May 5, 1997
Page Three

Date

The full date is usually placed below the letterhead at the left or right margin. It may also be centered below the letterhead. The date should include the full date: the day, month, and year. Since most correspondence is filed chronologically, a date is essential for the chronological file. Note that many offices date stamp correspondence when it is received in the office and file it according to that date.

Method of Delivery

At the left margin, below the date, is the method of delivery. This is usually required only if the manner of delivery is other than United States mail. Examples are as follows:

Via Federal Express
Via Hand Delivery
Via Facsimile

Recipient's Address Block

Below the date and method of delivery is the address block of the addressee. It is placed at the left margin. The address block should include:

- The name of the person to whom the letter is addressed
- The individual's title (if any)
- The name of the business (if applicable)
- The address

The following is an example of an address block:

Elizabeth Counter
President
Friendly Enterprises
139 Main Street
Friendly, NW 00065

Reference (Re:) Line

A reference line is usually placed at the left margin following the address block. The reference line briefly identifies the topic of the letter. Some firms require that the reference line include the case name and number if the letter concerns a pending lawsuit. The following is an example of a reference line:

Re: Request for production of documents
Smith v. Jones, Civil Action 97-1001

Salutation

Below the reference line is the salutation or greeting. Legal correspondence is generally formal in tone, and the greeting is normally formal. An example of a greeting follows:

Dear Ms. Counter:

You may use the first name if you know the addressee well. If in doubt, ask the supervisory attorney. If you do not know the name of the addressee, such as may be the case when the letter is addressed to a business, contact the business and ascertain the individual's name. The use of "To whom it may concern:" is very impersonal and invites a slow response. A person is likely to respond more quickly when he or she is specifically named.

Body

The body is the heart of the letter—what the letter is about. The body is usually composed of the three components listed in Figure 15–2.

Introduction

The body of the letter usually begins with an introductory sentence or paragraph (if necessary) that identifies or summarizes the main purpose of the letter.

For Example: "This letter is to advise you of the filing of a motion for summary judgment by the defendant. The hearing on the motion is scheduled to take place on March 6, 1997."

"This letter is to confirm our conversation today in which you stated that you would not be able to attend the hearing scheduled to take place on May 16, 1997."

Main Body

Following the introduction is the main body of the letter. The main body explains in detail the purpose of the letter. Craft the main body with care to ensure that you communicate the required information clearly and concisely. It may be necessary to use an outline when a letter covers multiple or complex matters. As with an office memorandum or court brief, the body may require several drafts.

You must always consider the audience when drafting the main body. If you are drafting the letter to a layperson, such as the client, avoid the use of legalese and define and explain clearly any legal terms that are used.

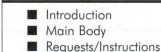

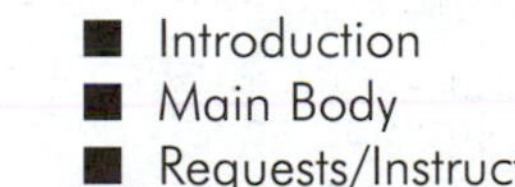

Figure 15–2

Components of the Body of a Letter

When writing to a layperson, consider the sophistication of the reader. Ask yourself:

- *"How familiar with legal matters is the reader?"*
- *"Does the reader often read material that involves complex subjects?"*

Although the addressee may not be familiar with the law, the individual may be highly educated or may often deal with complex or technical matters. In such cases, you may be able to craft the letter with greater complexity and present the subject matter with greater legal or technical detail. If the reader does not as a matter of course engage in a lot of complex or technical reading or is not familiar with such matters, then you should avoid including a detailed, complex discussion in the main body.

The content of the body will differ according to the type of letter you are drafting. The subsections of this chapter that address information, opinion, and demand letters discuss the differences in the format and content of the body of these types of correspondence.

Requests/Instructions

In the last section of the body, you should include any requests or instructions for the recipient.

For Example: "Please bring with you copies of the contract and any other written material related to the contract."

"Please keep a daily diary. Include in it a detailed description of all your daily activities, such as how long you sleep, what physical activities you engage in during the day, and so on."

In some instances, the paralegal may draft and *sign* a letter to the client. A paralegal may sign a letter that provides general information. *A paralegal may not sign a letter that gives a legal opinion or legal advice.* Most state laws and rules of ethics prohibit a paralegal from practicing law, and providing a legal opinion or legal advice constitutes the practice of law. Therefore, when preparing a letter that you or another paralegal will sign, be sure not to include a legal opinion or provide legal advice.

Closing

The closing follows the body of the letter. The closing usually consists of some standard statement. The following are examples of closings:

- "Thank you for your prompt consideration of this matter.
  Sincerely,"
- "Please contact me if you have any questions in regard to this matter.
  Very truly yours,"
- "Thank you for your assistance.
  Best Regards,"

Signature and Title

Following the closing is the signature and title of the person signing the letter. An example follows:

- "______________________________
  Sarah Smith
  Attorney at Law"

When the individual signing the letter is a paralegal, the paralegal status should be clearly indicated below the signature line, as in the following examples:

- "______________________________
  Jon Jones
  Paralegal"
- "______________________________
  Sarah Smith
  Paralegal"

Initials of Drafter

The final notation on the letter is a reference to the author of the letter and the typist. The author's initials are noted in all capitals, and the typist's are noted in lowercase letters—for example: JDR/mwt.

Enclosure Notation

Next, if enclosures, such as contracts, documents, and so on, are included with the letter, indicate their presence by typing "Enc." or "Encs." at the left margin following the signature.

- "__________________________
  Sarah Smith
  Attorney at Law
  Encs."

Others Receiving Copies

If other individuals are receiving copies of the letter, indicate this by typing "cc:" and the name of the individual(s) after the signature and title. This follows the enclosure notation if an enclosure notation is used. An example is as follows:

cc: Colin Smith
Mae Carrey

If you are uncertain who should receive copies, check with your supervisor.

Format Style

The basic format of a letter varies from firm to firm and is dictated by personal taste and style. Two fundamental styles are *full block* and *modified block*. In full block, everything but the letterhead is flush with the left margin. The information letter in the first example in the Application section is typed in full block format. In modified block, the date is centered, and the signature line can be just right of the center of the page or flush left. The first line of each paragraph is indented. The opinion letter in the second example in the Application section is presented in modified block format.

General Considerations—All Correspondence

Adopt the highest standards of accuracy, both substantive and stylistic, when drafting legal correspondence. As mentioned in the introduction, correspondence helps determine the image, reputation, and success of the law firm. In many situations, the information provided in the correspondence constitutes the practice of law and subjects the firm to possible liability for claims of legal malpractice. Therefore, the quality of the product is critically important and you should:

- *Take the utmost care to ensure that any legal research and analysis are error free.*
- *Make sure that the finished product is free from writing errors involving grammar, spelling, and so on.*
- *Be prepared to perform the number of edits and redrafts necessary to ensure the final product is professionally prepared.*

Letters should be drafted so clearly that they cannot be misinterpreted. A reader may not like the information conveyed in the letter and wish to intentionally misinterpret the contents. The discussion in the following sections is designed to assist in the preparation of letters that clearly convey information and are difficult to misinterpret.

TYPES OF CORRESPONDENCE

Although, as discussed in the previous section, the basic components of legal correspondence are the same, the content of the body of the correspondence varies according to the type of letter being drafted. There are many categories of legal correspondence, and the categorization is based upon the purpose that each category is designed to serve. Inasmuch as this text focuses on legal research and analysis, this section addresses law office correspondence that communicates the results of legal research and analysis. The three basic categories of letters that communicate this information are presented in Figure 15–3.

This section focuses on the body of these categories of letters and how each differs in the presentation of legal research and analysis. The following subsections address the preparation of letters where the recipient is a nonlawyer, since most of the correspondence a paralegal is called on to prepare is for that audience.

Information Letter

information letter

Correspondence that provides general legal information or background on a legal issue. It usually involves the communication of the results of legal research and analysis to a client or a third party.

A paralegal is often asked to draft a letter providing information to the client or other layperson. The components of an information letter usually include the elements mentioned in the Basic Components section of this chapter. The body of the information letter, however, varies according to the type of information conveyed. There are many types of information letters. Some of the types, and examples of parts of the body of these types, are the following:

- Letters that confirm an appointment or inform of the date and time of scheduled events.

For Example: "This letter is to advise you that the court hearing on the motion to modify child support will be held on May 6, 1997, in the courtroom of. . . ."

"This letter is to confirm our appointment at 9:00 A.M., May 22, 1997. . . ."

Figure 15–3

Types of Letters That Communicate the Results of Legal Research and Analysis

- Information Letters
- Opinion Letters
- Demand Letters

- Letters that inform the client of the current status of the case.

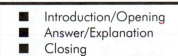

  For Example: "The defendants filed an answer on June 6, 1997. On June 14, 1997, we sent them a request to produce documents concerning the contract and are awaiting their response to that request. We will contact you when we receive their response."

- Letters that present the firm's bill.
- Letters that give the results of an investigation.

  For Example: "After performing a thorough investigation, we were unable to locate any witness who actually saw the accident. We interviewed the witnesses at the scene, canvassed the neighborhood, and contacted all the store owners in the area. If you happen to remember the license plate of any vehicle that passed by or have any additional information, please let us know. . . ."

- Letters that provide general legal information or background on a legal issue. This is the type of information being provided to Mr. Shine in the assignment at the beginning of the chapter. An example of an information letter is presented in the Application section of the chapter.

The information may be a summary of the law involved in the client's case or the requirements of a particular statute. This type of information letter is usually the most complex of the information letters and often involves communicating the results of legal research and analysis. The body of this type of information letter is discussed in the remainder of this subsection.

The body of an information letter that provides the results of legal research and analysis usually consists of the components listed in Figure 15–4.

Introduction/Opening

The introduction states the purpose of the letter.

For Example: "The purpose of this letter is to inform you of a request that has been filed by the defendant and the law the court will consider when addressing the request."

"The purpose of this letter is to inform you of a recent law that was passed which affects your business."

Answer/Explanation

This section presents the results of legal research and analysis.

For Example: "Section 97-355-21 of the corporation statutes was recently amended. Under the provisions of the amendment, you must file your annual report no later than twenty days after the end of the fiscal year. As you know, the statute prior to the amendment allowed forty days to file the report."

The body of the letter presented in the first example in the Application section provides a detailed illustration of this component of an information letter.

Closing

The closing of the letter is similar to the closing of any legal correspondence as discussed in the Basic Components section of this chapter.

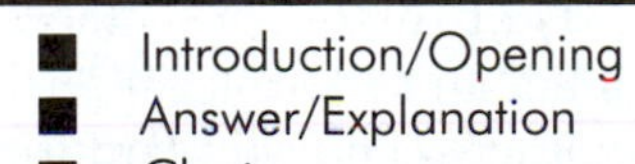
- Introduction/Opening
- Answer/Explanation
- Closing

Figure 15–4
Body of Information Letter—Recommended Format and Components

For Example: "Since you prepare the annual report for your corporation, I feel it is important that you be advised of the change in the law. If you have any questions, please contact me."

In some instances, especially when the answer/explanation is lengthy or complex, it may be necessary to include a summary or a conclusion in the closing. See the closing of the information letter in the first example in the Application section.

This type of information letter merely presents a summary of the law or the legal status of a case. It communicates basic information; it *does not give a legal opinion on a question or provide legal advice.* That role is performed by an opinion letter.

Opinion Letter

opinion letter
Correspondence, usually written to a client, that in addition to informing the reader of how the law applies to a specific question, provides legal advice.

An opinion letter is like an information letter in that it provides information concerning the law. It is different in that it often includes, in addition, an analysis of that information and provides a legal opinion or legal advice. The purpose is to inform the reader how the law applies to the facts. An opinion letter is usually generated by a question asked by the client or raised by the facts of the client's case. Therefore, the focus of this section is on opinion letters addressed to the client.

You may be assigned the task of researching, analyzing, and preparing an interoffice memorandum that addresses the question that will be answered in an opinion letter. The purpose of the assignment is usually to provide the attorney with the information necessary to prepare the letter. On occasion, you may be assigned the additional task of preparing a rough draft of the opinion letter. Many of the considerations involved in preparing an opinion letter are the same as those involved in preparing an office memorandum. When you are assigned the task of preparing the letter, refer to Chapters 12 and 13 in addition to this chapter for guidance.

An opinion letter provides the reader with a legal opinion and legal advice; therefore, *it constitutes the practice of law and must be signed by an attorney.* The attorney is subject to legal liability for harm that occurs as a result of the client acting upon erroneous information contained in the letter. If you are preparing the draft of an opinion letter, take great care to ensure that your research and analysis are accurate.

Since the purpose is to inform the client of the law and provide legal advice, the opinion letter is drafted in the same objective tone as the office memorandum. The difference is that the client is usually a layperson unfamiliar with legal terms and legal writing. When this is the case, you should avoid legalese and keep legal quotations and citations at a minimum. If the reader is familiar with the law and legal writing, you may use more legal terms, quotations, and citations. In some instances, the attorney may direct that the client be provided with the office memorandum rather than an opinion letter.

Although an opinion letter and office memorandum are similar in many respects, there are differences in format. An opinion letter follows a business format as discussed in the Basic Components section of this chapter, while an office memorandum follows a memo format as discussed in Chapters 12 and 13. The body of the letter includes the basic elements of the office memorandum, but the elements are presented with less technical detail and fewer legal terms.

As with most legal writing, there is no standard format for the body of an opinion letter. The body of most opinion letters, however, follows the format presented in Figure 15–5.

- Introduction/Opening
- Facts
- Answer/Conclusion
- Explanation
- Closing/Conclusion

Figure 15–5

Body of Opinion Letter—Recommended Format and Components

Introduction/Opening

The introduction establishes the focus of the letter and identifies the question or questions that will be answered. The opening usually begins with a reference to the question and the context within which the client raised the question.

For Example: "On January 2, 1996, you hired me to represent you in your criminal case. When we met in my office on that date, you asked me to determine whether we could obtain a suppression of the evidence (the heroin) seized when the police officers executed a search warrant by entering your residence unannounced."

Notice that the question is stated in broader terms than it would be in an office memorandum. You should draft the question in a manner sufficient for the client to understand the question. You do not have to state it as completely or as formally as discussed in Chapter 7. The Law + Question + Key Facts format does not have to be followed. In the preceding example, there is no reference to the rule of law.

You should include language in the introduction that indicates that the opinion and advice apply only to addressee and the specific facts included in the letter. You should also mention that the opinion is based on the law as of the date of the opinion.

For Example: "This opinion is provided for your use and solely for your benefit. It applies only to the facts presented in the fact section of this letter and the law as of the date of the letter."

Facts

Present the facts in an opinion letter in the same objective manner as in an office memorandum. Apply the techniques presented in Chapter 12 when preparing this section. Include only the key and background facts to keep the section as short as possible. See the fact section of the opinion letter presented in the second example in the Application section of this chapter.

Answer/Conclusion

This section presents a brief answer to the question. It is similar to the brief answer section of the office memorandum. Refer to the Brief Answer section of Chapter 12 when preparing this section. By placing the answer near the beginning of the letter, the reader immediately knows the result without having to read the explanation. This is helpful if the reader is busy and may not be able to read the explanation until a later time.

The answer should be clear, concise, and as short as possible. Since the answer is usually a legal opinion, you should state it as an opinion.

For Example: "The court will probably not suppress the evidence based upon the officers' failure to announce their presence prior to entering your residence when they executed the warrant."

Add any needed specifics or limitations after the answer.

For Example: "The outcome could be different if Officer Galen changes his testimony and states he did not see you holding a rifle in your front room when they approached the house. Officer Kaler stated that he did not see you in the front room as they approached the house. In light of Officer Kaler's statement, Officer Galen could change his statement."

Explanation

The explanation section is similar to the analysis section of an office memorandum. The difference is that the explanation must be crafted in a manner that is not so technical that the client has difficulty understanding it. Also, the explanation section is usually not as long or as complex as an analysis section of an office memorandum. When preparing this section, note the following guidelines.

- If there is more than one issue, discuss the issues in the order they are presented in the introduction.
- If possible, limit the letter to as few issues as possible, *i.e.,* two to three. If there are multiple issues, the letter may become too complex or long and the reader may have difficulty understanding or keeping track of the subject matter. Separate the issues, and prepare more than one letter if necessary.
- Draft the content with the legal sophistication of the reader in mind. The client may not be familiar with the law and technical writing, and an explanation that is as detailed as the analysis section of an office memorandum may not be appropriate. Keep quotations and citations to a minimum. Rather than quote, rephrase the statutory or case law in a manner that a layperson can understand. If you must use a legal term, make sure its meaning is clear. Define the legal terms that are used.
- Provide a complete explanation. The client must be fully informed. Do not omit important information because the client is unsophisticated in the law. Present all the key information in a manner that fully and clearly informs the client.

The following is an example of an explanation section of an opinion letter.

The Fourth Amendment to the United States Constitution and article II, section 9, of the state constitution prohibit "unreasonable searches and seizures." These amendments do not prohibit all searches and seizures, however, just those that are "unreasonable."

The law provides that anything seized as a result of an unreasonable search may not be admitted into evidence in a trial. The state supreme court has ruled that officers must announce their presence before entering a residence when executing a search warrant. The court has stated that an unannounced entry is unreasonable and violates the United States and state constitutions.

There are, however, exceptions to the rule that officers must announce their presence before executing a warrant. One exception is when the officers arrive at the place to be searched and there is evidence that the person or persons present at the scene are a danger to the officers. *Smith v. Jones* is a court case remarkably similar to your case. In this case, when the police arrived at the residence to be searched, they saw the defendant enter the house with a rifle in his hands. The state supreme court ruled that this evidence provided the officers with authority to execute the warrant and enter the residence to be searched without first announcing their presence.

Based upon the ruling in the *Smith v. Jones* case and the similarity between the facts of that case and the facts in your case, the trial court probably will not suppress the evidence seized at your residence and will allow its admission at trial.

Closing/Conclusion

The closing is usually not a separate section of an opinion letter. Rather, it is usually the last paragraph of the explanation section. It is similar to the closing of any legal correspondence as discussed in the Basic Components section of this chapter. In addition, in an opinion letter, the closing should summarize any action the client should take or what will occur next.

For Example: "I hope this letter answers your questions. Please note that, although the officers may have acted properly when they entered your residence unannounced, there is a question whether the warrant was properly issued in the first place. When we complete our investigation into this matter, we anticipate that we will file a motion to suppress the evidence because the warrant should not have been issued at all. We will discuss this at our appointment scheduled on Friday the ninth. Please contact me if you have any questions."

An example of an opinion letter is presented in the second example in the Application section of this chapter.

Demand/Advocacy Letter

Another basic type of letter you may be called upon to draft is a demand or advocacy letter. This type of letter is designed to persuade someone to take action favorable to the interests of the client or cease acting in a manner that is detrimental to the client. This may be as simple as demanding payment on a debt or as complex as requesting that a course of conduct be taken, such as the rehiring of an employee. In many instances, a demand letter will include a summary of the applicable law in support of the requested action. This section addresses the considerations involved in preparing a demand letter that includes a reference to the law and an analysis of the law.

demand/advocacy letter
Correspondence that is designed to persuade someone to take action favorable to the interests of the client or cease acting in a manner that is detrimental to the client.

You may be given an assignment to prepare an office memorandum summarizing the law that will be used as the basis for the demand letter and to prepare a draft of the letter. Like the opinion letter, a demand letter is signed by the attorney.

The basic format and components of a demand letter are similar to those discussed in the Basic Components section of this chapter, and like an opinion letter, there is no standard format for the demand letter. A major difference is that a demand letter is not designed to address a legal question but, rather, to encourage action or seek relief. Therefore, it does not contain an Answer/Conclusion section in the body because it does not address a question that requires a brief answer. The demand letter also differs from an opinion letter in that it is designed to advocate a position and persuade the reader and, therefore, is written in a persuasive manner.

The body of a demand letter follows the same basic format and is composed of elements similar to the body of the opinion letter (see Figure 15–6).

This section explores the differences between the body of a demand letter and the body of an opinion letter. The discussion focuses on demand letters sent to nonlawyers. The attorney will usually draft a demand letter that will be sent to another attorney.

Introduction/Opening

The introduction of a demand letter is somewhat different from the opening of an opinion letter. It begins with the identification of the writer or the client.

For Example: "Our office represents Mr. Jason Hill in the above-referenced case."
"Mr. Jason Hill has retained this office in regard to. . . ."

- Introduction/Opening
- Facts
- Explanation
- Closing/Conclusion

Figure 15–6
Body of Demand Letter—Recommended Format and Components

A statement of the purpose of the letter follows the identification. It establishes the focus of the letter and identifies the problem addressed and the relief sought.

For Example: "Your efforts to collect payment from Mr. Hill on his automobile loan are in violation of the Collections Act, and we demand that they cease immediately."

Facts

The content of the fact section is the same as in the opinion letter except that you should present the facts in a persuasive manner similar to the persuasive presentation of the facts in a court brief. See the Statement of Facts—Persuasive Presentation subsection of Chapter 14.

For Example: "On January 7, 1995, Mr. Hill signed a loan with your company to pay for the purchase of an automobile. From the date of the loan until two months ago, he has paid, on time and in full, every installment on the loan. For the past two months, due to the illness of his oldest child, Mr. Hill has been able to pay only one-half of the required monthly payment. He contacted your office on the fifth of last month and informed the loan officer that for the next three months he would be making reduced payments. He was informed that he should be making full payments.

"For the past three weeks, your collections department has telephoned Mr. Hill after 7 P.M. six nights a week demanding full payment. In each instance, Mr. Hill has politely informed the caller that he is paying all he can and requested that the calls cease. The calls have not ceased."

Explanation

This section presents the legal authority in support of the relief requested. Since the reader is a nonlawyer, you should draft the section with this in mind. Refer to the discussion in the Explanation subsection of the Opinion Letter section for guidance. This section of a demand letter differs from the explanation section of an opinion letter in that you should draft the section in a persuasive manner. The Argument—Persuasive Presentation subsection of Chapter 14 is helpful in this regard.

For Example: "The Collections Act provides that efforts to collect debts should be made in a reasonable manner. The state supreme court, in the case of *Irons v. Collections, Inc.*, ruled that telephone calls to a debtor's residence after 7 P.M. or more frequently than three times a week are unreasonable and violate the act if the debtor objects to the calls. Your office has contacted Mr. Hill after 7 P.M. six nights a week for the past three weeks. The calls have continued despite Mr. Hill's objections and requests that they cease."

Closing/Conclusion

Like the closing of an opinion letter, the closing of a demand letter is usually not a separate section. It is usually the last paragraph of the explanation section and is similar to the closing of any legal correspondence as discussed in the Basic Components section of this chapter. The closing should restate the relief requested and indicate what the next course of action may be.

For Example: "Therefore, your calls to Mr. Hill are clearly a violation of the Collections Act and must cease immediately. If the calls do not cease, we will take the appropriate steps necessary to obtain the relief provided in the act.

"If you have any questions in regard to this matter, please contact me."

KEY POINTS CHECKLIST: *Preparing Legal Correspondence*

- ❑ Prepare correspondence accurately and professionally. Letters may affect the reputation of the firm, and poorly drafted letters do not inspire the client's confidence.
- ❑ Draft the correspondence with the legal sophistication of the reader in mind. Avoid legalese, and if you must use legal terms, define them clearly.
- ❑ Keep legal citations and quotations to a minimum. Only use quotations if they are easy to understand and add clarity to the subject matter. Paraphrase the material if it is written in a manner that is difficult to comprehend.
- ❑ When drafting an opinion letter, be sure to indicate that the letter is limited to the facts of the case, based on the current law, and intended solely for the benefit of the addressee.
- ❑ If there are multiple issues, divide the subject into separate manageable topics. Prepare and send separate letters covering the topics.
- ❑ Do not include legal advice or recommend a course of action if the correspondence is to be signed by someone other than an attorney. Such information constitutes the practice of law and must be signed by an attorney.
- ❑ Keep a file of the letters and other documents you have prepared. Organize the file by topic, such as demand letters, opinion letters, and so on. Often, rather than starting a new letter, it is faster and easier to edit an old letter or use it as a guide for the correspondence you are drafting.

APPLICATION

This section contains two examples of legal correspondence that illustrate the application of the principles discussed in this chapter. The first example addresses the assignment presented at the beginning of the chapter. This assignment requires the preparation of an information letter by the paralegal, Pam Hayes. The second example illustrates an opinion letter. It is based on the same law used in the first example and on facts that are similar to those of the first example.

Example—Information Letter

The assignment introduced at the beginning of the chapter calls for the preparation of an information letter. In this example, the letter is presented in *full block* style.

Law Offices of Alice Black
2100 Main Street
Friendly, New Washington 00065
(200) 267-7000 • FAX 267-7001

April 29, 1997
Mr. Nick Shine
9100 2nd Street
Friendly, NW 00065

Re: Shine v. Blue Sky Ski Resort
Motion to dismiss for failure to state a claim

Dear Mr. Shine:

The purpose of this letter is to inform you of the status of your case and to summarize the law in regard to the motion that will be heard on May 17, 1997.

As you know, on April 6, we filed your complaint against Blue Sky Ski Resort. In the complaint, we claim that the resort was negligent for failing to post a sign warning skiers of the ice hazard you encountered. In order to prove a claim for negligence, one of the requirements we must establish is that the resort had a duty to warn skiers of the ice hazard.

On April 20, the resort filed a motion with the court asking that the court dismiss the case. A motion is a request submitted to the court asking the court to take some form of action. The court usually holds a hearing on a motion. At the hearing, the parties present their position on whether the request should be granted.

On May 17, 1997, the court will conduct a hearing on the resort's motion to dismiss. At that hearing, we anticipate the resort will claim that under the provisions of the Ski Safety Act, it does not have a duty to warn skiers of ice hazards. The resort will argue that ice hazards are the responsibility of skiers under the act and, therefore, it cannot be sued for negligence, since it had no duty to warn of the ice hazard.

In support of its argument that it does not have a duty to warn of ice hazards, the resort will rely on section 8B of the act. This section states that skiers are responsible for injuries that result from snow and ice conditions. Our position is that the resort does have a duty to warn of this type of hazard under section 7A of the act. That section provides that resorts have a duty to warn skiers of unusual conditions or hazards on ski runs.

It is unclear from the statute which section of the act applies in a situation such as yours. The state court of appeals, in the case of Aster v. White Mountain Resort, interpreted the act in a fact situation similar to yours. In this case, a skier, while skiing on a new ski run, hit a rock covered by snow. The court stated that resorts have a duty to warn of snow conditions if they are unavoidable and present an unobvious or latent hazard.

At the motion hearing, we will argue that the resort's motion to dismiss should be denied because the ice condition you encountered was unavoidable and latent, just as the snow condition was in Aster v. White Mountain Resort. We will further argue that the rule of law stated in that case provides that resorts have a duty to warn of hazards such as the one you encountered. Therefore, the resort can be sued for its negligence in failing to post a warning of the ice hazard.

The resort will probably argue that the ruling of the court of appeals in Karen v. High Mountain Pass should apply. In that case, a skier broke his leg after failing to negotiate a series of moguls that were present in the middle of a turn on a ski run. The court stated that skiers are responsible for snow and ice hazards, and moguls, even though unavoidable, are snow hazards easily observable and routinely present on most ski runs. We believe the court will not apply the ruling in the Karen case because that case involved a snow hazard that was observable and routinely encountered by skiers. In your case, the snow hazard was unobservable, unavoidable, and not routinely encountered by skiers.

We are optimistic that the court will rule in our favor and deny the motion. You are not required to attend the hearing, but you may attend if you wish. Please let us know if you plan to attend.

If you have any questions, please call.

Sincerely,

____

Pam Hayes
Paralegal

PAH/wkk

Example—Opinion Letter

The example in this section is based on the following fact situation. On January 6, 1997, the client, David Duggan, appeared for an initial interview at the law offices of Alice Black. Pam Hayes, the paralegal, conducted the interview. In the interview, Mr. Duggan stated that he was skiing on December 7, 1996, on an expert ski run at Red Mountain Ski Resort. He encountered a series of moguls near the top of the ski run. The moguls were difficult to ski, and he lost control, fell, and broke his left arm. There was no sign at the top of the run indicating the presence of difficult moguls on the run. He believes the resort should have posted a sign, well in advance of the moguls, warning of their presence. He wants to know if he can sue the resort for its failure to post a warning.

Alice Black assigned Pam Hayes the task of preparing a rough draft of an opinion letter to be sent to Mr. Duggan. The letter should inform him of the likelihood of successfully suing the resort for its failure to post a warning of the presence of the moguls. The governing law is chapter 70 of the New Washington Ski Safety Act. The governing case is *Karen v. High Mountain Pass,* 55 N. Wash. 462, 866 N.E. 995 (Ct. App. 1994). The relevant portions of the statute and case are introduced at the beginning of the Application section of Chapter 14. The opinion letter is presented in *modified block* format.

Law Offices of Alice Black
2100 Main Street
Friendly, New Washington 00065
(200) 267-7000 • FAX 267-7001

January 18, 1997

Via Facsimile and U.S. Mail
Mr. David Duggan
5501 Glenview Ave.
Friendly, NW 00065

Re: Possibility of a lawsuit against Red Mountain Ski Resort for failure to warn of moguls

Dear Mr. Duggan:

On January 6, 1997, we met in my office to discuss the possibility of suing Red Mountain Ski Resort for the ski injury you suffered on December 7, 1996. This opinion is based on the facts outlined in the fact section of this letter and the applicable law as of the date of the letter. This letter is solely for your benefit and limited to the facts discussed below. Please contact me if any of the facts are misstated or if you have additional information.

FACTS

On December 7, 1996, you were skiing on an expert run at Red Mountain Ski Resort. Near the top of the run, you encountered a series of moguls. The moguls were difficult to ski, and as a result, you lost control and broke your left arm. There were no signs posted on the run that warned skiers of the upcoming moguls.

ANSWER

Based upon the above facts, you probably cannot successfully sue Red Mountain Ski Resort for its failure to warn of the moguls. The only possible theory under which you could sue is negligence. You would claim that the resort was negligent for failing to warn of the upcoming moguls. Under the applicable state statute and the court opinions that interpret that statute, the resort does not have a duty to warn of the presence of moguls.

EXPLANATION

Chapter 70 of the New Washington statutes, the Ski Safety Act, governs the operation of ski resorts and establishes the duties of skiers and resort operators. Section 7A of the act requires resorts to warn of sections of trails "which present an unusual obstacle or hazard." Section 8B of the act states that a skier "expressly assumes the risk and legal responsibility for any injury to a person or property which results from . . . surface or subsurface snow or ice conditions. . . ."

The act does not discuss whether a mogul is a snow condition for which the skier is responsible. The state court of appeals, however, in the case of *Karen v. High Mountain Pass,* addressed the question of whether a resort has a duty to post a warning of the presence of moguls on a ski run. In this case, a skier broke his leg after failing to negotiate a series of moguls that were present in the middle of a turn on a ski run. The court stated that skiers are responsible for snow and ice hazards. The court noted that moguls, even though unavoidable, are snow hazards easily observable and routinely present on most ski runs. The court ruled that under the act, resorts have no duty to warn of snow hazards such as moguls.

The facts in your case are very similar to the facts in *Karen v. High Mountain Pass.* In your case, just as in that case, the injury occurred as a result of an encounter with moguls. It is apparent from section 8B of the statute, and the court's interpretation of that section in *Karen v. High Mountain Pass,* that skiers are responsible for injuries sustained as a result of encountering moguls on a ski run. Therefore, based on the statute and the court opinion in *Karen v. High Mountain Pass,* it is my opinion that it is highly unlikely that a lawsuit against Red Mountain Ski Resort for the injuries you sustained would be successful.

I hope this information answers your question. I regret that I am not able to provide a more favorable answer. If you have additional information concerning the accident or if you have any other questions, please contact me.

Sincerely,

____

Alice Black
Attorney at Law

ALB/wkk

Comments on Examples

In regard to the preceding examples, note that both letters:

- Present the subject matter clearly through the use of short sentences rather than complex sentences, which are often more difficult to follow and understand
- Present the law in an objective and professional manner
- Avoid legalese and discuss the material in a simple and clear manner. Although there are references to statutes and case law, a summary of the law is provided rather than a technical discussion. The legal points are simply phrased in lay terms.

In addition, the opinion letter clearly states at the outset that the opinion is limited to the current law and the facts provided by the client. Reference is made to the fact that the letter is intended solely for the benefit of the recipient.

SUMMARY

This chapter discusses the preparation of legal correspondence, referred to as letters in the chapter. The focus is on those letters that communicate the results of legal research and analysis. Letters are one of the primary forms of written communication directed to an audience outside the law office.

The following are fundamental components of all legal correspondence. There is no standard format; the content and style of presentation of these components vary according to personal and local preference. The basic contents of the components are discussed in the Basic Components section of the chapter.

- Letterhead/Heading
- Date
- Method of Delivery
- Recipient's Address Block
- Reference (Re:) Line
- Salutation
- Body
- Closing
- Signature and Title
- Initials of Drafter
- Enclosure Notation
- Others Receiving Copies

Letters that include the results of legal research and analysis fall into three basic categories that are based upon the purpose of the communication:

1. To provide information—information letters
2. To provide an opinion—opinion letters
3. To demand action—demand letters

These three types of letters differ primarily in the content of the body.

The body of an information letter presents an objective summary of the research and analysis without the inclusion of any legal opinion or advice. The body of an opinion letter, in addition to a summary of the law, usually provides an objective assessment of the application of the law to the facts and often recommends a course of action. Since it includes a legal opinion or legal advice, an opinion letter constitutes the practice of law and must be signed by an attorney. The body of an opinion letter closely resembles an office memorandum in that it is composed of the following elements:

- Introduction/Opening
- Facts
- Answer/Conclusion
- Explanation
- Closing/Conclusion

A demand letter is designed to persuade the reader to act in a manner that benefits the client, for example, to pay a debt. The body of a demand letter is similar to the body of an opinion letter. The major difference is that the law and analysis are drafted in a persuasive manner. Many of the considerations discussed in Chapter 14 involving persuasive writing apply to the preparation of the demand letter.

Since the recipient of legal correspondence is an individual outside the law office, the correspondence contributes to the image and reputation of the law firm. For this reason, and because legal liability attaches to some correspondence, it is of paramount importance that you draft an accurate and professional product.

EXERCISES

ASSIGNMENT 1

Describe the three types of correspondence discussed in this chapter and the purposes of each type.

ASSIGNMENT 2

Describe how the three types of correspondence are different.

ASSIGNMENT 3

For this exercise, refer to the assignment introduced at the beginning of Chapter 12 and the law relevant to that assignment presented in the Application section of Chapter 12. Assume the law firm represents Mrs. Findo. Draft an opinion letter to her informing her whether she can testify against her husband in light of the applicable Illinois statutory and case law.

ASSIGNMENT 4

For this exercise, refer to the assignment introduced at the beginning of Chapter 13 and the relevant law included in the Application section of that chapter. Assume you work for a law firm that represents the defendant.

A. Draft an information letter informing the defendant of what constitutes an arrest in the state of New Washington, and how the law has been interpreted to apply in search warrant situations.

B. Draft an opinion letter advising the defendant whether there is sufficient evidence to support charges of possession.

ASSIGNMENT 5

Assume the client, Mrs. Tatum, purchased a new microwave oven from Inki Appliances Company. There was no written or oral warranty given when the sale was made. The microwave stopped working one week after Mrs. Tatum took it home. She returned the microwave three days after it quit working. The owner of Inki Appliances refused to repair or replace the microwave or give Mrs. Tatum her money back. Prepare a demand letter to be sent to Inki Appliances. The letter is to be signed by your supervisory attorney, Alice Black. Use the letterhead presented in the Application section of this chapter. Mr. Terry Spear is the president and owner of Inki Appliances Company, and the address is 1001 Maple Drive, Friendly, NW 00065.

Statutory Law: Section 50-102-314 of the New Washington statutes provides that "a warranty that the goods shall be merchantable is implied . . . if the seller is a merchant with respect to the goods of that kind." Assume Mr. Spear is a merchant. Assume also that Mrs. Tatum did not misuse the microwave or in any other way cause it to quit working.

Case Law: The case on point is *Smith v. Appliance City,* 56 N. Wash. 162, 868 N.E. 997 (1995). In *Smith,* the New Washington supreme court ruled that the seller has three options when an implied warranty is breached: return the purchase price to the buyer, repair the merchandise, or replace the merchandise.

ASSIGNMENT 6

Refer to Assignment 4 in Chapter 13. Prepare an information letter to Mr. Canter informing him of the results of your research in regard to armed bank robbery.

ASSIGNMENT 7

Refer to Assignment 1 in Chapter 13. Draft an opinion letter to Mrs. Dixon informing her of the results of your research and the likelihood that the holographic will submitted by Mary Cary will be eligible for probate.

ASSIGNMENT 8

Refer to Assignment 5 in Chapter 13. Prepare a demand letter to Ms. Chavez informing her of the law concerning the unilateral reduction of child support when a child reaches the age of majority. Include in the letter a demand that she resume paying the full child support ordered by the court.

APPENDIX A

Court Opinions Referred to in the Text

INTRODUCTION

The court opinions in this appendix are presented in alphabetical order and not in the order in which they are referred to in the text. In order to save space, portions of some cases that are not relevant to specific assignments or the discussion presented in the text have been omitted. A series of three asterisks indicates that a portion of the opinion has been omitted.

Stephen Craig BEAM and Lori A. Beam, husband and wife, Respondents,

v.

John C. CULLETT, Appellant.

No. 77–1732; CA 15733.

Court of Appeals of Oregon.

Argued and Submitted June 18, 1980.
Decided Sept. 2, 1980.
Reconsideration Denied Oct. 7, 1980.

48 Or. App. 47, 615 P.2d 1196 (1980)

JOSEPH, Presiding Judge.

Plaintiff brought this action for fraud and breach of an implied warranty of fitness for a particular purpose. Plaintiff was in the business of hauling scrap automobile bodies from southern Oregon to a steel plaint in McMinnville. He bought a 1969 Ford Diesel truck from defendant to haul the scrap auto bodies. The truck had been used by defendant for approximately two and one-half years until the engine "blew up." Defendant had the engine rebuilt by a diesel engine mechanic. Plaintiff purchased the truck with the rebuilt engine for $10,000; there were no written warranties. After the truck was used for a brief period of time, the engine lost a rod bearing and the intake manifold was broken. This action followed.

The trial court, sitting without a jury, found in favor of defendant on the fraud claim; a judgment was entered against defendant for breach of an implied warranty of fitness for a particular purpose. Plaintiff was awarded damages of $7,000. Defendant appeals. He claims (1) that the court erred in entering judgment for plaintiff because an implied warranty of fitness for a particular purpose could not arise under the facts of this case and (2) that the court erred in assessing damages at $7,000.[1]

ORS 72.3150 provides for an implied warranty of fitness:

> "Where the seller at the time of contracting has reason to know any particular purpose for which the goods are required and that the buyer is relying on the seller's skill or judgment to select or furnish suitable goods, there is unless excluded or modified under ORS 72.3160 an implied warranty that the goods shall be fit for such purpose."

An implied warranty of fitness for a particular purpose arises then when two conditions are met: 1) the buyer relies on the seller's skill and judgment to select or furnish suitable goods; and 2) the seller at the time of contracting has rea-

1. The first assignment of error was preserved by defendant's motion for non-suit and motion for reconsideration. We need not reach the second assignment of error in light of our determination of the warranty issue.

son to know of the buyer's purpose and that the buyer is relying on his skill and judgment. *Controltek, Inc. v. Kwikee Enterprises, Inc.,* 284 Or. 123, 585 P.2d 670 (1978); *Valley Iron and Steel v. Thorin,* 278 Or. 103, 562 P.2d 1212 (1977).

The trial court found that defendant was advised that plaintiff intended to use the truck to haul scrap auto bodies. There was evidence to support that finding. No finding was made as to whether plaintiff-buyer relied on the defendant-seller's skill and judgment to select the truck or that defendant had reason to know of any reliance. The evidence was that plaintiff, who runs a junk yard, learned of defendant's truck being for sale from one of his employees. Plaintiff had had some experience with trucks, including driving, although usually not diesel trucks. He inspected the truck and drove it for a short distance. He was told by defendant that the engine had been rebuilt and was given the name of the mechanic who did the work. Defendant leases trucks, but does not drive them. He operates a well-drilling business and owns drilling rigs. He does not have any particular expertise concerning diesel trucks.

There was no evidence that plaintiff relied on defendant's judgment in selecting the truck he purchased. Defendant merely answered plaintiff's inquiries concerning the mechanic's work on the engine. While the needs of plaintiff were known to defendant, there was no showing that defendant offered to fulfill those needs, that plaintiff in fact relied on defendant's judgment or that defendant had reason to know of plaintiff's reliance, if any.

The existence of a warranty of fitness for a particular purpose depends in part on the comparative knowledge and skills of the parties. *Blockhead, Inc. v. Plastic Forming Company, Inc.,* 402 F.Supp. 1017, 1024 (D.Conn.1975); *Valley Iron and Steel v. Thorin, supra.* There can be no justifiable reliance by a buyer who has equal or superior knowledge and skill with respect to the product purchased by him. White and Summers, Uniform Commercial Code 298, § 9–9 (1972); *Valley Iron and Steel v. Thorin, supra.*

In the instant case, both parties had limited knowledge of diesel trucks. Absent evidence that plaintiff justifiably relied on defendant's judgment in selecting the truck to fulfill his hauling needs, there was no implied warranty of fitness for a particular purpose.

Reversed.

CASE

June F. BRITTON, Petitioner-Appellee,

v.

H.R. BRITTON, Respondent-Appellant.
No. 14577.

Supreme Court of New Mexico.
Oct. 17, 1983.
100 N.M. 424, 671 P.2d 1135 (1983)

OPINION

SOSA, Senior Justice.

Petitioner-Appellee, June Britton (Petitioner) filed a petition in the Bernalillo County District Court to reduce accrued and unpaid child support arrearages to judgment. The district court concluded that the divorce decree mandating child support was enforceable and that no statute of limitations period bars action on the arrearages. It did not allow H.R. Britton, Respondent, any offset. The court issued an order setting arrearages and a final judgment in the amount of $7900.00 without interest and did not award attorney's fees. Respondent appeals from the district court's determination awarding arrearages. Petitioner cross-appeals on the failure of the district court to award her attorney's fees.

The questions presented here are (1) whether the amended final divorce decree was unambiguous and therefore enforceable; (2) whether accrued and unpaid child support installments are deemed final judgments, thereby rendering action on them subject to a statute of limitations period; (3) whether a Respondent should have been allowed an offset against the arrearage judgment; (4) whether laches bars any recovery of the accrued child support installments; and (5) whether Petitioner should have been awarded attorney's fees for her presentation at the district court level. We affirm on all issues except the second.

FACTS

The parties were married on September 4, 1952. Four children issued from the marriage, all requiring specialized care and treatment due to varying degrees of developmental disability. By 1964 both the youngest and oldest child had been made wards of the state and committed to Los

Lunas Training School. These two children remained under the direct care and control of the Los Lunas facility at all times relevant to this case. The oldest child attained majority on June 27, 1971, the youngest on January 28, 1977.

The parties were divorced by final decree entered May 26, 1970 by Judge Edwin Swope of the Bernalillo County District Court. On June 28, 1971 a different judge entered an amended final decree which added the phrase "per month" after the one hundred dollar child support figure in the original final decree. The amendment was done *ex parte.* Respondent never moved the district court for a modification of the terms of either decree.

One of the twin children remained intermittently under Petitioner's direct care from the time of the divorce until the child was transferred to a group home in Albuquerque in January 1976. The other twin remained under the direct care of Petitioner through December 1972. Since that time he has voluntarily lived with Respondent.

ASSERTED AMBIGUITY

Respondent initially contends that the original final decree of May 26, 1970 was ambiguous and should not have been amended *ex parte.* The original final decree in relevant part awarded custody of all four children to Petitioner and also awarded her "one hundred dollars ($100)" in child support. The sole change made by the judge in the amended final decree was the addition of the phrase "per month" after the one hundred dollar child support figure.

The omission of the phrase "per month" was clearly a clerical mistake apparent on the face of the record. On Petitioner's timely motion this mistake was properly corrected without resort to extrinsic evidence pursuant to Rule 60(a) of the New Mexico Rules of Civil Procedure NMSA 1953, Section 21–1–1(60)(a) (Repl. Vol. 4, 1970), presently compiled as NMSA 1978, Civ.P.R. 60(a) (Repl.Pamp.1980). *Telephonic, Inc. v. Montgomery Plaza Co.,* 87 N.M. 407, 534 P.2d 1119 (Ct.App.1975); *see De Baca v. Sais,* 44 N.M. 105, 99 P.2d 106 (1940).

This simple amendment obviously did not purport to clear up any ambiguity that Respondent alleges existed regarding the exact amount of child support that was to apply to each minor child. Respondent asserts that he should have been afforded an opportunity to present parole evidence prior to modification so that the support terms could have been modified to apply to the twins only and to reflect the fact that another child had attained majority. In New Mexico, the duty of a parent to support a child continues until the child reaches the age of majority. NMSA 1978, §§ 28–6–1 and 28–6–6 (Repl.Pamp.1983); *Phelps v. Phelps,* 85 NM 62, 509 P.2d 254 (1973); *Coe's Estate,* 56 N.M. 578, 247 P.2d 162 (1952). The well-established general rule is that an undivided support award directed at more than one child is presumed to continue in force for the full amount until the youngest child reaches majority. Annot., 2 A.L.R.3d 596 (1965). We see no compelling reason to depart from this view.

Respondent's proper remedy, if indeed he though [sic] the final decree ambiguous and/or unjust, would have been to seek prospective modification of the decree on the basis of changed circumstances. We note as to the alleged ambiguity that Respondent at no time petitioned the district court for any modification of either decree. Respondent, having failed to timely petition for possible relief from this asserted ambiguity, cannot now seize upon the mere *ex parte* correction of a clerical error and expand this into an inquiry regarding his interpretation of his obligations under the final decree. We concluded that the decrees were not ambiguous in their terms, and thus were enforceable.

STATUTE OF LIMITATIONS

A hearing was held on Petitioner's December 15, 1981 motion to reduce accrued child support arrearages to judgment. Petitioner was awarded a judgment of $7900.00. The district court found that Respondent had not made any of the monthly child support payments required by the amended final decree. The $7900.00 figure was based on the calculation that the monthly payments should have been made during the seventy-nine months that elapsed between the entry of the original May 26, 1970 divorce decree and January 28, 1977, the date that the youngest child reached majority.

Respondent's central contention is that Petitioner's action to collect accrued arrearages at this late date is barred by the statute of limitations. He maintains that over eleven and one-half years had passed between May 1970 entry of the original final decree and Petitioner's December 1981 petition. Respondent primarily maintains that the seven year statute of limitations applicable to judgments in effect in December 1981 (formerly compiled as NMSA 1978, Section 37–1–2) should apply and bar any claim for arrearages that accrued seven years prior to the date Petitioner filed her petition.

Respondent's argument thus presents the question of whether accrued and unpaid periodic child support installments mandated in a new Mexico divorce decree are considered final judgments in New Mexico on the date they become due. This appears to be a case of first impression as the parties have not cited, and our research has not revealed, any New Mexico authority directly on point.

The applicability of any statute of limitations period will depend on the characterization of monthly child support installments as they become due. Both *Corliss v. Corliss,* 89 N.M. 235, 549 P.2d 1070 (1976), and *Slade v. Slade,* 81 N.M. 462, 468 P.2d 627 (1970), involved the characterization and enforcement of monthly child support provisions incorporated in *foreign* divorce decrees. In *Slade* this Court considered whether the New Mexico statute of limitations applicable to judgments applied to bar recovery of accrued child support arrearages under a Kansas divorce decree. Looking to Kansas law to determine the nature of a child support award, we concluded that the child support award was a judgment in installments. We further concluded that the seven year New Mexico statute of limitations then applicable to judgments (formerly compiled as NMSA 1953, Section 23–1–2 (Supp.1969)) applied and began to run on each monthly installment on the date it became due and unpaid. Accordingly, all uncollected installments that accrued more than seven years prior to the initiation of the action to collect the arrearages were deemed subject to the seven year statute of limitations applicable to judgments generally.

In considering the enforceability of a Missouri divorce decree, this Court in *Corliss* looked to Missouri law to determine whether child support awarded by the decree was subject to retroactive modification. This Court concluded that since Missouri courts had no power to modify or forgive accrued child support arrearages under a Missouri decree, New Mexico Courts could not do so.

Both *Slade* and *Corliss* lend support to a characterization of each monthly installment as a final judgment. In both cases, once the installment had become due, the amount payable was essentially deemed liquidated and, as with final judgments, not subject to retroactive modification. *Corliss* in particular concluded that child support arrearages would not be modified once accrued. Although this conclusion arose out of an application of Missouri law to a Missouri decree, the same characterization has obtained regarding New Mexico decrees.

In *Gomez v. Gomez,* 92 N.M. 310, 587 P.2d 963 (1978), *overruled on other grounds, Montoya v. Montoya,* 95 N.M. 189, 619 P.2d 1234 (1980), this Court considered whether weekly child support installment payments mandated in a New Mexico decree were modifiable once accrued. The then controlling New Mexico statute, NMSA 1953, Section 22–7–6(C) (Supp.1975) was compared with the substantially identical Missouri statute construed in *Corliss.* This Court held that, as with accrued Missouri installments, past due child support payments mandated in a New Mexico divorce decree were deemed not subject to retroactive modification.

Neither the reasoning nor the holding of *Gomez* bear out Petitioner's assertion that applying a statute of limitations to bar recovery of support installments is inconsistent with the proposition that such installments cannot be modified. Retroactive modification of child support awards is an issue distinct from the issue concerning the applicability of a statute of limitations period. Application of a statute of limitations merely bars the remedy on a stale claim without determining the underlying validity of that claim or modifying it in any way. See *Davis v. Savage,* 50 N.M. 30, 168 P.2d 851 (1946).

The fact of *Gomez* presented the question of retroactive modification of child support payments. It did not address the issue of a statute of limitations period as it would apply to the collection of accrued child support installments. As such, the holding is not determinative of the instant statute of limitations question. Furthermore, *Gomez* cites *Catlett v. Catlett,* 412 P.2d 942 (Okl. 1966) for the crucial proposition that accrued child support arrearages cannot be modified. While passing judgment on this question, the *Catlett* court also considered the applicability of the Oklahoma statute of limitations to a collection action for delinquent child support payments. In this regard the court stated:

> This apparently is a new question for the Oklahoma court but the rule appears to be well settled that where a divorce decree provides for the payment of alimony or support in installments the right to enforce payment accrues on each payment as it matures and the statute of limitations begins to run on each installment from the time fixed for its payment.

Id. at 946. The *Catlett* court thus properly viewed the application of a statute of limitations period as being compatible with its conclusion that accrued child support obligations were not modifiable.

Aside from Oklahoma, numerous other jurisdictions consider child support installments final judgments and hold that a statute of limitations begins to run on each installment as it becomes due. See 24 Am.Jur.2d *Divorce and Separation* § 863 (1966). In a number of decisions this construction has barred collection of child support installments accruing beyond the relevant limitations period. *See, e.g., Corbett v. Corbett,* 116 Ariz. 350, 569 P.2d 292 (App. 1977); *Bruce v. Froeb,* 15 Ariz.App. 306, 488 P.2d 662 (1971); *Hauck v. Schuck,* 143 Colo. 324, 353 P.2d 79 (1960); *Turinsky v. Turinsky,* 359 S.W.2d 114 (Tex.Civ.App.1962); *Seeley v. Park,* 532 P.2d 684 (Utah 1975). Indeed, rendering accrued child support installments individually subject to a limitations period appears to be the majority rule in the United States. Annot., 70 A.L.R.2d 1250 (1960); *cf.* 27B C.J.S. *Divorce* § 256 (1959) (outlining the analogous majority rule that as to judgments for alimony in installments, the pertinent statute of limitations begins to run on each installment as it falls due).

Since the installment obligations were clearly embodied in a final decree, they were a product of a precise judicial determination of Respondent's obligations. The authority is extensive and well-established that each monthly child support installment mandated in the final decree was a final judgment, not subject to retroactive modification.

Having determined that each installment was a final judgment, we turn to the question of which statute of limitations period should apply. We note at the outset that there is no special statute of limitations specified under child support or the enforcement provisions, respectively, of NMSA 1978, Section 40–4–7 or 40–4–19 (Repl.Pamp.1983).

In *Coe's Estate,* 56 N.M. 578, 247 P.2d 162 the ex-wife sought a judgment for arrearages pursuant to a divorce decree mandating undivided child support for the minor children under her custody. This Court first held that the child support order was a judgment in monthly installments granted only during the minority of the children, thereby precluding any accrual of liability after the youngest child reached majority. The next holding applied the general judgment statute of limitations then obtaining under former NMSA 1941, Section 27–102 to bar recovery since the claim was filed more than seven years after the youngest child reached majority.

Similarly, in *Slade* this Court considered the applicability of a statute of limitations period to an action on a Kansas decree mandating periodic child support payments. Having concluded, as we do here, that the mandated installments were judgments, we there applied the seven year judgment statute of limitations under former NMSA 1953, Section 23–1–2 (Supp.1969). *Slade* and *Coe's Estate* together provide clear authority for our application of the judgment statute of limitation. In addition, virtually all of the out-of-state decisions we have cited regarding construction of accrued installments as judgments have applied their statute which limits executions on judgments. *Corbett v. Corbett,* 116 Ariz. 350, 569 P.2d 292 and *Bruce v. Froeb,* 15 Ariz. App. 306, 488 P.2d 662 (both applying the general five year Arizona statute of limitations applicable to execution on judgments); *Hauck v. Schuck,* 143 Colo. 324, 353 P.2d 79 (applying twenty year limitations period pertaining to execution on judgments rendered in Colorado); *Turinsky v. Turinsky,* 359 S.W.2d 114 (applying general ten year Texas statute limiting execution on judgments); *Seeley v. Park,* 532 P.2d 684 (eight year statute of limitations pertaining to actions on judgments applies to suit for collection of accrued child support arrearages).

The judgment statute here strikes a reasonable balance between the competing interests of enforcing the supporting parent's right to periodic payments on the one hand and protecting the obligor parent from stale claims on the other.

The determination that accrued child support installments are final judgments of record results in the application of the longest possible statute of limitations period available to a collection action by the supporting parent. Application of the catchall four year limitations statute of NMSA 1978 Section 37–1–4 would provide for an inordinately short period in which a custodial parent could assert the child support claim. This would be clearly inimical to the best interests of the child, would place an undue burden on the custodial parent, and might encourage dilatory tactics on the part of obligor parents intent on avoiding their child support duties.

Accordingly, we hold that the judgment statute of limitations that was in effect at the time Petitioner filed her December 15, 1981 petition applies. This was the seven year statute codified at NMSA 1978, Section 37–1–2 (Orig.Pamp.). We note, however, that the judgment statute has since been amended and now provides for a fourteen year limitations period. NMSA 1978, § 37–1–2 (Cum.Supp.1983).

Applying the relevant seven year judgment statute of the facts of the instant case, we conclude that Petitioner is barred from recovering the installment arrearages that accrued more than seven years prior to her December 15, 1981 petition. The trial court was incorrect in awarding judgment based on a seventy-nine month arrearage period. The only installments which Petitioner may properly collect are those falling due between December 15, 1974, the last payment not barred by the judgment statute, and

January 28, 1977, the date that the youngest child attained majority—a period of twenty-five months. The trial court should have awarded judgment to Petitioner in the amount of $2500.00.

OFFSET

Respondent also asserts that he is entitled to an offset against any arrearages not barred by the statute of limitations. This offset claim is based in large part on the fact that Respondent has made substantial expenditures connected with the care and support of the son that has been living with him since December 1972. While it is entirely commendable that Respondent voluntarily undertook the responsibilities associated with the direct care and treatment of his son, we nevertheless cannot agree that Respondent's actions merit an offset under the circumstances of this case.

As we have previously concluded, the amended final decree clearly set forth Respondent's child support obligations and was fully enforceable at all time relevant herein. Respondent, as the obligor parent, cannot by his actions unilaterally alter the support obligations set forth in the decree. As we stated in our discussion concerning the asserted ambiguity of the decree, Respondent properly should have petitioned to modify the child support terms of the decree in light of this asserted change in circumstances. Modification of support obligations is strictly a matter to be determined by the courts. Not having pursued this avenue, Respondent cannot now claim an offset for his self-imposed expenditures, substantial though they may have been. *See Baures v. Baures,* 13 Ariz.App. 515, 478 P.2d 130 (1970) and authorities cited therein. As state in *Baures:*

> A father who is required to make periodic payments for the support of minor children has an opportunity to relieve himself of that liability by a petition to modify the decree *in futuro* but he cannot remain silent while the installments accrue and then claim credit for his voluntary acts. In view of the mandatory requirements of the divorce decree as to payments of the monthly support installments to appellant, although it is to appellee's credit that he cared for his [child], he was a volunteer and is not thereby relieved from the obligations of the decree.

Id. at 519, 478 P.2d at 134. The district court in the instant case properly disallowed any and all of Respondent's offset claims.

LACHES

Respondent next maintains that he has been prejudiced by Petitioner's delay in pursuing her action and that laches should therefore bar any claim for arrearages not barred by the statute of limitations. We find this contention without merit.

There is sufficient evidence to support the district court's determination that Respondent would not be unduly prejudiced by the judgment for arrearages. The standard review on appeal is whether substantial evidence reasonably supports the factual determinations of the trial court. *Toltec International, Inc. v. Village of Ruidoso,* 95 N.M. 82, 619 P.2d 186 (1980). Resolving all disputes and reasonable inferences in favor of the successful party below and refusing to reweigh the evidence, we conclude that the trial court properly determined that laches does not apply in this case.

ATTORNEY'S FEES

Petitioner contends that she should be awarded attorney's fees related to the instant appeal, and for her presentation at the district court level. The district court in its final order of August 30, 1982 did not include an award of attorney's fees at the level as Petitioner had requested but noted that all findings and awards not specifically included were denied. This should properly be interpreted as a finding against Petitioner on the attorney's fees issue. *See Maynard v. Western Bank,* 99 N.M. 135, 654 P.2d 1035 (1982). We have carefully reviewed the record and conclude that substantial evidence supports the district court's denial of attorney's fees. *Toltec International, Inc. v. Village of Ruidoso,* 95 N.M. 82, 619 P.2d 186; *Cave v. Cave,* 81 N.M. 797, 474 P.2d 480 (1970). Furthermore, we conclude that Petitioner does not merit attorney's fees for her instant cross-appeal.

The trial court is affirmed on all issues except that regarding the application of a statute of limitations period to an action on unpaid child support installments. The cause is remanded to the district court for further proceedings consistent with this opinion.

IT IS SO ORDERED.

RIORDAN and STOWERS, JJ., concur.

Dwonna Gayle Gwaltney
CARDWELL Appellant,

v.

Kenneth Wayne GWALTNEY, Appellee.

No. 87A01–9002–CV–80.
Court of Appeals of Indiana,
First District.
July 17, 1990.
556 N.E.2d 953 (Ind. Ct. App. 1990)

ROBERTSON, Judge.

The sole issue raised in this appeal is whether an individual should be absolved from paying child support because of his incarceration.

The underlying material facts show that the appellant Cardwell and the appellee Gwaltney were divorced with Gwaltney ordered to pay child support. About a year and one half later, Gwaltney filed a petition to modify the support order based upon the reason that he had spent a year in jail. Gwaltney sought to be absolved from the support which had accrued during that year and to have future support reduced. Cardwell and Gwaltney reached an agreement that, among other things, excused Gwaltney from paying support for the year he was imprisoned. The trial court approved the agreement; however, that agreement was challenged when the county prosecuting attorney appeared in the matter and sought to set aside the agreement because Cardwell had been a recipient of AFDC funds through the State and had assigned her support rights. The trial court refused to set aside the earlier agreements with this appeal resulting.

Even though the trial judge was prompted by equitable concerns when Gwaltney was excused from paying support the law is that any modification of a support order must act prospectively:

> In *Biedron v. Biedron* (1958), 128 Ind. App. 299, 148 N.E.2d 209, the Appellate Court of Indiana said, "in this state after support installments have accrued, the court is without power to reduce, annul or vacate such orders retrospectively, and therefore, the court committed error in attempting to do so." (Citations omitted). Therefore, payments must be made in the manner, amount, and at the times required by the support order embodied in the divorce decree until such order is modified or set aside. *Stitle v. Stitle,* (1964), 245 Ind. 168, 197 N.E.2d 174, Indiana does permit cancellation or modification of support orders as to future payments; but, all modifications operate prospectively. *Kniffen v. Courtney* (1971), 148 Ind.App. 358, 266 N.E.2d 72; *Haycraft v. Haycraft,* (1978), Ind.App. [176 Ind.App. 211], 375 N.E.2d 252.

Jahn v. Jahn (1979), 179 Ind.App. 368, 385 N.E.2d 488, 490. See also *O'Neil v. O'Neil* (1988), Ind.App., 517 N.E.2d 433 (transfer granted on other grounds).

Additionally, I.C. 31–2–11–12 provides:

> Modification of delinquent support payment.
>
> (a) Except as provided in subsection (b), *a court may not retroactively modify* an obligor's duty to pay a delinquent support payment.
>
> (b) A court with jurisdiction over a support order may modify an obligor's duty to pay a support payment that becomes due:
>
> (1) After notice of a petition to modify the support order has been given to each obligee; and
>
> (2) Before a final order concerning the petition for modification is entered. (Emphasis added.)

Although the Indiana Child Support Guidelines, effective October 1, 1989, were not officially in use at the time of the trial court's decision in this appeal, we are of the opinion that a part of the commentary to Ind. Child Support Guideline 2 takes into consideration existing statutes and case law as heretofore cited. That part of the commentary reads:

> Even in situations where the non-custodial parent has no income, Courts have routinely established a child support obligation at some minimum level. An obligor cannot be held in contempt for failure to pay support when he does not have the means to pay, but the obligation accrues and serves as a reimbursement to the custodial parent, or, more likely, to the welfare department if he later acquires the ability to meet his obligation.

We conclude that the trial court erred in retroactively excusing Gwaltney's support obligation for the time he was incarcerated.

Cause reversed and remanded for further action not inconsistent with this opinion.

Reversed and remanded.

RATLIFF, C.J., and CONOVER, J., concur.

COMMONWEALTH of Pennsylvania

v.

Adam DeMICHEL, Appellant.

Supreme Court of Pennsylvania.
April 22, 1971.
Rehearing Denied May 21, 1971.
442 Pa. 553, 277 A.2d 159 (1971)

OPINION OF THE COURT

ROBERTS, Justice.

Upon the basis of various lottery paraphernalia seized pursuant to a search warrant and introduced into evidence at trial, appellant Adam DeMichel was convicted of setting up and maintaining an illegal lottery and sentenced to undergo imprisonment for three to twelve months and to pay a fine of five hundred dollars plus costs. In this appeal from the judgment of sentence, appellant asserts that the evidence that led to his conviction was the fruit of an illegally executed search warrant. Upon reviewing the record we must agree.

Appellant was arrested on January 14, 1967, during a police search of his home at 707 Sears Street in Philadelphia. Also present at the time were appellant's wife and daughter. Upon initial entry into the house, the police observed appellant at a kitchen sink attempting to destroy rice paper, and in the course of the ensuing search they found and seized other sheets of rice paper containing several thousand lottery bets, other blank sheets of rice paper, lists of names, adding machine tape, and other lottery paraphernalia.

Prior to trial appellant filed a timely motion to suppress these items, and an evidentiary hearing was held on March 4, 1968. From testimony elicited at that hearing it appeared that five police officers armed with a search warrant arrived at the front of appellant's two story row house at 12:40 p.m. on January 14, 1967. All were dressed in plain clothes, and one of their number, Officer Daniel Creden, approached the front door alone carrying a cardboard box in an attempt to create the false impression of a deliveryman.

Corporal Frank Hall, another member of the raiding party, testified as follows concerning the execution of the search warrant:

"Q. Did * * * [appellant] admit you to the premises?
"A. No. We had to gain entrance.
"Q. How?
"A. We broke the door down.
"Q. With or without prior warning?
"A. With.

* * * * * *

"Q. What type of warning did you give to the occupants of the house before breaking in the door?
"A. I told him we were police officers, we had a warrant.
"Q. How much time elapsed between the time you said that and when you broke in the door, approximately?
"A. Approximately ten or fifteen seconds."

Upon cross-examination by appellant's counsel, Hall restated his version of the entry into the house but did not reaffirm that he *personally* gave any warnings to the occupants.[1]

At the conclusion of the hearing, appellant's counsel argued that the affidavit supporting the issuance of the search warrant was defective and that the police's method of entry into appellant's home was illegal. The hearing judge was unpersuaded and the motion for suppression denied.[2]

Appellant thereafter waived a jury, and his case proceeded to trial on May 16, 1968, before a different judge of the Philadelphia Court of Common Pleas. During the Commonwealth's case in chief, new and different evidence came to light concerning the execution of the search warrant. Corporal Hall again described the events surrounding the police's entry into appellant's house but failed to mention that he had given any warnings to the occupants, and Officer Creden, the policeman who actually knocked on appellant's door, gave the following testimony:

"Q. Now, sir, would you relate to the Court specifically in detail what occurred from the time you arrived at these premises until the time entry was made?

---

1. Instead, Hall used the pronoun "we":

"Q. And would you describe specifically, sir, the manner in which you attempted to gain entrance to these premises?

"A. We knocked on the door, and after hearing sound coming from inside the house *we* announced ourselves as police officers and that we had a warrant * * *."

* * * * *

"Q. What did you do?

"A. *We* announced ourselves as police officers and we had a search warrant * * *."

2. The question of the sufficiency of the affidavit is not pressed on this appeal.

277 A.2d—11

"A. Well, I guess we arrived around 12:40 p. m., I walked west on Sears Street, at 7th Street, I went up and knocked on the door. A few seconds, the blind was lifted up, and I announced that we were police. The blinds dropped, and we proceeded to knock the door down.

"Q. Within what period of time, sir?

"A. From the time that the blinds were dropped?

"Q. Yes, sir.

"A. Ten, five, I don't know how many seconds.

"Q. Seconds, sir?

"A. Well, as soon as the blinds dropped, I called the fellow officer who had the sledge hammer and knocked the door down."

* * * * * *

"Q. Just to make the record perfectly clear, when you first knocked, you did not say anything at all, did you?

"A. No. I just knocked.

"Q. And then, according to your testimony, someone lifted up the blinds?

"A. Yes, sir.

"Q. Could you tell whether that was male or female, sir?

"A. I couldn't tell. I believe there were curtains behind the blinds. I couldn't see who it was.

"Q. Then the blinds dropped, sir, is that correct?

"A. That is correct.

"Q. And then you made an announcement that you were police officers, is that correct, sir?

"A. No, it is not. While the blinds were up, I said, 'Open up, it is the police.'

"Q. *And that is all you said, sir?*

"A. *Yes.*" (Emphasis added.)

Appellant was adjudged guilty, but the trial judge granted his post trial motion in arrest of judgment on the ground that the evidence at trial demonstrated that the officer who executed the search warrant had not announced their purpose before resorting to forcible entry. The Superior Court, reasoning that a trial judge has no power to overrule the decision of a suppression hearing judge, reversed the order granting arrest of judgment and remanded the case for sentencing, 214 Pa.Super. 392, 257 A.2d 608. Following the imposition of sentence, appellant again appealed to the Superior Court. That court affirmed the judgment of sentence, 216 Pa.Super. 804, 263 A.2d 480, and we granted allocatur.

Preliminarily we note our disagreement with the Superior Court's apparent categorical holding that a trial judge is powerless to overrule the decision of a suppression hearing judge. While "[w]e impliedly held in Commonwealth v. Warfield, 418 Pa. 301, 211 A.2d 452 (1965) that the trial judge cannot reverse *on the same record* at trial the decision made after the pretrial suppression hearing * * *," Commonwealth v. Washington, 428 Pa. 131, 133 n. 2, 236 A.2d 772, 773 n. 2 (1968) (emphasis added), the same does not hold true when the trial judge's different ruling is based upon new and different evidence. When information comes to light after the suppression hearing clearly demonstrating that the evidence sought to be introduced by the Commonwealth is constitutionally tainted, no considertion [sic] of justice or interest of sound judicial administration would be furthered by prohibiting the trial judge from ruling it inadmissible. Although a favorable ruling at the suppression hearing relieves the Commonwealth of the burden of proving a second time at trial that its evidence was constitutionally obtained, the trial judge must exclude evidence previously held admissible at the suppression hearing when the defendant proves by a preponderance of new evidence at trial that the evidence sought to be introduced by the Commonwealth was obtained by unconstitutional means.[3]

Although we thus disagree with the Superior Court, we believe that the trial judge in the instant case erred in granting appellant's motion in arrest of judgment upon the basis of a finding that the police officers executing the search warrant did not properly announce their purpose before entering appellant's house. Officer Creden testified unequivocally at trial that *he* had made no announcement of purpose, but he did not state that his fellow officers were similarly mute or contradict Corporal Hall's suppression hearing testimony that Hall had made such an announcement of purpose. That being so, the record at trial in no way proves the absence of a proper police announcement of purpose.

3. At the time of appellant's trial, the method of pretrial litigation of the legality of searches and seizures was governed by Pa.R.Crim.P. 2001, 19 P.S. Appendix, which did not expressly speak to the question whether a trial judge could overrule the decision of the suppression hearing judge. Rule 2001 was superseded by a 1969 amendment to Pa.R.Crim.P. 323, which consolidated and made uniform the procedures relating to pretrial suppression of any evidence alleged to have been obtained in violation of a defendant's constitutional rights. Even this new consolidated rule recognized that there are some circumstances in which the trial judge should be free to exclude evidence previously held admissible.

> "If the [suppression hearing] court determines that the evidence is admissible, such determination shall be final, conclusive and binding at trial, *except upon a showing of evidence which was theretofore unavailable.* * * *"

Pa.R.Crim.P. 323(j) (emphasis added).

Despite the foregoing, we are nevertheless persuaded for other reasons that the search of appellant's home was illegally executed. It is settled in this Commonwealth that the Fourth Amendment prohibition against unreasonable searches and seizures demands that before a police officer enters upon private premises to conduct a search or to make an arrest he must, absent exigent circumstances, give notice of his identity and announce his purpose. Commonwealth v. Newman, 429 Pa. 441, 240 A.2d 795 (1968); United States ex rel. Manduchi v. Tracy, 350 F.2d 658 (3rd Cir.), cert. denied, 382 U.S. 943, 86 S.Ct. 390, 15 L.Ed.2d 353 (1965); United States ex rel. Ametrane v. Gable, 276 F.Supp. 555 (E.D. Pa.1967). The purpose of this announcement rule is that "* * * the dignity and privacy protected by the fourth amendment demand a certain propriety on the part of policemen even after they have been authorized to invade an individual's privacy. Regardless of how great the probable cause to believe a man guilty of a crime, *he must be given a reasonable opportunity to surrender his privacy voluntarily.*" United States ex rel. Ametrane v. Gable, supra, 276 F.Supp. at 559 (emphasis added). Accordingly, even where the police duly announced their identity and purpose, forcible entry in still unreasonable and hence violative of the Fourth Amendment if the occupants of the premises sought to be entered and searched are not first given an opportunity to surrender the premises voluntarily. See United States ex rel. Manduchi v. Tracy, 350 F.2d at 662.

The Commonwealth appears to concede this proposition of constitutional law but argues that the occupants of appellant's house were in fact given an adequate opportunity to open the door voluntarily. Corporal Hall and Officer Creden testified that they and the other officers began to break down the front door of appellant's house five to fifteen seconds after announcing their presence and purpose. We cannot deem this a reasonable sufficient period of time. In *Newman,* supra, for example, this Court stated that "a mere twenty second delay in answering the door cannot constitute support for a belief that evidence was being destroyed * * *." 429 Pa. at 448, 240 A.2d at 798. And in *Ametrane,* supra, the United States District Court for the Eastern District of Pennsylvania noted that "[e]ven if * * [the occupant] had known the officers to be policemen, he might have had countless legitimate reasons for taking a minute to answer the door." 276 F.Supp. at 559.

In both of the above cases the occupants were known by the police to be on the second floor whereas here Corporal Hall and Officer Creden testified that they saw someone peering at them through the blinds of a first story window located very near the front door. Given the close proximity of this person to the door, we are urged to conclude that a mere five to fifteen second delay was reasonable. But even in these circumstances this might be entirely innocent "for countless legitimate reasons." Appellant's wife, for example, testified that it was she who peered through the window and that her delay in responding was occasioned by her being attired in a nightgown and having to go to the kitchen to put on a robe. Regardless of the truth of her testimony, it serves to illustrate that a five to fifteen second delay was insufficient for the police to have formed a reasonable belief that the occupants of appellant's house did not intend to permit peaceable entry.

Finally, we are not persuaded that this case presents "exigent circumstances" suspending the ordinary requirement that the occupants of premises sought to be searched be given a reasonable opportunity to open the door voluntarily. The police officers involved were seeking to execute a warrant authorizing them to enter, search for and seize lottery paraphernalia, and from their prior experience with this type of mission they reasonably believed that some of the paraphernalia would be in the form of almost instantaneously destructible rice paper. However, as we stated in *Newman:*

> "The fact that some lottery paraphernalia is easily destroyed does not justify the suspension of the Fourth Amendment in all lottery prosecutions. One of the prices we have to pay for the security which the Fourth Amendment bestows upon us is the risk that an occasional guilty party will escape."

429 Pa. at 448, 240 A.2d at 798 (citation omitted). To excuse the police's failure to announce their purpose and presence and thereafter to allow a reasonable time for the voluntary surrender of the premises, there " * * * must be more than the presumption that the evidence *would* be destroyed because it *could* be easily done." State v. Mendoza, 104 Ariz. 395, 399, 454 P.2d 140, 144 (1969).

The testimony that appellant was found standing by a kitchen sink attempting to destroy rice paper is without significance.

> "It goes without saying that in determining the lawfulness of entry and the existence of probable cause we may concern ourselves only with what the officers had reason to believe *at the time of their entry.* Johnson v. United States, 333 U.S. 10, 17, 68 S.Ct. 367, 370–371, 92 L.Ed. 436 (1948). As the [Supreme] Court said in

United States v. Di Re, 332 U.S. 581, 595, 68 S.Ct. 222, 229, 92 L.Ed. 210 (1948), 'a search is not to be made legal by what it turns up. In law it is good *or bad* when it starts and does not change character from' what is dug up subsequently. (Emphasis added.)"

Ker v. California, 374 U.S. 23, 40 n. 12, 83 S.Ct. 1623, 1633 n. 12, 10 L.Ed.2d 726 (1963).

We hold that forcible entry in the circumstances of this case violated the standards of the Fourth Amendment and that the fruits of the ensuing search were improperly admitted at appellant's trial. Accordingly, the order of the Superior Court is reversed. The judgment of sentence is vacated and the case remanded for a new trial.

BELL, C. J., did not participate in the consideration or decision of this case.

* * * * * *

COHEN, J., did not participate in the decision of this case.

* * * * * *

POMEROY, J., filed a dissenting opinion, in which JONES, J., joins.

* * * * * *

EAGEN, J., concurs in the result.

* * * * * *

POMEROY, Justice (dissenting).

* * * * * *

CASE

COMMONWEALTH

v.

John J. SHEA.

No. 93–P–1066.

Appeals Court of Massachusetts, Plymouth.

Argued Sept. 12, 1994.
Decided Jan. 5, 1995.
Further Appellate Review Denied Feb. 28, 1995.

38 Mass. App. Ct. 7, 644 N.E.2d 244 (1995)

PERRETTA, Justice.

On the afternoon of June 15, 1991, the defendant and his friend invited two women who were sun bathing on the banks of the Charles River to board the defendant's boat and go for a ride. Once the women were aboard, the defendant headed out to the open sea. An hour later and about five miles off shore from Boston, he stopped the boat, disrobed, and made sexual remarks and advances toward the women. He ignored all requests that he dress and stop his offensive behavior. When the women demanded that he return them to Boston, he threw them overboard and drove away without a backward glance. The women were rescued after managing to swim within shouting distance of a sailboat. On evidence of these acts, a jury found the defendant guilty, as to each woman, of kidnapping, attempted murder, assault and battery by means of a dangerous weapon (the ocean), and indecent assault and battery. The defendant argues on appeal that the trial judge erroneously denied (1) his request for a continuance of the trial; (2) his motion in limine by which he sought to preclude the Commonwealth's use of a videotape showing the ocean from the perspective of the women in the water and the defendant on his boat; and (3) his motion for required findings of not guilty on all the indictments. Although we conclude that the ocean is not a dangerous weapon within the meaning of G.L. c. 265, § 15A, we affirm the kidnapping and attempted murder convictions.[1]

1. *The motion for a continuance.* Trial counsel was appointed to represent the defendant on August 29, 1991.[2] On February 21, 1992, he filed a motion seeking funds for a psychiatric evaluation of the defendant. The motion was allowed that same day, and the case was continued to April 21, 1992, "for trial." One week before the scheduled trial date, counsel sought a continuance of at least two months. The Commonwealth opposed the motion on numerous grounds, not the least of which was the fact that the victims had been receiving threatening mail and telephone calls. The judge denied the request and the defendant claims error. "[A] motion for continuance . . . lies within the sound discretion of the judge, whose action will not be disturbed unless there is a patent abuse of that discretion, which is to be determined in the circumstances of each case."

1. The defendant was also found guilty on two counts of indecent assault and battery. Because he assented to those convictions being placed on file, they are not before us. See *Commonwealth v. Delgado,* 367 Mass. 432, 438, 326 N.E.2d 716 (1975).

2. Appellate counsel was not trial counsel.

Commonwealth v. Bettencourt, 361 Mass. 515, 517–518, 281 N.E.2d 220 (1972). We relate the circumstances of the denial of the defendant's motion.

An affidavit and a letter from a psychiatrist, dated March 17, 1992, were attached to the motion for a continuance. It appears from these documents that the defendant's medical history indicated that he had suffered a series of head injuries from which he might have sustained brain trauma and that, according to the psychiatrist, the "charges now pending against him may reflect behavior caused by those head injuries." As further stated by the psychiatrist: "For a more conclusive answer to the question of the effect of Mr. Shea's head traumas to his alleged criminal acts, it would be necessary for him to undergo independent extensive neuropsychological testing and, in addition, have a BEAM study of the electrical activity of his brain."

As of April 14, 1992, the date of the hearing on the motion for a continuance, the BEAM study had been completed and the results reported to the psychiatrist. A copy of the report which had been submitted to the psychiatrist was also attached to the motion. The report recited the following conclusion of the BEAM study: "Overall this study is quite compatible with a history of multiple head injuries and suggests a generalized encephalopathy with irritable qualities falling just short of being a seizure disorder. The latter diagnosis, of course, should be made on clinical grounds."

It was not until the psychiatrist was called to testify at trial that the defendant's theory of defense took on a clarity: on the afternoon of June 15, 1991, he was experiencing a temporal lobe seizure which prevented him from formulating the specific intent necessary for criminal liability for his actions. At the time of the hearing on the motion, however, the trial judge was informed only that a continuance of two months was necessary so that in addition to the psychiatrist, various other named medical professionals could also review the results of the BEAM study and conduct psychoneurological testing of the defendant. Even were we to conclude that an adequate case for granting the motion had been made at that time, but see *Commonwealth v. Bettencourt,* 361 Mass. at 517–518, 281 N.E.2d 220, the defendant has failed to show that his defense was prejudiced by the denial of his request.

Although the defendant argues that the denial of the continuance prevented psychoneurological testing which would have allowed the psychiatrist to opine whether, at the time in question, the defendant was experiencing a temporal lobe seizure, the psychiatrist's testimony does not support the claim. The psychiatrist testified on voir dire that had additional psychoneurological testing been available, he could be more "definitive" or "conclusive" in his opinion concerning the defendant's potential for temporal lobe seizures.[3] The psychiatrist nonetheless could, and did, relate to the jury that it was his opinion, to the requisite degree of medical certainty, that the defendant's "history, test results, and behavior is consistent with a temporal lobe disorder."

As for the more immediate question of whether the defendant was experiencing a seizure at the time of the incident, the psychiatrist testified, on voir dire, that he could not say "with [a] high degree of certainty that at that moment on that boat, that type of episode occurred." Rather, he could state only that "this individual, with his condition, has a high potential for things like that happening." At no time was the psychiatrist asked whether psychoneurological testing could reveal to a reasonable degree of medical certainty whether a person who suffered from temporal lobe disorder had in fact experienced a seizure at a specific time in the past.

In sum, the defendant's temporal lobe disorder was fully presented to the jury. Although the defendant's expert and the expert for the Commonwealth agreed that the defendant's BEAM study indicated a temporal lobe abnormality, they sharply disagreed on the issue of whether the defendant's actions were consistent or inconsistent with a temporal lobe seizure. However, any weaknesses that the jury might have found in the testimony of the defendant's psychiatrist cannot, on the record before us, be attributed to a lack of psychoneurological testing and the denial of the continuance.

2. *The videotapes.* At trial, the Commonwealth was allowed to use two chalks, i.e., videotapes, to illustrate to the jury the victims' testimony concerning the condition of the ocean when the defendant threw them into the water and abandoned them. The first videotape depicted the victims' view from the water as they watched the defendant drive away, and the second showed how two people in the water would appear from the vantage point of the back of the boat as it drove away from them. The Commonwealth

3. The psychiatrist had reviewed some psychoneurological test results which were in the defendant's medical records. When asked by defense counsel whether he could be more conclusive in his opinion had "more extensive psychoneurological testing" been done, the psychiatrist responded ". . . [Y]es, everything that enhances helps become more definitive until ultimately, hopefully, you can become almost conclusive about it. I'm only saying I can't be conclusive, I can only render an opinion at this time."

argued that the tapes were relevant to the defendant's murderous intent. After an in camera viewing of the tapes, the trial judge ruled that the videos could be used as chalks. Immediately before the jury viewed the tapes, the trial judge instructed: "This is not offered for your consideration as evidence in this case. It is offered in the nature of what we refer to as a chalk to the extent that it may be of assistance to you in understanding the evidence that you have heard in view of the similarities, if any, and it's for you to determine if there are any similarities in the circumstances of the events of June 15, 1991." See generally Liacos, Massachusetts Evidence § 11.13.2 (6th ed. 1994) ("Chalks are used to illustrate testimony . . . they are not evidence in the ordinary sense of the word").

The defendant complains that the tapes were a prejudicial recreation of the crime, that they were not based upon the evidence, and that they were inflammatory. We see no abuse of discretion or other error in the trial judge's decision to allow the Commonwealth to use the videotapes as chalks.

" 'Whether the conditions were sufficiently similar to make the observation [offered by the demonstration] of any value in aiding the jury to pass upon the issue submitted to them [is] primarily for the trial judge to determine as a matter of discretion. [The judge's] decision in this respect will not be interfered with unless plainly wrong.' " *Commonwealth v. Chipman,* 418 Mass. 262, 270–271, 635 N.E.2d 1204 (1994), quoting from *Field v. Gowdy,* 199 Mass. 568, 574, 85 N.E. 884 (1908). See also *Terrio v. McDonough,* 16 Mass.App.Ct. 163, 173, 450 N.E.2d 190 (1983). To the extent the videotapes do not depict anyone being thrown from the boat into the ocean, they are not a recreation of the crime. The tapes otherwise essentially track the victims' testimony.

State police officers Earle S. Sterling and Leonard Coppengrath testified that at 9:30 A.M. on April 15, 1992, they and a number of their associates boarded a boat and proceeded to the point five miles off shore from Boston where the women had been pulled from the water. They described the weather conditions that day as well as the height of the waves and the temperature of the water. They had video cameras and other equipment with them. When they reached their destination, Sterling and another man, who was holding a camera, jumped overboard. Once in the water, the other man held the camera about two inches (the eye level of the victims) above the water, and filmed the boat as it drove off. Meanwhile, Coppengrath, who remained on the boat, focused a camera on the two men in the water as another one of the men slowly drove away.[4] After proceeding about one-half mile, the men in the water were no longer visible from the boat. Coppengrath then panned the "area from where we had come and to where we were heading and circled across the skyline of Boston towards the point in Hull which is the closest point of land to where we were."

There is no persuasive force to the defendant's argument that the Commonwealth's use of the videotapes was no more than a disguised inflammatory appeal to the jurors to put themselves in the place of the victims. See, e.g., *Commonwealth v. Sevieri,* 21 Mass.App.Ct. 745, 753–754, 490 N.E.2d 481 (1986). The Commonwealth was entitled to dispel any notion that the defendant's actions were no more than a sunny-day prank gone too far and that he returned for the victims but again departed when he saw them being pulled aboard the sailboat. When the defendant first threw one of the women into the water, she screamed that she did not know how to swim. He then jumped overboard, held her head under the water, and reboarded the boat for the second woman. Before he threw her into the water, she too told him that she could not swim. Having experienced the frigid temperature of the water and the height of the waves and having been told that the victims could not swim, the defendant drove away leaving the women in great peril. The videotapes show what that defendant saw and experienced, and they were relevant to the issue of whether he "did an act designed to result in death with the specific intent that death result." *Commonwealth v. Beattie,* 409 Mass. 458, 459, 567 N.E.2d 206 (1991). See also *Commonwealth v. Hebert,* 373 Mass. 535, 537, 368 N.E.2d 1204 (1977) ("An attempt to commit a crime necessarily involves an intent to commit that crime").[5] We have viewed the videotapes and conclude that the trial judge neither abused his discretion nor committed other error of law in allowing them to be seen by the jury. See *Commonwealth v. Chipman,* 418 Mass. at 271, 635

---

4. Although the victims testified that the defendant sped away in the boat, that testimony did not require preclusion of the use of the videotapes, see *Commonwealth v. Chipman,* 418 Mass. at 270–271, 635 N.E.2d 1204 (1994), especially in light of the trial judge's instructions to the jury prior to the viewing of the films. We also think it inconsequential that there was no evidence to show that the defendant turned to watch the victims as he drove off. The information being illustrated pertained to the water conditions and surroundings, which remained the same irrespective of any particular vantage point, and the defendant's awareness of them.

5. As the videotapes were illustrative on the issue of the defendant's intent, we need not consider whether, as the Commonwealth argues, they were also helpful to an understanding of the victims' state of mind, an issue of questionable relevancy. See *Commonwealth v. Zagranski,* 408 Mass. 278, 282–283, 558 N.E.2d 933 (1990).

N.E.2d 1204; *Terrio v. McDonough,* 16 Mass.App.Ct. at 173, 450 N.E.2d 190.

3. *Attempted murder and kidnapping.* It is the defendant's argument that the Commonwealth failed to prove that when he threw the women into the water and drove away, he specifically intended their death. Taking the evidence in the light most favorable to the Commonwealth, we see no error in the trial judge's denial of the defendant's motion for a required finding of not guilty on the indictments charging him with attempted murder by drowning. There was evidence to show that the defendant was five miles offshore with no boats in sight when he threw the women overboard. The water was fifty-two degrees, and the waves were one to two feet high. Because the defendant had jumped into the water to hold one of the woman under, he knew that it was cold and choppy. For all he knew, they could not swim.

This evidence of the defendant's conduct was sufficient to warrant the reasonable inference that he intended that the victims drown. See *Commonwealth v. Henson,* 394 Mass. 584, 591, 476 N.E.2d 947 (1985) ("[An] intent to kill may be inferred from the defendant's conduct"); *Commonwealth v. Dixon,* 34 Mass.App.Ct. 653, 656, 614 N.E.2d 1027 (1993) (attempted murder statute reaches act of throwing someone who cannot swim from a boat into water).[6]

In arguing that there was no evidence of kidnappings apart from the conduct incidental to the attempted murders, i.e., picking the women up and throwing them into the water, the defendant ignores the testimony of the victims. Both women related that after the defendant disrobed and made sexual advances towards them, they demanded that he return them to shore. He refused, continued with his offensive behavior, became angry over their reaction, and then threw them overboard. Moreover, the conduct which the jury reasonably could find as the basis for kidnapping, forcing the women to remain at sea while the defendant committed an indecent assault and battery upon them (see note one, *supra*), would not necessarily be based on the acts that constituted the attempted murders. See *Commonwealth v. Rivera,* 397 Mass. 244, 253–254, 490 N.E.2d 1160 (1986); *Commonwealth v. Sumner,* 18 Mass.App.Ct. 349, 352–353, 465 N.E.2d 1213 (1984).

4. *The dangerous weapon.* General Laws c. 265, § 15A, reads, in pertinent part: "Whoever commits assault and battery upon another by means of a dangerous weapon shall be punished. . . ." The sole argument made by the defendant in respect to the indictments charging him with assault and battery by means of a dangerous weapon is that the ocean is not a dangerous weapon within the meaning of § 15A.

We need not consider whether the specified weapon, the ocean, is dangerous per se or dangerous as used. See *Commonwealth v. Tarrant,* 367 Mass. 411, 416–417, 326 N.E.2d 710 (1975); *Commonwealth v. Appleby,* 380 Mass. 296, 303, 402 N.E.2d 1051 (1980). Although the ocean can be and often is dangerous, it cannot be regarded in its natural state as a weapon within the meaning of § 15A. See *Commonwealth v. Farrell,* 322 Mass. 606, 614–615, 78 N.E.2d 697 (1948), stating that the term "dangerous weapon" comprehends "any *instrument or instrumentality* so constructed or so used as to be likely to produce death or great bodily harm" (emphasis added); *Commonwealth v. Tarrant,* 367 Mass. at 417 n. 6, 326 N.E.2d 710, noting with approval the definition of dangerous weapon adopted in the Proposed Criminal Code of Massachusetts c. 263, § 3(i): " 'any firearm or other weapon, device, instrument, material or substance, *whether animate or inanimate,* which in the matter [in] which it is used *or is intended to be used* is capable of producing death or serious bodily injury' (emphasis added)";[7] *Commonwealth v. Appleby,* 380 Mass. at 308, 402 N.E.2d 1051, concluding that the "offense of assault and battery by means of a dangerous weapon under G.L. c. 265, § 15A, requires that the elements of assault be present . . . that there be a touching, however slight . . . that the touching be by means of the weapon . . . and that the battery be accomplished by use of an inherently dangerous weapon, or by use of *some other object* as a weapon, with the intent to *use that object* in a dangerous or potentially dangerous fashion" (emphasis added).

All the cases collected and cited in the discussion of dangerous weapons, per se and as used, in *Commonwealth v. Appleby,* 380 Mass. at 303–304, 402 N.E.2d 1051, share a common fact that is consistent with the definitions of "dangerous weapons" which speak in terms of "objects" or "instrumentalities." The commonality found in those cases

6. In deciding this issue, we need not, contrary to the defendant's argument, consider the testimony of his friend, that he was "eventually" able to persuade the defendant to turn back for the women and that with the aid of binoculars they were able to see the women about three-quarters of a mile away being pulled aboard a sailboat. See *Commonwealth v. Lydon,* 413 Mass. 309 312, 597 N.E.2d 36 (1992).

7. This definition tracks that of "deadly weapon" set out in § 210 of the Model Penal Code (1980), which, as noted in comment 5, was "designed to take account of the ingenuity of those who desire to hurt their fellows without encompassing every use of an ordinary object that could cause death or serious injury."

is that the object in issue, whether dangerous per se or as used, was an instrumentality which the batterer controlled, either through possession of or authority over it, for use of it in the intentional application of force. Because the ocean in its natural state cannot be possessed or controlled, it is not an object or instrumentality capable of use as a weapon for purposes of § 15A.

Our conclusion should not be construed to mean that there can never be criminal liability for causing physical harm to someone by subjecting them to a force of nature. We conclude only that for purposes of § 15A, the ocean, not being subject to human control, was not, in the instant case, an object or instrumentality which could be found by the jury to be a dangerous weapon. Accordingly, the defendant's motion for required findings of not guilty on the indictments charging him with assault and battery by means of a dangerous weapons should have been allowed.

5. *Conclusion.* It follows from what we have said that the judgments entered on the indictments charging kidnapping and attempted murder are affirmed. The judgments entered on the indictments charging assault and battery by means of a dangerous weapon are reversed, the verdicts are set aside and judgments for the defendant are to enter on those indictments.[8]

So ordered.

8. The Commonwealth has not argued that the defendant should, in any event, be resentenced on the lesser offense of assault and battery, presumably for the reason, if no other, that it would make no practical difference. The sentence imposed on the conviction for assault and battery by means of a dangerous weapon was to be served concurrently with that imposed on the attempted murder conviction.

Philip J. COOPER, Administrator Pendente Lite of the Estate of W.A. Bisson, Deceased, Plaintiff-Appellant,

v.

Charles AUSTIN, Defendant-Appellant.

Court of Appeals of Tennessee, Western Section, at Jackson.

Feb. 18, 1992.

Application for Permission to Appeal Denied by Supreme Court May 26, 1992.

837 S.W.2d 606 (Tenn. Ct. App. 1992)

CRAWFORD, Judge.

This is a will contest case involving a codicil to the Last Will and Testament of Wheelock A. Bisson, M.D., deceased. Phillip Cooper, Administrator *pendente lite* of the estate, is a nominal party only; the real parties in interest are the proponent of the codicil, Alois B. Greer, and the contestant, Charles Austin.

Dr. Bisson's will, which is not contested, was executed June 18, 1982. Dr. Bisson died in 1985, and shortly thereafter Greer filed a petition in probate court to admit the June 18, 1982, will and two codicils thereto dated August 20, 1984, and August 6, 1985, respectively, to probate as and for the Last Will and Testament of Wheelock A. Bisson, M.D. By order entered November 26, 1985, the probate court admitted the paper writings to probate as the Last Will and Testament of Dr. Bisson.

On May 20, 1986, Austin filed a petition in probate court to contest the two codicils[1], and, after answer to the petition by Greer, the probate court certified the contest to circuit court by order entered August 13, 1986.

No action was taken in circuit court until the administrator pendente lite filed a "Complaint to Establish Will and Codicil" on November 9, 1988. Austin's answer to the complaint, inter alia, denied that either codicil had been properly executed by the decedent or properly witnessed and further denied that the codicils had any legal validity or effect.

Greer filed a motion for summary judgment in October, 1990, seeking to have Austin's case dismissed on the grounds that it was barred by T.C.A. § 32–4–108 (1986), because it was brought more than two years from the entry of the order admitting the will to probate. The trial court denied this motion.

1. The codicil dated August 6, 1985, made no property disposition, but merely appointed Greer as executrix of the estate. During the course of the circuit court trial, the proponent withdrew this codicil from evidence. Since it is not involved in this appeal we will omit further reference to it in this Opinion.

On March 26, 1991, a jury trial was held on the issue of devisavit vel non as to the 1984 codicil. The 1982 will was introduced into evidence by stipulation, and Greer offered the 1984 codicil through the attesting witnesses.

In his 1982 will, Dr. Bisson left everything to his wife and if she predeceased him he left the majority of his estate to Austin. This disposition was changed by the 1984 codicil which provides:

CODICIL TO MY LAST WILL
AND TESTAMENT

I, Wheelock Alexander Bisson, M.D., of 2312 Park Avenue, Memphis, Shelby County, Tennessee, this August 20th, 1984. Bequeath that my adopted daughter, Alois B. Greer, receive a child's share of my estate which will consist of all real property, personal property, household furniture and any and all savings which I might have at the time of my demise.

/s/ Wheelock A. Bisson, M.D.
WHEELOCK ALEXANDER BISSON, M.D.

/s/ Michael E. Harrison
WITNESS

3907 Kerwin Dr. Memphis, Tenn. 38138
ADDRESS

/s/ Charles L. Harrison
WITNESS

4905 Sagewood, Mphs., TN. 38116
ADDRESS

Sworn to and subscribed before me this 20th day of August, 1984.

/s/ Lillie M. Thomas
NOTARY PUBLIC

My Commission Expires:
Jan. 5, 1987

On direct examination, Michael Harrison stated that he signed the codicil in the presence of Dr. Bisson. He then gave the following testimony regarding that signing:

Q. All right. When you got ready to sign did Dr. Bisson indicate to you what you were signing as a witness?
A. Yes. At the time I had no idea what a codicil was.
Q. All right.
A. But I did—I did witness it.

On cross examination, Michael Harrison gave the following testimony:

Q. All right. You didn't know what this document was now you've got in front of you at the time you signed it. Correct? This is one dated August, 1984.
A. I didn't understand your question.
Q. Well, Dr. Bisson didn't tell you what it was, he just said he needed a paper signed and notarized. Right?
A. He didn't tell me anything. I was asked to witness the document. He told Ms. Thomas. She notarized it, I was asked to witness it.
Q. At the time did you know what the document was—
A. No, sir.
Q. . . . that you were witnessing? Pardon me?
A. No, sir.
Q. And Dr. Bisson didn't tell you what it was?
A. No, sir.
Q. You didn't ask anybody what it was?
A. No, sir.

Charles Harrison, the other witness appearing on the 1984 codicil, testified on direct examination pertinent to the issue before us:

Q. All right. Do you recall the occasion when you signed this document?
A. Yes, sir.
Q. Okay. Will you give us the background as to how you came to be involved with this document at all?
A. On this particular day, the 20th of August, 1984, we were on our way back from Memorial Park—the rotunda at the Memorial Park Cemetery, and Dr. Bisson was seated on the front seat of the limousine with me.

And he said, when you get back, you know, to my place—which he referred that was his home—he said, when you get back to my place, he said, I have something I want you all to do for me. And so I said, well, okay, Doc. And that was that. And so the rest of the people that was in the limousine they were just carrying on casual conversation. So when we got back to his residence on Park Avenue we were letting them out of the limousines and he said, don't leave, come on in, I have something, you know, I want you to take care of for me. And so he asked me where was Ms. Thomas. I said, well, she's at the funeral home. He said, well, call her and tell her to come down here, I need her—you know, I need her here, you know, on this too. And so when we got inside—We came through the side entrance and we went up to his front office. And he said, I have this codicil that I want you all to notarize for me and witness, and that's how I came in contact with him.

Q. All right, sir. Now, at the time that this document was signed were you present?
A. Yes, sir.
Q. And did you see Dr. Bisson sign this document?
A. Yes, sir.
Q. Was your brother Michael also present?
A. Yes, sir.
Q. And all three of you were together at the time; is that correct?
A. Yes, sir.
Q. Ms. Thomas is on there as a notary. Was she also in the room or was she not?
A. No, she was in the room. Yes, sir.
Q. All right. And Dr. Bisson asked you all to sign this; is that correct?
A. Yes, sir.
Q. And all three of you signed it in each other's presence?
A. That's correct.

* * * * * *

The pertinent testimony from Charles Harrison on cross examination is:

Q. Now, Dr. Bisson didn't tell you what was in the document that you were signing. Correct?
A. No, he did not.
Q. And he didn't tell you what the document was?
A. Yes, sir, he did.
Q. Well, let me ask you. Do you recall giving a deposition, meaning when you came to my conference room up at my office January 14, 1987 and you swore to tell the truth, and there was a court reporter—it wasn't this woman, but another woman with a machine like that that took down your testimony? Do you recall that?
A. January the 14th of '87?
Q. Yes, sir.
A. I remember coming to your office, yes, sir.
Q. All right.
A. I don't remember the exact date, but I do remember coming to your office.
Q. Have you had a chance to look over this document—this deposition transcript?
A. No, sir.
Q. I asked you on page 40 at that time when you were under oath, I said—At line 3 you said, I just glanced over it. I didn't stop, I just glanced over it.
Question: (Line 5) Did Dr. Bisson tell you what was in it?
Answer: No, sir.
Question: Did he tell you what it was?
Answer: No, sir.
Was that your testimony at that time? Would you agree with me that your memory was probably better about this in January of 1987, which would be, what, four years ago?
A. I'm not playing with my memory, but I'd say that—well, you know, I—
Q. Would you accept that as the truth if that's what you said then?
A. Yes, sir.
Q. So Dr. Bisson didn't elaborate as to what the document was, he said I want you to witness a document. He had the document already. Right?
A. Right.
Q. You didn't give it to him?
A. No.
Q. Okay. And then he signed it and he said, okay, now you sign it, and that was it. Correct?
A. Yes, sir, basically. He didn't say sign it, he said witness it.
Q. Witness it. And then there wasn't any more conversation about it after you witnessed it, y'all got up and left. Correct?
A. Right.

On re-direct examination, Charles Harrison testified as follows:

Q. Mr. Harrison, be very careful now and think regarding both what you said previously and what you just said.

Are you absolutely certain that Dr. Bisson told you what it was he wanted you to witness?

A. MR. MITCHELL: Note my objection to the leading, Your Honor. He never testified he knew what it was.

THE COURT: He did testify, I believe, in his direct-examination. He said that Dr. Bisson said he had a codicil that he wanted witnessing.

MR. MITCHELL: Yes, sir, that's all he said.
Q. (BY MR. BEATY) Is that what you recall today as to what he said?
A. Yes, sir.

MR. BEATY: That's all I have.

Charles Harrison's re-cross examination is:

Q. But that was before you ever went in the room?
A. I beg your pardon.

Q. That was before you ever went into the room, that was when you were out in the car?
A. Right.
Q. When you went in the room he didn't say what it was or what was in it, just like you testified four years ago. Right?
A. Right.

Lillie Thomas, who appears as a notary public on the 1984 codicil, testified that all Dr. Bisson said in her presence was that he had a paper that he wanted her to notarize and that he said nothing in her presence about the paper being a will, a codicil or anything of that sort. We quote from the testimony:

Q. All right. And what did Dr. Bisson say about it in your presence?
A. He said I have a—he said a paper that I want you to notarize for me.
Q. All right. Did he use any language: will, codicil, anything of that sort?
A. No. He said a paper.
Q. All right. Did he sign it in your presence?
A. Yes, sir.
Q. Did he sign it in the presence of the other witnesses?
A. Yes, sir.
Q. Now Michael Harrison was present?
A. Yes, sir.
Q. And Charles Harrison, also; is that correct?
A. Yes, sir.

Following the testimony of these witnesses, counsel for Austin moved the court to disallow submission of the codicil to the jury on the grounds that the codicil's proponent, Mrs. Greer, had not met her burden of proof pursuant to T.C.A. § 32–1–104, regarding the manner in which a will must be executed.

The trial court granted Austin's motion and directed a verdict on the grounds that Ms. Greer had not proved the proper execution of the codicil. Accordingly, judgment was entered declaring that the last will and testament of Wheelock A. Bisson dated June 18, 1982, be admitted to probate without any codicils.

Greer has appealed and presents two issues for review. The first issue is whether the trial court erred in denying Greer's motion for summary judgment on the grounds that Mr. Austin's will contest was barred by T.C.A. § 32–4–108 (Supp. 1991) which provides:

All ***actions*** or ***proceedings*** to set aside the probate of any will, or petitions to certify such will for an issue of **devisavit vel non**, must be brought within two (2) years from entry of the order admitting the will to probate, or be forever barred, saving, however, to persons under the age of eighteen (18) years or of unsound mind at the time the cause of action accrues, the rights conferred by § 28–1–106. (Emphasis added.)

Greer contends that this statute bars Austin's action, because the 1984 codicil was admitted to probate by order entered November 26, 1985, and Austin filed no pleading in circuit court until he filed an answer to the complaint on December 2, 1988. Greer argues that the filing of the complaint in circuit court was the commencement of the action pursuant to Rule 3, Tennessee Rules of Civil Procedure, and because it was filed more than two years from the order of probate court admitting the will to probate, the action is barred by the two year statute of limitations in T.C.A. § 32–4–108.

We must respectfully disagree with Greer for several reasons. The statute itself is clear and unambiguous. It is confined to actions to set aside the probate of a will or to petitions to certify a will for an issue of devisavit vel non. Obviously, the proceedings contemplated by this statute are proceedings that take place in the probate court. It is equally clear that the proceeding in the circuit court on the issue of devisavit vel non after the case is certified from the probate court to the circuit court is in substance an original proceeding to probate the will, separate and distinct from any proceedings held in probate court. *Bearman v. Camatsos,* 215 Tenn. 231, 385 S.W.2d 91 (1964); *Arnold v. Marcom,* 49 Tenn.App. 161, 352 S.W.2d 936 (1961). In a proceeding of this nature, no particular form of pleading is required. All that is required is that the proponent shall offer it as a will and the contesting party shall deny it. See *Bowman v. Helton,* 7 Tenn.App. 325 (1928).

Finally, it has long been held in this state that the right of a contestant to resist the probate of a will is a preliminary matter and presents a separate and distinct issue from the issue of devisavit vel non, and that the order of the probate court sustaining or denying the right to contest the will in an appealable order. See *Winters v. American Trust Co.,* 158 Tenn. 479, 14 S.W.2d 740 (1929). T.C.A. § 32–4–108 clearly applies only to this separate action.

We hold that the statute of limitations set out in T.C.A. § 32–4–108 applies only to the proceeding filed in the probate court seeking to set aside the probate of a will or a certification for a will contest.

The second issue for review is whether the trial court erred in directing a verdict for the contestant Austin by refusing to allow the 1984 codicil to be submitted to the jury.

The rule for determining a motion for directed verdict requires the trial judge and the reviewing court on appeal to look to all of the evidence, taking the strongest legitimate view of it in favor of the opponent of the motion and allowing all reasonable inferences from it in his favor. The court must discard all countervailing evidence, and if there is then any dispute as to any material determinative evidence or any doubt as to the conclusion to be drawn from the whole evidence, the motion must be denied. *Tennessee Farmers Mut. Ins. Co. v. Hinson,* 651 S.W.2d 235 (Tenn. App. 1983).

The court should not direct a verdict if there is any material evidence in the record that would support a verdict for the plaintiff under any of the theories he had advanced. *See Wharton Transport Corp. v. Bridges,* 606 S.W.2d 521 (Tenn.1980).

The formal requirements for the execution of a will are set out in T.C.A. § 32–1–104 (1984), which provides:

> **Will other than holographic or nuncupative.**—The execution of a will, other than a holographic or nuncupative will, must be by the signature of the testator and of at least two (2) witnesses as follows:
>
> (1) The testator shall signify to the attesting witnesses that the instrument is his will and either:
>
> (A) Himself sign;
>
> (B) Acknowledge his signature already made; or
>
> (C) At his direction and in his presence have someone else sign his name for him; and
>
> (D) In any of the above cases the act must be done in the presence of two (2) or more attesting witnesses.
>
> (2) The attesting witness must sign:
>
> (A) In the presence of the testator; and
>
> (B) In the presence of each other.

Austin contended, and the trial court agreed, that Greer's proof failed to established that Dr. Bisson did "signify to the attesting witnesses that the [1984 codicil] is his will . . ." as required by the statute. Greer argues that the testimony of the attesting witnesses was sufficient to create an issue of fact for the jury as to whether Dr. Bisson so signified.

Austin relies primarily upon the case of *Lawrence v. Lawrence,* 35 Tenn.App. 648, 250 S.W.2d 781 (1951) which involved a will without an attestation clause and where the only surviving attesting witness testified both that the testatrix informed her that the instrument to be witnessed was the testatrix's will and also testified to the contrary by stating that she did not know that the instrument was a will. The Court of Appeals, in directing a verdict against the will, said:

> The meaning of this statute is clear, plain and unambiguous. When a testator calls upon persons to witness his will, " 'the testator shall signify to the attesting witnesses that the instrument in [sic] his will'." Surely it cannot be contended that this provision of the statute is doubtful of meaning. It simply means that the testator must state to the witnesses in substance that the paper writing is his will and that he wants them to sign it as witnesses.
>
> By the uncontradicted evidence before us that essential requisite of the execution of a valid will is lacking. The testatrix did not signify to the attesting witnesses that the instrument was the will of testatrix.

250 S.W.2d at 784.

Austin contends that the cases relied upon by Greer—*Whitlow v. Weaver,* 63 Tenn.App. 651, 478 S.W.2d 57 (Tenn.App. 1970); *Needham v. Doyle,* 39 Tenn.App. 597, 286 S.W.2d 601 (1955); and *Miller v. Thrasher,* 38 Tenn.App. 88, 251 S.W.2d 446 (1952), and *In re Estate of Bradley,* 817 S.W.2d 320 (Tenn.App.1991)—all involve wills which contained an attestation clause. He concedes that an attestation clause raises a strong presumption that the recitals therein contained are true and that contrary evidence raises a question for the jury. *Needham,* 286 S.W.2d at 601. We agree that these cases are distinguishable on their facts.

Greer also relies upon *Leathers v. Binkley,* 196 Tenn. 80, 264 S.W.2d 561 (1954). In *Leathers,* the will did not contain an attestation clause and the two attesting witnesses testified that they had signed the will in the presence of the testatrix and in the presence of each other. Neither witness testified specifically that the will had been declared by the testatrix to be her will at the time of the signing. In holding in favor of the will, the Court said:

> While it is true that neither Mr. Morrison nor Mrs. Gilmer remembered every detail of the signature and attestation of the will, the important fact in the record is that there was neither from Morrison, Mrs. Gilmer, nor the Notary Public, *a line of positive affirmative testimony that would support the allegations of the*

> *petition of contest, nor the verdict of the jury, that the will had not been regularly and legally executed in strict accordance with the requirements of Code, sec. 8089.4.*
>
> "Where, for instance, the subscribing witnesses testify that they do not recollect the circumstances, but do recognize their signatures, and declare that they would not have placed them to the instrument unless they had seen the testator sign it, or heard him acknowledge his signature, the due execution may be presumed." Sizer's Pritchard on Wills, sec. 336, p. 380.
>
> "In establishing the facts essential to the validity of the will by a preponderance of the evidence, proponents are, however, not obliged in all cases to prove each fact by direct evidence; but they may rely upon presumptions. There is, at the outset, no presumption that the alleged testator executed the will in question or any will; but when a paper propounded as a will is shown to have been signed by the alleged testator and the requisite number of witnesses, ***in the absence of any satisfactory evidence to the contrary*** the presumption is that all the formalities have been complied with." (Our Emphasis.) Page on Wills, Vol 2, sec. 755, p. 462.
>
> The forgoing statement is supported by cases from many jurisdictions, including Georgia, Illinois, Iowa, Missouri, Montana, New Jersey, New Mexico and South Carolina. Compare: Annotations, 47 L.R.A., N.S., 722; 76 A.L.R. 604; 14 L.R.A., N.S., 255; Ann.Cas. 426.

264 S.W.2d at 563. (Emphasis added.)

Austin asserts that *Leathers* is not controlling authority for the case at bar because in *Leathers* there was no positive affirmative testimony that the will had not been regularly and legally executed. We agree with Austin the *Leathers* turned on that point, so we must examine the testimony in the case at bar to determine if there is uncontroverted positive testimony that Dr. Bisson did not "signify to the attesting witnesses" that the 1984 instrument was his will or codicil.

In examining the testimony of the witnesses, we must look at the testimony in the best light and afford to it all legitimate inferences. With that direction in mind, we will examine the testimony.

Charles Harrison's testimony is to the effect that prior to the gathering of attesting witnesses, notary public and testator, testator told him that he, the testator, had "this codicil that I want you all to notarize for me and witness." He specifically pointed out that this statement by Dr. Bisson was made before the gathering for the signing of the instrument.

Michael Harrison's testimony indicates both that he was told by Dr. Bisson that it was a codicil to be witnessed and that Dr. Bisson did not tell him what it was that he was witnessing. He specifically testified that he did not know what the document was. These contradictory statements effectively eliminate any testimony from this witness on that fact. *Taylor v. Nashville Banner Pub. Co.,* 573 S.W.2d 476 (Tenn.App.1978) cert. den. 441 U.S. 923, 99 S.Ct. 2032, 60 L.Ed.2d 396 (1979); *Donaho v. Large,* 25 Tenn.App. 433, 158 S.W.2d 447 (1941).

Lillie Thomas, the notary public, testified that Dr. Bisson said he had a paper to be witnessed and he did not use any language such as will, codicil or anything of that sort. Dr. Bisson's statement was made at the time the parties gathered for the signing.

An examination of the witness' testimony indicates that there is uncontroverted affirmative proof that Dr. Bisson did not signify to at least one attesting witness that the instrument to be witnessed was his will or a codicil thereto. Therefore, the trial court correctly directed a verdict against the admission of the will.

The judgment of the trial court is affirmed and this case is remanded to the trial court for such further proceedings as may be necessary.

Costs of the appeal are assessed against the appellant.

TOMLIN, P.J. (W.S.), and HIGHERS, J., concur.

CASE

DEAN et al. v. DICKEY et al.
No. 4662.

Court of Civil Appeals of Texas. El Paso.
Sept. 28, 1949.

Rehearing Denied Oct. 26, 1949.
225 S.W.2d 999 (Tex. Civ. App. 1949)

MCGILL, Justice.

The sole question presented by this appeal is whether a typewritten instrument of testamentary character typed wholly by Trollis Dell Dickey on June 12, 1945, and intended by him to be his last will and testament, and signed by him and one witness in ink, is entitled to probate as the holographic will of the said Trollis Dell Dickey, Deceased. The trial court affirmed the order of the County Court denying probate of the instrument, and this appeal has been duly perfected.

The Statutes applicable on June 12, 1945, are the following: Vernon's Texas Civil Statutes:

Art. 8283: "Every last will and testament except where otherwise provided by law, shall be in writing and signed by the testator or by some other person by his direction and in his presence, and shall, if not wholly written by himself, be attested by two or more credible witnesses above the age of fourteen years, subscribing their names thereto in the presence of the testator."

Art. 8284: "Where the will is wholly written by the testator the attestation of the subscribing witnesses may be dispensed with."

Art. 3344: Sec. 4: "If the will was wholly written by the testator, by two witnesses to his handwriting, which may be made by affidavit taken in open court and subscribed to by the witnesses, or by deposition."

These Statutes construed together leave no room for doubt that the language employed in Art. 8283 "if not wholly written by himself"; in Art. 8284 "wholly written by the testator" and in Art. 3344, Sec. 4 "if the will was wholly written by the testator, by two witnesses to his handwriting", require that the words "wholly written" used in these Articles be construed to mean wholly written in the handwriting of the testator. Art. 8283 prescribes the requisites of a holographic will. Art. 8284 provides that when those requisites have been complied with, attestation by subscribing witnesses may be dispensed with, while Art. 3344, Sec. 4 prescribes the character of proof necessary to prove such will. To give the identical language "wholly written" used in these Statutes the meaning for which appellants contend would render Art. 8283 and Art. 3344, Sec. 4, inconsistent and repugnant, since such interpretation would make it impossible to prove a typewritten will in the manner prescribed by Art. 3344, Sec. 4, i.e., by two witnesses to the handwriting of the testator.

Appellants concede that this case is one of first impression in this State, and that the construction for which they contend is contrary to the overwhelming weight of authority in other jurisdictions where similar Statutes have been construed, citing 68 C.J., p. 719, Sec. 402, and 57 Am.Jur. p. 433, Sec. 634. The reason for the rule laid down by these authorities is ably stated in Re Dreyfus' Estate, 175 Cal. 417, 165 P. 941, L.R.A. 1917F, 391:

"From time immemorial, letters and words have been written with the hand by means of pen and ink or pencil of some description, and it has been a well-known fact that each individual who writes in this manner acquires a style of forming, placing, and spacing the letters and words which is peculiar to himself and which in most cases renders his writing easily distinguishable from that of others by those familiar with it or by experts in chirography who make a study of the subject and who are afforded an opportunity of comparing a disputed specimen with those admitted to be genuine. The provision that a will should be valid if entirely 'written, dated, and signed by the hand of the testator,' is the ancient rule on the subject. There can be no doubt that it owes its origin to the fact that a successful counterfeit of another's handwriting is exceedingly difficult, and that therefore the requirement that it should be in the testator's handwriting would afford protection against a forgery of this character."

See also: Adams' Ex'x v. Beaumont, 226 Ky. 311, 10 S.W.2d 1106; and McNeill v. McNeill, 261 Ky. 240, 87 S.W.2d 367, where the statutory language "wholly written" under construction is identical with that of ours. However, appellants contend that a different interpretation should be given to Articles 8283 and 8284, supra, for two reasons: First, because of Sec. 3, Art. 23:

"Definitions" of Title 1: "General Provisions" R.C.S., which provides:

" 'Written' or 'in writing' includes any representation of words, letters or figures, 'whether *by writing, printing or otherwise.*' " (Emphasis ours.)

Secondly: Because of the emergency clause of S.B. 328, enacted by the 50th Legislature, Acts of 1947, 50th Leg., Reg. Sess., Ch. 170, p. 275, which amended Articles 8283 and 8284 by substituting for the words "wholly written by himself" in Art. 8283, the words "wholly in the handwriting of the testator" and for the words "wholly written by the testator" in Art. 8284, the words "wholly written in the handwriting of the testator." The relevant portion of the emergency clause is "that under the present interpretation of the statute any form of writing including *typewriting, or printing or otherwise* (emphasis ours) is sufficient to constitute a will which leaves a dangerous and unsafe condition not properly protecting widows and orphans of this state". Section 3.

By the very terms of Art. 23, the meaning given the words "written or in writing" by Section 3 has no application where "a different meaning is apparent from the context". As above pointed out, Art. 8283–8284 and Art. 3344, Sec. 4, construed together leave no room for doubt as to the meaning of the words "wholly written" therein employed. Therefore, Art. 23, Sec. 3 has no application. For like reason, without application is the rule enunciated in Stanford et al v. Butler, 142 Tex. 692, 181 S.W.2d 269, loc. cit. 274(8, 9), 153 A.L.R. 1054:

> "* * * where a later act implies a particular construction of an existing law, and particularly where the existing law is ambiguous or its meaning uncertain, interpretation of the prior act by the Legislature as contained in the later act is persuasive when a court is called upon to interpret the prior law."

Articles 8283 and 8284, when construed with Art. 3344, Sec. 4, are not ambiguous, nor is their meaning uncertain. Furthermore, when S.B. 328 was enacted there had been no decision by any appellate court of this State construing Articles 8283 and 8284 as declared in the emergency clause. From the similarity of the language emphasized it is probable that the Legislature erroneously assumed that Art. 23, Sec. 3 was applicable and controlling in its construction of Articles 8283 and 8284. For this additional reason, the above quoted rule is inapplicable.

The judgment of the trial court is affirmed.

In re ESTATE OF Clifford P. KUSZMAUL, Deceased.

No. 85–647.

District Court of Appeal of Florida, Fourth District.

June 25, 1986.
491 So. 2d. 287 (Fla. Dist. Ct. App. 1986)

ON MOTION FOR REHEARING

LETTS, Judge.

The motion for rehearing is granted. The original opinion filed May 7, 1986, is withdrawn and we substitute the following:

This case involves the disposition of certain estate assets. The distribution hinges on whether a conformed copy of a will, found together with an original executed codicil, will suffice to uphold the provisions of that will and its codicil, despite the absence of the original executed last will and testament. The trial judge denied the petition for administration. Under the facts here presented, we disagree and reverse.

When the testator died, the interested parties fruitlessly searched for the original executed will, supposedly last seen in the decedent's possession. There is a dispute over where the copy of that will and the codicil were first located. It is conceded, however, that shortly after the testator died, a conformed copy of the will and the original of the executed codicil thereto, were found together among the decedent's personal possessions. The codicil stated in its concluding paragraph:

> THIRD. I hereby ratify and confirm my said Last Will and Testament except insofar as any part thereof is modified by this Codicil.

We begin by reaffirming our conclusion in *In the Estate of Parson,* 416 So.2d. 513, 515 (Fla. 4th DCA 1982) that there is a "presumption that a will which was in the possession of the testator prior to death and which cannot be located subsequent to death was destroyed by the testator with the intention of revoking it." We further continue to align ourselves with the proposition, also set forth in *Parson,* that "the presumption may only be overcome by competent and substantial evidence." *Id.* at 515. Unlike the trial judge, however, we are of the opinion that the facts of the case now before us yield competent and substantial evidence to overcome the presumption.

The proponents of the view that the instant will was revoked point to another decision of this court with somewhat similar facts. *See In re Estate of Baird,* 343 So.2d. 41 (Fla. 4th DCA 1977). However, there are important distinctions. In *Baird* the discovered executed codicil was not, so far as we can determine, accompanied by a copy of the will, as it was in the matter now before us. Further, while Mr. Kuszmaul, like Mr. Baird, showed continuing affection for the beneficiaries under the will, the former also wrote a letter to one of the beneficiaries under the will, after its execution, stating that property devised in that will would "someday . . . be yours."

We are of the opinion that the instant cause is more closely allied to the facts in the New York decision of *Will of Herbert,* 89 Misc.2d 340, 391 N.Y.S.2d 351 (1977) where the court held that the presumption was overcome because a copy of the will and the original codicil "were carefully kept together among [the testator's] personal possessions" and because it would be "unlikely that the testator intentionally revoked his will while retaining the codicil and a copy of the original will." *Id.* at 352.

We would also point to two Florida statutes not considered in *Baird.* The first of these is section 732.5105, Florida Statutes (1983) wherein it is stated that "the execution of a codicil referring to a previous will has the effect of republishing the will as modified by the codicil." True, that section does not set forth whether or not it is applicable if the executed original will cannot be found. However, the ensuing section 732.511, provides that even if a will has been revoked "it may be republished and made valid [by] . . . the execution of a codicil republishing it with the formalities required by this law for the execution of wills." The codicil before us now was executed with requisite formality.

In the sum of all that we have set forth above, we conclude that the presumption was overcome and the trial judge was in error.

REVERSED AND REMANDED IN ACCORDANCE HEREWITH.

DOWNEY and DELL, JJ., concur.

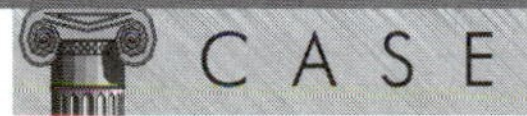

McCLAIN et al. v. ADAMS.

In re DOUGLASS' ESTATE.
No. 2340—7579.

Commission of Appeals of Texas, Section A.
Jan. 15, 1941.
146 S.W.2d 373 (Tex. Civ. App. 1941)

HICKMAN, Commissioner.

The subject matter of this litigation is an alleged nuncupative will. Annie Douglass, deceased, was the alleged testator; Willie Adams, defendant in error, was the proponent in the probate court; and Eliza McClain and others, plaintiffs in error, the next of kin of the deceased, were the contestants. The county court of Jefferson county sustained the contest and denied the probate. On appeal the district court of that county entered judgment admitting the alleged will to probate, which judgment was affirmed by the Court of Civil Appeals. 126 S.W.2d 61.

One of the requisites of a nuncupative will, as prescribed by article 3346, R.C.S., is that, "it be made in the time of the last sickness of the deceased." As we understand the position of plaintiffs in error, they concede that the trial court was warranted in finding that all other statutory requisites of a nuncupative will were met and complied with. Their sole contention here is that, as a matter of law, the words uttered by the deceased which are claimed to constitute her will were not uttered during her "last sickness" within the meaning of those words as used in the article above referred to. The case turns upon our decision of that single question and our statement will therefore be limited to such facts as are thought to be relevant thereto.

Annie Douglass, the alleged testator, died on September 8, 1934, at the age of more than sixty years. During the four years next preceding her death she had "spells". Dr. R. N. Miller, a witness for the proponent, began attending her professionally in June, 1934. In his opinion the original cause of her condition was malaria, but the immediate cause of her death was "aortic insufficiency," which he explained to be a weakened condition of the heart and aorta. The "spells" about which the other witnesses testified were in the nature of fainting spells brought about, according to the evidence as we understand it, by the general weakened condition of her heart. The words claimed to constitute a nuncupative will were spoken by the deceased at about 4:30 p.m. on Thursday, September 6, 1934. The proponent and four other witnesses were present in her bedroom at that time. One of the witnesses, Berttrue McDaniel, went to the home of the deceased to pay her some rent. He testified that he stayed there about two hours, and that while he was there she said to him:

> " 'Mr. McDaniels, I am feeling not very well at this time, and I know that I am going to die,' and says 'I want Willie Adams to have everything that I possess, and land and money.' She says 'She is the only one stood to me in my sick hour at my bedside.' Says, 'I haven't any relatives at all.' "
> "She called your name and said that?
> "Yes, sir, said 'Mr. McDaniels.' "
> Thereafter, on September 12, 1934, the witness committed the substance of the testimony to writing, his written memorandum being as follows:
> " 'Beaumont, Texas, Sept. 12, 1934.
> " 'On the 6 day of September, 1934, I was at Annie duglas home and she told me and others beside that at her death she wanted Willie Adams to have all that she had land and money and every thing else that she new she was going to die that she had no kin and she was the only one that sat at her bed side and waited on her and she wanted her to have all her estate at her death
> " 'Berttrue McDaniel.' "

He testified that when he went to the home of the deceased he found her in bed; that when he paid her the rent she handed him a receipt therefor which she had theretofore written. His testimony with regard to what occurred on the occasion is, in the main, corroborated by the other witnesses who were present at that time. There is practically no testimony concerning the condition of the deceased from Thursday afternoon until about noon on Saturday. The proponent testified that "she had taken the bed on a Thursday. Friday she was in and Thursday she taken the bed and stayed in bed from Thursday up to Friday." That testimony probably means that deceased did not leave her home on Friday but was in bed at least a part of that day. Shortly before noon on Saturday morning the deceased went to the home of a neighbor, Julia Keegans, to get Julia to pay a water bill for her which amounted to $1. Deceased had only a $5 bill with her and Julia was unable to change it. Deceased next went to a grocery store near by and purchased some bacon and a small sack of flour. She then returned to Julia's home and gave her $1 with which to pay the water bill. At that time she discovered that she had failed to bring the bill with her, whereupon Julia accompanied her home to get it. The deceased carried the bacon and Julia carried the flour. Shortly after reaching home the deceased became sick. Dr. Miller was later called and he came to see her about 6 o'clock that evening. She died some two hours or more thereafter.

All text-writers and opinions on the subject of what constitutes "last sickness" within the meaning of statutes relating to nuncupative wills seem to agree that the leading authority upon the question is Prince v. Hazleton, 20 Johns., N.Y., 502, 11 Am.Dec. 307. Of that case the author of Redfield On The Law of Wills, 4th Ed., in Vol. 1, ch. VI, Sec. 17a wrote: "* * * This subject came before the Court of Errors in New York, at an early day, * * * and is most exhaustively discussed by Chancellor Kent, and by Mr. Justice Woodworth. These opinions contain the substance of all the learning upon the subject of nuncupative wills, from the earliest days to that date and very little has occurred since, which could add much to the very full discussion which the subject there receives."

Our investigation has lead [sic] us to the conclusion that the foregoing is still an accurate statement of the situation. Nothing has been written to date, within our knowledge, which adds materially to the discussion contained in the majority and minority opinions in that case. In fact, there have been relatively few cases before the appellate courts in this generation in which a nuncupative will was offered for probate.

In the majority opinion Chancellor Kent announced this conclusion: "Upon the strength of so much authority, I feel myself warranted in concluding, that a nuncupative will is not good, unless it be made by a testator when he is in extremis, or overtaken by sudden and violent sickness, and has not time or opportunity to make a written will."

That has become known generally as the in extremis rule. The minority opinion in that case announced a somewhat more liberal rule of construction. From that decision two lines of decisions have emerged, one based upon the doctrine that the testator must be in extremis, as announced by Chancellor Kent in the majority opinion, and the other based upon the more liberal rule announced by Justice Woodworth in the dissenting opinion, that the testator need not actually be in extremis. The majority of the courts have adopted the Chancellor Kent doctrine. Schmitz v. Summers, 179 Miss. 260, 174 So. 569; O'Neill v. Smith, 33 Md. 569; Bellamy v. Peeler, 96 Ga. 467, 23 S.E. 387; Page v. Page, 2 Rob., Va., 424; Reese v. Hawthorn, 10 Grat., Va., 548. Annotations: 20 Am.Dec. 45; 9 A.L.R. 464; 13 L.R.A., N.S., 1092; 67 Am.St.Rep. 572.

The Court of Civil Appeals in its opinion in this case recognized the existence of both the rules above referred to, but concluded that Texas had not adopted the majority rule, and upon the theory that the minority rule was the more reasonable, it adopted and applied that rule. We cannot agree with its conclusions.

In the first place, this court has approved the rule of strict construction. While the facts in the cases below cited were not like those before us, still they presented situations calling upon the court to declare the rule of construction which should govern in cases like the instant one, and the court declared it in very clear language.

In Jones v. Norton, 10 Tex. 120, will be found the following: "* * * Nuncupative wills had their origin in the suddenness and urgency of the occasion, where there were present no means of making a formal written will, and no time for delay. And, among all civilized nations, where the necessity has been apparent, nuncupative wills have, under some regulations, been allowed. But the danger of fraud, in setting up such wills, has always exacted full and satisfactory proof of the existence of the necessity; and, where we have a statute regulating such wills, there is the same reason why we should require its conditions and requisites to be satisfactorily made out. * * *"

In Mitchell v. Vickers, 20 Tex. 377, it is stated: "Nuncupative wills are not favorites of the law. But as they are authorized by the statute, they must, when duly proved, be allowed and established. They are hedged round with numerous restrictions, to guard against the frauds for which oral wills offer so many facilities; and it is a well established rule, that strict proof is required of all the requisites prescribed by the law. ([Parsons v. Parsons] 2 Greenl. [Me.], 298; [In re Yarnall's Will] 4 Rawle [Pa.], 46 [26 Am.Dec. 115]; 20 Johns. 502; 1 Jarman on Wills, 89; Modern Probate of Wills, 304.) The provision of the statute (Hart.Dig. Art. 1113) is essentially a copy from the statute of frauds of the 29 Ch. 2, Sect. 19-21; and in substance the same provision is found in the codes of most of the other States; and everywhere a strict construction has been applied."

One of the authorities cited above, 20 Johns. 502, is the Prince-Hazleton case.

And in Watts v. Holland, 56 Tex. 54, Chancellor Kent's opinion in the Prince-Hazleton case, was cited in support of the following conclusion announced in the opinion: "* * * Wills of this kind, by the law, are allowed to exist, on its bare toleration, and under the shadow of its jealously; and the establishment of them is allowed, subject to exacting restrictions and conditions which correspond in degree with its fears of their dangerous qualities. * * *"

From the foregoing we conclude that early in the jurisprudence of this state the majority rule that the testator must be in extremis was approved by this court.

In the second place, we do not concur in the conclusion of the Court of Civil Appeals that the so-called liberal rule is the more reasonable. In Chancellor Kent's opinion, supra, written in 1822, reference was made to the fact that, in the ages of Henry the Eighth, Elizabeth and James reading and writing had become so widely diffused that nuncupative wills were confined to extreme cases. Under the view there expressed, which is the commonly accepted view, the more widely the ability to read and write becomes diffused, the less justification exists for recognizing nuncupative wills, except in cases of necessity. With the general diffusion of knowledge at this time, we can perceive of no reason why we should depart from or vary the terms of the rule of construction as heretofore pronounced by this court. The instant case appears to be free of the taint of fraud, but to adopt the rule pressed upon us would be to afford opportunity for fraud in many other cases.

Applying the approved rule to the facts of this case, it is obvious that Annie Douglass was not in extremis when she uttered the words claimed to constitute her will. Thereafter she had the time, ability and opportunity to prepare or have prepared a written will. About that there is no dispute in the record. Certain it is that she could have attended to that matter on Saturday morning when she was able to transact business and go in person to a store to purchase groceries. The probate court did not err in refusing to admit the alleged will to probate.

It is therefore ordered that the judgments of the district court and the Court of Civil Appeals both be reversed, and that judgment be here rendered that the alleged will be not admitted to probate. It is further ordered that upon receipt of the mandate of this court the district court certify this court's judgments to the county court for observance.

Opinion adopted by the Supreme Court.

The PEOPLE of the State of Illinois, Appellant,

v.

Robert SANDERS, Appellee.
No. 57801.
Supreme Court of Illinois.
Dec. 16, 1983.
99 Ill. 2d 262, 457 N.E.2d 1241 (1983)

SIMON, Justice:

The principal issued raised by this appeal is the construction and application to be given to the Illinois statute which prohibits husband and wife from testifying in criminal trials as to any communication or admission made one to the other or as to any conversation between them (Ill.Rev.Stat. 1981, ch. 38, par. 155–1). More precisely, the question is whether the privilege established by the statute is destroyed when the communication, admission or conversation in question is in the presence of children of the spouses (including a child of one of the spouses who is not the child of defendant) who are old enough to understand the content of the conversation. A secondary issue is whether the plain error rule (87 Ill.2d R. 615) should be applied to the admission of testimony about two conversations between spouses which may not have occurred in the presence of children but where no objection was advanced when all that was said in them was repeated in a third conversation which took place a few hours later and concerning which testimony was admissible.

A murder conviction of the defendant, Robert Sanders, in a jury trial in the circuit court of Cook County based in part upon the testimony of his wife was reversed by the appellate court (111 Ill.App.3d 1, 66 Ill.Dec. 761, 443 N.E.2d 687). We allowed the State's petition for leave to appeal (87 Ill.2d R. 315(a)).

During pretrial discovery, the defense filed a motion *in limine* to prevent the defendant's wife, Beverly Sanders, from testifying about conversations she had with her husband, the defendant. Shortly after it was filed, the public defender's office, which had been representing the defendant, was replaced by other appointed counsel, who represented the defendant at trial. Defendant's new attorney did not seek a ruling on the motion *in limine,* and that motion was never ruled upon. Neither did defendant's attorney object at trial to the wife's testimony.

She testified to three conversations with her husband which implicated him in the murder of which he was convicted. In the first conversation, which occurred the day before the murder, she testified the defendant told her while one or more of her children was present that he was going to rob the murder victim. The second conversation occurred in their bedroom in the early morning hours of the next day. During this conversation, at which no one else was present, the defendant gave his wife a ring and a watch which the woman who lived with the murder victim identified at trial as the victim's. The third conversation took place later that day. The defendant told her, she testified, that he had robbed the murder victim after striking him with a brick and tying him up. He also told her that he got the watch and ring during the robbery. This conversation, she said, was in the presence of their children.

The State argues that communications between spouses are privileged only when intended to be confidential. In this case the State contends the confidentiality of the first and third conversations was destroyed by the presence of their children. It contends that the second conversation was not confidential because the defendant must have expected that his wife would display the watch and ring he gave her by wearing them in public, and that he did not therefore intend his act to be confidential. The defendant argues that the record does not clearly show that their children were in the immediate presence of his wife and himself in a position to hear their first and third conversations, and that during the second communication he acted in reliance upon the expectation that what transpired would be confidential.

The starting point for our decision is the interpretation given in *People v. Palumbo* (1955), 5 Ill.2d 409, 125 N.E.2d 518, to the statute relating to the admissibility of interspousal communications (Ill.Rev.Stat.1981, ch. 38, par. 155–1). This court, in *Palumbo,* rejected the argument advanced by the defendant there that the statute covered all conversations between spouses, holding instead that the statutory privilege, like the similar common law privilege, applied only to conversations which were of a confidential character. The problem is to determine under what circumstances conversations between spouses are to be regarded as confidential in character. This court, in *Palumbo,* adopted the standards announced by the Supreme Court in *Wolfle v. United States* (1934), 291 U.S. 7, 14, 54 S.Ct. 279, 280, 78 L.Ed. 617, 620, a holding which the court 41 years later in *Trammel v. United States* (1980), 445 U.S. 40, 100 S.Ct. 906, 63 L.Ed.2d 186, said remained undisturbed, by adopting language from *Wolfle* which teaches the following: There is a presumption that interspousal communications are intended to be confidential. But if, because of the circumstances under which the communication took place, it appears that confidentiality was not intended, the communication is not to be regarded as privileged. In this regard, communications made in the presence of third persons are usually not regarded as privileged because they are not made in confidence. In *Palumbo* the communication testified to by the wife was regarded as not privileged because the entire conversation took place in the presence of a third person who, according to the wife, was trying to purchase narcotics from the husband, who was the defendant in the case.

We agree with the appellate court's conclusion that the evidence establishes that the third conversation took place in the presence of her sons, Robert who was 13, and two others who were 10 and 8 at the time. On cross-examination the wife repeated her direct testimony, which is quoted at length in the appellate court opinion, that the three children were present during the third conversation when the following exchange took place:

"Q. Did you know anything about Curtiss Lovelace?
A. Only what my husband had told me.
Q. You say he was bragging when he told you this?
A. Yes.
Q. He wasn't nervous, was he?
A. Not until he found out the man was dead.
Q. When he first told you was he nervous or bragging?
A. Not nervous.
Q. Pacing around the room?
A. No, he wasn't.
Q. Excited?
A. No.
Q. Who was present when this conversation occurred?
A. Robert, Albert and Pee Wee.
Q. They were all there?
A. Yes."

Following this exchange there was another reference during her cross-examination to the presence of the wife's oldest son:

"Q. And that day of the events that you have testified to, October the 14th, that day you had just finished a fight with your husband, right?
A. Yes.
Q. Did he threaten your son, Robert, in any way at that time?
A. No.
Q. But during all of these conversations, Robert, your son, was present, right?
A. Yes, he was."

The question presented in this case is whether the communications fell outside the ambit of the statute's protection because of the presence of the children. We have found no Illinois case holding that the confidentiality of a conversation between a husband and wife is preserved when it takes place in the presence of children. The appellate court appears to have exhaustively researched the subject and concluded, as we do, that the great weight of authority is that the presence of children of the spouses destroys confidentiality unless they are too young to understand what is being said. (See, *e.g., Master v. Master* (1960), 223 Md. 618, 166 A.2d 251; *Freeman v. Freeman* (1921), 238 Mass. 150, 130 N.E. 220; *Fuller v. Fuller* (1925), 100 W.Va. 309, 130 S.E. 270; McCormick, *Evidence* sec. 80, at 166 (2d ed. 1972); 97 C.J.S. *Witnesses* sec. 271, at 777 (1957).) Nothing in the record indicates that Robert, then 13 years old, was not old enough or sufficiently bright to understand the conversation at which he was present, particularly inasmuch as the wife's testimony indicates that some of it was directed to him. In these circumstances, under the rule followed in this State, his presence rendered the conversation ineligible for the protection of the statutory privilege.

The defendant argues that this court should recognize a privilege, which he concedes does not presently exist in Illinois, between parents and children which would include conversations between spouses at which their children are present. Courts in a few other jurisdictions have cloaked communications between parent and child with a privilege. (*In re Agosto* (D.Nev.1983), 553 F.Supp. 1298; *People v. Fitzgerald* (1979), 101 Misc.2d 712, 422 N.Y.S.2d 309.) The source of all privileges currently applicable in Illinois, with the exception of the attorney-client privilege which has a long-standing common law existence, is statutory. (See Ill.Rev.Stat. 1981, ch. 51, par. 5.1, Ill.Rev.Stat.1981, ch. 38, par. 104–14 (physician-patient); Ill.Rev.Stat.1981, ch. 51, par. 48.1 (clergymen); Ill.Rev.Stat.1981, ch. 91½, par. 810 (therapist-client); Ill.Rev.Stat.1981, ch. 111, par. 5533 (accountants); Ill.Rev.Stat.1981, ch. 51, par. 5.2 (rape crisis personnel-victims); Ill.Rev.Stat.1981, ch. 48, par. 640 (public officers, regarding unemployment compensation).) We decline, therefore, to introduce an additional privilege by judicial authority which would be applicable to communications between parents and children. Even if we were to initiate this type of privilege, to assist the defendant here we would have to extend it to children of only one spouse, for Robert, the oldest and presumably the most discerning of the children and who was privy at least to the third conversation, was the son of the wife and not the defendant. The statute by its terms does not contemplate such a stretch. Were we to recognize such a privilege under our judicial authority, it would be impossible to contain it logically from spreading to conversations with other relatives in whom a person might normally confide, or even to close friends.

Moreover, we are constrained not only by the legislature's lack of interest in extending an interspousal communications privilege to communications between parent and child, but also by the fact that evidentiary privileges of this sort exclude relevant evidence and thus work against the truthseeking function of legal proceedings. In this they are distinct from evidentiary rules, such as the prohibition against hearsay testimony, which promote this function by insuring the quality of the evidence which is presented. The privilege at issue here results not from a policy of safeguarding the quality of evidence at trial but from a policy of promoting family harmony independent of what might occur in a trial at some future date. The Supreme Court in *Trammel v. United States* (1980), 445 U.S. 40, 50, 100 S.Ct. 906, 912, 63 L.Ed.2d 186, 195, has stated:

> "Testimonial exclusionary rules and privileges contravene the fundamental principle that ' "the public . . . has a right to every man's evidence." ' *United States v. Bryan* [(1950), 339 U.S. 323, 331, 70 S.Ct. 724, 730, 94 L.Ed. 884, 891.] As such, they must be strictly construed and accepted 'only to the very limited extent that permitting a refusal to testify or excluding relevant evidences has a public good transcending the normally predominant principle of utilizing all rational means for ascertaining truth.' *Elkins v. United States* [(1960), 364 U.S. 206, 234, 80 S.Ct. 1437, 1454, 4 L.Ed.2d 1669, 1695] (Frankfurter, J., dissenting)."

See also 8 J. Wigmore, *Evidence* sec. 2285, at 527–28 (1961).

The expansion of existing testimonial privileges and acceptance of new ones involves a balancing of public policies which should be left to the legislature. A compelling reason is that while courts, as institutions, find it easy to perceive value in public policies such as those favoring the admission of all relevant and reliable evidence which directly assist the judicial function of ascertaining the truth, it is not their primary function to promote policies aimed at broader social goals more distantly related to the judiciary. This is primarily the responsibility of the legislature. To the extent that such policies conflict with truth seeking or other values central to the judicial task, the balance that courts draw might not reflect the choice the legislature would make.

The defendant argues, however, that inasmuch as the Federal courts have recognized the right of privacy to be of constitutional dimension in the context of certain functions which are intimately associated with the family, we should hold that communications of a confidential nature between a parent and his child enjoy an evidentiary privilege under the Constitution which did not exist under the common law. The defendant points out that in *In re Agosto* (D.Nev.1983), 553 F.Supp. 1298, and *People v. Fitzgerald* (1979), 101 Misc.2d 712, 422 N.Y.S.2d 309, courts have recognized the sort of constitutionally based privilege sought to be invoked here.

We need not decide here, and we do not decide, whether the decisions in *In re Agosto* or *People v. Fitzgerald* were sound, for the question in both of these cases was whether a parent or a child could be compelled against his will to testify against the other. (See also *In re A & M* (1978), 61 A.D.2d 426, 403 N.Y.S.2d 375 (same).) The testimony in the instant case, by contrast, was given by the defendant's wife, without protest and apparently of her own free will, after she was approached and requested to give it by an assistant State's Attorney.

We find this difference to be significant. Both *Agosto* and the New York courts, in holding that a constitutional privilege protected the communications there at issue, relied heavily on conjecture that a family member who is forced to testify against her will would face the unpleasant choice of aiding the criminal conviction of a loved one, perjuring herself on the stand, or risking a citation for contempt of court for refusing to testify, and the belief that the harshness of this choice has the effect of sundering the family relationship. (*In re Agosto* (D.Nev.1983), 553 F.Supp. 1298, 1309–10, 1326; *In re A & M* (1978), 61 A.D.2d 426, 432–33, 403 N.Y.S.2d 375, 380.) Such a fear is without foundation where, as in this case, the witness who is a family member volunteers her testimony; the voluntariness of the act is strong evidence that the choice the witness faced was an easy one for her to make. We conclude that even if the Constitution bestows a privilege on communications between a parent and a child, an issue which we do not decide here, that privilege may be waived by the testifying witness acting alone. Compare *United States v. Penn* (9th Cir. 1980), 647 F.2d 876, 882 (rejecting a challenge to a child's voluntary testimony based on due process, on which the right to privacy depends).

Although they were the subject of the motion *in limine* which was never ruled upon, no objection was advanced at trial when the wife testified about the first and second conversations. Under *Palumbo* the Illinois statute preventing testimony by either spouse concerning confidential communications between them creates only a privilege, and a privilege may be waived by the holder of it, in this case the husband. (See Comment, *Marital Privileges,* 46 Chi.-Kent L.Rev. 71, 82–83 (1969).) Therefore, in order to affirm the appellate court's reversal of the conviction, we would have to conclude that the court properly applied the plain error doctrine (87 Ill.2d R. 615) in holding that testimony regarding the first two conversations was improperly admitted. We believe the appellate court erred in reaching that conclusion.

The plain error doctrine is properly applied only when the question of guilt is close and the evidence in question might have significantly affected the outcome of the case (*People v. Jackson* (1981), 84 Ill.2d 350, 359, 49 Ill.Dec. 719, 418 N.E.2d 739; *People v. Pickett* (1973), 54 Ill.2d 280, 283, 296 N.E.2d 856), or where the error alleged is so substantial as to reflect on the fairness or impartiality of the trial regardless of how closely balanced the evidence is (*People v. Baynes* (1981), 88 Ill.2d 225, 233–34, 244, 58 Ill.Dec. 819, 430 N.E.2d 1070; *People v. Roberts* (1979), 75 Ill.2d 1, 14, 25 Ill.Dec. 675, 387 N.E.2d 331). The third conversation which we conclude, as the appellate court did, was properly admitted, incorporated substantially all of what was said in the first two conversations. The defendant, in the third conversation, discussed the robbery of the murder victim, said he hit him over the head with a brick, displayed several items of clothing taken from the victim, and referred to the watch and ring he had given his wife earlier that day. Thus, even conceding that no one overheard the first two conversations and that they were privileged and should have been excluded had timely objections been made, in practical effect they did no more than duplicate the incriminating content of the third conversation which was properly admitted. For that reason, the testimony which narrated the defendant's conversation and conduct during the first two conversations was not prejudicial. It added nothing to the third conversation that was needed by the prosecutor to implicate the defendant, and after the third conversation was in evidence, the evidence as to the defendant's guilt was no longer closely balanced.

Nor do we regard any errors that might have been made concerning the admissibility of the first and second conversations as depriving the accused of the substantial means of enjoying a fair and impartial trial (*People v. Roberts* (1979), 75 Ill.2d 1, 14, 25 Ill.Dec. 675, 387 N.E.2d 331; citing *People v. Burson* (1957), 11 Ill.2d 360, 370–71, 143 N.E.2d 237, see *People v. Whitlow* (1982), 89 Ill.2d 322, 342, 60 Ill. Dec. 587, 433 N.E.2d 629), as the admission of polygraph evidence does (see *People v. Baynes* (1981), 88 Ill.2d 225, 244, 58 Ill.Dec. 819, 430 N.E.2d 1070). As we have noted, the husband-wife testimonial privilege operates not to purge a trial of unreliable evidence but to withhold relevant and often highly reliable evidence from the trier of fact. The decision whether to apply the plain error doctrine where the evidence is not close is one of grace. (*People v. Roberts* (1979), 75 Ill.2d 1, 14, 25 Ill.Dec. 675, 387 N.E.2d 331; *People v. Burson* (1957), 11 Ill.2d 360, 370–71.) We believe it should not have been applied here, for the fairness and impartiality of the *trial* was not substantially compromised by the errors, if any took place. See *People v. Roberts* (1979), 75 Ill.2d 1, 14–15, 25 Ill.Dec. 675, 387 N.E.2d 331.

The defendant has raised a number of other issues, none of which were considered by the appellate court because of its erroneous reversal of the conviction on the ground of improper use of privileged communications. The judgment of the appellate court is reversed and the cause is remanded to that court for disposition of the issues raised by the defendant but not reached by its original decision. See *People v. Simpson* (1977), 68 Ill.2d 276, 284, 12 Ill.Dec. 234, 369 N.E.2d 1248.

Reversed and remanded, with directions.

Peter STANLEY, Sr., Petitioner,

v.

State of ILLINOIS.
No. 70–5014.

Argued Oct. 19, 1971.
Decided April 3, 1972.
405 U.S. 645 (1972)

Mr. Justice WHITE delivered the opinion of the Court.

Joan Stanley lived with Peter Stanley intermittently for 18 years, during which time they had three children.[1] When Joan Stanley died, Peter Stanley lost not only her but also his children. Under Illinois law, the children of unwed fathers become wards of the State upon the death of the mother. Accordingly, upon Joan Stanley's death, in a dependency proceeding instituted by the State of Illinois, Stanley's children[2] were declared wards of the State and placed with court-appointed guardians. Stanley appealed, claiming that he had never been shown to be an unfit parent and that since married fathers and unwed mothers could not be deprived of their children without such a showing, he had been deprived of the equal protection of the laws guaranteed him by the Fourteenth Amendment. The Illinois Supreme Court accepted the fact that Stanley's own unfitness had not been established but rejected the equal protection claim, holding that Stanley could properly be separated from his children upon proof of the single fact that he and the dead mother had not been married. Stanley's actual fitness as a father was irrelevant. In re Stanley, 45 Ill.2d 132, 256 N.E.2d 814 (1970).

Stanley presses his equal protection claim here. The State continues to respond that unwed fathers are presumed unfit to raise their children and that it is unnecessary to hold individualized hearings to determine whether particular fathers are in fact unfit parents before they are separated from their children. We granted certiorari, 400 U.S. 1020, 91 S.Ct. 584, 27 L.Ed.2d 631 (1971), to determine whether this method of procedure by presumption could be allowed to stand in light of the fact that Illinois allows married fathers—whether divorced, widowed, or separated—and mothers—even if unwed—the benefit of the presumption that they are fit to raise their children.

I

At the outset we reject any suggestion that we need not consider the propriety of the dependency proceeding that separated the Stanleys because Stanley might be able to regain custody of his children as a guardian or through adoption proceedings. The suggestion is that if Stanley has been treated differently from other parents, the difference is immaterial and not legally cognizable for the purposes of the Fourteenth Amendment. This Court has not, however, embraced the general proposition that a wrong may be done if it can be undone. Cf. Sniadach v. Family Finance Corp. of Bay View, 395 U.S. 337, 89 S.Ct. 1820, 23 L.Ed.2d 349 (1969). Surely, in the case before us, if there is delay between the doing and the undoing petitioner suffers from the deprivation of his children, and the children suffer from uncertainty and dislocation.

It is clear, moreover, that Stanley does not have the means at hand promptly to erase the adverse consequences of the proceeding in the course of which his children were declared wards of the State. It is first urged that Stanley could act to adopt his children. But under Illinois law, Stanley is treated not as a parent but as a stranger to his children, and the dependency proceeding has gone forward on the presumption that he is unfit to exercise parental rights. Insofar as we are informed, Illinois law affords him no priority in adoption proceedings. It would be his burden to establish not only that he would be a suitable parent but also that he would be the most suitable of all who might want custody of the children. Neither can we ignore that in the proceedings from which this action developed, the "probation officer," see App. 17, the assistant state's attorney, see *id.*, at 29–30, and the judge charged with the case, see *id.*, at 16–18, 23, made it apparent that Stanley, unmarried and impecunious as he is, could not now expect to profit from adoption proceedings.[3] The Illinois Supreme Court apparently recognized some or all of these considerations, because it did not suggest that Stanley's case was undercut by his failure to petition for adoption.

1. Uncontradicted testimony of Peter Stanley, App. 22.

2. Only two children are involved in this litigation.

3. The Illinois Supreme Court's opinion is not at all contrary to this conclusion. That court said: "[T]he trial court's comments clearly indicate the court's willingness to consider a *future* request by the father for *custody and guardianship.*" 45 Ill.2d 132, 135, 256 N.E.2d 814, 816. (Italics added.) See also the comment of Stanley's counsel on oral argument: "If Peter Stanley could have adopted his children, we would not be here today." Tr. of Oral Arg. 7.

Before us, the State focuses on Stanley's failure to petition for "custody and control"—the second route by which, it is urged, he might regain authority for his children. Passing the obvious issue whether it would be futile or burdensome for an unmarried father—without funds and already once presumed unfit—to petition for custody, this suggestion overlooks the fact that legal custody is not parenthood or adoption. A person appointed guardian in an action for custody and control is subject to removal at any time without such cause as must be shown in a neglect proceeding against a parent. Ill.Rev.Stat., c. 37, § 705–8. He may not take the children out of the jurisdiction without the court's approval. He may be required to report to the court as to his disposition of the children's affairs. Ill.Rev.Stat., c. 37, § 705–8. Obviously then, even if Stanley were a mere step away from "custody and control," to give an unwed father only "custody and control" would still be to leave him seriously prejudiced by reason of his status.

We must therefore examine the question that Illinois would have us avoid: Is a presumption that distinguishes and burdens all unwed fathers constitutionally repugnant? We conclude that, as a matter of due process of law, Stanley was entitled to a hearing on his fitness as a parent before his children were taken from him and that, by denying him a hearing and extending it to all other parents whose custody of their children is challenged, the State denied Stanley the equal protection of the laws guaranteed by the Fourteenth Amendment.

II

Illinois has two principal methods of removing nondelinquent children from the homes of their parents. In a dependency proceeding it may demonstrate that the children are wards of the State because they have no surviving parent or guardian. Ill.Rev.Stat., c. 37, §§ 702–1, 702–5. In a neglect proceeding it may show that children should be wards of the State because the present parent(s) or guardian does not provide suitable care. Ill.Rev.Stat., c. 37, §§ 702–1, 702–4.

The State's right—indeed, duty—to protect minor children through a judicial determination of their interests in a neglect proceeding is not challenged here. Rather, we are faced with a dependency statute that empowers state officials to circumvent neglect proceedings on the theory that an unwed father is not a "parent" whose existing relationship with his children must be considered.[4] "Parents," says the State, "means the father and mother of a legitimate child, or the survivor of them, or the natural mother of an illegitimate child, and includes any adoptive parent," Ill.Rev.Stat., c. 37, § 701–14, but the term does not include unwed fathers.

Under Illinois law, therefore, while the children of all parents can be taken from them in neglect proceedings, that is only after notice, hearing, and proof of such unfitness as a parent as amounts to neglect, an unwed father is uniquely subject to the more simplistic dependency proceeding. By use of this proceeding, the State, on showing that the father was not married to the mother, need not prove unfitness in fact, because it is presumed at law. Thus, the unwed father's claim of parental qualification is avoided as "irrelevant."

In considering this procedure under the Due Process Clause, we recognize, as we have in other cases, that due process of law does not require a hearing "in every conceivable case of government impairment of private interest." Cafeteria and Restaurant Workers Union etc. v. McElroy, 367 U.S. 886, 894, 81 S.Ct. 1743, 1748, 6 L.Ed.2d 1230 (1961). That case explained that "[t]he very nature of due process negates any concept of inflexible procedures universally applicable to every imaginable situation" and firmly established that "what procedures due process may require under any given set of circumstances must begin with a determination of the precise nature of the government function involved as well as of the private interest that has been affected by governmental action." *Id.*, at 895, 81 S.Ct., at 1748; Goldberg v. Kelly, 397 U.S. 254, 263, 90 S.Ct. 1011, 1018, 25 L.Ed.2d 287 (1970).

The private interest here, that of a man in the children he has sired and raised, undeniably warrants deference and, absent a powerful countervailing interest, protection. It is plain that the interest of a parent in the companionship, care, custody, and management of his or her children "come[s] to this Court with a momentum for respect lacking when appeal is made to liberties which derive merely from shifting economic arrangements." Kovacs v. Cooper, 336 U.S. 77, 95, 69 S.Ct. 448, 458, 93 L.Ed. 513 (1949) (Frankfurter, J., concurring).

The Court has frequently emphasized the importance of the family. The rights to conceive and to raise one's children have been deemed "essential," Meyer v. Nebraska, 262 U.S. 390, 399, 43 S.Ct. 625, 626, 67 L.Ed. 1042 (1923), "basic

4. Even while refusing to label him a "legal parent," the State does not deny that Stanley has a special interest in the outcome of these proceedings. It is undisputed that he is the father of these children, that he lived with the two children whose custody is challenged all their lives, and that he has supported them.

civil rights of man," Skinner v. Oklahoma, 316 U.S. 535, 541, 62 S.Ct. 1110, 1113, 86 L.Ed.1655 (1942), and "[r]ights far more precious . . . than property rights," May v. Anderson, 345 U.S. 528, 533, 73 S.Ct. 840, 843, 97 L.Ed. 1221 (1953). "It is cardinal with us that the custody, care and nurture of the child reside first in the parents, whose primary function and freedom include preparation for obligations the state can neither supply nor hinder." Prince v. Massachusetts, 321 U.S. 158, 166, 64 S.Ct. 438, 442, 88 L.Ed. 645 (1944). The integrity of the family unit has found protection in the Due Process Clause of the Fourteenth Amendment, Meyer v. Nebraska, *supra,* 262 U.S. at 399, 43 S.Ct. at 626, the Equal Protection Clause of the Fourteenth Amendment, Skinner v. Oklahoma, *supra,* 316 U.S., at 541, 62 S.Ct., at 1113, and the Ninth Amendment, Griswold v. Connecticut, 381 U.S. 479, 496, 85 S.Ct. 1678, 14 L.Ed.2d 510 (1965) (Goldberg, J., concurring).

Nor has the law refused to recognize those family relationships unlegitimized by a marriage ceremony. The Court has declared unconstitutional a state statute denying natural, but illegitimate, children a wrongful-death action for the death of their mother, emphasizing that such children cannot be denied the right of other children because familial bonds in such cases were often as warm, enduring, and important as those arising within a more formally organized family unit. Levy v. Louisiana, 391 U.S. 68, 71–72, 88 S.Ct. 1509, 1511, 20 L.Ed.2d 436 (1968). "To say that the test of equal protection should be the 'legal' rather than the biological relationship is to avoid the issue. For the Equal Protection Clause necessarily limits the authority of a State to draw such 'legal' lines as it chooses." Glona v. American Guarantee & Liability Ins. Co., 391 U.S. 73, 75–76, 88 S.Ct. 1515, 1516, 20 L.Ed.2d 441 (1968).

These authorities make it clear that, at the least, Stanley's interest in retaining custody of his children is cognizable and substantial.

For its part, the State has made its interest quite plain: Illinois has declared that the aim of the Juvenile Court Act is to protect "the moral, emotional, mental, and physical welfare of the minor and the best interests of the community" and to "strengthen the minor's family ties whenever possible, removing him from the custody of his parents only when his welfare or safety or the protection of the public cannot be adequately safeguarded without removal . . ." Ill.Rev.Stat., c. 37, § 701–2. These are legitimate interests, well within the power of the State to implement. We do not question the assertion that neglectful parents may be separated from their children.

But we are here not asked to evaluate the legitimacy of the state ends, rather, to determine whether the means used to achieve these ends are constitutionally defensible. What is the state interest in separating children from fathers without a hearing designed to determine whether the father is unfit in a particular disputed case? We observe that the State registers no gain towards its declared goals when it separates children from the custody of fit parents. Indeed, if Stanley is a fit father, the State spites its own articulated goals when it needlessly separates him from his family.

In Bell v. Burson, 402 U.S. 535, 91 S.Ct. 1586, 29 L.Ed.2d 90 (1971), we found a scheme repugnant to the Due Process Clause because it deprived a driver of his license without reference to the very factor (there fault in driving, here fitness as a parent) that the State itself deemed fundamental to its statutory scheme. Illinois would avoid the self-contradiction that rendered the Georgia license suspension system invalid by arguing that Stanley and all other unmarried fathers can reasonably be presumed to be unqualified to raise their children.[5]

5. Illinois says in its brief, at 21–23,

"[T]he only relevant consideration in determining the propriety of governmental intervention in the raising of children is whether the best interests of the child are served by such intervention.

"In effect, Illinois has imposed a statutory presumption that the best interests of a particular group of children necessitates some governmental supervision in certain clearly defined situations. The group of children who are illegitimate are distinguishable from legitimate children not so much by their status at birth as by the factual differences in their upbringing. While a legitimate child usually is raised by both parents with the attendant familial relationships and a firm concept of home and identity, the illegitimate child normally knows only one parent—the mother. . . .

". . . The petitioner has premised his argument upon particular factual circumstances—a lengthy relationship with the mother . . . a familial relationship with the two children, and a general assumption that this relationship approximates that in which the natural parents are married to each other.

". . . Even if this characterization were accurate (the record is insufficient to support it) it would not affect the validity of the statutory definition of parent. . . . The petitioner does not deny that the children are illegitimate. The record reflects their natural mother's death. Given these two factors, grounds exist for the State's intervention to ensure adequate care and protection for these children. This is true whether or not this particular petitioner assimilates all or none of the normal characteristics common to the classification of fathers who are not married to the mothers of their children."

It may be, as the State insists, that most unmarried fathers are unsuitable and neglectful parents.[6] It may also be that Stanley is such a parent and that his children should be placed in other hands. But all unmarried fathers are not in this category: some are wholly suited to have custody of their children.[7] That much the State readily concedes, and nothing in this record indicates that Stanley is or has been a neglectful father who has not cared for his children. Given the opportunity to make his case, Stanley may have been seen to be deserving of custody of his offspring. Had this been so, the State's statutory policy would have been furthered by leaving custody in him.

Carrington v. Rash, 380 U.S. 89, 85 S.Ct. 775, 13 L.Ed.2d 675 (1965), dealt with a similar situation. There we recognized that Texas had a powerful interest in restricting its electorate to bona fide residents. It was not disputed that most servicemen stationed in Texas had no intention of remaining in the State; most therefore could be deprived of a vote in state affairs. But we refused to tolerate a blanket exclusion depriving all servicemen of the vote, when some servicemen clearly were bona fide residents and when "more precise tests," *id.*, at 95, 85 S.Ct., at 779, were available to distinguish members of this latter group. "By forbidding a soldier ever to controvert the presumption of nonresidence," *id.*, at 96, 85 S.Ct., at 780, the State, we said, unjustifiably effected a substantial deprivation. It viewed people one-dimensionally (as servicemen) when a finer perception could readily have been achieved by assessing a serviceman's claim to residency on an individualized basis.

> "We recognize that special problems may be involved in determining whether servicemen have actually acquired a new domicile in a State for franchise purposes. We emphasize that Texas is free to take reasonable and adequate steps, as have other States, to see that all applicants for the vote actually fulfill the requirements of bona fide residence. But [the challenged] provision goes beyond such rules. '[T]he presumption here created is . . . definitely conclusive—incapable of being overcome by proof of the most positive character.' " *Id.*, at 96, 85 S.Ct., at 780.

"All servicemen not residents of Texas before induction," we concluded, "come within the provision's sweep. Not one of them can ever vote in Texas, no matter" what their individual qualifications. *Ibid.* We found such a situation repugnant to the Equal Protection Clause.

Despite *Bell* and *Carrington,* it may be argued that unmarried fathers are so seldom fit that Illinois need not undergo the administrative inconvenience of inquiry in any case, including Stanley's. The establishment of prompt efficacious procedures to achieve legitimate state ends is a proper state interest worthy of cognizance in constitutional adjudication. But the Constitution recognizes higher values then speed and efficiency.[8] Indeed, one might fairly

---

See also Illinois' Brief 23 ("The comparison of married and putative fathers involves exclusively factual differences. The most significant of these are the presence or absence of the father from the home on a day-to-day basis and the responsibility imposed upon the relationship"), *id.*, at 24 (to the same effect), *id.*, at 31 (quoted below in n. 6), *id.*, at 24–26 (physiological and other studies are cited in support of the proposition that men are not naturally inclined to childrearing), and Tr. of Oral Arg. 31 ("We submit that both based on history or [*sic*] culture the very real differences . . . between the married father and the unmarried father, in terms of their interests in children and their legal responsibility for their children, and the statute here fulfills the compelling governmental objective of protecting children . . .").

6. The State speaks of "the general disinterest of putative fathers in their illegitimate children" (Brief 8) and opines that "[i]n most instances the natural father is a stranger to his children." Brief 31.

7. See In re T., 8 Mich.App. 122, 154 N.W. 2d 27 (1967). There is a panel of the Michigan Court of Appeals in unanimously affirming a circuit court's determination that the father of an illegitimate son was best suited to raise the boy, said:

> "The appellants' presentation in this case proceeds on the assumption that placing Mark for adoption is inherently preferable to rearing by his father, that uprooting him from the family which he knew from birth until he was a year and a half old, secretly institutionalizing him and later transferring him to strangers is so incontrovertibly better that no court has the power even to consider the matter. Hardly anyone would even suggest such a proposition if we were talking about a child born in wedlock.
>
> "We are not aware of any sociological data justifying the assumption that an illegitimate child reared by his natural father is less likely to receive a proper upbringing than one reared by his natural father who was at one time married to his mother, or that the stigma of illegitimacy is so pervasive it requires adoption by strangers and permanent termination of a subsisting relationship with the child's father." *Id.*, at 146, 154 N.W.2d, at 39.

8. Cf. Reed v. Reed, 404 U.S. 71, 76, 92 S.Ct. 251, 254, 30 L.Ed.2d 225 (1971). "Clearly the objective of reducing the workload on probate courts by eliminating one class of contests is not without some legitimacy. . . . [But to] give a mandatory preference to members of either sex over members of the other, merely to accomplish the elimination of hearings on the merits, is to make the very kind of arbitrary legislative choice forbidden by the Equal Protection Clause of the Fourteenth Amendment." Carrington v. Rash, 380 U.S. 89, 96, 85 S.Ct. 775, 780 (1965), teaches the same lesson. ". . . States may not casually deprive a class of individuals of the vote because of some remote administrative benefit to the State. Oyama v. [State of] California, 332 U.S. 633, 68 S.Ct. 269, 92 L.Ed. 249. By forbidding a soldier ever to controvert the presumption of nonresidence, the Texas Constitution imposes an invidious discrimination in violation of the Fourteenth Amendment."

say of the Bill of Rights in general, and the Due Process Clause in particular, that they were designed to protect the fragile values of a vulnerable citizenry from the overbearing concern for efficiency and efficacy that may characterize praiseworthy government officials no less, and perhaps more, than mediocre ones.

Procedure by presumption is always cheaper and easier than individualized determination. But when, as here, the procedure forecloses the determinative issues of competence and care, when it explicitly disdains present realities in deference to past formalities, it needlessly risks running roughshod over the important interests of both parent and child. It therefore cannot stand.[9]

Bell v. Burson held that the State could not, while purporting to be concerned with fault in suspending a driver's license, deprive a citizen of his license without a hearing that would assess fault. Absent fault, the State's declared interest was so attenuated that administrative convenience was insufficient to excuse a hearing where evidence of fault could be considered. That drivers involved in accidents, as a statistical matter, might be very likely to have been wholly or partially at fault did not foreclose hearing and proof in specific cases before licenses were suspended.

We think that Due Process Clause mandates a similar result here. The State's interest in caring for Stanley's children is *de minimis* if Stanley is shown to be a fit father. It insists on presuming rather than proving Stanley's unfitness solely because it is more convenient to presume than to prove. Under the Due Process Clause that advantage is insufficient to justify refusing a father a hearing when the issue at stake is the dismemberment of his family.

III

The State of Illinois assumes custody of the children of married parents, divorced parents, and unmarried mothers only after a hearing and proof of neglect. The children of unmarried fathers, however, are declared dependent children without a hearing on parental fitness and without proof of neglect. Stanley's claim in the state courts and here is that failure to afford him a hearing on his parental qualifications while extending it to other parents denied him equal protection of the laws. We have concluded that all Illinois parents are constitutionally entitled to a hearing on their fitness before their children are removed from their custody. It follows that denying such a hearing to Stanley and those like him while granting it to other Illinois parents in inescapably contrary to the Equal Protection Clause.[10]

The judgment of the Supreme Court of Illinois is reversed and the case is remanded to that court for proceedings not inconsistent with this opinion. It is so ordered.

Reversed and remanded.

Mr. Justice POWELL and Mr. Justice REHNQUIST took no part in the consideration or decision of this case.

Mr. Justice DOUGLAS joins in Parts I and II of this opinion.

Mr. Chief Justice BURGER, with whom Mr. Justice BLACKMUN concurs, dissenting.

9. We note in passing that the incremental cost of offering unwed fathers an opportunity for individualized hearings on fitness appears to be minimal. If unwed fathers, in the main, do not care about the disposition of their children, they will not appear to demand hearings. If they do care, under the scheme here held invalid, Illinois would admittedly at some later time have to afford them a properly focused hearing in a custody or adoption proceeding.

Extending opportunity for hearing to unwed fathers who desire and claim competence to care for their children creates no constitutional or procedural obstacle to foreclosing those unwed fathers who are not so inclined. The Illinois law governing procedure in juvenile cases. Ill.Rev.Stat., c. 37, § 704-1 et seq., provides for personal service, notice by certified mail, or for notice by publication when personal or certified mail service cannot be had or when notice is directed to unknown respondents under the style of "All whom it may Concern." Unwed fathers who do not promptly respond cannot complain if their children are declared wards of the State. Those who do respond retain the burden of proving their fatherhood.

10. Predicating a finding of constitutional invalidity under the Equal Protection Clause of the Fourteenth Amendment on the observation that a State has accorded bedrock procedural rights to some, but not to all similarly situated, is not contradictory to our holding in Picard v. Connor, 404 U.S. 270, 92 S.Ct. 509, 30 L.Ed.2d 438 (1971). In that case a due process, rather than an equal protection, claim was raised in the state courts. The federal courts were, in our opinion, barred from reversing the state conviction on grounds of contravention of the Equal Protection Clause when that clause had not been referred to for consideration by the state authorities. Here, in contrast, we dispose of the case on the constitutional premise raised below, reaching the result by a method of analysis readily available to the state court.

For the same reason the strictures of Cardinale v. Louisiana, 394 U.S. 437, 89 S.Ct. 1161, 22 L.Ed.2d 398 (1969), and Hill v. California, 401 U.S. 797, 91 S.Ct. 1106, 28 L.Ed.2d 484 (1971), have been fully observed.

STATE of Maine

v.

David BENNER.

Supreme Judicial Court of Maine.

Submitted on Briefs Jan. 3, 1995.

Decided Feb. 10, 1995.

654 A.2d 435 (Me. 1995)

CLIFFORD, Justice.

David Benner appeals from a conviction for assault, 17–A M.R.S.A. § 207 (1983 & Supp.1994),[1] following a jury trial in Superior Court (Washington County, *Mills,* J.). On appeal Benner contends, *inter alia,* that the trial court erred in giving a cautionary instruction on how the jury should consider the hearsay testimony of the investigating state trooper, and that there was insufficient evidence to support the jury's verdict. Finding no error, we affirm the conviction.

The evidence at trial revealed the following. The victim testified that Benner is her boyfriend, and at the time of the alleged assault, she was living with him. On the night of September 11, 1993, she was home alone with Benner; they were arguing and she wanted him out of the house. The victim stated that she called the state police and complained that Benner had hit her. She also testified that she told the investigating trooper that Benner had struck her on the hand with either an ax handle or a broom stick. She testified that she had said that Benner had hit her only because she wanted him out of her house and not because he had actually hit her. She further testified that the injury to the back of her hand occurred because she was drunk and had fallen.

State Trooper Raymond Bessette testified that while on patrol on the night of September 11, 1993, he received a call from the dispatcher that the victim called to complain that Benner had struck her. When Bessette arrived at the home, he observed the victim to be visibly distraught, scared, and quite nervous, and that she had an injury to the back of her hand. She also had watery eyes. He did not, however, observe her to be under the influence.

In order to impeach her credibility, and without objection by the defendant,[2] Bessette further testified as to what the victim had told him that night. Before Bessette did so, however, Benner requested the jury be instructed that the statements "can be used for impeachment value, but not as substantive evidence." The court cautioned the jury as follows:

> [T]he Trooper is now going to testify about statements that were made to him by [the victim], and that testimony is offered to impeach her testimony, the statements that she has testified about. It is not offered for the truth of the matter asserted.

The defendant did not object to the instruction. The jury returned a verdict of guilty and the court accordingly entered a judgment of conviction.

I.

Benner contends that the trial court's cautionary instruction to the jury prior to Trooper Bessette's testimony was inadequate. Although he concedes that the court's instruction is a correct statement of the law, and that he failed to object, he avers that the trial court committed reversible error by failing to give a full explanation of the instructions. We disagree.

Because Benner did not object to the instruction when it was given, we review the charge only for obvious error affecting his substantial rights. *State v. McCluskie,* 611 A.2d 975, 978 (Me.1992); *see* M.R.Crim.P. 30(b). Giving an instruction that is a correct statement of the law does not rise to the level of obvious error. Jurors are presumed to understand the instruction. *See State v. Naoum,* 548 A.2d 120, 123 (Me.1988). While it would have been more helpful for the trial court to have given a more detailed instruction on the limited purposes for which the hearsay testimony was admitted, *see* D. Alexander, *Maine Jury Instruction Manual* § 6-24 (2d ed. 1990), the cautionary instruction actually given was not obvious error.

II.

Benner further contends that the evidence presented at trial was insufficient to support a judgment of conviction. The standard to determine if evidence at trial was sufficient to support the jury's verdict is "whether, based on the evidence viewed in the light most favorable to the prosecution, any trier of fact rationally could find beyond a reasonable doubt every element of the offense charged." *State v. Barry,* 495 A.2d 825, 826 (Me.1985).

1. 17–A M.R.S.A. § 207(1) (1983) provides that "[a] person is guilty of assault if he intentionally, knowingly, or recklessly causes bodily injury or offensive physical contact to another."

2. Benner did not argue for the exclusion of the statements because the probative value of Bessette's testimony as to the victim's statement was substantially outweighed by the danger of unfair prejudice. *See* M.R.Evid. 403.

The affirmative evidence supporting a guilty verdict includes the following. The victim was home alone with Benner; the two were having an argument; the victim made a complaint; when the trooper arrived, the victim was distraught, scared, and nervous; the trooper observed the back of the victim's hand to be swollen; Benner was intoxicated; the trooper testified that the victim was sober.

Although the victim testified at the trial that Benner had not hit her and that she sustained her injuries while drunk by falling into a wall, her testimony was substantially impeached by her own testimony [3] and that of Trooper Bessette. It was reasonable for the jury to disregard her denials. As we have previously stated, "the weight of the evidence and the determination of witness credibility are the exclusive province of the jury." *State v. Glover,* 594 A.2d 1086, 1088 (Me.1991). Therefore, her testimony alone does not mandate a conclusion that the evidence was insufficient.

Although the conviction in this case was based substantially on circumstantial evidence, a conviction may be grounded on such evidence. *State v. Ingalls,* 554 A.2d 1272, 1276 (Me.1988). Indeed, a conviction based solely on circumstantial evidence is not for that reason less conclusive. *State v. LeClair,* 425 A.2d 182, 184 (Me.1981). The factfinder is allowed to draw all reasonable inferences from the circumstantial evidence. *State v. Crosby,* 456 A.2d 369, 370 (Me.1983). Viewing the evidence in the light most favorable to the State, the jury could have rationally inferred that Benner had assaulted the victim.[4]

The entry is:

Judgment affirmed.

All concurring.

3. The victim's trial testimony that she told police that Benner hit her was hearsay. It normally would not be admissible for the truth of the matter asserted, but would be admissible to impeach the victim's trial testimony that Benner did not strike her. M.R.Evid. 801, 802. In this case, however, because there was no objection to the victim's statement that she told the police that Benner had hit her, there was no instruction that the testimony could be considered for impeachment only. It is not wholly unreliable and its admission was not obvious error.

4. Benner also contends that the court's instruction on the elements of assault constituted error. Our review of the instructions, to which Benner did not object, reveals no error. See *State v. Griffin,* 459 A.2d 1086, 1091–92 (Me.1983); 17–A M.R.S.A. § 2(5) (1983).

CASE

UNITED STATES, Petitioner

v.

Alberto Antonio LEON et al.

No. 82–1771.

Argued Jan. 17, 1984.
Decided July 5, 1984.
Rehearing Denied Sept. 18, 1984.
468 U.S. 897 (1984)

Justice WHITE delivered the opinion of the Court.

This case presents the question whether the Fourth Amendment exclusionary rule should be modified so as not to bar the use in the prosecution's case in chief of evidence obtained by officers acting in reasonable reliance on a search warrant issued by a detached and neutral magistrate but ultimately found to be unsupported by probable cause. To resolve this question, we must consider once again the tension between the sometimes competing goals of, on the one hand, deterring official misconduct and removing inducements to unreasonable invasions of privacy and, on the other, establishing procedures under which criminal defendants are "acquitted or convicted on the basis of all the evidence which exposes the truth." *Alderman v. United States,* 394 U.S. 165, 175, 89 S.Ct. 961, 967, 22 L.Ed.2d 176 (1969).

I

In August 1981, a confidential informant of unproven reliability informed an officer of the Burbank Police Department that two persons known to him as "Armando" and "Patsy" were selling large quantities of cocaine and methaqualone from their residence at 620 Price Drive in Burbank, Cal. The informant also indicated that he had witnessed a sale of methaqualone by "Patsy" at the residence approximately five months earlier and had observed at that time a shoebox containing a large amount of cash that belong to "Patsy." He further declared that "Armando" and "Patsy" generally kept only small quantities of drugs at their residence and stored the remainder at another location in Burbank.

On the basis of this information, the Burbank police initiated an extensive investigation focusing first on the

Price Drive residence and later on two other residences as well. Cars parked at the Price Drive residence were determined to belong to respondents Armando Sanchez, who had previously been arrested for possession of marihuana, and Patsy Stewart, who had no criminal record. During the course of the investigation, officers observed an automobile belonging to respondent Richardo Del Castillo, who had previously been arrested for possession of 50 pounds of marihuana, arrive at the Price Drive residence. The driver of that car entered the house, exited shortly thereafter carrying a small paper sack, and drove away. A check of Del Castillo's probation records led the officers to respondent Alberto Leon, whose telephone number Del Castillo had listed as his employer's. Leon had been arrested in 1980 on drug charges, and a companion had informed the police at the time that Leon was heavily involved in the importation of drugs into this country. Before the current investigation began, the Burbank officers had learned that an informant had told a Glendale police officer that Leon stored a large quantity of methaqualone at his residence in Glendale. During the course of this investigation, the Burbank officers learned that Leon was living at 716 South Sunset Canyon in Burbank.

Subsequently, the officers observed several persons, at least one of whom had prior drug involvement, arriving at the Price Drive residence and leaving with small packages; observed a variety of other material activity at the two residences as well as at a condominium at 7902 Via Magdalena; and witnessed a variety of relevant activity involving respondents' automobiles. The officers also observed respondents Sanchez and Stewart board separate flights for Miami. The pair later returned to Los Angeles together, consented to a search of their luggage that revealed only a small amount of marihuana, and left the airport. Based on these and other observations summarized in the affidavit, App. 34, Office Cyril Rombach of the Burbank Police Department, an experienced and well-trained narcotics investigator, prepared an application for a warrant to search 620 Price Drive, 716 South Sunset Canyon, 7902 Via Magdalena, and automobiles registered to each of the respondents for an extensive list of items believed to be related to respondents' drug-trafficking activities. Officer Rombach's extensive application was reviewed by several Deputy District Attorneys.

A facially valid search warrant was issued in September 1981 by a State Superior Court Judge. The ensuing searches produced large quantities of drugs at the Via Magdalena and Sunset Canyon addresses and a small quantity at the Price Drive residence. Other evidence was discovered at each of the residences and in Stewart's and Del Castillo's automobiles. Respondents were indicted by a grand jury in the District Court for the Central District of California and charged with conspiracy to possess and distribute cocaine and a variety of substantive counts.

The respondents then filed motions to suppress the evidence seized pursuant to the warrant.[1] The District Court held an evidentiary hearing and, while recognizing that the case was a close one, see *id.,* at 131, granted the motions to suppress in part. It concluded that the affidavit was insufficient to establish probable cause,[2] but did not suppress all of the evidence as to all of the respondents because none of the respondents had standing to challenge all of the searches.[3] In response to a request from the Government, the court made clear that Officer Rombach had acted in good faith, but it rejected the Government's suggestion that the Fourth Amendment exclusionary rule should not apply

1. Respondent Leon moved to suppress the evidence found on his person at the time of his arrest and the evidence seized from his residence at 716 South Sunset Canyon. Respondent Stewart's motion covered the fruits of searches of her residence at 620 Price Drive and the condominium at 7902 Via Magdalena and statements she made during the search of her residence. Respondent Sanchez sought to suppress the evidence discovered during the search of his residence at 620 Price Drive and statements he made shortly thereafter. He also joined Stewart's motion to suppress evidence seized from the condominium. Respondent Del Castillo apparently sought to suppress all of the evidence seized in the searches. App. 78–80. The respondents also moved to suppress evidence seized in the searches of their automobiles.

2. "I just cannot find this warrant sufficient for a showing of probable cause.

* * *

"There is no question of the reliability and credibility of the informant as not being established.

"Some details given tended to corroborate, maybe, the reliability of [the informant's] information about the previous transaction, but if it is not a stale transaction, it comes awfully close to it; and all the other material I think is as consistent with innocence as it is with guilt.

"So I just do not think this affidavit can withstand the test. I find, then, that there is no probable cause in this case for the issuance of the search warrant . . . ." *Id.,* at 127.

3. The District Court concluded that Sanchez and Stewart had standing to challenge the search of 620 Price Drive; that Leon had standing to contest the legality of the search of 716 South Sunset Canyon; that none of the respondents has established a legitimate expectation of privacy in the condominium at 7902 Via Magdalena; and that Stewart and Del Castillo each had standing to challenge the searches of their automobiles. The Government indicated that it did not intend to introduce evidence seized from the other respondents' vehicles. *Id.,* at 127–129. Finally, the court suppressed statements given by Sanchez and Stewart. *Id.,* at 129–130.

where evidence is seized in reasonable good-faith reliance on a search warrant.[4]

The District Court denied the Government's motion for reconsideration, *id.*, at 147, and a divided panel of the Court of Appeals for the Ninth Circuit affirmed, judgt. order reported at 701 F.2d 187 (1983). The Court of Appeals first concluded that Officer Rombach's affidavit could not establish probable cause to search the Price Drive residence. To the extent that the affidavit set forth facts demonstrating the basis of the informant's knowledge of criminal activity, the information included was fatally stale. The affidavit, moreover, failed to establish the informant's credibility. According, the Court of Appeals concluded that the information provided by the informant was inadequate under both prongs of the two-part test established in *Aguilar v. Texas,* 378 U.S. 108, 84 S.Ct. 1509, 12 L.Ed.2d 723 (1964), and *Spinelli v. United States,* 393 U.S. 410, 89 S.Ct. 584, 21 L.Ed.2d 637 (1969).[5]

* * *

We have concluded that, in the Fourth Amendment context, the exclusionary rule can be modified somewhat without jeopardizing its ability to perform its intended functions. Accordingly, we reverse the judgment of the Court of Appeals.

II

Language in opinions of this Court and of individual Justices has sometimes implied that the exclusionary rule is a necessary corollary of the Fourth Amendment, *Mapp v. Ohio,* 367 U.S. 643, 651, 655–657, 81 S.Ct. 1684, 1689, 1691–1692, 6 L.Ed.2d 1081 (1961); *Olmstead v. United States,* 277 U.S. 488, 462–463, 48 S.Ct. 564, 567, 72 L.Ed. 944 (1928), or that the rule is required by the conjunction of the Fourth and Fifth Amendments. *Mapp v. Ohio, supra,* 367 U.S., at 661–662, 81 S.Ct., at 1694–1695 (Black, J., concurring); *Agnello v. United States,* 269 U.S. 20, 33–34, 46 S.Ct. 4, 6–7, 70 L.Ed. 145 (1925). These implications need not detain us long. The Fifth Amendment theory has not withstood critical analysis or the test of time, see *Andresen v. Maryland,* 427 U.S. 463, 96 S.Ct. 2737, 49 L.Ed.2d 627 (1976), and the Fourth Amendment "has never been interpreted to proscribe the introduction of illegally seized evidence in all proceedings or against all persons." *Stone v. Powell,* 428 U.S. 465, 486, 96 S.Ct. 3037, 3048, 49 L.Ed.2d 1067 (1976).

A

The Fourth Amendment contains no provisions expressly precluding the use of evidence obtained in violation of its commands, and an examination of its origin and purposes makes clear that the use of fruits of a part unlawful search or seizure "work[s] no new Fourth Amendment wrong." *United States v. Calandra,* 414 U.S. 338, 354, 94 S.Ct. 613, 623, 38 L.Ed.2d 561 (1974). The wrong condemned by the Amendment is "fully accomplished" by the unlawful search or seizure itself, *ibid.*, and the exclusionary rule is neither intended nor able to "cure the invasion of the defendant's rights which he has already suffered." *Stone v. Powell, supra,* 428 U.S., at 540, 96 S.Ct., at 3073 (WHITE, J., dissenting). The rule thus operates as "a judicially created remedy designed to safeguard Fourth Amendment rights generally through its deterrent effect, rather than a personal constitutional right of the party aggrieved." *United States v. Calandra, supra,* 414 U.S., at 348, 94 S.Ct., at 620.

* * *

The substantial social costs exacted by the exclusionary rule for the vindication of Fourth Amendment rights have long been a source of concern. "Our cases have consistently recognized that unbending application of the exclusionary sanction to enforce ideals of governmental rectitude would impede unacceptably the truth-finding functions of judge and jury." *United States v. Payner,* 447 U.S. 727, 734, 100 S.Ct. 2439, 2445, 65 L.Ed.2d 468 (1980). An objectionable collateral consequence of this interference with the criminal justice system's truth-finding function is that some guilty defendants may go free or receive reduced

4. "On the issue of good faith, obviously that is not the law of the Circuit, and I am not going to apply that law.

"I will say certainly in my view, there is not any question about good faith. [Officer Rombach] went to a Superior Court judge and got a warrant; obviously laid a meticulous trail. Had surveilled for a long period of time, and I believe his testimony—I think he said he consulted with three Deputy District Attorneys before proceeding himself, and I certainly have no doubt about the fact that that is true." *Id.*, at 140.

5. In *Illinois v. Gates,* 462 U.S. 213, 103 S.Ct. 2317, 76 L.Ed.2d 527 (1983), decided last Term, the Court abandoned the two-pronged *Aguilar-Spinelli* test for determining whether an informant's tip suffices to establish probable cause for the issuance of a warrant and substituted in its place a "totality of the circumstances" approach.

sentences as a result of favorable plea bargains.[6] Particularly when law enforcement officers have acted in objective good faith or their transgressions have been minor, the magnitude of the benefit conferred on such guilty defendants offends basic concepts of the criminal justice system. *Stone v. Powell,* 428 U.S., at 490, 96 S.Ct., at 3050. Indiscriminate application of the exclusionary rule, therefore, may well "generat[e] disrespect for the law and administration of justice." *Id.,* at 491, 96 S.Ct., at 3051. Accordingly, "[a]s with any remedial device, the application of the rule has been restricted to those areas where its remedial objectives are thought most efficaciously served." *United States v. Calandra, supra,* 414 U.S., at 348, 94 S.Ct., at 670; see *Stone v. Powell, supra,* 428 U.S., at 486–487, 97 S.Ct., at 3048–3049; *United States v. Janis,* 428 U.S. 433, 447, 96 S.Ct. 3021, 3028, 49 L.Ed.2d 1046 (1976).

* * *

III

A

Because a search warrant "provides the detached scrutiny of a neutral magistrate, which is a more reliable safeguard against improper searches than the hurried judgment of a law enforcement officer 'engaged in the often competitive enterprise of ferreting out crime,' " *United States v. Chadwich,* 433 U.S. 1, 9, 97 S.Ct. 2476, 2482, 53 L.Ed.2d 538 (1977) (quoting *Johnson v. United States,* 333 U.S. 10, 14, 68 S.Ct. 367, 369, 92 L.Ed. 436 (1948)), we have expressed a strong preference for warrants and declared that "in a doubtful or marginal case a search under a warrant may be sustainable where without one it would fall." *United States v. Ventresca,* 380 U.S. 102, 106, 85 S.Ct., 741, 744, 13 L.Ed.2d 687 (1965). See *Aguilar v. Texas,* 378 U.S., at 111, 84 S.Ct., at 1512. Reasonable minds frequently may differ on the question whether a particular affidavit establishes probable cause, and we have thus concluded that the preference for warrants is most appropriately effectuated by according "great deference" to a magistrate's determination. *Spinelli v. United States,* 393 U.S., at 419, 89 S.Ct., at 590. See *Illinois v. Gates,* 462 U.S., at 236, 103 S.Ct., at 2331; *United States v. Ventresca, supra,* 380 U.S., at 108–109, 85 S.Ct., at 745–746.

Deference to the magistrate, however, is not boundless. It is clear, first, that the deference accorded to a magistrate's finding of probable cause does not preclude inquiry into the knowing or reckless falsity of the affidavit on which that determination was based. *Franks v. Delaware,* 438 U.S. 154, 98 S.Ct. 2674, 57 L.Ed.2d 667 (1978).[12] Second, the courts must also insist the magistrate purport to "perform his 'neutral and detached' function and not serve merely as a rubber stamp for the police." *Aguilar v. Texas, supra,* 378 U.S., at 111, 84 S.Ct., at 1512. See *Illinois v. Gates, supra,* 462 U.S., at 239, 103 S.Ct., at 2332. A magistrate failing to "manifest that neutrality and detachment demanded of a judicial officer when

6. Researchers have only recently begun to study extensively the effects of the exclusionary rule on the disposition of felony arrests. One study suggests that the rule results in the nonprosecution or nonconviction of between 0.6% and 2.35% of individuals arrested for felonies. Davies, A Hard Look at What We Know (and Still Need to Learn) About the "Costs" of the Exclusionary Rule: The NIJ Study and Other Studies of "Lost" Arrests, 1983 A.B.F.Res.J. 611, 621. The estimates are higher for particular crimes the prosecution of which depends heavily on physical evidence. Thus, the cumulative loss due to nonprosecution or nonconviction of individuals arrested on felony drug charges is probably in the range of 2.8% to 7.1%. *Id.,* at 680. Davies' analysis of California data suggests that screening by police and prosecutors results in the release because of illegal searches or seizures of as many as 1.4% of all felony arrestees, *id.,* at 650, that 0.9% of felony arrestees are released, because of illegal searches or seizures, at the preliminary hearing or after trial, *id.,* at 653, and that roughly 0.5% of all felony arrestees benefit from reversals on appeal because of illegal searches. *Id.,* at 654. See also K. Brosi, A Cross-City Comparison of Felony Case Processing 16, 18–19 (1979); U.S. General Accounting Office, Report of the Comptroller General of the United States, Impact of the Exclusionary Rule on Federal Criminal Prosecutions 10–11, 14 (1979); F. Feeney, F. Dill, & A. Weir, Arrests Without Convictions: How Often They Occur and Why 203–206 (National Institute of Justice 1983); National Institute of Justice, The Effects of the Exclusionary Rule: A Study in California 1–2 (1982); Nardulli, The Societal Cost of the Exclusionary Rule: An Empirical Assessment, 1983 A.B.F.Res.J. 585, 600. The exclusionary rule also has been found to affect the plea-bargaining process. S. Schlesinger, Exclusionary Injustice: The Problem of Illegally Obtained Evidence 63 (1977). But see Davies, *supra,* at 668–669; Nardulli, *supra,* at 604–606.

Many of these researchers have concluded that the impact of the exclusionary rule is insubstantial, but the small percentages with which they deal mask a large absolute number of felons who are released because the cases against them were based in part on illegal searches or seizures. "[A]ny rule of evidence that denies the jury access to clearly probative and reliable evidence must bear a heavy burden of justification, and must be carefully limited to the circumstances in which it will pay its way by deterring official unlawlessness." *Illinois v. Gates,* 462 U.S., at 257–258, 103 S.Ct., at 2342 (WHITE, J., concurring in judgment). Because we find that the rule can have no substantial deterrent effect in the sorts of situations under consideration in this case, see *infra,* at 3417–3419, we conclude that it cannot pay its way in those situations.

* * *

12. Indeed, "it would be an unthinkable imposition upon [the magistrate's] authority if a warrant affidavit, revealed after the fact to contain a deliberately or recklessly false statement, were to stand beyond impeachment." 438 U.S., at 165, 98 S.Ct., at 2681.

presented with a warrant application" and who acts instead as "an adjunct law enforcement officer" cannot provide valid authorization for an otherwise unconstitutional search. *Lo-Ji Sales, Inc. v. New York,* 442 U.S. 319, 326–327, 99 S.Ct. 2319, 2324–2325, 60 L.Ed.2d 920 (1979).

Third, reviewing courts will not defer to a warrant based on an affidavit that does not "provide the magistrate with a substantial basis for determining the existence of probable cause." *Illinois v. Gates,* 462 U.S., at 239, 103 S.Ct., at 2332. "Sufficient information must be presented to the magistrate to allow that official to determine probable cause; his action cannot be a mere ratification of the bare conclusions of others." *Ibid.* See *Aguilar v. Texas, supra* 378 U.S., at 114–115, 84 S.Ct., at 1513–1514; *Giordenello v. United States,* 357 U.S. 480, 78 S.Ct. 1245, 2 L.Ed.2d 1503 (1958); *Nathanson v. United States,* 290 U.S. 41, 54 S.Ct. 11, 78 L.Ed.159 (1933).[13] Even if the warrant application was supported by more than a "bare bones" affidavit, a reviewing court may properly conclude that, notwithstanding the deference that magistrates deserve, the warrant was invalid because the magistrate's probable-cause determination reflected an improper analysis of the totality of the circumstances, *Illinois v. Gates, supra,* 462 U.S., at 238–239, 103 S.Ct., at 2332–2333, or because the form of the warrant was improper in some respect.

Only in the first of these three situations, however, has the Court set forth a rationale for suppressing evidence obtained pursuant to a search warrant; in the other areas, it has simply excluded such evidence without considering whether Fourth Amendment interests will be advanced. To the extent that proponents of exclusion rely on its behavioral effects on judges and magistrates in these areas, their reliance is misplaced. First, the exclusionary rule is designed to deter police misconduct rather than to punish the errors of judges and magistrates. Second, there exists no evidence suggesting that judges and magistrates are inclined to ignore or subvert the Fourth Amendment or that lawlessness among these actors requires application of the extreme sanction of exclusion.[14]

Third, and most important, we discern no basis, and are offered none, for believing that exclusion of evidence seized pursuant to a warrant will have a significant deterrent effect on the issuing judge or magistrate.[15] Many of the factors that indicate that the exclusionary rule cannot provide an effective "special" or "general" deterrent for individual offending law enforcement officers[16] apply as well to judges or magistrates. And, to the extent that the rule is thought

---

13. See also *Beck v. Ohio,* 379 U.S. 89, 85 S.Ct. 223, 13 L.Ed.2d 142 (1964), in which the Court concluded that "the record . . . does not contain a single objective fact to support a belief by the officers that the petitioner was engaged in criminal activity at the time they arrested him." *Id.,* at 95, 85 S.Ct., at 227. Although the Court was willing to assume that the arresting officers acted in good faith, it concluded that:

> " '[G]ood faith on the part of the arresting officers is not enough,' *Henry v. United States,* 361 U.S. 98, 102, 80 S.Ct. 168, 171, 4 L.Ed.2d 134. If subjective good faith alone were the test, the protections of the Fourth Amendment would evaporate, and the people would be 'secure in their persons, houses, papers, and effects,' only in the discretion of the police." *Id.,* at 97, 85 S.Ct., at 228.

We adhere to this view and emphasize that nothing in this opinion is intended to suggest a lowering of the probable-cause standard. On the contrary, we deal here with the remedy to be applied to a concededly unconstitutional search.

14. Although there are assertions that some magistrates become rubber stamps for the police and others may be unable effectively to screen police conduct, see, *e.g.,* 2 W. LaFave, Search and Seizure § 4.1 (1978); Kamisar, Does (Did) (Should) The Exclusionary Rule Rest on a "Principled Basis" Rather than an "Empirical Proposition"?, 16 Creighton L.Rev. 565, 569–571 (1983); Schroeder, Deterring Fourth Amendment Violations: Alternatives to the Exclusionary Rule, 69 Geo.L.J. 1361, 1412 (1981), we are not convinced that this is a problem of major proportions. See L. Tiffany, D. McIntyre, & D. Rotenberg, Detection of Crime 119 (1967); Israel, Criminal Procedure, the Burger Court, and the Legacy of the Warren Court, 75 Mich.L.Rev. 1319, 1414, n. 396 (1977); P. Johnson, New Approaches to Enforcing the Fourth Amendment 8–10 (Working Paper, Sept. 1978), quoted in Y. Kamisar, W. LaFave, & J. Israel, Modern Criminal Procedure 229–230 (5th ed. 1980); R. Van Duizend, L. Sutton, & C. Carter, The Search Warrant Process, ch. 7 (Review Draft, National Center for State Courts, 1983).

15. As the Supreme Judicial Court of Massachusetts recognized in *Commonwealth v. Sheppard,* 387 Mass. 488, 506, 441 N.E.2d 725, 735 (1982):

> "The exclusionary rule may not be well tailored to deterring judicial misconduct. If applied to judicial misconduct, the rule would be just as costly as it is when it is applied to police misconduct, but it may be ill-fitted to the job-created motivations of judges. . . . [I]deally a judge is impartial as to whether a particular piece of evidence is admitted or a particular defendant convicted. Hence, in the abstract, suppression of a particular piece of evidence may not be as effective a disincentive to a neutral judge as it would be to the police. It may be that a ruling by an appellate court that a search warrant was unconstitutional would be sufficient to deter similar conduct in the future by magistrates."

But see *United States v. Karathanos,* 531 F.2d 26, 33–34 (CA2), cert. denied, 428 U.S. 910, 96 S.Ct. 3221, 49 L.Ed.2d 1217 (1976).

16. See, *e.g., Stone v. Powell,* 428 U.S., at 498, 96 S.Ct., at 3054 (BURGER, C.J., concurring); Oaks, Studying the Exclusionary Rule in Search and Seizure, 37 U.Chi.I.Rev. 665, 709–710 (1970).

to operate as a "systemic" deterrent on a wider audience,[17] it clearly can have no such effect on individuals empowered to issue search warrants. Judges and magistrates are not adjuncts to the law enforcement team; as neutral judicial officers, they have no stake in the outcome of particular criminal prosecutions. The threat of exclusion thus cannot be expected significantly to deter them. Imposition of the exclusionary sanction is not necessary meaningfully to inform judicial officers of their errors, and we cannot conclude that admitting evidence obtained pursuant to a warrant while at the same time declaring that the warrant was somehow defective will in any way reduce judicial officers' professional incentives to comply with the Fourth Amendment, encourage them to repeat their mistakes, or lead to the granting of all colorable warrant requests.[18]

B

If exclusion of evidence obtained pursuant to a subsequently invalidated warrant is to have any deterrent effect, therefore, it must alter the behavior of individual law enforcement officers or the policies of their departments. One could argue that applying the exclusionary rule in cases where the police failed to demonstrate probable cause in the warrant application deters future inadequate presentations or "magistrate shopping" and thus promotes the end of the Fourth Amendment. Suppressing evidence obtained pursuant to a technically defective warrant supported by a probable cause also might encourage officers to scrutinize more closely the form of the warrant and to point out suspected judicial errors. We find such arguments speculative and conclude that suppression of evidence obtained pursuant to a warrant should be ordered only on a case-by-case basis and only in those unusual cases in which exclusion will further the purposes of the exclusionary rule.[19]

We have frequently questioned whether the exclusionary rule can have any deterrent effect when the offending officers acted in the objectively reasonable belief that their conduct did not violate the Fourth Amendment. "No empirical researcher, proponent or opponent of the rule, has yet been able to establish with any assurance whether the rule has a deterrent effect. . . ." *United States v. Janis,* 428 U.S., at 452, n. 22, 96 S.Ct., at 3031, n. 22. But even assuming that the rule effectively deters some police misconduct and provides incentives for the law enforcement profession as a whole to conduct itself in accord with the Fourth Amendment, it cannot be expected, and should not be applied, to deter objectively reasonable law enforcement activity.

As we observed in *Michigan v. Tucker,* 417 U.S. 433, 447, 94 S.Ct. 2357, 2365, 41 L.Ed.2d 182 (1974), and reiterated in *United States v. Peltier,* 422 U.S., at 539, 95 S.Ct., at 2318:

> "The deterrent purpose of the exclusionary rule necessarily assumes that the police have engaged in wilful, or at the very least negligent, conduct which has deprived the defendant of some right. By refusing to admit evidence gained as a result of such conduct, the courts hope to instill in those particular investigating officers, or in their future counterparts, a greater deal of care toward the rights of an accused. Where the official action was pursued in complete good faith, however, the deterrence rationale loses much of its force."

The *Peltier Court* continued, *id.,* at 542, 95 S.Ct., at 2320:

> "If the purpose of the exclusionary rule is to deter unlawful police conduct, then evidence obtained from a search should be suppressed only if it can be said that the law enforcement officer had knowledge, or may

17. See, *e.g., Dunaway v. New York,* 442 U.S. 200, 221, 99 S.Ct. 2248, 2261, 60 L.Ed.2d 824 (1979) (STEVENS, J., concurring); Mertens & Wasserstrom, The Good Faith Exception to the Exclusionary Rule: Deregulating the Police and Derailing the Law, 70 Geo.L.J. 365, 399–401 (1981).

18. Limiting the application of the exclusionary sanction may well increase the care with which magistrates scrutinize warrant applications. We doubt that magistrates are more desirous of avoiding the exclusion of evidence obtained pursuant to warrants they have issued than of avoiding invasions of privacy.

Federal magistrates, moreover, are subject to the direct supervision of district courts. They may be removed for "incompetency, misconduct, neglect of duty, or physical or mental disability." 28 U.S.C. § 631(i). If a magistrate serves merely as a "rubber stamp" for the police or is unable to exercise mature judgment, closer supervision or removal provides a more effective remedy than the exclusionary rule.

19. Our discussion of the deterrent effect of excluding evidence obtained in reasonable reliance on a subsequently invalidated warrant assumes, of course, that the officers properly executed the warrant and searched only those places and for those objects that it was reasonable to believe were covered by the warrant. Cf. *Massachusetts v. Sheppard,* 468 U.S. 981, 989, n. 6, 104 S.Ct. 3424, 3429, n. 6, 82 L.Ed.2d 737 ("[I]t was not unreasonable for the police in this case to rely on the judge's assurances that the warrant authorized the search they had requested").

properly be charged with knowledge, that the search was unconstitutional under the Fourth Amendment."

See also *Illinois v. Gates,* 462 U.S., at 260–261, 103 S.Ct., at 2344 (WHITE, J., concurring in judgment); *United States v. Janis, supra,* 428 U.S., at 459, 96 S.Ct., at 3034; *Brown v. Illinois,* 422 U.S., at 610–611, 95 S.Ct., at 2265–2266 (POWELL, J., concurring in part).[20] In short, where the officer's conduct is objectively reasonable,

> "excluding the evidence will not further the ends of the exclusionary rule in any appreciable way; for it is painfully apparent . . . the officer is acting as a reasonable officer would and should act in similar circumstances. Excluding the evidence can in no way affect his future conduct unless it is to make him less willing to do his duty." *Stone v. Powell,* 428 U.S., at 539–540, 96 S.Ct., at 3073–3074 (WHITE, J., dissenting).

This is particularly true, we believe, when an officer acting with objective good faith has obtained a search warrant from a judge or magistrate and acted within its scope.[21] In most such cases, there is no police illegality and thus nothing to deter. It is the magistrate's responsibility to determine whether the officer's allegations establish probable cause and, if so, to issue a warrant comporting in form with the requirements of the Fourth Amendment. In the ordinary case, an officer cannot be expected to question the magistrate's probable-cause determination or his judgment that the form of the warrant is technically sufficient. "[O]nce the warrant issues, there is literally nothing more the policeman can do in seeking to comply with the law." *Id.,* 428 U.S., at 498, 96 S.Ct., at 3054 (BURGER, C.J., concurring). Penalizing the officer for the magistrate's error, rather than his own, cannot logically contribute to the deterrence of Fourth Amendment violations.[22]

We conclude that the marginal or nonexistent benefits produced by suppressing evidence obtained in objectively reasonable reliance on a subsequently invalidated search warrant cannot justify the substantial costs of exclusion. We do not suggest, however, that exclusion is always inappropriate in cases where an officer has obtained a warrant and abided by its terms. "[S]earches pursuant to a warrant

20. We emphasize that the standard of reasonableness we adopt is an objective one. Many objections to a good-faith exception assume that the exception will turn on the subjective good faith of individual officers. "Grounding the modification in objective reasonableness, however, retains the value of the exclusionary rule as an incentive for the law enforcement profession as a whole to conduct themselves in accord with the Fourth Amendment." *Illinois v. Gates,* 462 U.S., at 261, n. 15, 103 S.Ct., at 2344, n. 15 (WHITE, J., concurring in judgment); see *Dunaway v. New York,* 442 U.S., at 221, 99 S.Ct., at 2261 (STEVENS, J., concurring). The objective standard we adopted, moreover, requires officers to have a reasonable knowledge of what the law prohibits. *United States v. Peltier,* 442 U.S. 531, 542, 95 S.Ct. 2313, 2320, 45 L.Ed.2d 374 (1975). As Professor Jerold Israel has observed:

> "The key to the [exclusionary] rule's effectiveness as a deterrent lies, I believe, in the impetus it has provided to police training programs that make officers aware of the limits imposed by the fourth amendment and emphasize the need to operate within those limits. [An objective good-faith exception] is not likely to result in the elimination of such programs, which are now viewed as an important aspect of police professionalism. Neither is it likely to alter the tenor of those programs; the possibility that illegally obtained evidence may be admitted in borderline cases is unlikely to encourage police instructors to pay less attention to fourth amendment limitations. Finally, [it] should not encourage officers to pay less attention to what they are taught, as the requirement that the officer act in 'good faith' is inconsistent with closing one's mind to the possibility of illegality." Israel, *supra* n. 14, at 1412–1413 (footnotes omitted).

21. According to the Attorney General's Task Force on Violent Crime, Final Report (1981), the situation in which an officer relies on a duly authorized warrant

> "is a particularly compelling example of good faith. A warrant is a judicial mandate to an officer to conduct a search or make an arrest, and the officer has a sworn duty to carry out its provisions. Accordingly, we believe that there should be a rule which states that evidence obtained pursuant to and within the scope of a warrant is prima facie the result of good faith on the part of the officer seizing the evidence." *Id.,* at 55.

22. To the extent that Justice STEVENS' conclusions concerning the integrity of the courts, *post,* at 3454–3455, rest on a foundation other than his judgment, which we reject, concerning the effects of our decision on the deterrence of police illegality, we find his argument unpersuasive. "Judicial integrity clearly does not mean that the courts must never admit evidence obtained in violation of the Fourth Amendment." *United States v. Janis,* 428 U.S. 433, 458, n. 35, 96 S.Ct. 3021, 3034, n. 35, 49 L.Ed.2d 1046 (1976). "While courts, of course, must ever be concerned with preserving the integrity of the judicial process, this concern has limited force as a justification for the exclusion of highly probative evidence." *Stone v. Powell,* 428 U.S., at 485, 96 S.Ct., at 3048. Our cases establish that the question whether the use of illegally obtained evidence in judicial proceedings represents judicial participation in a Fourth Amendment violation and offends the integrity of the courts

> "is essentially the same as the inquiry into whether exclusion would serve a deterrent purpose. . . . The analysis showing that exclusion in this case has no demonstrated deterrent effect and is unlikely to have any significant such effect shows, by the same reasoning, that the admission of the evidence is unlikely to encourage violations of the Fourth Amendment."

United States v. Janis, supra, 428 U.S., at 459, n. 35, 96 S.Ct., at 3034, n. 35.

Absent unusual circumstances, when a Fourth Amendment violation has occurred because the police have reasonably relied on a warrant issued by a detached and neutral magistrate but ultimately found to be defective, "the integrity of the courts is not implicated." *Illinois v. Gates, supra,* 462 U.S., at 259, n. 14, 103 S.Ct., at 2343, n. 14 (WHITE, J., concurring in judgment). See *Stone v. Powell,* 428 U.S., at 485, n. 23, 96 S.Ct., at 3048, n. 23; *id.,* at 540, 96 S.Ct., at 3073 (WHITE, J., dissenting); *United States v. Peltier,* 442 U.S. 531, 536–539, 95 S.Ct. 2313, 2317–2318, 45 L.Ed.2d 374 (1975).

will rarely require any deep inquiry into reasonableness," *Illinois v. Gates,* 462 U.S., at 267, 103 S.Ct., at 2347 (WHITE, J., concurring in judgment), for "a warrant issued by a magistrate normally suffices to establish" that a law enforcement officer has "acted in good faith in conducting the search." *United States v. Ross,* 456 U.S. 798, 823, n. 32, 102 S.Ct. 2157, 2172, n. 32, 72 L.Ed.2d 572 (1982). Nevertheless, the officer's reliance on the magistrate's probable-cause determination and on the technical sufficiency of the warrant he issues must be objectively reasonable, cf. *Harlow v. Fitzgerald,* 457 U.S. 800, 815–819, 102 S.Ct., 2727, 2737–2739, 73 L.Ed.2d 396 (1982),[23] and it is clear that in some circumstances the officer[24] will have no reasonable grounds for believing that the warrant was properly issued.

Suppression therefore remains an appropriate remedy if the magistrate or judge in issuing a warrant was misled by information in an affidavit that the affiant knew was false or would have known was false except for his reckless disregard of the truth. *Franks v. Delaware,* 438 U.S. 154, 98 S.Ct. 2674, 57 L.Ed.2d 667 (1978). The exception we recognize today will also not apply in cases where the issuing magistrate wholly abandoned his judicial role in the manner condemned in *Lo-Ji Sales, Inc. v. New York,* 442 U.S. 319, 99 S.Ct. 2319, 60 L.Ed.2d 920 (1979); in such circumstances, no reasonably well trained officer should rely on the warrant. Nor would an officer manifest objective good faith in relying on a warrant based on an affidavit "so lacking in indicia of probable cause as to render official belief in its existence entirely unreasonable." *Brown v. Illinois,* 422 U.S., at 610–611, 95 S.Ct., at 2265–2266 (POWELL, J., concurring in part); see *Illinois v. Gates, supra,* 462 U.S., at 263–264, 103 S.Ct., at 2345–2346 (WHITE, J., concurring in the judgment). Finally, depending on the circumstances of the particular case, a warrant may be so facially deficient—*i.e.,* in failing to particularize the place to be searched or the things to be seized—that the executing officers cannot reasonably presume it to be valid. Cf. *Massachusetts v. Sheppard,* 468 U.S., at 988–991, 104 S.Ct. at 3428–3430.

In so limiting the suppression remedy, we leave untouched the probable-cause standard and the various requirements for a valid warrant. Other objections to the modification of the Fourth Amendment exclusionary rule we consider to be insubstantial. The good-faith exception for searches conducted pursuant to warrants is not intended to signal our willingness strictly to enforce the requirements of the Fourth Amendment, and we do not believe that it will have this effect. As we have already suggested, the good-faith exception, turning as it does on objective reasonableness, should not be difficult to apply in practice. When officers have acted pursuant to a warrant, the prosecution should ordinarily be able to establish objective good faith without a substantial expenditure of judicial time.

Nor are we persuaded that application of a good-faith exception to searches conducted pursuant to warrants will preclude review of the constitutionality of the search or seizure, deny needed guidance from the courts, or freeze Fourth Amendment law in its present state.[25] There is no need for courts to adopt the inflexible practice of always deciding whether the officers' conduct manifested objective good faith before turning to the question whether the Fourth Amendment has been violated. Defendants seeking suppression of the fruits of allegedly unconstitutional searches or seizures undoubtedly raise live controversies

23. In *Harlow,* we eliminated the subjective component of the qualified immunity public officials enjoy in suits seeking damages for alleged deprivations of constitutional rights. The situations are not perfectly analogous, but we also eschew inquiries into the subjective beliefs of law enforcement officers who seize evidence pursuant to a subsequently invalidated warrant. Although we have suggested that, "[o]n occasion, the motive with which the officer conducts an illegal search may have some relevance in determining the propriety of applying the exclusionary rule," *Scott v. United States,* 436 U.S. 128, 139, n. 13, 98 S.Ct. 1717, 1724, n. 13, 56 L.Ed.2d 168 (1978), we believe that "sending state and federal courts on an expedition into the minds of police officers would produce a grave and fruitless misallocation of judicial resources." *Massachusetts v. Painten,* 389 U.S. 560, 565, 88 S.Ct. 660, 663, 19 L.Ed.2d 770 (1968) (WHITE, J., dissenting). Accordingly, our good-faith inquiry is confined to the objectively ascertainable question whether a reasonably well trained officer would have known that the search was illegal despite the magistrate's authorization. In making this determination, all of the circumstances—including whether the warrant application had previously been rejected by a different magistrate—may be considered.

24. References to "officer" throughout this opinion should not be read too narrowly. It is necessary to consider the objective reasonableness, not only of the officers who eventually executed a warrant, but also of the officers who originally obtained it or who provided information material to the probable-cause determination. Nothing in our opinion suggests, for example, that an officer could obtain a warrant on the basis of a "bare bones" affidavit and then rely on colleagues who are ignorant of the circumstances under which the warrant was obtained to conduct the search. See *Whiteley v. Warden,* 401 U.S. 560, 568, 91 S.Ct. 1031, 1037, 28 L.Ed.2d 306 (1971).

25. The argument that defendants will lose their incentive to litigate meritorious Fourth Amendment claims as a result of the good-faith exception we adopt today is unpersuasive. Although the exception might discourage presentation of insubstantial suppression motions, the magnitude of the benefit conferred on defendants by a successful motion makes it unlikely that litigation of colorable claims will be substantially diminished.

which Art. III empowers federal courts to adjudicate. As cases addressing questions of good-faith immunity under 42 U.S.C. § 1983, compare *O'Connor v. Donaldson,* 422 U.S. 563, 95 S.Ct. 2486, 45 L.Ed.2d 396 (1975), with *Procunier v. Navarette,* 434 U.S. 555, 566, n. 14, 98 S.Ct. 855, 862, n. 14, 55 L.Ed.2d 24 (1978), and cases involving the harmless-error doctrine, compare *Milton v. Wainwright,* 407 U.S. 371, 372, 92 S.Ct. 2174, 2175, 33 L.Ed.2d 1 (1972), with *Coleman v. Alabama,* 399 U.S. 1, 90 S.Ct. 1999, 26 L.Ed.2d 387 (1970), make clear, courts have considerable discretion in conforming their decision-making processes to the exigencies of particular cases.

If the resolution of a particular Fourth Amendment question is necessary to guide future action by law enforcement officers and magistrates, nothing will prevent reviewing courts from deciding that question before turning to the good-faith issue.[26] Indeed, it frequently will be difficult to determine whether the officers acted reasonably without resolving the Fourth Amendment issue. Even if the Fourth Amendment question is not one of broad import, reviewing courts could decide in particular cases that magistrates under their supervision need to be informed of their errors and so evaluate the officers' good faith only after finding a violation. In other circumstances, those courts could reject suppression motions posing no important Fourth Amendment questions by turning immediately to a consideration of the officers' good faith. We have no reason to believe that our Fourth Amendment jurisprudence would suffer by allowing reviewing courts to exercise an informed discretion in making this choice.

IV

When the principles we have enunciated today are applied to the facts of this case, it is apparent that the judgment of the Court of Appeals cannot stand. The Court of Appeals applied the prevailing legal standards to Officer Rombach's warrant application and concluded that the application could not support the magistrate's probable-cause determination. In so doing, the court clearly informed the magistrate that he had erred in issuing the challenged warrant. This aspect of the court's judgment is not under attack in this proceeding.

Having determined that the warrant should not have issued, the Court of Appeals understandably declined to adopt a modification of the Fourth Amendment exclusionary rule that this Court had not previously sanctioned. Although the modification finds strong support in our previous cases, the Court of Appeals' commendable self-restraint is not to be criticized. We have now reexamined the purposes of the exclusionary rule and the propriety of its application in cases where officers have relied on a subsequently invalidated search warrant. Our conclusion is that the rule's purposes will only rarely be served by applying it in such circumstances.

In the absence of an allegation that the magistrate abandoned his detached and neutral role, suppression is appropriate only if the officers were dishonest or reckless in preparing their affidavit or could not have harbored an objectively reasonable belief in the existence of probable cause. Only respondent Leon has contended that no reasonably well trained police office could have believed that there existed probable cause to search his house; significantly, the other respondents advance no comparable argument. Officer Rombach's application for a warrant clearly was supported by much more than a "bare bones" affidavit. The affidavit related the results of an extensive investigation and, as the opinions of the divided panel of the Court of Appeals make clear, provided evidence sufficient to create disagreement among thoughtful and competent judges as to the existence of probable cause. Under these circumstances, the officers' reliance on the magistrate's determination of probable cause was objectively reasonable, and application of the extreme sanction of exclusion is inappropriate.

Accordingly, the judgment of the Court of Appeals is

Reversed.

Justice BLACKMUN, concurring.

The Court today holds that evidence obtained in violation of the Fourth Amendment by officers acting in objectively reasonable reliance on a search warrant issued by a neutral and detached magistrate need not be excluded, as a matter of federal law, from the case in chief of federal and state criminal prosecutions. In so doing, the Court writes another chapter in the volume of Fourth Amendment law opened by *Weeks v. United States,* 232 U.S. 383, 34 S.Ct. 341, 58 L.Ed. 652 (1914). I join the Court's opinion in this case and the one in *Massachusetts v.*

26. It has been suggested, in fact, that "the recognition of a 'penumbral zone,' within which an inadvertent mistake would not call for exclusion, . . . will make it less tempting for judges to bend fourth amendment standards to avoid releasing a possibly dangerous criminal because of a minor and unintentional miscalculation by the police." Schroeder, *supra* n. 14, at 1420–1421 (footnote omitted); see Ashdown, Good Faith, the Exclusionary Remedy, and Rule-Oriented Adjudication in the Criminal Process, 24 Wm. & Mary L.Rev. 335, 383–384 (1983).

Sheppard, 468 U.S. 981, 104 S.Ct. 3424, 82 L.Ed.2d 737 (1984), because I believe that the rule announced today advances the legitimate interests of the criminal justice system without sacrificing the individual rights protected by the Fourth Amendment. I write separately, however, to underscore what I regard as the unavoidably provisional nature of today's decision.

As the Court's opinion in this case makes clear, the Court has narrowed the scope of the exclusionary rule because of an empirical judgment that the rule has little appreciable effect in cases where officers act in objectively reasonable reliance on search warrants. See *ante,* at 3419–3420. Because I share the view that the exclusionary rule is not a constitutionally compelled corollary of the Fourth Amendment itself, see *ante,* at 3412, I see no way to avoid making an empirical judgment of this sort, and I am satisfied that the Court has made the correct one on the information before it. Like all courts, we face institutional limitations on our ability to gather information about "legislative facts," and the exclusionary rule itself has exacerbated the shortage of hard data concerning the behavior of police officers in the absence of such a rule. See *United States v. Janis,* 428 U.S. 433, 448–453, 96 S.Ct. 3021, 3029–3031, 49 L.Ed.2d 1046 (1976). Nonetheless, we cannot escape the responsibility to decide the question before us, however imperfect our information may be, and I am prepared to join the Court on the information now at hand.

What must be stressed, however, is that any empirical judgment about the effect of the exclusionary rule in a particular class of cases necessarily in a provisional one. By their very nature, the assumptions on which we proceed today cannot be cast in stone. To the contrary, they now will be tested in the real world of state and federal law enforcement, and this Court will attend to the results. If it should emerge from experience that, contrary to our expectations, the good-faith exception to the exclusionary rule results in a material change in police compliance with the Fourth Amendment, we shall have to reconsider what we have undertaken here. The logic of a decision that rests on untested predictions about police conduct demands no less.

If a single principle may be drawn from this Court's exclusionary rule decisions, from *Weeks* through *Mapp v. Ohio,* 367 U.S. 643, 81 S.Ct. 1684, 6 L.Ed.2d 1081 (1961), to the decisions handed down today, it is that the scope of the exclusionary rule is subject to change in light of changing judicial understanding about the effects of the rule outside the confines of the courtroom. It is incumbent on the Nation's law enforcement officers, who must continue to observe the Fourth Amendment in the wake of today's decisions, to recognize the double-edged nature of that principle.

CASE

UNITED STATES of America.

Plaintiff-Appellee,

v.

Gilbert MARTINEZ–JIMENEZ,
Defendant-Appellant.

No. 87–5305.
United States Court of Appeals,
Ninth Circuit.

Submitted Oct. 4, 1988.
Decided Jan.3, 1989.
864 F.2d 664 (9th Cir. 1989).

NELSON, Circuit Judge:

Gilbert Martinez–Jimenez appeals his conviction following a bench trial on one count of armed bank robbery in violation of 18 U.S.C. § 2113(a) & (d). He contends that the trial court erred in concluding that the toy gun that he held during the bank robbery was a "dangerous weapon" as defined by 18 U.S.C. § 2113(d). We affirm the judgment of the district court.

PROCEDURAL BACKGROUND

On July 14, 1987 a federal grand jury in the Central District of California returned a three-count indictment that charged the appellant and an accomplice, Joe Anthony De La Torre, with armed bank robbery in violation of 18 U.S.C. § 2113(a) & (d) and with carrying a firearm during a crime of violence in violation of 18 U.S.C. § 924(c). At a bench trial the appellant and his accomplice were found guilty of armed bank robbery as charged in count one and not guilty of carrying a firearm during a crime of violence, as charged in counts two and three.

FACTS

On June 19, 1987, at approximately 12:55 p.m., Martinez–Jimenez and De La Torre entered a bank in

Bellflower, California. While De La Torre took cash from a customer and two bank drawers, Martinez–Jimenez remained in the lobby and ordered that the people in the bank lie "face down on the floor." During this time Martinez–Jimenez was holding an object that eyewitnesses thought was a handgun. These persons included two bank employees and a customer who was familiar with guns because he owned handguns, had handled weapons while in military service, and occasionally used weapons at firing ranges. The three witnesses testified that the object was a dark revolver about eight or nine inches long and that it caused them to fear for the safety of themselves and of those around them.

At trial, De La Torre testified that neither he nor Martinez–Jimenez had operable firearms when they entered the bank. He testified that Martinez–Jimenez had a toy gun that he and Martinez–Jimenez had purchased at a department store a few hours prior to the robbery. De La Torre also testified that he hid the toy gun in his closet after the robbery, that neither he nor Martinez–Jimenez wanted the bank employees to believe that they had a real gun, and that they did not want the bank employees to be in fear for their lives. Martinez–Jimenez testified that he had carried the toy gun because he felt secure with it and that during the robbery he held it down toward his leg in order to hide it so that people would not see it. The defense introduced into evidence a toy gun. Martinez–Jimenez testified that the gun used in the robbery was the toy gun introduced into evidence. It was stipulated that De La Torre's attorney had received the toy gun offered as the gun used in the robbery from De La Torre's mother.

Based upon observation of the bank robbery photographs and the toy gun, the court concluded that Martinez–Jimenez possessed a toy gun during the course of the bank robbery and that he had kept the toy gun pointed downwards by his side during the course of the bank robbery. On the basis of his display of the toy gun in the course of the robbery, Martinez–Jimenez was convicted under section 2113(d) which provides an enhanced penalty for use of a "dangerous weapon" during a bank robbery.

STANDARD OF REVIEW

The question presented is whether a toy gun is a "dangerous weapon" within the meaning of the federal bank robbery statute. Interpretation of a statute presents a question of law reviewable de novo. *United States v. Wilson,* 720 F.2d 608, 609 n. 2 (9th Cir.1983), *cert. denied,* 465 U.S. 1034, 104 S.Ct. 1304, 79 L.Ed.2d 703 (1984); *United States v. Moreno–Pulido,* 695 F.2d 1141, 1143 (9th Cir.1983).

DISCUSSION

A robber may be guilty of an armed bank robbery under section 2113(d) if he uses a dangerous weapon or device in the commission of the crime. The instrumentality does not have to be a firearm. The use, or unlawful carrying, of a firearm in a bank robbery is a more serious offense punishable separately under section 924(c). In this case, the appellant carried a toy replica of a firearm that simulated the appearance but not the weight of a genuine firearm. The toy gun did not fit the statutory definition of a firearm under 18 U.S.C. § 921(a)(3). However, it did fall within the meaning of a "dangerous weapon or device" under section 2113(d). Section 2113(d) states that

> Whoever, in committing, or in attempting to commit, any offense defined in subsections (a) and (b) of this section, assaults any person, or puts in jeopardy the life of any person by the use of a dangerous weapon or device, shall be fined not more than $10,000 or imprisoned not more than twenty-five years, or both.

In *McLaughlin v. United States,* 476 U.S. 16, 106 S.Ct. 1677, 90 L.Ed.2d 15 (1986), the Supreme Court found that a defendant who used an unloaded handgun was convicted properly under section 2113(d) because the unloaded handgun was a dangerous weapon under the statute. *Id.* at 17, 106 S.Ct. at 1677–78. Prior to *McLaughlin* this circuit, and other circuits, had assumed that section 2113(d) was violated only by the use of a loaded operable gun. *United States v. Terry,* 760 F.2d 939, 942 (9th Cir.1985); see also *Parker v. United States,* 801 F.2d 1382, 1384 n. 2 (D.C.Cir.1986), *cert. denied,* 479 U.S. 1070, 107 S.Ct. 964, 93 L.Ed.2d 1011 (1987).

The *McLaughlin* opinion stated:

> Three reasons, each independently sufficient, support the conclusion that an unloaded gun is a "dangerous weapon." First, a gun is an article that is typically and characteristically dangerous; the use for which it is manufactured and sold is a dangerous one, and the law reasonably may presume that such an article is always dangerous even though it may not be armed at a particular time or place. *In addition, the display of a gun instills fear in the average citizen; as a consequence, it creates an immediate danger that a violent response will ensue.* Finally, a gun can cause harm when used as a bludgeon.

McLaughlin, 476 U.S. at 17–18, 106 S.Ct. at 1677–78 (footnote omitted) (emphasis added).

The *McLaughlin* opinion recognizes that the dangerousness of a device used in a bank robbery is not simply a function of its potential to injure people directly. Its dangerousness results from the greater burdens that it imposes upon victims and law enforcement officers. Therefore an unloaded gun that only simulates the threat of a loaded gun is a dangerous weapon. The use of a gun that is inoperable and incapable of firing also will support a conviction under section 921(a)(3) and section 2113(d). *United States v. York,* 830 F.2d 885, 891 (8th Cir.1987), *cert. denied,* ___ U.S. ___, 108 S.Ct. 1047, 98 L.Ed.2d 1010 (1988); see also *United States v. Goodheim,* 686 F.2d 776, 778 (9th Cir.1982)

These cases reflect a policy that the robber's creation of even the appearance of dangerousness is sufficient to subject him to enhanced punishment. Other cases have given effect to this policy by holding that the trier of fact may infer that the instrument carried by a bank robber was a firearm based only on witness testimony that it appeared to be genuine. *Parker,* 801 F.2d at 1283–84; *United States v. Harris,* 792 F.2d 866, 868 (9th Cir.1986). *McLaughlin* validates this policy but eliminates the inefficiencies associated with the inference process.

A robber who carries a toy gun during the commission of a bank robbery creates some of the same risks as those created by one who carries an unloaded or inoperable genuine gun. First, the robber subjects victims to greater apprehension. Second, the robber requires law enforcement agencies to formulate a more deliberate, and less efficient, response in light of the need to counter the apparent direct and immediate threat to human life. Third, the robber creates a likelihood that the reasonable response of police and guards will include the use of deadly force. The increased chance of an armed response creates a greater risk to the physical security of victims, bystanders, and even the perpetrators. Therefore the greater harm that a robber creates by deciding to carry a toy gun is similar to the harm that he creates by deciding to carry an unloaded gun.

The *McLaughlin* opinion examined the floor debate on the provision that became section 2113(d) and concluded that Congress was concerned with the potential of an apparently dangerous article to incite fear. *McLaughlin,* 476 U.S. at 18 n. 3, 106 S.Ct. at 1678 n. 3. The House debate on the provision that became section 2113(d) indicates that an ersatz wooden gun used in a bank robbery would satisfy the statutory meaning of a dangerous weapon or device. *See* 78 Cong.Rec. 8132 (1934). If Congress intended that an ersatz wooden gun would fall within the statute, by analogy an ersatz plastic gun should fall within the statute. Congress' intent focused on the nature of the effect that the robber creates, not the specific nature of the instruments that he utilizes.

Appellant concedes that *McLaughlin* applies to the use of an inherently dangerous weapons such as an unloaded firearm but argues that it does not apply to a harmless instrumentality of a crime, such as a toy gun, unless the defendant used the instrumentality in an assaultive manner. The trial court found that the replica was a "totally plastic and extremely light" toy gun, and that Martinez–Jimenez had held it downward by his side and not towards any of the bank employees or customers. Therefore the defendant urges that his manner of displaying this particular toy gun avoids *McLaughlin's* definition of a dangerous weapon because it would not have instilled fear in an average citizen and would not have created a danger of a violent response.

We disagree. A bank robber's use of a firearm during the commission of the crime is punishable even if he does not make assaultive use of the device. He need not brandish the firearm in a threatening manner. *United States v. Mason,* 658 F.2d 1263, 1270–71 (9th Cir.1981). His possession of the weapon is an integral part of the crime. *United States v. Moore,* 580 F.2d 360, 362 (9th Cir.), *cert. denied,* 439 U.S. 970, 99 S.Ct. 463, 58 L.Ed.2d 430 (1978). By analogy, a bank robber's use of a replica or simulated weapon violates section 2113(d) even if he does not make assaultive use of the device. His possession of the instrument during the commission of the crime evidences his apparent ability to commit an assault. The appellant's possession of the toy gun facilitated the crime and increased its likelihood of success. The appellant testified that he carried the toy gun because he "felt secure with it." This suggests that he may not have begun the robbery without it.

Section 2113(d) is not concerned with the way that a robber displays a simulated or replica weapon. The statute focuses on the harms created, not the manner of creating the harm. The record shows substantial evidence that the appellant's possession of the toy gun created fear and apprehension in the victims. Appellant argues that we should put aside this testimony because it was based upon the witnesses' mistaken assessment of the apparent threat. Appellant's argument fails because, during a robbery, people confronted with what they believe is a deadly weapon cannot be expected to maintain a high level of critical perception.[1]

By extension, appellant also argues that the toy gun did not jeopardize the life of any person because it did not increase the police's burden to interdict the crime during its commission or aftermath and could not have provoked the police's use of a deadly response that could have endangered others. This argument fails because the police must formulate a response to an apparently armed robber during the course of the crime, not after it. They must confront the risk that a replica or simulated gun creates before knowing that it presents no actual threat. These confrontations often lead to gunfire and casualties. *See, e.g.,* L.A. Times, Oct. 18, 1988, § 2, at 3, col. 1 (San Diego County ed.); *id.,* May 13, 1988, § 2, at 2, col. 5 (home ed.).

CONCLUSION

The values of justice, administrability, and deterrence require the rule that a robber's use of a replica or simulated weapon that appears to be a genuine weapon to those present at the scene of the crime, or to those charged with responsibility for responding to the crime, carries the same penalty as the use of a genuine weapon. In this case appellant avoided the harsher penalties associated with use of a firearm in violation of section 924(c) by proving that he only had simulated the use of a firearm. However, the appellant's decision to bluff did not eliminate the harms that Congress intended to address in section 2113(d).

AFFIRMED.

1. The recent trend in toy and replica manufacturing to duplicate precisely the outward appearance of genuine weaponry compounds the difficulty and risk of making any distinction. *See* N.Y. Times, Oct. 16, 1988, § 4, at 7, col. 1. This trend has led some state and local governments to enact bans on realistic toy guns. *See* N.Y. Times, Aug. 5, 1988, § A, at col. 1; L.A. Times, Apr. 29, 1988, § 1, at 2, col. 6 (home ed.). Congress has held hearings on a federal ban. 134 *Cong.Rec.* D 1084 (daily ed. Aug. 11, 1988).

CASE

Stephen Alan WOLCOTT,
Petitioner-Appellant,

v.

Sandra Lee WOLCOTT,
Respondent-Appellee.

No. 9308.
Court of Appeals of New Mexico
March 5, 1987.

Certiorari Denied April 9, 1987.
105 N.M. 608, 735 P.2d 326 (Ct. App. 1987)

OPINION

FRUMAN, Judge.

Our opinion, previously filed on February 3, 1987, is withdrawn and the following opinion is substituted therefor.

Husband appeals from the denial of his post-divorce motions to reduce or abate his child support obligations and to terminate or abate his alimony obligation. Husband relied upon his voluntary change of employment, which resulted in a major reduction of his income, as the substantial change of circumstances justifying his motions. In denying these motions, the trial court found that husband had not acted in good faith with regard to his support obligations when he changed employment.

Husband's issues on appeal are: "1. Whether the voluntary career change of a professional never justifies modification of his support obligation, even if undertaken in good faith." and 2. Whether there is substantial evidence to support the trial court's finding that husband was not acting in good faith when he changed specialty.

As the first issue is presented in the abstract, it would require an advisory opinion on review. This court does not give advisory opinions. *In re Bunnell,* 100 N.M. 242, 668 P.2d 1119 (Ct.App.1983). Although the first issue will not be directly addressed, it will be generally considered in our review of the second issue. We affirm the trial court on the second issue.

FACTS

Following their marriage of thirteen years, the parties were divorce in December 1983. Pursuant to the marital settlement agreement incorporated into the decree of dissolution, husband was to pay $1,500 monthly for the support of the three minor children, and $300 monthly for alimony for a period of five years. At the time of the divorce, husband was a physician specializing in obstetrics and gynecology in Albuquerque.

For a number of years husband had considered changing his specialty to psychiatry. In March 1985, he was accepted in a psychiatric residency program in Washington, D.C. Husband closed his Albuquerque office in June 1985 and commenced his residency the following month. The duration of the program is three to four years, and during this period, husband's annual gross income will range from approximately $21,000 to $24,000. This salary is approximately one-fourth of his annual gross income during the several years prior to and the year following the divorce.

In June 1985, husband unilaterally reduced his combined monthly child support and alimony payment from $1,800 to $550, contrary to the terms of the marital settlement agreement and without judicial approval or forewarning his former spouse.

DISCUSSION

Husband contends that the denial of his motion for reduction of support payments was erroneously based on the trial court's finding of a lack of good faith in changing his speciality and that there was not substantial evidence to support this finding.

To justify modification in the amount of child support already awarded, there must be evidence of a "substantial change of circumstances which materially affects the existing welfare of the child and which must have occurred since the prior adjudication where child support was originally awarded." *Henderson v. Lekvold,* 95 N.M. 288, 291, 621 P.2d 505, 508 (1980). See *Spingola v. Spingola,* 91 N.M. 737, 580 P.2d 958 (1978). A similar change in circumstances of the supported spouse must be shown before the request may be granted as to alimony. See *Brister v. Brister,* 92 N.M. 711, 594 P.2d 1167 (1979). The recipient's actual need for support is the essential criterion. See *Weaver v. Weaver,* 100 N.M. 165, 667 P.2d 970 (1983); *Brister v. Brister.*

Husband, as the petitioner for the modification, had the burden of proving to the trial court's satisfaction that circumstances had substantially changed and, thereby, justified his requests. See *Smith v. Smith,* 98 N.M. 468, 649 P.2d 1381 (1982); *Spingola v. Spingola.* Any change in support obligations is a matter within the discretion of the trial court, and appellate review is limited to a determination of whether that discretion has been abused. *Henderson v. Lekvold.* If substantial evidence exists to support the trial court's findings, they will be upheld. See *Chavez v. Chavez,* 98 N.M. 678, 652 P.2d 228 (1982). Cf. *Pitcher v. Pitcher,* 91 N.M. 504, 576 P.2d 1135 (1978).

The common trend in various jurisdictions is that a good faith career change, resulting in a decreased income, *may* constitute a material change in circumstances that warrants a reduction in a spouse's support obligation. See *Thomas v. Thomas,* 281 Ala. 397, 203 So.2d 118 (1967); *Graham v. Graham,* 21 Ill.App.3d 1032, 316 N.E.2d 143 (1974); *Schuler v. Schuler,* 382 Mass. 366, 416 N.E.2d 197 (1981); *Giesner v. Giesner,* 319 N.W.2d 718 (Minn.1982); *Fogel v. Fogel,* 184 Neb. 425, 168 N.W.2d 275 (1969); *Nelson v. Nelson,* 225 Or. 257, 357 P.2d 536 (1960); *Anderson v. Anderson,* 503 S.W.2d 124 (Tex.Civ.App. 1973); *Lambert v. Lambert,* 66 Wash.2d 503, 403 P.2d 664 (1965). Likewise, where the career change is not made in good faith, a reduction in one's support obligations will not be warranted. See *In re Marriage of Ebert,* 81 Ill.App.3d 44, 36 Ill.Dec. 415, 400 N.E.2d 995 (1980) (evidence of a desire to evade support responsibilities); *Moncada v. Moncada,* 81 Mich. App. 26, 264 N.W.2d 104 (1978) (no evidence that husband acted in bad faith or with willful disregard for the welfare of his dependents); *Bedford v. Bedford,* 49 Mich. App. 424, 212 N.W.2d 260 (1973) (husband voluntarily avoided re-employment opportunities); *Nelson v. Nelson* (no evidence that the sale of a medical practice and assumption of clinic duties, resulting in a decrease in income, was made to jeopardize the interests of the children); *Commonwealth v. Saul,* 175 Pa.Super. 540, 107 A.2d 182 (1954) (husband literally gave away assets available for support payments). *See generally* Annot., 89 A.L.R.2d 1 at 54 (1963).

Husband challenges the trial court's findings that: (1) at the time husband entered the marital settlement agreement, he had planned to terminate his private practice and return to school, but did not so advise wife; (2) although wife may have had prior knowledge of husband's future employment desires, she had no reason to believe that he would effect a career change upon entering the settlement agreement, if it interfered with the support obligations he was assuming; and (3) husband was not acting in good faith with regard to his child support and alimony obligations when he voluntarily made his career change.

The record contains both direct and reasonably inferred evidence from the testimony of the parties to support the first two challenged findings. The third finding is supported by evidence of husband's disregard for several financial obligations undertaken by him in the marital settlement agreement, by his failure or inability to make a full disclosure of his income and assets to wife and the court, and by his self-indulgence with regard to his own lifestyle and personal necessities without regard to the necessities of his children and his former spouse. We find this evidence sufficient to support the trial court's decision to deny husband's petition for a modification of his child support obligation.

Husband also argues that, during their marriage, wife was willing to make changes in the family's lifestyle as would be necessary to accommodate his career change. Because of this, husband contends that his career change following the divorce does not indicate a lack of good faith. Husband did not, however, request a finding as to this contention, and his failure to do so waives any merit the argument may have. See *Worland v. Worland,* 89 N.M. 291, 551 P.2d 981 (1976).

In the determination of alimony, the recipient's actual need for support is the focal point. See *Brister v. Brister.* While husband did request a finding as to wife's employment and there was testimony as to her employment, there was also testimony indicating her continued need for alimony. We find this evidence sufficient to support the trial court's decision to continue wife's alimony.

Although husband asserts that his voluntary career change was made entirely in good faith, without a disregard of the welfare of his children and former spouse, this change does not automatically mandate a reduction in his support obligation. See *Spingola v. Spingola.* The decision as to reducing or maintaining the support obligation rests within the trial court's discretion. *Id.*

We recognize that the "responsibilities of begetting a family many times raise havoc with dreams. Nevertheless, the duty [to support] persists, with full authority in the State to enforce it." *Romano v. Romano,* 133 Vt. 314, 316, 340 A.2d 63, 63 (1975).

Based upon our review of the record we conclude that the decision of the trial court does not constitute an abuse of its discretion. Its decision is affirmed.

IT IS SO ORDERED.

DONNELLY, C.J., and ALARID, J., concur.

APPENDIX B

Appellate Court Brief

INTRODUCTION

The brief of the appellee in the case of *Frank Lewis v. the U.S. Attorney, U.S. Marshal and New Mexico Department of Corrections* is presented in this appendix. The brief was filed in the United States Court of Appeals for the Tenth Circuit. The legal research, legal analysis, and initial drafts of this brief were performed by Gardner Miller. Mr. Miller received his Associate of Applied Science degree in Legal Assistant Studies from Albuquerque Technical-Vocational Institute, a community college. He works as a paralegal in the Criminal Division of the United States Attorney's office for the District of New Mexico.

The Tenth Circuit Court of Appeals decided this case on the briefs submitted to the court (there was no oral argument). The decision was in favor of the appellee (United States Government).

UNITED STATES COURT OF APPEALS

TENTH CIRCUIT

NO. 94-2275

FRANK LEWIS,

Petitioner-Appellant,

vs.

U.S. Attorney, U.S. Marshal and
New Mexico Department of Corrections,

Respondents-Appellees.

APPEAL FROM THE UNITED STATES DISTRICT COURT
FOR THE DISTRICT OF NEW MEXICO

BRIEF OF APPELLEE

ORAL ARGUMENT IS NOT REQUESTED

JOHN J. KELLY
United States Attorney

LARRY GOMEZ
Assistant U.S. Attorney
P.O. Box 607
Albuquerque, New Mexico 87103
(505) 766-3341

Attorneys for Appellee

January, 1995

TABLE OF CONTENTS

TABLE OF CASES AND OTHER AUTHORITIES

TABLE OF CASES

TABLE OF CASES, cont.

PAGE

TABLE OF OTHER AUTHORITIES

PRIOR OR RELATED APPEALS

The United States informs this Court, pursuant to 10th Cir. R. 28.2(a), that there are no prior or related appeals in this case.

STATEMENT OF ISSUES PRESENTED FOR REVIEW

This appeal is a review of the District Court's denial of appellant's Habeas Petition, and presents the following issues for review:

POINT I:

WHETHER THE DISTRICT COURT SHOULD HAVE DISMISSED APPELLANT'S HABEAS PETITION FOR LACK OF JURISDICTION?

POINT II:

WHETHER THE DISTRICT COURT ACTED PROPERLY IN DENYING APPELLANT'S HABEAS PETITION ON THE MERITS AND DISMISSING THE PETITION WITH PREJUDICE?

STATEMENT OF THE CASE

On March 15, 1993, Petitioner-Appellant Frank Lewis (herein after referred to as Lewis) filed a *pro se* Petition for Writ of Habeas Corpus under 28 U.S.C. § 2254 for a person in state custody.[1] (Doc. 1). On March 25, 1993, United States Magistrate Judge William Deaton issued an Order appointing Tova Indritz, the Federal Public Defender, to represent Lewis. (Doc. 4).

On May 25, 1993, Lewis filed an Amended Petition (Doc. 5) with numerous exhibits. The government filed its Answer on July 20, 1993, requesting that Lewis' Amended Petition be dismissed for lack of jurisdiction. (Doc. 8). Lewis then filed a Memorandum Brief in support of his Amended Petition on September 27, 1993. (Doc. 12). Because this Memorandum Brief restructured Lewis' habeas petition under 28 U.S.C. § 2241 and § 2255, revamped old arguments, requested new remedies and introduced new exhibits, it was, for all practical purposes, a new habeas petition. Without being ordered to do so, the government responded to Lewis' Memorandum Brief on December 13, 1993. (Doc. 14).

On October 4, 1994, United States Magistrate Judge Lorenzo Garcia issued his proposed findings and recommended disposition of Lewis' habeas petition. (Doc. 17). Lewis filed

---

[1] The following day, March 16, 1993, the New Mexico Department of Corrections transferred Lewis into Federal custody.

his objections to Judge Garcia's findings and recommended disposition on October 17, 1994 (Doc. 18).

On November 8, 1994, Senior United States District Judge Juan Burciaga adopted Judge Garcia's proposed findings and recommended disposition and ordered that Lewis' action be dismissed with prejudice. (Doc. 19). Lewis timely filed a notice of appeal of Judge Burciaga's Order on November 22, 1994. (Doc. 20).

STATEMENT OF THE FACTS

The facts underlying Lewis' habeas petition are not in dispute. They are summarized from the record as follows:

On February 27, 1985, Lewis pled guilty in New Mexico State District Court for the Second Judicial District (Bernalillo County) to two crimes he committed on December 22, 1983. One was the felony offense of heroin possession and the other was the misdemeanor offense of possession of drug paraphernalia. (Doc. 5, Petitioner's Exhibit 1).

As a result of these convictions, on May 17, 1985, State District Judge Burt Cosgrove sentenced Lewis to the custody of the New Mexico Department of Corrections for a term of 6-1/2 years. The court also ordered Lewis to turn himself in to state authorities at 9:00 a.m. on May 21, 1985 to begin serving his sentence. On June 4, 1985, about two weeks after Lewis started serving his sentence, a federal grand jury indicted him on four counts of heroin trafficking. The first two counts charged Lewis with possession with intent to distribute heroin and distribution of heroin on or about August 18, 1983. The other two counts charged that Lewis committed the same offenses on or about August 25, 1983. (Doc. 5, Petitioner's Exhibit 2).

On April 29, 1986, as a consequence of the federal indictment, United States District Judge Juan Burciaga issued a Writ of Habeas Corpus Ad Prosequendum commanding the Warden of the New Mexico State Penitentiary to deliver Lewis into federal custody so that he could be prosecuted on the federal drug charges. (Doc. 5, Petitioner's Exhibit 5).

On May 23, 1986, pursuant to a plea agreement, Lewis pled guilty to Count IV of the Indictment (heroin distribution). In return, the government agreed to dismiss the other three counts against him and not seek a sentence enhancement under 21 U.S.C. § 851, based on his prior state drug conviction. The agreement also stated there was no agreement that "a specific sentence is the appropriate disposition of this case." (Doc. 5, Petitioner's Exhibit 3).

Judge Burciaga accepted Lewis' guilty plea and, on July 18, 1986, sentenced Lewis to eight years imprisonment to be followed by a special parole term of three years. After imposing the sentence, the court dismissed the remaining counts against Lewis. The Judgment was entered on the docket on July 28, 1986. (Doc. 5, Petitioner's Exhibit 4).

Lewis was returned to the state's custody on July 23, 1986. (Doc. 12, Petitioner's Exhibit 16 at 3).

Five months later, on December 22, 1986, Lewis escaped from the New Mexico state penitentiary and also kidnapped someone. The record does not show when he was apprehended. However, on January 12, 1988, Lewis was convicted in state district Court (Thirteenth Judicial District, Valencia County) for the felony offenses of Escape from the penitentiary and

Kidnapping. On April 11, 1988, the state district court sentenced Lewis to the custody of the New Mexico Corrections Department for 19 years for these convictions. The court then suspended eight years of the sentence and ordered the remaining eleven years to be served in the state penitentiary, "consecutive to any other state or federal time that he is now serving or served." (Doc. 5, Petitioner's Exhibit 6). According to an affidavit from Lewis' attorney at this sentencing, State District Court Judge Mayo T. Boucher actually wanted the new eleven-year sentence to be concurrent with Lewis' existing state and federal sentences. (Doc. 5, Petitioner's Exhibit 9).

Consequently, the state district court for Valencia County issued a series of Amended Judgments regarding Lewis' latest state sentence. The first, filed August 27, 1990, ordered the sentence to run concurrently with the eight-year federal sentence, but consecutively to the original state sentence of 6 1/2 years. (Doc. 5, Petitioner's Exhibit 7). The second, filed October 31, 1990, made Lewis' latest sentence run concurrently with both his original state sentence and his federal sentence. (Doc. 5, Petitioner's Exhibit 8). The Third Amended Judgment, filed September 10, 1992, retained the basic nineteen-year sentence, but suspended half of it (9-1/2 years) instead of the eight years that had been previously suspended. It again ordered the state sentence to be served concurrently with the federal sentence, this time specifying the underlying case number, and ordered Lewis to be remanded to the custody of the U.S. Marshal's Office for transfer to a federal prison to serve his federal sentence. (Doc. 5, Petitioner's Exhibit 10). A year earlier, New Mexico prison officials had given Lewis written notification that the U.S. Marshal's Office, on the advice of the U.S. Attorney's Office, would not take him into federal custody until he had been paroled or discharged from the state. (Doc. 5, Petitioner's Exhibit 12). The Fourth (and final) Amended Judgment was filed on January 7, 1993. It again specified that Lewis' state sentence for escape and kidnapping run concurrently with his federal sentence to be served and ordered Lewis' immediate transfer to federal custody. (Doc. 5, Petitioner's Exhibit 11).

As a result of his federal sentence, a federal detainer had been lodged against Lewis while he was incarcerated at the New Mexico state penitentiary. However, despite the state court judgment ordering his transfer to federal custody, the U.S. Marshal's Office refused to take him into custody until he had been released from all his state sentences. (Doc. 12, Petitioner's Exhibit 17 at 2).

Upon being paroled from his final state sentence, Lewis was transferred to federal custody on March 16, 1993 and began serving his federal sentence. (Doc. 12, Petitioner's Exhibit 15 at 2). On April 30, 1993, Lewis arrived at his present place of incarceration, the Federal Correctional Institution (FCI) at Florence, Colorado. (Doc. 12, Petitioner's Exhibit 16 at 3).

After his arrival at FCI Florence, Lewis sought to receive credit against his sentence through a Request for Administrative Remedy. His request was denied, as was his appeal of that denial. (Doc. 12, Petitioner's Exhibits 14 and 15). Lewis then pursued the habeas petition which was denied by the federal district court.

POINT I

LEWIS' HABEAS PETITION SHOULD HAVE BEEN DISMISSED BY THE DISTRICT COURT FOR LACK OF JURISDICTION.

STANDARD OF REVIEW: Jurisdictional issues are reviewed de novo. United States v. 51 Pieces of Real Property, 17 F.3d 1306, 1309 (10th Cir. 1994).

It is well settled that jurisdictional issues are important enough that they may be raised at any time during the proceedings. McGrath v. Kristensen, 340 U.S. 162, 167 (1950); United States v. Siviglia, 686 F.2d 832, 835 (10th Cir. 1981), cert. denied 461 U.S. 918 (1983); Bledsoe v. Wirtz, 384 F.2d 767, 769 (10th Cir. 1967).

28 U.S.C. § 2242 provides that a habeas petition shall state "the name of the person who has custody over him" (i.e. the petitioner). Likewise, 28 U.S.C. § 2243 states: "The writ, or order to show cause shall be directed to the person having custody of the person detained." As the Supreme Court noted: "The writ of habeas corpus does not act upon the prisoner who seeks relief, but upon the person who holds him in what is alleged to be unlawful custody." Braden v. 30th Judicial Circuit Court of Kentucky, 410 U.S. 484, 494-5 (1973). The Braden Court then quoted from In the Matter of Jackson, 15 Mich. 417, 439-440 (1867), characterizing the quotation as a "classic statement":

> 'The important fact to be observed in regard to the mode of procedure upon this writ is, that it is directed to, and served upon, not the person confined but his jailer. The

> officer or person who serves it does not unbar the prison doors and set the prisoner free, but the court relieves him by compelling the oppressor to release his constraint. The whole force of the writ is spent upon the respondent'.

410 U.S. at 495.

When the habeas petitioner is incarcerated, the only appropriate respondent to his habeas petition is the warden of the facility where he is incarcerated. Guerra v. Meese, 786 F.2d 414, 417 (D.C. Cir. 1986) ("Until they are paroled . . . the proper respondents are the wardens of the federal facilities at which the prisoners are confined."). Guerra was expressly reaffirmed in Chatman-Bey v. Thornburgh, 864 F.2d 804, 810-11 (D.C. Cir. 1988) ("[T]he proper defendant in federal habeas cases is the warden."). See also Joyner v. Henman, 755 F.Supp. 982, 984 (D.Kan. 1991) (Proper respondent for petitioner's habeas action is the warden at USP Leavenworth because he is the petitioner's present custodian). The "custodian", for habeas corpus purposes, is the person having day-to-day control of the prisoner and is the only one who can produce "the body" of the habeas petitioner. Guerra, supra at 416.

The record clearly shows that Lewis was delivered to FCI Florence on April 30, 1993. (Doc. 12, Petitioner's Exhibit 16 at 3). On May 25, 1993, Lewis (through his appointed counsel) filed his Amended Petition. (Doc. 5). In this Amended Petition, Lewis acknowledged that "he is currently in the custody of the Bureau of Prisons at Florence, Colorado. (Doc.

5 at 4). Yet, the respondent to his Amended Petition was not his present custodian, the warden of FCI Florence. Instead, Lewis named as respondents: the U.S. Attorney, (for the District of New Mexico), the U.S. Marshal (for the same District) and the New Mexico Department of Corrections.

A similar situation occurred in Billiteri v. United States Board of Parole, 541 F.2d 938 (2d Cir. 1976). There, instead of naming as respondent the Warden of USP Lewisburg, Pennsylvania where he was confined, the petitioner named the parole board which had denied his release. In dismissing his petition, the Billiteri Court declared:

> It would have imposed no great hardship on Billiteri to have brought his action against the Warden in the Middle District of Pennsylvania, as he should have done. As he did not, the present case must be dismissed for lack of jurisdiction over an application for a writ of habeas corpus . . .

541 F.2d at 948-49.

Recently, the Ninth Circuit in Stanley v. California Supreme Court, 21 F.3d 359 (9th Cir. 1994), addressed the same situation as here where there were two habeas petitions with multiple respondents, but none of them were the petitioner's custodian:

> A petitioner for habeas corpus relief must name the state officer having custody of him or her as the respondent to the petition . . . . Failure to name the petitioner's custodian as a respondent deprives federal courts of personal jurisdiction. (Citations omitted). . . . Neither of Stanley's two petitions named his custodian as a respondent

> and <u>therefore</u> the district lacked jurisdiction. (Emphasis added).

21 F.3d at 360.

In its initial Answer to Lewis' Amended Petition, the government sought to have the petition dismissed for lack of jurisdiction. (Doc. 8). The district court never ruled on this request, but impliedly rejected it by addressing the merits of Lewis' Amended Petition as presented in his Memorandum Brief.

For the reasons stated herein, this Court, as a matter of law, should remand the case with instructions to dismiss for lack of jurisdiction.

POINT II

IN DECIDING ON THE MERITS OF LEWIS' HABEAS PETITION THE DISTRICT COURT ACTED PROPERLY IN DENYING THE PETITION AND DISMISSING IT WITH PREJUDICE.

STANDARD OF REVIEW: This Court reviews de novo a district court's decision to deny habeas relief. Sinclair v. Herman, 986 F.2d 407, 408 (10th Cir.), cert. denied, ____ U.S. ____, 114 S.Ct. 129 (1993).

As an introductory note, it is recognized that, should this court indeed remand the case with instructions to dismiss for lack of jurisdiction, Lewis may be tempted to file another habeas petition under 28 U.S.C. § 2241 in perhaps a different forum. In that event, an opinion from this Court which also discusses the merits of Lewis' contentions would prove very useful.

The thrust of Lewis' habeas petition was that he was entitled to receive credit against his federal sentence because the U.S. Marshal's Service, on advice from the U.S. Attorney, ignored the custody transfer orders issued by a New Mexico district court. In his Memorandum Brief (Doc. 12), Lewis introduced a second stratagem under 28 U.S.C. § 2255 for obtaining the credit he sought. It was to request that Judge Burciaga (who had imposed his federal sentence) recommend nunc pro tunc that New Mexico State Correctional Facilities be designated as the location for serving his federal sentence. In his Order Adopting the Magistrate's Findings and Dismissing Action with Prejudice, Judge Burciaga expressly declined to make such a recommendation. (Doc. 19). Because the decision was clearly within Judge Burciaga's discretion, this avenue for obtaining the desired credit is permanently blocked.

As previously stated, Lewis' main complaint centers around the conduct of the U.S. Marshals. By ignoring the repeated custody transfer orders of a state district judge, they ensured that Lewis would not start serving his federal sentence until he had been paroled from his second state sentence. This also defied the state district court's Orders that Lewis' second state sentence be served concurrently with his imposed but unserved federal sentence.

A somewhat similar situation existed in Del Guzzi v. United States, 980 F.2d 1269 (9th Cir. 1992). The federal marshals in that case also created a consecutive sentence by refusing to accept custody of the defendant until he had completed his state sentence. In Del Guzzi, however, the expectation of concurrent sentences was shared by all parties concerned before the state sentence was imposed and may have even contributed to its length (the statutory maximum). Nonetheless, the court upheld the marshal's actions, stating it had "no authority to violate the statutory mandate that federal authorities need only accept prisoners upon completion of their state sentence and need not credit prisoners with time spent in state custody." Del Guzzi, 980 F.2d at 1271.

In his proposed findings and recommended disposition, Magistrate Judge Garcia found the following guidance from Judge Norris' concurring opinion in Del Guzzi to be "highly instructive." (Doc. 17 at 9).

> While Del Guzzi will get no relief from this court, I hope his case will serve as a lesson to those who are in a position to guard against future cases of this sort. State sentencing judges and defense attorneys in state proceedings should be put on notice. Federal prison officials are under no obligation to, and may well refuse to, follow the recommendation of state sentencing judges that a prisoner be transported to a federal facility. Moreover, concurrent sentences imposed by state judges are nothing more than recommendations to federal officials. Those officials remain free to turn those concurrent sentences into consecutive sentences by refusing to accept the state prisoner until completion of the state sentence and refusing to credit the time the prisoner spent in state custody.

980 F.2d at 1272-73.

To counter this harsh reality, Lewis contends that a prisoner should not be made to suffer because ministerial officers, such as federal marshals, failed to execute a court order. Among the cases Lewis relies upon to support this contention are: Kiendra v. Hadden, 763 F.2d 69 (2d Cir. 1985); United States v. Croft, 450 F.2d 1094 (6th Cir. 1971) and Smith v. Swope, 91 F.2d 260 (9th Cir. 1937). As Magistrate Judge Garcia noted, these cases are easily distinguishable because they involved federal marshals failing to execute orders issued by federal courts, not state courts. (Doc. 17 at 7-9).

Lewis also attempts to find support in Tenth Circuit case law. He cites Bloomgren v. Belaski, 948 F.2d 688, 690 (10th Cir. 1991) for the proposition that "a federal prisoner is entitled to credit for time spent in state prison on an unrelated charge 'if the continued state confinement was exclusively the product of such action by federal law enforcement officials as to justify treating the state jail as the practical equivalent of the federal one'." (Appellant's Brief-in-Chief at 9, 20).

What Lewis fails to mention is that this exception was being applied to the pretrial state time served by Bloomgren on bailable offenses; Bloomgren had been denied bail in accordance with a federal arrest warrant that had been lodged against him after his arrest by state officials. Bloomgren, 948 F.2d at 689-90. In contrast, all of Lewis' state prison time was the direct result of his convictions and sentences imposed by state district courts.

In fact, Bloomgren supports the government's case. Bloomgren had committed his bailable state offenses while on a federal appeal bond from an earlier federal conviction. That conviction became final while Bloomgren was serving a state sentence from yet another set of offenses. Although the state sentencing judge had ordered Bloomgren's state sentence to be concurrent with his unserved federal sentence, the federal marshals refused to take him into custody until he had been paroled from his state sentence. Bloomgren, 948 F.2d at 290-91. The Bloomgren court held:

> Bloomgren thus served his federal sentence after his state sentence, rather than serving them concurrently as anticipated by the state court. Nonetheless, Bloomgren is not entitled to credit on his federal sentence for time spent incarcerated on state charges. The federal government has no duty to take on in Bloomgren's situation into custody. See Smith v. United States Parol Comm'n, 875 F.2d 1361, 1364 (9th Cir. 1989).

948 F.2d at 691.

If the federal government did have such a duty, then merely by ordering concurrent sentences and custody transfers, state courts could require the federal government to assume the costs of incarcerating any state prisoner facing a previously imposed federal sentence.

In imposing Lewis' federal sentence, by not recommending that New Mexico corrections facilities be designated as Lewis' place of federal confinement, Judge Burciaga made it clear that he intended for Lewis' federal sentence to be consecutive to his first state sentence.[2] The Bloomgren Court declared:

> The determination by federal authorities that Bloomgren's federal sentence would run consecutively to his state sentence is a federal matter which cannot be overridden by a state court provision for concurrent

---

[2] In his Memorandum Brief, Lewis acknowledged that Judge Burciaga intended that Lewis serve his federal sentence after his existing state sentence. (Doc. 12 at 19).

> sentencing on a subsequently-obtained state conviction.

948 F.2d at 691.

Also, in Salley v. United States, 786 F.2d 546, 548 (2d Cir. 1986), another federal circuit court observed: "There is no reason why the (United States) district court's sentence, which was prior in time, must give way to that of the State court." (Citations omitted).

Another case in which U.S. Marshals ignored a state judge's order for concurrent sentences was Lionel v. Day, 430 F.Supp. 384 (W.D. Okla. 1976). In Lionel, as here, consecutive sentences resulted and federal prison officials refused to grant the petitioner credit for time spent in state custody. In upholding their decision, the Lionel court declared: "Obviously no comment or order by a state judge can control the service of a federal sentence." 430 F. Supp. at 386.

As established by these cases, the comment by U.S. Marshal John Sanchez that "state court judges cannot dictate when a federal sentence begins" is a correct statement of the law. (Affidavit of Cathleen M. Catanach, Doc. 12, Petitioner's Exhibit 17 at 2). The portions of the Amended Judgments which directed Lewis to be transferred into federal custody (and thus begin serving his federal sentence) were invalid; therefore, the marshals were free to ignore such orders.

A crucial part of Lewis' claim is the theory that, once Lewis was paroled from his first state sentence on December 9,

1989, the state lost its jurisdiction over Lewis and Lewis was now subject to federal jurisdiction by virtue of his federal arrest and conviction that occurred "before the Valencia County case even arose." (Appellant's Brief-in-Chief at 10).

The government's position is based on the fact that Lewis' first state sentence was clearly still in force on April 11, 1988 when his second state sentence was imposed. Therefore, Lewis' second state sentence merely extended the time the State had jurisdiction over Lewis. This also was the conclusion reached by Magistrate Judge Garcia. (Doc. 17 at 6).

The authority for this proposition lies in another Tenth Circuit case, McIntosh v. Looney, 249 F.2d 62 (10th Cir. 1957), cert. denied 355 U.S. 935 (1958), which the appellant has relied upon for support.[3] McIntosh was serving a six-month sentence in a Missouri county jail when, pursuant to a Writ of Habeas Corpus Ad Prosequendum, he was sentenced in federal district court for violation the federal kidnapping statute. He received a five-year sentence, to begin upon completion of his misdemeanor sentence. He was returned to the county jail and, while still serving his six-month sentence, he assaulted a jailer there. McIntosh's misdemeanor sentence was still in

---

[3] McIntosh agreed with the "ministerial officer malfeasance" exception propounded by Smith, calling it the "academic premise" for the claims in its case. McIntosh, 249 F.2d at 64. However, the Court then described why the marshal's actions in its case were proper. (Id.)

force when he was indicted in state court for the assault, pled guilty, and received a five-year sentence. It also was to begin when he completed his misdemeanor sentence. When McIntosh finally completed his six-month sentence, he was taken from the county jail to the Missouri penitentiary to serve his second state sentence. Only after his second state sentence was completed on October 11, 1956 was McIntosh transferred into federal custody to begin serving his federal sentence. McIntosh, 249 F.2d at 63.

Like Lewis, McIntosh claimed the State had lost its jurisdiction over him upon completion of his first state sentence and that the federal marshals had a duty to take into custody at that time to begin serving his federal sentence. Id. at 64. In rejecting his claim, the McIntosh Court declared:

> The State of Missouri . . . had continuous jurisdiction and custody of appellant until October 11, 1956, at which time state jurisdiction and the right to custody were terminated . . . . Appellant's incarceration was continuous and under a single and proper authority, that of the State of Missouri. (Id.).

The Court then compared its case to Harrell v. Shuttleworth, 200 F.2d 490 (5th Cir. 1952). There, while serving a state sentence, a federal court sentenced the prisoner to a federal sentence to begin upon completion of his state sentence. Before completion of the state sentence, the prisoner received an additional state sentence for an offense committed at the state prison. The Harrell Court held that federal sentence did not begin to run upon completion of the first state sentence. The comparison which the McIntosh court made was as follows:

> In Harrell, the state sentences overlapped. In the instant case they were consecutive. The effect was the same -- continuous jurisdiction and custody under a single sovereign authority. (Emphasis added).

249 F.2d at 64.

In recognition of the State of New Mexico's jurisdiction over Lewis and Judge Burciaga's intent that Lewis' federal sentence be consecutive, a federal detainer was lodged against Lewis at the New Mexico State Penitentiary. It was not linked to a specific conviction or sentence and it could be executed only after New Mexico had released Lewis from all his state sentences, thereby relinquishing its jurisdiction over him. This occurred on March 16, 1993 and Lewis was transferred into federal custody on that date.

In his Appeal Brief, Lewis acknowledges that 18 U.S.C. § 3568 (since repealed)[4] governed the calculation of federal sentences imposed for crimes committed prior to November 1, 1987. (Appellant's Brief-in-Chief at 12).

This statute clearly stated "The sentence of imprisonment . . . shall commence to run from the date on which

---

[4] 18 U.S.C. § 3568 (1982) (repealed effective November 1, 1987 by P.L. 98-473, Title II §§ 212(a)(2), 98 Stat. 1987, 2031 (1984), reenacted in part, 18 U.S.C. § 3585 (1988).

such person is received at the penitentiary, reformatory, or jail for service of such sentence."

Although Lewis decries applying § 3568 "mechanistically", there is no other way to apply it. Federal courts have uniformly interpreted the plain language of § 3568 as precluding the calculation of the time served on a federal sentence from any date other than the one on which the prisoner was delivered into federal custody. See, e.g., Thomas v. Whalen, 962 F.2d 358, 363 (4th Cir. 1992); Meagher v. Clark, 943 F.2d 1277, 1282 (11th Cir. 1991); Thomas v. Brewer, 923 F.2d 1361, 1367 (9th Cir. 1991); Scott v. United States, 434 F.2d 11, 21 (5th Cir. 1970).

Title 18 U.S.C. § 3568 also stated that, in order to receive credit against a federal sentence for state time served, the offense underlying the state sentence must be "in connection with the offense or acts for which (the federal) sentence was imposed." Lewis' federal sentence was for drug trafficking while his second state sentence (for which he seeks credit against his federal sentence) was for escape and kidnapping. Thus, the statute itself precludes the credit Lewis seeks. See Bloomgren, supra at 690, citing to Goode v. McCune, 543 F.2d 751, 753 (10th Cir. 1976) (no credit for time spent in state custody where state time was attributable to state charges only).

In effect, Lewis' pleadings are an attempt to obtain double credit for much of the time he was incarcerated by the State of New Mexico. In Bruss v. Harris, 479 F.2d 392, 394 (10th Cir. 1973), the court addressed a similar claim:

> We attach no significance to the fact that the state sentence ran concurrently with the previously imposed federal sentence. Petitioner owed a debt to two sovereigns, and each had a right to exact its debt independently of the other. The petitioner's claim is that after having received credit from one sovereign he is entitled to double credit.

Lastly, Lewis decries the perceived unfairness and unjustness of his plight resulting from federal marshals actions. Lewis was convicted of five distinct crimes for which he was sentenced to a total of more than 33 years imprisonment. Even if he serves every day of his federal sentence, his total time of incarceration (even counting the time he was a fugitive) will be less than 16 years.

CONCLUSION AND STATEMENT CONCERNING ORAL ARGUMENT

For the reasons stated above, Lewis' habeas petition was properly denied. Oral argument is not necessary in this case and the matter should be submitted on the briefs of the parties.

Respectfully submitted,

JOHN J. KELLY
United States Attorney

LARRY GÓMEZ
Assistant U.S. Attorney
P.O. Box 607
Albuquerque, NM 87103
(505) 766-3341

CERTIFICATE OF SERVICE

I HEREBY CERTIFY that the Brief of Appellee was served upon Defendant-Appellant, Frank Lewis, by mailing two true and correct copies to his Attorney of record, Tova Indritz, at her address of record, Post Office Box 449, Albuquerque, New Mexico, 87102, this 27th day of January, 1995.

Larry Gómez

LARRY GÓMEZ
Assistant U.S. Attorney
P.O. Box 607
Albuquerque, NM 87103
(505) 766-3341

APPENDIX C

Overview of Legal Citation

INTRODUCTION

Whenever a reference is made in legal writing to the law (primary authority) or a nonlaw source a court may rely on (secondary authority), the source of the reference should be identified. This reference is called a *citation.*

A citation provides the information necessary to allow the reader to locate the reference, *i.e.,* the specific statute, court opinion, law review, encyclopedia, and so on. Citations are usually required in office legal memorandums and court briefs. They also may be included in general legal correspondence or other documents when there is reference to a legal authority.

It is essential that the information included in a citation is correct. It is useless to refer a reader to a source of information and incorrectly identify the location of the source. The reader who takes the time to look up the authority and does not locate the reference at the page or volume indicated in the citation will not be pleased. There are several additional reasons why it is important that your citations be correct:

- A citation that is incorrect in either form or content sends the message that the drafter is not careful. If there are errors in citations, the reader may wonder if there are also errors in the substance of the research.
- Errors in documents submitted to a court may cause the judge to question the competence of the attorney and the quality and content of the research and analysis. Court rules require proper form, and improper citation exhibits a disregard for those rules.
- Opposing counsel may question the ability of the attorney to mount an effective opposition and be less inclined to settle a case.
- A paralegal's professional reputation is determined by the quality of his or her work product. A paralegal's research and analysis skills become suspect if research sources are not properly presented.

The precision of a citation and the manner of its presentation are critical elements of legal writing. The main guide and source of authority on legal citations is *The Bluebook, A Uniform System of Citation* published by the Harvard Law Review Association. It presents the rules and proper format for citing constitutions, statutes, regulations, rules, cases, and other legal sources such as legal encyclopedias, law reviews, and so on. Note that it is also necessary to check the local court rules whenever preparing a document to be submitted to a court. The court rules may require a citation format that differs from *The Bluebook* format.

The following discussion and examples present a brief summary of rules and citation forms for specific authorities. The discussion and examples are based upon *The Bluebook: A Uniform System of Citation* (16th ed. 1996).

PRIMARY AUTHORITY

Constitutions

Constitutions usually consist of articles and amendments. The citation form for a constitution consists of the abbreviated name of the constitution, the article, and the section.

For Example: U.S. Const. art. IV, § 3; N.M. Const. art. IV, § 1.

In the first example, the elements of the citation are as follows:

1. U.S. Const.—the abbreviated name
2. art. IV—the article
3. § 3—the section number

Statutes

Statutory citations include the following:

1. Numbers representing the specific topic, section, and subsection
2. The abbreviated name of the publication, code, or statute
3. The year of the publication or supplement

Federal Statutes

The federal statutes of general public interest are printed in three separate publications:

1. *United States Code* (U.S.C.)
2. *United States Code Annotated* (U.S.C.A.) (West Publishing Company)
3. *United States Code Service* (U.S.C.S.) (Lawyers Cooperative Publishing)

The official code is the *United States Code* (U.S.C.)

For Example: 15 U.S.C. § 7 (1988).

In this example, the elements of the citation are as follows:

1. 15—the volume number
   § 7—the section number
2. U.S.C.—the abbreviated name of the code
3. (1988)—the year of the publication or supplement

The popular name of the statute is not required but may be included.

For Example: Robinson-Patman Act, 15 U.S.C. § 7 (1988).

State Statutes

The citation form for state statutes varies from state to state. *The Bluebook* and local court rules should be consulted for the proper citation format.

For Example: N.M. Stat. Ann. § 36-1-1 (Michie 1978).

In this example, the elements of the citation are as follows:

1. § 36-1-1—the chapter, article, and section number
2. N.M. Stat. Ann.—the name of the statutes
3. (Michie 1978)—the name of the publisher and the year of the edition of the statutes

Procedural Rules

Citations to procedural rules should include the following:

1. The abbreviated name identifying the rule
2. The number of the rule

For Example: Fed. R. Civ. P. 4 (rule 4 of the Federal Rules of Civil Procedure); Fed. R. Evid. 407 (rule 407 of the Federal Rules of Evidence); Fed. R. Crim. P. 18 (rule 18 of the Federal Rules of Criminal Procedure); Fed. R. App. P. 4 (rule 4 of the Federal Rules of Appellate Procedure)

Administrative Law

The components of administrative rule/regulation citations are the following:

1. The title (topic or agency) number in the code publication
2. The abbreviated name of the publication (*Code of Federal Regulations*—C.F.R.; *Federal Register*—Fed. Reg.)
3. The section number or page number of the regulation/rule
4. The year of the publication

For Example: 27 C.F.R. § 20.235 (1988); 48 Fed. Reg. 37,315 (1983).

In these examples, the elements of the citations are as follows:

1. 27 and 48—the title (topic or agency) number in the publication
2. C.F.R. and Fed. Reg.—the abbreviated name of the publication
3. § 20.235 and 37,315—the section number or page number of the regulation or rule
4. 1988 and 1983—the year of the publication

Case Law—Court Opinions

Citations to federal and state cases are similar in form. A discussion of the elements of a case and a case citation is presented in Chapter 4. The components of a case citation are the following:

1. The case name
2. The reporter in which the case is published (the volume number, abbreviation of the case reporter, and page number where the case begins)
3. The parallel (unofficial) publication, if any (the volume number, abbreviation of the parallel publication, and page number where the case begins)
4. The abbreviation for the court issuing the opinion unless the issuing court is included in the reporter abbreviation
5. The year of the decision

Federal Court Decisions

The following is an example of a citation to a United States Supreme Court decision.

For Example: *United States v. Matlock,* 415 U.S. 164 (1974).

In this example, the elements of the citation are as follows:

1. *United States v. Matlock*—case name
2. 415 U.S. 164—the reporter in which the case is published: 415 is the volume number, 164 is the page number, and U.S. is the abbreviation of the case reporter
3. No parallel publication is included in this citation.
4. The court issuing the opinion is not identified because it is apparent from the citation. *The United States Reports* publishes the opinions of the United States Supreme Court. Notice that in the next two examples the identity of the court issuing the opinion is included (9th Cir. and N.D. Ill.).
5. 1974—the year of the decision

The following two examples are examples of citations to decision of the United States Court of Appeals and the United States District Court respectively.

For Example: *United States v. Martinez-Jiminez,* 864 F.2d 664 (9th Cir. 1989); *United States v. Central R.R.,* 436 F. Supp. 739 (N.D. Ill. 1990).

State Court Decisions

The following is an example of a citation to a New Mexico supreme court decision.

For Example: *Britton v. Britton,* 100 N.M. 424, 671 P.2d 1135 (1983).

In this example, the elements of the citation are as follows:

1. *Britton v. Britton*—case name
2. 100 N.M. 424—the reporter in which the case is published: 100 is the volume number, 424 is the page number, and N.M. is the abbreviation of the case reporter
3. 671 P.2d 1135—the parallel (unofficial) publication: 671 is the volume number, 1135 is the page number, and P.2d is the abbreviation of the parallel publication
4. The court issuing the opinion is not identified because it is apparent from the citation. The decision was rendered by the New Mexico supreme court. If a court other than the New Mexico supreme court issued the decision, the initials of the court would be included with the year of the opinion, for example: (Ct. App. 1983).
5. 1983—the year of the decision

KEY POINTS CHECKLIST: *Case Citations*

- ❑ If you have any questions concerning case citation, consult *The Bluebook* or the applicable local court rules.
- ❑ Case names should be italicized. If they cannot be italicized, they should be underscored.
- ❑ Case names should include the last names of the plaintiff and defendant.

For Example: *Correct:* *Smith v. Jones*
Incorrect: *Mary Smith v. John Jones*

- ❑ If there are multiple plaintiffs and defendants, use the last name of the plaintiff and defendant listed first.
- ❑ If there is a parallel citation, it is normally included in the citation. *The Bluebook* should

be consulted for the rules governing parallel citations.

- ❑ A parallel citation may not be available because the state does not publish an official case reporter or the opinion is so recent that one is not available. When this occurs, the case should be cited as follows: *Beam v. Cullett,* 615 P.2d 1196 (Or. Ct. App. 1980).

Note the abbreviation "Or. Ct. App." before the date in the parentheses. This abbreviation refers to the state court that issued the decision. In this instance, the court is the Oregon court of appeals. If the highest court in Oregon issued the decision, then only "Or." would be included in the parentheses. This lets the reader know which state and which state court issued the opinion.

If it is clear from the citation which state issued the decision, as illustrated by "N.M." in the citation for the *Britton* case above, it is not necessary to include a reference to the state next to the date of the opinion.

The general rule is that the court rendering the opinion will be indicated only if it is not the highest court in the state.

For Example: If the New Mexico court of appeals issued the opinion in the *Britton* case, it would be indicated next to the year of the opinion: (Ct. App. 1983). If the New Mexico supreme court rendered the decision, there would be no reference to a court next to the year of the opinion: (1983).

- ❑ When citing or quoting information contained on a specific page of a case, you must show the page as follows: *Vestron, Inc. v. Lowell,* 347 U.S. 483, 487 (1965).
- ❑ The short form *"Id."* may be used when a full citation of the quoted or referred to material is given immediately above. In other words, this short form is used where there is no other citation between the full citation and *Id.*

For Example: "The case on point is *Britton v. Britton,* 100 N.M. 424, 671 P.2d 1135 (1983). In this case, the court addressed several issues involving child custody. In regard to undivided custody orders, the court stated 'When. . . .' *Id.* at 425."

In this example, if there was a reference to another case between the full citation of *Britton* and the quote from *Britton,* the use of *Id.* would not be appropriate.

- ❑ According to *The Bluebook, supra* should not be used in reference to cases, statutes, or constitutions. Its use is appropriate when referring to legislative hearings, books, periodicals, services, treatises, regulations, and so on. Consult *The Bluebook* for the proper use of *supra.*
- ❑ Whenever you are quoting material, refer to *The Bluebook* for guidance.

SECONDARY AUTHORITY

Annotated Law Reports

The components of an *Annotated Law Reports* (A.L.R.) citation are the following:

1. The full name of the author
2. The word "Annotation"
3. The title (underscored or italicized)
4. The volume number
5. The abbreviated name of the publication
6. The page number where the annotation begins
7. The year of publication

For Example: Michael J. Weber, Annotation, *Application of Statute of Limitations to Actions for Breach of Duty in Performing Services of Public Accountant,* 7 A.L.R.5th 852 (1992).

In this example, the elements of the citation are as follows:

1. Michael J. Weber—the full name of the author
2. The word "Annotation"

3. *Application of Statute of Limitations to Actions for Breach of Duty in Performing Services of Public Accountant*—the title (italicized or underscored)
4. 7—the volume number
5. A.L.R.5th—the abbreviated name of the publication
6. 852—the page number where the annotation begins
7. 1992—the year of publication

Legal Dictionary

A legal dictionary citation should include the following:

1. The full name of the dictionary (no abbreviations, with underscoring or italics)
2. The page of the definition
3. The edition and year of publication

For Example: *Black's Law Dictionary* 451 (7th ed. 1992).

In this example, the elements of the citation are as follows:

1. *Black's Law Dictionary*—the full name of the dictionary (no abbreviations, with underscoring or italics);
2. 451—the page of the definition
3. 7th ed. 1992—the edition and year of publication

Legal Encyclopedia

A citation to a legal encyclopedia should contain the following:

1. The volume number of the encyclopedia
2. The abbreviated name of the encyclopedia, usually either Am. Jur. 2d or C.J.S. (no underscoring or italics)
3. The topic name (underscored or italicized)
4. The section symbol and section number within the article
5. The year of publication

For Example: 88 C.J.S. *Trial* § 105 (1980); 59A Am. Jur. 2d *Partnership* § 925 (Supp. 1995).

In these examples, the elements of the citations are as follows:

1. 88 and 59A—the volume number of the encyclopedia
2. C.J.S. and Am. Jur. 2d—the abbreviated name of the encyclopedia
3. *Trial* and *Partnership*—the topic name (italicized or underscored)
4. § 105 and § 925—the section symbol and section number within the article
5. (1980) and (Supp. 1995)—the year of publication

Law Review/Journal Citations

The following are the components of a law review or journal citation:

1. The full name of the author
2. The title of the article (underscored or italicized)
3. The volume number
4. The abbreviated title of the periodical
5. The page number where the article begins
6. The year of the publication

For Example: Patricia W. Bennett, *After* White v. Illinois: *Fundamental Guarantees to a Hollow Right to Confront Witnesses,* 40 Wayne L. Rev. 159 (1993).

In this example, the elements of the citation are as follows:

1. Patricia W. Bennett—the full name of the author
2. *After* White v. Illinois: *Fundamental Guarantees to a Hollow Right to Confront Witnesses*—the title of the article (italicized or underscored)
3. 40—the volume number
4. Wayne L. Rev.—the abbreviated title of the periodical
5. 159—the page number where the article begins
6. (1993)—the year of the publication

Restatements

A citation to a Restatement should include the following components:

1. The full name of the Restatement and the edition
2. The section number of the Restatement
3. The year of the publication

For Example: Restatement (Second) of Judgments § 28 (1982).

In this example, the elements of the citation are as follows:

1. Restatement (Second) of Judgments—the full name of the Restatement and the edition
2. § 28—the section number
3. (1982)—the year of the publication

Treatises/Books

Treatise and book citations should include the following:

1. The volume number if there is more than one volume
2. The full name of the author or editor if a name is given
3. The full title of the publication as it appears on the title page (italicized or underscored)
4. The number of the section, paragraph, or page if you are referring to a specific section, paragraph, or page
5. The edition or series number of the book if it is not the first edition
6. The year of publication

For Example: 6A Richard R. Powell, *Powell on Real Property* ¶ 899 (Patrick J. Rohan ed. 1994).

In this example, the elements of the citation are as follows:

1. 6A—the volume number
2. Richard R. Powell—the full name of the author
3. *Powell on Real Property*—the full title of the publication as it appears on the title page (italicized or underscored)
4. ¶ 899—the number of the paragraph
5. (Patrick J. Rohan ed.)—the edition
6. 1994—the year of publication

GLOSSARY

active voice See *voice.*

adjective A word that modifies a noun or pronoun. An adjective usually describes a noun or pronoun (a *red* car).

administrative law Rules, regulations, orders, and decisions adopted by administrative agencies that have the authority of law.

advocacy To support or urge the adoption of a position through the use of an argument.

advocacy letter See *demand/advocacy letter.*

affirm A decision of an appellate court that upholds the decision of the trial court.

agreement Words that are related must agree in number (singular/plural) and gender (feminine/masculine/neuter) (*e.g., Workers* must wear *their* helmets. *Mary* must wear *her* helmet).

antecedent A word, clause, or phrase referred to by a pronoun. In the following sentence, the word *workers* is the antecedent for the pronoun *their.* The *workers* put on *their* helmets.

apostrophe (') A mark that serves to indicate possession (Mary's hat) or to form a contraction (can't).

appeals court A court that reviews the decision of a trial court or other lower court to determine and correct any error that may have been made.

appellant The party who files an appeal. On appeal, the appellant argues that the lower court made an error that entitles the appellant to relief.

appellate court brief An external memorandum of law submitted to a court of appeals. It presents the legal analysis, authority, and argument in support of a position that the lower court's decision or ruling was either correct or incorrect. It is often referred to as an appellate brief.

appellee The party who opposes the appeal. On appeal, the appellee usually argues that the lower court did not make an error that entitles the appellant to relief.

authority Anything a court may rely on when deciding an issue. It includes the law, such as constitutions and statutes, and nonlaw sources, such as legal encyclopedias and treatises.

background facts Facts presented in a court opinion, case brief, or legal memorandum that put the key facts in context. They give an overview of a factual event and provide the reader with the overall context within which the key facts occurred.

brackets ([ ]) Marks used to show changes in or additions to quotations, usually for the purpose of providing clarification to the quotation or indicating an error in the original quotations. ("The privilege [against self-incrimination] allows an individual to remain silent.")

brief See *appellate court brief; case brief;* and *trial court brief.*

brief answer A section of a memorandum of law that presents a brief, precise answer to the issue(s) addressed in the memo.

canons of construction The rules and guidelines courts use when interpreting statutes.

caption In an opinion, the caption consists of the names of the parties to a lawsuit and their court status (*e.g.,* Eddie RAEL, Plaintiff-Appellee v. Emillio CADENA and Manuel Cadena, Defendants-Appellants).

case brief A written summary identifying the essential components of a court opinion.

case law See *common law/case law.*

case law analysis The analytical process engaged in to determine if and how a decision in a court opinion either governs or affects the outcome of a client's case.

cause of action The legal basis upon which a lawsuit is based (*e.g.,* negligence). To state a claim in a lawsuit means to allege facts in support of each element of the cause of action (*e.g.,* in a negligence case, there must be facts alleged in support of each of the elements of negligence—duty, breach of duty, proximate cause, and damages).

certiorari See *writ of certiorari.*

citation Information that allows the reader to locate where a reference can be found. In case law, the term refers to the volume number, page number, and name of the reporter where a case may be found.

cite See *citation.*

collateral estoppel—doctrine of The doctrine prevents a party in a lawsuit from relitigating an issue that has been decided in a previous lawsuit.

colon (:) A punctuation mark used to introduce or call attention to information that follows. (The statutory requirements are the following: the will must be witnessed by two witnesses. . . .)

comma (,) The most frequently used punctuation mark. It is used to separate parts of a sentence.

common law/case law The body of law created by courts. It is composed of the general legal rules, doctrines, and principles adopted by courts when interpreting existing law or when creating law in the absence of controlling enacted law.

concurring opinion A judicial opinion that agrees with the majority holding in a case but for different or additional reasons than those presented by the majority.

constitution A governing document adopted by the people that establishes the framework for the operation of the government, defines the powers of the government, and guarantees the fundamental rights of the people.

contraction A word formed by combining two words: *can't* (cannot), *isn't* (is not).

counteranalysis The process of discovering and considering the counterargument to a legal position or argument; the process of anticipating the argument the opponent is likely to raise in response to the analysis of an issue. It is the identification and objective evaluation of the strengths and weaknesses of a legal argument.

counterargument The argument in opposition to a legal argument or position. The argument the opponent is likely to raise in response to the analysis of an issue.

court opinion The statement of a court of its decision reached in a case, the rule that applies, and the reasons for the court's decision.

court rules Procedural rules adopted by a court that govern the litigation process. Court rules often govern the format and style of documents submitted to the court.

dangling modifier A modifier that does not modify any other part of a sentence.

dash (—) A mark used in a sentence to emphasize something, set off lists, briefly summarize materials containing commas, or show an abrupt change of thought or direction. (The items located at the scene—the knife, the drugs, and the scarf—have disappeared from the evidence room.)

defendant The party against whom a lawsuit is brought.

demand/advocacy letter Correspondence that is designed to persuade someone to take action favorable to the interests of the client or cease acting in a manner that is detrimental to the client.

dissenting opinion A judicial opinion in a case that disagrees with the majority opinion.

district court In many states, the district court is the trial court of general jurisdiction. See also *United States district court.*

ejusdem generis A cannon of construction that provides that whenever a statute contains a specific list followed by a general term, the general term is interpreted to be limited to other things of the same class or kind as the list.

element An essential component of a law, rule, principle, or doctrine. In order for a law, rule, and so on to apply, the requirements of each element must be met. (The elements of negligence are duty, breach of duty, proximate cause, and damages. For a claim of negligence to prevail, the plaintiff must establish that the defendant had a duty, the defendant breached the duty, the breach of duty was the cause of the incident, and the plaintiff was damaged as a result of the breach.)

ellipsis The use of three dots to indicate the omission of part of a quotation (*e.g.,* "The statute provides that contractors are responsible for . . . the preparation of work orders. . . .")

enacted law The body of law adopted by the people or legislative bodies, including constitutions, statutes, ordinances, and administrative rules and regulations.

expanded outline See *outline—expanded.*

expressio unius A canon of construction that provides that if a statute contains a list of items covered by the statute, everything else is excluded.

external memorandum A memorandum of law that is designed for use outside the law office (*e.g.,* memoranda submitted to a court, such as briefs in support of motions; memoranda designed for other external use, such as for clients or opposing attorneys).

fact Information concerning some thing, action, event, or circumstance.

general jurisdiction A court of general jurisdiction has the power, with few exceptions, to hear and decide any matter brought before it.

headnotes Summaries of the points of law discussed in a court opinion prepared by the publisher of the opinion.

holding The court's application of the rule of law to the legal question raised by the facts of a case. The court's answer to the legal issue in a case.

hyphen (-) A mark used to form compound modifiers and compound nouns (*e.g.,* well-known, ex-judge).

in personam jurisdiction See *personal jurisdiction.*

infinitive A verb form that functions as a noun or as an auxiliary verb (*e.g.,* to argue, to leave). A *split infinitive* refers to the placement of an adverb between *to* and the verb in an infinitive (*e.g.,* to *completely* understand).

information letter Correspondence that provides general legal information or background on a legal issue. It usually involves the communication of the results of legal research and analysis to a client or a third party.

intellectual honesty In the context of legal analysis, intellectual honesty means to research and analyze a problem objectively. This includes analyzing all aspects of a problem free of preconceived notions, personal views, and emotions.

interoffice memorandum of law See *office legal memorandum.*

IRAC An acronym commonly used in reference to the legal analysis process. It is composed of the first letter of the descriptive term for each step of the process—*I*ssue, *R*ule, *A*nalysis/*A*pplication, *C*onclusion. The standard legal analysis process is the identification of the issue, followed by the presentation of the governing rule of law, the analysis/application of the rule of law, and the conclusion.

irrelevant facts Those facts that are coincidental to an event but are not of significant legal importance in a case.

issue The precise legal question raised by the specific facts of a dispute.

issue—comprehensive/narrow statement A complete statement of the issue that includes the specific law, legal question, and key facts.

issue—short/broad statement A broad formulation of the issue that usually does not include reference to the specific facts of the case or the applicable law.

jurisdiction The court's authority to hear and resolve specific disputes. Jurisdiction is usually composed of *personal jurisdiction* (authority over persons) and *subject matter jurisdiction* (authority over the types of cases a court may hear and decide).

key fact(s) The legally significant facts of a case that raise the legal question of how or whether the law governing the dispute applies. The facts upon which the outcome of the case is determined. They are the facts that establish or satisfy the elements of a cause of action and are necessary to prove or disprove a claim. A key fact is a fact that is so essential that, if it were changed, the outcome of the case would probably change.

key facts—groups Individual facts that, when considered as a group, are key facts. Individual facts that when treated as a group may determine the outcome of a case.

key facts—individual A key fact that, if it were changed, the outcome of the case would be affected or changed.

key numbers West Publishing Company has divided all areas of American law into various topics and subtopics. Each area is identified by a topic name, and each specific topic or subtopic is assigned a number called a key number.

law The enforceable rules that govern individual and group conduct in a society. The law establishes standards of conduct, the procedures governing standards of conduct, and the remedies available when the standards are not adhered to.

legal analysis The process of identifying the issue or issues presented by a client's facts and determining what law applies and how it applies. The process of applying the law to the facts of a case. It is an exploration of how and why a specific law does or does not apply.

legal issue See *issue.*

legal writing process A systematic approach to legal writing. An organized approach to legal research, analysis, and writing. It is composed of three stages: prewriting, writing, and postwriting.

legislative history The record of legislation during the enactment process. It is composed of committee reports, transcripts of hearings, statements of legislators concerning the legislation, and any other material published for legislative use in regard to the legislation.

limited jurisdiction A court of limited jurisdiction is limited in the types of cases it may hear and decide.

majority opinion The opinion in a court decision of the majority of judges.

mandatory authority Any authority or source of law that a court must rely on or follow when reaching a decision (*e.g.,* a decision of a higher court in the jurisdiction on the same or a similar issue).

memorandum of law A written analysis of a legal problem. It is an informative document that summarizes the research and analysis of the legal issue or issues raised by the facts of a case. It contains a summary of the law and how the law applies in the case.

modifier A word or phrase that provides a description of the subject, verb, or object in a sentence.

nominalization A noun created from a verb (*e.g.,* realization from the verb realize).

nouns Words that refer to persons, places, things, or qualities.

office legal memorandum A legal memorandum prepared for office use. It presents an objective legal analysis of the issue(s) raised by the facts of the client's case and usually includes the arguments in favor of and in opposition to the client's position. It is often referred to by other names, such as interoffice legal research memorandum, office research memorandum, and interoffice memorandum of law.

on all fours A prior court opinion in which the key facts and applicable rule of law are identical or nearly identical with those of the client's case or the case before a court.

on point A term used to refer to a prior court opinion in which the facts are sufficiently similar to the facts of the client's case or the case before the court for the prior court opinion to apply as precedent. A case is on point if the similarity between the key facts and rule of law or legal principle of the court opinion and those of the client's case is sufficient for the court opinion to govern or provide guidance to a later court in deciding the outcome of the client's case.

opinion The written statement by the court expressing how it ruled in a case and the reasons for its ruling.

opinion letter Correspondence, usually written to a client, that in addition to informing the reader of how the law applies to a specific question, provides legal advice. It informs the reader how the law applies and advises which steps should be taken.

outline The skeletal structure and organizational framework of a writing.

outline—expanded An outline that has been expanded so that it may be used in the prewriting stage. The use of an expanded outline allows the integration of all research, analysis, and ideas into an organized outline structure while research and analysis are being conducted. It facilitates the preparation of a rough draft.

paragraph A group of sentences that address the same topic.

parallel citation When a court opinion is printed in more than one reporter, each citation is a parallel citation to the other citation or citations. (*E.g., "Britton v. Britton,* **100 N.M. 424, 671 P.2d 1135** (1983). The parallel citations are in bold.)

parentheses ( ) Marks used to add to a sentence information that is outside the main idea of the sentence or of lesser importance.

pari materia A canon of construction that provides that statutes dealing with the same subject should be interpreted consistently.

party A plaintiff or defendant in a lawsuit.

passive voice See *voice*.

persuasive authority Any authority a court is not bound to consider or follow but may consider or follow when reaching a decision (*e.g.,* a decision of a court in another state on the same or a similar issue, secondary authority, and so on).

personal jurisdiction The authority of the court over the parties to resolve a legal dispute involving the parties.

plain meaning rule A canon of construction that provides that if the meaning of a statute is clear on its face, it will be interpreted according to its plain meaning and the other canons of construction will not be applied by the court.

plaintiff The party who starts (files) a lawsuit.

point heading A summary of the position advocated in the argument section of a trial or appellate brief.

postwriting stage The stage in the legal writing process where an assignment is revised, edited, and assembled in final form.

precedent An earlier court decision on an issue that applies to govern or guide a subsequent court in its determination of an identical or similar issue based upon identical or similar facts. A court opinion is precedent if there is a sufficient similarity between the key facts and rule of law or legal principle of the court sopinion and the matter before the subsequent court.

predicate A verb, its modifiers, and the object of the verb, such as a direct object (if necessary). The predicate of a sentence provides information concerning the subject of a sentence. (*E.g.,* "Tom **ran to the store.**" The predicate of the sentence is in bold.)

prewriting stage The stage in the legal writing process where the assignment is organized, researched, and analyzed.

primary authority Authority that is composed of the law (*e.g.,* constitutions, statutes, and court opinions).

prior proceedings The events that occurred in the litigation in a lower court or administrative hearing.

punctuation Marks or characters used in writing to make the meaning clear and easy to understand (*e.g.,* period [.], comma [,], semicolon [;], and colon [:]).

purpose clause A statutory section that includes the purpose the legislative body intended to accomplish when drafting the statute.

quotation (" ") Marks used to identify and set off quoted material. (Mary said, "I do not believe it is true.")

re *Re* means in the matter of, about, or concerning. It is usually placed at the beginning of the reference line in a memo or correspondence.

remand A decision of an appellate court that sends the case back to the trial court for further action.

reverse A decision of an appellate court that disagrees with the decision of the trial court.

salutation The part of a letter that presents the greeting (Dear Ms. Jones).

scope A statutory section that states what is specifically covered and not covered by the statute.

secondary authority Any source of law a court may rely on that is not the law (*e.g.,* legal treatises, restatements of the law, and legal encyclopedias).

semicolon (;) A punctuation mark used to separate major elements of complex sentences, or to separate items in a series if the items are long or if one of the items has internal commas. (The shareholders held their meeting at noon; the board of directors met immediately thereafter.)

sentence The fundamental building block of writing. It is composed of a group of words that convey a single thought. It is usually a statement in which the actor (subject) performs some action or describes a state of being (the predicate).

short title The name by which a statute is known (*e.g.,* Uniform Commercial Code—Sales).

split infinitive See *infinitive*.

squinting modifier A modifier located in a position in a sentence that makes it unclear whether it modifies the word that precedes it or the word that follows it. (*E.g.,* "The report that was prepared *routinely* indicated that the structure was unsafe." It is unclear whether *routinely* refers to the report being prepared routinely or the report routinely indicated the structure was unsafe).

stare decisis A basic principle of the common law system that requires a court to follow a previous decision of that court or a higher court when the current decision involves issues and facts similar to those involved in the previous decision. The doctrine that provides that precedent should be followed.

statement of facts The section of a memorandum of law that presents the factual context of the issue(s) addressed in the memorandum.

statutes Laws passed by legislative bodies that declare rights and duties, or command or prohibit certain conduct.

statutory analysis The interpretation and application of statutory law. The process of determining if a statute applies to a specific fact situation, how it applies, and the effect of that application.

statutory elements The specific conditions or components of a statute that must be met for the statute to apply.

statutory law The body of law composed of laws passed by legislative bodies. The term includes laws or ordinances passed by any legislative body.

subject A noun or pronoun that is the actor in a sentence. (*E.g.,* "**Tom** ran to the store." The subject of the sentence is in bold.)

subject matter jurisdiction The types or kinds of cases the court has the authority to hear and decide.

topic sentence The sentence that identifies the subject of a paragraph. It introduces the subject and provides the focus of a paragraph.

trial court The court where the matter is heard and decided. Testimony is taken, the evidence is presented, and the decision is reached in the trial court.

trial court brief An external memorandum of law submitted to a trial court. It presents the legal authority and argument in support of a position advocated by an attorney, usually in regard to a motion or issue being addressed by the court. It is often referred to as a trial brief.

United States district court The trial court of general jurisdiction in the federal judicial system.

United States supreme court The final court of appeals in the federal system and the highest court in the United States.

verbs Words that express action, a state of being or feeling, or a relation between two things. (*E.g.,* "Tom **ran** to the store." The verb in this sentence is in bold.)

voice The relationship of the subject to the action of the sentence. *Active voice*—the subject of the sentence is performing the action in the sentence. (The automobile hit the child.) *Passive voice*—the subject of the sentence is acted upon. (The child was hit by the automobile.)

writ of certiorari A writ from a higher court asking a lower court for the record of a case. A petition for a writ of certiorari is a request filed by a party in a lawsuit that a higher court review the decision of a lower court.

writing stage The stage in the legal writing process where research, analysis, and ideas are assembled into a written product.

INDEX

I

J

K

L

M

N

O